Changing Perspectives on the Archaeology of the Central Mississippi River Valley

Changing Perspectives on the Archaeology of the Central Mississippi River Valley

Edited by
Michael J. O'Brien and Robert C. Dunnell

The University of Alabama Press
Tuscaloosa and London

Copyright © 1998
The University of Alabama Press
Tuscaloosa, Alabama 35487-0380
All rights reserved
Manufactured in the United States of America

∞
The paper on which this book is printed meets the minimum requirements of American National Standard for Information Science-Permanence of Paper for Printed Library Materials, ANSI Z39.48-1984.

Library of Congress Cataloging-in-Publication Data

Changing perspectives on the archaeology of the Central Mississippi
  River Valley / edited by Michael J. O'Brien and Robert C. Dunnell.
      p.   cm.
  This volume originated from the 1993 annual meeting of the
  Society for American archaeology in St. Louis.
  Includes bibliographical references and index.
  ISBN 0-8173-0909-8 (paper : alk. paper)
   1. Mississippian culture.   2. Excavations (Archaeology)—
Mississippi River Valley—History.   3. Mississippi River Valley—
Antiquities.   I. O'Brien, Michael J. (Michael John), 1950-   .
II. Dunnell, Robert C., 1942-   . III. Society for American
Archaeology. Meeting (1993 : St. Louis, Mo.)
E99.M6815C53   1998
977'.01—dc21   97-35595

British Library Cataloguing-in-Publication Data available

Contents

Figures — vii
Tables — xii
Preface and Acknowledgments — xv

1. A Brief Introduction to the Archaeology of the Central Mississippi River Valley — 1
   Michael J. O'Brien and Robert C. Dunnell

2. An Examination of Mississippian-Period Phases in Southeastern Missouri — 31
   Gregory L. Fox

3. Pottery, Radiocarbon Dates, and Mississippian-Period Chronology Building in Western Kentucky — 59
   Paul P. Kreisa

4. An Overview of Walls Engraved Pottery in the Central Mississippi Valley — 80
   David H. Dye

5. Graves Lake: A Late Mississippian–Period Village in Lauderdale County, Tennessee — 99
   Robert C. Mainfort, Jr., and Michael C. Moore

6. Landscape Change and Settlement Location in the Cairo Lowland of Southeastern Missouri — 124
   Robert H. Lafferty III

7. Nonsite Survey in the Cairo Lowland of Southeastern Missouri — 148
   Patrice A. Teltser

8. Powers Fort: A Middle Mississippian–Period Fortified Community in the Western Lowlands of Missouri — 169
   Timothy K. Perttula

9. The Langdon Site, Dunklin County, Missouri — 200
   Robert C. Dunnell

10. Moon: A Fortified Mississippian-Period Village in Poinsett County, Arkansas — 225
    David W. Benn

11. Variability in Crowley's Ridge Gravel 258
    Patrick T. McCutcheon and Robert C. Dunnell

12. Blade Technology and Nonlocal Cherts: Hopewell(?) Traits at the Twenhafel Site, Southern Illinois 281
    Carol A. Morrow

13. Prehistoric Diet in the Central Mississippi River Valley 299
    Diana M. Greenlee

Notes 325

References 329

Contributors 375

Index 379

Illustrations

Figures

1-1. Map of the central Mississippi River valley showing physiographic features and locations mentioned in the text — 2

1-2. Map of the central Mississippi River valley showing the distribution of different kinds of surface sediments — 6

1-3. In situ mandible of a Pleistocene-age llama, Buffalo Slough, Dunklin County, Missouri — 9

1-4. Aerial photograph taken in 1950 of southern Dunklin County, Missouri, showing the contact between the Malden Plain and the Little River Lowland to the east — 11

1-5. Aerial photograph taken in 1967 showing ridge-and-swale topography in Cross County, Arkansas, that is typical of the modern Mississippi River meander belt — 12

1-6. Map of a portion of the central Mississippi River valley showing locations of archaeological sites mentioned in the text — 14

2-1. Map of southeastern Missouri showing physiographic features and locations of archaeological sites mentioned in the text — 32

2-2. Cluster analysis of Brainerd-Robinson coefficients of ceramic assemblages from sites surface collected by Stephen Williams — 47

2-3. Averaged Euclidian distances of sites surface collected by Stephen Williams — 48

2-4. Results of multidimensional scaling (two dimensions) of surface-collected ceramic assemblages from twenty-six sites surveyed by Stephen Williams — 49

2-5. Cluster analysis of Brainerd-Robinson coefficients of excavated ceramic assemblages from fourteen sites in southeastern Missouri and one in northeastern Arkansas (Parkin) — 53

2-6. Results of multidimensional scaling (two dimensions) of excavated ceramic assemblages from fourteen sites in southeastern Missouri and one in northeastern Arkansas (Parkin) — 54

2-7. Cluster analysis of Brainerd-Robinson coefficients of excavated ceramic assemblages from fourteen sites in southeastern Missouri and one in northeastern Arkansas (Parkin), with Neeley's Ferry Plain and Bell Plain sherds removed — 55

2-8. Results of multidimensional scaling (two dimensions) of excavated ceramic assemblages from fourteen sites in southeastern Missouri and one in northeastern Arkansas (Parkin), with Neeley's Ferry Plain and Bell Plain sherds removed — 56 viii | *Figures*

3-1. Map of western Kentucky showing locations of Mississippian-period sites mentioned in the text — 61

3-2. Comparison of Mississippian-period phases for western Kentucky proposed by Barry Lewis and Kit Wesler — 62

3-3. Radiocarbon dates from Rowlandtown, Twin Mounds, Adams, and Turk, in order of listing in Table 3-2 — 67

3-4. Cluster-analysis dendrogram of ceramic assemblages from Adams, Turk, Twin Mounds, and Rowlandtown — 71

3-5. Multidimensional-scaling scatterplot of ceramic assemblages from Adams, Turk, Twin Mounds, and Rowlandtown — 72

3-6. Geographic and temporal trends in percentages of Wickliffe Thick and Kimmswick Fabric-Impressed sherds in western-Kentucky assemblages — 74

3-7. Geographic and temporal trends in percentages of Mississippian decorated-pottery types in western-Kentucky assemblages — 75

3-8. Geographic and temporal trends in percentages of Old Town Red and total decorated pottery in western-Kentucky assemblages — 76

4-1. Distribution of Walls Engraved, *var. Walls*, and Walls Engraved, *var. Hull*, sherds in the central Mississippi River valley — 86

4-2. Distribution of Walls Engraved, *var. Walls*, and Walls Engraved, *var. Hull*, vessels in the central Mississippi River valley — 87

4-3. Vessel forms associated with Walls Engraved designs — 94

4-4. Scroll types found on Walls Engraved vessels — 96

5-1. Map of western Tennessee and environs showing locations of sites mentioned in the text — 100

5-2. Topographic setting of Graves Lake (40LA92) and site 40LA83, Lauderdale County, Tennessee — 101

5-3. Topographic map of Graves Lake showing grid lines and tested localities — 104

5-4. House 2 area at Graves Lake showing locations of burial pits, hearths, miscellaneous features, and post molds — 105

5-5. House 3 area at Graves Lake showing locations of burial pits, miscellaneous features, post molds, and several artifacts — 107

5-6. Ceramic vessels from Graves Lake — 112

5-7. Distribution of surface-collected shell-tempered sherds by weight (grams per 10 × 10-meter unit) at Graves Lake — 115

5-8. Distribution of surface-collected primary flakes by weight (grams per 10 × 10-meter unit) at Graves Lake — 116

5-9. Distribution of surface-collected chert cobbles by weight (grams per 10 × 10-meter unit) at Graves Lake — 117

5-10. Radiocarbon determinations for Graves Lake (calibrated using CALIB 2.0) — 119

6-1. Map of the Cairo Lowland, southeastern Missouri, showing the location of the New Madrid Floodway and sampling areas relative to major physiographic features and modern soil associations   125

6-2. Map of the northern portion of the New Madrid Floodway project area showing the locations of Mississippi River channels mapped and labeled by Harold Fisk   129

6-3. Map of the northern portion of the New Madrid Floodway showing the areas surveyed   130

6-4. Map of the northern portion of the New Madrid Floodway showing the proposed reconstruction of the landscape about 2000 B.C. (Late Archaic period) and the distribution of sites across the landscape   133

6-5. Map of the northern portion of the New Madrid Floodway showing the proposed reconstruction of the landscape about A.D. 500 (early Late Woodland period) and the distribution of sites across the landscape   137

6-6. Map of the northern portion of the New Madrid Floodway showing the proposed reconstruction of the landscape about A.D. 1000 (Early Mississippian period) and the distribution of sites across the landscape   138

6-7. Map of the southern portion of the New Madrid Floodway showing the distribution of sites on Barnes and Sugar Tree ridges   140

6-8. Map of the southern portion of the New Madrid Floodway showing the proposed reconstruction of the landscape about 1000 B.C. (terminal Late Archaic period) and the distribution of sites on Barnes and Sugar Tree ridges that contained Poverty Point objects   141

6-9. Map of the southern portion of the New Madrid Floodway showing the proposed reconstruction of the landscape about A.D. 1 (Middle Woodland period) and the distribution of sites on Barnes and Sugar Tree ridges that contained sand-tempered pottery   142

6-10. Map of the southern portion of the New Madrid Floodway showing the proposed reconstruction of the landscape about A.D. 1000 (Early Mississippian period) and the distribution of sites on Barnes and Sugar Tree ridges that contained shell-tempered pottery   143

7-1. Map showing the locations of the Sandy Woods site, the Cairo Lowland, and major physiographic features in southeastern Missouri   149

7-2. Nineteenth-century map of the Sandy Woods site, prepared by W. B. Potter for the Academy of Science of St. Louis, showing the locations of mounds, enclosures, and house depressions   152

7-3. Outlines of the three fields surveyed around Sandy Woods, superimposed on soil data from the Scott County soil survey   156

7-4. Survey map of Field CB at Sandy Woods   157

7-5. Survey map of Field JM at Sandy Woods   158

7-6. Survey map of Field RM at Sandy Woods   159

7-7. Comparison of artifact density (artifacts per 4 × 4-meter unit) across the clusters identified in the survey around Sandy Woods   *160*

7-8. Biface-to-debitage ratios for assemblages from fields RM, JM, and CB at Sandy Woods   *162*

7-9. Pottery-to-debitage ratios for assemblages from fields RM, JM, and CB at Sandy Woods   *163*

8-1. Location of Powers Fort relative to physiographic features in southeastern Missouri   *170*

8-2. Map of the sand-ridge system in the Little Black River watershed in the vicinity of Powers Fort showing locations of Powers-phase sites   *171*

8-3. Plan map of Powers Fort made by Col. Philetus W. Norris for the Bureau of (American) Ethnology, Division of Mound Exploration   *174*

8-4. Cross section of Mound 1 at Powers Fort as depicted by Col. Philetus W. Norris   *175*

8-5. Topographic map of Powers Fort showing mounds, surface-collected areas, locations of excavations in the 1960s, and burials 2 through 6   *177*

8-6. Plan maps of excavated burials at Powers Fort   *179*

8-7. Plan map of Structure 1 at Powers Fort   *182*

8-8. Large sherd and vessels from Powers Fort   *192*

8-9. Locations of large Middle Mississippian–period sites in southeastern Missouri that contain mounds and/or palisades   *196*

8-10. Plan of the internal structure of Powers Fort   *198*

9-1. Map of the central Mississippi Valley showing locations of physiographic features and archaeological sites mentioned in the text   *201*

9-2. Stephen Williams's map of the Langdon site, 1954   *204*

9-3. The 1985–1987 Langdon topographic map showing the location of recent investigations   *206*

9-4. June 1937 Soil Conservation Service black-and-white aerial photograph showing Langdon as a walled rectangle   *208*

9-5. Soil Conservation Service black-and-white aerial photographs showing the Langdon site in November 1950 and July 1959   *210*

9-6. Artifact frequencies along the south-to-north transect west of the road at Langdon   *212*

9-7. Magnetic transect across the northernmost mound in the three-mound structure at Langdon   *213*

9-8. Grain-size and chemical characteristics of a core through the northernmost mound in the three-mound structure at Langdon   *214*

9-9. Projectile points from Langdon   *218*

9-10. Plain shell-tempered rimsherds from Langdon   *219*

9-11. Whole vessels from Langdon   *220*

10-1.	Map of the central Mississippi River valley showing physiographic features and the location of Moon and other archaeological sites mentioned in the text	226
10-2.	Environmental setting of Moon and Priestly based on modern soil surveys and General Land Office survey notes	228
10-3.	Excavation plan of Moon (November 1989) superimposed on the 10-meter grid	230
10-4.	Density (objects per 10 × 10-meter unit) of surface-collected artifacts in all classes at Moon	233
10-5.	Density (objects per 10 × 10-meter unit) of surface-collected shell-tempered sherds at Moon	236
10-6.	Density (objects per 10 × 10-meter unit) of surface-collected daub at Moon	235
10-7.	Locations of projectile points and other lithic artifacts in 10 × 10-meter surface-collection units at Moon	236
10-8.	The excavated Moon community pattern superimposed on the 10 × 10-meter grid	237
10-9.	Plan of all features at Moon	239
10-10.	Plan of rectangular Structure 15 at Moon showing the location of carbon smears, pits, and post molds	240
10-11.	Plan of the Moon site showing locations of structures, courtyards 1 and 2, and radiocarbon-dated wood samples	242
10-12.	Excavation plans of square wall-trench structures 1030/1042 and 1036 at Moon	245
10-13.	Locations of structures with deep basins and courtyards 1 and 2 at Moon	247
10-14.	Locations of burned structures and courtyards 1 and 2 at Moon	248
11-1.	Map of the central Mississippi River valley showing the locations of physiographic features, chert-gravel sources that were sampled, and sites mentioned in the text	259
11-2.	Research design used to examine Crowley's Ridge gravels	261
11-3.	Plots of impact-testing results by rock groundmass	276
11-4.	Plots of impact-testing results by solid inclusions	277
11-5.	Plots of impact-testing results by void inclusions	278
11-6.	Plots of impact-testing results by solid-inclusion distributions	279
11-7.	Plots of impact-testing results by void-inclusion distributions	280
12-1.	Map of western Illinois and eastern Missouri showing the locations of Twenhafel and chert quarries mentioned in the text	282
12-2.	Identification protocol used to sort chert artifacts from Twenhafel	290
12-3.	Line graph showing general technological trends in assemblages from Twenhafel	293

13-1. Map of the central Mississippi River valley, showing the locations of previously acquired and newly acquired stable-carbon-isotope data 302

13-2. Plot showing previously acquired stable-carbon-isotope ratios versus estimated age 303

13-3. Plot showing the percent yield for the two independent replicate extractions 317

13-4. Atomic carbon/nitrogen ratios of "collagen" plotted against the mean extract yield of replicate extractions 318

13-5. Carbon and nitrogen concentrations in "collagen" plotted against the mean extract yield of replicate samples 319

13-6. Newly (and previously) acquired stable-carbon-isotope ratios versus estimated age 322

13-7. Variance in stable-carbon-isotope ratios versus number of individuals for four central Mississippi Valley skeletal samples 323

Tables

2-1. Southeastern Missouri Mississippian-period phases, cultural periods, and ceramic types 34

2-2. Archaeological sites forming the data base for statistical comparisons 39

2-3. Provenience of analytical units for Crosno 42

2-4. Similarity matrix of Brainerd-Robinson coefficients of analytical units derived from excavations at Crosno 44

2-5. Similarity matrix of Brainerd-Robinson coefficients of twenty-five surface-collected sites and the excavated Crosno assemblage 46

2-6. Similarity matrix of Brainerd-Robinson coefficients of excavated ceramic assemblages from fourteen sites in southeastern Missouri and one in northeastern Arkansas 51

3-1. Frequencies and percentages of selected ceramic types from four Mississippian sites in western Kentucky 65

3-2. Radiocarbon dates from Rowlandtown, Twin Mounds, Adams, and Turk 66

4-1. Sites in the central Mississippi Valley producing Walls Engraved sherds 88

4-2. Sites in the central Mississippi Valley producing Walls Engraved vessels 90

5-1. Frequencies of shell-tempered sherds from Graves Lake and Richardson's Landing 109

5-2. Calibrated radiocarbon dates from Graves Lake 118

5-3. Frequencies of interior beveling on rimsherds from sites in western Tennessee and southeastern Missouri 120

Tables | xiii

6-1. Numbers of hectares surveyed and sites found in high- and low-probability areas in the northern portion of the New Madrid Floodway — *131*

6-2. Radiocarbon dates from archaeological sites in the New Madrid Floodway — *135*

6-3. Frequencies of components identified during the New Madrid Floodway Survey — *144*

6-4. Frequencies and weights of artifacts from test units at Rinaud — *145*

7-1. Frequency of eroded sherds from Cluster RMA by temper — *166*

8-1. Position, orientation, age, sex, and associated artifacts of Powers Fort burials — *180*

8-2. Vertical distribution of cultural materials in Structure 1 at Powers Fort — *184*

8-3. Concentration indices of excavated artifacts from Structure 1 at Powers Fort — *184*

8-4. Frequencies of shell-tempered sherds and other ceramic items from Powers Fort — *188*

8-5. Occurrence of vessel forms, rim and body decoration, and appendages and bases in the Powers Phase ceramic assemblages — *189*

8-6. Decorative elements on shell-tempered pottery from Powers Fort — *190*

8-7. Percentages of raw materials in lithic assemblages from five surface-collected areas at Powers Fort — *193*

8-8. Lithic artifacts from excavated contexts at Powers Fort — *194*

8-9. Powers Phase lithic tools from surface contexts at Powers Fort — *195*

10-1. Radiocarbon dates from Moon — *231*

10-2. Decorated pottery and special artifacts from Moon — *251*

11-1. Dimensions and attributes for the rock physical-properties classification — *264*

11-2. Results of *t*-tests for gravel collections comparing size to rock physical-properties-classification dimensions — *268*

11-3. Chi-square results comparing archaeological assemblages to nearest gravel sample along rock physical-properties-classification dimensions — *273*

11-4. Brainerd-Robinson coefficients for rock physical-properties-classification dimensions comparing archaeological assemblages and gravel samples — *274*

11-5. Mean and standard deviation of failure loads and weight loss for Crowley's Ridge gravel specimens — *275*

12-1. Frequencies of lithic pieces by period at Twenhafel — *292*

12-2. Technological use of Cobden/Dongola chert through time at Twenhafel — *294*

12-3. Percentage of Cobden/Dongola chert used in each technology by period at Twenhafel   294

12-4. Frequencies of items of Crescent and Grimes Hill chert in each technology by period at Twenhafel   295

13-1. Summary of skeletal specimens from southeastern Missouri included in the analysis   314

13-2. Collagen-extract yield, percent carbon, percent nitrogen, and carbon/nitrogen ratios for new samples from southeastern Missouri   316

13-3. $\delta 13C$ Values for new skeletal samples from southeastern Missouri   321

Preface and Acknowledgments

This volume had its origin in a 1993 Society for American Archaeology symposium. That year the annual meeting was held in St. Louis, and given the venue, it seemed appropriate to focus at least one set of papers on current research in the Mississippi Valley. Although that region played a critical role in the development of American archaeology—the work conducted there became something of a paradigm—it was our impression that the region was still known for its earlier contributions, even though current research had begun to move away from that model, both methodologically and substantively. In proposing a seminar on the archaeology of the central Mississippi Valley, it was our intention to bring some of those changes to the notice of a broad audience.

The present volume is not, however, a more permanent version of the 1993 symposium. Several papers originally presented were dropped as the volume developed, and all chapters have been modified extensively. Although complete coverage of a region as large as the central Mississippi Valley is impossible, as is summarizing the myriad approaches that have been taken toward understanding the prehistoric record, we solicited a number of new works in an attempt to provide a more representative aspect to the collection as a whole. Regrettably, some potential contributors were unable to participate in either the symposium or the present volume.

More than half the chapters focus almost exclusively on that portion of the archaeological record that dates after A.D. 900, traditionally the beginning of what commonly is referred to as the Mississippian period. Perhaps this is to be expected, since, as we note in Chapter 1, it has been this portion of the record, with its mounds and cemeteries, that has long attracted the interest of prehistorians. Certainly more has been written about that part of the central Mississippi Valley record than about all the other parts combined, and there is no reason to expect that trend to change in the immediate future. However, to present somewhat of a more balanced view of the record, we deliberately sought contributions from several archaeologists working with materials from other periods. The chapters that were finally included cover diverse topics—distributions of artifacts across the landscape, internal configurations of large fortified settlements, human-bone chemistry, and ceramic technology, to name a few—and all incorporate the results of new fieldwork and/or analysis. We decidedly did not want simple recapitulations of older material. In essence, one strength of the volume is the diversity of topics covered and the potential avenues for further research suggested by the various authors.

Another strength—at least we see it that way—stems from the manner in which we handled certain production mechanics. Our intent from the start was to produce a volume that did not look like, nor read like, a willy-nilly assemblage of loosely connected papers. The reader will notice, for example, that all maps in the various chapters carry the same kinds of information and that each can be referenced to the base map presented in Chapter 1. Likewise, the manner in which the chapters themselves were edited was based on establishing consistency. We ended up walking a fine line between editing for style and editing for substance, which in many instances required us to ask the authors to rethink some of their positions. We do not necessarily agree with some of the conclusions presented herein, but we firmly believe that all the authors make reasonable arguments and that their contributions are important to understanding the tremendous variation evident in the archaeological record of the central Mississippi River valley.

As with the production of any book, a number of people need to be thanked for their contributions to the process. We greatly appreciate the help and encouragement we received from the University of Alabama Press, specifically from Judith Knight. For their input and attention to detail, we thank Kris Wilhelmsen, who generated many of the line drawings and all of the physiographic maps, and Dan Glover, who made corrections to various maps and also generated several of the line drawings. We greatly appreciate the capable editorial help supplied by Jennifer Smith Glover and Dan Glover, each or both of whom read numerous drafts of the chapters, converted chapters from one word-processing program to another, looked up missing references, and proofread the final manuscript. We thank Mary D. Dunnell for her editing work and Lee Lyman for his comments on the introductory chapter. E. J. O'Brien read the manuscript in its entirety and made numerous suggestions on how to improve wording and avoid needless repetition. Consistency in such things as legends and captions and agreement between text and figures are due in large part to his eye for detail. Kathy Cummins copy edited the final manuscript, and we appreciate her excellent work. Finally, we thank two anonymous reviewers, both of whom suggested numerous changes that greatly improved the manuscript.

Changing Perspectives on the Archaeology of the Central Mississippi River Valley

1 | A Brief Introduction to the Archaeology of the Central Mississippi River Valley
Michael J. O'Brien and Robert C. Dunnell

THE CHAPTERS IN this volume summarize a series of recent investigations of the archaeological record of the central Mississippi River valley, which, following Morse and Morse (1983; see also Williams 1956), we take to be that portion of the greater Mississippi Alluvial Valley (Fisk 1944) lying between the Arkansas River and its deposits on the south and Thebes, Illinois, on the north (Figure 1-1). This is not a wholly arbitrary area, even though the southern boundary of the central valley is less marked than the northern, eastern, and western boundaries (see below). North of Thebes, the Mississippi flows in a narrow valley only a few kilometers wide and deeply incised into Paleozoic bedrock. South of Thebes, the river occupies a major structural depression—the Mississippi Embayment—that is filled largely with poorly consolidated or unconsolidated sediments of Cretaceous and later age. There, the valley often is 200 kilometers wide; its eastern and western boundaries are Paleozoic bedrock, deeply buried by loess in the east.

One would be hard pressed to find another region of the United States, unless it is the Southwest, that has witnessed such a long-standing interest on the part of prehistorians. Given the high visibility of segments of its archaeological record—especially mounds—why *wouldn't* the region attract the attention of those interested in the past? Alban Jasper Conant, an amateur prehistorian writing in the *Transactions of the Academy of Science of St. Louis* in 1878, prosaically characterized the southeastern Missouri portion of the valley as an archaeologist's paradise:

> There is, doubtless, now no richer field for archaeological research in this great basin of the Mississippi Valley than is to be found in [southeastern] Missouri. The wonderful extent and variety of the ancient works and monuments therein, the relics they disclose, the huge burial mounds filled with the bones of the dead, disposed in orderly array, as though by loving hands, along with vessels of pottery of graceful forms and varied patterns, often, too, skillfully ornamented,—all bear witness to a settled and permanent condition of society and government and obedience to law, and to certain convictions of a future life. (Conant 1878:353)

Once people with an interest in antiquities began poking in and around the mounds, they were immediately rewarded for their efforts. By the end of the

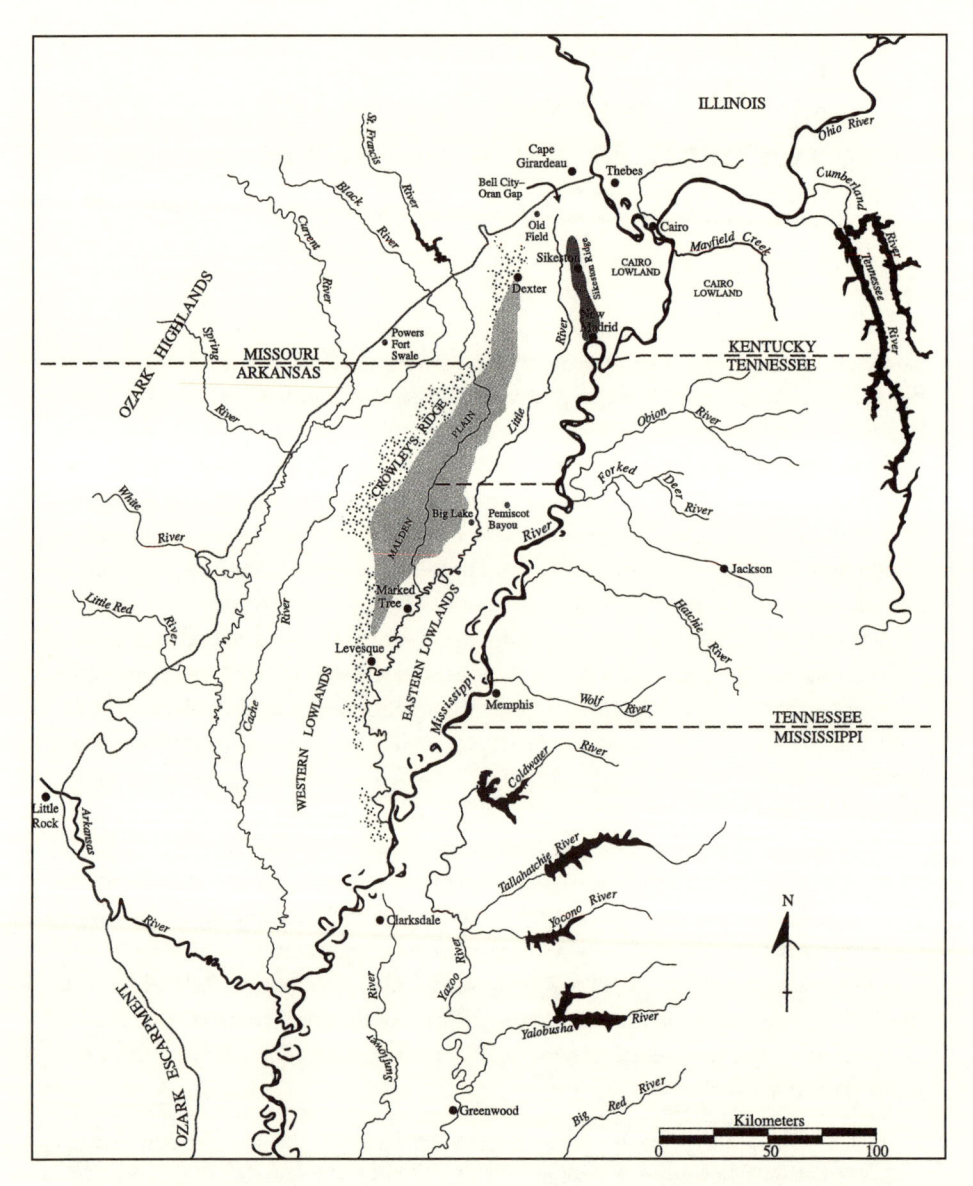

Figure 1-1. Map of the central Mississippi River valley showing physiographic features and locations mentioned in the text.

nineteenth century, thousands of magnificent ceramic bowls, bottles, and jars that had lain hidden in the large prehistoric cemeteries along the Mississippi and St. Francis rivers and neighboring streams such as Little River and Pemiscot Bayou had been mined, many of them ending up in museums in the East. In a very real sense, it is a wonder that anything was left of the archaeological record of the central Mississippi Valley by the beginning of the twentieth century. Perhaps it is testament to the incredible wealth of the record that even today, after more than a century of indiscriminate digging coupled with new farming technologies, especially those related to land leveling, there are still large segments of the record that are in reasonable condition.

The chapters in this volume demonstrate that not only is there still a considerable amount to be learned about the archaeological record of the central Mississippi Valley but also that the methods and techniques that are being used to study the record have changed dramatically over the past half century. If one peruses the literature on the archaeology of the region, it appears that the culture-history paradigm that long guided Americanist archaeology everywhere (Lyman et al. 1997) is still quite at home. Culture history has a revered place in Americanist archaeology (see Lyman et al. 1997 for an extensive review), one important aspect of which is the chronological ordering of archaeological materials. Many of the issues that were central to Americanist archaeology during the period 1940 to 1970 were brought to the table as a direct result of fieldwork conducted in the central Mississippi Valley (O'Brien and Lyman n.d.). Archaeologists working in the region, like most of their counterparts working in areas to the south and east, did not take part in the processual debates of the 1960s and 1970s (Dunnell 1990). Although many factors played a role in this conservatism, one stands out: the Mississippi Valley had been an important and early donor to the culture-history paradigm; thus, archaeologists working in the region either had played a direct role in creating the paradigm or were students of those who had. Many students of the original creators continued to work in the valley after receiving their degrees, and they continued in the same vein as their predecessors, adding new data to the growing pile rather than reinterpreting old facts.

Most archaeologists working in the central Mississippi Valley are comfortable with the culture-history framework provided them—a framework first worked out by Philip Phillips in collaboration with James Ford and James Griffin (Phillips et al. 1951) (see below) and later modified through Phillips's collaboration with Gordon Willey (Phillips and Willey 1953; Willey and Phillips 1955, 1958). Likewise, they are comfortable with the pottery types first described by Phillips, Ford, and Griffin (1951) and later modified by Phillips (1958, 1970). If the pottery types described by Phillips, Ford, and Griffin (1951) can be used to bring chronological order to archaeological phenomena, and if the phases proposed by Phillips (1970) have a usefulness in keeping track of things both chronologically and spatially, then why should they not continue to be used? No one has ever said that units such as phases and pottery types have no use. What a few archaeologists *have* said (e.g., Fox 1992; O'Brien 1994a, 1995; O'Brien and Fox 1994a, 1994b; O'Brien and Lyman n.d.) is that modern usage of the units in some cases far exceeds what the creators of the units had in mind. Continued use of the units with little or no reflection as to their original intended purposes has, in our minds, had a rather palling effect on the archaeology of the central Mississippi Valley. For the most part, the chapters included here bypass extended discussion of types and phases in favor of other aspects of archaeological analysis. Some of the chapters document that archaeological attention is beginning to move beyond time-and-space systematics; others question many of the long-held assumptions about time and space and look toward refining our understanding of those two dimensions.

We find it difficult to evaluate work being done today without an awareness of how that work mirrors or differs from what was done previously. Our purpose in this chapter is threefold: (1) to summarize the who, what, when, and where of various research efforts; (2) to mention some of the major issues with which investigators wrestled; and (3) to show how some of the work reported in the various chapters included here has readdressed those issues. We make no attempt to chronicle all the myriad pieces of research that have been carried out between Thebes, Illinois, and the mouth of the Arkansas River: for extended discussions see Dye and Cox (1990), Morse and Morse (1983), and McNutt (1996). Our choice of what to include is highly selective, but we believe it accurately reflects the history of archaeological research in the region.

Because the unique character of the Mississippi Alluvial Valley intrudes into this history, we preface the historical account with a brief description of the physical environment. Analysis of the landscape has long been of importance to archaeologists working in the central Mississippi Valley, and several contributors to this volume continue this tradition and examine selected features of the landscape and the differential use of those features by prehistoric humans. We focus here on only one component of the physical environment, namely, fluvial regimes. These not only structured prehistoric use of the region but also have had profound effects on the archaeological record itself.

Physical Setting

The modern Mississippi River hugs the eastern margin of the valley from Thebes southward, moving out of sight of the loess bluffs only south of Memphis (Figure 1-1). A major feature of the central valley—one that sets it apart in striking fashion from the lower valley—is Crowley's Ridge—a loess-capped Tertiary monadnock with a north-south trend that divides the alluvial valley into two segments. The portion between the ridge and the Mississippi River comprises a series of lowlands (e.g., the Cairo Lowland and the Little River Lowland) collectively referred to as the Eastern Lowlands; similarly, the portion between Crowley's Ridge and the Ozark Highlands comprises several lowlands (e.g., Morehouse Lowland) that collectively are known as the Western Lowlands (Figure 1-1). The Eastern Lowlands cover the greater percentage of the St. Francis River basin—an extensive drainage area that extends from the northern terminus of the Mississippi Alluvial Valley south to Helena, Arkansas. Except for a small area in the extreme northern Western Lowlands that is drained by the St. Francis, drainage west of Crowley's Ridge is controlled by numerous tributaries of the White River (Figure 1-1).

The kinds and ages of the various sediments in the central valley (Figure 1-2) are products of where the ancestral Mississippi and Ohio rivers happened to be at various times during the Pleistocene and early Holocene—of channel positions that in large part were controlled by the enormous volumes of water those rivers carried into the embayment during interstadials. Harold Fisk, in his monumental *Geological Investigation of the Alluvial Valley of the Lower Mississippi River* (1944), attempted to provide a history of the valley by mapping and dating all physiographic features from just north of Cairo, Illinois, south to the Gulf of Mexico. Although Fisk produced a series of excellent maps of the valley, some of his channel reconstructions were speculative, and his chronological positioning of the channels, in terms of both absolute and relative time, was based on faulty assumptions (Autin et al. 1991; Saucier 1981). More-recent mapping of portions of the valley (e.g., Saucier 1994; Saucier and Snead 1989) (Figure 1-2) has modified Fisk's sequence of events and greatly altered the timing he suggested for those events.

Fluvial Regimes

Understanding the geomorphological history of the Mississippi Alluvial Valley is predicated on recognizing the presence of two different fluvial regimes, the braided stream and the meander-belt stream, which left dissimilar evidence of their history across the landscape. That evidence, in the form of sediments and landforms, is important from an archaeological standpoint, since knowledge of how the landscape changed through time provides clues not only as to where prehistoric materials might be found but also as to where they might *not* be found. For example, recent analysis of prehistoric-site locations in Pemiscot County, Missouri, documented that few archaeological remains dating to the pre-Christian era have been found in the eastern half of the county, not because the area was uninhabited during that period but because the processes associated with an active floodplain have either removed or buried them (O'Brien 1994b). Archaic (pre–ca. 600 B.C.) and Early Woodland (600–250 B.C.) remains that are found occur on topographic highs that have escaped removal by channel erosion or burial from overbank deposits. This pattern characterizes the situation in much of the central Mississippi Valley.

THE BRAIDED-STREAM REGIME

Extensive evidence of braided-stream courses, which are complex features composed of master channels and an interlocking series of gathering channels

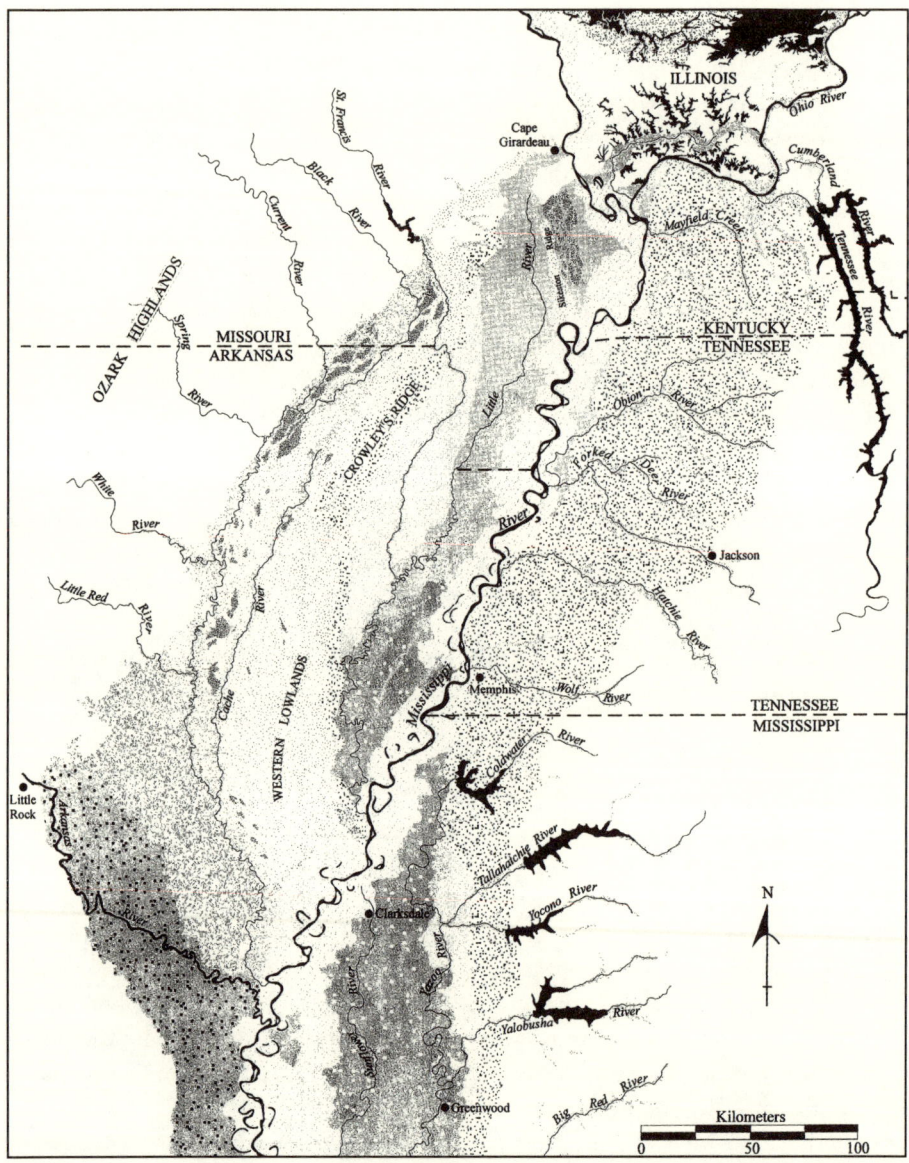

Figure 1-2. Map of the central Mississippi River valley showing the distribution of different kinds of surface sediments. The structure of the valley and the ages of the sediments, with the exception of those comprising Crowley's Ridge, are the result of varied positions of the ancestral Mississippi and Ohio rivers during the Pleistocene (1.65 million–10,900 years ago) and Holocene (after 10,900 years ago) epochs. Crowley's Ridge is a Tertiary-age monadnock capped by more-recent loess. In general, older sediments occur at greater distance from the modern channel of the Mississippi River. One ancient surface that figures prominently in several chapters in this volume is the Malden Plain, shown as the light-gray area abutting most of the eastern base of Crowley's Ridge. (Map after Lineback 1979.)

HOLOCENE

Water - open water streams, rivers, lakes, and reservoirs.

Recent Alluvium - Recent alluvium undifferentiated on smaller streams [Ha].

Modern Mississippi River Meander Belt - Area of channel deposition related to lateral migration of recent Mississippi River courses; a complex of four older meander belts are mapped as the Mississippi River Meander Belt Complex [Hmm1] {c}.

Mississippi River Meander Belt Complex - Areas of channel deposition related to lateral migration of past Mississippi River courses; a complex of five meander belts are recognized but only the Modern Mississippi River Meander Belt is distinguished from this complex [Hmm2-5].

Arkansas River Meander Belt Complex - Areas of channel deposition related to lateral migration of past and present Arkansas River courses; a complex of seven meander belts are recognized but not mapped individually [Hma1-7].

Wisconsin Lake Deposits - Areas of lacustrine deposition in proglacial lakes and slack-water lakes in valleys tributary to major river valleys; deposits in older lakes of a thin to medium cover of silt (Richland Loess or Peoria Loess); identified as Carmi Member of Equality Formation {ec}.

PLEISTOCENE

Wisconsin Glacial Outwash - Includes well-sorted and well-bedded sand and gravel; deposits in valleys; mostly glacial outwash in former valley trains and terrace remnants of former valley trains; generally has a thin covering of Richland or Peoria Loess; identified as Mackinaw Member of Henry Formation {hm}.

Late Wisconsin Valley Train - Level 1 - Terraced outwash deposits of braided streams deposited during the late Wisconsin glaciation; Level 1 is younger and lower in elevation than Level 2 [Pvl1].

Late Wisconsin Valley Train - Level 2 - Terraced outwash deposits of braided streams deposited during the late Wisconsin glaciation; Level 2 is older and higher in elevation than Level 1 [Pvl2].

Sand Dune Fields - Eolian sand deposits on valley trains [Ps].

Early Wisconsin Valley Train - Terraced outwash deposits of braided streams deposited during the early Wisconsin glaciation; five levels are recognized but not mapped individually [Pvel-5].

Prairie Complex - A diverse depositional sequence of the Mississippi River, its tributaries, and coastal plain streams; includes terraces, fluvial (meander belt and braided stream), colluvial, estuarine, deltaic, and marine units deposited over a considerable length of time during the late Pleistocene (Wisconsin to Sangamon) [Pp].

Illinoian Glacial Till - Areas of hard, compact sandy till with sand and gravel; identified as the Vandalia Till Member of the Glasford Formation {gv}.

TERTIARY

Upland Complex - Fluvial deposits from both glacial and non-glacial sources [Pu].

Tertiary and Older Formations - Undifferentiated [T].

Note: Square brackets [ ] contain designations of Saucier and Sneed (1989) while curvilinear brackets { } contain designations of Lineback (1979).

and dispersal channels, is found in the Western Lowlands (Royall et al. 1991; Saucier 1974; Smith and Saucier 1971) as the result of the ancestral Mississippi River and in the Little River Lowland as the result of both the ancestral Ohio and Mississippi rivers. Braided surfaces, or valley trains (Figure 1-2), comprise outwash sediments derived from midcontinental glaciers that formed throughout the Pleistocene (Autin et al. 1991; Saucier 1974; Teller 1987, 1990). The oldest exposed valley-train surface in the Western Lowlands is located east of the extreme southwestern edge of Crowley's Ridge and probably dates in excess of 120,000 years (Autin et al. 1991; Rutledge et al. 1985) (Figure 1-2). Older braided-stream deposits in the Eastern Lowlands are (1) a narrow strip along the base of the northern half of Crowley's Ridge and (2) Sikeston Ridge, a discontinuous projection southward from just east of the Bell City–Oran Gap in Crowley's Ridge to New Madrid, Missouri (Figure 1-1).

A radiocarbon chronology of sediments from corings in Powers Fort Swale near the base of the Ozark Escarpment in Butler County, Missouri (Figure 1-1), establishes the dating of the permanent shift of the Mississippi River to the east of Crowley's Ridge (Royall et al. 1991). In the swale, "the last deposition of fine sand layers by 11,500 yr [ago] marks the termination of glacial meltwater flow through the Western Lowlands, after which full meltwater flow was funneled east of Crowley's Ridge" (Royall et al. 1991:167–68).

At least two northeast-southwest-trending braided surfaces connected with the displaced Mississippi River are exposed in the Morehouse and Little River lowlands. The more western of the two, the Malden Plain, extends in an arc shape from the base of Crowley's Ridge at Dexter, Missouri, to near Levesque, Arkansas, a distance of approximately 175 kilometers (Figure 1–1). Primary drainage of the surface today is provided by the St. Francis River. The eastern braided surface extends from the northern wall of the alluvial valley, through the Bell City–Oran Gap, to Marked Tree, Arkansas, a distance of approximately 170 kilometers (Figure 1-1). When the Mississippi River shifted its course east of Crowley's Ridge and began to drain the Little River Lowland, it created its own outwash fan and braided drainage pattern, in the process reworking earlier sediments and eradicating previous northeast-southwest-trending Ohio River channels. After the Mississippi again changed course and moved into the channel occupied by the Ohio River (see below), underfit streams such as the Little River developed to drain the abandoned braided-stream surface in a southerly pattern. But as Saucier (1964:6 [unpaginated]) noted, "The establishment of the [Mississippi] river in its present meander belt did not mean the end of Mississippi River sedimentation in the [area east of Crowley's Ridge], however. For long periods of time, the Little River system served as an outlet for [Mississippi River] floodwaters that entered the upper end. . . . Its well-developed natural levees and other meander belt features attest to its role in carrying sediment-laden floodwaters of the Mississippi River."

East of Crowley's Ridge, the braided-stream deposits have been partially

Figure 1-3. In situ mandible of a Pleistocene-age llama (*Palaeolama mirifica*), Buffalo Slough, Dunklin County, Missouri. Virtually the entire skeleton, save the cranium, was discovered by Woodrow Long of Senath, Missouri, after dredging by the U.S. Army Corps of Engineers in 1990. The llama was excavated by Russell W. Graham of the Illinois State Museum in 1990. Graham (1990:207) notes that previous to this discovery, the stout-legged llama was known only from the Gulf Coastal Plain of Florida and Texas and one site in southern California. Parts of at least two mastodons (*Mammut americanum*) were found by local people farther south along Buffalo Slough. A nearly complete mastodon skeleton is reported to have been found within a kilometer of the *Palaeolama* location during another dredging episode in the 1950s. (Photograph courtesy of W. Long and R. W. Graham.)

eroded by the meandering of the modern Mississippi (see below). In the northern part of the valley, surface sediments of the Malden Plain (Figure 1-1) comprise braided-stream deposits that are somewhat younger (less than ca. 13,300 years ago) than those of the Western Lowlands and thus lack any substantial loess (Guccione and Rutledge 1990; Guccione et al. 1988). The large braided-stream channels, which contain older sediments, are well known locally for their terminal Pleistocene fauna (e.g., mastodon [*Mammut americanum*] and llama [*Palaeolama mirifica*]) (Figure 1-3); the uppermost part of the fill in one such channel, Buffalo Slough in Dunklin County, Missouri, yielded an uncorrected radiocarbon age of 10,890 × ±130 years ago (D. F. Morse, pers. comm., 1990). Inasmuch as the surface of the braided-stream deposits has a steeper gradient than the surface of those created by the meandering Mississippi, the erosional escarpment that forms the boundary between the two is more marked in the north (ca. 5 meters high) and gradually disappears in northeastern Arkansas.

Because the Malden Plain blocked access to the St. Francis for Mississippi floodwaters, a vast backswamp developed in the Little River Lowlands (Figure 1-1) so that while this area is shallowly underlain by braided-stream deposits, the surface deposits are much younger (less than 6000 years old). Surface deposits consist of uniform, fine-grained "gumbos," broken only by the natural levees of the usually incompetent drainage (e.g., Little River and Pemiscot Bayou) (Figure 1-4). In northern Arkansas, this featureless terrain is replaced by ridge-and-swale topography characteristic of recent meander belts (Figure 1-5). Thus, in the northern half of the region, the Western Lowlands and Crowley's Ridge provide surfaces that were exposed in the Late Pleistocene, whereas the Malden Plain provides a slightly later surface. The ages of meander-belt surfaces are highly variable, but except for local monadnocks, they are considerably younger, of mid-Holocene age.

THE MEANDER-BELT REGIME

The second great diversion event occurred when the Mississippi River breached the Commerce Hills near Thebes, Illinois, and captured the Ohio River south of Cairo, Illinois. Several minimum ages of this last movement east by the Mississippi are available (Figure 1-1), based on radiocarbon chronology of sediments: 8810 years ago from the Old Field site, located in the Bell City–Oran Gap (King and Allen 1977); 9050 years ago from Big Lake, Arkansas (Guccione 1987; Guccione et al. 1988; Scott and Aasen 1987); and 8530 years ago from Pemiscot Bayou just south of the Missouri-Arkansas line (Guccione 1987; Guccione et al. 1988; Scott and Aasen 1987). Saucier (1981:16) stated "emphatically that at no time in the last 9000 years have the Mississippi and Ohio rivers flowed in separate channels farther south than a point only 16 km south of Cairo, Illinois."

After the Mississippi River began flowing through Thebes Gap, the combined Mississippi-Ohio converted to a meandering regime, the result of disequilibrium between sediment load and discharge brought about by a change in sediment type (from coarse, glacially derived sands and gravels to a mixed load) (Saucier 1964, 1968, 1970). The exceedingly complex history of the Mississippi River meander belt is a result of 9000 years of channel migrations across the floodplain, in which older channels were abandoned during periods of flooding, older channels were cut off by newer ones, and new levees were built up over previous levees and channels.

Previous Archaeological Investigations

The authors of the following chapters present detailed background of their particular geographic areas relative to previous archaeological investigations; here we examine in general fashion several methodological issues and how prehistorians over the past century and a half have approached examination of the

Figure 1-4. Aerial photograph (1:20,000 scale) taken in 1950 of southern Dunklin County, Missouri, showing the contact between the Malden Plain (A) and the Little River Lowland (B and C) to the east. The terminal Pleistocene-age Malden Plain clearly shows the ancient braided-stream deposits and topography; the Little River Lowland, underlain by the same material as the surface of the Malden Plain, is veneered by Holocene-age backwater organic, clayey sediments that give the lowland a uniform appearance except where Little River channels and natural levees (C) and monadnocks of the earlier braided-stream material (visible as light spots near the western boundary) poke through the veneer. The lines extending from the *upper right* to *lower center* are part of the extensive system of drainage ditches completed early in the twentieth century. (Photograph courtesy of the U.S. Soil Conservation Service.)

archaeological record in one of the archaeologically richest areas in the United States. Because the majority of authors in this book either focus specifically on southeastern Missouri or mention various sites in the region, we use early investigations there as examples of the kinds of work that was done throughout the central Mississippi Valley. Readers interested in particular aspects of research should consult Dunnell (1985a), Dye and Cox (1990), Klinger (1977a), McNutt (1996), Meltzer and Dunnell (1992), O'Brien (1994a), and Smith (1985, 1990a, 1990b). Those interested in more in-depth coverage of the history of re-

Figure 1-5. Aerial photograph (1:20,000 scale) taken in 1967 showing ridge-and-swale topography in Cross County, Arkansas, that is typical of the modern Mississippi River meander belt. The St. Francis River is in the northwest corner. (Photograph courtesy of the U.S. Soil Conservation Service.)

search in the central Mississippi Valley should see Morse and Morse (1983), O'Brien (1996), and Phillips (1970).

The Nineteenth Century

Two issues dominated Americanist archaeology in the nineteenth century and spawned an array of fieldwork designed to address them. The first was the antiquity of human beings in North America—an issue that, while of considerable interest, does not concern us here since it played only a minor role in the Mississippi Valley. The second issue was the authorship of the tens of thousands of mounds and other earthworks characteristic of the trans-Appalachian region. Explorations conducted in southeastern Missouri proliferated in the last quarter of the nineteenth century. For example (Figure 1-6), Horatio Rust (1877) excavated several mounds at Sandy Woods (Teltser, Chapter 7) and sites at unknown locations; Caleb Croswell (1878) worked at Matthews and Sandy Woods; Conant (1878) excavated at Sikeston; and J. W. Foster (1864) and Thomas Beckwith (1887) excavated mounds at Beckwith's Fort. Lilbourn, the largest of the southeastern-Missouri palisaded mound centers, was excavated by G. C. Swallow of the University of Missouri (Figure 1-6). He made brief reports of what he recovered (1858) and described his excavations in a manuscript that accompanied his artifact collection when it was donated to the Peabody Museum (Harvard) (see Putnam 1875a, 1875b).[1] The work of Rust, Croswell, Conant, Beckwith, Swallow, and others was conducted on a fairly large scale, but it produced little in the way of useful information concerning the archaeological record of the sites. With few exceptions, artifact descriptions were vague and intrasite provenience almost never was reported.

THE ACADEMY OF SCIENCE OF ST. LOUIS MOUND SURVEY

There was, however, one major exception to collecting expeditions organized for fun and profit, and its product stands in direct contrast to the other results. In December 1876, the Academy of Science of St. Louis reorganized its committee on mound exploration into a formal archaeology section, and four years later the unit released a two-section report on five large mound centers in and around New Madrid County. The first section, "Archaeological Remains in Southeastern Missouri," was written by W. B. Potter (1880), and the second section, "The Ancient Pottery of Southeastern Missouri," was written by Dr. Edward Evers (1880). Potter's maps and descriptions of the mound sites—Sikeston, East Lake,[2] Matthews, Lilbourn, and Sandy Woods (Figure 1-6)—are unduplicated in terms of what they tell us about the configuration of large Middle Mississippian-period fortified communities in the region. As Teltser points out in Chapter 7, Potter's maps in some cases provide the only evidence that the communities were fortified, since erosion and agricultural activities have subsequently obliterated surface evidence of embankments and ditches.

14 | O'Brien and Dunnell

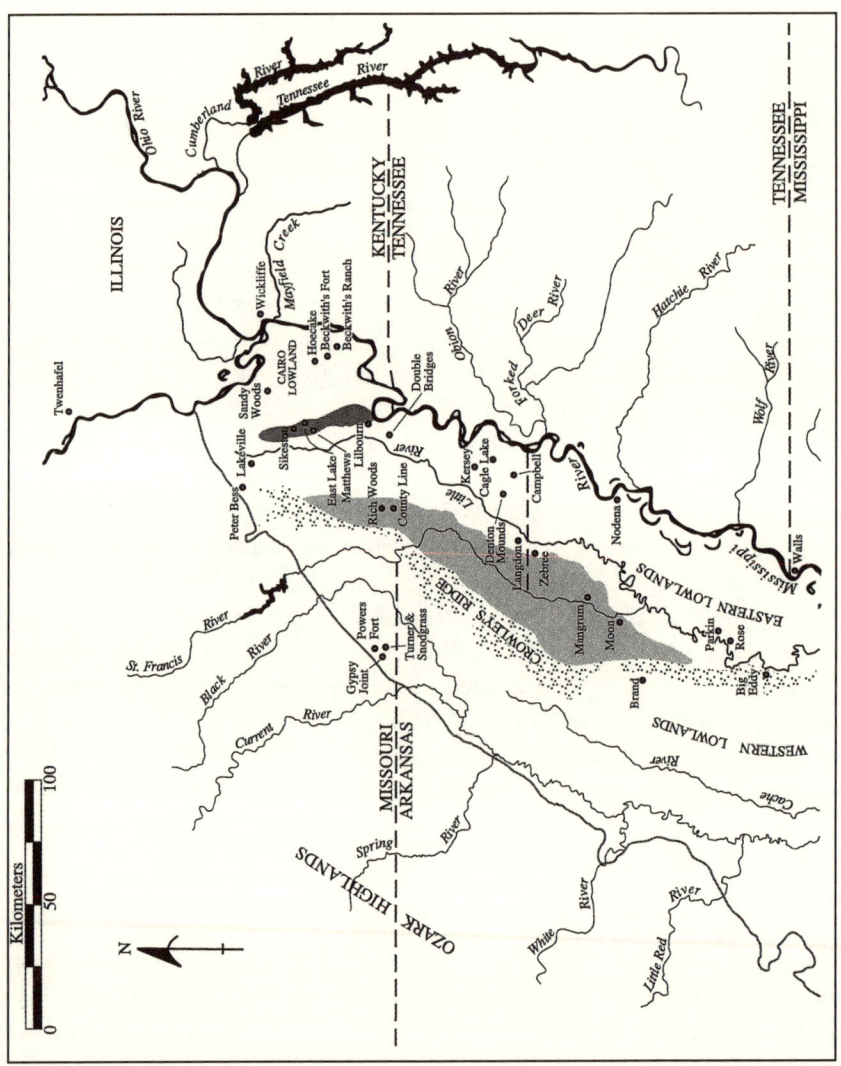

Figure 1-6. Map of a portion of the central Mississippi River valley showing locations of archaeological sites mentioned in the text.

Potter's report is a study that contrasts with others of the period, not only in terms of what is contained in his short monograph but also in terms of what it does not contain. The purpose of the reports by the archaeology section, which is stated in the preface (unattributed, but probably authored by Potter, the section head), is clear: "These papers [Potter's and Evers's] are intended not so much to express the theories and opinions of individual members of the Section, as to be the means of furnishing to those interested in the archaeology of the country, a reliable statement of facts connected with the occurrence of prehistoric remains in this important region."

THE DIVISION OF MOUND EXPLORATION

The Bureau of (American) Ethnology was founded within the Smithsonian Institution in 1879, and John Wesley Powell was selected as director. The Division of Mound Exploration was formed within the bureau in 1881, and the following year Cyrus Thomas was appointed as its head. Thomas published the "Report on the Mound Explorations of the Bureau of Ethnology" in 1894, which details the mound explorations carried out by members of his crews as they worked their way over two dozen states in the Midwest and East. Information demanded by Thomas of his crews included "topography of the immediate locality, the form, characters, and dimensions of the works and their relations to one another" (Thomas 1894:21). Diagrams of excavations often accompanied the descriptions, and in rare instances Thomas included drawings of artifacts.

The Twentieth Century

It is difficult to summarize archaeological work that was going on in the greater southeastern United States during the initial decades of the twentieth century and not discuss the work of Clarence B. Moore, who for a quarter century or so—from the 1890s to the second decade of the twentieth century— explored various rivers and bayous in search of burial mounds, in the process excavating several thousand skeletons and recovering thousands of ceramic vessels and other artifacts. He sponsored his own fieldwork and underwrote the production costs of twenty reports dealing with the excavations, which appeared in the *Journal of the Academy of Natural Sciences of Philadelphia*. The reports are rather sketchy, but the accompanying field photographs and artifact illustrations are excellent.

Moore spent four field seasons between 1908 and 1916 in the central Mississippi Valley, exploring mounds along the Arkansas, Yazoo, Sunflower, St. Francis, White, and Black rivers, as well as those along the Mississippi (Moore 1910, 1916). Northeastern Arkansas, with its prominent Late Mississippian-period mounds and accompanying cemeteries, was already well known for its beautiful pottery, and that region received the bulk of Moore's attention. He did, however, spend a few weeks in 1916 exploring several mound groups in Pemiscot, New Madrid, and Mississippi counties in southeastern Missouri. Moore's major work in Missouri was conducted at what he termed the Davis place (now known as Double Bridges) (Figure 1-6), a mound group on the north bank of Portage Open Bay (Moore called it Open Bayou), a crevasse channel of the Mississippi River that forms the dividing line between Pemiscot and New Madrid counties.

Much of what we know about prehistoric material culture in the central

Mississippi Valley stems from Moore's investigations. His work, along with the pottery treatises of William Henry Holmes (1886, 1903), called attention to the region and formed the basis for many of the projects initiated several decades later. Morse and Morse (1983:21) noted that "it has become almost traditional to deplore the work of Moore, because of his emphasis on recovery of fine specimens from burials," but they also pointed out that he kept excavation records, cataloged his materials, and donated his collections to museums. In many regards, Moore's treatment of artifacts was ahead of its time. For example, he occasionally had physical and chemical analyses done to identify materials—what we might term the earliest American archaeometry.

Little archaeological activity took place in the northern half of the central Mississippi Valley in the four decades following Moore's brief explorations—a situation that was not paralleled in areas to the south and east. If anything, the 1930s and 1940s were the heyday of archaeology in the southeastern United States, fueled in large part by the interest of avocationalists (see below) but to an even larger degree by the sudden availability of federal funds to salvage archaeological remains threatened with destruction by large public projects, chiefly impoundments on the Tennessee River and its tributaries (see Lyon 1996 for an excellent overview).

Lack of professional involvement did not mean that no fieldwork at all was done in the region. If anything, the 1930s heralded the emergence of amateur archaeology in the central Mississippi Valley. Three important sites were the focus of activities by avocational archaeologists during the 1930s—Wickliffe, in Ballard County, Kentucky, and Upper Nodena and Middle Nodena, in Mississippi County, Arkansas (Figure 1-6). Throughout the decade, Fain King excavated in and around the five mounds at Wickliffe, roofing over exposed burials in order to use them as a lure for tourists to visit the "Ancient Buried City." King published no documentation of his work, though that unfortunate situation has been partly remedied by Kit Wesler's recent reports (e.g., Wesler 1991). Between 1932 and 1941, Dr. James K. Hampson excavated portions of Upper Nodena and Middle Nodena, in the process inviting the University of Arkansas Museum and the Alabama Museum of Natural History to join him. More than 1200 graves and some sixty-five house patterns were uncovered during the course of the work, but except for Morse's (1989) summary of the excavations and Powell's (1989) analysis of some of the human remains, no report exists on these important late prehistoric sites.

THE LOWER MISSISSIPPI ALLUVIAL VALLEY SURVEY

The lull in professional attention to the vast archaeological resources in the valley ended in 1939 with the initiation of an ambitious survey-and-excavation project that was to leave a lasting mark not only on the archaeology of the central Mississippi Valley but also on Americanist archaeology generally. The final report, entitled *Archaeological Survey in the Lower Mississippi Alluvial Valley, 1940–1947* and co-authored by Phillips, Ford, and Griffin (1951), may well be the most important work relative to the archaeology of the entire southeastern United States produced between 1941 and 1960 (Dunnell 1985a). Because of the volume's centrality to the growth of the culture-history paradigm in general and because it set the stage for almost all subsequent fieldwork conducted in the Mississippi Valley to date, we discuss it here in some detail.

The authors of the report were explicit about the objectives of the project:

> The purpose of the Survey was to investigate the northern two-thirds of the alluvial valley of the Lower Mississippi River—roughly from the mouth of the Ohio to Vicksburg, Mississippi, an area long regarded as one of the principal blind spots in the archaeology of the Southeast. This is not altogether due to lack of work in the area, or to the character of such work, but rather to the fact that it had so far failed to reveal anything concerning the earlier pre-Mississippian cultures. The need for a comprehensive survey had been repeatedly voiced at Midwestern and Southeastern conferences and various suggestions made for carrying out such a project. (Phillips et al. 1951:v)

During the course of the nine-year project (1940–1948), crews spent a total of seven months in the field locating and mapping sites, making surface collections, and conducting test excavations. The amount of data compiled for the final report was, and still is, truly impressive. It would be difficult to find a more comprehensive discussion of ceramic types—Griffin's specialty as director of the Ceramic Repository at the University of Michigan—or a more thorough correlation of ceramic types by excavation level—Phillips's specialty. The most significant contribution, in fact a legacy, of the Phillips, Ford, and Griffin report is the extraordinary number of ceramic types that were described, most for the first time. More than a decade earlier, Southeastern archaeologists had come to some agreement on how pottery types were to be formulated and described (e.g., Ford and Griffin 1937, 1938), but most of the types that were beginning to appear in print prior to 1951 were not applicable to the central Mississippi Valley.

A critical break with earlier approaches to pottery types is represented by three facets of the work of Phillips, Ford, and Griffin. First, although they remained ambiguous about what pottery types were "types of," similar to others of the time (e.g., Newell and Krieger 1949), the classification of Phillips, Ford, and Griffin was designed to be applied to sherds as opposed to pots. Second, through Ford's seriations, their work was quantitative rather than qualitative (Lyman et al. 1997; O'Brien and Lyman n.d.). Third, they included surface collections in their analysis instead of focusing entirely on excavated materials—again, following a tradition begun in the Mississippi Valley by Ford (e.g., 1936).

Phillips, Ford, and Griffin (1951:426) acknowledged the usefulness of their typological system: "Our classification cannot be too bad or it would not have produced the consistent patterning of types through time that is shown in the seriation and stratigraphic analyses"—but they also acknowledged dissatisfaction:

> The archaeologist who thinks he has achieved a final classification of anything is a rare and probably untrustworthy individual. Most of the shortcomings of our classification have been fully exposed in the type descriptions. Our guess is that very few of our types will stand up when more and better material is available. Many of them will break down into more specialized groups, a few (we may hope) will be combined into more general groups. It is not likely that the total number of types will be reduced. The outlook for the Southeast as a whole, so long as present typological methods remain in favor, is not pleasant to contemplate. Where we are now counting types in tens, they will be counted in hundreds. (Phillips et al. 1951:426)

The authors did a remarkable job of predicting future developments in the archaeology of the central Mississippi Valley.

Types were recognized by Phillips, Ford, and Griffin (1951:64) as composites of various separate characters—paste, vessel form, surface treatment, and decoration—and the authors reasoned that each character had its own history (see Ford 1938; Ford and Griffin 1937, 1938). Just as selecting the "characters" around which to construct a typological system was viewed as a trial-and-error exercise, so too was the decision about where to draw the line between one type and another. Ford supplied a rather sophisticated, if characteristically cryptic, rationalization of pottery classification:

> Each community that had reached a certain level of sophistication in pottery-making will be found to have been maintaining side by side several different vessel styles [read *types*]. . . . Between these centers, styles vary and trend toward those of other centers in rough proportion to the distances involved, subject of course to ethnic distributions and geographic factors. Thus we have in mind the concept of a continuously evolving regional pottery tradition, showing a more or less parallel development in and around a number of centers, each of which employs a number of distinct but related styles, each style in turn being in process of change both areally and temporally. With this remarkably unstable material, we set out to fashion a key to the prehistory of the region. Faced with this three-dimensional flow, which seldom if ever exhibits "natural" segregation, and being obliged to reduce it to some sort of manageable form, we arbitrarily cut it into units. Such *created units of the ceramic continuum* are called *pottery types*. (Phillips et al. 1951:62–63)

This was, and in many respects still is, the philosophy behind creation of the ceramic types used to bring chronological order to the vast archaeological record of the central Mississippi Valley. Phillips, Ford, and Griffin clearly recognized the inherent problems in the typological system they constructed and constantly warned archaeologists of the dangers in blindly accepting the system. They also provided one of the most insightful comments on ceramic typologies ever written:

> Exigencies of language require us to think and talk about pottery types as though they had some sort of independent existence. "This sherd *is* Baytown Plain." Upon sufficient repetition of this statement, the concept Baytown Plain takes on a massive solidity. The time comes when we are ready to fight for dear old Baytown. What we have to try to remember is that the statement really means something like this: "This sherd sufficiently resembles material which *for the time being* we have elected to call Baytown Plain." Frequent repetition of this and similar exorcisms we have found to be extremely salutary during the classificatory activities. (Phillips et al. 1951:66)

Unfortunately, as Fox documents in Chapter 2, archaeologists since the time Phillips, Ford, and Griffin published their monograph have forgotten to repeat the "exorcism" quoted above. Types, which Phillips, Ford, and Griffin (especially Ford) viewed as arbitrary constructions, came to be treated as "real," empirical, units that had been discovered as opposed to created.

With the publication of *Archaeological Survey in the Lower Mississippi Alluvial Valley,* Americanist archaeology in general, and certainly that of the Mississippi Valley specifically, was elevated to a different level. The authors were forthright, often blunt, about problems not only with their data—for example, biases in the sherd collections—but also with their analytical methods. They dramatically overhauled the chronological position of archaeological cultures, especially that of Hopewell, which was pushed further back in time so that there were at least 500 years between it and the beginning of the Mississippian period—enough time in which to fit, at least in the central Mississippi Valley, the Late Baytown (Woodland) period. Hopewell itself no longer was thought of as a panregional phenomenon but rather, as Griffin (1946) had earlier suggested, as one of several Middle Woodland–period manifestations. For the Mississippi Valley sequence, Phillips, Ford, and Griffin used the designation Early Baytown for the Middle Woodland period, aligning it with Marksville to the south (Ford 1935a, 1935b, 1936; Ford and Willey 1940, 1941).

If it did nothing else, the massive synthesis compiled by Phillips, Ford, and Griffin indeed demonstrated that "the archaeology of the Lower Mississippi Valley, and eastern North America generally, is even more interesting, and perhaps more important" (Phillips et al. 1951:457) than even the authors had realized previously. Griffin (1985:7) later noted that his collaboration with Phillips and Ford was fruitful, "even if some lemons appeared in the publication." Perhaps because of the amount of time they spent together, Phillips, Ford, and Griffin each knew the methodological strengths and weaknesses of the other two as well as what their individual biases were. They were clear in their disagreements, which gives their volume its unique flavor. However, investigators who came after them adopted their conclusions apparently without reading the disagreements, in the process either ignoring or failing to consider warnings plainly registered by one or more of the trio. What had started life as a well-thought-out, if sometimes internally inconsistent, methodology became a disjointed series of techniques often poorly applied.

CONTINUATION OF THE ALLUVIAL VALLEY SURVEY

The volume by Phillips, Ford, and Griffin was followed by a number of studies that extended coverage of their survey area. In 1949 the University of Michigan established the Central Mississippi Valley Archaeological Survey to investigate the area between the mouth of the Illinois River and approximately the Missouri-Arkansas line (Griffin and Spaulding 1952). Five years later, Stephen Williams completed a doctoral dissertation (Yale University) entitled *An Archeological Study of the Mississippian Culture in Southeast Missouri* (Williams 1954), which was a compilation of information gathered during several field seasons of surface collection and excavation in several areas of southeastern Missouri, undertaken as an outgrowth of the Griffin-Spaulding project. In the course of his analysis, Williams established a series of time-space units (discussed below) that as Morse and Morse (1983:27) noted "are the basis for those still used in southeast Missouri today," just as Phillips, Ford, and Griffin's had been for the region to the south. Thus, by 1954, the entire central Mississippi Valley was integrated theoretically.

Stimulated by Ford (1936), chronologies based largely on percentage stratigraphy and correlation of excavated levels at different sites (Ford 1935b; Ford and Quimby 1945; Ford and Willey 1940) began to appear, so that by the 1940s any system that did not take time into account was rapidly becoming anachronistic. The Lower Mississippi Alluvial Valley Survey provided the context and much of the substance of the new system, which was based on phase recognition (see below). Seriations were limited to "local" areas (e.g., Ford 1952; Phillips et al. 1951); thus, in terms of cultural content, the implicit organization was by period *and* area. Williams's (1954) treatise was the first to incorporate the new system per se. To Phillips, Ford, and Griffin, periods were arbitrary segments of the temporal continuum. However, without Ford's materialist influence, Williams adopted Phillips's essentialist ontology and relied on typological comparison in order to create phases. Soon after, Williams's (1954) phases came to be viewed as "real" rather than simply tools of description created by the archaeologist.

Phillips's essentialist stance was laid out in two papers in *American Anthropologist* (Phillips and Willey 1953; Willey and Phillips 1955) that later were revised and combined as *Method and Theory in American Archaeology* (Willey and Phillips 1958). The papers, and later the book, consolidated archaeological practice, in essence providing a cultural-historical cookbook for carving up the archaeological record in terms of time, space, and form. Willey and Phillips added time and space to cultural content, thus changing the older *focus* (McKern 1939, 1940) into *phase*, which they defined as "an archaeological unit possessing traits sufficiently characteristic to distinguish it from all other units similarly conceived, whether of the same or other cultures or civilizations, spatially limited to the order of magnitude of a locality or region and chronologically limited to a brief span of time" (Willey and Phillips 1958:22).

Willey and Phillips (1958:23–24) pointed out that a phase has "no appropriate scale independent of the cultural situation in which it is applied. . . . [P]hases may have very considerable and highly variable spatial and temporal dimensions." At one level, phases are "practical and intelligible unit[s] of study" (Willey and Phillips 1958:22), but, as Fox points out in Chapter 2, once they take on lives of their own, they are difficult to modify. One of the problems in central Mississippi Valley archaeology has been the incredible growth in phase names since the 1950s—a growth that has not followed the slow, deliberate procedure envisioned by Willey and Phillips. Instead, the nomenclature has grown like Topsy, with the vexing result that the literature is replete with phase names, the majority of which have lasted only a short time before being replaced.

Williams applied the initial formulation of Phillips and Willey (1953) to his materials from southeastern Missouri. Assignments of individual components (exclusively sites) to the phases were based almost entirely on the occurrence of sherds, which Williams either placed in the types described by Phillips, Ford, and Griffin (1951) or created new types for. Williams used his interpretation of the Phillips, Ford, and Griffin typological system to introduce numerous ceramic types not previously described. These were important additions to the list of types because they were in most cases northern variants not recognized in the survey of Phillips, Ford, and Griffin. Williams's essentialist thinking on phases, as on pottery types, was clear: "the O'Bryan Ridge phase is not considered *the first phase in the region,* but since only very scattered remains seem to indicate a prior occupation, they will be discussed later" (Williams 1954:31; emphasis added). Here Williams was referring to a phase as a real entity, comprising real artifacts, as opposed to an arbitrary construct.

Williams, like Phillips, Ford, and Griffin, might not have intended his phases and types to remain unrefined, but archaeologists for the most part accepted his designations uncritically. The constructions became so ingrained in archaeological thinking over the next several decades that they became the centerpieces of two syntheses of regional chronology for the central Mississippi River valley, that by Phillips (1970) and that by Morse and Morse (1983). The first serious challenge to the validity of the central Mississippi Valley phases was by Gregory Fox (1992; see also O'Brien and Fox 1994a), almost four decades after publication of Williams's dissertation. Fox continues the challenge in

Chapter 2. No serious challenge to the pottery types has appeared, in large part because they do what Ford and others intended them to do—tell time—and, for the most part, they do it fairly well.

THE GENESIS OF FEDERAL ARCHAEOLOGY

As noted earlier, Depression-era federal archaeology had limited impact in the central Mississippi Valley. This was not so with the second iteration, however, which was ushered in by federal highway-construction programs in the 1960s. The federal highway salvage program was initiated in New Mexico in 1954 (Jennings 1985; Ritchie 1961), and two years later the Federal Aid Highway Act was passed, which authorized states to expend federal funds on archaeological surveys and testing in advance of interstate-highway construction. The first project in Missouri was a study of archaeological sites in two southeastern Missouri counties, New Madrid and Pemiscot, that lay in the proposed corridor of Interstate 55, one of the major midcontinental north-south arteries. Thirty sites were found in the corridor, and two of them were tested during 1964 and 1965 (Marshall 1965, 1966). One of these, Kersey (O'Brien and Marshall 1994) (Figure 1-6), provided the basis of much of what is known of early Mississippian-period life in the meander-belt portion of the central Mississippi River valley.

Beginning in the 1960s, archaeologists (e.g., Ford et al. 1972; McGimsey and Davis 1977; Medford 1972; Williams 1967) became concerned about the increased destruction of sites in the central Mississippi Valley through agricultural activities. The destruction of archaeological sites in southeastern Missouri and northeastern Arkansas (McGimsey and Davis 1968; Medford 1972) has been of massive proportions, with little nonurban land remaining unaltered. Compounding the problem in southeastern Missouri has been the excavation of a complex system of large ditches to drain the St. Francis–Little River basin. Although not readily quantified, the magnitude of the damage to the archaeological record has been immense. McGimsey and Davis (1968) estimated that by the middle of the 1960s more than a quarter of the known archaeological sites in the Arkansas portion of the Mississippi Valley had been destroyed by land leveling. The effect on the low-density nonsite record (Teltser, Chapter 7) must have been equally as great.

Between 1966 and 1968, the University of Missouri, under the Inter-Agency Archaeological Salvage Program, conducted a salvage operation in three Missouri counties in the alluvial valley, Mississippi, New Madrid, and Pemiscot. Twenty-two sites were examined during the three-year program, which was directed by J. R. Williams (1967, 1968, 1972). These included Hoecake in Mississippi County and Denton Mounds and Cagle Lake in Pemiscot County (Figure 1-6), the latter two of which are Late Mississippian–period sites located along Pemiscot Bayou. These sites, along with at least a dozen others in the immediate vicinity, represent the remains of communities that existed until at least the sixteenth century, on the basis of Spanish goods found at several of them. Analysis of the materials produced through decades of pothunting (O'Brien 1994a) has given us some understanding of the range in variation of material items, but Williams's (1968, 1972) excavations produced the only information on architectural details. Also, with the exception of Leo Anderson's work at Campbell (Chapman and Anderson 1955) (Figure 1-6), another Late Mississippian-period site that has figured prominently in the literature (Holland 1991; O'Brien and Holland 1994), Williams's detailed and thoughtful analyses of excavated sherds have produced the only baseline for ceramic-type frequencies from excavated midden deposits at Pemiscot Bayou sites.

It was Williams's (1967) work at Hoecake that was perhaps his most important contribution to our understanding of central Mississippi Valley prehistory. In 1966, archaeological materials were spread over an area of roughly 200 acres, and Williams (1967:24) stated that only one mound was left undisturbed. In 1963 a house and two mounds on the site were excavated (Anonymous 1964; Marshall 1988; Marshall and Hopgood 1964), one of which produced three tombs containing fourteen individuals. The tombs were lined with split cane and covered with logs. Williams's excavations uncovered the remains of eleven houses plus numerous other architectural features. Of particular interest from a historical point of view was Williams's documentation at Hoecake of a phenomenon mentioned earlier by Stephen Williams (1954) relative to southeastern Missouri pottery-bearing sites—the paucity of "pure" shell-tempered or clay-tempered ceramic assemblages (see also Hopgood 1969a). What typically is found are sherds of each temper type and, frequently, individual sherds that contain both types of temper.

Although J. R. Williams organized the new materials by the Willey-Phillips system and used many of the pottery types described by Phillips, Ford, and Griffin (1951) and Stephen Williams (1954), he did not buy into many of the assumptions these constructs implied to their inventors, which gives his work a surprisingly up-to-date look. Adding to this look was his stance on migration—a concept encouraged by essentialist interpretations of the phase concept (Lyman et al. 1997). He stated simply that "we know nothing about possible human migrations or cultural diffusion into and out of the area" (Williams 1967:156; see also Williams 1974). Such cautious opinion was rarely repeated in much of the later archaeological work in the central Mississippi River valley.

Williams produced excellent reports that attempted to integrate the findings into emerging pictures of prehistoric life in the alluvial valley (see also Klippel 1969; Williams 1964, 1974). In fact, the reports are among the best ever produced on Missouri prehistory. Without them, our knowledge particularly of the Mississippian-period occupation of the meander-belt portion of the Mississippi River valley would not be nearly what it is, since few projects in the region were undertaken after 1968. The salvage program related to land leveling in southeastern Missouri was terminated in the late 1960s as funding within the National Park Service was shifted to other projects.

CONSOLIDATION AND DESCRIPTION

Stephen Williams's (1954) work was the first practical application of the new phase formulation of Phillips and Willey (1953), but unification of the archaeological systematics of the central (and lower) Mississippi Valley was done by Phillips in *Archaeological Survey in the Lower Yazoo Basin, Mississippi, 1949–1955* (Phillips 1970). The impact of Phillips's contribution can hardly be overestimated relative to the central portion of the Mississippi Valley, in large part because he "revised" the ceramic types of Phillips, Ford, and Griffin, bringing them more in line with his type-variety concept (Phillips 1958). Phillips's changes erased most of Ford's influence from the classification (O'Brien and Lyman n.d.), in the process returning ceramic classification to an essentialist exercise in which types were treated as empirical discoveries rather than as archaeological constructs. This is nowhere more evident than in the absence of sorting criteria for numerous types and varieties. More important, borrowing from Williams (1954) for southeastern Missouri, Phillips (1970:861–974) converted the period/area structure of Phillips, Ford, and Griffin (1951) to the phase structure for the entire lower Mississippi Valley from Cairo, Illinois, to the Gulf of Mexico. With the phase structure largely in place by 1970, the general pattern in central-valley research has been to fill in the boxes represented by the phases with substantive detail. The focus of new work shifted south to Arkansas, where the Arkansas Archeological Survey, established in 1967 (Klinger 1982a), and its cultural resource management (CRM) studies combined to supply the main motor for fieldwork throughout the 1970s and 1980s. CRM changed forever the structure of archaeological research in the region by compelling a shift from what might be labeled "go-where-you-please" survey and excavation to specific-area investigations—in CRM, the impact area determines where work is done—and by forcing consideration of a much broader range of archaeological phenomena than just big "sites" (O'Brien 1996). The first serious examinations in the Crowley's Ridge physiographic province (Padgett 1977) were, for example, a direct consequence of this new orientation.

The manner in which the new opportunities presented by CRM were to be exploited was heavily influenced, not only in the local area (e.g., Klinger 1982a) but nationally as well, by the Cache River project carried out in the Western Lowlands by Michael Schiffer and John House (1975, 1977a, 1977b). The importance of this project to CRM regional designs and to the kinds of questions addressed by subsequent CRM work (e.g., Morse 1975) is unquestioned. Further, the data base it created for the Western Lowlands remains unmatched to the present. Many of the CRM studies were limited in scope and made but modest contributions to central-valley archaeology (e.g., Klinger 1977a; Klinger and Mathis 1978), but major excavations at such sites as Mangrum, in Craighead County, Arkansas (Klinger 1982a), fleshed out particular phases. Similar studies continue to dominate new fieldwork in the region (e.g., Benn 1990, 1992, Chapter 10).

Although CRM studies tended to dominate work in northeastern Arkansas during the 1970s, several important studies were not contract related. Albert Goodyear's (1974) study of the Dalton-age Brand site in Poinsett County (Figure 1-6) was the first detailed study of any preceramic component in the central Mississippi Valley, though earlier surveys (e.g., Redfield 1971) and excavations (e.g., Redfield and Moselage 1970) documented the richness of the preceramic record. Also prominent among these non-CRM projects was Phyllis Morse's (1981, 1990) study of the Parkin phase. In addition to bringing together the results of disparate investigations of an important site, Parkin (Figure 1-6), she carried out a survey of the surrounding region, which contained sites that she placed in the phase. Similarly, Dan Morse (1973b, 1990) pulled together bits and pieces of information on the earlier work at the Upper Nodena and Middle Nodena sites in Mississippi County.

Archaeologists were not inactive in southeastern Missouri during this period. Two projects in particular made important contributions—the Powers Phase Project and the Lilbourn salvage project. The former was a long-term examination by University of Michigan personnel of Mississippian-period settlement along the Little Black River in western Butler County. The genesis of the project lay in the discovery by James Price in the early 1960s of several burned structures on a series of sand ridges at the foot of the Ozark Highlands. Price subsequently excavated a small portion of one site, Turner (Figure 1-6), in 1966 (Price 1969) and found that the village had burned, which appeared to have effectively sealed the house floors and everything that was on them at the time. The remarkable state of preservation of Turner and its potential for addressing numerous questions about Mississippian life in the central Mississippi Valley were obvious, and between 1966 and 1976 it and another village, Snodgrass (Figure 1-6), were excavated almost in their entirety (Price 1973; Price and Griffin 1979). Also, more than 200 square kilometers of the Little Black River drainage was surveyed, and eighty Mississippian-period sites were located (Price 1974, 1978).

While the above-mentioned work was going on in the Western Lowlands, University of Missouri personnel were working at Beckwith's Fort, the largest fortified settlement in southeastern Missouri, and at Lilbourn, the second-largest fortified settlement. In 1970–1971, Lilbourn received extensive excavation prior to destruction of part of the site in advance of expansion of a vocational-technical school (Chapman et al. 1977). Excavations revealed a complicated archaeological signature, comparable to that at Beckwith's Fort (Chapman et al.

1977; Price and Fox 1990), with numerous examples of houses having been erected on top of other houses and burial pits placed through earlier burials. Few of the tens of thousands of artifacts have been analyzed, though available data suggest that the center was contemporaneous with other large fortified communities in the Cairo Lowland. Radiocarbon dates span the period from about A.D. 1100 to A.D. 1370.

Summary

In many respects, the archaeology of the central Mississippi River valley has been the victim of its own successes. The pathbreaking study of Phillips, Ford, and Griffin (1951) laid the foundation for what became, in the hands of Phillips and Willey (1953; Willey and Phillips 1955, 1958), *the* way of doing culture history. The concept central to culture history, the archaeological phase, was applied there first and most uniformly. Yet in the process, many of the innovative features in the system of Phillips, Ford, and Griffin, traceable mostly to Ford, were lost to a rigid essentialist interpretation of the original program (Lyman et al. 1997; O'Brien and Lyman n.d.). That so much of the archaeology of such a large region came to be investigated within this paradigm made it almost impossible to differentiate the artificial constructs from the empirical reality they were intended to describe. Progress became adding new bits to the same old structure instead of reexamining the structure itself. Cultural-resource management demanded a broadening of the archaeological purview—for example, small sites had to be addressed and sampling designs had to be formulated—but even this redirection, important as it was, did not carry with it much of a critical examination of some of the underlying presumptions that carried over from the halcyon days of culture history. The methods that Phillips, Ford, and Griffin (1951) had used to measure time—*the* innovative feature of their work—had come undone at the hands of Phillips and his successors so that culture history of the 1960s and 1970s was a hodgepodge of ill-advised assumptions and approaches. For reasons we mentioned earlier, the central Mississippi Valley escaped the onslaught of new archaeology, though there were more than a few instances of an interest or two being piqued by cultural reconstructionism. But for the most part, archaeologists working in the valley were unmolested by such interests, preferring to remain in the culture-history tradition of their predecessors.

In several respects, most of the chapters in this volume represent a break with that tradition. For example, in Chapter 2, Fox demonstrates that the phases used in the northern part of the region are based on unsystematic comparisons of ceramic assemblages. One result of his analysis (see also Fox 1992; O'Brien and Fox 1994a, 1994b) is clear demonstration that phenomena once treated as being the same are more similar to phenomena treated as being different. Fox finds that the phases in current use in southeastern Missouri are neither classes nor groups but are inconsistent sets of assemblages, the only rationale for which is historical usage. This finding should be of considerable interest to archaeologists who have employed the phases.

Kreisa (Chapter 3) finds much the same thing in his analysis of ceramic assemblages from western Kentucky. Although there are distinct differences between pre–A.D. 1250 and post–A.D. 1250 assemblages, there is little apparent segregation of assemblages dating A.D. 1250–1350 and those postdating A.D. 1350. Although the potential of spatial variation in the frequencies of historical types was recognized by Phillips, Ford, and Griffin (1951), especially by Ford—see his *Measurements of Some Prehistoric Design Developments in the Southeastern States* (Ford 1952; see also Deetz and Dethlefsen 1965)—the use of essentialist phases encouraged workers to overlook these issues. Kreisa's analysis demonstrates that there is considerably more variation in western-Kentucky assemblages than has been admitted previously, a point that calls into immediate question the validity of traditional interpretations of pottery types as time markers.

It has become customary to assign ceramic assemblages containing sherds of historical types such as Walls Engraved, Campbell Appliqué, and Parkin Punctated to the Late Mississippian period, though until recently there has been little attempt to either date the types directly or, since the time of Phillips (1970), to analyze geographic differences in how designs were placed on vessel exteriors. The contributions by Dye (Chapter 4) and Mainfort and Moore (Chapter 5) are primarily efforts to establish useful chronological markers for the Late Mississippian period, in Dye's case by examining spatial differences in Walls Engraved vessels and in Mainfort and Moore's case by radiometrically dating a small ceramic assemblage from western Tennessee.

Phillips, Ford, and Griffin (1951) discussed in considerable depth the dynamic nature of the central Mississippi Valley floodplain and even used Fisk's (1944) reconstructed channel positions to date sites. Despite this start, few efforts have been made to understand how prehistoric groups responded to the constantly changing physical environment and to document the effects of changes to the floodplain on the archaeological record. Lafferty's intensive survey of a portion of the Cairo Lowland, summarized in Chapter 6, is an effort in this direction. Despite the long history of archaeological research in the Cairo Lowland, small sites have been overlooked—a result primarily of the attraction the large palisaded mound centers have long held for prehistorians. Lafferty's work is the first systematic analysis of site locations relative both to time and physiographic features.

In Chapter 7, Teltser examines the archaeological record around Sandy Woods, a palisaded mound center that received considerable attention during the nineteenth century (e.g., Potter 1880; Rust 1877). Her use of methods designed to detect low-density archaeological phenomena shows that a different picture of Mississippian-period settlement systems emerges than that derived solely from "big" sites. This allows her to reevaluate Stephen Williams's (1980, 1982, 1990) argument that the northern half of the central Mississippi Valley was depopulated beginning sometime in the second half of the fourteenth century. The argument, as she correctly notes, has been framed in terms of the persistence or abandonment of sites with mounds and large population aggregates. Importantly, those involved in the debate have failed to consider that populations can be distributed in a variety of ways across the landscape. Consequently, Teltser suggests that the late-prehistoric record be approached in terms of demographic reorganization. In that context, abandonment is only one of several possibilities.

Despite the importance and influence of the Powers Phase Project in the archaeology of the central Mississippi Valley, the "paramount" settlement, Powers Fort (Figure 1-6), has not been reported since the nineteenth century (Thomas 1894), and then only briefly. In Chapter 8, Perttula examines the internal configuration of Powers Fort, which at a little more than 4 hectares is the smallest of the fortified mound centers in southeastern Missouri. Perttula's systematic examination of features contained within the palisade and analysis of artifacts from limited excavation and surface collections comprise the first modern statement on the site. His contribution is all the more important in light of the considerable effort that has been expended at contemporary nonmound sites in the Little Black River drainage of the Western Lowlands (e.g., Price 1973, 1974, 1978; Price and Griffin 1979).

Chapter 9 contains Dunnell's analysis of the surface structure of Langdon (Figure 1-6), a fortified mound center on the edge of the Malden Plain in Dunklin County, Missouri. Although a major center by all criteria, it escaped the attention of early prehistorians and even in more recent times has received only passing mention. Perhaps because he did not realize that it was palisaded, J. R. Williams (1964) did not even mention the site in his survey of fortified centers in southeastern Missouri. Dunnell points out the error in the common assumption that all of the fortified mound centers are more or less the same in terms of form. Langdon, as opposed to the large centers in the Cairo Lowland, for example, contains a main mound that is tall relative to its basal width—a feature that makes it similar to settlements located farther south in the St. Francis basin. The artifact assemblage, however, has more in common with Cairo Lowland assemblages than it does with those from the St. Francis sites. An important aspect of Dunnell's chapter is the amount of information that can be learned about these complex centers through the use of nondestructive field methods such as aerial photography, coring, and controlled surface collection.

In Chapter 10, Benn reports the results of analysis of material from Moon (Figure 1-6), a small, palisaded Mississippian-period settlement in Poinsett County, Arkansas. His contribution is significant from several standpoints. Knowledge of the second-order communities in Mississippian settlement systems has been limited to the Powers-phase communities of Turner and Snodgrass. Moon, comparable to those communities in size, displays an organization that is quite distinct; thus, Benn's work represents a clear caveat regarding the use of superficial similarity to generalize about "Mississippian" settlement.

Chapters 11 and 12 focus on lithic material—a much neglected aspect of the archaeological record in the central Mississippi Valley. In Chapter 11, McCutcheon and Dunnell explore the size and composition of gravels from locations on Crowley's Ridge, the nearest source of lithic raw material for groups residing in much of the Eastern Lowlands. Finished products of Crowley's Ridge gravels, as well as the by-products of stone-tool manufacture, are ubiquitous on sites in the valley, but to date there has been little attention paid to the kinds of raw materials that were being selected. This contrasts with increasing attention paid to imported cherts (e.g., Mill Creek and Kaolin) that appeared in the region during the Mississippian period (e.g., Dunnell et al. 1994; O'Brien 1994a).

In Chapter 12, Morrow examines lithic material from Twenhafel (Figure 1-6), located in extreme southwestern Illinois on the alluvial plain near the junction of the Big Muddy River and the Mississippi. Twenhafel is a large, complex site that, perhaps because of its twenty-five mounds, has received considerable attention by prehistorians from at least the 1880s (e.g., Thomas 1894). Artifacts from the site document that it was used from at least the Early Woodland period through at least the Middle Mississippian period, though it is the heavy Middle Woodland–period occupation that historically has received the most attention. Classic Middle Woodland "Hopewell" materials recovered from Twenhafel include figurines, copper artifacts, sheet mica, galena cubes, marine-shell artifacts, quartz and obsidian chips, and large numbers of prismatic blades manufactured from nonlocal cherts. Morrow addresses the function of the prismatic blades in the socioeconomic system in place at Twenhafel.

Traditional takes on prehistoric subsistence in the central Mississippi Valley have focused on plant and animal remains and have assumed simple correlations with phases; that is, *a* phase has *a* corresponding form of subsistence. Thus, Mississippian phases represent groups of farmers (witness Chapman's [1980] use of the term *Village Farmer tradition, Early Mississippi period*), and data from one or a few localities are generalized to larger cultural-historical units. In Chapter 13, Greenlee reviews the data available on stable-carbon isotopes for the central valley (e.g., Boutton et al. 1991; Greenlee 1991; Greenlee and Dunnell 1990, 1993; Lynott et al. 1986) and adds a number of new analyses. Again, a picture of variability, not uniformity, emerges. With this beginning, it is possible to suggest hypotheses about subsistence changes that can be tested and the results used to structure future research.

In summary, the chapters included here represent fresh looks at old problems in central Mississippi Valley archaeology. At one level, they document in objective fashion that the archaeological record of the region is exceedingly rich and varied—a fact not lost on nineteenth-century antiquarians and one that has been borne out repeatedly ever since. At a second level, the studies plainly indicate that some of the work conducted previously actually masked that variation through the methods used and the assumptions made about how and why the variation came to be expressed the way it was in the archaeological record. This set of studies is offered as an initial step toward clarifying the nature of some of that variation.

2 | An Examination of Mississippian-Period Phases in Southeastern Missouri
Gregory L. Fox

MODERN (post-1940) archaeological research in southeastern Missouri (Figure 2-1), and indeed in the central Mississippi River valley, has focused primarily on classificatory-historical problems (e.g., Lafferty and Price 1996; Phillips et al. 1951; Williams 1954), though more-recent studies by Dunnell (1982, 1988), Dunnell and Feathers (1991), Feathers (1990b), Holland (1991), O'Brien (1994a), Teltser (1988, 1993), and others have attempted to go beyond those classification-oriented studies and better document the tremendous variation that exists in the region's archaeological record. Still, the majority of archaeologists working in the area are culture historians, and they continue to base their conclusions on intuitive and untested interpretations of archaeological phenomena, many of which were formulated three or more decades ago. Two classificatory units, phases and pottery types, are integral to the interpretive framework that has grown up around the archaeology of the Mississippian period in southeastern Missouri. Understanding not only the history behind these units but also their limitations and how they have been applied is integral to assessing the accuracy of various cultural-historical interpretations. This chapter is a critical examination of phase constructions that have been proposed for southeastern Missouri. Although I focus specifically on that area, I suspect the findings have broad applicability to the central Mississippi Valley.

My examination of Mississippian-period phases in southeastern Missouri was stimulated by two realities. First, despite forty years of archaeological research in the region, the initial classifications of cultural phenomena made by Stephen Williams in the early 1950s (Williams 1954) have remained essentially unchanged. Second, researchers working in the area (e.g., Klippel 1969; Marshall 1965; J. R. Williams 1967, 1968, 1972) have difficulty assigning many archaeological components to the existing phases. Stephen Williams recently asserted that his original definitions of the four phases in southeastern Missouri—Cairo Lowland, Nodena, Malden Plain, and Pemiscot Bayou—were based on more data than were generated from his excavations at Crosno (23MI1), located in Mississippi County, and from his surface collections of other sites in southeastern Missouri.[1] A review of the literature, examination of artifacts in museums and private collections, and discussions with other archae-

32 | Fox

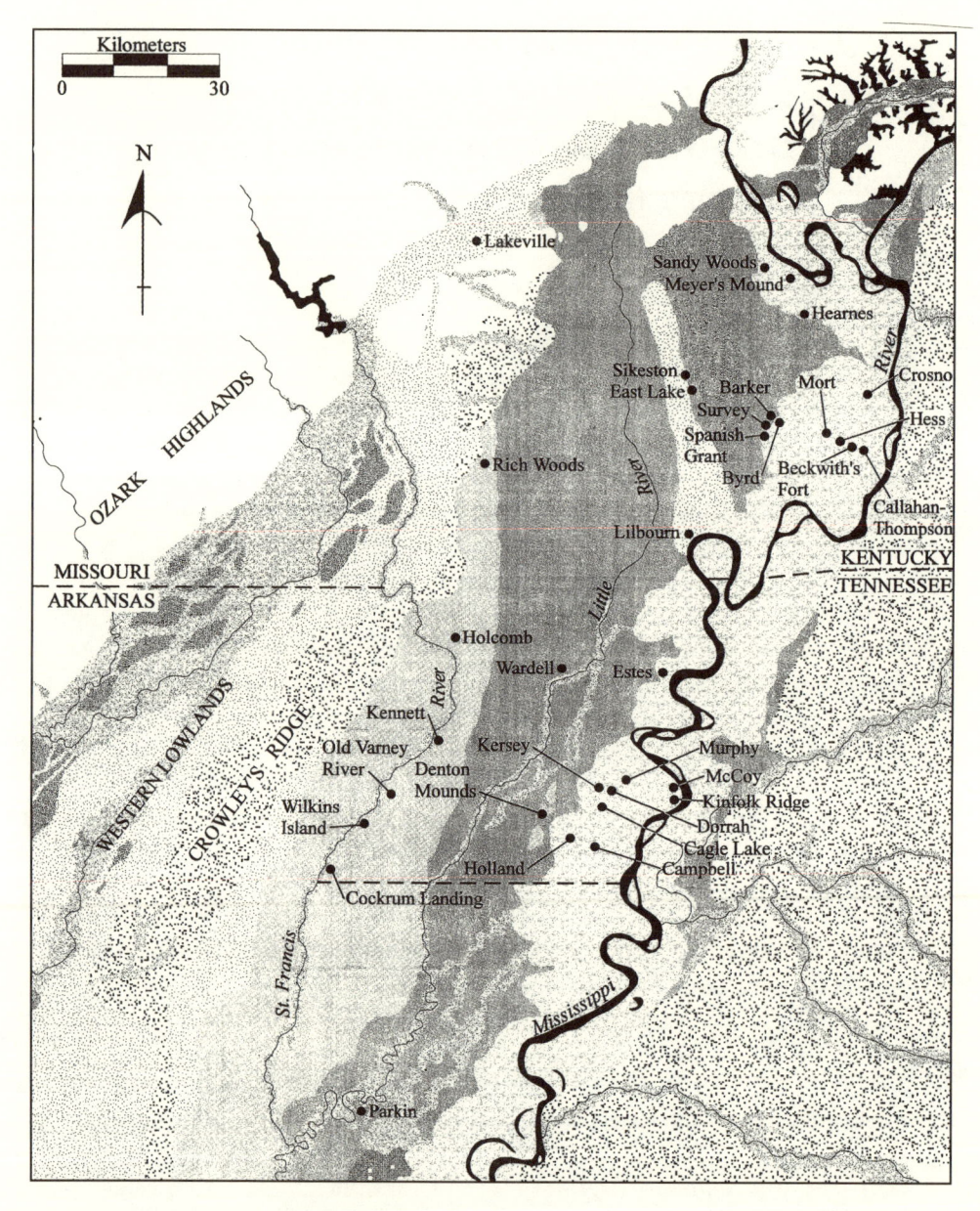

Figure 2-1. Map of southeastern Missouri showing physiographic features and locations of archaeological sites mentioned in the text.

ologists were also involved. Regardless of the impact of these activities, archaeological interpretation in the region is still based on the phases Williams (1954) presented in his dissertation.

Over the succeeding decades, archaeologists (e.g., Klippel 1969; Marshall 1965; Smith 1990; J. R. Williams 1967, 1968, 1972) embraced the four-phase system and added a few pieces here and there, but the system has not been evaluated through a detailed comparative analysis, a consistent application of chronometric controls, or the use of statistical methods. Here I use statistical procedures rather than intuitive groupings to reexamine the type-frequency information, derived from surface collections and excavations, which Williams (1954) and subsequent researchers (e.g., Chapman and Anderson 1955; Klinger 1977b; Lewis 1982; Marshall 1965; Smith 1990; J. R. Williams 1968) used to define Mississippian-period phases and to assign assemblages to those phases.

But what *is* a phase? Is it a *group* of similar assemblages—"similar" being based on some qualitative feel that assemblages are somehow similar—or is it a *class* of assemblages that share a set of necessary and sufficient traits that serve to distinguish any particular phase from all other phases (e.g., Dunnell 1971; Rouse 1964)? Williams's formulations for southeastern Missouri might be interpreted either way. Since he never explained this element of his conceptual scheme, it is necessary to evaluate his phases as both groups and classes.

Williams's Phases: Groups or Classes?

In his dissertation, Williams (1954) provided the first modern categorization of Mississippian-period phases in southeastern Missouri. For all intents and purposes, subsequent phase designations that have been proposed for the area (e.g., Marshall 1965) are simply variations on that original system (Table 2-1). The Cairo Lowland phase, originally based on Williams's (1954) excavations at Crosno and on his review of museum collections, can be considered the archetypical phase in the region, since all other phases are defined primarily on the absence of Cairo Lowland ceramic markers and secondarily on the presence of other pottery types in site assemblages. Williams, closely following Phillips and Willey (1953), defined a phase as follows:

> A space-time-culture unit possessing traits sufficiently characteristic to distinguish it from all other units similarly conceived whether of the same or other cultural traditions geographically limited to a locality or region and chronologically limited to a relatively brief span of time. Often initially defined on the strength of one component with the expectation that others will be found. In most cases, phase probably equals "society." (1954:25)

The question remains, however, did Williams's actual formulations follow his stated definition? In other words, did his phases possess traits "sufficiently

Table 2-1. Southeastern Missouri Mississippian-Period Phases, Cultural Periods, and Ceramic Types

Phase Name	Cultural Period	Diagnostic Pottery Types	Pottery-Type Reference
Malden Plain[a]	Early Mississippian	Neeley's Ferry Plain Varney Red Filmed Shell-tempered cordmarked	Phillips et al. (1951) Williams (1954) Williams (1954)
Big Lake[b]	Early Mississippian	Neeley's Ferry Plain Varney Red Filmed	Phillips et al. (1951) Williams (1954)
Hayti[c]	Early Mississippian	Neeley's Ferry Plain Grassy salt pan Varney Red Filmed salt pan Varney Red Filmed Wickliffe Incised Wickliffe Cordmarked Wickliffe Plain Combed and cordmarked Neeley's Ferry Plain	Phillips et al. (1951) Williams (1954) Williams (1954) Williams (1954) Phillips et al. (1951)
Beckwith[d]	Early Mississippian	Clay-tempered Bell Plain Wickliffe Thick O'Byam Incised	 Williams (1954) Williams (1954)

Table 2-1. (cont.)

Bryant[e]	Early Mississippian	Matthews Incised	Phillips (1970)
		Unknown	
Cairo Lowland[a]	Early and Middle Mississippian	Kimmswick Fabric-Impressed	Type cluster
		Wickliffe series	Williams (1954)
		O'Byam Incised	Williams (1954)
		Bell Plain, *var. New Madrid*	Phillips (1970)
		Matthews Incised, *var. Matthews*	Phillips (1970)
		Matthews Incised, *var. Beckwith*	Phillips (1970)
		Matthews Incised, *var. Manly*	Phillips (1970)
		Old Town Red	Phillips et al. (1951)
		O'Byam Incised, *var. O'Byam*	Phillips (1970)
		Kimmswick Fabric-Impressed, *var. Kimmswick*	Phillips (1970)
		Wickliffe Thick, *var. Wickliffe*	Phillips (1970)
		Mound Place Incised	Phillips et al. (1951)
		Nashville Negative Painted, *var. Sikeston*	Phillips (1970)
Pemiscot Bayou[a]	Middle Mississippian	Parkin Punctated	Phillips et al. (1951)
		Barton Incised	Phillips et al. (1951)
		Old Town Red	Phillips et al. (1951)

Table 2-1. (cont.)

	Neeley's Ferry Plain	Phillips et al. (1951)
	Shell-tempered incised, punctated, and noded	
Nodena[a]	Late and Middle Mississippian	
	Ranch Incised	Phillips et al. (1951)
	Vernon Paul Appliquéd	Phillips et al. (1951)
	Fortune Noded	Phillips et al. (1951)
	Parkin Punctated	Phillips et al. (1951)
	Pecan Point–type headpots	Phillips et al. (1951)
	Tail-riding effigy pots	
Campbell[f]	Late Mississippian–Protohistoric	
	Nodena Red-and-White	Phillips et al. (1951)
	Kent Incised	Phillips et al. (1951)
	Barton Incised	Phillips et al. (1951)
	Ranch Incised	Phillips et al. (1951)
	Rhodes Incised	Phillips et al. (1951)
	Fortune Noded	Phillips et al. (1951)
	Walls Engraved	Phillips et al. (1951)
	Campbell Punctated	Chapman and Anderson (1955)
	Matthews Incised	Phillips (1970)
	Hollywood White Filmed	Phillips et al. (1951)

Table 2-1. (cont.)

		Carson Red-on-Buff	Phillips et al. (1951)
		Old Town Red	Phillips et al. (1951)
		Parkin Punctated	Phillips et al. (1951)
Armorel[g]	Late Mississippian–Protohistoric	Well-executed Bell Plain	Phillips et al. (1951)
		Late Parkin Punctated	Phillips et al. (1951)
		Campbell Appliquéd	Chapman and Anderson (1955)
		Fortune Noded	Phillips et al. (1951)

[a]S. Williams (1954).
[b]Morse and Morse (1977).
[c]Marshall (1965).
[d]Phillips (1970).
[e]J. R. Williams (1967).
[f]G. P. Smith (1990).
[g]S. Williams (1980).

characteristic to distinguish [them] from all other units similarly conceived?" And, if his phases are truly classes, then the members of a phase *must* share a *unique* set of traits, phrased as some set of "in-use historical types" (e.g., those in Phillips et al. 1951), none of which is shared with members of any other phase. If, on the other hand, we interpret Williams's phases as groups, then the members of a phase *must* be more similar to one another, measured in terms of in-use historical types, than any one is to a member of another phase. This is an assemblage-scale application of what Cowgill (1982) called object clustering. Consequently, for Williams's phases to be legitimate, they must conform to one or the other sets of expectations. I examine Williams's phases in this light. Confirming that his phases conform to one or the other expectations does not, of course, imply their usefulness; rather, such an exercise determines only whether his constructions meet the specifications of phases. The value of phases themselves to modern work has been challenged (Lyman et al. 1997; O'Brien 1995, 1996; O'Brien and Fox 1994a) and is an issue not addressed here.

To assess the similarity between and among the multiple phases and components defined by Williams (1954) and others (e.g., Marshall 1965), I undertook a comparison of ceramic assemblages using data derived from published and manuscript sources and from collections housed at the Museum of Anthropology, University of Missouri–Columbia. Only frequencies of in-use historical types (e.g., those in Chapman and Anderson 1955; Phillips 1970; Phillips et al. 1951; Williams 1954) were used (Table 2-1). The data base, which was compiled from information on surface-collected and excavated sherds from thirty-four sites (thirty-three in Missouri and one in Arkansas), is summarized in Table 2-2.

Comparisons of the ceramic assemblages listed in Table 2-2 are based on the use of Robinson's Index of Agreement (the Brainerd-Robinson coefficient of similarity [BR]) to measure assemblage similarity (Robinson 1951). Frequency data for twenty-five pottery types were used to calculate similarity scores using the following formula:

$$BR = 200 - \sum_{i=1}^{N} |p_{iA} - p_{iB}|$$

In effect, the formula says to sum the absolute values of differences in percentages of ceramic types in two assemblages and then to subtract that sum from 200. The method provides a pairwise similarity coefficient ranging from 0 (no similarity) to 200 (identical in every respect). Consequently, a small cumulative difference between assemblages A and B will produce a high coefficient, and a large difference will produce a low coefficient (for more information see Cowgill 1990; Robinson 1951).

In order to determine whether the original four phases could be identified from the BR matrices or from the original ceramic-frequency data, cluster analyses were performed on those data. Cluster analysis is a multivariate procedure

Table 2-2. Archaeological Sites Forming the Data Base for Statistical Comparisons

Site	Sample Source	Reference	Phase
23MI1 (Crosno)	Pooled sample	S. Williams (1954)	Cairo Lowland
23MI2 (Beckwith's Fort)	Surface collection	S. Williams (1954)	Cairo Lowland
23MI7 (Hearnes)	Surface collection	S. Williams (1954)	Cairo Lowland
23MI10 (Meyer's Mound)	Surface collection	S. Williams (1954)	Cairo Lowland
23MI30 (Survey)	Surface collection	S. Williams (1954)	Cairo Lowland
23MI31 (Spanish Grant)	Surface collection	S. Williams (1954)	Cairo Lowland
23MI33 (Barker)	Surface collection	S. Williams (1954)	Cairo Lowland
23MI53 (Byrd)	Excavated pooled sample	J. R. Williams (1968)	Cairo Lowland
23MI55 (Hess)	Excavated pooled sample	Lewis (1982)	Cairo Lowland
23MI69 (Mort)	Excavated pooled sample	J. R. Williams (1968)	Cairo Lowland
23MI71 (Callahan–Thompson)	Excavated pooled sample	Lewis (1982)	Cairo Lowland
23NM38 (Lilbourn)	Surface collection	S. Williams (1954)	Cairo Lowland
23NM68 (Sikeston)	Surface collection	S. Williams (1954)	Cairo Lowland
23NM69 (East Lake)	Surface collection	S. Williams (1954)	Cairo Lowland
23PM2 (Holland)	Surface pooled sample	Marshall (1965)	Pemiscot Bayou
23PM5 (Campbell)	Multiple samples	Chapman and Anderson (1955), Holland (1991), S. Williams (1954)	Nodena, Armorel, Cairo Lowland
23PM11 (Dorrah)	Pooled sample	UMC Museum	Pemiscot Bayou

Table 2-2. (cont.)

23PM13 (Cagle Lake)	Multiple samples	S. Williams (1954), UMC Museum	Nodena
23PM15 (Kinfolk Ridge)	Surface collection	S. Williams (1954)	Pemiscot Bayou
23PM21 (McCoy)	Pooled sample	J. R. Williams (1968)	Nodena, Armorel
23PM28 (Wardell)	Surface collection	S. Williams (1954)	Pemiscot Bayou
23PM40 (Estes)	Surface collection	S. Williams (1954)	Pemiscot Bayou
23PM42 (Kersey)	Excavated pooled sample	Marshall (1965)	Hayti, Pemiscot Bayou
23PM43 (Murphy)	Multiple samples	S. Williams 1954, UMC Museum	Hayti, Pemiscot Bayou, Nodena, Armorel
23PM549 (Denton Mounds)	Excavated pooled sample	J. R. Williams (1972)	Nodena, Armorel
23DU2 (Kennett)	Surface collection	S. Williams (1954)	Malden Plain
23DU4 (Holcomb)	Surface collection	S. Williams (1954)	Malden Plain
23DU5 (Old Varney River)	Surface collection	S. Williams (1954)	Malden Plain
23DU12 (Cockrum Landing)	Surface collection	S. Williams (1954)	Malden Plain
23DU13 (Wilkins Island)	Surface collection	S. Williams (1954)	Malden Plain
23SO1 (Rich Woods)	Surface Surface collection	S. Williams (1954)	Cairo Lowland
23SO111 (Lakeville)	Surface collection	S. Williams (1954)	Cairo Lowland
23ST26 (Sandy Woods)	Surface collection	S. Williams (1954)	Cairo Lowland
3CS29 (Parkin)	Excavated pooled sample	Klinger (1977b)	Parkin, Armorel

Note: UMC, University of Missouri–Columbia.

used to detect groupings in data; the procedure seeks to classify a set of objects into subgroups when neither the number nor members of that subgroup is known. The procedures were run on the SYSTAT software (Wilkinson et al. 1992) using the broad class of clustering ("join") to produce a hierarchical cluster represented as a dendrogram. Dendrograms represent the linkage of each object or group of objects: "the 'root' of the tree is the linkage of all clusters into one set, and the ends of the branches lead to each separate object" (Wilkinson et al. 1992:21). The specific procedure used was Euclidean distance (root mean squared distance), done with an average-linkage method.

Comparison of Williams's Analytical Units from Crosno

The obvious place to begin any statistical evaluation of phase designations based on ceramic collections is Crosno, which Williams (1954) assigned to the Cairo Lowland phase. I rely on the ceramic-type frequencies in the analytical units used by Williams (1954) to order the pottery he excavated and to define both an Early Mississippian–period (ca. A.D. 900–1200) component and a Late Mississippian–period (ca. A.D. 1400–1540) component (the dates are mine; Williams assigned no dates to the periods). Williams referred to his ceramic ordering as a seriation when in fact it was simply a presentation of stratigraphically ordered frequencies of ceramic types. Although Williams acknowledged the site was not excavated with the express purpose of performing that "seriation" but rather with the intent of defining architectural features and obtaining a sample of artifacts (Williams 1954:109), stratigraphic analysis *was* performed and influenced the definition of the Cairo Lowland phase. Table 2-3 lists the provenience of Williams's analytical units. Williams (1954:108) noted that his analytical units were not of equal size and did not necessarily follow the site's stratigraphic sequence.

BR coefficients of similarity were calculated for all pairs of analytical units (AU) (Table 2-4). Similarity coefficients range from a high of 197 to a low of 159. The most similar pair (BR = 197) comprises AU 10 and AU 11 from Excavation Section 2, representing depths below surface of 0.5 to 1.0 feet and 0.5 to 1.5 feet. The high similarity score is no surprise since the units overlap vertically. The least-similar coefficients result from comparisons made between other units and AU 23, the deepest unit (3.5 to 4.0 feet, in Excavation Section 3). This coefficient is somewhat surprising since AU 23 contains all horizon markers of the Cairo Lowland phase as defined by Williams (1954)—Kimmswick Fabric-Impressed, the Wickliffe series (Plain, Cordmarked, Thick, and Incised), and O'Byam Engraved—and does not contain any Crosno/Cahokia Cordmarked sherds (a marker of the Early Mississippian–period occupation). Virtually all other pottery types are absent in this AU. Interestingly, this deep AU is most similar to two units (AU 9 and AU 10) that were closest to the surface (AU 9 had a depth below surface of 0.0 to 1.0 feet, and AU 10 had a depth below surface of 0.5 to

Table 2-3. Provenience of Analytical Units for Crosno

Analytical Unit	Excavation Section	Level	Depth below Surface (feet)
1	1	1–4	0.0–2.0
2	1	2	0.5–1.0
3	1	3	1.0–1.5
4	1	4	1.5–2.0
5	1	5	2.0–2.5
6	1	5–6	2.0–3.0
7	1	6–7	2.5–3.5
8	2	1	0.0–0.5
9	2	1–2	0.0–1.0
10	2	2	0.5–1.0
11	2	2–3	0.5–1.5
12	2	3	1.0–1.5
13	2	3–4	1.0-2.0
14	2	4	1.5–2.0
15	2	5	2.0–2.5
16	2	6–7	2.5–3.0
17	3	1–2	0.0–1.0
18	3	3–4	1.0–2.0
19	3	4	1.5–2.0
20	3	5	2.0–2.5
21	3	6	2.5–3.0
22	3	6–7	2.5–3.5
23	3	8	3.5–4.0

Source: Data from S. Williams (1954).

1.0 feet), suggesting that the excavated Crosno assemblage represented in Williams's (1954) units is primarily a mixture of sherds from different periods and thus there is no basis for identifying distinct Early Mississippian–period and Late Mississippian–period components.

Phase Designation: Williams's Cairo Lowland–Phase Sites

In his descriptions of Mississippian phases, Williams (1954) provided lists of in-use historical pottery types that represented traits of the four phases. These markers were presented to identify assemblages that "belonged" to particular phases. It is unclear whether the ceramic-trait lists (McKern's [1939] determinants) were intended to define groups of assemblages or classes of assemblages. The overlapping character of the trait lists makes a class interpretation of phase highly unlikely. In fact, inspection of the "Diagnostic Pottery Types" column in Table 2-1 makes it abundantly clear that Williams's phases are *not* classes: there is no set of necessary and sufficient traits that serves to distinguish each phase. Diagnostic pottery types often are common to more than one phase. If such traits are removed, some phases (e.g., Big Lake) are left with no criteria at all. Consequently, I focus attention throughout the remainder of this chapter on whether Williams's phases can be construed as groups.

How well does Crosno (23MI1), the archetype site of the Cairo Lowland phase, compare to other sites assigned to that phase by Williams (1954)? Results of the statistical evaluation of this "most profusely documented phase in the Lower Mississippi Valley, if not the entire Southeast" (Phillips 1970:925) are paralleled in other evaluations of Williams's phases (see Fox 1992; O'Brien and Fox 1994b). In order to calculate a BR similarity matrix (not shown) for all the ceramic assemblages identified by Williams as components of the Cairo Lowland phase, it was necessary to produce a composite assemblage for Crosno. This was accomplished by combining into a pooled sample all of Williams's AUs and surface collections from Crosno that contained Mississippian-period ceramics. (BR analysis of the individual AUs with the surface-collected assemblages produced results similar to those presented below.)

The highest coefficient in the matrix is 193 (Sikeston [23NM68] and Sandy Woods [23ST26]), and the lowest is 102 (Barker [23MI33] and Beckwith's Fort [23MI2]). Comparisons of all identified components with the archetypical Crosno sample result in scores ranging from a low of 114 (with Beckwith's Fort [23MI2]) to a high of only 140 (with Meyer's Mound [23MI10]). These coefficients represent cumulative-percentage differences of 30 to 43 percent. In fact, comparisons of ceramic assemblages with the archetype assemblage have the lowest overall set of BR scores of any other column or row in the matrix. The archetype, Crosno, appears to be considerably different (in the neighborhood of a cumulative 30-percent difference) from all other sites assigned by Williams to the Cairo Lowland phase.

The matrix indicates that the sites identified by Williams as belonging to the Cairo Lowland phase are not necessarily a cohesive group if they are considered strictly on the basis of ceramic-assemblage composition. In fact, in terms of a cumulative-percentage difference, there is nearly a 46-percent difference (91 BR points) between the highest and lowest coefficients. Consequently, given the original interpretation that the assemblages are from like or similar components, intergroup variation among Williams's surface-collected sites assigned to the Cairo Lowland phase and the excavated archetype site appears to be extremely great.

44 | Fox

Table 2-4. Similarity Matrix of Brainerd–Robinson Coefficients of Analytical Units Derived from Excavations at Crosno

	1	2	3	4	5	6	7	8	9	10	11	12	13	14	15	16	17	18	19	20	21	22
2	185																					
3	191	184																				
4	193	190	190																			
5	195	186	189	192																		
6	188	185	195	188	188																	
7	171	165	175	169	168	176																
8	192	179	191	186	191	189	174															
9	178	172	183	176	176	183	190	182														
10	180	174	184	179	178	186	187	184	196													
11	182	175	186	181	180	186	187	186	195	197												
12	187	178	189	184	185	189	181	191	190	193	193											
13	193	184	195	191	191	193	174	193	182	185	187	188										
14	191	178	192	184	189	189	176	196	185	187	187	191	193									
15	192	185	193	191	190	192	176	192	183	184	187	191	192	191								
16	188	180	192	185	187	191	180	189	187	185	188	191	194	193	191							
17	190	186	195	192	190	195	174	191	183	185	187	190	195	191	193	192						
18	191	182	193	189	188	193	178	192	186	188	190	193	191	193	194	192	194					
19	185	175	186	180	185	184	172	192	181	182	183	187	188	190	187	186	185	184				
20	188	179	192	186	186	191	181	189	188	189	191	193	191	192	191	195	192	195	184			
21	180	182	185	183	180	186	173	180	177	177	178	179	186	181	182	185	187	182	177	184		
22	183	177	187	181	181	189	183	187	188	190	191	193	185	188	188	187	187	192	182	192	184	
23	165	159	170	163	164	171	182	169	186	185	183	178	169	172	170	173	170	173	169	176	167	176

Source: Data from S. Williams (1954).
Note: Numbers along the left-hand side and base of the matrix refer to the analytical units used by S. Williams (1954) (see Table 2-3).

Table 2-5 is a master matrix of BR coefficients that result from comparison of all of Williams's original surface-collected ceramic assemblages to the excavated archetype assemblage from Crosno. This matrix illustrates the intersite variation in Williams's original survey sample. Williams defined other phases in large part by comparing various assemblages against that from Crosno; column 1 in the matrix illustrates the variation among individual site assemblages compared to that archetype. Cluster analysis of the BR coefficients in the matrix was performed using the Euclidean-distance average-linkage method. The resulting dendrogram (Figure 2-2) suggests that three clusters are present in the matrix. Cluster 2 contains two subclusters, with Subcluster A containing assemblages from Holcomb (23DU4), Wardell (23PM28), Cockrum Landing (23DU12), Kennett (23DU2), Rich Woods (23SO1), Barker (23MI33), Lakeville (23SO111), Sandy Woods (23ST26), and Sikeston (23NM68). These assemblages were assigned variously by Williams (1954) to the Malden Plain, Pemiscot Bayou, and Cairo Lowland phases. Subcluster B contains ceramic assemblages from Estes (23PM40), East Lake (23NM69), Lilbourn (23NM38), and Kinfolk Ridge (23PM15). Assemblages in this subcluster were assigned by Williams (1954) to the Pemiscot Bayou and Cairo Lowland phases. Cluster 3 contains ceramic assemblages from McCoy (also known as Chute [23PM21]), Meyer's Mound (23MI10), Cagle Lake (also known as Persimmon Grove [23PM13]), Campbell (also known as Cooter [23PM5]), Murphy (23PM43), Survey (23MI30), Hearnes (also known as Charleston [23MI7]), and Spanish Grant (23MI31). These assemblages were assigned by Williams (1954) to the Pemiscot Bayou, Nodena, and Cairo Lowland phases. The ceramic assemblage from Beckwith's Fort (23MI2) is an outlier at increased distance to Cluster 3. Old Varney River (23DU5) and Kersey (also known as Canady [23PM42]) represent a distinct cluster (Cluster 1) in the dendrogram. This is not surprising, since the ceramic assemblages from the two sites are considered to date to the Early Mississippian period (see Marshall 1965; Williams 1954).

An averaged Euclidean-distance cluster analysis also was calculated to assess whether any of Williams's surface-collected ceramic assemblages could be sorted into clusters strictly on the basis of ceramic-type frequencies. The resulting dendrogram (Figure 2-3) suggests only a single cluster with one outlier (Crosno). Thus, Williams's phases clearly fail as groups. Had they been groups, correspondence of phase and cluster would have obtained at some level. Instead, assignments are arranged randomly across clusters.

In order to make every effort to identify something that might justify Williams's phase assignments, I used SYSTAT multidimensional scaling (Figure 2-4), a procedure for fitting a set of points in a space such that distances between any two points correspond as closely as possible to dissimilarities between sets of objects. Because multidimensional scaling operates on dissimilarities, statistical-distribution assumptions are unnecessary. The two large clusters evident

46 | Fox

Table 2-5. Similarity Matrix of Brainerd–Robinson Coefficients of Twenty-Five Surface-Collected Sites and the Excavated Crosno Assemblage

	1	2	3	4	5	6	7	8	9	10	11	12	13	14	15	16	17	18	19	20	21	22	23	24	25
2	118																								
3	167	141																							
4	146	158	172																						
5	161	102	146	134																					
6	180	129	166	159	166																				
7	172	112	156	149	184	181																			
8	169	118	165	159	169	188	181																		
9	173	108	148	142	186	179	193	175																	
10	164	99	146	138	189	167	186	170	188																
11	159	94	141	135	191	165	182	173	185	194															
12	105	93	105	105	107	105	113	106	105	110															
13	168	103	148	140	192	172	190	174	192	194	190	106													
14	172	106	142	134	187	173	185	167	191	186	184	105	188												
15	156	133	176	175	146	169	159	171	152	147	146	107	151	144											
16	170	110	157	151	167	180	179	184	172	167	169	109	171	164	174										
17	158	93	40	34	90	163	181	172	184	194	198	110	190	184	146	168									
18	168	116	163	157	177	186	192	190	185	181	177	105	182	177	167	146	177								
19	119	109	124	123	110	120	128	116	111	113	181	114	107	123	125	112	120								
20	158	142	176	182	149	172	161	172	155	149	148	107	153	146	190	168	147	168	123						
21	160	137	175	178	149	174	164	174	156	153	149	105	155	149	184	166	149	172	120	190					
22	156	116	163	157	147	168	159	170	153	148	147	107	152	144	176	170	147	167	122	173	168				
23	153	152	182	189	141	165	155	165	148	146	140	105	147	142	180	156	140	163	124	187	183	162			
24	156	147	175	189	145	170	160	170	153	149	146	105	151	145	183	161	145	169	120	192	189	167	191		
25	160	95	141	134	192	165	183	169	185	195	196	107	191	185	146	166	197	177	109	148	147	149	147	140	
26	158	93	140	134	167	163	165	173	165	170	170	140	166	165	146	168	170	165	143	147	149	147	145	145	167
	1	2	3	4	5	6	7	8	9	10	11	12	13	14	15	16	17	18	19	20	21	22	23	24	25

Source: Data from S. Williams (1954).

Note: 1, Crosno (23MI1); 2, Beckwith's Fort (23MI2); 3, Meyer's Mound (23MI10); 4, Spanish Grant (23MI31); 5, Barker (23MI33); 6, Lilbourn (23NM38); 7, Sikeston (23NM68); 8, East Lake (23NM69); 9, Sandy Woods (23ST26); 10, Kennett (23DU2); 11, Holcomb (23DU4); 12, Old Varney River (23DU5); 13, Rich Woods (23SO1); 14, Lakeville (23SO111); 15, Cagle Lake (23PM13); 16, Kinfolk Ridge (23PM15); 17, Wardell (23PM28); 18, Estes (23PM40); 19, Kersey (23PM42); 20, Murphy (23PM43); 21, Campbell (23PM5); 22, McCoy (23PM21); 23, Hearnes (23MI7); 24, Survey (23MI30); 25, Cockrum Landing (23DU12); 26, Wilkins Island (23DU13).

Mississippian Phases in Missouri | 47

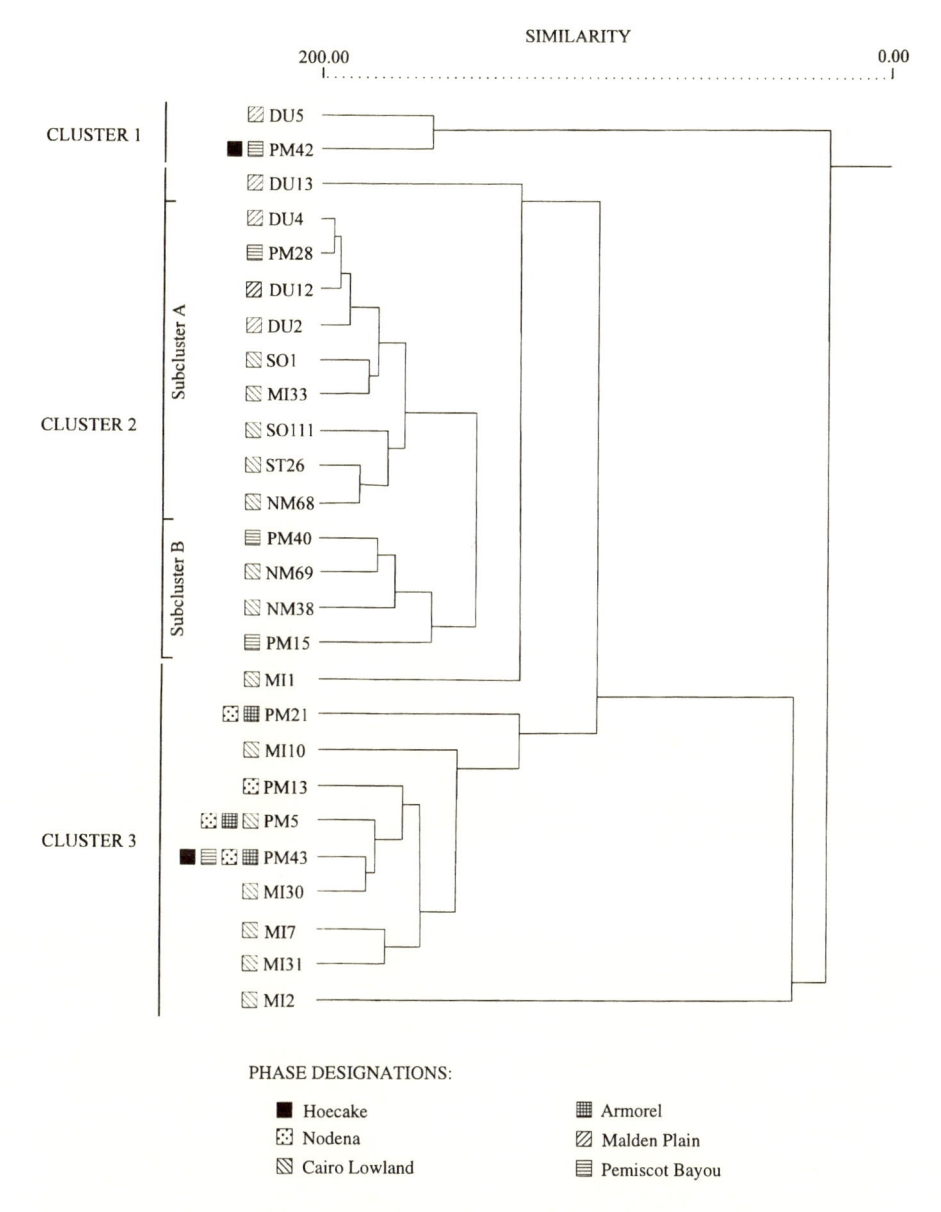

SIMILARITY
200.00   0.00

CLUSTER 1
- ▨ DU5
- ■ ≡ PM42

CLUSTER 2

Subcluster A
- ▨ DU13
- ▨ DU4
- ≡ PM28
- ▨ DU12
- ▨ DU2
- ▧ SO1
- ▧ MI33
- ▧ SO111
- ▧ ST26
- ▧ NM68

Subcluster B
- ≡ PM40
- ▧ NM69
- ▧ NM38
- ≡ PM15

CLUSTER 3
- ▧ MI1
- ⊞ ▦ PM21
- ▧ MI10
- ⊞ PM13
- ⊞ ▦ ▧ PM5
- ■ ≡ ⊞ ▦ PM43
- ▧ MI30
- ▧ MI7
- ▧ MI31
- ▧ MI2

PHASE DESIGNATIONS:

■ Hoecake   ▦ Armorel
⊞ Nodena   ▨ Malden Plain
▧ Cairo Lowland   ≡ Pemiscot Bayou

Figure 2-2. Cluster analysis of Brainerd-Robinson coefficients of ceramic assemblages from sites surface collected by Stephen Williams (1954) (see Table 2-2 for site names).

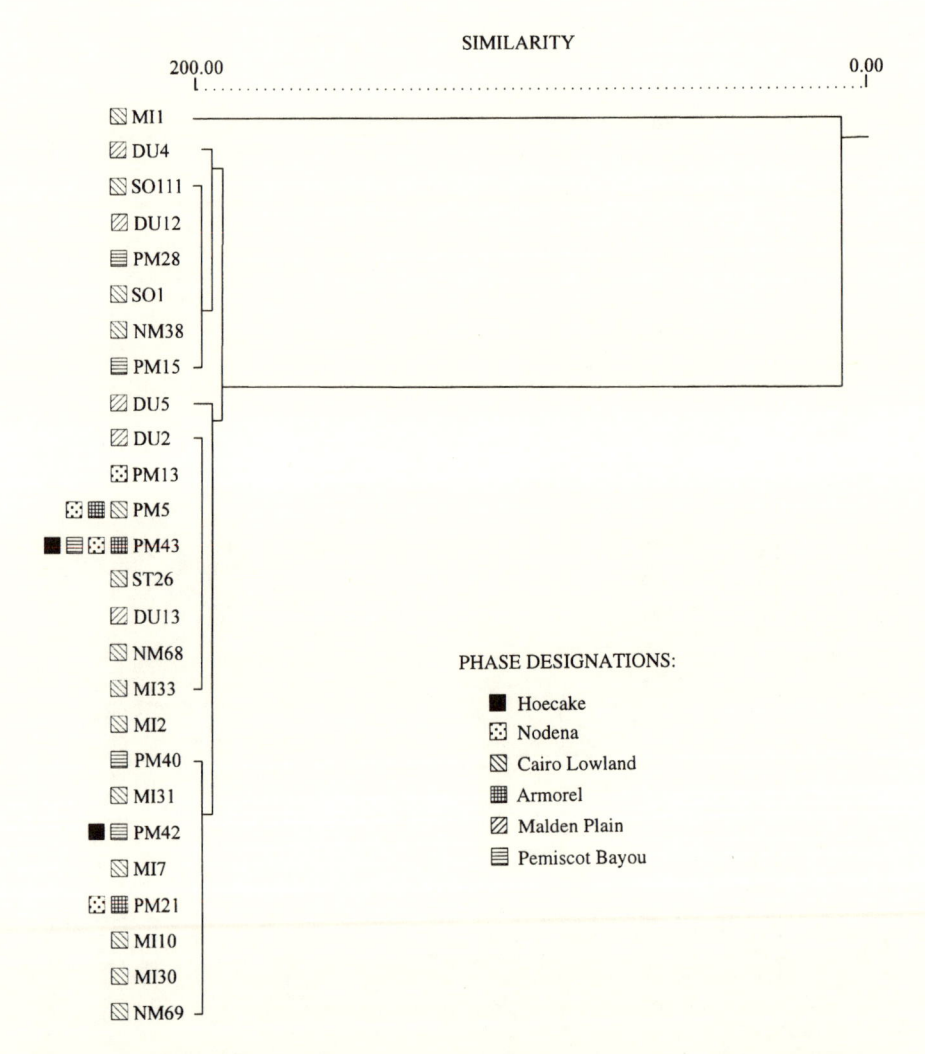

```
                        SIMILARITY
        200.00                                          0.00
          └ . . . . . . . . . . . . . . . . . . . . . . . . . . . ┘
    ▨ MI1
    ▨ DU4
    ▨ SO111
    ▨ DU12
    ≡ PM28
    ▨ SO1
    ▨ NM38
    ≡ PM15
    ▨ DU5
    ▨ DU2
    ▦ PM13
  ▦▤▨ PM5
■≡▦▤ PM43
    ▨ ST26
    ▨ DU13
    ▨ NM68
    ▨ MI33
    ▨ MI2
    ≡ PM40
    ▨ MI31
  ■≡ PM42
    ▨ MI7
  ▦▤ PM21
    ▨ MI10
    ▨ MI30
    ▨ NM69
```

                              PHASE DESIGNATIONS:
                              ■ Hoecake
                              ▦ Nodena
                              ▨ Cairo Lowland
                              ▤ Armorel
                              ▨ Malden Plain
                              ≡ Pemiscot Bayou

Figure 2-3. Averaged Euclidian distances of sites surface collected by Stephen Williams (1954).

in Figure 2-2 are represented in Figure 2-4, as are the outliers—Beckwith's Fort (23MI2) (B), Crosno (23MI1) (A), and the two Early Mississippian–period sites Old Varney River (23DU5) (L) and Kersey (23PM42) (S). A fifth site, Wilkins Island (23DU13 [represented by Z in Figure 2-4]), also appears as an outlier.

To assess the effects of plainwares (Neeley's Ferry Plain and Bell Plain) on the statistical evaluations, the same procedures—BR and multidimensional scaling—were performed on the data after deleting the plainware categories.[2] The BR matrix without plainwares (not shown) has a noticeably different appearance from that of the matrix that includes Neeley's Ferry Plain and Bell

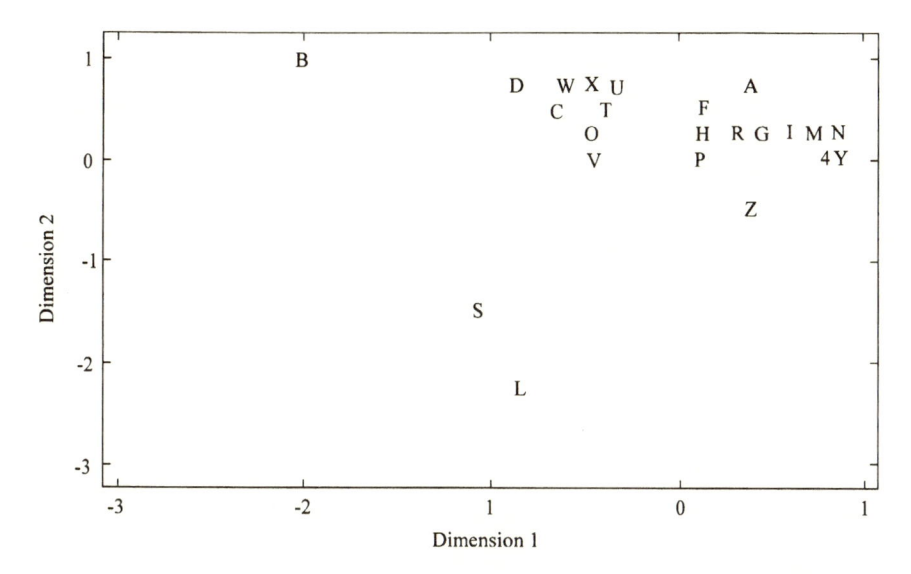

Figure 2-4. Results of multidimensional scaling (two dimensions) of surface-collected ceramic assemblages from twenty-six sites surveyed by Stephen Williams (1954) (from Fox 1992). Key to sites: A, Crosno (23MI1); B, Beckwith's Fort (23MI2); C, Meyer's Mound (23MI10); D, Spanish Grant (23MI31); F, Lilbourn (23NM38); G, Sikeston (23NM68); H, East Lake (23NM69); I, Sandy Woods (23ST26); L, Old Varney River (23DU5); M, Rich Woods (23SO1); N, Lakeville (23SO111); O, Cagle Lake (23PM13); P, Kinfolk Ridge (23PM15); R, Estes (23PM40); S, Kersey (23PM42); T, Murphy (23PM43); U, Campbell (23PM5); V, McCoy (23PM21); W, Hearnes (23MI7); X, Survey (23MI30); Y, Cockrum Landing (23DU12); Z, Wilkins Island (23DU13); 4, Barker (23MI33), Kennett (23DU2), Holcomb (23DU4), and Wardell (23PM28).

Plain. The BR matrix contains four coefficients of 200, representing identical assemblages. These scores, however, simply represent assemblages wherein only one ceramic type (e.g., Varney Red Filmed) is present in each collection after removal of the plainwares; they are not discussed further. Malden Plain–phase assemblages, when plainwares are removed, score between 0 and 168. The highest coefficient (168) occurs between Holcomb (23DU4) and Old Varney River (23DU5) and between Holcomb and Wilkins Island (23DU13). All other Malden Plain–assemblage comparisons score below 134 (compare with Table 2-5). The Pemiscot Bayou–phase sites fare somewhat better, with three coefficients above 140. Comparisons between assemblages from Kinfolk Ridge (23PM15) and Murphy (23PM43) (BR = 140), and between assemblages from Wardell (23PM28) and Kersey (23PM42) (BR = 186), indicate there may be some cohesion to those particular groupings (see O'Brien and Fox 1994b). When plainwares are removed, the highest coefficient between assemblages assigned to the Nodena phase— Campbell (23PM5), Cagle Lake (23PM13), Murphy (23PM43), and McCoy

(23PM21)—is only 126, with the other coefficients falling below 63 (see O'Brien and Fox 1994b).

Using ceramic-type-frequency data, an averaged Euclidean-distance cluster analysis of ceramic assemblages without plainwares also was run (not shown) to determine whether the phase assignments could be replicated by cluster analysis. Because of the high degree of similarity among many components, the resulting dendrogram is not readily interpreted as indicating clusters. There are two clear outliers—Crosno (23MI1) and Old Varney River (23DU5). The remainder of the components are, again, assigned willy-nilly to the Cairo Lowland, Malden Plain, Nodena, and Pemiscot Bayou phases. In summary, no clear segregation of sites by phase is evident in the BR scores, in the cluster analysis of those scores, or in the cluster analysis of the ceramic-type frequencies. Hence, we must conclude that none of the current phases, as defined by in-use historical ceramic types, is a cohesive unit sufficiently distinct to be categorized as a phase.

BR coefficients of similarity calculated on Williams's (1954) surface collections appear to reveal a diverse group of ceramic assemblages when plainwares are included. When sherds of the two plainware types are removed, assemblages assigned to individual phases also do not appear to represent homogeneous, cohesive groups, even though ceramic types ostensibly used to identify phases are now major parts of the assemblages. In part, sample size and temporal differences might be contributing to the problems of interpreting the analytical results. However, if the excavated and surface assemblages represent samples from like components, cluster analysis employing either the BR scores or the ceramic-type frequencies should have produced clusters of ceramic assemblages similar to the groups of sites Williams assigned to the individual phases. This simply is not the case.

A Comparison of Excavated Assemblages from Southeastern Missouri

Williams (1954) was not the only archaeologist to assign sites to the phases he defined. Virtually all other archaeologists working in southeastern Missouri have used his model to classify assemblages, components, and sites. The following analysis of larger excavated assemblages is presented to exhaust possibilities that might justify Williams's phases. The following evaluations were done with only large, excavated, pooled samples of ceramics. Fifteen excavated sites were identified in the literature as having samples of sufficient size for comparison. Of these, five are in Mississippi County, Missouri; eight are in Pemiscot County, Missouri; one is in Dunklin County, Missouri; and one is in Cross County, Arkansas. Other excavated materials exist, but generally those samples are small or are presented in such a way that they could not be used in this analysis.

The BR matrix (Table 2-6) calculated for this sample of fifteen sites resulted

Table 2-6. Similarity Matrix of Brainerd–Robinson Coefficients of Excavated Ceramic Assemblages from Fourteen Sites in Southeastern Missouri and One in Northeastern Arkansas

2	133													
3	153	170												
4	159	118	142											
5	167	118	143	172										
6	96	139	139	86	88									
7	107	166	150	97	99	168								
8	166	131	160	156	158	130	130							
9	92	122	127	80	84	137	135	111						
10	94	94	97	92	96	97	100	100	150					
11	105	134	138	95	97	159	155	139	156	121				
12	162	120	144	154	155	116	125	166	92	92	112			
13	105	106	110	106	107	96	105	114	150	186	125	105		
14	170	133	157	170	179	107	118	175	102	91	116	163	105	
15	122	155	159	112	114	152	157	148	157	124	175	121	38	132
	1	2	3	4	5	6	7	8	9	10	11	12	13	14

Note: 1, Crosno (23MI1) (S. Williams 1954); 2, Callahan–Thompson (23MI71) (Lewis 1982); 3, Hess (23MI55) (Lewis 1982); 4, Mort (23MI69) (J. R. Williams 1968); 5, Byrd (23MI53) (J. R. Williams 1968); 6, McCoy (23PM21) (J. R. Williams 1968); 7, Cagle Lake (23PM13) (J. R. Williams 1972); 8, Denton Mounds (23PM549) (J. R. Williams 1972); 9, Holland (23PM2) (Marshall 1965); 10, Kersey (23PM42) (Marshall 1965); 11, Campbell (23PM5) (UMC Museum collections); 12, Parkin (3CS29) (Klinger 1977b); 13, Old Varney River (23DU5) (S. Williams 1954); 14, Dorrah (23PM11) (UMC Museum collections); 15, Murphy (23PM43) (UMC Museum collections). UMC, University of Missouri–Columbia.

in a correlation matrix that contrasts with previous matrices. Similarity coefficients range from a high of 186 to a low of 80. Only one score—that between Old Varney River (23DU5) and Kersey (23PM42)—is above 180, fifteen are between 160 and 179, twenty-two are between 140 and 159, and sixty-seven are below 140 (more than a 30-percent cumulative-frequency difference). (The large number of low BR scores is expected, as the comparisons are made across proposed phases, time, and geographic space.) High coefficients are not restricted to assemblage comparisons within bounded geographic regions (the phases) as originally defined by Williams (1954). The highest coefficient (186) is between an assemblage assigned to the Malden Plain phase (that from Old Varney River [23DU5]) and an assemblage assigned to the Pemiscot Bayou phase (Kersey [23PM42]). Both assemblages have an Early Mississippian–period component, and one (Kersey) also has small Middle Mississippian– and Late Mississippian–period components.

Six coefficients of 160 or higher link assemblages from Pemiscot County to assemblages from Mississippi County (Dorrah [23PM11] to Byrd [23MI53], Crosno [23MI1], and Mort [23MI69]; Cagle Lake [23PM13] to Callahan-Thompson [23MI71]; and Denton Mounds [23PM549] to Crosno and Hess [23MI55]). Three coefficients of 160 or higher link assemblages from Pemiscot County (Dorrah [23PM11] to Denton Mounds [23PM549]; Cagle Lake [23PM13] to McCoy [23PM21]; and Murphy [23PM43] to Campbell [23PM5]). Three coefficients of 160 or higher link assemblages from Mississippi County (Byrd [23MI53] to Mort [23MI69] and Crosno [23MI1], and Hess [23MI55] to Callahan-Thompson [23MI71]). Two coefficients of 160 or higher link the Parkin (3CS29 [Cross County, Arkansas]) assemblage to Pemiscot County assemblages (Denton Mounds [23PM549] and Dorrah [23PM11]). Finally, one coefficient of 160 or higher (162) links the Parkin (3CS29) assemblage to that from Crosno (23MI1). These assemblages are the largest samples currently available for analysis from southeastern Missouri (excluding the assemblage from Parkin) and are constantly used in the literature to compare and assign ceramic assemblages to phases. The assemblages also provide virtually the entire comparative material on which current Mississippian-period prehistory in southeastern Missouri is based (see Chapman 1980; Morse and Morse 1983; Price and Price 1990; Smith 1990).

Cluster analysis of BR coefficients of excavated assemblages with plainwares included produced three clusters (Figure 2-5). Cluster 1 contains assemblages from Mort (23MI69), Byrd (23MI53), Dorrah (23PM11), Denton Mounds (23PM549), Crosno (23MI1), and Parkin (3CS29). These assemblages were previously assigned variously to the Cairo Lowland, Nodena, Pemiscot Bayou, Parkin, and Armorel phases. Cluster 2 contains assemblages from Hess (23MI55), Callahan-Thompson (23MI71), Cagle Lake (23PM13), McCoy (23PM21), Campbell (23PM5), Murphy (23PM43), and Holland (23PM2). Previous phase assignments of the ceramic assemblages represented in Cluster 2 include the Cairo Lowland, Nodena, Armorel, and Pemiscot Bayou phases. Cluster 3 contains only two assemblages—those from Kersey (23PM42) and Old Varney River (23DU5). On the basis of published ceramic-type frequencies, Old Varney River is a single-component, Early Mississippian–period site; Kersey, as mentioned previously, has a major Early Mississippian–period component as well as a minor later component. Ceramic assemblages from two sites—Campbell (23PM5) and Parkin (3CS29)—are included in distinct clusters, even though they often have been identified in the literature (e.g., Williams 1954, 1980) as components of the same phase. Campbell is considered by Williams (1980) to be the type site of the Armorel phase and Parkin a member of that phase. Morse (1981, 1990), however, places it in the Parkin phase. Multidimensional scaling of the similarity matrix (Figure 2-6) illustrates a fairly tight cluster (*A, D, E, H, L, N*) representing Cluster 1 in Figure 2-5. Cluster 2 (*C, B, G, F, I, K, O*) is not so closely linked, and Cluster 3 is separate and isolated in the plot.

Mississippian Phases in Missouri | 53

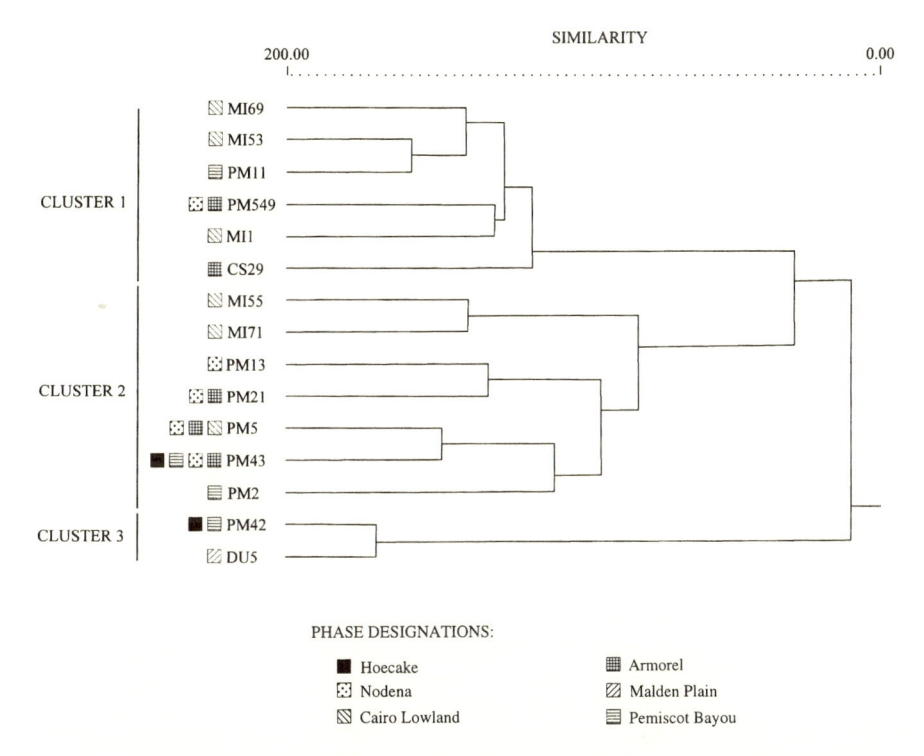

```
                              SIMILARITY
              200.00                                          0.00
              |...................................................|
              ▨ MI69  ─────┐
              ▨ MI53  ───┐ │
              ≡ PM11  ───┤ ├─┐
CLUSTER 1     ⬚▦ PM549 ───┘ │ │
              ▨ MI1   ──────┘ ├──────────────┐
              ▦ CS29  ────────┘              │
              ▨ MI55  ─────┐                 │
              ▨ MI71  ───┐ │                 │
              ⬚ PM13  ───┤ ├─┐               │
CLUSTER 2     ⬚▦ PM21  ───┘ │ ├──────┐        │
              ⬚▦▨ PM5   ─────┘ │      ├───────┤
              ■≡⬚▦ PM43  ───────┘      │       │
              ≡ PM2   ────────────────┘       │
CLUSTER 3     ■≡ PM42  ───┐                    │
              ▧ DU5   ───┴────────────────────┘
```

PHASE DESIGNATIONS:

■ Hoecake   ▦ Armorel
⬚ Nodena   ▧ Malden Plain
▨ Cairo Lowland   ≡ Pemiscot Bayou

Figure 2-5. Cluster analysis of Brainerd-Robinson coefficients of excavated ceramic assemblages from fourteen sites in southeastern Missouri and one in northeastern Arkansas (Parkin) (from Fox 1992).

As with the other BR matrices, a separate matrix was calculated without the two plainware types (not shown), and as with the previous analyses in which plainwares were excluded, this matrix consistently produced lower BR coefficients. Only nine comparisons resulted in scores above 140 (less than a 30-percent cumulative-frequency difference in assemblage composition). Surprisingly, only one pair of Cairo Lowland–phase assemblages (those from Crosno [23MI1] and Byrd [23MI53]) has a BR coefficient above 140. The two Early Mississippian–period sites (Old Varney River [23DU5] and Kersey [23PM42]) retain their high coefficient (191). The remaining high correlations are all confined to Pemiscot County sites.

Cluster analysis of the BR coefficients of assemblages with the plainwares removed (Figure 2-7) indicates three clusters that join at a greater distance than the clusters derived from the assemblages containing plainwares. Cluster 1 contains assemblages from Callahan-Thompson (23MI71), Hess (23MI55), Crosno (23MI1), and Byrd (23MI53), which were previously assigned to the Cairo Lowland phase. The assemblage from Mort (23MI69) might be considered as an outlier since its inclusion in Cluster 1 would merge the otherwise distinct clusters 2 and 3 as a single group. Clusters 2 and 3 are linked at the same distance as

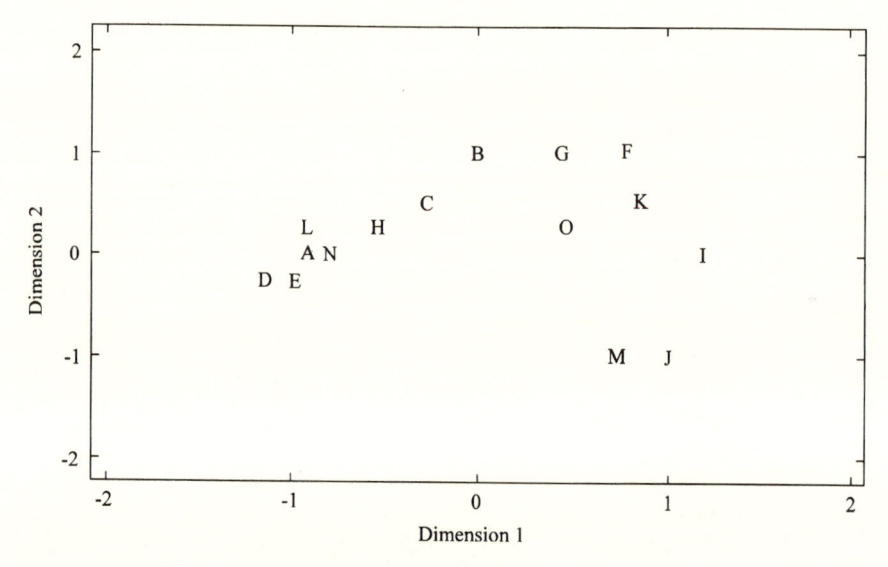

Figure 2-6. Results of multidimensional scaling (two dimensions) of excavated ceramic assemblages from fourteen sites in southeastern Missouri and one in northeastern Arkansas (Parkin) (from Fox [1992] and O'Brien and Fox [1994b]). Key to sites: A, Crosno (23MI1); B, Callahan-Thompson (23MI71); C, Hess (23MI55); D, Mort (23MI69); E, Byrd (23MI53); F, McCoy (23PM21); G, Cagle Lake (23PM13); H, Denton Mounds (23PM549); I, Holland (23PM2); J, Kersey (23PM42); K, Campbell (23PM5); L, Parkin (3CS29); M, Old Varney River (23DU5); N, Dorrah (23PM11); O, Murphy (23PM43).

Cluster 1. Cluster 2 contains four assemblages—those from Dorrah (23PM11), Parkin (3CS29), Cagle Lake (23PM13), and McCoy (23PM21), which were previously assigned to no fewer than three phases—Pemiscot Bayou, Nodena, and Armorel. Cluster 3 contains assemblages from Campbell (23PM5), Denton Mounds (23PM549), Murphy (23PM43), Holland (23PM2), Kersey (23PM42), and Old Varney River (23DU5). Assemblages in this cluster previously were assigned to the Malden Plain, Big Lake, Nodena, Armorel, Campbell, Hayti, and Pemiscot Bayou phases.

The assignment of four Cairo Lowland-phase assemblages to a single cluster is the only occurrence of such correspondence in all the analyses performed. It is not symmetrical, however, since not all Cairo Lowland assemblages are assigned to that cluster. Nor is it general, since clusters 2 and 3 have mixed-phase membership. Cluster 1 represents a cluster of BR coefficients in which, first, the plainwares were removed and, second, the average BR coefficient among and between the assemblages is below 116.

Cluster analysis of the ceramic-type frequencies without plainwares (not shown) produced a single cluster with several outliers. Such arrangements are not usually regarded as meaningful, an interpretation supported by the inclusion of Old Varney River (23DU5) but the exclusion of Kersey (23PM42) in the

Mississippian Phases in Missouri | 55

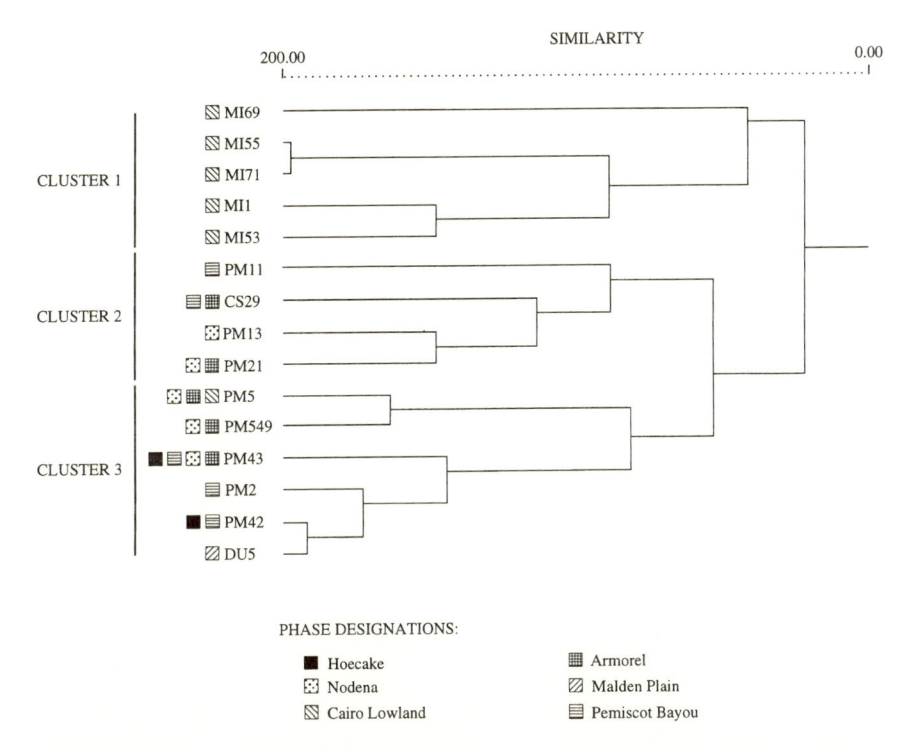

```
                                    SIMILARITY
                200.00                                                  0.00
                L........................................................I

              ▧ MI69  ─────────────────────────────┐
              ▧ MI55  ┐                            │
CLUSTER 1     ▧ MI71  ┘├──┐                        │
              ▧ MI1   ───┤                         │
              ▧ MI53  ───┘                         │
              ▤ PM11  ─────┐                       │
              ▤▦ CS29 ─────┤                       │
CLUSTER 2     ▦ PM13  ─────┤                       │
              ▦▤ PM21 ─────┘                       │
              ▦▤▧ PM5  ──┐                         │
              ▦▤ PM549 ──┤                         │
CLUSTER 3     ■▤▦▤ PM43 ──┤                        │
              ▤ PM2    ──┤                         │
              ■▤ PM42  ──┤                         │
              ▨ DU5    ──┘
```

PHASE DESIGNATIONS:

■ Hoecake   ▤ Armorel
▦ Nodena   ▨ Malden Plain
▧ Cairo Lowland   ▤ Pemiscot Bayou

Figure 2-7. Cluster analysis of Brainerd-Robinson coefficients of excavated ceramic assemblages from fourteen sites in southeastern Missouri and one in northeastern Arkansas (Parkin), with Neeley's Ferry Plain and Bell Plain sherds removed (from Fox 1992).

cluster (they were closely linked in previous analyses discussed here). Even so, it is worth noting that the eleven assemblages—from Callahan-Thompson (23MI71), Old Varney River (23DU5), Denton Mounds (23PM549), Campbell (23PM5), Cagle Lake (23PM13), Holland (23PM2), Hess (23MI55), Byrd (23MI53), Dorrah (23PM11), Mort (23MI69), and Parkin (3CS29)—join as a cluster. Assemblages in the macrocluster have been assigned by various investigators to the Cairo Lowland, Nodena, Armorel, Campbell, Malden Plain, and Pemiscot Bayou phases (Parkin is assigned to the Parkin phase by Morse [1981, 1990]). The cluster of Cairo Lowland–phase assemblages is not replicated when the ceramic-type frequencies are subjected to cluster analysis.

Multidimensional scaling of the BR matrix of excavated assemblages without plainwares produced the plot in Figure 2-8. Once sherds of Neeley's Ferry Plain and Bell Plain are removed, the Mississippi County sites group in a more definable cluster than they do when those types are included. All five Mississippi County sites (*A* through *E*) lie to the left of the centerline and well away from the Pemiscot Bayou–Parkin–Old Varney River group, though Williams's (1954) archetype ceramic assemblage, that from Crosno (*A*), is the farthest dis-

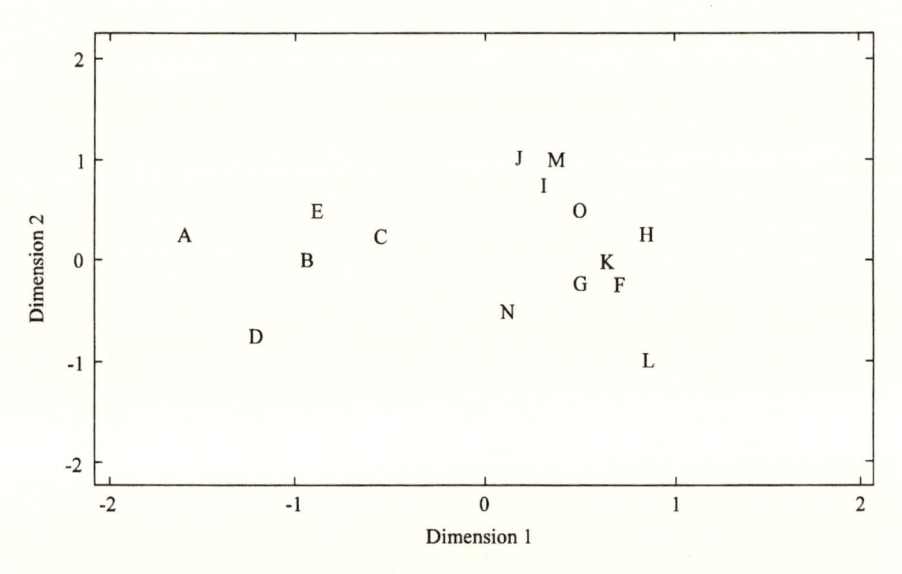

[Scatter plot with Dimension 1 on x-axis (-2 to 2) and Dimension 2 on y-axis (-2 to 2), showing letter-labeled points A through O]

Figure 2-8. Results of multidimensional scaling (two dimensions) of excavated ceramic assemblages from fourteen sites in southeastern Missouri and one in northeastern Arkansas (Parkin), with Neeley's Ferry Plain and Bell Plain sherds removed (from Fox [1992] and O'Brien and Fox [1994b]). Note the separation between the five Mississippi County sites on the left and the more southern (and for the most part later) sites on the right. Compare the distribution seen in Figure 2-6. Key to sites: *A*, Crosno (23MI1); *B*, Callahan-Thompson (23MI71); *C*, Hess (23MI55); *D*, Mort (23MI69); *E*, Byrd (23MI53); *F*, McCoy (23PM21); *G*, Cagle Lake (23PM13); *H*, Denton Mounds (23PM549); *I*, Holland (23PM2); *J*, Kersey (23PM42); *K*, Campbell (23PM5); *L*, Parkin (3CS29); *M*, Old Varney River (23DU5); *N*, Dorrah (23PM11); *O*, Murphy (23PM43).

tance away from another Mississippi County assemblage. The Pemiscot Bayou sites (*F* through *K*) form a cluster to the right of the centerline, along with Old Varney River (23DU5 [*M*]) and Parkin (3CS29 [*L*]). Sites often cited in the literature (e.g., O'Brien 1994a) as being very late—Campbell (23PM5 [*K*]), Cagle Lake (23PM13 [*G*]), and McCoy (23PM21 [*F*])—cluster together tightly, as do Old Varney River (23DU5 [*M*]), Holland (23PM2 [*I*]), and Kersey (23PM42 [*J*]). Interestingly, Parkin (*L*), a supposed component of the Armorel phase (Williams 1980), lies well away from Campbell (*K*), another Armorel component (Williams 1980).

Summary

Current phase constructions in southeastern Missouri are clearly not based on any general principles. Rather, a phase is "defined" from an archetypical component, and all subsequent assemblages are compared to that component. In the absence of a perfect match, those assemblages are assigned to new phases using a vague notation of similarity. The new phases become archetypes for assemblages that contain the new requisite traits (in southeastern Missouri this was originally phrased [Williams 1954] as the absence of Cairo Lowland–phase traits). Those new phases are considered axiomatic by their originators, when in fact they are anecdotal.

BR coefficients of similarity calculated to evaluate the similarities of ceramic assemblages from southeastern Missouri illustrate the ad hoc nature of the development of cultural phases in the region. What appeared to the original investigators to be cohesive, congruent sets of pottery types often exhibit minimal similarity in terms of pottery-type frequencies. Cluster analysis, a multivariate procedure designed to detect natural groupings in data, consistently failed to segregate either the BR coefficients or the pottery-type-frequency data into the sets of assemblages created by Williams (1954) and others. When the plainware categories are removed, those same assemblages often exhibit little statistical similarity whatsoever. Cluster analysis of the BR matrices and of ceramic-type-frequency data and the multidimensional-scaling procedures were intended to examine (1) whether assemblages assigned to existing phases would cluster and (2) the nature of those clusters. These examinations failed to produce clusters comprising assemblages assigned to a single phase. The sole exception is the cluster of four excavated assemblages assigned to the Cairo Lowland phase (see Figure 2-7). However, this coincidence is best explained as a chance occurrence, given the number of cluster analyses performed.

Although the Cairo Lowland phase has been considered to be "without a question the most profusely documented phase in the Lower Mississippi Valley, if not the entire Southeast" (Phillips 1970:925), statistical comparisons of ceramic assemblages assigned to that phase do not support this contention. Cairo Lowland components are not closely similar and do not consistently generate high BR coefficients. Rather, BR coefficients illustrate considerable differences among both the surface-collected and excavated assemblages. This is particularly true when the plainware types are removed from the assemblages. On the other hand, comparisons of sites assigned to the Pemiscot Bayou phase, considered "one of our weakest Mississippian formulations" (Phillips 1970:929), produce numerous high BR coefficients and continue to produce high scores when plainwares are removed from the assemblages (see O'Brien and Fox 1994a for an expanded discussion of the Pemiscot Bayou assemblages).

Discussion

Variation in the Mississippian-period archaeological record from southeastern Missouri is immense. Past attempts to order that variation in terms of the dimensions of time, space, and content are based on unsystematic comparisons of assemblages of varying degrees of similarity in terms of pottery-type frequency. However, if we are to advance our knowledge of the archaeological record, we must first illustrate the flaws in existing attempts to carve up the record; of primary importance is demonstrating that phenomena once thought to be the same are now known to vary in their levels of similarity. Phases for southeastern Missouri were developed implicitly from the essentialist concept of the archetype or type site. Continued use of the phase concept without a critical examination of the underlying nature of the classification system employed to define the phases has led to an acceptance of the system as reality.

As presented here, the problem, as well as its solution, is deceptively simple and involves answering three questions: Are the phases groups, are they classes, or are they neither? It might be argued that several things work against our ability to answer these questions. For example, many of the sites under consideration are multicomponent, and the assemblages being analyzed are derived from mixed contexts. Differing sample sizes might influence our analysis as well. Although these problems limit what can be said about the results of the analyses, the same problems were present when the original phases were defined. Consequently, they have no bearing on the use of these analyses to test the validity of the phase formulations. (Expanded discussions of sample size problems, pottery-type identification, and other factors influencing the phase constructions can be found in Fox 1992; Lyman et al. 1997; and O'Brien and Fox 1994a, 1994b.)

It is clear that the absence of an explicit set of necessary and sufficient traits required for membership precludes treating any of the phases as classes. The evaluation of Williams's phases as groups is more complex. Cluster analyses failed to demonstrate that the phases are internally coherent, externally contrastive groups. If Williams's phases are legitimate groups, the analysis presented here should have produced consistently high BR coefficients among members of the same phase and low coefficients between assemblages assigned to different phases. The analyses did not produce this result. In addition, cluster analysis should have produced clusters of assemblages that corresponded to phase assignments. It did not. As a result, I suggest the phases proposed by Williams (1954) and others (Klippel 1969; Marshall 1965; Phillips 1970; Smith 1990; J. R. Williams 1967, 1968, 1972) are neither groups nor classes but rather are inconsistent sets of assemblages. I further submit that the only rationale for their continued existence is historical usage.

Although archaeologists' early efforts to classify archaeological phenomena dating to the Mississippian period in southeastern Missouri are no worse (perhaps even better) than those in other areas, we should not be constrained by those initial interpretations. At this point we should begin to build a new set of data based on a more rigorous paradigm. That paradigm should be based on documentation of all variation within and between assemblages, not on casual reference to broad similarities.

3 | Pottery, Radiocarbon Dates, and Mississippian-Period Chronology Building in Western Kentucky
Paul P. Kreisa

As A CONSEQUENCE of the initiation of stratigraphic excavation as a field technique after the turn of the twentieth century, archaeologists recognized that changes in how artifacts were made, and in some cases decorated, could be used to order the remains of past cultures chronologically. Most often in eastern North America, because of their durability, these remains consisted of projectile points and pieces of broken pottery. Chronological ordering was ordinal until after World War II and the development of radiocarbon dating. With the advent of processual archaeology in the 1960s, chronology came to be viewed as the foundation for addressing more encompassing questions concerning prehistoric cultures and less as an end in and of itself.

Whereas the chronological aspect of phase construction has received a great deal of attention, much less attention has been focused on developing appropriate measures of the spatial extent of phases, even though geographic variation in late-period pottery in the Southeast has long been recognized (e.g., Holmes 1903). No doubt the largest-scale survey and subsequent analysis of Mississippian pottery ever conducted was that of Phillips, Ford, and Griffin (1951) in the lower Mississippi River valley. A key component of that monumental effort was the geographic analysis of pottery performed by James A. Ford and included in the final report (Phillips et al. 1951; see also Ford 1952). One interesting, and perhaps debatable, assumption of that analysis was that in any large region, cultural (and hence ceramic?) continuity was to be expected as a normal state of affairs (Phillips et al. 1951:220). Ford (1952) recognized that the pottery types used to create chronologies in the Mississippi River valley varied systematically in space, and, employing comparisons of ceramic seriations, he identified five regions for the lower Mississippi River valley. Despite this history, archaeologists building chronologies routinely ignore spatial variation in stylistic or cultural-historical types.

The basic manner in which chronologies are constructed has changed little since the first use of radiocarbon dating. Many chronologies still suffer from small sample sizes, dependence on data from single locales, and lack of association between radiocarbon dates and artifacts. Many of these problems become magnified when the proposed chronologies are regional in nature. Interestingly, in those instances in which these problems are overcome, a complex relation between artifacts and chronology, even within a spatially restricted area, is evident (e.g., Kelly, Finney et al. 1984; Milner et al. 1984). This chapter examines the effect of spatial variation relative to competing chronologies in the Ohio-Mississippi confluence region, with specific reference to the Mississippian period in western Kentucky, an area in which I have conducted extensive field research (e.g., Kreisa 1988, 1991; Kreisa and Edging 1990).

Prior to the late 1970s, chronologies for the Mississippian period (post–A.D. 900) in western Kentucky and surrounding regions lacked detail and a solid foundation in radiocarbon dating. A decade of intensive excavations at a number of sites has yielded large ceramic assemblages with associated radiocarbon dates that have been used to address these deficiencies. With the acknowledgment that ceramic chronologies based on associated radiocarbon dates form a foundation for addressing a range of questions concerning the development of Mississippian societies, a number of chronologies and associated phase sequences have been proposed (e.g., Butler 1991; Clay 1979, 1984; Clay et al. 1991; Lewis 1990, 1991; Muller 1986; Wesler 1989, 1991b). Despite, or more accurately because of, the increase in the number of dated ceramic assemblages, Mississippian-period chronology continues to be a source of debate. An interesting and vital area of inquiry is the identification of the *basis* of differences in the interpretation of that chronology.

I review two models of Mississippian-period chronology proposed for the Mississippi River section of western Kentucky, both of which depend heavily on proportional representation of individual types in sherd assemblages. My primary goal is to evaluate the adequacy (or, conversely, the inadequacy) of the two pottery-based chronologies for the region. Secondarily, I examine possible reasons for patterning in the ceramic data. The analysis of spatial variation is based on stratigraphic excavations conducted by members of the Western Kentucky Project of the University of Illinois at Urbana-Champaign at four sites: Rowlandtown, Twin Mounds, Turk, and Adams (Figure 3-1).

Mississippian-Period Chronologies in Western Kentucky

The confluence region of the Mississippi and Ohio rivers has seen the construction of many Mississippian-period ceramic chronologies, most, if not all, of which have provided starting points for much of the research currently in progress in the central Mississippi Valley. Two of the best known are Orr's (1951) Kincaid chronology and Williams's (1954) scheme based on excavations at Crosno in Mississippi County, Missouri (Fox, Chapter 2). Farther to the east, Clay (1961, 1963a, 1963b) detailed a ceramic-based Woodland- and Mississippian-period chronology for the Tennessee-Cumberland region. Other schemes have touched on the Mississippian period, such as those proposed for southeast-

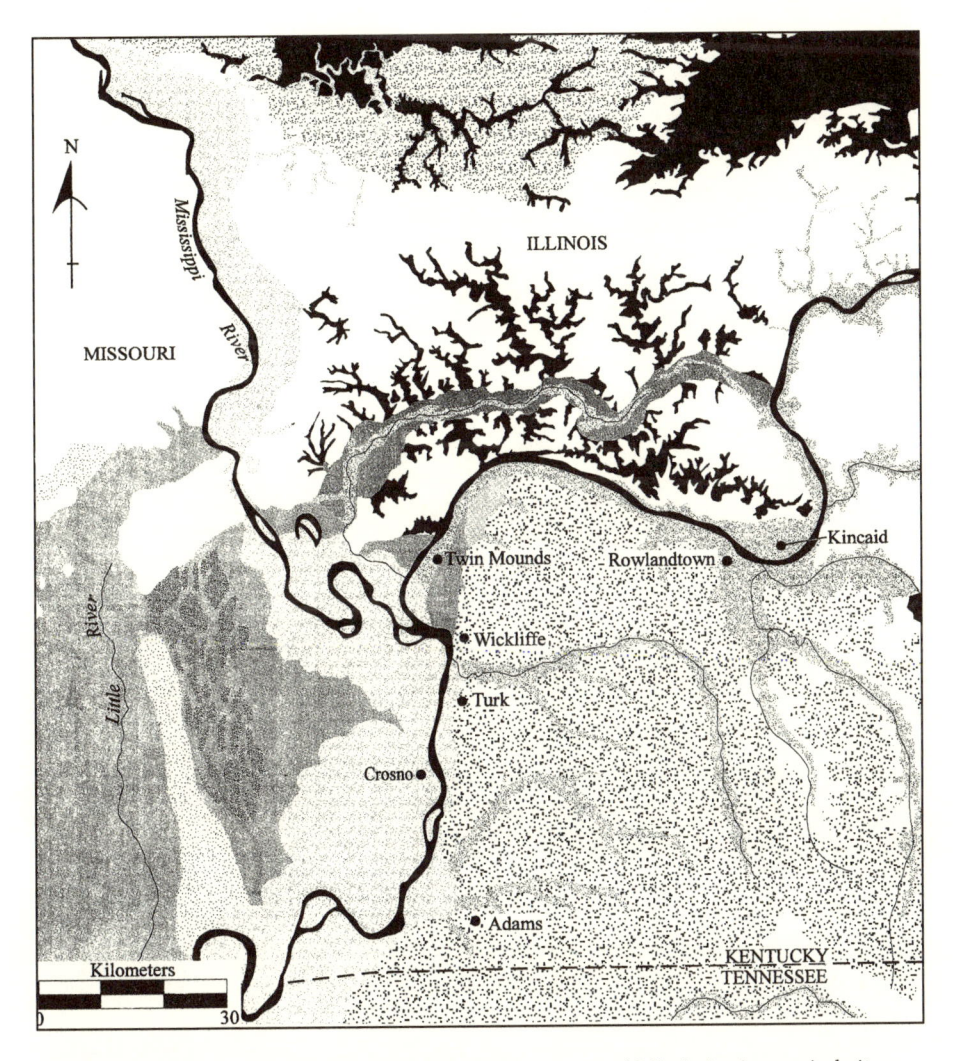

Figure 3-1. Map of western Kentucky showing locations of Mississippian-period sites mentioned in the text.

ern Missouri by Hopgood (1969a), Lafferty and Price (1996), Marshall (1965), and Williams (1967, 1968, 1974).

Currently, there are two principal Mississippian-period chronological sequences for the Mississippi River section of western Kentucky (Figure 3-2). Lewis (1986, 1990, 1991) proposed a four-phase sequence in which temporal parameters are given precedence over cultural parameters. Alternatively, Wesler (1989, 1991b; see also Clay et al. 1991) proposed a three-phase sequence based on his research at Wickliffe Mounds in which cultural differences are given precedence over temporal differences. Although not discussed in this analysis,

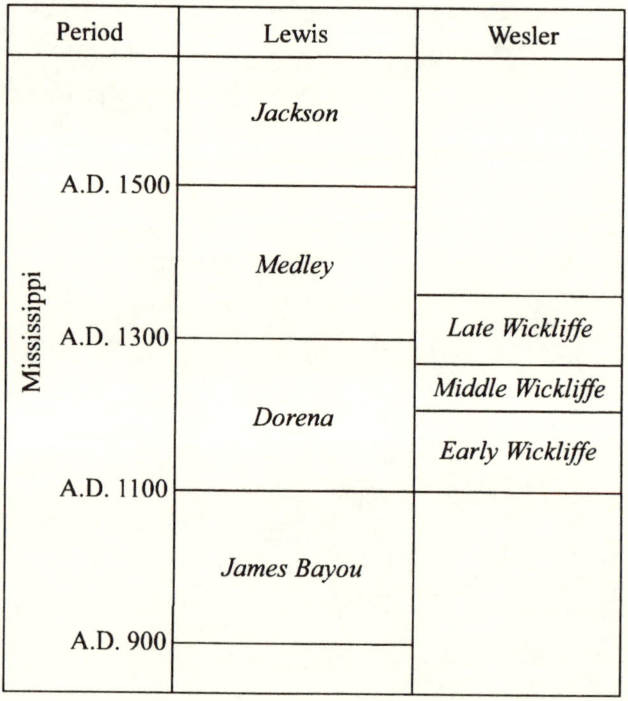

Period		Lewis	Wesler
Mississippi		*Jackson*	
	A.D. 1500		
		Medley	
	A.D. 1300		Late Wickliffe
		Dorena	Middle Wickliffe
			Early Wickliffe
	A.D. 1100		
		James Bayou	
	A.D. 900		

Figure 3-2. Comparison of Mississippian-period phases for western Kentucky proposed by Barry Lewis and Kit Wesler. Wesler's phases are derived primarily from his analysis of materials from the Wickliffe site in Ballard County, Kentucky. Thus he makes no mention of phases not represented by materials from that site.

there are several alternative sequences for the Black Bottom of southern Illinois and the Tennessee-Cumberland rivers region to the east (e.g., Butler 1991; Clay 1979, 1984; Clay et al. 1991; Muller 1986; Riordan 1975).

The methodological basis of Lewis's (1990, 1991) four-phase Mississippian-period chronology differs from that of Willey and Phillips (1958) in at least one significant way. Lewis created a system in which the Mississippian period and its phases are laid out in arbitrary 200-year increments, with the temporal units not viewed as inherent in the archaeological data but rather defined by the archaeologist. In this construct, *Mississippian* is a cultural unit largely divorced from temporal parameters. Lewis (1990, 1991) chose this approach in the belief that when Mississippian is viewed as both a time period and a culture, it takes on stage-like characteristics that confound our efforts to investigate culture change.

The earliest Mississippian phase in Lewis's scheme is James Bayou (A.D. 900–1100). Sherds used as hallmarks are either grog or grog and shell tempered and are mainly unslipped and plain surfaced, though red slipping is also a common surface treatment. Settlements consist of large villages, some of which may have a mound or two, and smaller habitation sites. Ceramic assemblages that characterize the succeeding Dorena phase (A.D. 1100–1300) exhibit the following features: plain, utilitarian vessels are common; red-slipped surfaces decrease in frequency; bottles and plates are added as new vessel forms; and the first decorated vessels are present—those of types such as Matthews Incised (Griffin, in Walker and Adams 1946), O'Byam Incised, *var. Adams,* Mound Place Incised (Phillips et al. 1951:147–48), and Nashville Negative Painted (Griffin, in Phillips 1940; Phillips et al. 1951:174–75). The appearance of towns also characterizes the Dorena phase; they are often 10 hectares or larger, with a central plaza and eight or more mounds, and at times they are palisaded.

The Medley phase (A.D. 1300–1500) exhibits an increase in the amount of decorated pottery, which often comprises 3 to 4 percent of assemblages (Lewis 1991). Hence, there is an increase in the number of pottery types used to place components in the phase as compared to the number of types for the Dorena phase. It has been suggested that populations became concentrated in larger settlements after A.D. 1300, though the number of different site types remained similar to that characterizing the Dorena phase (Kreisa 1990). The fourth Mississippian phase, Jackson (A.D. 1500–1700), has been a point of contention among researchers (e.g., Eisenberg 1989; Wesler 1991a; Williams 1990), and I do not discuss it here.

Wesler (1989, 1991b; see also Clay et al. 1991) proposed an alternative chronology based on his analysis of pottery from Wickliffe. The chronology began as an internal site ordering (Wesler 1989), but more recently it has been applied across a larger portion of western Kentucky (e.g., Wesler 1991b). Wesler developed the chronology because of shortcomings he perceived in the Lewis chronology, namely a lack of flexibility needed to pursue (1) a detailed chronological sequence with phases spanning less than 200 years and (2) redefinition of the chronology as new data become available.

Wesler (1989, 1991b) proposed a three-phase sequence (Figure 3-2): Early Wickliffe, A.D. 1100–1200; Middle Wickliffe, A.D. 1200–1250; and Late Wickliffe, A.D. 1250–1350 (Clay et al. 1991; Wesler 1989, 1991b). Mississippi Plain (Griffin 1949; Griffin, in Walker and Adams 1946:91), Bell Plain (Phillips et al. 1951:122–26), Kimmswick Fabric-Impressed (Orr 1951; Walker and Adams 1946:91), and Wickliffe Thick (Williams 1954) are present in all three phases. Also proposed as characterizing all phases are Matthews Incised, Mound Place Incised, and Barton Incised (Phillips et al. 1951:114–19). Early Wickliffe pottery assemblages have relatively high percentages of Old Town Red (Phillips et al. 1951:129–32); higher, in fact, than the percentage of all incised sherds combined. Wesler (1989, 1991b) also used Ramey Incised (Griffin 1949) as a criterion for including a component in the Early Wickliffe phase. In Middle Wickliffe assemblages, sherds of Old Town Red decrease in percentage and are about as common as incised pottery. One key marker for the middle phase is the decorated type O'Byam Incised, *var. Adams* (Lewis 1986:40–43). Late Wickliffe assemblages are characterized by greater percentages of incised sherds than of Old Town Red sherds. Plates of O'Byam Incised, *var. O'Byam* (Phillips 1970; Williams 1954), and sherds of Nashville Negative Painted, *vars. Angel* and *Nashville* (Phillips et al. 1951:173–77), are present, as are more exotic types from the south such as Winterville (Phillips 1970:172–74), Leland Incised (Phillips et al. 1951:137–40), and Owens Punctated (Phillips et al. 1951:136–37).

On the face of it, these two chronologies are at once very similar and very different. Wesler constructed his ceramic chronology essentially from deposits at Wickliffe, whereas Lewis used data predominantly from Adams and Turk in western Kentucky (Figure 3-1) and from Callahan-Thompson and Hess in the Cairo Lowland of Missouri (Lewis 1982, 1990, 1991) (Figure 2-1). Both researchers note a trend toward increasing percentages of decorated pottery and decreasing percentages of red-slipped pottery through time. But, in contrast to Lewis, Wesler has no pre-A.D. 1100 or post-A.D. 1350 chronological segments for western Kentucky, yet the ceramic attributes of his A.D. 1250–1350 Late Wickliffe phase are similar to those of the A.D. 1300–1500 Medley phase of Lewis. Wesler considers the initial appearance of decorated pottery, especially material placed in Barton Incised, to be as much as fifty to a hundred years earlier than the date set by Lewis, and he uses nonlocal types such as Ramey Incised, Winterville Incised, and Leland Incised to construct his chronology. In contrast, Lewis postulates a decrease in the percentage of Kimmswick Fabric-Impressed and Wickliffe Thick through time, whereas Wesler does not indicate that any significant changes occurred in the popularity of those types.

Current Analysis

I do not add here to these competing models of the local Mississippian-period chronology for western Kentucky. Instead, I attempt to identify possible reasons for the differences between the chronologies. I use sherds (Table 3-1) and radiocarbon dates (Table 3-2) from four Mississippian sites in western Kentucky—Adams, Turk, Twin Mounds, and Rowlandtown (Figure 3-1)—as a data base. The scale of analysis is limited to sherds from excavation units with associated radiocarbon dates that fall between roughly A.D. 1150 and A.D. 1450. I have chosen these four sites because all were excavated by members of the University of Illinois Western Kentucky Project, which thus reduces problems caused by differences in excavation technique and pottery analysis.

The four sites form a north-south transect across western Kentucky (Figure 3-1). From north to south the sites are Rowlandtown, a single-mound site with a 3-hectare village area (Kreisa 1991); Twin Mounds, with two mounds, a plaza, and an 8-hectare village area (Kreisa 1988); Turk, with eight mounds, a plaza,

Table 3-1. Frequencies and Percentages of Selected Ceramic Types from Four Mississippian Sites in Western Kentucky

Site	Mississippi Plain n	%	Bell Plain n	%	Wickliffe Thick n	%	Kimmswick Fabric-Impressed n	%	Matthews Incised n	%	O'Byam Incised n	%	Other Decorated n	%	Old Town Red n	%	Total
Pre–A.D. 1250																	
Twin Mounds	105	70	29	19	1	1	12	8	0	0	0	0	1	1	3	2	151
Turk	148	66	56	25	7	3	7	3	2	1	0	0	1	<1	2	1	223
Adams	671	70	196	20	34	4	35	4	13	1	5	1	2	<1	2	<1	958
A.D. 1250–1350																	
Rowlandtown	2410	94	122	5	2	<1	19	1	1	<1	2	<1	2	<1	6	<1	2564
Twin Mounds	1239	77	283	18	9	1	59	4	3	<1	2	<1	6	<1	5	<1	1606
Turk	847	71	298	25	22	2	15	1	6	1	3	<1	0	0	1	<1	1192
Adams	1778	61	772	27	149	5	81	3	57	2	43	1	14	<1	4	<1	2898
Post–A.D. 1350																	
Rowlandtown	3298	93	216	6	0	0	21	1	7	<1	0	0	11	<1	5	<1	3558
Twin Mounds	3099	79	751	19	15	<1	25	1	32	1	7	<1	6	<1	8	<1	3943
Turk	573	70	195	24	16	2	19	2	8	1	5	1	1	<1	7	1	824
Adams	367	62	161	27	26	4	19	3	9	2	5	1	3	1	4	1	594

Table 3-2. Radiocarbon Dates from Rowlandtown, Twin Mounds, Adams, and Turk

Site	RCYBP[a]	Minimum[b]	Calibrated Age	Maximum
Rowlandtown	540 ± 70	1320	1410	1440
Twin Mounds	630 ± 70	1295	1310, 1355, 1385	1405
	770 ± 70	1220	1280	1295
Adams	610 ± 70	1300	1320, 1340, 1395	1410
	700 ± 70	1275	1295	1385
	820 ± 70	1170	1230	1280
	610 ± 70	1295	1320, 1340, 1395	1410
	900 ± 70	1030	1165	1225
Turk	710 ± 90	1250	1290	1390
	700 ± 70	1275	1295	1385
	910 ± 70	1030	1160	1220
	710 ± 70	1275	1290	1380
	490 ± 70	1405	1435	1455
	630 ± 70	1290	1310, 1355, 1385	1405
	630 ± 70	1290	1310, 1355, 1385	1405

[a]RCYBP, Radiocarbon years before present.
[b]Minimum and maximum ranges presented are 1 standard deviation of the calibrated age; all dates rounded to the nearest 5/0.

and a 3-hectare village area (Edging 1990); and Adams, with seven mounds, a plaza, and an 8-hectare village area (Lewis 1986). Physiographically, Rowlandtown is situated on the edge of the uplands on a secondary stream terrace south of the Ohio River, and Twin Mounds is situated on the floodplain of the Ohio River, north of its confluence with the Mississippi. To the south, Turk is on a spur of the Mississippi River bluff crest, and Adams is on a terrace remnant where Bayou de Chien empties onto the floodplain.

Analytical Units

Analytical units used in this investigation consist of groupings of stratigraphic and arbitrary excavation levels that are associated with, or bracketed by, radiocarbon dates. All radiocarbon dates have been corrected following Stuiver and Reimer (1993) and are presented with one-sigma ranges (Table 3-2; Figure 3-3 [all dates are rounded to the nearest 5/0]). Ceramic data from the

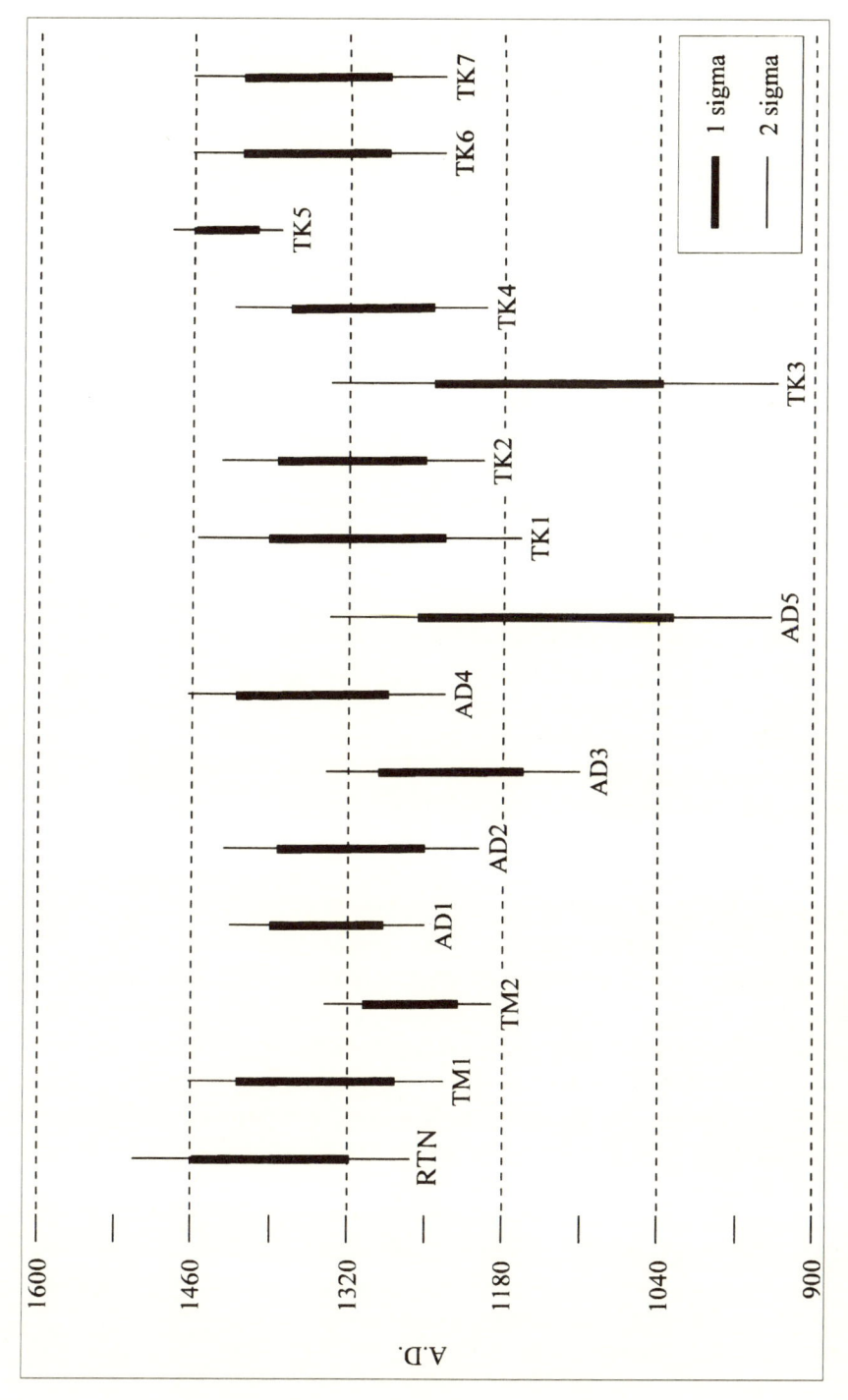

Figure 3-3. Radiocarbon dates from Rowlandtown, Twin Mounds, Adams, and Turk, in order of listing in Table 3-2 (calibrated using Stuiver and Reimer 1993).

stratigraphic and arbitrary excavation levels were incorporated here only if they were associated with, or bracketed by, radiocarbon dates *and* if the deposits did not contain evidence of animal burrows. In cases in which it was recognized that later pits intruded into earlier deposits, samples from the pits were kept separate from those from outside the pits. The ceramic data were first divided into three temporal segments. One set of calibrated dates has ranges between roughly A.D. 1200 and 1300, and another set clusters between A.D. 1300 and 1400. Taking the centerpoints of these ranges, A.D. 1250 and A.D. 1350, respectively, results in a three-fold temporal division: early, or pre–A.D. 1250; middle, or A.D. 1250–1350; and late, or post–A.D. 1350. On the basis of comparisons with other chronologies (e.g., Lewis 1990; Wesler 1991b), the deposits should not predate A.D. 1100, nor should they postdate A.D. 1450.

Data from Rowlandtown were derived from Unit 2, which produced sherds from A.D. 1250–1350 and from post–A.D. 1350 (Table 3-1). Unit 2 was excavated in a village midden area south of the mound. The deposits consisted of several distinct house-construction sequences (Kreisa 1991). The initial 30 centimeters included both intact and disturbed midden deposits. The remains of a burned house, consisting of a daub layer and charred logs, occurred at 30 centimeters below surface. A radiocarbon date from one of the charred logs was assayed at 540 ± 70 B.P., placing the ceramic assemblage into the post–A.D. 1350 sample (Table 3-2). The house layer sealed lower deposits that extended from 30 to 70 centimeters below ground surface and that consisted of a midden, a house basin, and associated wall trenches and post molds. Sherds from that zone do not appear to predate A.D. 1250 and were placed in the A.D. 1250–1350 sample.

Twin Mounds data are from Unit 1 (Kreisa 1988), which produced sherds from all three time segments (Table 3-1). The first 48 centimeters below the surface consisted largely of undifferentiated midden, though two pit features filled with sherds were identified. At about 48 centimeters below surface, more pits and a row of post molds were identified; charcoal recovered from one of the post molds yielded a radiocarbon date of 630 ± 70 B.P. (Table 3-2). The material above the pits was placed in the post–A.D. 1350 sample. Below the 48-centimeter level were three discrete levels of midden into which pits had been excavated. At 175 centimeters below surface, two wall trenches were encountered. A sample of wood charcoal from one wall trench dated to 770 ± 70 B.P. (Table 3-2). Thus the three discrete midden zones are bracketed by calibrated dates of roughly A.D. 1280 to A.D. 1385, placing the material into the A.D. 1250–1350 sample. At 175 centimeters below ground surface, a hard-packed floor sealed all lower deposits. A midden and house basin were found below this level, extending to a depth of 216 centimeters below ground surface.

Data from Turk are from units 1, 2, and 4 (Edging 1990) (Table 3-2). One occupation postdates A.D. 1350, three fall between A.D. 1250 and A.D. 1350, and two predate A.D. 1250. Unit 1 contained deposits dating A.D. 1250–1350 and pre–

A.D. 1250. Two midden zones were defined, with the initial 40 centimeters of deposit dated by a charred-wood sample from 30 centimeters below surface that produced a calibrated date range of A.D. 1250–1390 (710 ± 90 B.P.). The second midden zone, from 40 to 60 centimeters below surface, contained a carbonized-wood sample that produced a calibrated date range of A.D. 1030–1220 (910 ± 70 B.P.). Unit 2 contained two midden zones into which later pits had been excavated. The initial midden zone extended 30 centimeters below surface. A date of 710 ± 70 B.P., or A.D. 1275–1380 (calibrated), was obtained from carbonized wood recovered from the interface of this and the lower midden zone, which extended from 30 to 60 centimeters below surface. This date allowed for a division of the unit between the upper, A.D. 1250–1350, midden and the lower, pre–A.D. 1250, midden.

Superimposed on both was Feature 4, a structural post-and-pit complex that produced a date of 630 ± 70 B.P., or a calibrated date of A.D. 1290–1405. Sherds from the feature were placed in the post–A.D. 1350 group. Unit 4 similarly contained two midden zones. The upper zone, extending from the surface to a depth of 40 centimeters, was differentiated from the lower zone (40 to 95 centimeters) by textural characteristics. Within the lower of the two zones, a radiocarbon assay of 630 ± 70 B.P., or A.D. 1290–1405, was obtained from wood charcoal.[1] Sherds from the lower zone were placed in the A.D. 1250–1350 group, and sherds from the upper zone were placed in the post–A.D. 1350 group. Additional support for this placement comes from Feature 6, an oval pit identified within the upper midden. A radiocarbon assay of wood charcoal from that pit yielded a date of 490 ± 70 B.P., or A.D. 1405–1455.

Data on Adams come from units 1 through 5 (Lewis 1986) and consist of one provenience postdating A.D. 1350, two dating A.D. 1250–1350, and two predating A.D. 1250 (Table 3-2). Unit 1 deposits dated A.D. 1250–1350, with a break between a later Mississippian midden and an earlier Baytown midden identified at 60 centimeters below surface. A charcoal sample from 50 centimeters below surface dated 700 ± 70 B.P., or A.D. 1275–1385 (calibrated). Unit 2 deposits consisted of a midden zone that extended 60 centimeters below surface and that postdated A.D. 1350. A wood-charcoal sample found at 50 centimeters below surface dated 610 ± 70 B.P., or A.D. 1295–1410 (calibrated). Unit 3 deposits, which extended to 55 centimeters below surface, consisted of a series of midden and house-floor zones that dated prior to A.D. 1250. A charcoal sample from 30 to 35 centimeters below surface dated to 820 ± 70 B.P., providing a range of A.D. 1230–1280 (calibrated). Unit 4 sherds from the uppermost 45 centimeters of deposit (one of two strata defined) were placed in the pre–A.D. 1250 sample. A radiocarbon assay of charcoal from a wall-trench feature at the transition between the two strata produced a date of 900 ± 70 B.P., or A.D. 1030–1225 (calibrated). Finally, Unit 5 deposits between 0 and 50 centimeters below surface dated between A.D. 1250 and A.D. 1350. In that unit, between the base of the plow zone and the intact deposits, a feature consisting of a collapsed daub wall and burned beams produced a date of 610 ± 70 B.P., or A.D. 1295–1410 (calibrated).

Analytical Methods

Two methods—cluster analysis (Wilkinson et al. 1992) and multidimensional scaling (Wilkinson et al. 1992)—were used to search for structure within the eleven temporally and geographically categorized assemblages. The variables used for both routines consisted of the percentages of ceramic types presented in Table 3-1. I used cluster analysis to produce groups of assemblages based on similarity of ceramic-type percentages, and I used multidimensional scaling to identify variables that account for the clustering of assemblages into discrete groups (Fox, Chapter 2). Here, cluster analysis links assemblages in a particular order using a specific measure of similarity. A number of different cluster analyses were performed, using both hierarchical agglomerative and hierarchical divisive techniques (Aldenderfer and Blashfield 1984). An ordering of samples as presented in Figure 3-4 was obtained from most of the techniques employed.

Multidimensional scaling, on the other hand, is a technique that measures dissimilarities among sets of values to produce a spatial configuration of points (Kruskal and Wish 1978). Therein, dissimilar assemblages should be farther apart than assemblages that are more alike in terms of ceramic-type percentages. A calculation of stress reveals whether the number of dimensions plotted represents the data adequately; low stress values indicate an adequate representation.

Results

On the basis of a visual inspection of Figure 3-4, I identified four groups of analytical samples in descending order of similarity: Cluster 1—all early, middle, and late assemblages from the Turk and Adams sites; Cluster 2—early assemblage from Twin Mounds; Cluster 3—middle and late assemblages from Twin Mounds; and Cluster 4—middle and late assemblages from Rowlandtown. For the most part, the northern sites of Twin Mounds and Rowlandtown are at the top of the dendrogram and are separate from the southern sites, which cluster together at the bottom of the dendrogram. The clusters suggest a divergence of northern and southern assemblages, with additional differences between the northern sites of Twin Mounds and Rowlandtown. Interestingly, the early Twin Mounds assemblage is more similar to the southern assemblages than it is to any later assemblage from either Twin Mounds or Rowlandtown. In general, the cluster analysis provides support that geographic variation exists within the Mississippian assemblages of western Kentucky, though temporal variation exists as well.

Figure 3-5 depicts the multidimensional-scaling scatterplot with the ana-

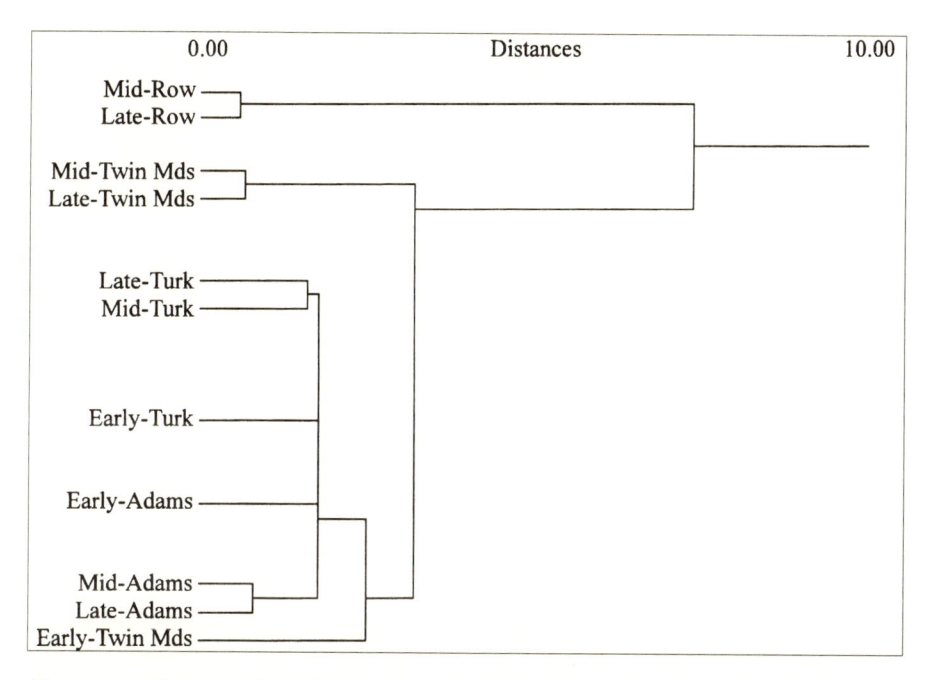

Figure 3-4. Cluster-analysis dendrogram of ceramic assemblages from Adams, Turk, Twin Mounds, and Rowlandtown.

lytical units grouped according to the clusters defined by the cluster analysis. The two-dimensional plot produced a stress level of .00627, indicative of a good representation of the data. Most variation appears to be represented in Dimension 1, which I interpret as representing south-to-north ceramic variation. It is interesting to note that the early, middle, and late Adams and Turk assemblages appear to be more similar to one another, regardless of time period, than they are to similarly dated assemblages from Twin Mounds and Rowlandtown. I interpret Dimension 2 as representing time.

The pottery percentages presented in Table 3-1 can also be used to interpret the multidimensional-scaling scatterplot. Regarding Dimension 1, to the left on the plot, the southern assemblages are characterized by relatively low percentages of Mississippi Plain and high percentages of Bell Plain, Wickliffe Thick, Kimmswick Fabric-Impressed, and Old Town Red. The opposite is true of the northern assemblages, which are located to the right on the plot (Figure 3-5). For Dimension 2, the lower, or earlier, assemblages have relatively low percentages of decorated sherds and Wickliffe Thick and higher percentages of Kimmswick Fabric-Impressed and Old Town Red (Figure 3-5). The opposite is true for the upper, or later, assemblages.

I discuss below several ceramic types—Wickliffe Thick, Kimmswick Fabric-Impressed, O'Byam Incised, Matthews Incised, and Old Town Red—that

72 | Kreisa

[Scatterplot with Dimension 1 (x-axis, -1.5 to 2.0) and Dimension 2 (y-axis, -0.8 to 0.4)]

Cluster 1: points 1, 2, 3, 4, 5, 6
Cluster 2: point 7
Cluster 3: points 8, 9
Cluster 4: points 10, 11

Late
High % Decorated
High % Wickliffe Thick
Low % Kimmswick F.I.
Low % Old Town Red

South
High % Bell Plain
High % Decorated
High % Old Town Red
High % Wickliffe Thick
High % Kimmswick F.I.
Low % Mississippi Plain

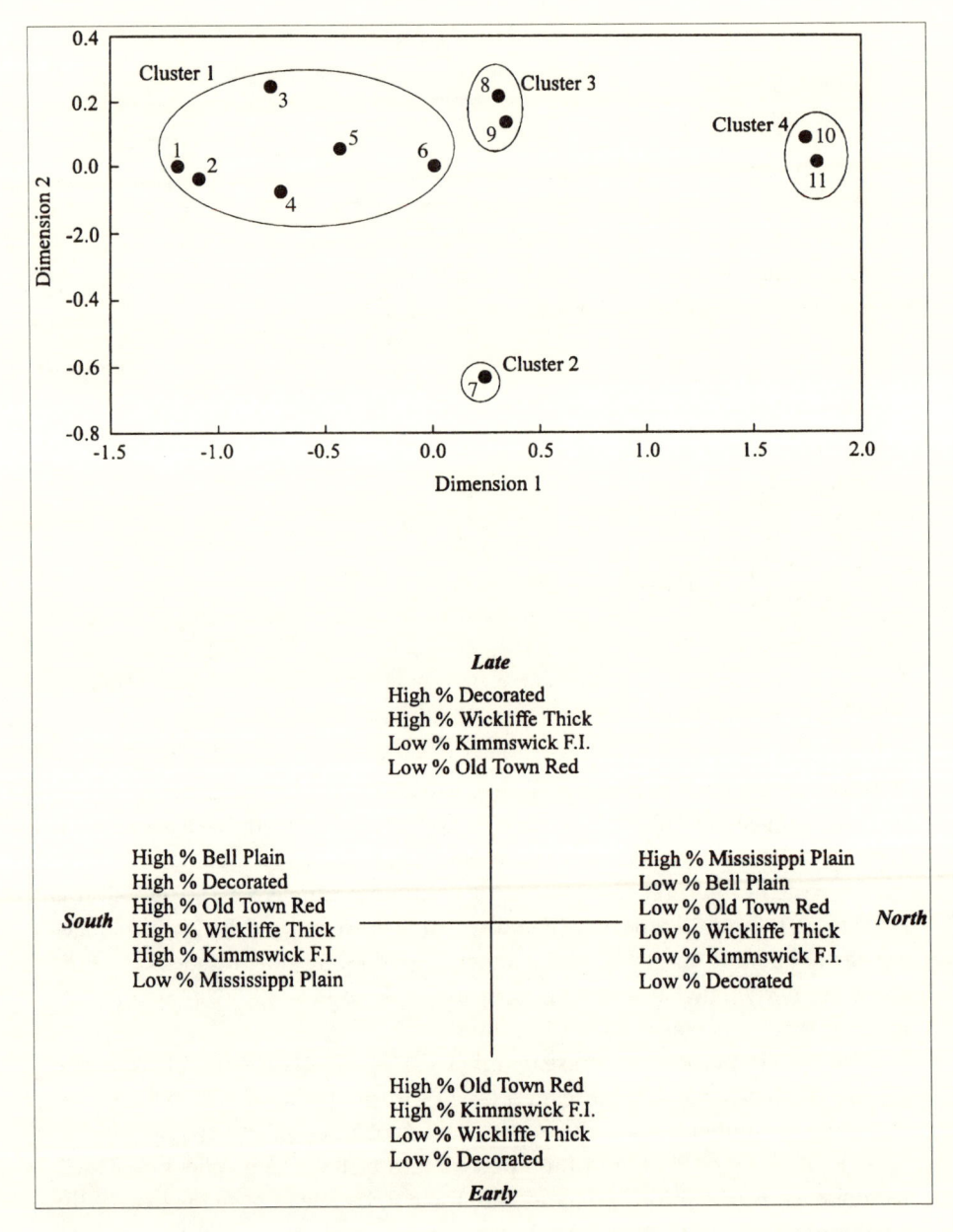

North
High % Mississippi Plain
Low % Bell Plain
Low % Old Town Red
Low % Wickliffe Thick
Low % Kimmswick F.I.
Low % Decorated

High % Old Town Red
High % Kimmswick F.I.
Low % Wickliffe Thick
Low % Decorated
Early

Figure 3-5. Multidimensional-scaling scatterplot of ceramic assemblages from Adams, Turk, Twin Mounds, and Rowlandtown: *1*, Adams (middle); *2*, Adams (late); *3*, Turk (middle); *4*, Turk (early); *5*, Turk (late); *6*, Adams (early); *7*, Twin Mounds (early); *8*, Twin Mounds (late); *9*, Twin Mounds (middle); *10*, Rowlandtown (late); *11*, Rowlandtown (middle).

contribute to temporal variation. This discussion focuses on differential rates of ceramic change between regions, different rates of introduction of key temporal indicators, and a comparison of types of change relative to time and space.

Relative to pre–A.D. 1250 assemblages, similar proportions of Wickliffe Thick and Kimmswick Fabric-Impressed (Figure 3-6) occur in the southern assemblages, and greater proportions of Kimmswick Fabric-Impressed dominate the northern assemblages. There is considerable spatial variation in the proportions of Kimmswick Fabric-Impressed in the A.D. 1250–1350 assemblages, whereas Wickliffe Thick contributes higher percentages to the southern assemblages. Relative to the post–A.D. 1350 assemblages, the percentages of both Wickliffe Thick and Kimmswick Fabric-Impressed are greater in the south than they are in the north. The histograms presented in Figure 3-6 can be interpreted to indicate not only spatial variation but temporal variation as well.

Although decorated pottery exhibits a general increase in frequency through time, the rate appears to vary geographically. For example, no sherds of O'Byam Incised or of Matthews Incised, both of which are considered to be important temporal markers in the region, occur in the pre–A.D. 1250 northern assemblages (Figure 3-7), and only small amounts are found at southern sites. (All of the O'Byam Incised sherds are of O'Byam Incised, *var. Adams.*) Sherds of these types contribute only small percentages to the A.D. 1250–1350 northern assemblages and relatively larger percentages to the contemporaneous southern assemblages. After A.D. 1350, geographic variation is pronounced. Both types comprise small proportions of assemblages in the north but greater proportions in the south. The incorporation of these types into assemblages occurred relatively early in the south but later in the north.

Wesler (1989, 1991b) believes the ratio of red-slipped sherds to decorated sherds is significant chronologically. Sherds of Old Town Red occur more frequently than decorated sherds in pre–A.D. 1250 northern assemblages, though in contrast, decorated sherds are more frequent than Old Town Red in southern assemblages (Figure 3-8). Old Town Red sherds decrease in proportion north to south, whereas decorated sherds increase. This pattern deviates from that expected by Wesler (1989, 1991b) in that pre–A.D. 1250 sites should exhibit higher percentages of Old Town Red sherds than decorated sherds. Relative to A.D. 1250–1350 assemblages, Old Town Red sherds are similar in percentage to decorated sherds at Rowlandtown, whereas at all other sites the percentage of decorated sherds is greater than the percentage of Old Town Red sherds. The ratio of the two types during this period is similar to what Wesler (1989, 1991b) proposes, except in the Rowlandtown assemblage. Finally, post–A.D. 1350 assemblages have a higher proportion of total decorated sherds to Old Town Red sherds, as proposed by Wesler. It appears that the dominance of decorated pottery over Old Town Red pottery occurred prior to A.D. 1150 in the south, but did not occur until after A.D. 1350 in the north.

74 | Kreisa

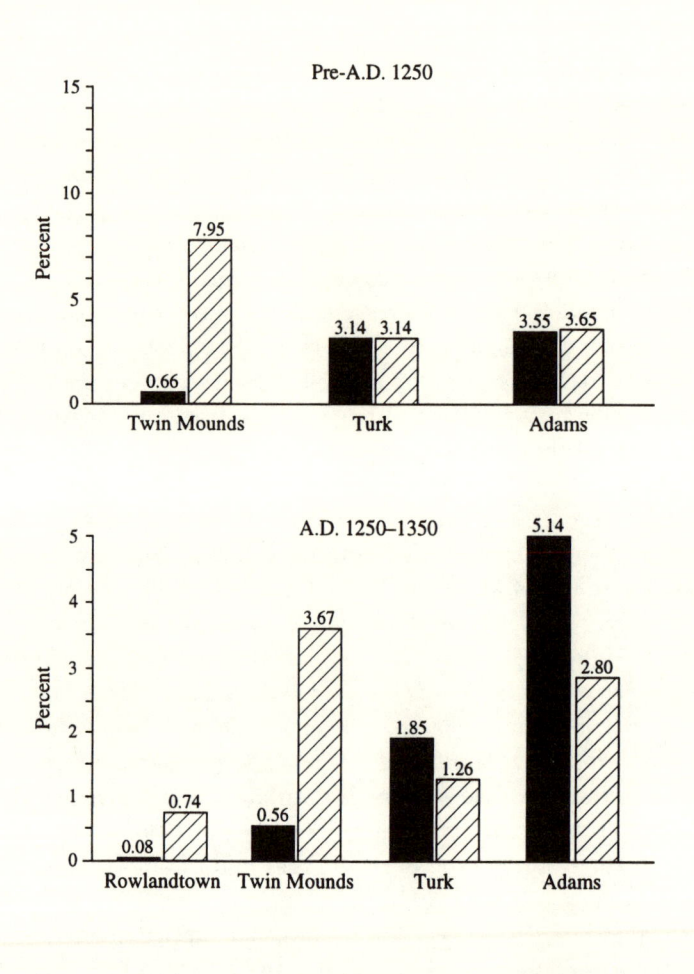

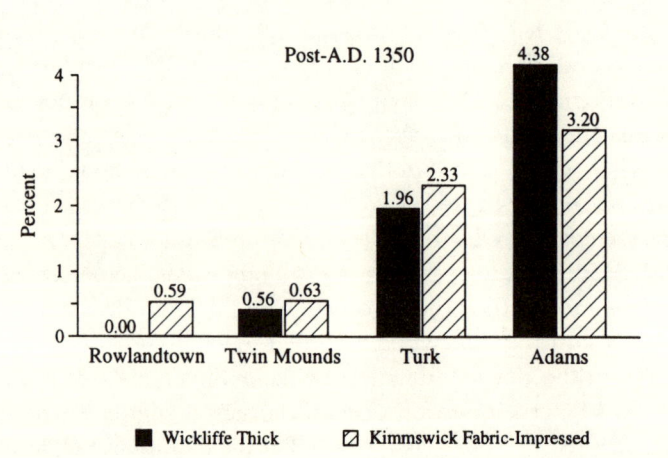

Figure 3-6. Geographic and temporal trends in percentages of Wickliffe Thick and Kimmswick Fabric-Impressed sherds in western-Kentucky assemblages.

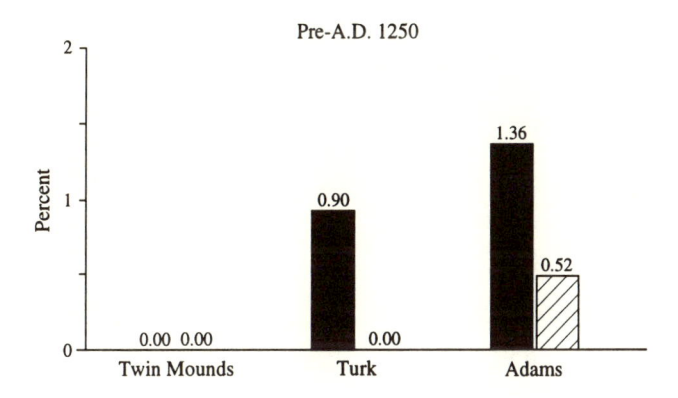

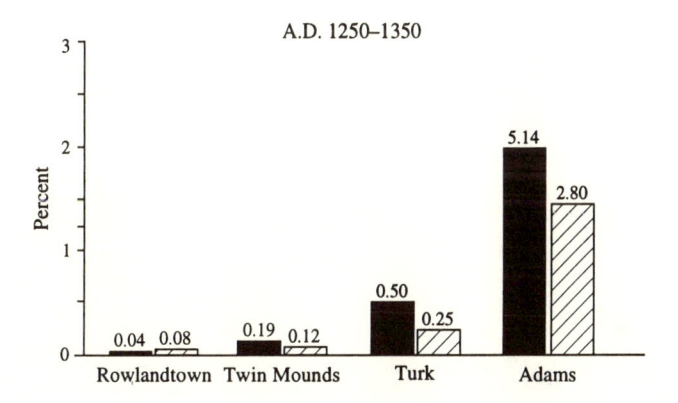

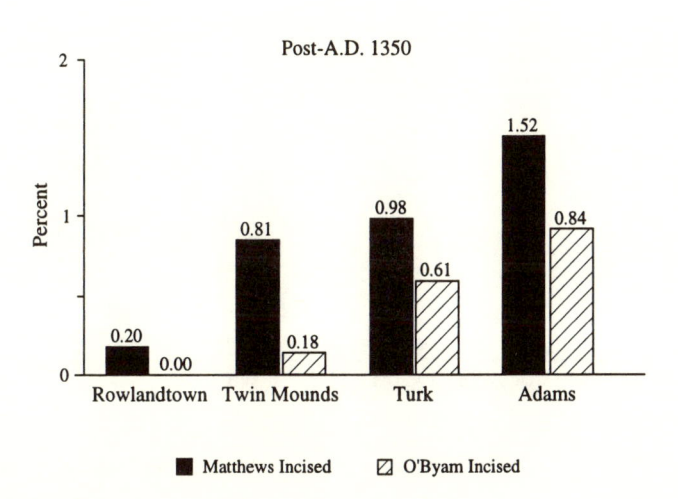

Figure 3-7. Geographic and temporal trends in percentages of Mississippian decorated-pottery types in western-Kentucky assemblages.

76 | Kreisa

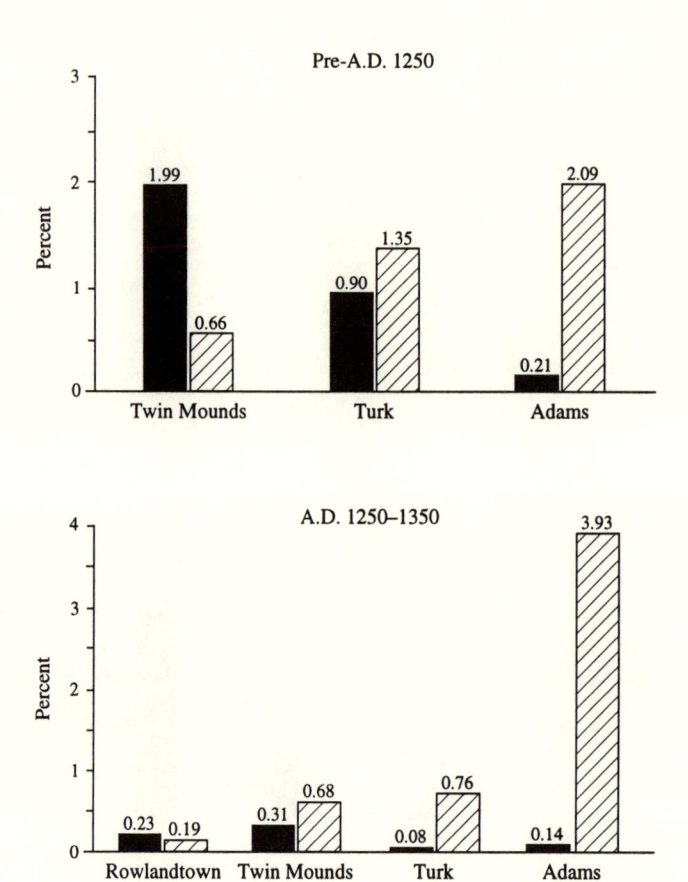

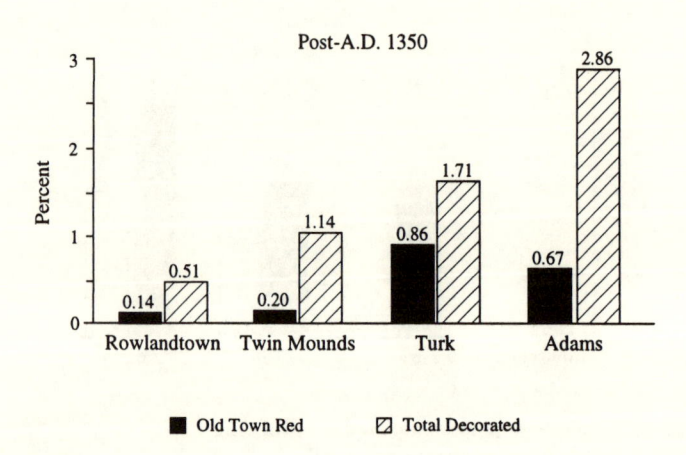

Figure 3-8. Geographic and temporal trends in percentages of Old Town Red and total decorated pottery in western-Kentucky assemblages.

Discussion

The premise of this chapter is that (1) there is significant geographic variation in Mississippian ceramic assemblages of western Kentucky and (2) this has influenced, and perhaps can even explain, some portion of the divergence in regional chronologies. Results of the cluster analysis and multidimensional-scaling analysis presented in the preceding section suggest that spatial or geographic variation *is* present in the Mississippian assemblages of western Kentucky and that this, along with temporal factors, in part determines the structure of ceramic assemblages. Relative frequencies of pottery types, including Mississippi Plain, Bell Plain, Old Town Red, Wickliffe Thick, Kimmswick Fabric-Impressed, and various types of decorated pottery vary from north to south in the region. However, relative frequencies of several pottery types also vary temporally; especially important in this regard are Wickliffe Thick, Kimmswick Fabric-Impressed, Old Town Red, and several types of decorated pottery. This temporal and spatial variation has implications not only for the construction of western-Kentucky chronologies but also for chronology and phase building in general.

The multidimensional-scaling scatterplot (Figure 3-5) indicates that whereas there is a difference between pre–A.D. 1250 and post–A.D. 1250 assemblages, little segregation of A.D. 1250–1350 and post–A.D. 1350 assemblages is apparent. It indicates there are (1) relatively few ceramic markers that differentiate pre–A.D. 1250 and post–A.D. 1250 assemblages and (2) fewer yet that consistently separate A.D. 1250–1350 assemblages from post–A.D. 1350 assemblages. With regard to the four ceramic groups noted earlier as exhibiting temporal variation in western Kentucky, discrepancies between the Lewis and Wesler chronologies and the data base analyzed here can be identified. Both Lewis and Wesler suggest the manufacture of Old Town Red vessels declined through time. The data presented here generally support this proposition, though at Adams and Turk percentages of Old Town Red sherds actually increase in post–A.D. 1350 assemblages. Regarding the ratio of decorated sherds to Old Town Red sherds, greater variation than has been suggested actually exists in the assemblages. Decorated sherds are predominant in the southern assemblages that postdate A.D. 1150, but a similar pattern is not evident in the northern assemblages until after A.D. 1350. More specifically, vessels of O'Byam Incised and Matthews Incised appeared earlier, perhaps by as much as a hundred years, in the south than in the north. Throughout the sequence, sherds of decorated types in general, and of O'Byam Incised and Matthews Incised in particular, are most common at Adams, the southernmost site discussed here, and no O'Byam Incised sherds have ever been found at Rowlandtown, the northernmost locality discussed here. Both Lewis and Wesler place the initial appearance of those two decorated types after A.D. 1100 and more specifically for O'Byam Incised, after A.D. 1200. Data presented here on the appearance of those types generally agree with the chronologies of Lewis and Wesler, though my analysis notes that the two types appeared earlier in the south and later in the north.

Lewis (1986) has suggested that the contributions of Kimmswick Fabric-Impressed and Wickliffe Thick to regional assemblages decreased through time. My analysis demonstrates that the percentage contribution of Kimmswick Fabric-Impressed was very stable through time in southern assemblages and decreased in northern assemblages. Wickliffe Thick decreased through time in northern assemblages, whereas its frequency was more variable in southern assemblages. At Turk, Wickliffe Thick appears to have decreased after A.D. 1250, whereas at Adams it increased. In general, Kimmswick Fabric-Impressed was predominant over Wickliffe Thick in the north but never in the south. In contrast, at southern sites Wickliffe Thick was as popular as or even more popular than Kimmswick Fabric-Impressed. The great variation, both regionally and subregionally, in the percentages of these two types brings into question their usefulness as temporal markers in a large-scale, regional chronology.

Turning from the discussion of the data presented to support the contention that geographic variation is present in western-Kentucky Mississippian ceramic assemblages, I need to comment on the potential reasons for this variation. Such variation has been noted to be associated with a number of factors, including stylistic preference, historic precedent, factors akin to random drift, and social or political boundaries, among others (e.g., Dunnell 1978; Plog 1980; Rice 1987). The cause of the spatial variation noted above in western Kentucky remains undiscovered, but any or all of the factors mentioned above, or others, could have played a part. As one potential avenue of investigation, it is interesting to note that two decades ago, Clay (1976) postulated that a number of different Mississippian polities and political structures were present in western Kentucky, and recent research has tended to support this view (Clay 1991; Kreisa 1995; see also Butler 1977). The differences in ceramic "evenness" and the timing of the introduction of new pottery types between the northern and southern sites could be mirroring a division between polities in western Kentucky. If ceramic variation in western Kentucky was based on factors other than stylistic preference or random drift, this would have implications for the creation of chronologies in western Kentucky. For instance, if multiple political spheres were present, regional chronologies that subsume geographic or temporal variation would mask, rather than identify, the ceramic data needed to support such a contention.

Finally, this analysis of ceramic diversity in the Mississippian assemblages of western Kentucky has implications for the construction of phases in that region, provided one sees some usefulness to such an exercise. Willey and Phillips (1958) defined a phase as an archaeological unit *distinguishable from all other such units,* being both spatially and temporally delimited. Unfortunately, as Fox points out in Chapter 2, archaeologists working in the central Mississippi Valley have not always clearly defined the necessary and sufficient traits required to establish usable phases. Clearly, the data reviewed above possess the variation necessary on a subregional scale to allow for the construction of phases. To accomplish this task, renewed emphasis on both site-specific and regional comparative analyses is needed. Single-site or period-like constructs, while not invalid chronologies, by their very nature are unable to encompass the variation inherent in multiple ceramic assemblages. It is the recognition and explanation of the source of this variation that allows a greater understanding of the Mississippian societies of western Kentucky.

The results of the analysis presented here also imply that the reliability of Mississippian chronologies can be lessened by a number of factors. Geographic variation impacts the accuracy of such constructs, but once identified, this variation may yield insights into other aspects of the Mississippian world. Further, such temporal and geographic variation present in assemblages can be impacted by the methods used by archaeologists to construct chronologies—witness the problems inherent in Mississippian-period phases in southeastern Missouri (Fox, Chapter 2). To enhance the accuracy of chronologies, archaeologists must continue to control for sample size, use a number of assemblages, adequately date those assemblages, and, perhaps most important, *identify the geographic limits of accuracy for the proposed chronology.* Emphasis on these issues will not only result in chronologies of greater accuracy but also might allow archaeologists to identify ceramic discontinuities, with their explanation providing another fruitful area of research into the development of Mississippian societies in the central Mississippi Valley.

4 | An Overview of Walls Engraved Pottery in the Central Mississippi Valley
David H. Dye

ENGRAVED POTTERY, particularly of the type known as Walls Engraved, has been used over the past forty years as a Late Mississippian–period (post–A.D. 1400) ceramic marker in the central Mississippi River valley (Griffin 1952; Morse and Morse 1983; O'Brien 1994a; Phillips 1939, 1970; Phillips et al. 1951; Rands 1956; Williams 1954). Various observations have been made concerning motif variation within the type (Childs 1993; House 1993a; Phillips and Brown 1978:198–202; Rands 1956), but to date there have been no systematic efforts to evaluate the spatial and temporal range of individual variants. This chapter addresses that topic in three-step fashion. I first provide a brief historical background and overview of late Mississippian engraved pottery in the central Mississippi Valley, I then outline the spatial and temporal distribution of Walls Engraved sherds and vessels, and finally I examine variation in one engraved motif, the scroll.

Engraved types other than Walls Engraved have been identified in the central Mississippi Valley. One of these is O'Byam Incised (Phillips 1970:144; Williams 1954:222–23), a type that technically should be called O'Byam Incised/Engraved (see below). The type occupies an earlier temporal position and to some extent a slightly more northern spatial position than Walls Engraved, though there may well be some overlap in geographic distribution between the types. The engraved Caddo vessels to the west, while contemporary with Walls Engraved vessels, are sufficiently different in both vessel form and motif that they can be regarded as of a distinct ceramic tradition.

One local type, Rhodes Incised (Phillips 1970:157; Phillips et al. 1951:127), exhibits a "trailed," or scroll, motif also found on Walls Engraved vessels, and, as Phillips (1970:157) stated, the former type is "firmly welded into the local ceramic tradition" of the so-called Walls complex. Phillips divided Rhodes into two varieties. One, Rhodes Incised, *var. Rhodes,* occurs on flattened, globular jars that have arcaded rims. If they are undecorated, such jars are placed in the type Mississippi Plain, *var. Neeley's Ferry* (Phillips 1970:133–34). The other variety, Rhodes Incised, *var. Horn Lake,* is restricted to "bowls, bottles, and effigy forms, but not usually found on jars" (Phillips 1970:157). Unlike the Rhodes variety, these vessels have a fine shell-tempered paste comparable to Bell Plain, *var. Bell*

(Phillips 1970:59). In addition, the execution of the motif is on a "drier" surface than that found on the Rhodes variety. Such vessels may represent unfired but dried surfaces that were incised to resemble engraving. Thus, Rhodes motifs could be applied on surfaces that were wet and pliable (Rhodes Incised, *var. Rhodes*), dry and unfired (Rhodes Incised, *var. Horn Lake*), or postfired (Walls Engraved, *var. Walls*). Interestingly, Rhodes Incised, *var. Horn Lake*, vessel forms (bottles and bowls) and paste (finely crushed shell) fit more comfortably within the description of Walls Engraved than within Rhodes Incised, *var. Rhodes*—not a particularly unusual situation relative to central Mississippi Valley typology (O'Brien and Dunnell, Chapter 1). Phillips's (1970:127) illustration of a high-shouldered jar as an example of Rhodes Incised, *var. Horn Lake*, further supports the close association (relative to decorative similarity) of that variety with Walls Engraved (see below).

Engraving in the central Mississippi Valley, especially for Walls Engraved pottery, usually occurs on fine-paste, shell-tempered bottle exteriors and bowl interiors. Designs are characterized by a thin line usually applied to a fired and smoothed, often polished or burnished, surface. Lines incised into unfired-vessel surfaces are often difficult to distinguish from postfired engraved lines (Phillips 1970:101; Shepard 1956:198). Some types, such as L'eau Noire Incised (Phillips 1970:100–104) and O'Byam Incised (Phillips 1970:144), have a wide latitude in treatment, grading from fine-line to broad-line engraving/incising, but Walls Engraved designs, regardless of whether they were applied on an unfired or fired vessel, were executed with use of a fine-pointed instrument. Put more precisely, the type Walls Engraved is defined in large part by the occurrence of fine-line engraving as opposed to broad-line engraving.

Sherds and vessels of Walls Engraved are rare occurrences in much of the central Mississippi Valley. For example, in the Lower Mississippi Survey sherd counts (Phillips 1970; Phillips et al. 1951), Walls Engraved sherds usually comprised less than 1 percent of ceramic assemblages. Phillips (1939:603) noted that engraved pottery was an "extreme minority factor in Eastern Arkansas, 1.75% in the present series." His sample presumably was based on complete vessels.

Historical Background

Engraved vessels from the Mississippi Valley began to attract scholarly attention in the late nineteenth century with the work of William Henry Holmes, an artist who later turned to archaeology, eventually becoming chief of the Bureau of American Ethnology (Meltzer and Dunnell 1992). In his classic papers on Mississippi Valley and Southeastern pottery, Holmes (1884a, 1884b, 1886, 1903) illustrated vessels from the Davenport Academy of Sciences and the Smithsonian Institution to define pottery regions on the basis of minor stylistic differences in form and design (O'Brien and Dunnell, Chapter 1; Teltser, Chapter 7). Large accumulations of vessels, especially the collections of Capt. Wilfrid P. Hall (Griffin 1981) and Capt. C. W. Riggs (Brose 1980), were Holmes's primary sources of information.

Inspired in part by Holmes's publications and in part by his own examination of Riggs's collection (Brose 1980), Clarence B. Moore excavated numerous sites throughout the greater Southeast (Brigham 1936). His illustrations and discussions of engraved vessels were published in the *Journal of the Academy of Natural Sciences of Philadelphia*. The first archaeologist to provide contextual information on Mississippi Valley engraved pottery, Moore (1910, 1911) based his discussions on his eastern-Arkansas fieldwork, which took place at Rose Mound on the St. Francis River during the winter of 1909-1910 and at Bradley, Pecan Point, and Rhodes on the Mississippi River during the winter of 1910-1911.

In addition to the work of Moore, amateur and professional excavations undertaken in northeastern Arkansas, southwestern Tennessee, and northwestern Mississippi during the first four decades of the twentieth century produced numerous examples of engraved pottery. For example, a physician from Mississippi County, Arkansas, James K. Hampson, excavated a number of sites along the Mississippi River in northeastern Arkansas and western Tennessee (Morse 1973b; Williams 1957). His primary efforts were directed to the sites of Upper Nodena and Middle Nodena, where several engraved vessels were found (see below). During Hampson's early work at the Nodena sites, another physician, Julius A. Davies, began accumulating a large collection of vessels from what is believed to be the Walls (Harris) site in DeSoto County, Mississippi (Pugh and McNutt 1991). Calvin Brown, a geologist by training and a professor of Romance languages by vocation, illustrated several of Davies's Walls Engraved vessels in his *Archaeology of Mississippi* (Brown 1926). In 1932, the University of Arkansas Museum, under the direction of Samuel C. Dellinger (Hoffman 1981), and the Alabama Museum of Natural History, under the direction of Walter B. Jones, David L. DeJarnette, James DeJarnette, and James Hayes (Morse 1973b:33-40), conducted excavations at several sites in northeastern Arkansas, including Upper Nodena and Middle Nodena, that resulted in the recovery of engraved vessels.

The Davies, Hampson, and other collections have served as the basis for considerable archaeological research on engraved vessels (e.g., Childs 1993; Phillips 1939, 1970; Phillips et al. 1951; Rands 1956), which I summarize below in more or less chronological order. Phillips (1939) illustrated several "polished drab incised" vessels in the University of Arkansas Museum collections and stated that the postfired "incised" pottery was intrusive from the south, where engraved pottery was more common. He also pointed out that engraving was more abundant in the Mississippi River area than in the St. Francis area, where painted vessels were more common (Phillips 1939:605). Phillips (1939:605, 632) also remarked on the close relation between the engraved vessels from the Mississippi Valley and those from Moundville, Alabama—a point to which I return later.

Based on James A. Ford's (1936) earlier work, Phillips, Ford, and Griffin (1951), in detailing results of their archaeological survey in the lower Mississippi Valley between 1940 and 1947, established a ceramic typology still widely used today. James B. Griffin, principal author of the pottery section, wrote the first description of the type Walls Engraved. He placed all central Mississippi Valley engraved vessels in two categories, Walls Engraved and Hull Engraved. He named the former after the Walls site (see above) and the latter after either the Hull Brake site or the small community of Hull Brake, both in Coahoma County, Mississippi.

Griffin described Walls Engraved as fine-line engraving applied to the exteriors of fine-paste (Bell Plain) vessels. He noted that engraving appeared to be rare in the St. Francis subarea, with the exception of "a few inept examples" (Phillips et al. 1951:128), and appeared to be concentrated in the Memphis subarea, particularly in the Walls–Pecan Point complex, throughout the Mississippian period. Only three out of seventy-four sherds of Walls Engraved in surface collections made by Phillips, Ford, and Griffin were found south of Helena, Arkansas. The others were localized in the Memphis area. Griffin, reiterating Phillips, called attention to the close resemblance in vessel shape, design motif, and design-application technique of Walls Engraved vessels and some vessels from Moundville in Alabama. Decoration was noted to be primarily a series of cross-hatched spiral bands, sometimes embellished with cross-hatched triangles, which gave a "crested" effect (Phillips et al. 1951:127–29). Less commonly found on Walls Engraved vessels were esoteric iconographic motifs of the Southern Cult (Waring and Holder 1945), or the Southeastern Ceremonial Complex (Galloway 1989; Howard 1968). These latter motifs included winged and entwined rattlesnakes, woodpeckers in flight, severed human heads, defleshed forearm bones, hands, maces or war clubs, and a variety of other motifs including triskeles, swastikas, and concentric festoons.

Griffin characterized Hull Engraved as fine-line engraving on the interiors of fine-paste (Bell Plain) bowls (Phillips et al. 1951:129). On Hull Engraved bowls, the engraver typically placed groups of parallel, concentric arcs that abutted other similar groups to form fish-scale-like, imbricate patterns. Griffin noted that two bowl shapes were present: a simple curve-sided vessel and a carinated, or shouldered, vessel. The distribution of Hull Engraved bowls was restricted to the Memphis subarea, where they were believed to date slightly earlier than Walls Engraved vessels.

Phillips (1970:169–71) restructured the typological relation between Walls Engraved and Hull Engraved by subsuming the latter as a variety of the former. Thus, Walls Engraved became Walls Engraved, *var. Walls*, and Hull Engraved became Walls Engraved, *var. Hull*. He reiterated Griffin's characterization of Walls Engraved as fine-line engraving applied to the exterior of fine, polished bottles and to the interior of simple- and flared-rim, carinated bowls. Bands and zones of cross hatching played a major role in Walls Engraved, *var. Walls*, but not in Walls Engraved, *var. Hull*. Phillips found that Walls Engraved, *var. Hull*, bowls occurred with higher relative frequency below the mouth of the St. Francis River than did vessels of Walls Engraved, *var. Walls*, which were more common north of the St. Francis River in the Memphis subarea. He called attention to two other sorting criteria: (1) Walls Engraved, *var. Hull*, bowls often contained shell-temper particles that were so small as to be almost invisible and (2) the surface color of sherds and vessels of that variety were of "the lighter shades of buff and reddish buff" (Phillips 1970:170).

More recently, illustrations of engraved vessels have appeared in several popular publications. In his volumes illustrating vessels from the central Mississippi Valley, Hathcock (1976, 1983, 1988) included a number of engraved vessels. His discussions included descriptions, site provenience, and vessel measurements. Westbrook (1982) also illustrated several Walls Engraved vessels in his publication resulting from a ceramic exhibit held at the Arkansas Arts Center in Little Rock in 1982.

But is it possible, within the broad type, to isolate variants that are more-precise chronological markers? Connected to this question is the issue of how widely we want to expand the description of Walls Engraved, which I discussed above, and how much stock we want to place on stylistic similarity between designs on Walls Engraved vessels and designs on vessels that have been placed in other ceramic traditions. Recall that Phillips (1939) noted similarities between late prehistoric engraved vessels from the central Mississippi Valley—what we now call Walls Engraved—and engraved vessels from Moundville. Later, Rands (1956), in response to the widespread and often uncritical application of the concept of the Southern Cult, argued that archaeologists should be measuring similarities between areas quantitatively instead of with the use of simple trait lists. He concluded that although there appeared to be some shared participation in religious thought throughout the Southeast, there was little reason to suspect a close connection between such types as Walls Engraved and Moundville Engraved. More recently, Phillips and Brown (1978:198–202) examined similarities between Walls Engraved motifs and those found on vessels from Moundville and on shell artifacts from Spiro, Oklahoma. They pointed out the thematic and stylistic diversity in central Mississippi Valley engraved vessels and argued that there are close thematic similarities between Walls Engraved bottles and bowls and engraved marine shell from Spiro but that there is little similarity between Walls Engraved and Moundville Engraved vessels.

Spatial and Temporal Distribution

Morse and Morse (1983) view Walls Engraved as a rare but important ceramic marker for the Late Mississippian period and suggest it and other late forms of ceramic decoration (e.g., painting) appeared by A.D. 1250 in the Cairo Lowland phase of southeastern Missouri. Phillips (1970:925), however, specifically stated that Walls Engraved, *var. Walls*, made its appearance in the time following the Cairo Lowland phase. The exact timing of its appearance is problematic. Received wisdom is that it first appeared sometime in the mid-fourteenth century and became widespread, albeit still rare, by the beginning of the fifteenth century (Morse and Morse 1983:280, 285). At the other end of the temporal spectrum, Walls Engraved was found in apparently good context at the Otto Sharpe site in Lake County, Tennessee, in a ceramic assemblage dating well into the seventeenth century (Lawrence and Mainfort 1992; Mainfort and Moore, Chapter 5). If this is the case, then Walls Engraved in the central Mississippi Valley dates between the mid-fourteenth and the early to mid-seventeenth centuries.

To better understand the distribution of Walls Engraved in the central Mississippi Valley, I examined sherds and vessels from seventy-six sites in the region (Figures 4-1 and 4-2 and Tables 4-1 and 4-2). An important component of the data set consists of sherds collected between Perryville, Missouri (Tier 1), and Greenville, Mississippi (Tier 18), during the Peabody Museum (Harvard) Lower Mississippi Survey (Phillips 1970; Phillips et al. 1951). Additional distributional data are included for western Tennessee, based on the Tennessee Division of Archaeology records, and for southeastern Missouri (Chapman and Anderson 1955; O'Brien 1994a; Williams 1968).

In general, distributional studies such as the one undertaken here—especially studies that use older collections—are fraught with sampling problems. In this study, for example, a bias is inherent in the sherd counts, which are predominantly from large sites rather than from a cross section of site sizes (size, presumably, being related in some way to settlement type). Likewise, the complete vessels, excavated by archaeologists as well as by pothunters, are also from large sites, especially those with mounds and deep, multicomponent middens.

The sample includes sherds from forty-eight sites (Table 4-1). Eight sites produced sherds of both varieties of Walls Engraved; thirty-one produced sherds only of Walls Engraved, *var. Walls*, and nine produced sherds only of Walls Engraved, *var. Hull*. Most assemblages are represented by fewer than five sherds; therefore, I use presence/absence instead of attempting to use relative

86 | Dye

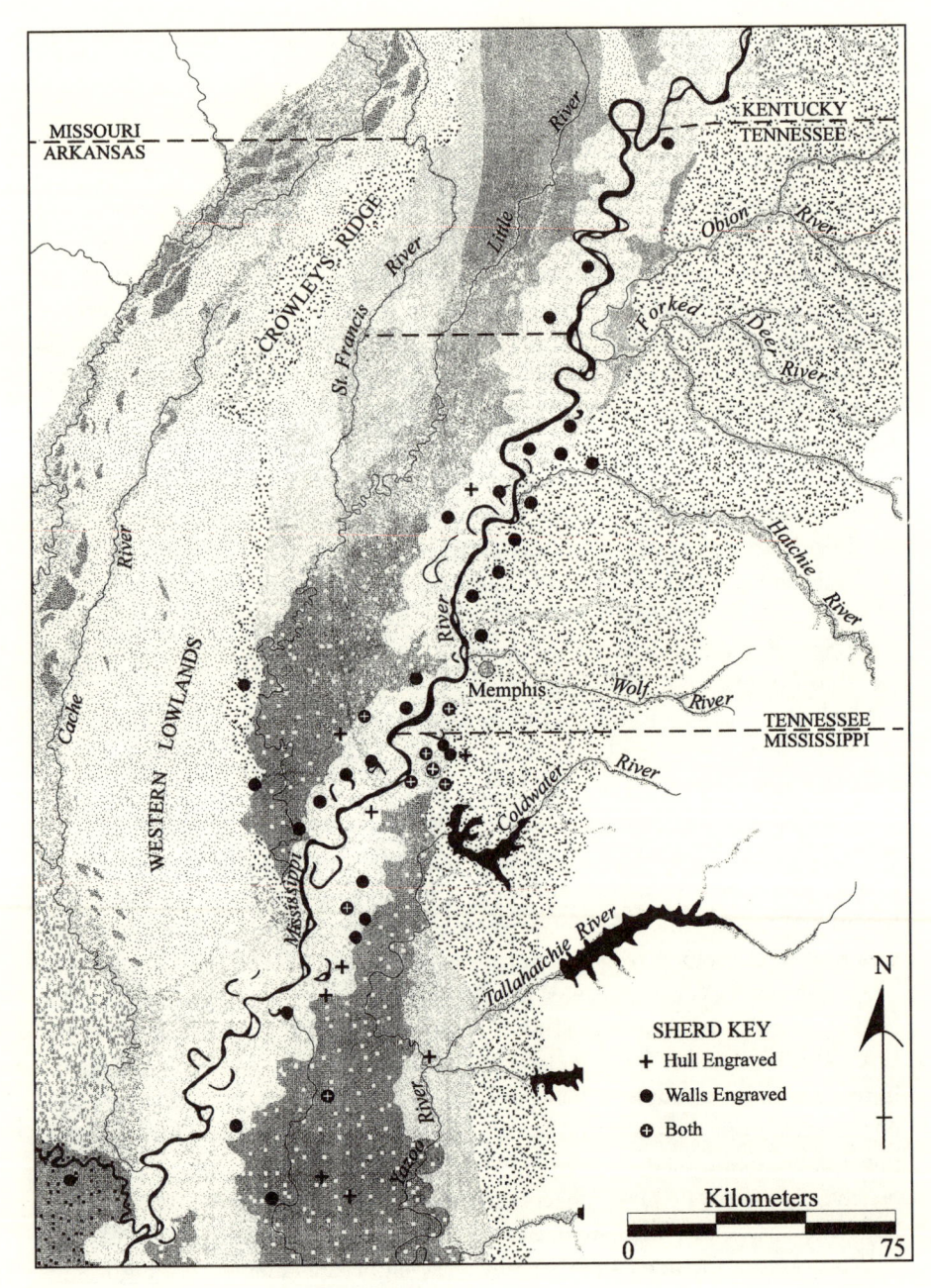

Figure 4-1. Distribution of Walls Engraved, *var. Walls*, and Walls Engraved, *var. Hull*, sherds in the central Mississippi River valley.

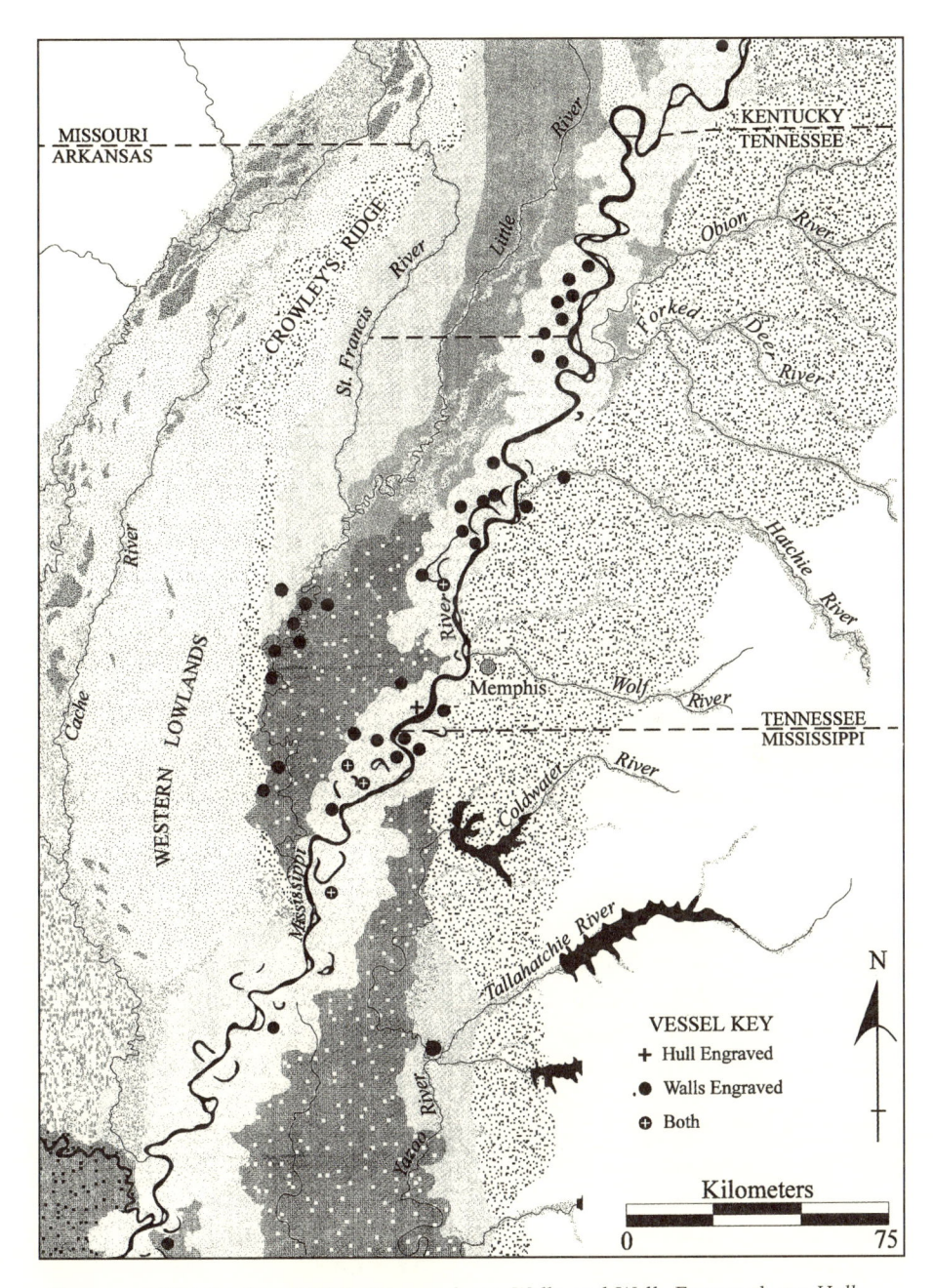

Figure 4-2. Distribution of Walls Engraved, *var. Walls,* and Walls Engraved, *var. Hull,* vessels in the central Mississippi River valley.

Table 4-1. Sites in the Central Mississippi Valley Producing Walls Engraved Sherds

Site Number[a]	Site Name	LMS Number[b]	Variety
03AR004	Menard	17-K-01	Walls
03CT001	Mound Place	12-P-01	Walls
03CT003	Brackinseik (Rhodes)	12-O-06	Walls
03CT008	Beck	13-O-07	Walls
03CT030	Belle Meade	13-O-05	Walls
03CT034	Pouncey	12-O-02	Hull
03CT034	Pouncey	12-O-02	Walls
03LE008	Kent	13-N-04	Walls
03LE011	Clay Hill	13-N-07	Walls
03LE017	Starkley	13-N-16	Walls
03MS004	Upper Nodena	10-Q-01	Walls
03MS013	Carson Lake	10-P-01	Hull
03MS015	Notgrass	10-O-04	Walls
03SF043	Huber	13-O-03	Walls
03SF044	New Bethel	13-O-06	Hull
22BO509	Stokes Bayou	16-M-06	Walls
22BO532	Merigold	17-N-01	Walls
22CO504	Salomon	15-O-01	Hull
22C0510	Barbee	15-O-02	Hull
22CO511	Parchman	15-N-05	Hull
22CO518	Montgomery	15-N-06	Hull
22CO529	Myer	16-N-10	Walls
22DS500	Walls (Harris)	13-P-01	Walls
22DS500	Walls (Harris)	13-P-01	Hull
22DS501	Lake Cormorant	13-P-08	Hull
22DS501	Lake Cormorant	13-P-08	Walls
22DS511	Dogwood Ridge	13-P-04	Walls
22DS512	Owens	14-O-02	Walls
22DS513	Norfolk	13-P-07	Walls
22DS514	Cheatham	13-P-06	Walls
22DS516	Irby	13-P-10	Hull
22DS516	Irby	13-P-10	Walls
22DS517	Woodlyn	13-P-11	Walls
22DS517	Woodlyn	13-P-11	Hull
22QU529	Cox	16-P-06	Hull

Table 4-1. (cont.)

22SU511	Long Lake	17-N-12	Hull
22SU516	Powell Bayou	17-O-09	Hull
22TU500	Hollywood (Bowdre)	13-O-10	Walls
22TU504	Commerce	13-O-11	Walls
22TU504	Commerce	13-O-11	Hull
22TU520	West (Hood)	14-O-10	Walls
22TU520	West (Hood)	14-O-10	Hull
23PM005	Campbell (Cooter)	08-Q-07	Walls
23PM021	Chute (McCoy)	08-R-03	Walls
40LA002	Porter		Walls
40LA004	Jones Bayou		Walls
40LA092	Graves Lake		Walls
40LA109	Fullen		Walls
40LK004	Otto Sharpe		Walls
40SY001	Chucalissa (Fuller)	12-P-02	Hull
40SY001	Chucalissa (Fuller)	12-P-02	Walls
40SY028	Jeter		Walls
40SY075	Rast	11-Q-02	Walls
40TP002	Richardson's Landing	10-Q-10	Walls
40TP010	Bishop	10-R-01	Walls
40TP012	Wilder		Walls

[a]03, Arkansas; 22, Mississippi; 23, Missouri; 40, Tennessee.
[b]Lower Mississippi Survey (see Phillips 1970; Phillips et al. 1951).

frequencies. The distribution of Walls Engraved, *var. Walls,* sherds extends from the Kentucky-Tennessee border on the north to the mouth of the St. Francis River (Arkansas) on the south. Walls Engraved, *var. Hull,* sherds, on the other hand, tend to be concentrated in an area from south of Memphis to the mouth of the Arkansas River (Figure 4-1).

The sample of engraved vessels contains 115 specimens from forty-two sites (Table 4-2). The vessel distribution suggests that Walls Engraved, *var. Walls,* occurs over a relatively large area within the valley, whereas Walls Engraved, *var. Hull,* is restricted to the southern and eastern portions of the valley. However, note that the sample of Walls Engraved, *var. Hull,* vessels consists of only five specimens, four of which came from sites on the west side of the Mississippi River. Most Walls Engraved, *var. Hull,* sherds in the sample came from sites on the east side of the river. Sites that produced Walls Engraved, *var. Hull,* vessels

Table 4-2. Sites in the Central Mississippi Valley Producing Walls Engraved Vessels

Site Number[a]	Site Name	LMS Number[b]	Vessel Shape	Neck Type[c]	Variety
03CS024	Neeley's Ferry	11-N-04	Carinated bottle		Walls
03CS027	Rose Mound	12-N-03	Subglobular bottle	SW	Walls
03CS027	Rose Mound	12-N-03	Subglobular bottle	SW	Walls
03CS027	Rose Mound	12-N-03	Flared-rim beaker		Walls
03CS028	Togo (Star Woods)		Subglobular bottle	SW	Walls
03CS029	Parkin	11-N-01	Subglobular bottle	TN	Walls
03CS078	Twist	11-N-16	Subglobular bottle	TW	Walls
03CT003	Brackinseik (Rhodes)	12-O-06	Simple bowl		Hull
03CT003	Brackinseik (Rhodes)	12-O-06	Carinated bottle		Walls
03CT007	Bradley	11-P-02	Effigy bottle		Walls
03CT007	Bradley	11-P-02	Simple bowl		Hull
03CT007	Bradley	11-P-02	Unidentified bottle	TW	Walls
03CT007	Bradley	11-P-02	Subglobular bottle	SW	Walls
03CT008	Beck	13-O-07	Subglobular bottle	SW	Walls
03CT008	Beck	13-O-07	Carinated bottle		Walls
03CT008	Beck	13-O-07	Subglobular bottle	SW	Walls
03CT008	Beck	13-O-07	Carinated bottle		Walls
03CT008	Beck	13-O-07	Carinated bottle		Walls
03CT008	Beck	13-O-07	Subglobular bottle	SW	Walls
03CT008	Beck	13-O-07	Subglobular bottle	SW	Walls
03CT010	Young	12-O-07	Carinated bottle		Walls
03CT010	Young	12-O-07	Subglobular bottle	SW	Walls
03CT013	Banks	11-P-08	Subglobular bottle	SW	Walls
03CT013	Banks	11-P-08	Effigy bottle		Walls
03CT013	Banks	11-P-08	Subglobular bottle	SW	Walls
03CT013	Banks	11-P-08	Subglobular bottle	SW	Walls
03CT018	Barton Ranch	11-O-10	Subglobular bottle	SW	Walls
03CT030	Belle Meade	13-O-05	Flared-rim beaker		Walls
03CT030	Belle Meade	13-O-05	Subglobular bottle	SW	Walls
03CT030	Belle Meade	13-O-05	Subglobular bottle	SW	Walls
03CT030	Belle Meade	13-O-05	Subglobular bottle	TW	Walls
03CT030	Belle Meade	13-O-05	Carinated bottle		Walls
03CT030	Belle Meade	13-O-05	Simple bowl		Hull
03CT030	Belle Meade	13-O-05	Subglobular bottle	SW	Walls
03CT030	Belle Meade	13-O-05	Subglobular bottle	SW	Walls
03CT030	Belle Meade	13-O-05	Subglobular bottle	SW	Walls
03CT030	Belle Meade	13-O-05	Subglobular bottle	SW	Walls

Table 4-2. (cont.)

03CT033	Edmondson	12-O-11	Subglobular bottle	TW	Walls
03CT033	Edmondson	12-O-11	Flared-rim bowl		Walls
03CT033	Edmondson	12-O-11	Subglobular bottle	SW	Walls
03LE008	Kent	13-N-04	Straight-sided bowl		Walls
03LE011	Clay Hill	13-N-07	Subglobular bottle	SW	Walls
03LE011	Clay Hill	13-N-07	Carinated bottle		Walls
03LE015	Grant	13-M-11	Subglobular bottle	SW	Walls
03LE015	Grant	13-M-11	Carinated bottle		Walls
03MS004	Upper Nodena	10-Q-01	Subglobular bottle	SW	Walls
03MS004	Upper Nodena	10-Q-01	Carinated bottle		Walls
03MS004	Upper Nodena	10-Q-01	Subglobular bottle	SW	Walls
03MS004	Upper Nodena	10-Q-01	Unidentified bottle		Walls
03MS004	Upper Nodena	10-Q-01	Subglobular bottle	SW	Walls
03MS004	Upper Nodena	10-Q-01	Subglobular bottle	SW	Walls
03MS004	Upper Nodena	10-Q-01	Subglobular bottle	SW	Walls
03MS004	Upper Nodena	10-Q-01	Subglobular bottle	TW	Walls
03MS005	Chickasawba (Gosnell)	09-Q-02	Subglobular bottle	TN	Walls
03MS005	Chickasawba (Gosnell)	09-Q-02	Effigy bowl		Walls
03MS006	Friends	11-P-11	Subglobular bottle	SW	Walls
03MS006	Friends	11-P-11	Subglobular bottle	TN	Walls
03MS008	Bell	10-P-02	Subglobular bottle	?	Walls
03MS017	Turnage (Ellis Ridge)	10-Q-03	Subglobular bottle	SW	Walls
03MS017	Turnage (Ellis Ridge)	10-Q-03	Subglobular bottle	SW	Walls
03MS017	Turnage (Ellis Ridge)	10-Q-03	Subglobular bottle	SW	Walls
03MS018	Crosskno		Subglobular bottle	TW	Walls
03MS018	Crosskno		Subglobular bottle	TW	Walls
03MS060	Golden Lake (Rhodes)	10-P-14	Subglobular bottle	SW	Walls
03MS078	Pecan Point	11-P-06	Subglobular bottle	SW	Walls
03MS078	Pecan Point	11-P-06	Simple bowl		Walls
03MS078	Pecan Point	11-P-06	Subglobular bottle	SW	Walls
03MS078	Pecan Point	11-P-06	Subglobular bottle	SW	Walls
03MS078	Pecan Point	11-P-06	Subglobular bottle		Walls
03SF004	Nickel	13-N-15	Carinated bottle		Walls
03SF004	Nickel	13-N-15	Carinated bottle		Walls
03SF004	Nickel	13-N-15	Subglobular bottle	SW	Walls
03SF005	Sycamore Bend	13-O-15	Simple bowl		Hull
03SF009	Bid Eddy	12-N-04	Unidentified bottle		Walls
22BO503	Neblett Landing	18-L-01	Carinated bottle		Walls
22CO601	Humber-McWilliams	15-N-12	Subglobular bottle	TN	Walls
22CO601	Humber-McWilliams	15-N-12	Effigy bowl		Walls
22DS500	Walls (Harris)	13-P-01	Subglobular bottle	SW	Walls

Table 4-2. (cont.)

22DS500	Walls (Harris)	13-P-01	Unidentified bottle		Walls
22DS500	Walls (Harris)	13-P-01	Subglobular bottle	SW	Walls
22DS500	Walls (Harris)	13-P-01	Subglobular bottle	SW	Walls
22DS500	Walls (Harris)	13-P-01	Subglobular bottle	SW	Walls
22DS500	Walls (Harris)	13-P-01	Subglobular bottle	TW	Walls
22DS500	Walls (Harris)	13-P-01	Subglobular bottle	?	Walls
22DS500	Walls (Harris)	13-P-01	Subglobular bottle	SW	Walls
22DS500	Walls (Harris)	13-P-01	Simple bowl		Walls
22DS509	Edgefield	13-P-02	Subglobular bottle	?	Walls
22DS509	Edgefield	13-P-02	Subglobular bottle	TW	Walls
22TU520	West (Hood)	14-O-10	Simple bowl		Hull
22TU520	West (Hood)	14-0-10	Subglobular bottle	TW	Walls
23MI002	Towosahgy (Beckwith's Fort)	06-T-01	Straight-sided bowl		Walls
23PM005	Campbell (Cooter)	08-Q-07	Subglobular bottle	SW	Walls
23PM005	Campbell (Cooter)	08-Q-07	Subglobular bottle	TW	Walls
23PM005	Campbell (Cooter)	08-Q-07	Subglobular bottle	?	Walls
23PMOO?	Stateline		Subglobular bottle	SW	Walls
23PM013	Kersey (Persimmon Grove)	08-Q-04	Beaker		Walls
23PM043	Murphy Mound (Caruthersville)	08-R-01	Subglobular bottle	SW	Walls
23PM043	Murphy Mound (Caruthersville)	08-R-01	Subglobular bottle	SW	Walls
23PM043	Murphy Mound (Caruthersville)	08-R-01	Subglobular bottle	SW	Walls
23PM056	Brooks		Subglobular bottle	SW	Walls
23PM056	Brooks		Subglobular bottle	TW	Walls
23PM056	Brooks		Subglobular bottle	SW	Walls
23PM056	Brooks		Subglobular bottle	TW	Walls
23PM059	Berry		Subglobular bottle	TW	Walls
23PM059	Berry		Subglobular bottle	TW	Walls
40SY001	Chucalissa (Fuller)	12-P-02	Subglobular bottle	SW	Walls
40SY001	Chucalissa (Fuller)	12-P-02	Effigy bowl		Walls
40SY001	Chucalissa (Fuller)	12-P-02	Subglobular bottle	SW	Walls
40SY001	Chucalissa (Fuller)	12-P-02	Flask		Walls
40SY001	Chucalissa (Fuller)	12-P-02	Subglobular bottle	SW	Walls
40SY001	Chucalissa (Fuller)	12-P-02	Subglobular bottle	SW	Walls
40SY001	Chucalissa (Fuller)	12-P-02	Subglobular bottle	SW	Walls
40SY001	Chucalissa (Fuller)	12-P-02	Effigy bowl		Walls
40TP001	Hatchie	10-Q-12	Subglobular bottle	TW	Walls
40TP010	Bishop	10-R-01	Subglobular bottle	SW	Walls

[a]03, Arkansas; 22, Mississippi; 23, Missouri; 40, Tennessee.
[b]Lower Mississippi Survey (see Phillips 1970; Phillips et al. 1951).
[c]SW, Short neck, wide orifice; TW, tall neck, wide orifice; TN, tall neck, narrow orifice.

are Brackinseik, Bradley, Belle Meade, and Sycamore Bend in Arkansas (the latter three around Horseshoe Lake) and West in Mississippi.

To summarize the data on engraved sherds and vessels, the distribution of Walls Engraved, *var. Walls,* and Walls Engraved, *var. Hull,* is virtually the same with respect to plots of sherds and vessels, with two exceptions. First, the distribution of sherds of Walls Engraved, *var. Hull,* indicates a more southerly orientation for interior engraving on bowls than the Walls Engraved, *var. Walls,* sherd distribution suggests. Second, the distribution of Walls Engraved, *var. Walls,* vessels indicates they occur in the Pemiscot Bayou and Parkin regions of southeastern Missouri and northeastern Arkansas, respectively. Collectively, this information supports the notion that the distribution of Walls Engraved vessels extends from southeastern Missouri to the mouth of the Arkansas River, but what is noteworthy is that the distribution is densest immediately west and south of Memphis, as indicated by Griffin (1952:236), Phillips (1970:169–71), and Phillips, Ford, and Griffin (1951:127–29).

The densest concentrations of engraved vessels occur in six locales: (1) the Pemiscot Bayou sites of Brooks, Campbell, and Murphy Mound (O'Brien 1994a; Price and Price 1990); (2) the Wilson, Arkansas, sites of Upper Nodena, Turnage, and Pecan Point (Morse 1973b, 1989, 1990); (3) the Lake Wapanocca, Arkansas, sites of Banks and Bradley (Perino 1966); (4) the Parkin site of Rose Mound (Morse 1981, 1990); (5) the Horseshoe Lake, Arkansas, sites of Belle Meade, Beck, and Nickel (Smith 1990); and (6) the Walls sites of Walls and Chucalissa (Nash 1972; Smith 1990). We might have expected other sites to make the above list, especially those, like Parkin, that have received extensive excavation over the past century (Moore 1910; Morse 1981, 1990). Parkin has produced but a single Walls Engraved vessel, while the nearby site of Rose Mound has produced three. My guess is that such differences are attributable in large part to sampling error.

The vessels can be divided into eleven vessel forms (Figure 4-3), four of which are of particular interest here: (1) tall-neck, narrow-orifice bottles (Figure 4-3, *a*); (2) tall-neck, wide-orifice bottles (Figure 4-3, *b*); (3) short-neck, wide-orifice bottles (Figure 4-3, *c*); and (4) high-shouldered jars (Figure 4-3, *e*). In fact, 80 percent of the sample is composed of bottles and jars. Beakers (Figure 4-3, *f* and *g*) make up 4 percent of the sample, flasks (Figure 4-3, *d*) 1 percent, bowls (Figure 4-3, *h* through *j*) 4 percent, and effigy vessels (Figure 4-3, *k*) 11 percent. As noted previously, all five bowls in the sample are of the type Walls Engraved, *var. Hull.*

Despite the conventional name, high-shouldered jars do not appear to be functionally related to jars; rather, they are more akin to bottles. The classic Mississippian-period jar, with its everted rim, often exhibits evidence of exposure to fire (e.g., soot on the shoulder and exfoliation on the outer surfaces), internal damage from stirring, and accretional buildup of organic residues on the inside. High-shouldered jars, on the other hand, rarely if ever exhibit such signs of

94 | Dye

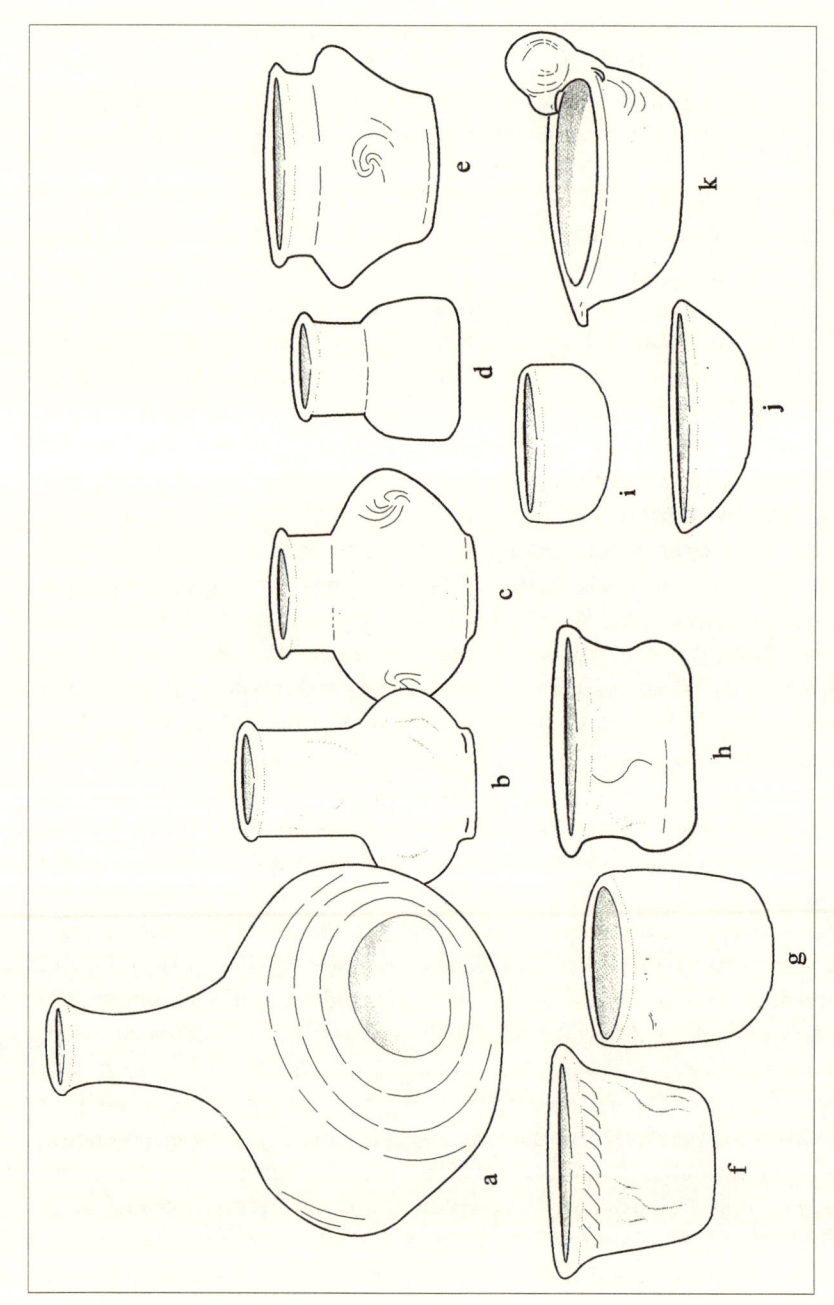

Figure 4-3. Vessel forms associated with Walls Engraved designs: *a*, subglobular, tall-neck, narrow-orifice bottle; *b*, subglobular, tall-neck, wide-orifice bottle; *c*, subglobular, short-neck, wide-orifice bottle; *d*, flask; *e*, high-shouldered jar; *f*, flared-rim beaker; *g*, straight-side beaker; *h*, flared-rim bowl; *i* and *j*, simple bowls; *k*, effigy bowl.

cooking-related activities. Also, they have flat bases onto which intricate designs often were engraved, as if the motifs were meant to be seen. One vessel in particular suffered extensive damage to a complex design on the base from predepositional abrasion. The standard Mississippian jar rarely has a flat base, nor is the base decorated. Thus, high-shouldered jars should more appropriately be termed carinated bottles with short necks and wide orifices.

The distribution of subglobular bottles and carinated bottles is interesting from several standpoints. First, the distribution of subglobular bottles extends from southeastern Missouri to just south of Memphis. Second, subglobular bottles with short necks and wide orifices occur with higher frequency in the Horseshoe Lake and Walls areas than in other areas. Third, subglobular bottles with tall necks and wide orifices occur with the highest frequency in the Pemiscot Bayou district of southeastern Missouri. Fourth, subglobular bottles with tall necks and narrow orifices are found throughout the region except in the Horseshoe Lake and Walls locales. I propose that the distribution of neck forms associated with Walls Engraved vessels reflects the *general* distribution of those neck forms independent of whether they occur on engraved vessels. Fifth, the high-shouldered jar has a distribution that is localized to the Horseshoe Lake area and is rare in other areas.

The Scroll Motif

Three basic decorative modes occur on Walls Engraved vessels: (1) an imbricate design on bowl interiors (Walls Engraved, *var. Hull*), (2) zoomorphic or anthropomorphic motifs on vessel exteriors (Walls Engraved, *var. Walls*), and (3) scroll motifs on vessel exteriors (Walls Engraved, *var. Walls*). The one I am primarily concerned with here is the scroll. Holmes (1886:419) provided a succinct description of the scroll motif, a design composed of "four elaborate, interlinked scrolls, comprising a number of lines, and bordered by wing-like, triangular figures, filled in with reticulated lines." The four volute centers are sometimes slightly concave (Holmes 1886:420).

I subdivide Walls Engraved scrolls into five varieties: (1) single cross-hatched bands (Figure 4-4, *a*), (2) bordered cross-hatched bands (Figure 4-4, *b*), (3) double cross-hatched bands (Figure 4-4, *c*), (4) plain (noncross-hatched) bands (Figure 4-4, *d*), and (5) Rhodes-like (noncross-hatched) bands (Figure 4-4, *e*). The fifty-two vessels that contain the scroll motif occur in the Walls, Horseshoe Lake, Nodena, and Pemiscot Bayou areas and are most commonly short, wide-orifice, subglobular bottles or carinated bottles (high-shouldered jars).

Single-band scrolls ($n = 4$), consisting of two parallel lines embracing a zone of cross hatching, are rare (8 percent of all scroll-motif vessels), occurring on vessels from only three sites along the Mississippi River: Pecan Point, Walls, and Beck (two vessels). *Bordered-band* scrolls ($n = 17$) are simple, two-line bands with

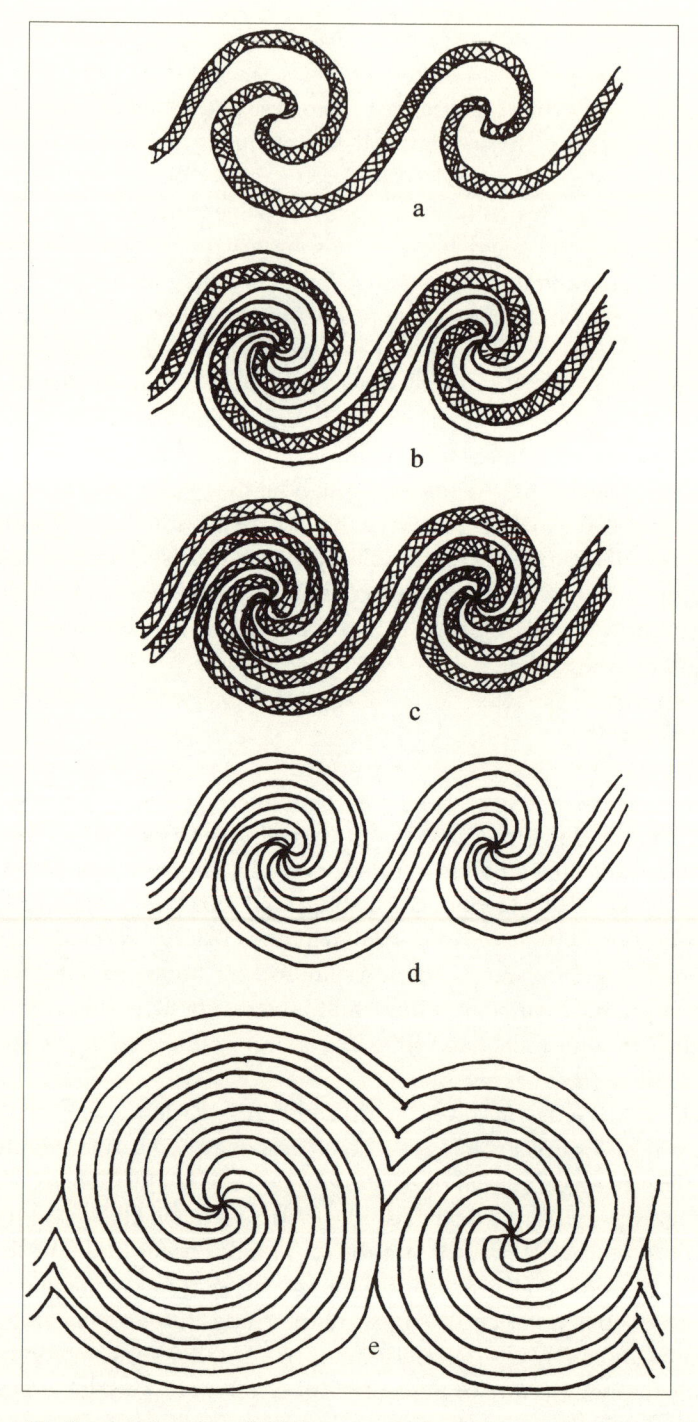

Figure 4-4. Scroll types found on Walls Engraved vessels: *a*, single band; *b*, bordered band; *c*, double band; *d*, plain band; *e*, Rhodes-like band.

the addition of a single line engraved on either side of the band. Sometimes the engraver cross hatched the area between the conjoined lines, which gives the appearance of a double band. Bordered-band scrolls occur on short-neck, wide-orifice bottles from thirteen sites in the Memphis area and on a variety of vessel forms from Rose Mound, Bradley, Upper Nodena, and Chickasawba in Arkansas (one vessel per site). *Double-band* scrolls ($n = 9$) consist of two single cross-hatched bands running parallel to each other. Like other scroll motifs, the bands radiate from a centroid to form a swastika. Often the double-band scroll is bordered on one side by a single line. The motif occurs on subglobular bottles with short necks and wide orifices and on carinated bottles. Vessels containing double-band scrolls do not appear to be as localized in distribution as vessels with bordered bands, though more than half the vessels come from the Walls–Horseshoe Lake area of southwestern Tennessee, northwestern Mississippi, and northeastern Arkansas. *Plain scrolls* ($n = 12$) consist of from three to five lines radiating from a centroid (Figure 4-4, *d,* shows four lines). The motif occurs on subglobular bottles with wide mouths and either tall or short necks. Six vessels in the sample came from sites in the Nodena area, three from sites in the Walls area, and one each from sites in the Parkin, Horseshoe Lake, and Pemiscot Bayou areas. *Rhodes-like* scrolls ($n = 10$)—actually whorls or volutes linked by three to five lines—do not contain the cross-hatched points or fins characteristic of the cross-hatched and plain scrolls, and, unlike the plain scroll, the whorl occupies the greater portion of the vessel body. Rhodes-like scrolls often have unconnected lines about the whorls, giving the impression that the designs are larger than they are. The motif is found on subglobular bottles with wide orifices and either tall or short necks. Half of the vessels with Rhodes-like scrolls came from the Pemiscot County, Missouri, sites of Brooks, Campbell, and Stateline (see O'Brien 1994a).

Conclusion

Late prehistoric inhabitants of the central Mississippi River valley engraved ceramic bottles and bowls with a variety of highly individualized designs, including imbrications, "feathered" scrolls, and representational motifs incorporating anthropomorphic and zoomorphic forms. In general, these designs are not portrayed in other decorative formats such as incising, appliquéing, and painting (with the exception of the scroll or swastika design on Carson Red-on-Buff, Nodena Red-and-White, and Avenue Polychrome vessels). Walls Engraved vessels, including those of Walls Engraved, *var. Walls,* and Walls Engraved, *var. Hull,* appear to have a contiguous distribution covering southeastern Missouri, northeastern Arkansas, western Tennessee, and northwestern Mississippi. On the basis of the sample presented here, Walls Engraved is found in greatest relative frequency at those sites in the meander-belt zone of the Mississippi River immediately west and south of Memphis. The temporal position of Walls Engraved is believed to span the late fourteenth century to the mid to late seventeenth century and to be to some extent contemporary with that of engraved vessels from Moundville. Future archaeological studies in the Midsouth, and the central Mississippi Valley in particular, will, we can hope, broaden our understanding of the temporal and spatial dimensions of Walls Engraved, especially of its individual variants.

Acknowledgments

I thank S. Williams for graciously making available the site files of the Peabody Museum (Harvard) Lower Mississippi Survey. I also thank R. C. Mainfort, Jr., for sharing his West Tennessee Survey data. D. F. and P. A. Morse have offered considerable help over the years, as have numerous collectors and museum curators, especially C. Fletcher, J. C. Roberts, and C. Wharey. C. Koeppel provided help with the tables, T. Foster prepared Figures 4-1 through 4-3, and M. E. Taylor provided the drawings in Figure 4-4 from her rubbings of Walls Engraved vessels. I also thank M. J. O'Brien, R. C. Dunnell, and C. H. McNutt for their comments and suggestions.

5 | Graves Lake
A Late Mississippian–Period Village in Lauderdale County, Tennessee

Robert C. Mainfort, Jr., and
Michael C. Moore

GRAVES LAKE (40LA92) is located within Lower Hatchie National Wildlife Refuge, approximately 5 kilometers north of the mouth of the Hatchie River in Lauderdale County, Tennessee (Figure 5-1). The site occupies a low, mesa-like erosional remnant that rises approximately 10 meters above the surrounding bottomland at the southern terminus of the First Chickasaw Bluff system (Figure 5-2). Like much of the loess-bluff system in western Tennessee, the local soil association is Memphis silt loam, which is well suited to row-crop agriculture (Monteith 1990), and the site area has been under cultivation for more than fifty years. King Pond (known locally as Graves Lake), a seasonally flooded marsh that probably represents an abandoned meander scar of the Hatchie River, is located immediately east of the site; the Mississippi River flows about 400 meters to the west. Other notable late prehistoric sites in the vicinity of Graves Lake include Hatchie (40TP1), a moundless Late Mississippian–period community on the south bank of the Hatchie River (Mainfort 1991; Smith 1990) (Figure 5-1); site 40LA95, a large substructural platform mound in the Hatchie River floodplain several kilometers to the east (Mainfort 1991); and site 40LA83, apparently a small mound or mound complex that may have been visited by Clarence B. Moore (1916:493) earlier in the century (Figure 5-2).

Investigations at Graves Lake were prompted by the actions of a maintenance worker who mistakenly made several passes with a road grader along the eastern edge of the site in 1990. The refuge manager and one of us (RCM) subsequently prepared a plan that addressed not only the immediate problem of how to mitigate the damage already done to the site but also the long-term problem of how best to protect and manage the archaeological resource. Fieldwork was conducted by the Tennessee Division of Archaeology (TDOA) late in 1990 and was based on preservation, not specifically on collection of archaeological materials. However, the results represent an important contribution to our understanding of the Late Mississippian–period (post–A.D. 1400) archaeological record in the central Mississippi River valley.

Much of what is known about that period is derived from fieldwork con-

100 | Mainfort and Moore

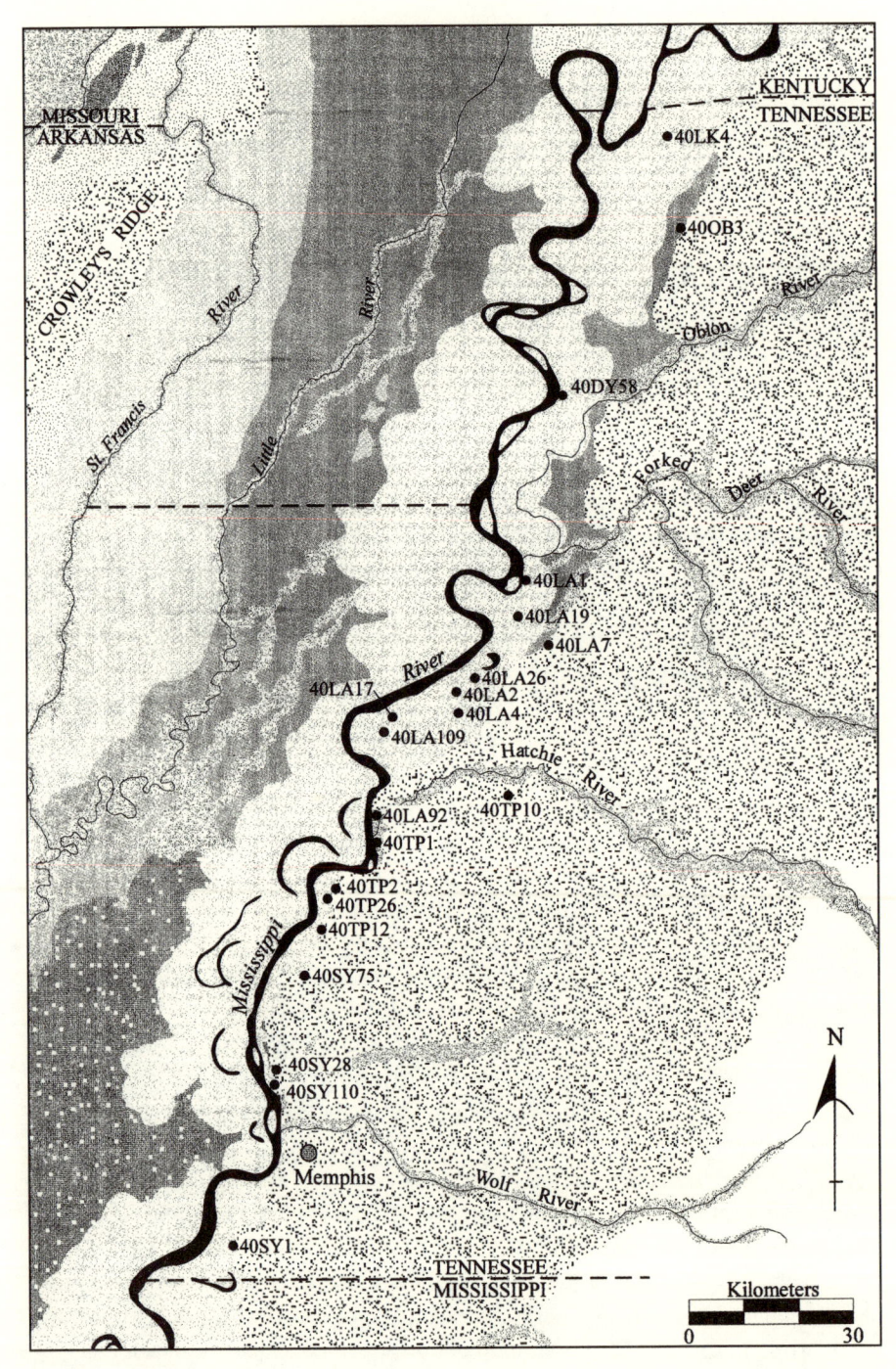

Figure 5-1. Map of western Tennessee and environs showing locations of sites mentioned in the text.

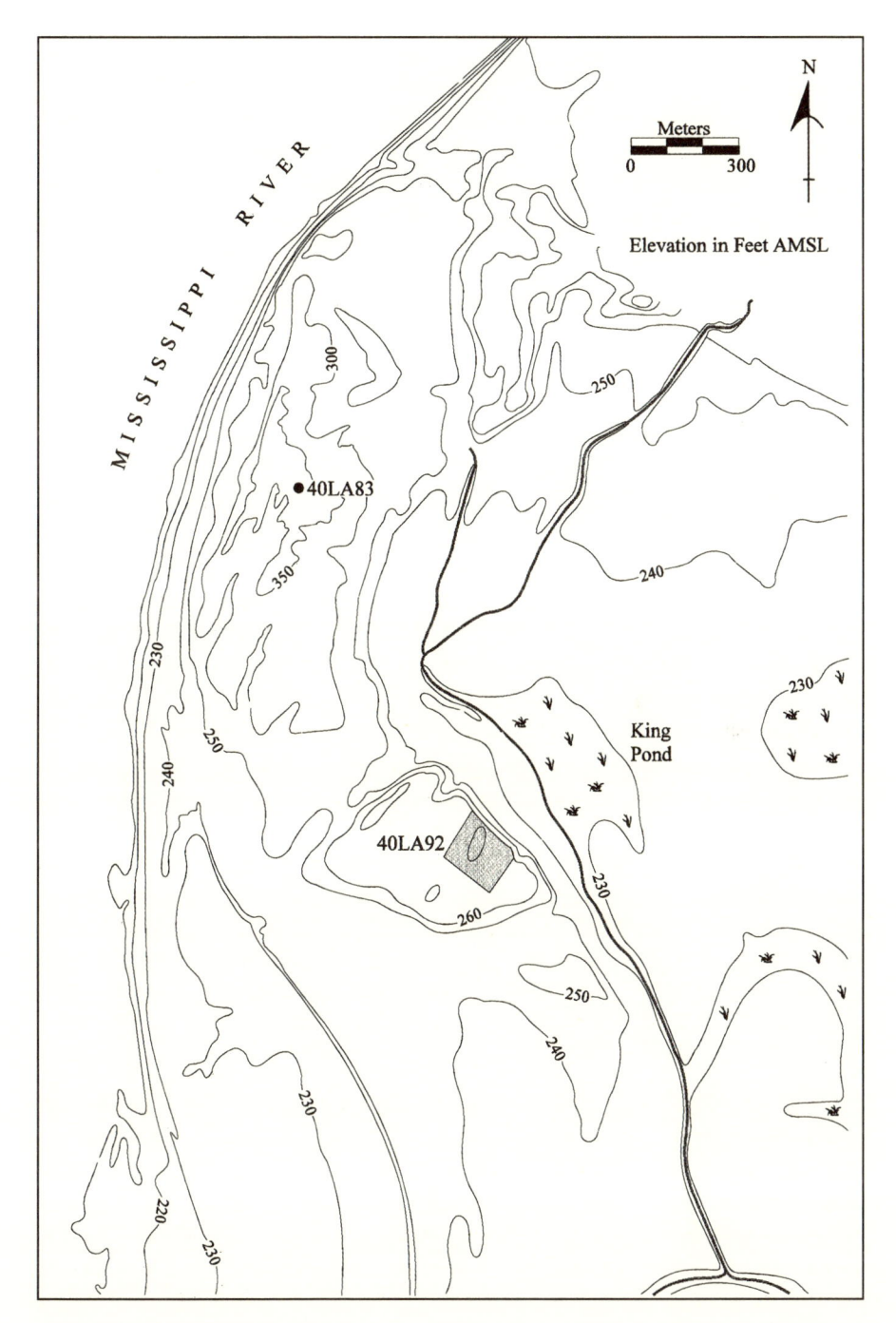

Figure 5-2. Topographic setting of Graves Lake (40LA92) and site 40LA83, Lauderdale County, Tennessee.

ducted in southeastern Missouri (e.g., Chapman and Anderson 1955; O'Brien 1994a; Price and Price 1990; Williams 1954) and northeastern Arkansas (e.g., D. F. Morse 1989, 1990; P. A. Morse 1981, 1990; Morse and Morse 1983). Although sites in western Tennessee often are mentioned in overviews of the Late Mississippian period (e.g., Williams 1980), the references have lacked specificity. The Graves Lake archaeological record presents an opportunity to address specific questions regarding the use of the east side of the Mississippi River by Late Mississippian groups.

Fieldwork

The first objective of our work at Graves Lake was to examine the northeastern slope of the site. Severe natural erosion in that area apparently had been exacerbated by the former landowner, who reportedly had made several bulldozer cuts near the bluff crest, exposing human skeletal remains in the process. That area had been cursorily examined by TDOA several years earlier. Our initial investigation consisted of a general surface collection made across the entire northeastern slope, up to and including a bulldozed field road at the bluff crest. Areas that exhibited minor concentrations of daub and other cultural materials were shovel skimmed, but no evidence of intact subsurface cultural deposits was found at those localities.

Moderate rainfall exposed additional cultural material on the slope of the elevated area, particularly along the uppermost portion, and one major daub concentration was recorded. Because the area would require disking and/or plowing prior to the planting of grass seed, limited excavations were conducted within the daub concentration to assess possible impacts from plowing. An irregularly shaped area measuring approximately 9 × 2 meters, eventually designated House 3 (Figure 5-3), was exposed, revealing a number of posts and several pits beneath a 10- to 25-centimeter-thick layer of daub (discussed below).

Controlled Surface Collection

A major objective of the project was to determine approximate site boundaries, both for National Register of Historic Places purposes and for management of the site area by the U.S. Fish and Wildlife Service. Staff from TDOA addressed this objective in part by conducting a controlled surface collection of the site. Approximately one month prior to the beginning of fieldwork in 1990, vegetation covering the site and adjacent areas was cut with a brush-hog. Ground cover was relatively short at the time of cutting, which made it impossible to bale the cut materials; this limited surface visibility in several units during surface collection. Approximately 20 percent of the top of the erosional remnant, including all of the presumed site area, was disked to a depth of roughly 15 to 20 centimeters. Although deeper disking or plowing might have produced larger artifact collections, we wanted to minimize damage to the site.

A grid consisting of 182 10-meter-square units was established over most of the disked area (Figure 5-3). Collection-unit size was based on several factors, with the greatest weight given to practical considerations. First, since the principal objective of the controlled surface collection was to provide a reasonable estimate of site boundaries for land-management purposes, a smaller unit size was deemed unnecessary. Second, establishing a 10 × 10-meter grid was considerably less labor intensive than establishing, say, a 5 × 5-meter grid; our limited budget and reliance on volunteers ruled out use of a smaller grid interval. Third, although it is difficult to demonstrate that a specific unit size is optimal for distributional studies of surface-collected artifacts (but see Jermann 1981), it has been shown (e.g., Odell and Cowan 1987) that distributional studies of surface collections based on small grid intervals produce spurious aggregations of artifacts (but see Lewarch and O'Brien 1981).

The grid system was deliberately aligned along a low ridge intuitively believed to align with the main axis of the site (23°37'20" east of magnetic north). After approximately 5 centimeters of rain had fallen on the site, a surface collection of all grid units was conducted by a crew of TDOA staff members and three volunteers from the Department of Anthropology, University of Memphis.

After initial experimentation, collection time was limited to five minutes per unit. In every instance, this procedure allowed crew members to collect virtually all surface material in each unit. Although artifact recovery in low-density units probably was somewhat inflated and recovery in high-density units probably slightly decreased, such potential sampling biases were not of great relevance to our main objective. All visible artifacts, with the exception of daub, were collected. Apparent concentrations of daub, some appearing to represent individual houses, were flagged during surface collection for further investigation. Subsequent rainfall revealed the distribution of daub to be much more continuous than we originally suspected, suggesting that the "concentrations" observed during the surface collection were a product of collecting conditions on particular days. Interestingly, subsequent rainfall exposed very little additional cultural material, with the exception of daub.

Test Excavations

Limited subsurface testing was conducted at several localities, with emphasis on (1) determining the nature and extent of archaeological materials and (2) assessing damage caused by road grading and subsequent erosion. The road-grader cut extended along the entire northeastern side of the site and continued across the erosional remnant (Figure 5-3). The width of the impact area averaged approximately 9 meters, and the depth of disturbance was 15 to 30 centimeters. Fortunately, the grader blade had not been set to cut a level surface, so the great-

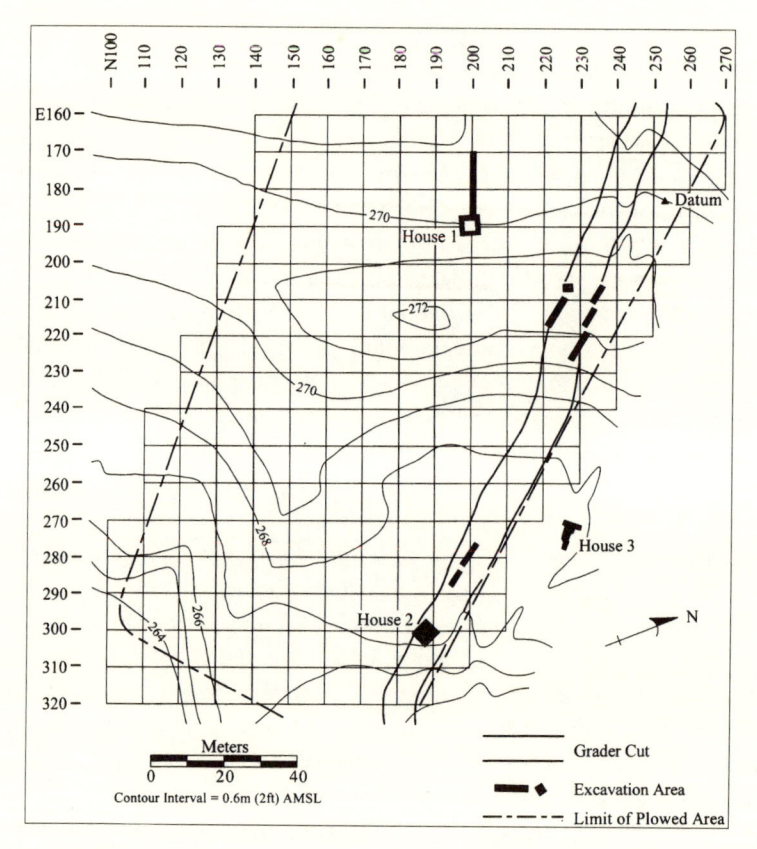

Figure 5-3. Topographic map of Graves Lake showing grid lines and tested localities.

est damage occurred along the outer margins of the impact area; deposits near the center received only minor damage.

Test excavations were undertaken at seven localities within and adjacent to the road-grader cut, as well as within the House 3 area near (and probably within) the field road cut by the former landowner (Figure 5-3). A complete assessment of damage was beyond the scope of the Archaeological Resources Protection Act (ARPA) permit under which we were working, and we focused attention on localities recorded as possible features. Depths of undisturbed cultural deposits ranged from virtually zero in unit N230/E210 and vicinity to more than 60 centimeters below surface in unit N200/E230. Deposits in the latter area included a substantial amount of midden that apparently was redeposited prehistorically by erosion. It quickly became evident that a considerable number of human burials were present within the area. Rather than cause additional disturbance to human remains, testing within the impact area was suspended, with the exception of work conducted in the area of House 2 (Figure 5-3).

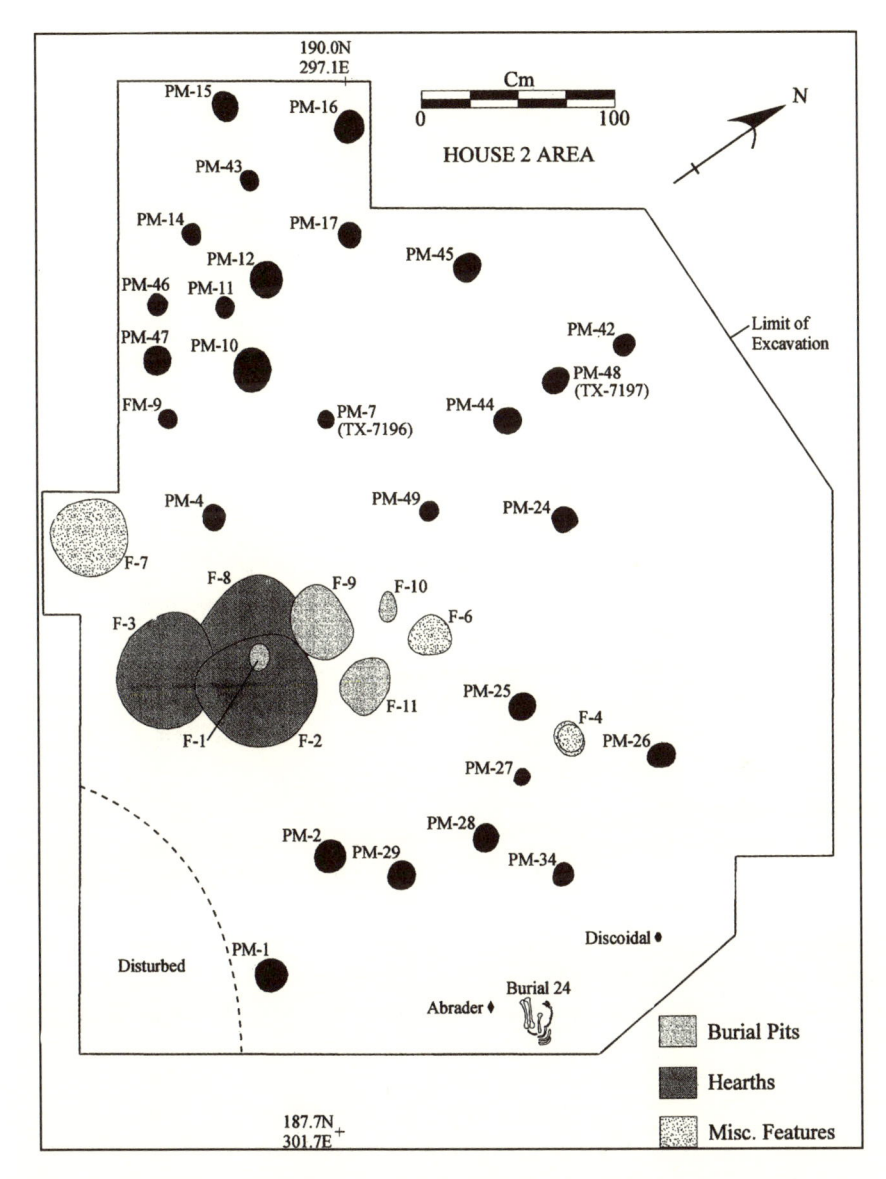

Figure 5-4. House 2 area at Graves Lake showing locations of burial pits, hearths, miscellaneous features, and post molds (labeled *PM*).

HOUSE 2

A heavy concentration of daub interpreted as a prehistoric house was exposed in the road-grader cut near the northeastern edge of the site. That locality, designated House 2, was partially excavated, disclosing the remains of a house that apparently had been rebuilt three times (Figure 5-4). Excavation revealed ten pits and twenty-seven post molds within an area measuring approximately 5 × 4 meters. Although possible alignments were evident among several groups of post molds, no walls could be identified with confidence, and no indications of wall trenches were observed. In addition to the interpretive difficulties posed by three inferred rebuilding episodes, precise definition of the structure was also hampered by incomplete excavation and by disturbance from both the road grader and erosion, particularly in the southwestern portion of the house.

Three shallow, superimposed hearths (features 2, 3, and 8) were located in the southwestern quadrant of the excavation area. These ash-filled basins were 52 to 60 centimeters in diameter and 6 to 16 centimeters deep. Feature 8 represented the earliest hearth, followed in time by Feature 3 and then by Feature 2 (Figure 5-4). A portion of Feature 8 was preserved under Feature 2 at the same depth as the base of Feature 3. Intruding into Feature 2 was a small pit covered with a portion of a Barton Incised, *var. Kent* (Phillips 1970:46) jar, under which were found the remains of an infant (Feature 1). Feature 10, located about 40 centimeters east of Feature 8, was virtually identical to Feature 1 and also contained part of a Barton Incised, *var. Kent*, jar. Two somewhat larger pits (features 9 and 11) also contained infant remains; a small untempered plain-surface vessel was associated with the latter feature. Upon identification of human skeletal remains, excavation of the features ceased, in accordance with provisions of the ARPA permit. The functions of the remaining features (4, 6, and 7) are unknown, as there were few associated artifacts.

The disarticulated remains of an adult (Burial 24) were partially exposed in the southeastern quadrant of the excavation area. Nearby was a sandstone abrader, but previous disturbance rendered its association with the burial uncertain. A fragment of a large hematite discoidal was located near the southeastern edge of the excavated area at approximately the same elevation as the presumed structure floor. A Bell Plain (Phillips et al. 1951:122–26) bowl and several concentrations of pottery sherds were found in the daub rubble overlying the floor.

HOUSE 3

House 3 was recorded initially as a daub concentration near the top of the northeastern slope of the erosional remnant, north of House 2 (Figure 5-3). The former landowner reportedly had bulldozed the area. The excavation area measured approximately 9 meters southeast-northwest by 2 meters northeast-southwest, with a total excavated area of 20 square meters. Beneath a 10- to 25-centimeter layer of daub thirteen post molds, three storage or refuse pits, and four human burials were exposed (Figure 5-5). Discovery of the burials (25, 26, 27, and 28) caused excavation to be suspended in the large northwestern portion of the tested area and limited the overall extent of investigations in the locality.

Limited excavations in the House 3 area did not permit a definitive assessment of the house-related features and posts encountered. Nine post molds were

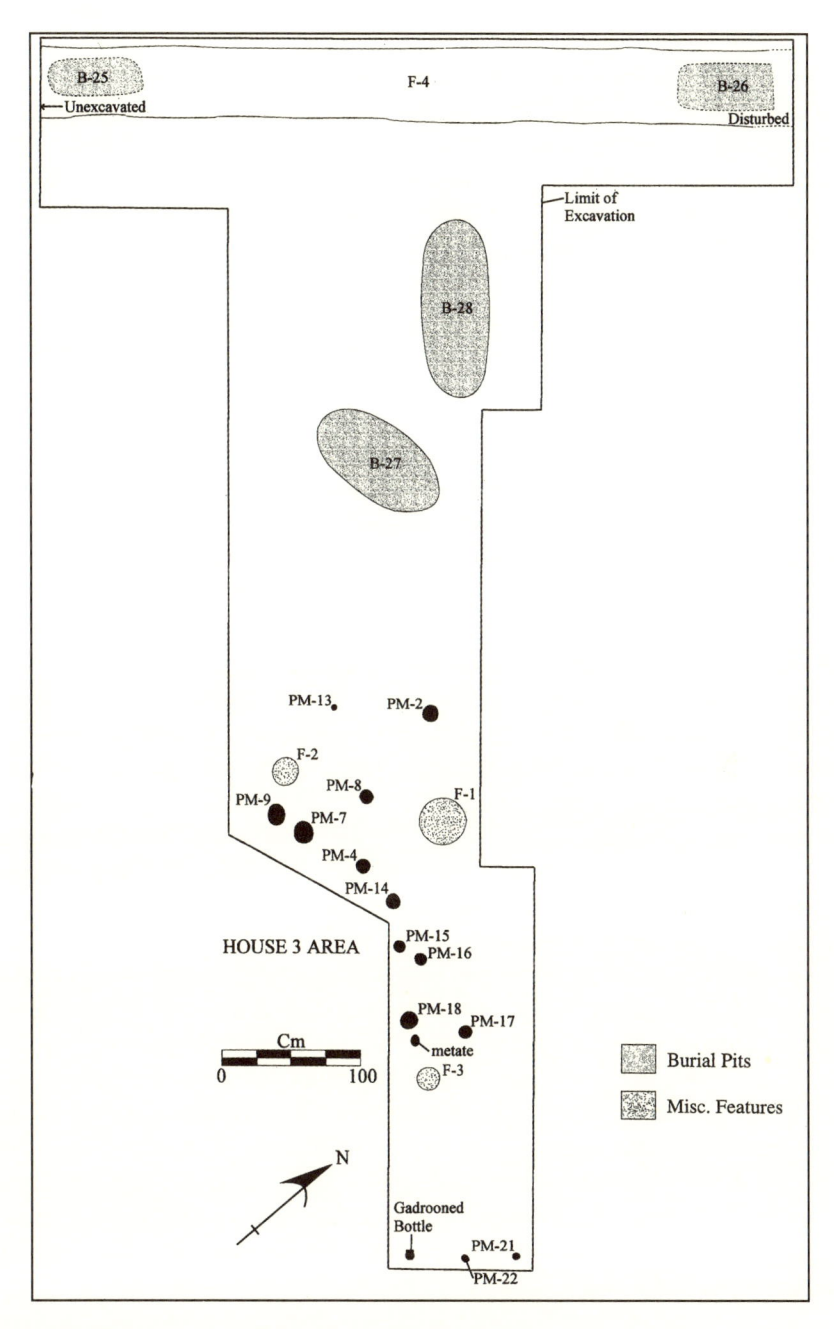

Figure 5-5. House 3 area at Graves Lake showing locations of burial pits, miscellaneous features, post molds (labeled *PM*), and several artifacts.

located in a linear arrangement and presumably represented a section of a house wall. As in the case of House 2, we found no evidence of wall trenches. Several of the more isolated posts, notably post molds 21 and 22 (Figure 5-5), might have been part of a second structure. A probable hearth, Feature 1, was represented by a shallow basin with a fired base; no artifacts were recovered from the fill. A smaller basin (Feature 2) also lacked artifacts. Feature 3 appeared to be a small pit, 18 centimeters deep. Evidence of an apparent floor was observed throughout most, but not all, of the excavated area near the posts and features. Part of a large, heavily worn metate was recovered from the presumed floor adjacent to Feature 3, and a section of a gadrooned bottle was found in the rubble immediately above the floor.

ADDITIONAL TEST EXCAVATIONS

A series of contiguous 50-centimeter-wide trenches was cut along the N200 grid line between points E171 and E195 to determine whether a palisade marking the edge of the village was present. No indications of a palisade were encountered, but the tests revealed the relatively undisturbed remains of a Mississippian-period house at a depth of approximately 30 centimeters below surface between units E187 and E193.5. Test excavations were expanded to confirm identification of the house (designated House 1) and to define its limits (Figure 5-3), but no attempt was made to expose the structure floor or associated features. Charcoal samples were recovered from several probable posts that extended into the daub rubble above the floor.

To the west of House 1, we observed a marked falloff in the density of cultural material, and no additional cultural features were located. The plow zone appeared to extend to an average depth of 25 centimeters below surface within the trenches, though several possible plow scars were observed as deep as 30 centimeters. A series of small shovel tests (30 × 30 centimeters) was placed at 20-meter intervals along the N200 and E200 grid lines to determine the depth of cultural deposits across the site and to aid in site-boundary definition. The shovel tests were excavated to subsoil, and profiles were recorded for each test unit. Intact midden was observed at points N170/E200, N210/E200, N200/E190, N200/E210, and N200/E290 (Figure 5-3); no indications of midden were noted at points N250/E200, N200/E250, or N200/E270. The remaining test units yielded ambiguous results. Two small test units were placed in a low rise located southwest of the site that resembled a mound remnant (Figure 5-2), though excavation suggested it was a natural feature.

Pottery

We recovered 2278 prehistoric sherds during the 1990 fieldwork at Graves Lake.[1] Other sherds were collected during initial visits to the site in 1987. Vir-

Table 5-1. Frequencies of Shell-Tempered Sherds from Graves Lake and Richardson's Landing

Ceramic Type	Graves Lake (1987)	Graves Lake (1990)[a]	Richardson's Landing
Mississippi Plain	185	1329	492
Bell Plain	222	776	514
Parkin Punctated, *var. Parkin*	9	40	8
Parkin Punctated, *var. Castile*	1	0	0
Parkin Punctated, *var. unspecified*	0	1	0
Barton Incised, *var. Barton*	3	10	2
Barton Incised, *var. Kent*	1	10	0
Barton/Kent Incised	13	3	0
Ranch Incised	11	19	1
Old Town Red	8	38	23
Nodena Red-and-White	2	2	1
Hollywood White Filmed	0	8	0
Unidentified decorated	7	39	22
Rhodes Incised	2	1	1
Walls Engraved	0	1	3
Vernon Paul Appliquéd	3	0	0
Campbell Appliquéd	3	0	0
Kent Incised and Ranch Incised	1	0	0
Pouncey Ridge Pinched	0	1	0
Total	471	2278	1067

[a]The 1990s totals include only sherds recovered during the controlled surface collection at Graves Lake.

tually all the material included in the earlier collection was obtained from eroded localities along the northeastern slope; that area was not included in the 1990 work in order to avoid causing additional erosional damage. The notable differences between the two collections (Table 5-1)—for example, the higher frequency in the 1990 collection of sherds of the type Bell Plain and of sherds of several decorated types—might be partly attributable to the reported occurrence of numerous graves in the 1987 collection area. Radiocarbon determinations presented below suggest that use of the 1987 collection area might postdate major use of other portions of the site.

All but a fraction of the sherds are representative of the Late Mississippian–

period occupation of the site; the remainder date to the Tchula (Early Woodland) and Baytown (Middle Woodland–Late Woodland) periods. The type-varieties used here, with few exceptions, are based on descriptions presented in Phillips (1970). In some instances, notably in the case of Ranch Incised, the terminology of Phillips et al. (1951) has been retained. Variety names are not used in describing shell-tempered plainwares because no truly distinctive variety definitions have been formulated for the study area. Most of the Mississippi Plain (Griffin 1949; Griffin, in Walker and Adams 1946:91) sherds from Graves Lake could be subsumed under the description of *var. Chucalissa* (Lumb and McNutt 1988). Several researchers have experienced difficulties in consistently sorting Bell Plain, *vars. Bell* and *Nickel,* as described by Lumb and McNutt (1988). Because the inclusion of crushed potsherds in Bell Plain paste has no apparent temporal significance at Chucalissa (cf. Lumb and McNutt 1988), all sherds containing finely crushed shell were classified as Bell Plain without varietal distinctions.

The combined 1987 and 1990 assemblage from Graves Lake (n = 2749) contains 1514 sherds of Mississippi Plain (55 percent) (Table 5-1). Virtually all identifiable rimsherds represent bowls or jars; most are too small to permit conclusive identification of vessel form. Many lips exhibit interior beveling (see below). The combined assemblage also produced 998 Bell Plain sherds (36 percent). Exteriors of these sherds are generally, but not always, smoothed or burnished. Bowls and/or jars are the dominant vessel forms, though several bottles are represented. Appliqué strips of various styles, below and parallel to the vessel lip, are relatively common, as is interior lip beveling.

As is typical at Late Mississippian–period sites in the central Mississippi Valley, Parkin Punctated (Phillips et al. 1951:110–14) is the most common decorated ceramic type in the Graves Lake assemblage (n = 51). With only two exceptions, all sherds are classified as Parkin Punctated, *var. Parkin* (Phillips 1970:151). One exception is a sherd of Parkin Punctated, *var. Castile* (Phillips 1970:151); the second exception is not easily accommodated under current type-variety nomenclature. Among Barton Incised sherds, thirteen examples are of Barton Incised, *var. Barton,* and eleven are of Barton Incised, *var. Kent;* many specimens cannot be identified to variety because of their small sizes.

Although Phillips (1970) reduced Ranch Incised to variety status, other researchers (e.g., Lumb and McNutt 1988) believe that the original type designation has greater utility. Because in contrast to types such as Parkin Punctated and Barton Incised, the Ranch motif has no pre-Mississippian precedents, we believe the original type status is justified. Decoration consists of wet-paste-incised "fish-scale" curvilinear designs, almost exclusively on a Mississippi Plain paste. The relative frequency of this type in the Graves Lake assemblage is noteworthy (n = 30). Among painted ceramics are forty-six sherds of Old Town Red (Phillips et al. 1951:129–32) and four Nodena Red-and-White (Phillips et al. 1951:133–34) specimens; some white-filmed sherds classified here as Hollywood

White Filmed (Phillips et al. 1951:134) probably came from red-and-white vessels.

Minority shell-tempered types include Vernon Paul Appliqué (Phillips et al. 1951:120) ($n = 3$), Campbell Appliqué (Chapman and Anderson 1955:42–44) ($n = 3$), Rhodes Incised (Phillips et al. 1951:127) ($n = 3$), and single examples of Pouncey Ridge Pinched (Phillips 1970:154–55) and Walls Engraved (Phillips et al. 1951:127–29). The presence of sherds of the former two appliquéd types is particularly significant, as those types are characteristic of post–A.D. 1540 assemblages in southeastern Missouri and the Reelfoot Lake area of western Tennessee (e.g., Chapman and Anderson 1955; Holland 1991; Lawrence and Mainfort 1995; O'Brien 1994a). All six appliquéd sherds were collected in 1987, probably from the extreme northeastern margin of the site. Their provenience is important in light of two post–de Soto–period radiocarbon determinations from this general area (see below).

A number of whole or partially restorable vessels were recovered (Figure 5-6), among the more distinctive examples of which are two Mississippi Plain helmet-shaped bowls. The larger of these, which was damaged by the road grader, is 18 centimeters in diameter and 7 centimeters high. The rim is flared, with a notched, appliquéd strip below the everted lip. The smaller, complete, example exhibits four equally spaced appliquéd handles. Helmet-shaped bowls are considered to be excellent late-period markers (Curren 1984; Williams 1980).

A pair of Bell Plain bird-effigy vessels, differing only in size, was associated with Burial 25 in the House 3 area. The heads exhibit small, flattened, semi-pointed beaks and coffee-bean-shaped eyes encircled by incised lines that continue down the necks; holes were placed in the back and in the middle of the necks. Broad lines were incised on the upper surfaces of the flattened tails; two holes were pierced through the tails near the midpoints. Also recovered from the House 3 area were a small Barton Incised, *var. Kent*, jar that exhibits a herringbone motif and Parkin Punctated handles; a basal fragment of a Bell Plain gadrooned bottle; a heavily decorated Barton Incised, *var. unspecified* (cf. *Arcola* [Phillips 1970:45]) jar; and a Bell Plain bottle with a slightly flaring neck. A privately owned Rhodes Incised "cat-serpent" vessel from the site (D. F. Morse and L. White, pers. comm., 1991), is illustrated by Hathcock (1988; the provenience is given as "Gray's Lake site").

A relatively small number of pre-Mississippian sherds was recovered during the controlled surface collection. These consisted of ten sherds of Baytown Plain, *var. Tishomingo* (Mainfort 1994); two of Baytown Plain, *var. Forked Deer* (Mainfort 1994); twenty-one of Baytown Plain, *var. unspecified* (Phillips et al. 1951:76–82); five of Mulberry Creek Cordmarked, *var. unspecified* (Haag 1939; Phillips et al. 1951:82–87); and single specimens of Cormorant Cord-Impressed (Phillips et al. 1951:73), Baldwin Plain, and Furrs Cordmarked (Cotter and Corbett 1951). Most of the sherds probably represent one or more Middle Woodland

Figure 5-6. Ceramic vessels from Graves Lake: *top,* Barton Incised, *var. Kent,* jar (*left*) and helmet-shaped bowl (*right*); *middle,* Bell Plain bowls; *bottom,* Bell Plain bottle (*left*) and Barton Incised, *var. unspecified,* jar (*right*). Barton Incised jar is roughly one-eighth actual size; all others are roughly one-quarter actual size.

components at the site; the Baytown Plain, *var. Forked Deer,* and Cormorant Cord-Impressed specimens indicate a minor Tchula occupation. Also of probable Tchula-period or earlier origin are seven baked-clay-object fragments.

Lithic Material

A total of 8028 lithic artifacts—including chipped and ground tools, knapping debris, and unmodified cobbles—was recovered during the 1990 investigations. Frequency data are presented below; more detailed descriptions of artifact classes can be found in Mainfort (1992). Roughly one-third of the lithic sample consists of unmodified cobbles of chert, quartzite, sandstone, limestone, and limonite, more than two-thirds of which appear to have been thermally altered. Projectile points are all subtriangular to triangular types such as Madison ($n = 9$), Nodena ($n = 8$), and Sand Mountain ($n = 1$) (Cambron and Hulse 1983; Justice 1987). These types are typically associated with late prehistoric occupations, and their presence is consistent with the ceramic assemblage from the site. Several triangular arrow points classified here as Madison exhibit an overall length that is greater than that normally associated with specimens of that type. They are quite similar to points recovered from Otto Sharpe (40LK4), a seventeenth-century site that has also yielded a number of snub-nosed end scrapers and sherds with distinctive vertical appliqué strips (Lawrence and Mainfort 1995; O'Brien et al. 1995). Future research should address whether those elongated triangular points are better treated as a variety of Madison or whether they represent a separate form diagnostic of late-period occupations.

Among the scraping tools from Graves Lake is a single snub-nosed end-scraper fragment, a tool form that is characteristic of protohistoric sites in the central Mississippi Valley (Brain 1988; Mainfort 1991; Price and Price 1990; Williams 1980). The assemblage also includes several crude end and side scrapers, a moderate number of unifacially retouched flakes, spokeshaves, and a graver. Several forms of drills ($n = 6$), including examples with expanded and round to parallel bases, also were collected. Ground specimens from the surface collection include two discoidals, three celt/hoe fragments, and five hoe-rejuvenation flakes. Numerous hammerstones and a pitted "nutting" stone also were recovered.

Lithic-Resource Identification

More than 99 percent of the flaked artifacts were made from local cherts obtained from gravel deposits along the nearby Mississippi River (see Stallings 1989). This material generally is fine grained, opaque, and nonlustrous. Off-white, tan, and dull yellow are the most common colors of chert, with shades of gray, red, blue, and black also represented. Small quantities of Mill Creek and Dover chert are present in the surface collection, which is not an unexpected occurrence at late prehistoric sites. Mill Creek chert was extensively used during the Mississippian period for the production of agricultural implements (Bareis and Porter 1984; Cobb 1989; Dunnell et al. 1994; Morse and Morse 1983). This material comes from southern Illinois, approximately 200 kilometers north of Graves Lake, where it occurs as nodules and flat boulders, both of which are excellent forms for the manufacture of large tools (Brown et al. 1990).

Dover chert has traditionally been viewed as coming from Stewart County, Tennessee, roughly 175 kilometers northeast of the project area (Marcher 1962), but recent research has identified outcrops in Houston, Humphreys, and Dickson counties, Tennessee (K. Smith, pers. comm., 1991). Dover chert circulated widely during the Mississippian period and was often used for producing large hoes and celts as well as exotic implements such as some of those in the Duck River cache from Tennessee (Bass 1984; Winters 1981).

Ground and pecked artifacts were primarily made from local sandstone and limestone. All celt/hoe fragments were made of an unidentified chert that may have originated near the site.

Human Burials

Twenty-four human burials were recorded during test excavations within the grader cut (four individuals were associated with House 2), and four additional burials were located in the House 3 area. As noted previously, information on human remains is limited, because, when they were encountered, skeletal material was uncovered only to the extent necessary to identify the remains as human, to determine the extent of disturbance, and, if possible, to determine skeletal orientation. Nine skeletons of adults were extended (supine), one was apparently bundled, and one may have been disarticulated; eight individuals were represented by only one or a few bones. Remains of five subadults were extended, and three were bundled or disarticulated; the remains of one individual were too fragmentary to determine burial position.

Artifact-Density Distributions

We used the Transform computer program (Spyglass 1991) to create a series of surface-artifact-density maps (Figures 5-7 through 5-9). Shell-tempered ceramics were heavily concentrated along the low ridge defined by the 271-foot contour line (Figures 5-3 and 5-7); the distribution of primary flakes (Figure 5-8) and chert cobbles (Figure 5-9) more or less mirrored the distribution of sherds. A high density of daub also occurred on the ridge, and that topographic feature may be reasonably interpreted as the product of successive episodes of house construction and destruction. Bell Plain and decorated Mississippian ceramics are often associated with specialized contexts (particularly mortuary areas) in the central Mississippi Valley, but no distinctive spatial patterning was evident in the Graves Lake surface collection. In fact, the distribution of decorated ceramics (both by individual types and as a group) closely corresponded to the distribution of Mississippi Plain sherds.

Sherds representing pre-Mississippian occupation of Graves Lake occurred in low frequency across much of the area, with a minor concentration centered on unit N130/E270. At least two pre-Mississippian occupations appear to have been present, the earlier of which is represented by Baytown Plain, *var. Forked Deer*, Cormorant Cord-Impressed, and several baked-clay-object fragments. Sand, clay, and mixed sand-and-clay (Tishomingo paste) wares constitute the

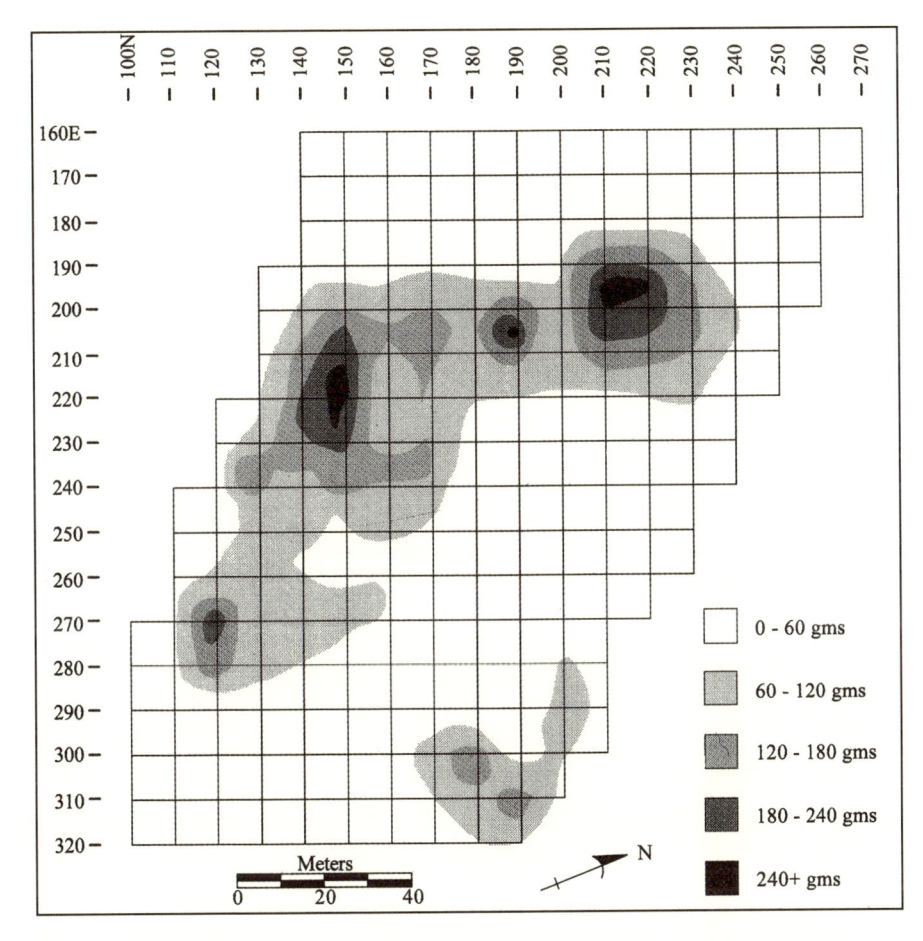

Figure 5-7. Distribution of surface-collected shell-tempered sherds by weight (grams per 10 × 10-meter unit) at Graves Lake. Shapes of the distributions in Figures 5-7 through 5-9 do not conform exactly to collection-unit boundaries because the Transform program interpolates values in calculating boundaries.

remainder of the pre-Mississippian ceramic assemblage and probably represent one or more additional early occupations.

Distributional analysis of functionally related lithic-artifact classes was also performed, but no distinct functional areas are apparent in the data. Distributions of all lithic categories are relatively isomorphic and, moreover, closely mirror the distribution of pottery (Figures 5-7 through 5-9). This finding suggests that lithic manufacture and use was fairly homogeneous among households and that no specialized lithic-activity areas were present at the site. The minor concentration of primary flakes in unit N140/E280 may have been associated with a Woodland component (Figure 5-8), inasmuch as a minor concentration of pre-Mississippian pottery was also present in the unit.

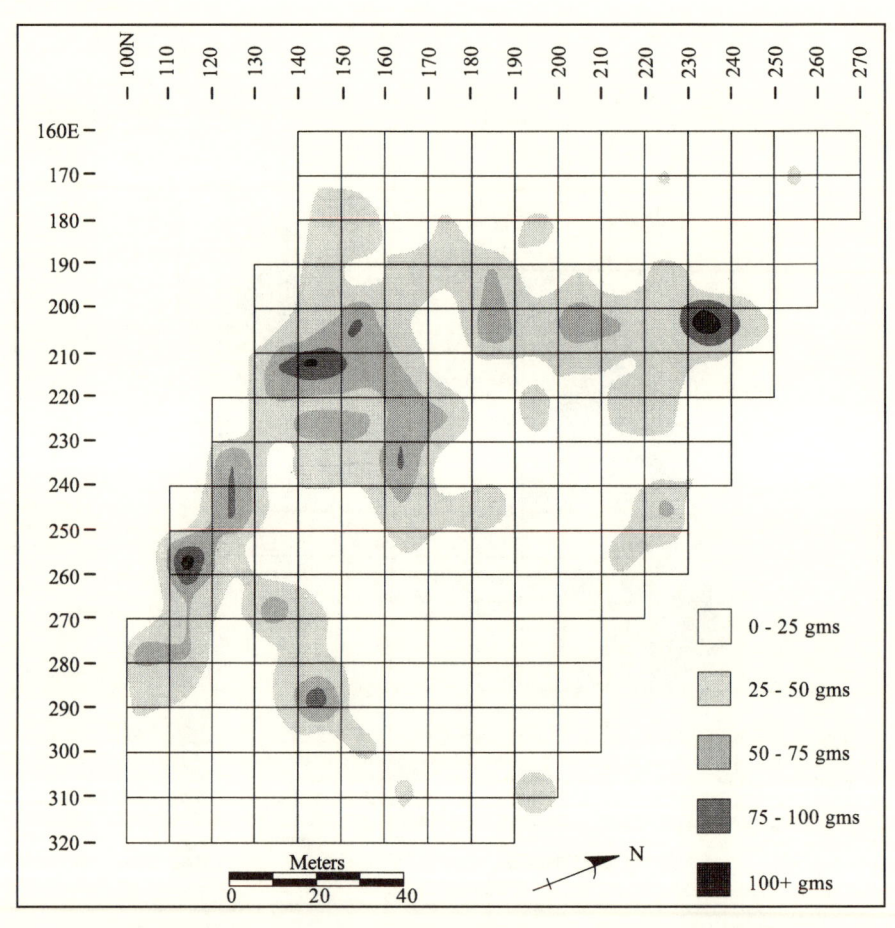

Figure 5-8. Distribution of surface-collected primary flakes by weight (grams per 10 × 10-meter unit) at Graves Lake.

Radiocarbon Determinations

Seven radiocarbon determinations were obtained for the late prehistoric/protohistoric component at Graves Lake (Table 5-2 and Figure 5-10 [all dates in Table 5-2 are rounded to the nearest 5/0]), including two each from houses 1 through 3. Limited testing of the House 1 locality yielded two large wood-charcoal samples that produced radiocarbon ages of 520 ± 60 B.P. (TX-7194) and 480 ± 50 B.P. (TX-7195). The respective calibrated dates (obtained with CALIB 2.0 [Stuiver and Becker 1986]) are A.D. 1330 (1415) 1435 and A.D. 1410 (1430) 1440; the average calibrated date for House 1 is A.D. 1410 (1425) 1435. Wood-charcoal samples from two possible posts associated with the House 2 area produced radiocarbon ages of 390 ± 70 B.P. (TX-7196) and 500 ± 70 B.P. (TX-

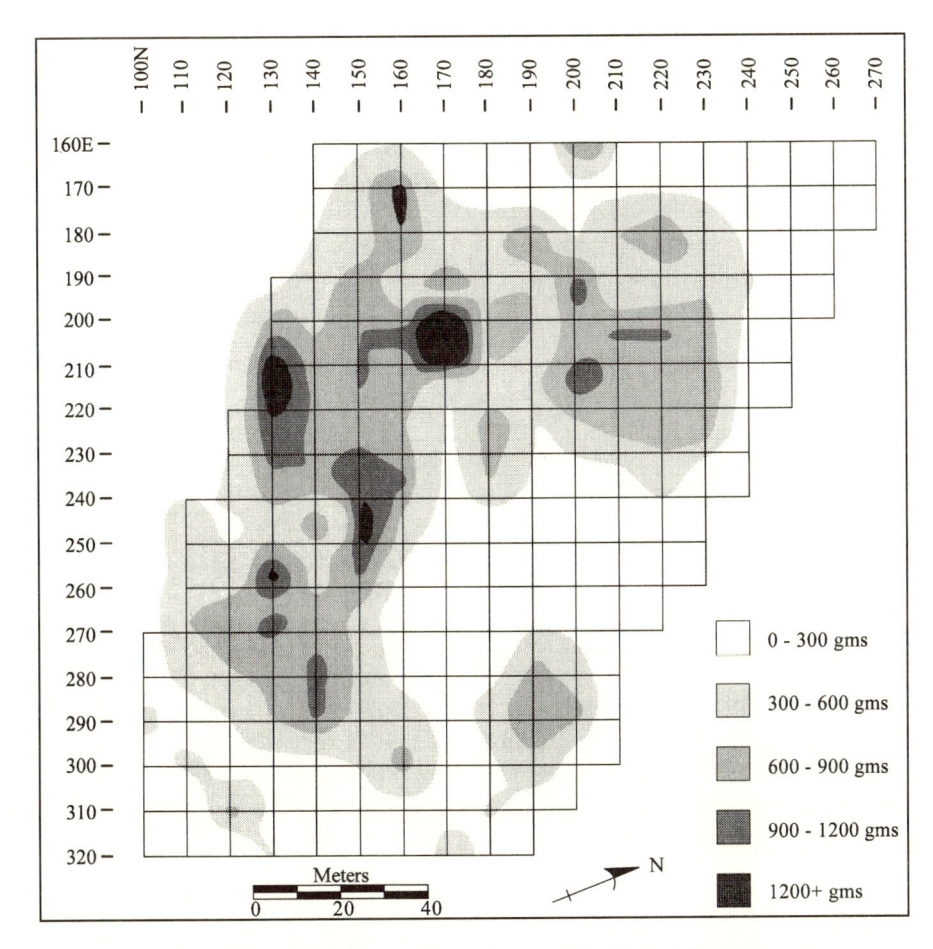

Figure 5-9. Distribution of surface-collected chert cobbles by weight (grams per 10 × 10-meter unit) at Graves Lake.

7197), representing calibrated dates of A.D. 1435 (1455) 1630 and A.D. 1330 (1420) 1440, respectively. Averaging yields a calibrated date of A.D. 1425 (1440) 1455.

Two large wood-charcoal samples from posts in the House 3 area yielded radiocarbon ages of 320 ± 50 B.P. (TX-7486) and 310 ± 50 B.P. (TX-7487); the associated calibrated dates are A.D. 1485 (1525, 1565, 1630) 1645 and A.D. 1490 (1530, 1555, 1635) 1650, respectively. An average calibrated date of A.D. 1495 (1525, 1560, 1630) 1640 was obtained by combining these two age estimates; at one sigma, there is a .78 probability (determined with CALIB 2.0) of the actual date of the sample falling between A.D. 1515 and A.D. 1600. A small wood-charcoal sample collected approximately 3 meters southeast of Burial 1 during initial inspection of the impact area (1988) returned a radiocarbon age of 280 ± 60 B.P. (TX-6079), which calibrates to A.D. 1515 (1640) 1660. As a result of

Table 5-2. Calibrated Radiocarbon Dates from Graves Lake

Sample[a]	Weight	Provenience	Uncorrected Date (B.P.)	Calibrated Date (1 Sigma)[b]
TX-6079	14.0 g	3 m SE of burial 1	280 ± 60	A.D. 1515 (1640) 1660
TX-7194	20.0 g	House 1, post	520 ± 60	A.D. 1330 (1415) 1435
TX-7195	17.0 g	House 1, post?	480 ± 50	A.D. 1410 (1430) 1440
TX-7196	24.0 g	House 2, PM 7	390 ± 70	A.D. 1435 (1455) 1630
TX-7197	30.0 g	House 2, PM 48	500 ± 70	A.D. 1330 (1420) 1440
TX-7486	19.5 g	House 3, PM 18	320 ± 50	A.D. 1485 (1525, 1565, 1630) 1645
TX-7487	28.0 g	House 3, PM 17	310 ± 50	A.D. 1490 (1530, 1555, 1635) 1650

Note: PM, Post mold.
[a]All dates on wood charcoal.
[b]Minimum and maximum ranges presented are 1 standard deviation of the calibrated age; all dates rounded to the nearest 5/0.

erosion, that collection locality could not be precisely relocated during the 1990 field season.

The radiocarbon dates could represent two distinct periods in the occupational history of Graves Lake, though all of the dates overlap around A.D. 1450 at two sigma. Four calibrated dates (those from the House 1 and House 2 areas) cluster tightly around A.D. 1430. This appears to be consistent with the presumed dates of the sherds in the surface collection, particularly when considered in light of similar sherds and calibrated dates for the penultimate summit structure at Chucalissa (cf. Lumb and McNutt 1988; Mainfort 1991), located in southern Memphis. The three remaining dates, especially those from the House 3 area, suggest that the site was occupied (continuously?) during or slightly after the time of the de Soto entrada; that is, around A.D. 1540. Certain recovered artifact types are consistent with such an interpretation, namely the helmet-shaped bowls, the gadrooned bottle, Campbell Appliqué and Vernon Paul Appliqué sherds, large triangular points, and the fragment of a snub-nosed scraper (Lawrence and Mainfort 1995; Williams 1980).

Despite intensive, long-standing interest in the Late Mississippian period in the central Mississippi Valley, there is an appalling lack of published (or even of unpublished) radiocarbon dates for that general time. The dates from Graves Lake provide the best chronometric anchors for late ceramic types in the region.

Pottery-Rim Modes as Chronometric Indicators

House (1991, 1993b; see also Phillips et al. 1951) recently suggested that interior-beveled rims are characteristic of post–A.D. 1450 occupations in the Kent-

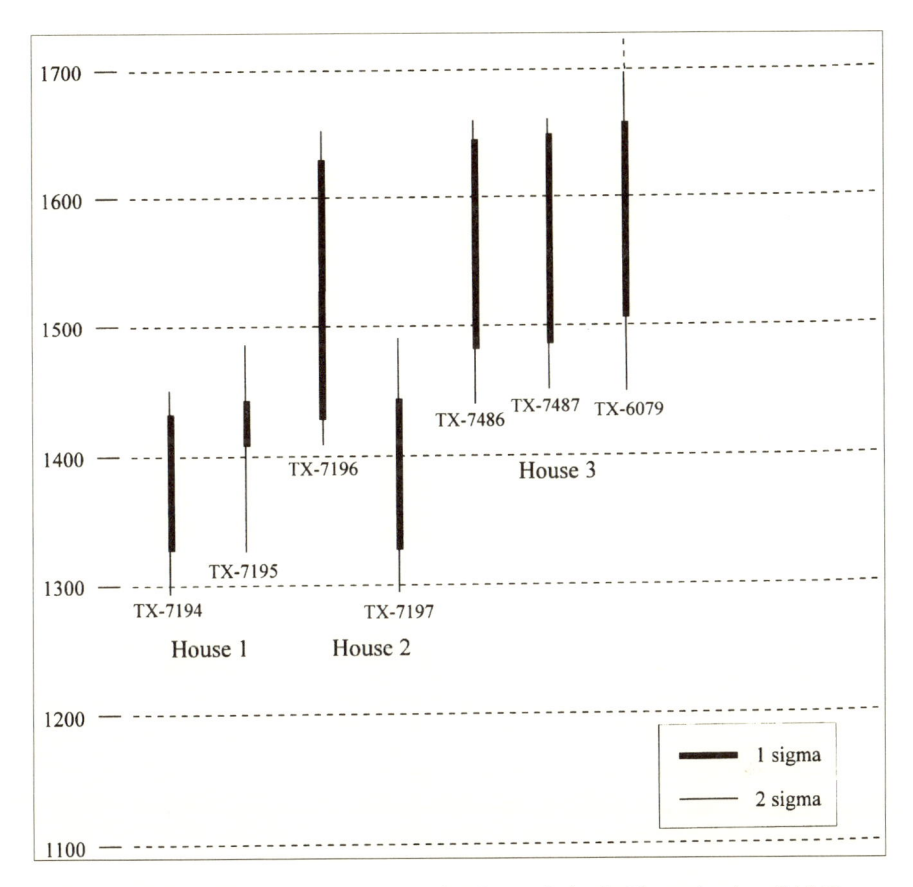

Figure 5-10. Radiocarbon determinations for Graves Lake (calibrated using CALIB 2.0 [Stuiver and Becker 1986]).

phase area of eastern Arkansas, along the lower St. Francis River. In particular, House argued that the "Memphis rim mode" is associated with Kent II and Kent III occupations but is absent in the Kent I temporal segment. Analysis of rimsherds from Graves Lake focused on, but was not limited to, recording variation in interior-rim beveling. As presented in Table 5-3, four categories, ranging from no bevel to sharp bevel, were used in analyzing all rims from the surface collections. In this exercise, beveling was defined as an outflared flattening of the lip interior that resulted in the creation of an obvious angle of inflection (essentially a "shoulder") between the vessel interior and the beveled area. This use appears to be somewhat more restrictive than House's Memphis rim mode, which does not necessarily require such a well-defined break between the beveled area and the unmodified vessel interior (e.g., House 1993b:28, figure 6a). A *sharp bevel* refers to an angle approaching (and even exceeding, in some instances) approximately 40 degrees (cf. House 1993b:figure 6, *b* and *c*); this often

Table 5-3. Frequencies of Interior Beveling on Rimsherds from Sites in Western Tennessee and Southeastern Missouri

Site	Sharp Bevel n	Sharp Bevel %	Moderate Bevel n	Moderate Bevel %	Slight Bevel n	Slight Bevel %	No Bevel n	No Bevel %	Total
Berry (23PM59)	151	32	152	32	77	16	93	20	473
Campbell (23PM5)	30	26	42	37	20	17	23	20	115
Bishop (40TP10)	2	10	8	40	2	10	8	40	20
Sweat (40LA26)	29	22	36	27	8	6	59	45	132
40LA17	2	13	5	33		0	8	53	15
Graves Lake (40LA92)	24	12	44	22	23	11	112	55	203
Dry Arm (40LA19)	7	23	5	17	1	3	17	57	30
Jones Bayou (40LA4)	16	17	11	11	9	9	60	63	96
Wilder (40TP12)	18	14	18	14	7	6	84	66	127
Fullen (40LA109)	12	11	9	8	13	12	77	69	111
Rast (40SY75)	9	11	12	14	4	5	59	70	84
Hatchie (40TP1)	11	16	6	9	1	1	52	74	70
Richardson's Landing (40TP2)	8	7	8	7	11	10	88	77	115
Jeter (40SY28)	3	9	2	6		0	28	85	33
Porter (40LA2)	5	5	2	2	9	8	95	86	111

produces outflaring on the rim exterior. Rims recorded as *slight bevel* exhibit characteristic flattening and a distinct, but small, angle of inflection.

Slightly fewer than half the analyzed rims from Graves Lake exhibit some degree of interior beveling. Roughly one-third (those tabulated as sharp and moderate bevel) fall within the range of House's Memphis rim mode. Intuitively, the frequency of beveled rims at Graves Lake originally appeared to be higher than that at many late-period sites in the central Mississippi Valley. Analysis of rimsherds from other major Late Mississippian sites in western Tennessee (Mainfort 1991) indicates that this impression is essentially correct, though the incidence of beveled rims at several sites exceeds that in the Graves Lake assemblage. Importantly, sites with the highest frequency of beveled rims also have yielded artifacts indicative of the latest temporal placement. For example, sherds or vessels with vertical appliqués are reported from Graves Lake, Bishop, and Sweat (40LA26), whereas snub-nosed end scrapers occur only at Graves Lake and Bishop (Mainfort 1991).

It appears, therefore, that the frequency of beveled rims has temporal significance within the area under consideration. To test this proposition, surface collections from Campbell and Berry, both located in Pemiscot County, Missouri (O'Brien 1994a), were analyzed. Both are well-known late-period sites, and Campbell, the key site in Williams's (1980) formulation of the Armorel phase, has produced Spanish (O'Brien 1994a) and perhaps French artifacts (D. F. Morse

1990). As shown in Table 5-3, Campbell and Berry exhibit the highest percentages of beveled rims of any analyzed site, and thus the proposition that the frequency of interior beveling increases over time is strongly supported by the data from Campbell and Berry.

This conclusion has some interesting implications for the chronological positions of several sites listed in Table 5-3. Graves Lake and Hatchie (40TP1), located only 3 kilometers to the south of Graves Lake, have long been viewed as representing sequent occupations by a single sociopolitical group. On the basis of the incidence of beveled rims, Graves Lake, the smaller of the two sites, appears to postdate Hatchie. A cluster of sites to the north—Porter (40LA2), Jones Bayou (40LA4), and Sweat (40LA26)—presents another instructive case (Figure 5-1). Again, we have a group of late-period sites in close proximity that probably were occupied sequentially (Mainfort 1991). Reference to Table 5-3 clarifies the situation, because data there indicate that Porter is the earliest of the three and Sweat the latest. The latter is also the smallest site and lacks an associated mound. Although a comprehensive analysis is beyond the scope of this chapter, preliminary results presented here strongly suggest that late-period sites in the central Mississippi Valley can be chronologically ordered on the basis of the frequency of rim beveling.

Supplemental Data from Richardson's Landing

As a small step toward alleviating the dearth of radiocarbon dates bemoaned above, we take this opportunity to present three radiocarbon dates on wood charcoal obtained during minor testing by TDOA at Richardson's Landing (40TP2), located several kilometers west of the Second Chickasaw Bluff system in the Mississippi River floodplain of Tipton County, Tennessee, and approximately 10 kilometers south of Graves Lake (Figure 5-1). The site is perhaps best known through Williams's work with collections in the Hampson Museum in Wilson, Arkansas (e.g., Williams 1980). We have examined a number of late-period vessels bearing variants of the provenience "Richardson's Landing" in the Hampson collection. These include "Richardson's Landing," "Harris site at Richardson's Landing," "1 mile south of Richardson's Landing," and "3 miles south of Richardson's Landing." Either or both of the first two designations might represent what we refer to as Richardson's Landing; the others probably represent site 40TP26 and Wilder (40TP12), respectively (see Figure 5-1). Two of the vessels illustrated by Williams (1980:figure 2, K and Q) are in all likelihood from site 40TP26. Other vessels in the Hampson collection that may be from Richardson's Landing proper include a Bell Plain bottle with appliquéd hands and long bones, a gadrooned Bell Plain bottle, a "cat-serpent" bowl, a Bell Plain bottle with an appliquéd ogee motif, and a Bell Plain stirrup bottle.

Long rumored to have been destroyed, Richardson's Landing was relocated by TDOA in 1989. In 1990 several surface collections were made and minor testing was conducted (Mainfort 1991). On the basis of surface indications, the site covers approximately a hectare. Lithic artifacts in the collections include ten Nodena points (including several examples of Nodena, *var. Banks*), five Madison points, a number of flaked adzes or gouges, and a ground basalt celt. Sherd counts from several general surface collections at Richardson's Landing are presented in Table 5-1. Although there are some general similarities with the collections from Graves Lake, the relatively low frequency of decorated sherds (especially of the types Parkin Punctated and Barton Incised) in the Richardson's Landing collection might be noteworthy.

Two radiocarbon assays were obtained from wood-charcoal samples associated with the remains of a house near the center of the site. The ages are 530 ± 70 B.P. (TX-7198) and 460 ± 70 B.P. (TX-7199); the associated calibrated dates are A.D. 1325 (1412) 1435 and A.D. 1410 (1435) 1465. The calibrated average of these two dates is A.D. 1410 (1425) 1440. A third radiocarbon determination was made on wood charcoal from an ash-filled pit found immediately below the plow zone, in which a large segment of a Mississippi Plain salt pan was found. The uncorrected age is 460 ± 70 B.P. (TX-6967), which is calibrated to A.D. 1410 (1435) 1465.

Obviously, the three radiocarbon dates for Richardson's Landing derive from only two features at a moderately large site; thus, they should be interpreted with caution. Indeed, it appears unlikely that these dates accurately reflect the age of some of the whole vessels mentioned above. Nonetheless, the partial contemporaneity of Richardson's Landing and Graves Lake seems securely established.

Concluding Remarks

Field research at Graves Lake was directed primarily toward addressing specific resource-management concerns. Preservation and stabilization of the site, not the accumulation of artifacts, was the desired outcome. Nonetheless, a considerable body of data pertaining to the Late Mississippian period in the central Mississippi Valley was obtained. Our use of controlled surface collection to define site boundaries was largely successful and revealed that cultural material was concentrated along a low rise on the west side of the site. Concentrations of daub along that rise were interpreted as the remains of houses. Excavation of the House 2 and House 3 areas (Figure 5-3) indicated that not all houses at the site were located on the rise. The marked drop in artifact frequencies immediately to the east of the ridge raises the question of whether a central plaza is present.

Seven radiocarbon determinations were obtained from Graves Lake and suggest the site was occupied between A.D. 1430 (calibrated) and A.D. 1550 (calibrated). It is not clear that occupation was continuous during the period represented, and there is some indication of distinct spatial patterning over time. The radiocarbon dates and the artifact assemblage constitute some of the best available chronometric controls for the central Mississippi Valley during the late prehistoric and protohistoric periods. Such temporal and typological control is a necessary precondition for meaningful assessments of regional depopulation associated with early European contacts in the New World (see Ramenofsky 1987).

Acknowledgments

Fieldwork at Graves Lake was conducted under ARPA permit No. 01-TN-1-90 issued by the U.S. Fish and Wildlife Service, Atlanta. The interpretations and opinions expressed herein are solely the responsibility of the authors and do not necessarily represent the views of the service or its representatives. We thank R. Walling, W. Lawrence, S. Chapman, T. Pugh, C. McNutt, Jr., G. P. Smith, N. Fielder, J. Moore, D. F. Morse, P. Stripling, M. Nichols, M. Kwas, H. Smith, M. Norton, and M. Williams for assisting in various phases of the project and C. McNutt and S. Williams for reviewing the manuscript. Pottery illustrations in Figure 5-6 were prepared by S. Chapman.

6 | Landscape Change and Settlement Location in the Cairo Lowland of Southeastern Missouri
Robert H. Lafferty III

BETWEEN 1989 AND 1993, Mid-Continental Research Associates, Inc., of Springdale, Arkansas, under contract with the Memphis District of the U.S. Army Corps of Engineers, conducted surveys and limited excavation of archaeological sites in the New Madrid Floodway of southeastern Missouri (Figure 6-1). The floodway is located in the Cairo Lowland, a region bounded on the east by the Mississippi River and on the west by Pleistocene-age terrace deposits of the ancestral Mississippi and Ohio river systems. The floodway, which includes portions of Mississippi and New Madrid counties, occupies more or less the eastern half of the Cairo Lowland and is bounded by the Birds Point–New Madrid Set Back Levee, which abuts a levee of the Mississippi River on the north and Pleistocene-age Sikeston Ridge on the south.

Established in 1929, the floodway was designed to relieve flooding in Cairo, Illinois, and cities downriver. When the Mississippi River reached a critical level in 1936, roughly 600 meters of the frontline levee opposite Cairo was dynamited, and floodwaters from the Mississippi inundated the basin, in the process creating an enormous scoured area near the blown section known as Tom Bird Blue Hole (Figure 6-1). The diversion fulfilled its intended purpose; floodwaters around Cairo receded by an estimated half meter. Current operating plans are more drastic, calling for dynamiting some 3.7 kilometers of levee if needed. The higher water velocity that would result from this breach, which would be roughly six times as great as that in 1936, is projected not only to create enormous blue holes but also to remove the plow zone from most, if not all, of the land throughout the floodway. Such an event would have catastrophic effects on archaeological resources. It is safe to say that if the floodway is ever used, the results of the fieldwork discussed here will be the only information available for a sizable portion of the archaeological record of Mississippi County.

The floodway survey focused primarily on areas of projected high water velocity following a levee breach. The survey covered 2900 hectares of the 100,000-hectare floodway, and 250 sites were located. Presented here is a summary of some of the significant results of the project, which are detailed elsewhere (Lafferty et al. 1995). For present purposes, I concentrate on two areas: (1) the northernmost section of the floodway, from Birds Point to O'Bryan Ridge, and (2) a

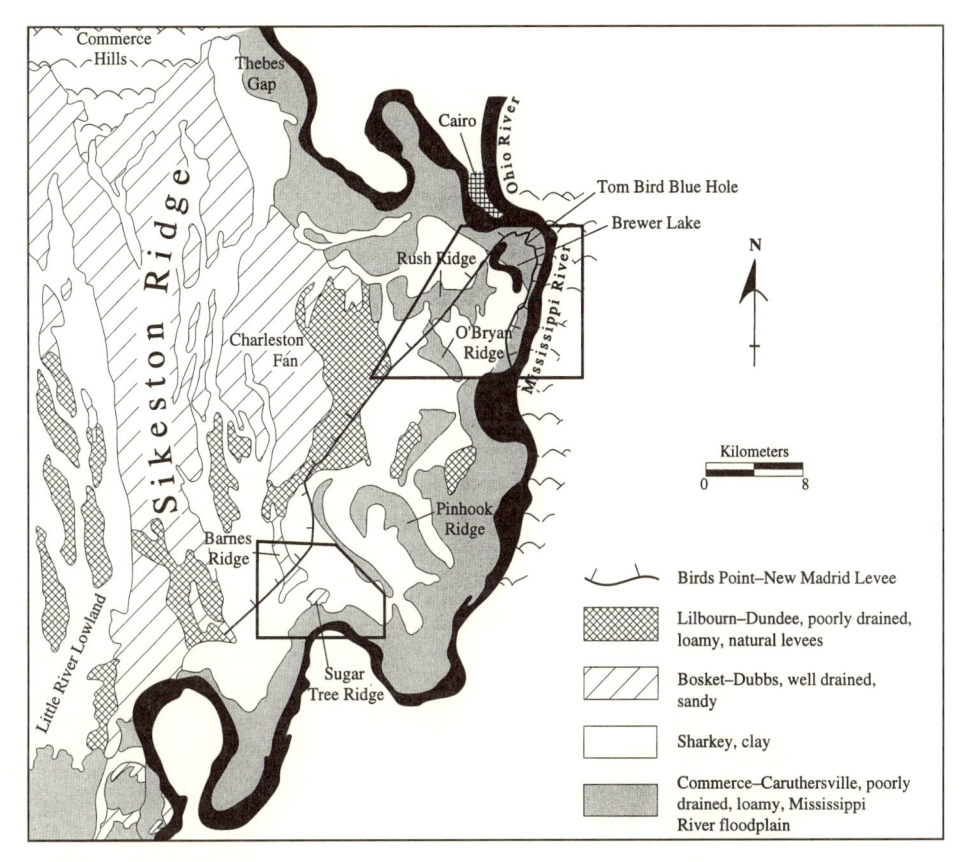

Figure 6-1. Map of the Cairo Lowland, southeastern Missouri, showing the location of the New Madrid Floodway and sampling areas relative to major physiographic features and modern soil associations. The floodway boundary is defined by the Mississippi River on the east and south and by the Birds Point–New Madrid Levee on the north and west. Most of the landscape within the floodway is of Holocene age and is tied to the Mississippi River meander-belt regime; that to the north and west comprises features and sediments associated with the ancestral Mississippi River braided-stream regime.

section in the south-central portion of the floodway that contains Barnes and Sugar Tree ridges (Figure 6-1).

Previous Research

The Cairo Lowland has long been known for the significance and the diversity of its archaeological record. The earliest professional archaeological work in the lowland and its environs was done as part of the mound-exploration project of the Bureau of (American) Ethnology during the 1880s (Thomas 1894), but this was preceded (and succeeded) by decades of sometimes frenzied activities (e.g., Croswell 1878; Fowke 1910; Moore 1910; Potter 1880; Putnam 1875a, 1875b [see also Williams 1988]) that resulted in the removal of tens of thousands of ceramic vessels from the many mounds in the region. Oftentimes, the vessels were sent to museums in the East, but in other cases they ended up in private collections. In some instances, data generated from examination of the vessels were used to define major prehistoric ceramic units (see particularly Holmes 1884b, 1903), and, as Fox points out in Chapter 2, these early conceptualizations still structure currently used chronological orderings of archaeological materials (e.g., Chapman 1952, 1980; Ford and Willey 1941; Griffin 1952).

Following the Bureau of American Ethnology investigations, there was a hiatus in professional work in the region until the 1940s, when Winslow Walker and Robert Adams began their investigations in New Madrid County (Adams and Walker 1942; Walker and Adams 1946), which encompasses the southwestern portion of the floodway. Their excavation program centered on the Matthews site, a large Mississippian-period settlement located on Sikeston Ridge. Walker and Adams's work in New Madrid County was contemporary with a much larger effort—the Lower Mississippi Survey—that began in 1939 and had as its sampling universe that portion of the Mississippi Alluvial Valley from the mouth of the Ohio River south to Vicksburg, Mississippi (Phillips et al. 1951; Williams 1954; see also Griffin and Spaulding 1952). This work continued in some locations into the succeeding decades (e.g., Phillips 1970). The authors of the final report of the Lower Mississippi Survey (Phillips et al. 1951) defined numerous ceramic types on the basis of their examination of specimens from the region, and those types, with only minor revision (e.g., Phillips 1970), are still used today. Slightly later, Stephen Williams (1954) expanded the list of ceramic types and used the types to assign Cairo Lowland sites that he excavated and/or surface collected to phases (Fox, Chapter 2).

Beginning in the 1960s, the tempo and scope of archaeological work increased significantly. Numerous survey-and-testing projects were done across southeastern Missouri and northeastern Arkansas in advance of land leveling and federally funded construction projects (e.g., Cande and Lafferty 1991; Hopgood 1969a; Klinger and Mathis 1978; Lafferty et al. 1984, 1985, 1987; LeeDecker 1979; Marshall 1965, 1966; Morse and Morse 1977; P. A. Morse 1979; Price 1976a; Price et al. 1978; Williams 1967, 1968, 1972, 1974). Generally referred to as cultural-resource management studies, these projects greatly increased the number of known sites from all time periods. Most of the projects were geared toward survey and testing and were seldom of a scope capable of generating large assemblages of artifacts from intact contexts. Nevertheless, an extensive body of data on surface preservation, depositional characteristics of site context, and preservation variation on a range of different sites accumulated.

In terms of the discussion here, perhaps the most important project was the University of Missouri's Landleveling Salvage Project conducted in the late 1960s and early 1970s (Williams 1967, 1968, 1972; see also Cottier and Southard 1977; Hopgood 1969b; Lewis 1974, 1982; Williams 1971, 1974). Several small sites and several mounds in the Pinhook Ridge area (Figure 6-1) were excavated, including several dating to the Baytown (Woodland) and Mississippian periods. Radiocarbon dates from the land-leveling and related projects still form the basis for the chronological ordering of archaeological remains in the region (Lafferty and Price 1996).

Concurrent with these survey-and-testing projects were a number of larger-scale excavation programs—for example, those undertaken at Lilbourn (Chapman et al. 1977; Cottier 1977a, 1977b; Cottier and Southard 1977), in New Madrid County, and Beckwith's Fort (Cottier 1972; Price and Fox 1990), in Mississippi County, the two largest of several fortified centers in the Cairo Lowland (Williams 1964)—that have greatly expanded our understanding of the Mississippian portion of the archaeological record. Excavations at Lilbourn and Beckwith's Fort produced numerous radiocarbon dates that added to the sequence established by dates obtained through the land-leveling project.

Despite the amount of work undertaken in Mississippi and New Madrid counties, our knowledge of the prehistoric record of southeastern Missouri is woefully inadequate for addressing modern archaeological concerns. Previous work has tended to focus on mound centers and other large sites that contain highly visible archaeological signatures and not on the smaller sites that once were so abundant across the region. As a result, we know quite a bit about the development of large, nucleated settlements and less about the histories of smaller communities. Also, because of the visibility of sites dating to the Mississippian period, previous work has tended to emphasize them and to neglect earlier portions of the record. The project discussed here was viewed as an opportunity to redress some of the bias against smaller, pre–Mississippian-period sites.

Of particular interest, not only from an intellectual standpoint but also from that of good resource management, was documenting the distribution of sites across a few large, thoroughly surveyed areas as opposed to surveying a larger number of smaller blocks randomly scattered across the impact area. As I point out below, two sample areas, one in the northern part of the impact zone and a smaller one in the southern part, were surveyed intensively. Also of interest was the location of sites of varying age relative (1) to various landforms, particularly Pleistocene ridges in the modern meander belt, which are rare features in the Mississippi Alluvial Valley, and (2) to former channels of the Mississippi as it moved around in its post-Pleistocene meander-belt location east of Sikeston Ridge (O'Brien and Dunnell, Chapter 1). Numerous archaeologists since the mid-1940s (e.g., Ford et al. 1955; Phillips et al. 1951; Scully 1953) have used Harold Fisk's (1944) meander-belt maps as a means of dating sites. As

Saucier (1964, 1968, 1974, 1994; Saucier and Snead 1989) and others (Autin et al. 1991) have repeatedly shown, Fisk's estimates of when certain prehistoric channels were occupied were well off the mark, as were parts of his developmental history of the alluvial valley. However, in the portion of the valley just south of Cairo, his *relative* chronology of specific channels, which was constructed in large part by inspection of aerial photographs, is remarkably consistent with modern interpretations. It is the relative sequence—and only the relative sequence—that I use in this chapter.

The New Madrid Floodway Project

The only archaeological work conducted in the immediate impact zones of the New Madrid Floodway within the past decade and a half consisted of three small, linear surveys of northern portions of the area (McNerney 1978; Nixon 1982; Sturdevant 1981). Data from those surveys, together with data from previous examinations of the Cairo Lowland, were used to develop a predictive model of site location (Niemczycki 1987) that I subsequently used in structuring initial investigation of the impact areas. I examine some of the elements of the model below in terms of its success in predicting the locations of sites in the Birds Point–O'Bryan Ridge location (Figure 6-1). I then turn attention to the evolution of the exceedingly complex landscape in that northern portion of the survey area and the relation between landform and the location of archaeological sites. Finally, I examine the distribution of sites on two relatively stable landforms—Barnes Ridge and Sugar Tree Ridge—in the southern portion of the floodway (Figure 6-1).

Birds Point–O'Bryan Ridge

The northern portion of the floodway is a complex mosaic of intersecting channel scars and ridges (Figure 6-2), the latter corresponding to natural-levee remnants and point-bar deposits. Selection of locations for survey was based on a prediction of Niemczycki's (1987) model, namely that locales containing "well-drained" soils, especially Bosket-Dubbs soil (Figure 6-1), had the highest probability of containing sites (Figure 6-3). In addition to high-probability areas, 480 hectares in the Tom Bird Blue Hole impact area were surveyed, as were an additional carefully selected 300 hectares of low-probability areas comprising poorly drained soils (Figure 6-1). Surveys were extended systematically along the edges of high-probability areas to include any low-probability areas that were in the same agricultural field. In many cases, particularly on the southern edges of Fisk Meander Channels (FMC) 1 through 3 (Fisk 1944) (Figure 6-2), the transition from light-colored sandy soils to gray Sharkey clay was obvious. Localities containing the latter were low lying and often waterlogged, and in many cases had only recently been drained. Much of the area

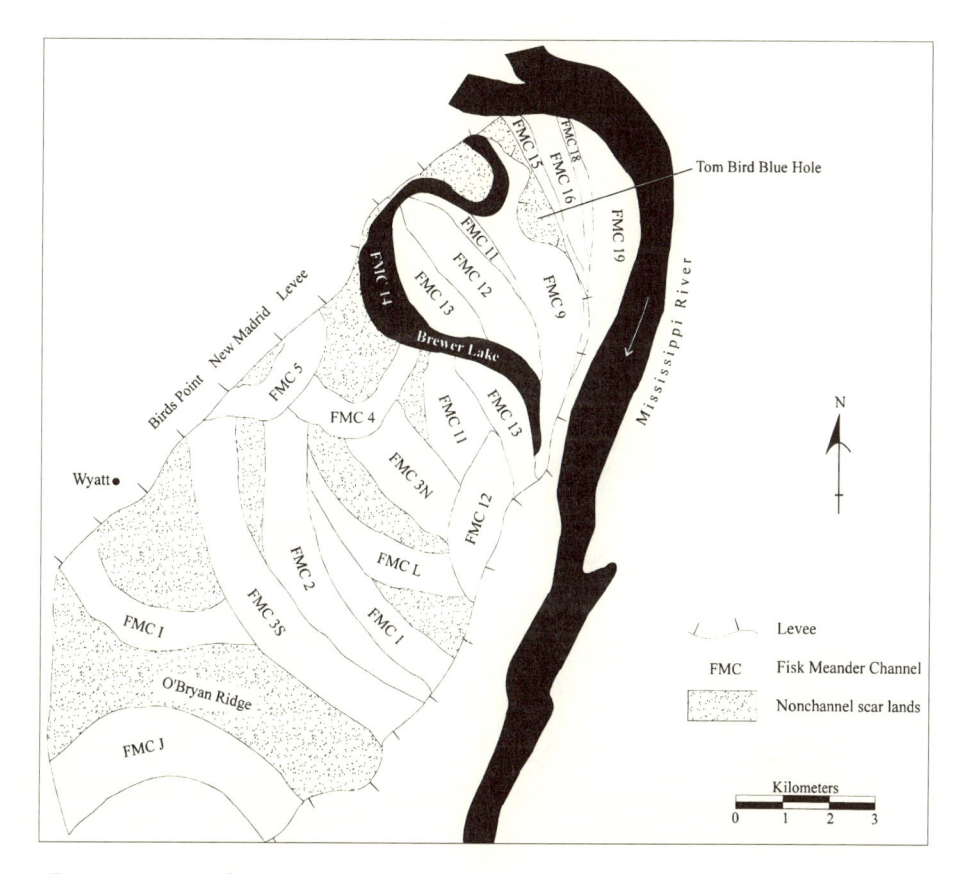

Figure 6-2. Map of the northern portion of the New Madrid Floodway project area showing the locations of Mississippi River channels mapped and labeled by Harold Fisk (1944). The oldest channel shown is FMC I, followed by FMC J and then by FMC L. Numbered channels are younger, beginning with FMC 1 (oldest) and ending with FMC 19 (youngest).

north of O'Bryan Ridge had been land leveled. Low-probability, land-leveled areas shown in Figure 6-3 were surveyed; 160 hectares of high-probability, land-leveled area on the north-central section of O'Bryan Ridge were not surveyed. Table 6-1 summarizes the amount and percentage of area surveyed and lists the numbers of sites each contained.

If the predictive model is accurate, the proportion of prehistoric sites found in the high-probability areas should be higher than that in the low-probability areas, provided that equal amounts of both strata were examined under the same conditions and with the same intensity. Survey intensity was similar in both types of areas, but almost four times as much land was surveyed in high-probability areas as in low-probability areas. Table 6-1 lists the number of sites per hectare; note that high-probability areas contained one site per roughly 9.7

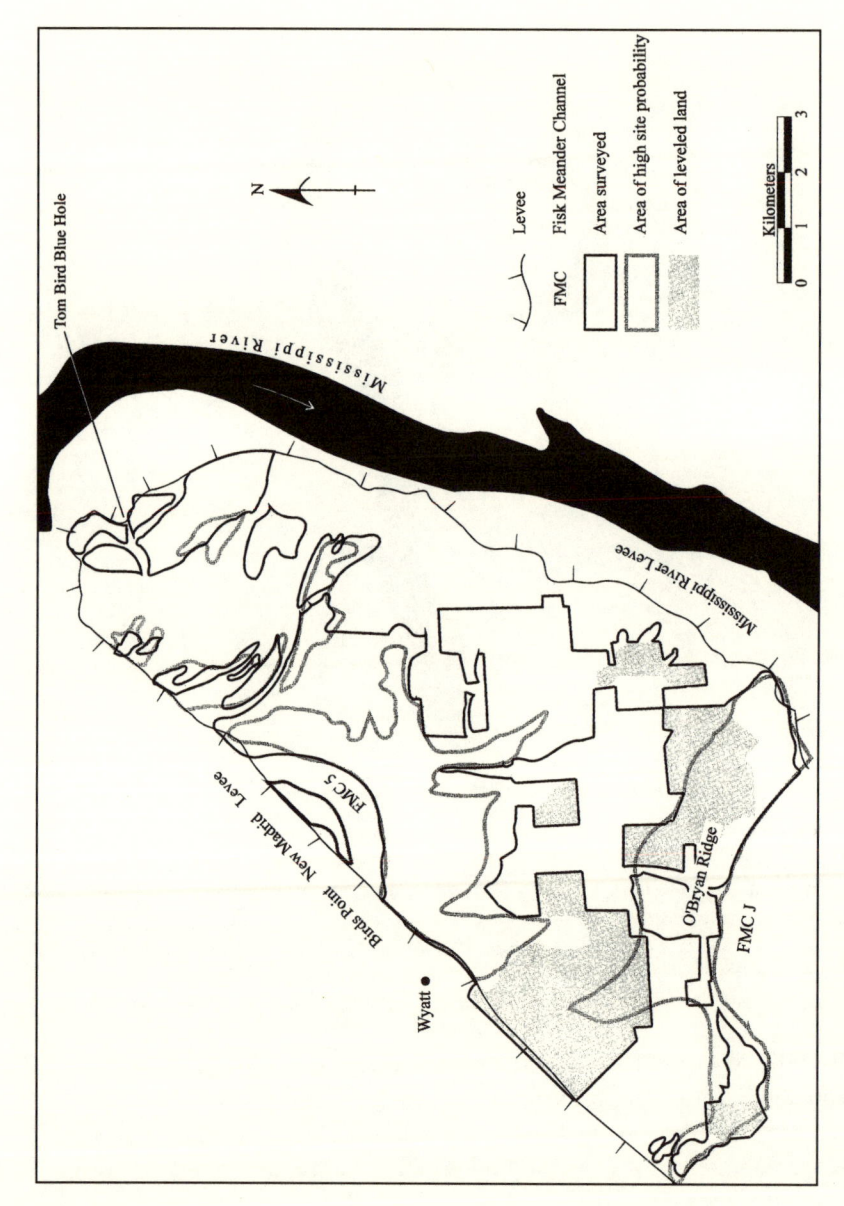

Figure 6-3. Map of the northern portion of the New Madrid Floodway showing the areas surveyed. High-probability areas are designated on the basis of a previously designed model of site location (Niemczycki 1987) based on modern soil associations.

Table 6-1. Numbers of Hectares Surveyed and Sites Found in High- and Low-Probability Areas in the Northern Portion of the New Madrid Floodway

Area Surveyed	Hectares	Percentage	Sites	Percentage
High Probability	1134	78.9	117	83.6
Low Probability	304	21.1	23	16.4
Total	1438	100.0	140	100.0

hectares and low-probability areas contained one site per roughly 13.2 hectares. Chi-square tests (Lafferty et al. 1995:92–94) demonstrated that there was no significant difference ($p = .10$) between high- and low-probability areas in terms of the number of sites each contained.

Modern soil associations might not be particularly good predictors of site location, but elevation *is* a good predictor, which is not surprising given the nature of the terrain. By subtracting 74 hectares of the topographically highest land from the low-probability stratum as defined by soils data and adding them to the high-probability stratum, ten sites are added to the 117 sites listed in Table 6-1 as occurring in high-probability areas. The discovery rate changes very little for the high-probability areas—from one site per 9.6 hectares to one site per 9.4 hectares—but the rate for the low-probability areas decreases dramatically—from one site per 13.2 hectares to one site per 17.7 hectares. Now, the chi-square distribution is significant ($p = .01$). Interestingly, two of the largest sites found during the survey, Nally (23MI644) and Hillhouse (23MI699) (discussed below), are located in high-relief areas that soil associations estimate as being of low probability. In general, the findings support Williams's (1956:55) contention that permanent settlements in the region were founded in locations that "remained dry under foot the year round."

LANDSCAPE EVOLUTION

The landscape evolution discussed below relative to the northern portion of the study area is based on three lines of evidence: (1) Fisk's (1944) relative sequence of Mississippi River meander-belt channels; (2) radiocarbon dates from sediment cores; and (3) pollen and sediment-size analysis (Cummings 1994; Porter and Guccione 1994). Careful analysis of Fisk's (1944) reconstruction of Mississippi River meander channels from Birds Point south to O'Bryan Ridge (Figure 6-2) led Porter and Guccione (1994) to conclude that the reconstruction is essentially correct in a relative (not an absolute) sense. Relevant to this landscape is the fact that FMC 3S cuts FMC 1, FMC 2, and FMC I; the position of FMC 3N is not clear relative to those of FMC 1 through 3S and FMC J. However,

FMC 1 through 3 are all truncated by FMC 4 and FMC 5. It also is clear that FMC 4 is truncated by the mass of channel scars northeast of Brewer Lake.

Sediments in the project area were deposited during the Pleistocene and Holocene by the ancestral Ohio and Mississippi rivers. During the Pleistocene, the relict braided surface—a portion of which is exposed in the west-central portion of the floodway (Figure 6-1)—was laid down by the ancestral Ohio, which throughout the Pleistocene periodically carried glacial meltwater and enormous amounts of coarse sediments (O'Brien and Dunnell, Chapter 1). The Charleston Fan (Figure 6-1) was deposited sometime after 12,000 years ago, when the Mississippi finally broke through Thebes Gap (Figure 6-1) and captured the Ohio below Cairo, Illinois. O'Bryan Ridge was deposited next, perhaps when the Mississippi was in FMC I (Figure 6-2). The inversion of silts and clays in two dated pollen cores from the north and south sides of O'Bryan Ridge (Figure 6-4) indicates that the Mississippi River was occupying FMC J around 5000 B.C. FMC 1, located north of O'Bryan Ridge, was occupied at about the same time. By about 2000 B.C., FMC 1 and FMC 2 were silted in, and Late Archaic Poverty Point sites were located on top of those former channels and near the then-active FMC 3S. Around A.D. 1, the river was in either FMC 4 or FMC 5. Occupation of FMC 12 through 19 appears to have taken place over the past 1300 years.

The above reconstruction has implications for the ages of sites present in the northern part of the floodway. Given the extremely dynamic nature of the Mississippi River, archaeological sites that date earlier than the Late Archaic period are unlikely to be present. For example, O'Bryan Ridge, an early landform, was heavily dissected by later river meanders that left only the core of the ridge. Although it is possible that early sites on the ridge are buried under more-recent sediments, it is more likely that they were nearer the then-active river channels and hence were eroded by FMC 3S, FMC I, and FMC J. The only evidence of pre–Late Archaic occupation or use of the region is an Early Archaic point (ca. 7000–5000 B.C.) found on O'Bryan Ridge.

Late Archaic sites (ca. 3000–600 B.C.) are restricted to O'Bryan Ridge and to FMC 1 and FMC 2 (Figure 6-4). O'Bryan Ridge was the highest point of land in the northern part of the project area during the Late Archaic period, though sediment analysis from the New Madrid core (Figure 6-4) indicates the western end of the ridge was a swamp. FMC I at that time probably was an oxbow lake (Porter and Guccione 1994). Rush Ridge (Figure 6-1) was separated from O'Bryan Ridge by the Mississippi River. During the Late Archaic period, the confluence of the Mississippi and Ohio rivers was to the south of O'Bryan Ridge. A small section of land northeast of FMC 3N containing Late Archaic sites is a remnant of the older surface. Several radiocarbon dates are relevant to the landscape reconstruction for the Late Archaic period.[1] Two dates are from carbonized wood removed from the Moxley Well in FMC 3S (Figure 6-4) at depths of

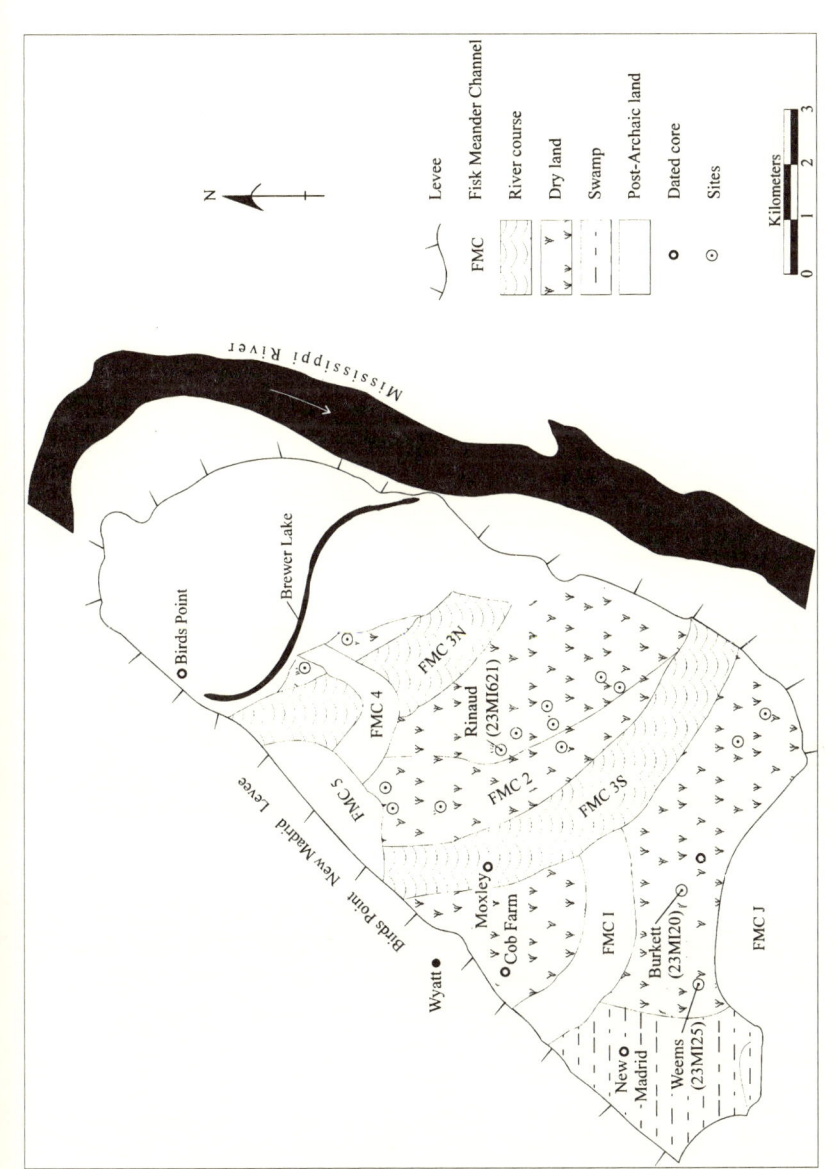

Figure 6-4. Map of the northern portion of the New Madrid Floodway showing the proposed reconstruction of the landscape about 2000 B.C. (Late Archaic period) and the distribution of sites across the landscape. The blank area labeled *post-Archaic land* undoubtedly once contained sites, but they were destroyed by subsequent erosion by the Mississippi River as it meandered across the area. The reconstruction is based on site location, pollen and sediment samples, and radiocarbon dating of carbonized material from the sediment cores (Cummings 1994; Porter and Guccione 1994).

24.4 and 30.5 meters. The calibrated-date ranges (at two sigma) (Stuiver and Reimer 1993) suggest that FMC 3S was an active channel between 3100 B.C. and 3900 B.C. A radiocarbon date from the Rinaud site (23MI621) (Figure 6-4 and Table 6-2) indicates that by about 2450 B.C., FMC 2 was dry land inhabited by Archaic peoples.

During the Baytown, or Woodland, period (ca. 600 B.C.–A.D. 900), there was a major change in the hydrological regime of the Mississippi River. More sites were located in and along FMC 3N and along FMC 3S (Figure 6-5), which probably was an oxbow lake. The Mississippi-Ohio confluence had moved north of its former position and was somewhere between Brewer Lake and its present location. It appears likely, given the density of artifacts at the Nally (23MI644) and Hillhouse (23MI699) sites (Figure 6-5), that the course of the river was in Brewer Lake during some of the Woodland period.

Sometime during the Mississippian period (post–A.D. 900), the Mississippi-Ohio confluence moved near to its current location. There appears to have been significant settlement along the escarpment near what had been Brewer Lake (Figure 6-4), and small Mississippian communities appeared along the abandoned FMC 5 (see Figure 6-2 for location). The lack of such components around FMC 3N suggests it was filled in by about A.D. 1000. North of Brewer Lake is a series of meander channels that date to the Mississippian period. The area has classic ridge-and-swale topography, and the lack of sites there is surprising. Only two Mississippian sites were found north of Brewer Lake, both just to the southwest of Birds Point on FMC 9. The Moxley site (23MI633) (Figure 6-6) produced a radiocarbon date of A.D. 1235–1405 (dates rounded to the nearest 5/0) for wood charcoal from a pit located 30 to 50 centimeters below the surface. The test unit containing the pit was located on a slope, about a meter below the crest; shell-tempered sherds were found eroding out of the slope at a point a meter lower than the test unit. The site location suggests that the Mississippi-Ohio confluence migrated to its present location sometime after about A.D. 1300.

Barnes and Sugar Tree Ridges

Barnes Ridge and its outlier, Sugar Tree Ridge (Figure 6-1), are remnants of the Pleistocene braided surface and, in the southern part of the project area, are the nearest locations of Pleistocene-age deposits to the current channel of the Mississippi River. In contrast to the northern part of the project area, many of the sites in the southern portion apparently were continuously occupied, or were reoccupied, from at least the Late Archaic period into the Mississippian period (Figure 6-7). The southern sites averaged 2.75 components/site, compared with the northern-site average of 1.45 components/site. In addition to the well-known La Plant site (23NM51) (Chapman 1980; Griffin and Spaulding 1952; Hopgood 1969b; Toth 1977, 1979), there are at least five large, stratified middens within the project area. These are described on the Archaeological Sur-

Table 6-2. Radiocarbon Dates from Archaeological Sites in the New Madrid Floodway

Lab Number	Site Number	Provenience	^{14}C Age (Years B.P.)	Calibrated Age[a]	Associated Artifacts
Beta 41307	23MI621	Control column 80 cmbs	3920+\-100	2850 (2450) 2050 B.C.	PPO to 44 cmbs
Beta 44368	23NM575	Feature 6 10–20 cmbs	2170+\-60[b]	380 (190) 40 B.C.	PPO; fabric-impressed, punctated sand-tempered sherds; cordmarked grog-, grog-and-sand-, and sand- tempered sherds
Beta 41309	23NM575	Test Unit 4 10–20 cmbs	1860+\-70	A.D. 80 (140) 340	Grog- and sand-tempered sherds
Beta 44367	23NM575	Test Unit 3 60–70 cmbs	1140+\-60	A.D. 720 (890) 1010	Grog- and sand-tempered sherds
Beta 40327	23NM176	Feature 8 48–57 cmbs	930+\-80	A.D. 975 (1120) 1280	Shell bead; grog- and grog-and-sand-tempered sherds in unit, 42–70 cmbs
Beta 44366	23NM575	Test Unit 3 40–50 cmbs	890+\-50	A.D. 1025 (1170) 1275	Grog-, sand-, and grog-and-sand-tempered sherds
Beta 40325	23NM176	Feature 2 12–23 cmbs	890+\-90	A.D. 990 (1170) 1290	Grog-, sand-, and shell-tempered sherds
Beta 40326	23NM176	Feature 5-6 42–52 cmbs	880+\-80	A.D. 1010 (1180) 1290	Grog- and shell-tempered sherds
Beta 41310	23NM566	Test Unit 1 35 cmbs	740+\-70	A.D. 1175 (1280) 1400	Shell- and grog-and-shell-tempered sherds

Table 6-2. (cont.)

Beta 41306	23MI633	Test Unit 1 20–30 cmbs	690+\-60	A.D. 1235 (1300) 1405	Shell-tempered sherds
Beta 44369	23NM176	Test Unit 1 32–42 cmbs	580+\-70	A.D. 1290 (1400) 1610	Grog-, shell-, and grog-and-shell-tempered sherds
Beta 44370	23NM176	Test Unit 1 22–32 cmbs	520+\-60	A.D. 1320 (1430) 1610	Grog-, shell-, and grog-and-shell-tempered sherds
Beta 40329	23NM178	Feature 1 10–28 cmbs	290+\-100	A.D. 1430 (1640) 1955	Grog-, shell-, and grog-and-shell-tempered sherds
Beta 41311	23NM566	Feature 2 42–52 cmbs	170+\-60	A.D. 1645 (1800) 1955	Shell-tempered and red-filmed shell-tempered sherds

Note: cmbs, Centimeters below surface; PPO, Poverty Point objects.
[a]Calibrations done with CALIB 3.03 (Stuiver and Reimer 1993). Minimum and maximum ranges presented are 2 standard deviations of the calibrated age; all dates rounded to the nearest 5/0.
[b]$13_C/14_C$ corrected.

Landscape Change in Cairo Lowland | 137

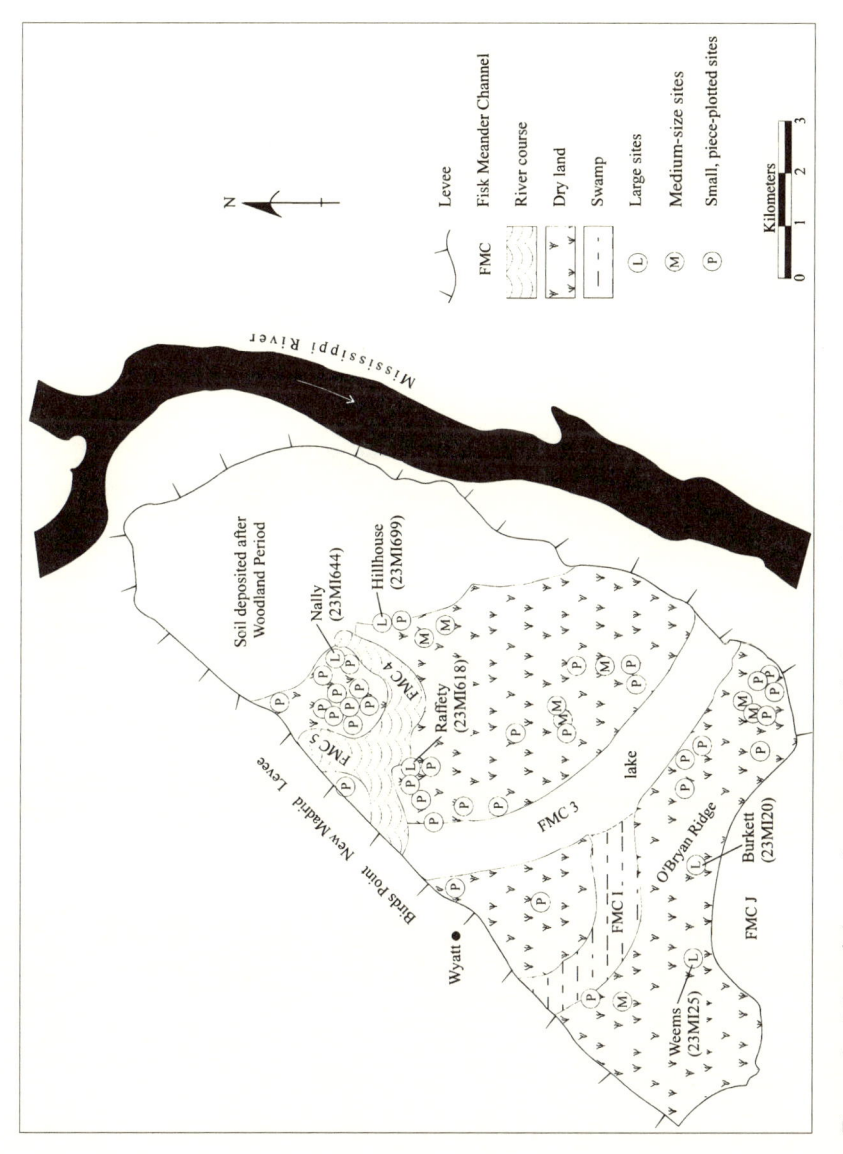

Figure 6-5. Map of the northern portion of the New Madrid Floodway showing the proposed reconstruction of the landscape about A.D. 500 (early Late Woodland period) and the distribution of sites across the landscape.

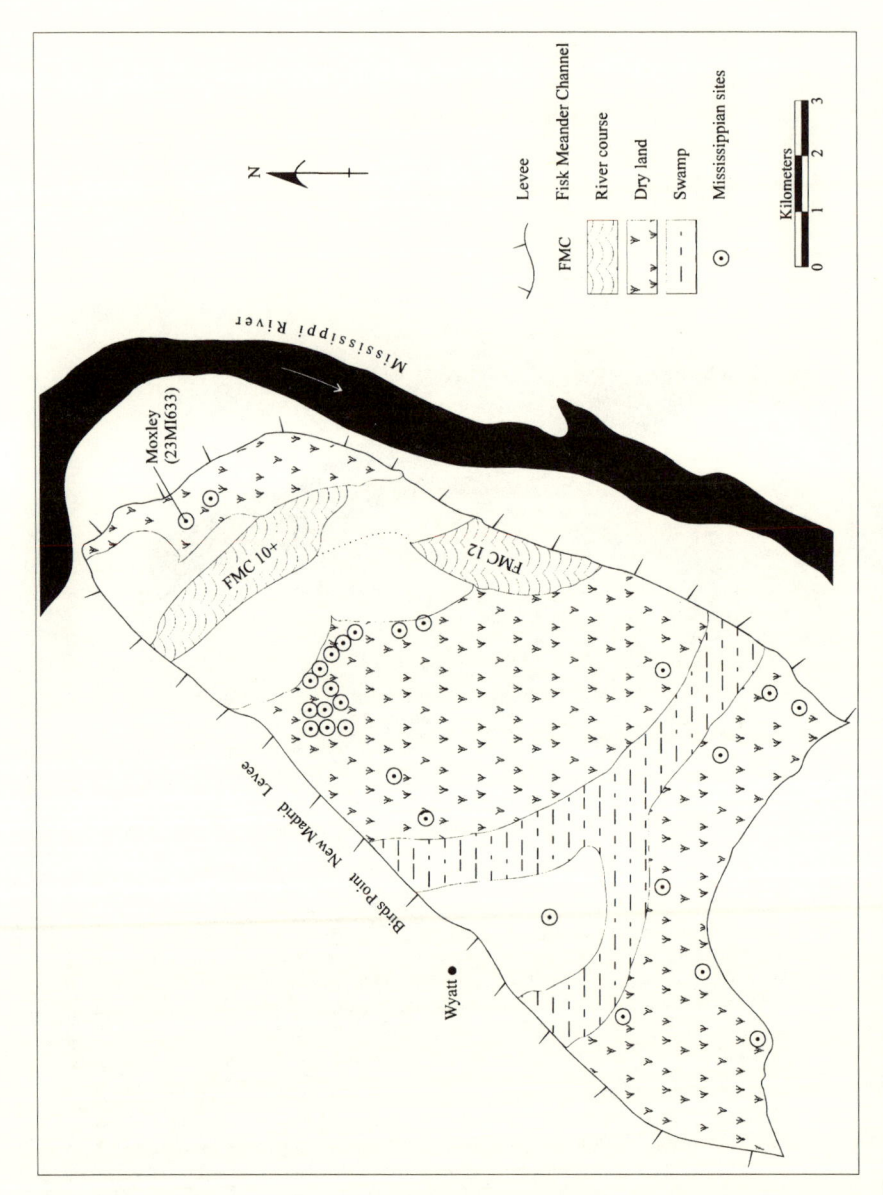

Figure 6-6. Map of the northern portion of the New Madrid Floodway showing the proposed reconstruction of the landscape about A.D. 1000 (Early Mississippian period) and the distribution of sites across the landscape.

vey of Missouri site forms as sand dunes, and they have the appearance of small Middle Eastern tells (Figure 6-7). The three such sites that were tested during the project contained Poverty Point objects to a depth of a meter or more, at which point excavations were halted because of the instability of test-unit walls. At least ten similar sites exist outside the floodway and are arranged linearly along the center of Barnes Ridge and adjacent to the more poorly drained Sharkey and Alligator clays to the west.

The sequence of channels adjacent to Barnes and Sugar Tree ridges is clear, but the ages of the channels have not been established. Based on the distribution of ridge sites that contain Poverty Point objects, it appears that FMC F (Figure 6-8) was cut during or before the Late Archaic period. Fourteen sites, seven of which were buried under later deposits, produced Late Archaic artifacts. The presence of Woodland sites on the southern edges of Barnes and Sugar Tree ridges (Figure 6-9) suggests that FMC 7 through 10 represent the course of the Mississippi River between about A.D. 1 and A.D. 1000. All sites on the southern edges of both ridges contain Woodland and Mississippian components (Figure 6-10). I infer that FMC F and FMC J were either swamps or lakes during the Mississippian period. Single-component Woodland sites and some small Mississippian sites lay adjacent to the swamps or lakes.

Settlement Location through Time

What did the survey of the northern and southern parts of the New Madrid Floodway tell us in terms of the prehistoric settlement pattern? Two obvious conclusions can be drawn. First, the environment is a complex mosaic of landforms associated with an active meandering river. Throughout the Holocene, the Mississippi meandered across much of the Cairo Lowland, leaving behind natural levees and point-bar deposits as well as inactive channels that gradually evolved from lakes and swamps into sediment-filled depressions. The complexity of the landscape makes dating individual features difficult at best. Second, the archaeological record is skewed in favor of sites dating later in the sequence. As the Mississippi meandered across the landscape, it destroyed older sites located on lower elevations or buried them under new sediments. On the other hand, the river constantly created new topographic highs that provided prime spots for settlement location. Below I summarize what we know about changes in settlement location through time.

Late Archaic Period

Using Poverty Point fired-clay objects as temporal markers, I identified thirty Late Archaic sites during survey and testing (Table 6-3). Sites of this age occur on O'Bryan Ridge, in FMC 1 and FMC 2, and along FMC 3S. Sites range in size from small surface-artifact scatters with a few pits filled with Poverty

140 | Lafferty

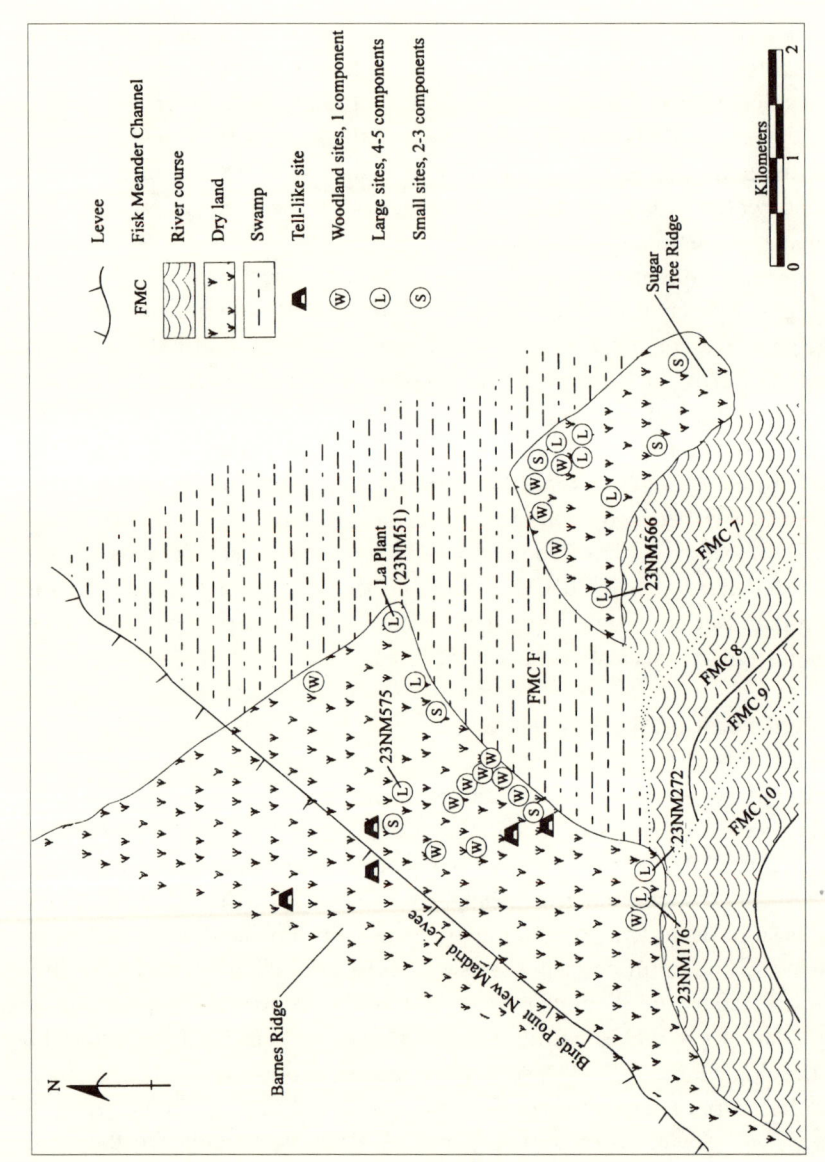

Figure 6-7. Map of the southern portion of the New Madrid Floodway showing the distribution of sites on Barnes and Sugar Tree ridges.

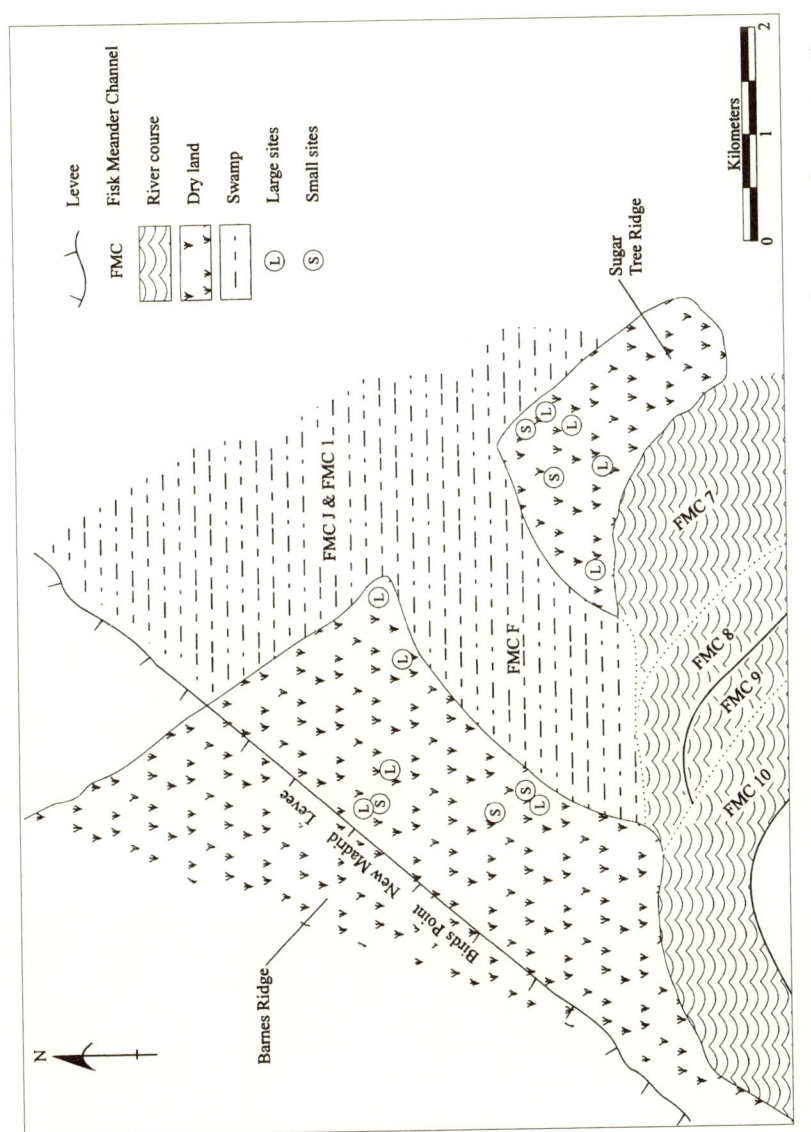

Figure 6-8. Map of the southern portion of the New Madrid Floodway showing the proposed reconstruction of the landscape about 1000 B.C. (terminal Late Archaic period) and the distribution of sites on Barnes and Sugar Tree ridges that contained Poverty Point objects.

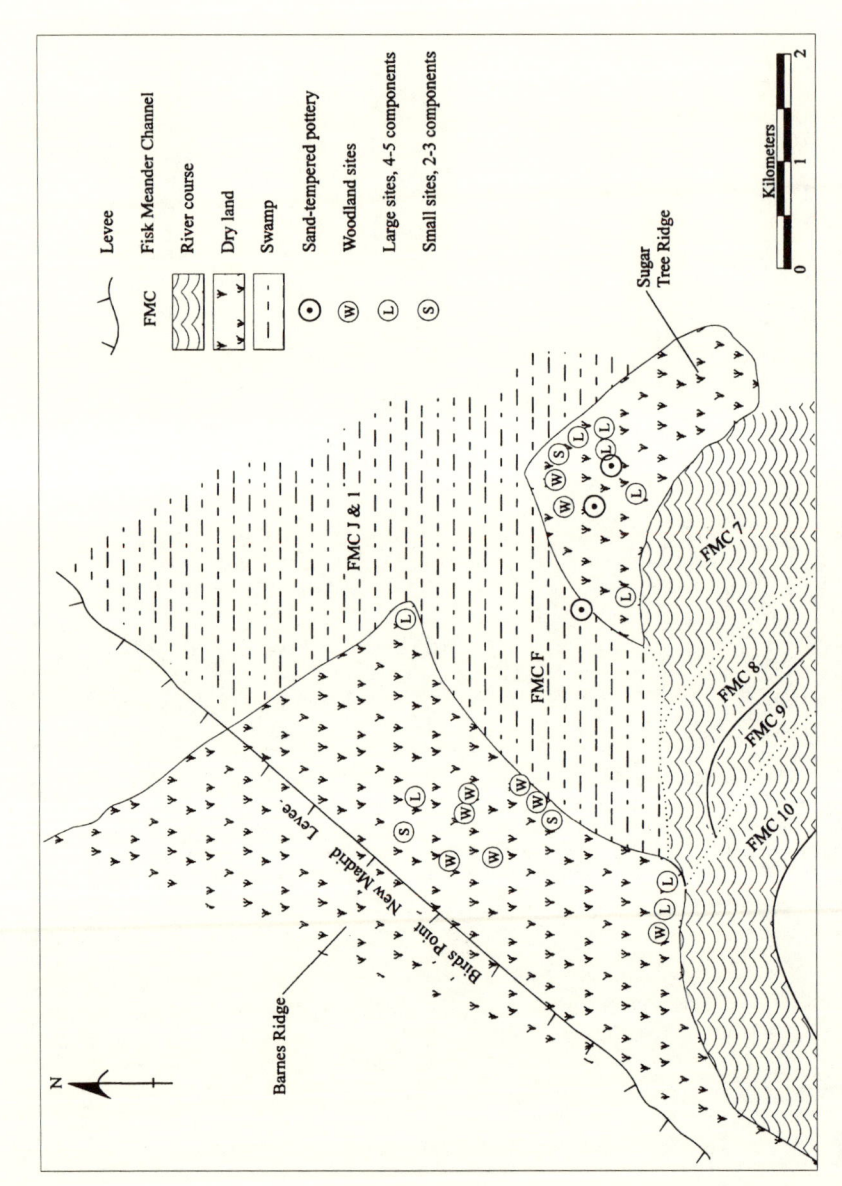

Figure 6-9. Map of the southern portion of the New Madrid Floodway showing the proposed reconstruction of the landscape about A.D. 1 (Middle Woodland period) and the distribution of sites on Barnes and Sugar Tree ridges that contained sand-tempered pottery.

Figure 6-10. Map of the southern portion of the New Madrid Floodway showing the proposed reconstruction of the landscape about A.D. 1000 (Early Mississippian period) and the distribution of sites on Barnes and Sugar Tree ridges that contained shell-tempered pottery.

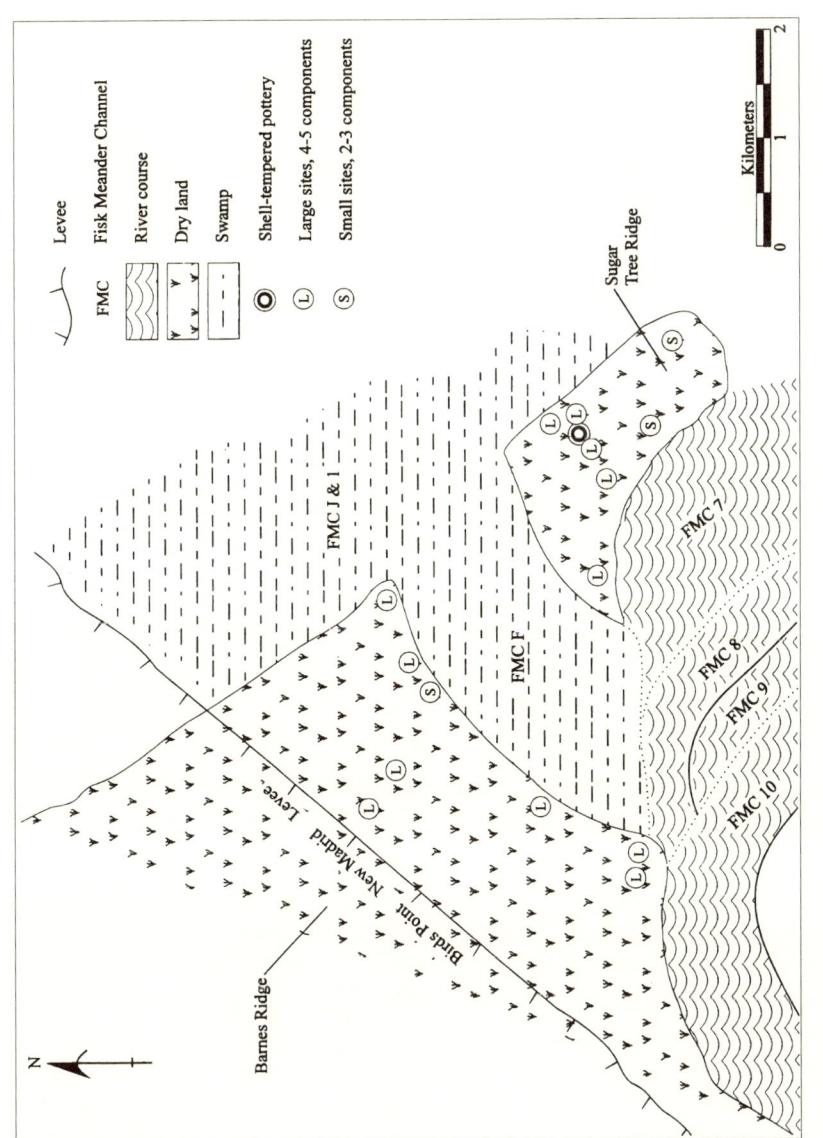

Table 6-3. Frequencies of Components Identified during the New Madrid Floodway Survey

Location	Late Archaic	Woodland	Mississippian	Unidentified Prehistoric	Total
Northern portion					
Birds Point	0	0	2	1	3
Rush Ridge	12	42	18	10	82
O'Bryan Ridge	4	24	8	17	53
Subtotal	16	66	28	28	138
Southern portion					
Barnes Ridge	8	18	8	0	34
Sugar Tree Ridge	6	20	9	0	35
Subtotal	14	38	17	0	69
Total	30	104	45	28	207

Point objects to buried middens that cover as much as a half hectare and contain large pits. Importantly, some Late Archaic components had no surface visibility and were found as a result of excavation. Rinaud (23MI621) (Figure 6-4) is one such Late Archaic site. There, 123 artifacts were recovered from a 2-hectare area. Control columns and a test unit indicated the presence of a dense midden (Table 6-4) with large, deep (more than 135 centimeters) pits distributed over half a hectare. No temporally diagnostic artifacts from any other period were found, so we assume the deposit dates to the Late Archaic period.

Sand-tempered pottery was found at forty-four sites in the project area. Pottery containing sand as temper was manufactured for at least a millennium—perhaps much longer—in the Cairo Lowland, and for it to be useful as a more-precise temporal marker one needs to examine various stylistic and technological features of individual sherds. The small size of the sherds recovered from most sites in the floodway precludes much detailed analysis, but I mention their occurrence because of the significant correlation ($p < .05$) between sites containing sand-tempered pottery and those containing Poverty Point objects. Some sand-tempered sherds may be contemporary with the Poverty Point objects; others probably date much later, pointing out that Woodland-period groups used the same landforms that their predecessors had.

Table 6-4. Frequencies and Weights of Artifacts from Test Units at Rinaud

	\multicolumn{8}{c}{Depth (cm)}		
	0–14		14–24		24–34		34–44		Total	
Artifact Type	n	weight	n	weight	n	weight	n	weight	n	weight
Interior flakes	4	1.1	5	1.6	0	0	0	0	9	2.7
Shatter	6	32.7	3	1.6	0	0	0	0	9	34.3
Fire-cracked rock	0	0	—	82.4	0	0	0	0	—	82.4
Pottery, grog tempered	1	1.9	0	0	0	0	1	1.8	2	3.7
Fired clay	—	27.3	—	147.0	—	8.4	—	36.5	—	219.2
Poverty Point objects	0	0	18	195.6	6	236.9	1	33.7	25	466.2
Bone	0	0	14	1.3	0	0	4	0.4	18	1.7
Charcoal	0	0	18	0.9	0	0	0	0	18	0.9
Hematite	0	0	0	0	1	42.4	0	0	1	42.4
Total	11	63.0	58	430.4	7	287.7	6	72.4	82	853.5
Volume (m^3)		0.1		0.1		0.1		0.1		0.4
Density (artifacts/m^3)		110.0		580.0		70.0		60.0		205.0

Note: Weight given in grams.

Woodland Period

Clay-tempered Baytown Plain (Phillips et al. 1951:76–82) and Mulberry Creek Cordmarked (Phillips et al. 1951:82–87) pottery was found on 104 sites and is used here as a marker for Woodland-period occupation. Some of the surface-artifact scatters assigned to the Woodland period cover less than a tenth of a hectare; others range in size up to 4 hectares. Five of the largest sites—Burkett (23MI20), Weems (23MI25), Raffety (23MI618), Nally (23MI644), and Hillhouse (23MI699)—are located in the northern part of the project area. They are the only localities in the project area that produced artifacts from the Late Archaic period through the Mississippian period, and all five sites contained the most diverse assemblages of artifacts of any of the sites surveyed. Three of them—Raffety (23MI618), Nally (23MI644), and Hillhouse (23MI699)—are located at the juncture of FMC 4 and the edge of the older escarpment. Weems and Burkett, two of the most extensively examined sites in the Cairo Lowland (e.g., Chapman 1980; Griffin and Spaulding 1952; Hopgood 1967; J. R. Williams 1967, 1968; S. Williams 1954), are located on the south side of O'Bryan Ridge.

Based on a set of 1-foot-contour maps of the floodway published by the U.S. Army Corps of Engineers in 1931, three of the large sites, Weems, Burkett, and Nally, had at one time what appear to be small mounds. Remnants of the topographic highs lack characteristics of natural depositional features (M. J. Guccione, pers. comm., 1993) and probably do mark the locations of former mounds. J. R. Williams (1974:23) reported that at one time Weems did contain mounds and that Burkett perhaps had mounds. The owner of the land on which Burkett is located reported to me that what he believes to have been a mound was accidentally destroyed in 1989 and that he observed broken ceramic vessels on the leveled surface beneath the mound.

Mississippian Period

Forty-five Mississippian components—twenty-seven in the northern part of the project area (Figure 6-6) and eighteen in the southern part—were identified, a substantial decrease from the 104 identified Woodland components. Shell-tempered and shell-and-clay-tempered sherds were used as chronological markers for the Mississippian period. Twenty-six of the components in the northern portion exhibited low artifact density and relatively few classes of material. Components in the southern portion, especially those on Barnes and Sugar Tree ridges, were substantially larger than those in the northern portion and contained large numbers of classes and numerous subsurface features, including a house basin at 23NM566. Interestingly, radiocarbon dates (Table 6-2) suggest that, especially in the Barnes Ridge and Sugar Tree Ridge portion of the Cairo Lowland, clay temper was in use well into the thirteenth century and perhaps even later.

Summary

This survey of selected portions of the New Madrid Floodway indicates that at least part of the Cairo Lowland was occupied (or used intermittently) from at least the Late Archaic period through the Mississippian period. The meandering Mississippi River obliterated much of the pre–Late Archaic–period landscape, so we know almost nothing about occupation of the region prior to about 3000 B.C. From that date on, there was a steady progression in the intensity of use of the region. Apparently, prime localities were reused throughout the succeeding four-plus millennia of prehistoric tenure in the Cairo Lowland. At least five localities contain components from all three major archaeological periods represented in the floodway, and undoubtedly others—probably many others—have gone undetected. The project has shown us much about the archaeological record in the region, but extensive excavations on a range of site types— defined to this point by size, artifact density, and number of artifact classes present—are needed to address the nature of settlement.

One thing, however, is apparent at this point: the archaeological record of the Cairo Lowland is exceedingly complex. As I mentioned at the outset of this chapter, previous work in the region was biased in favor of large sites, and as a result we knew very little about the smaller sites in the Cairo Lowland, especially those that are pre-Mississippian in age. The presence of relatively high Pleistocene- and early Holocene-age sediments east of Sikeston Ridge (Figure 6-1) ensured not only that prehistoric groups of Archaic and Woodland age made use of the region but also that portions of the archaeological record were protected from subsequent meandering of the Mississippi River. It appears that the project area discussed here represents an excellent laboratory in which to examine several aspects of human occupation of the Mississippi Valley. Despite the action of the Mississippi during the past several thousand years and land-modifying activities of the past hundred years, the record is still in reasonable shape. Such will not be the case, however, if extremely high water in the Mississippi one day forces the blowing of the levee.

7 | Nonsite Survey in the Cairo Lowland of Southeastern Missouri
Patrice A. Teltser

THE CAIRO LOWLAND of southeastern Missouri (Figure 7-1), located in what Holmes (1886, 1903) defined as the Middle Mississippi region, has long been of interest to antiquarians and archaeologists because of its relatively high density of mound centers and large "towns" (Conant 1878; Croswell 1878; Evers 1880; Potter 1880; Putnam 1875b; Swallow 1858; Thomas 1894). Notwithstanding the problematic nature of defining what is meant by the archaeological term *Mississippian* (Muller 1983; Muller and Stephens 1991; Smith 1978b; Teltser 1988), it is in the Middle Mississippi region that many of the traits commonly used to identify this cultural-historical unit have their so-called classic expression (Griffin 1952, 1967; Morse and Morse 1983).

Despite a long history of work in the region, major gaps and severe biases in our knowledge of the region obscure understanding of the prehistoric developments in even their most basic outline. For example, the ceramic sequence, which provides the backbone of many working regional chronologies, is largely derived from areas outside the region (Fox, Chapter 2). Although there are some general trends in ceramic changes for large portions of the Mississippi Valley, they do not provide the kind of temporal control required for current archaeological questions. This is a problem particularly for Woodland materials, which represent a period of some 1500 years (ca. 600 B.C.–A.D. 900) and yet remain poorly differentiated chronologically.

Understanding the Mississippian-period record in the central Mississippi River valley is likewise hindered by fundamental gaps and severe biases in current knowledge.[1] It is commonly believed that sometime during the fourteenth century A.D., permanent settlement of a large portion of the region came to an end (Morse and Morse 1983; Price and Price 1990; Williams 1980, 1982, 1990). This notion of widespread abandonment of much of the central Mississippi Valley was first introduced in the 1970s (Price 1976b; see also Williams 1980, 1982), and since that time, substantial population decline or abandonment has been postulated for the American Bottom (Milner 1990; Milner et al. 1984) and lower Ohio Valley of Illinois (Muller 1986) and for the southeastern Missouri lowlands west of Crowley's Ridge (Price 1978; Price and Griffin 1979; see also Perttula, Chapter 8).

Relative to the archaeological record of some areas, particularly the low-

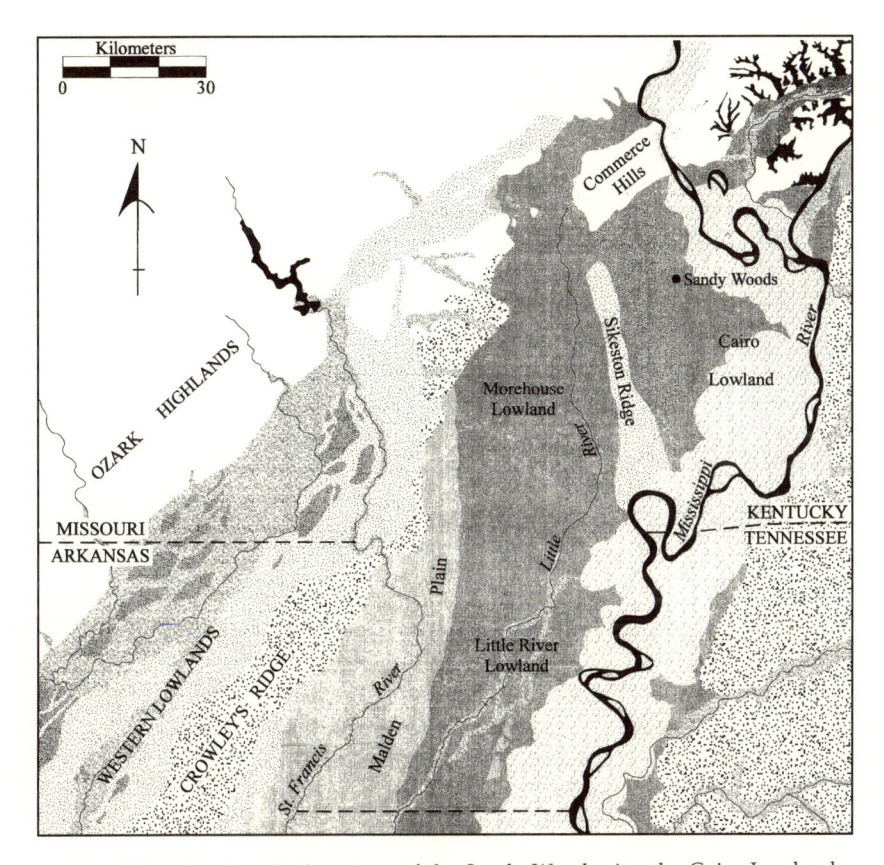

Figure 7-1. Map showing the locations of the Sandy Woods site, the Cairo Lowland, and major physiographic features in southeastern Missouri.

lands of southeastern Missouri east of Crowley's Ridge, the Vacant Quarter hypothesis, as this phenomenon is now widely known, has, as Kreisa points out (Chapter 3), become a surprisingly contentious issue (Lewis 1984, 1988, 1990; O'Brien 1994a; Teltser 1988; Wesler 1991a). While on one level it is an empirical question about the timing and persistence of "permanent" settlements in the area, the Vacant Quarter hypothesis has come to involve a somewhat more complex set of issues based partly on how the ceramic sequence of the region is interpreted and partly on insufficient understanding of the range of spatial and temporal variation of materials dating from the fourteenth century and later (Kreisa, Chapter 3).

In reviewing this debate, it is clear that the Vacant Quarter hypothesis, like any historical sketch, is based on current understanding of the range of spatial and temporal variation in the record and how our knowledge of that variation is structured by explanatory frameworks. This is particularly clear when we consider some basic assumptions of the debate and the terms in which it is conducted. Perhaps the most important feature is that archaeological knowledge of the southeastern Missouri lowlands, and virtually all work conducted in the region (including my own [Teltser 1988:76]), is site-oriented and biased toward large sites with mounds. This bias is widely acknowledged (e.g., Lewis 1984, 1990; Morse and Morse 1983), but what seems less well appreciated is how it has structured current interpretations and the formulation of working hypotheses.

Much speculation about the nature of Mississippian-period social organization assumes that settlement systems were organized hierarchically. Variation in site size and configuration has been well documented for many regions (e.g., various papers in Smith 1978b), but the inferential basis for contemporary occupation of those sites and systemic interaction among specific settlements is less secure (Benn, Chapter 10). Further, it is not clear that all mound centers are associated with large population aggregates as implied by the hierarchical model (Teltser 1988).

Explanations of change in the Mississippian record currently emphasize the establishment, consolidation, and fragmentation of competing centers or polities, which correspond to documented, or in some instances hypothetical, occupational histories of the mound sites (e.g., Anderson 1990; Chapman 1980; Milner 1990; Morse and Morse 1983; Wesler 1992). These models, conceived primarily in sociopolitical terms, also assume that Mississippian settlement systems were hierarchical. While these scenarios reflect an important shift away from assuming that all Mississippian mound sites are part of a single systemic entity, they still assume that all smaller manifestations of the Mississippian record are either early—that is, they predate major mound construction—or contemporary with, and tied to, the large centers.

My purpose is not to argue that the mounds and large population aggregates are not important to the Mississippian record (for they surely are) or that sociopolitical processes were not operative in some proximal sense. It is significant, however, that the basis of current debate is phrased solely in terms of the persistence or abandonment of sites with mounds and large population aggregates and that those in the debate fail to consider that populations can be distributed in a variety of ways across the landscape. It is quite possible that large population aggregates and mound building were indeed confined to the thirteenth and fourteenth centuries in the Cairo Lowland, followed by population dispersion. This would have created a late prehistoric record that appears very different and far less visible when only the large aggregated centers are monitored. Consequently, I suggest that we approach the late prehistoric record in terms of demographic reorganization. In this context, abandonment is only one of a variety of possibilities.

Regardless of theoretical orientation, most would agree that understanding change in the archaeological record is a regional-scale issue. Given the bias in favor of large sites, a major goal of my ongoing survey work in the region is to broaden our knowledge about the range of variation in the archaeological record. In designing this work, questions regarding developments at the end of the Mississippian period were accommodated. Consequently, the survey does not make three common assumptions: (1) that the only relevant record is confined to mounds or large population aggregates; (2) that the entire Mississippian-period record in a given area represents a single systemic entity; or (3) that the later part of the Mississippian sequence necessarily includes mound building or population aggregation. Ultimately, by not making assumptions about the nature of the record, this kind of survey also has the potential to correct many other gaps in our knowledge of the region, particularly in regard to an all but ignored Woodland record, which, despite preliminary studies (e.g., Williams 1974), is known primarily (though certainly not exclusively) by the mound site of Hoecake in Mississippi County (Marshall 1988; Marshall and Hopgood 1964; Williams 1967, 1974) (Figure 1-6).

The Study Area

Since most archaeologists would agree that the large mound sites are in some way important to understanding change in the Mississippian record, and seeing my research as an attempt to understand the context of those features in terms of a demographic history of the region, I chose as my survey area in the northern Cairo Lowland one of the well-known locales—the Sandy Woods site (Figure 7-1). Sandy Woods was at one time a large settlement, on the order of 16 hectares or more, with a ditch and wall enclosing nine mounds.

I chose the Sandy Woods vicinity for four reasons. First, the site was initially recorded in the late nineteenth century and has a fairly prominent place in the mound-related literature of the time (e.g., Houck 1908; Potter 1880; Rust 1877), though it is conspicuously absent in Thomas's (1894) report on investigations by the Bureau of (American) Ethnology. There are contradictions in some of those descriptions, but there are also consistent elements that have since been verified (e.g., J. R. Williams 1968; S. Williams 1949). Potter's (1880) map and description supply helpful information about the presence and general orientation of such features as a fortification wall, enclosing ditch, and nine mounds (Figure 7-2). There also are well-known collections of pottery from the site at the Peabody Museum (Yale), obtained from Horatio Rust (see Potter 1880; Rust 1877).

Second, the site is in reasonably good condition (by current standards), such that some aspects of its overall structure can be obtained. Many of the large mound sites reported in the nineteenth century no longer exist as such (Rich Woods, in Stoddard County, Missouri, being perhaps the best example [Leeds 1979]), and Sandy Woods has had its share of degradation over the past century. In the Charleston area, mining of prehistoric sites for pottery reached rather legendary proportions in the late nineteenth century (Thomas 1894), and by

152 | Teltser

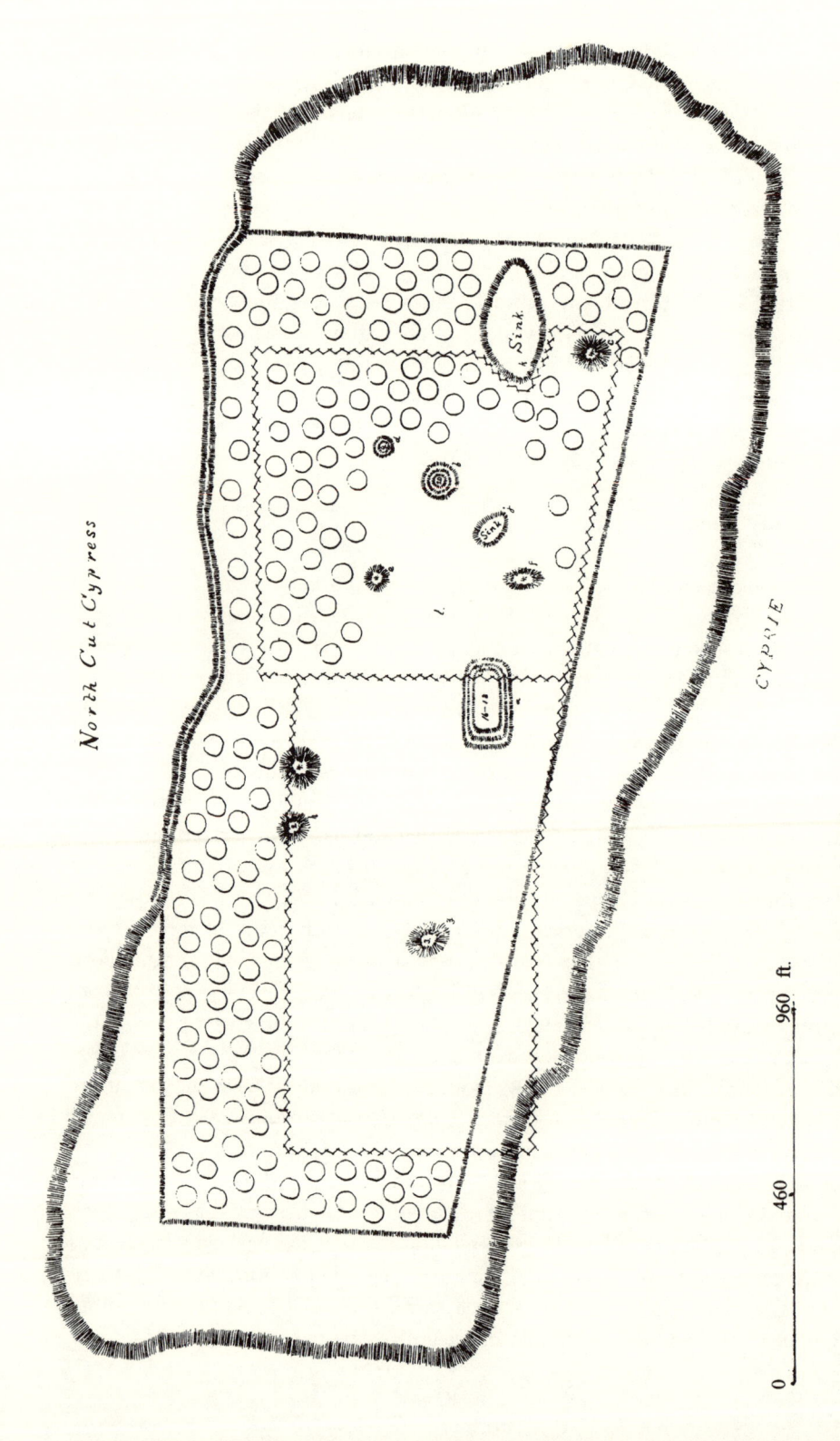

Figure 7-2. Nineteenth-century map of the Sandy Woods site, prepared by W. B. Potter for the Academy of Science of St. Louis, showing the locations of mounds, enclosures, and house depressions (from Potter 1880).

1950 all nine mounds at Sandy Woods had been either modified by plowing or leveled. Stephen Williams (1954) reported that the largest conical mound was leveled in 1949 and at the same time more than a meter was removed from the central pyramidal mound. Even so, enough of the site appears intact so that the locations of major features are still discernible from the ground as well as from aerial photographs taken in 1952, after the last episode of major land alteration.

Third, the area has been subject to less land-leveling activity than have other localities, especially those in counties to the south, where farmers have converted their fields to rice cultivation (Leeds 1979; Medford 1972). Judgments regarding the extent of current land leveling in the Sandy Woods locality are purely subjective, formed after interviewing landowners.

Fourth, in the northern section of the Cairo Lowland there are major portions of older, sandy, braided-stream surfaces (Figure 1-2). Such surfaces are characterized by irregular, erosional, and depositional topography (Fisk 1944) created when ancient braided channels of the Mississippi River reworked alluvial deposits from even more ancient channels of the Ohio River. Sometime after 12,000 years ago, when the Mississippi River abandoned its course in this area for its current channel (King and Allen 1977; O'Brien and Dunnell, Chapter 1), the river shifted from a braided to a meandering regime (O'Brien 1994a; Saucier 1974). Since that time, the smaller, underfit river systems in the area have tended to follow the low-lying areas between the older sandy channel bars. Consequently, more-recent deposition has been quite localized. An advantage to working with surfaces of that age lies in the potential of obtaining a longer portion of the prehistoric sequence from the surface record than can be found in areas to the south, where far more of the older surfaces have been buried under recent alluvium.

Strategy and Tactics

With the exception of Lafferty's work (Chapter 6), previous survey efforts in the Cairo Lowland have been sporadic and nonsystematic at best. The region is agricultural but lacks large tracts of publicly owned land, the managers of which would be responsible for inventorying cultural resources. Of course, there has been significant land alteration in the form of land leveling, but these activities do not fall under federal or state regulations. Because landholdings have been within private ownership for several generations, land parcels are small and are owned by many different individuals. Tenants may cluster their fields, but crop scheduling varies from one field to the next. In short, textbook strategies for obtaining a regionally representative sample of surface artifacts cannot be applied. Instead, it is necessary to survey where permission and visibility allow and to keep one's sights set on the necessary longer-term goal of obtaining samples that both include materials from the full range of microenvironments and exhibit redundancy in composition.

My work requires a strategy and set of tactics that make as few assumptions as possible about the nature of the archaeological record. For example, the tactics must allow for the existence of very small settlements, often referred to as "hamlets" or "farmsteads." These classes of settlements are often claimed to be ubiquitous (Morse and Morse 1983:253) but are poorly documented, especially in the Cairo Lowland (Lafferty, Chapter 6). Should such settlements be present in the region, obtaining samples from them would be important for determining the relations between more dispersed segments of the Mississippian population and those that are aggregated. Are the settlements contemporary, are they confined to specific time periods, or do they persist throughout the sequence as fairly stable segments of the population? Further, there is no way to predict the size of such settlements. Minimum settlement sizes estimated for other areas vary widely (e.g., compare estimates by various authors in Smith 1978b), though it is doubtful that methods have been comparable.

I chose a field strategy that employs nonsite methods. Such an approach allows for documentation of the widest range of archaeological contexts and at the same time makes the fewest assumptions about the nature and size of potentially relevant archaeological features (Dancey 1973; Dunnell and Dancey 1983; Rossignol and Wandsnider 1992). The set of tactics is derived from years of work and experience with surface and plow-zone contexts of southeastern Missouri (Dunnell 1984, 1985b, 1988, 1992; Dunnell and Simek 1995; Teltser 1988, 1992). Continuing the use of such tactics also provides the basis for establishing some degree of comparability in results across regions.

Specific tactics used in the survey involve a pedestrian survey with individuals spaced at 5-meter intervals, or along every fifth crop row. Surveyors flag all observed artifacts. A cluster of artifacts is defined as two or more artifacts within 10 meters of each other. When a cluster is encountered, the first and last artifacts observed are flagged. After a field is surveyed in this manner, the status of each flagged artifact is established. A 10-meter-radius search is conducted around each isolated artifact to ascertain whether it is part of a cluster; clusters of flags are reexamined to determine the boundaries of each cluster using the 10-meter rule. Isolated artifacts are assigned a field number, mapped, and collected. Cluster boundaries are also mapped.

Generally, all artifacts observed within a set of boundaries are collected as a cluster. This procedure was modified in one case (Cluster RMJ, see below) where there was a high density of both prehistoric and historical-period material. At that location, all prehistoric materials observed were collected along every fourth crop row, representing a 25-percent sample. In several cases (clusters CBA, CBB, and RMA, see below), a grid was established for systematic, controlled surface collection. At those locations, 4 × 4-meter collection units were used, and all artifacts observed within every other unit were collected.

It is important to point out that the clusters defined during fieldwork are observational units and have no behavioral significance. Because the surfaces examined are quite ancient, determining whether any spatial aggregate of artifacts represents an assemblage of temporally associated artifacts is a chronological question, answered on the basis of analytical decisions very different from spatial association (Dunnell 1992; Jones and Beck 1992).

Preliminary Findings

The preliminary findings presented here are confined to assessment of the sampling strategy and the general nature of the archaeological record as these topics pertain to biases in our knowledge of the prehistory of the Cairo Lowland. I focus on three fields in close proximity to each other (Figure 7-3), all south of the Sandy Woods mound group and on the west side of what was formerly known as North Cut Swamp (now North Cut Ditch). The fields are shown in the figure superimposed on data taken from the 1981 soil survey for Scott County (Festervand 1981). To simplify, I have dichotomized soils with sandy texture and those with silty and clayey texture (Figure 7-3). These correspond tightly with depositional history, surface age, and elevation. Sandy soils are located on remnants of the older sandy channel bars, and silty and clayey soils are located in lower-lying areas that have received more-recent deposition (see above).

Five general statements can be made about the archaeological record. First, the prehistoric record in the region is truly ubiquitous, though only one field was surveyed for which the farmer knew beforehand that a "site" was present. This small cluster, termed *A* (Figure 7-4), was located at the south end of Field CB and was highly visible because it was represented by an extremely high density of artifacts and was situated on an erosional feature (locally referred to as a "sand-blow") that, because of moisture differential, caused the crops to grow unevenly. Such erosional features are common in the area, and this context accounts for most, if not all, of the previously recorded sites in the immediate vicinity. Typically, these features are remnants of former sandy channel bars and are composed of Scotco Sand soils (Festervand 1981). Aerial photographs taken in the late 1930s, before the area was completely cleared of timber, show that these features were tree-covered but that the cover was more sparse than on the surrounding terrain. After clearing, the topographic highs were subject to erosion from southwestern-prevailing winds. Many of the features are now set aside from cultivation (although Cluster CBA is cultivated), and the surfaces have been slightly deflated, creating lag deposits of artifacts. The visibility of Cluster CBA and the density of its artifacts were similar to those of the previously recorded sites in the area; however, the site is smaller. I conducted a con-

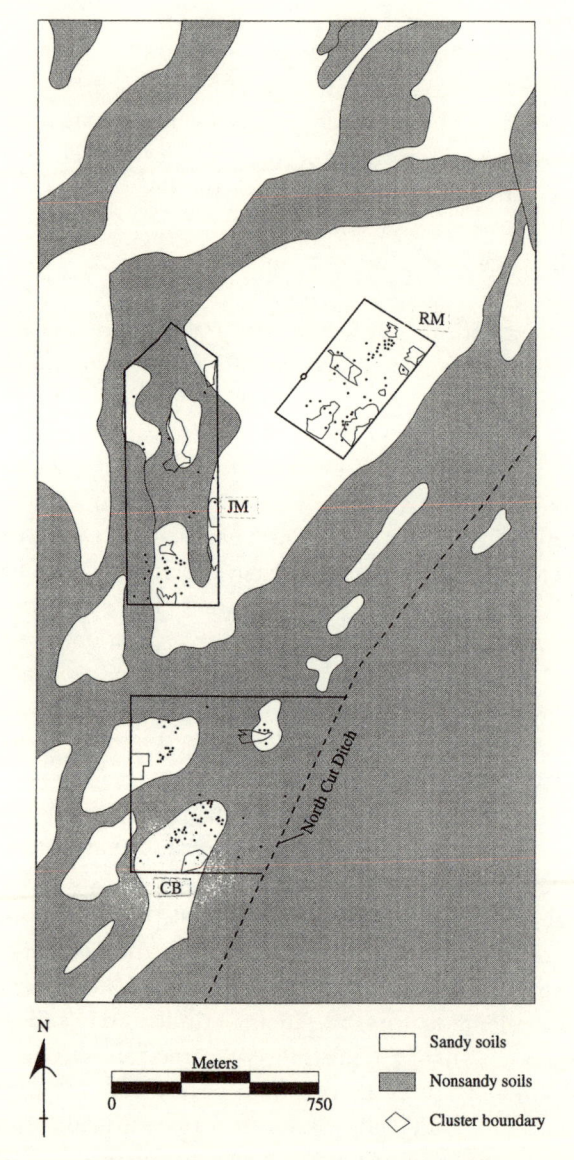

Figure 7-3. Outlines of the three fields surveyed around Sandy Woods, superimposed on soils data from the Scott County soil survey (Festervand 1981).

trolled surface collection of the location (see Figure 7-4, where the collection grid is superimposed on the cluster boundaries) and also identified two lower-density clusters and an offsite record (Figure 7-4).

In the centrally located field, JM (Figure 7-5), six relatively low-density clusters were identified, as well as an offsite record. In the northeastern field, RM

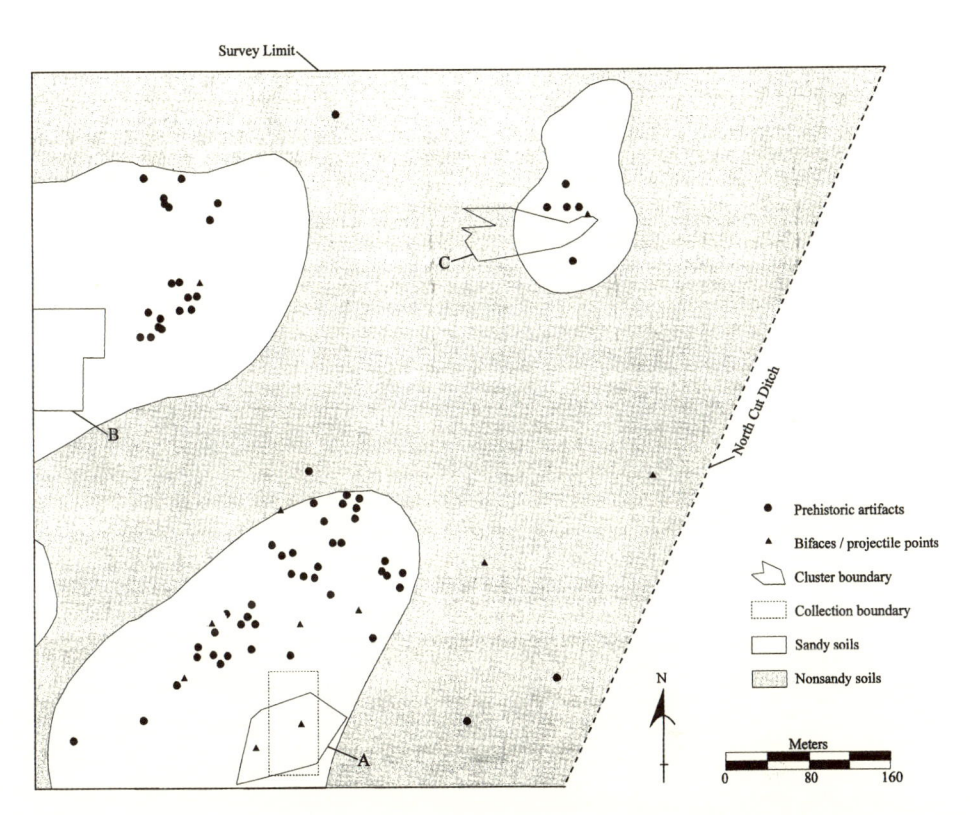

Figure 7-4. Survey map of Field CB at Sandy Woods (grid for systematic controlled surface collection is superimposed on Cluster A and serves as boundaries for Cluster B).

(Figure 7-6), seven clusters were identified in addition to an offsite record. Cluster J was a relatively high-density cluster that contained both prehistoric and historical-period material. Given its prominent position—on a sandy rise—and the density of artifacts present, it probably would be recorded as a site following usual conventions. Another controlled surface collection was conducted on part of Cluster A because it contained material of Mississippian age (e.g., shell-tempered pottery).

Comparing the artifact density across the clusters identified in the survey only begins to illustrate the kind of biases in our knowledge of the area (Figure 7-7). Density estimates were calculated as the number of artifacts observed and collected in a cluster divided by the area within the boundaries. The estimate for Cluster RMJ is based on a 25-percent sample and should be considered an extremely conservative estimate inasmuch as the calculation does not include historical-period materials. The estimates for clusters RMA, CBA, and CBB are based on 50-percent samples of the collected portions of those clusters, so the

158 | *Teltser*

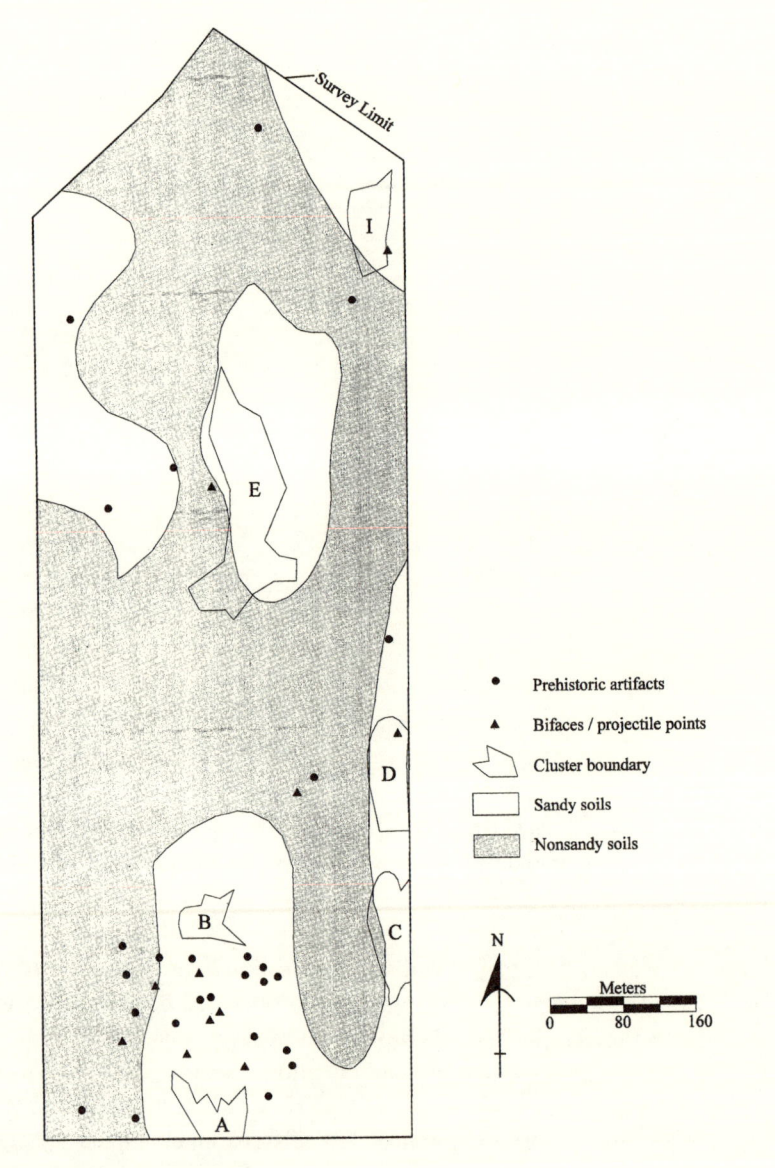

Figure 7-5. Survey map of Field JM at Sandy Woods.

area has been adjusted accordingly. If the density of a cluster such as CBA is used as a standard for the kind of archaeological features represented in the state site files, then it should be quite clear that significant portions of the record in the region remain unaccounted for.

The second observation is that the presence of archaeological material corresponds closely to land form and topography. This was expected and is easily

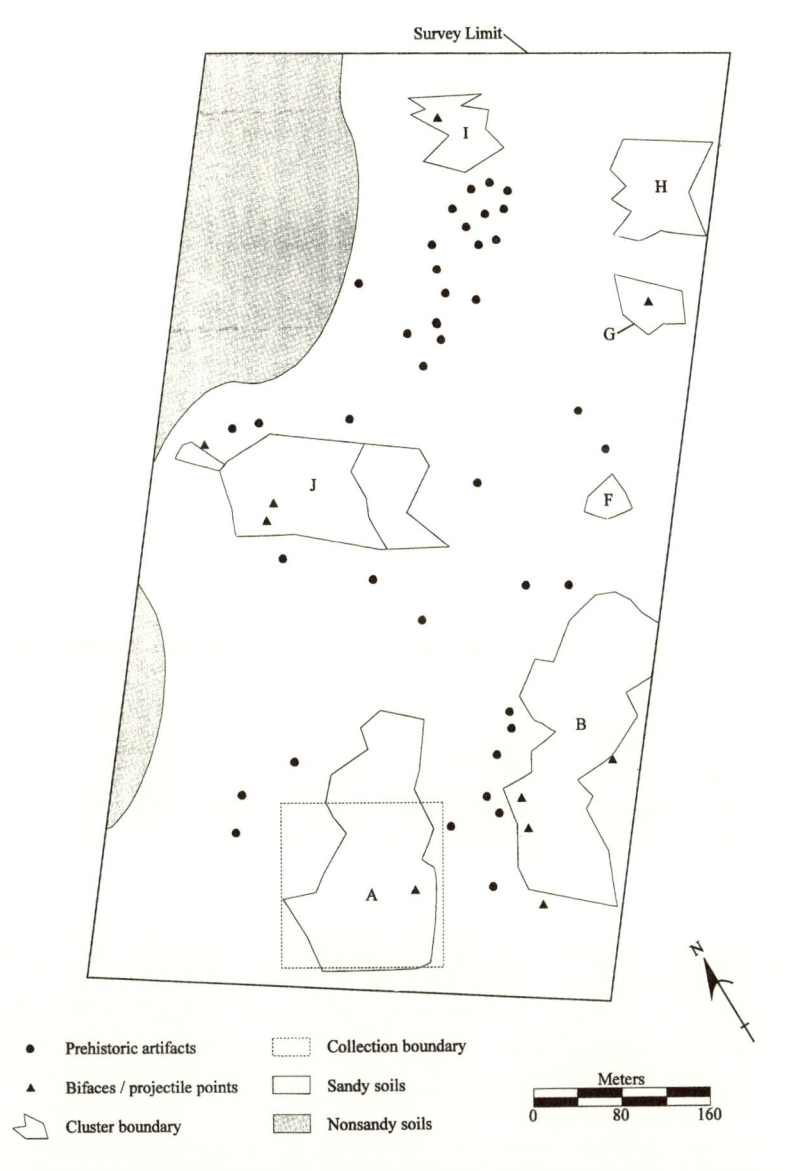

Figure 7-6. Survey map of Field RM at Sandy Woods (grid for systematic controlled surface collection is superimposed on Cluster A).

explained in terms of the poorly drained nature of the low-lying areas. Prehistoric materials, however, are not confined exclusively to higher areas or to discrete clusters. This was also expected, given the results of work conducted in other areas of southeastern Missouri using similar recovery methods (e.g., Dunnell 1985b, 1992; Dunnell and Simek 1995; Teltser 1988).

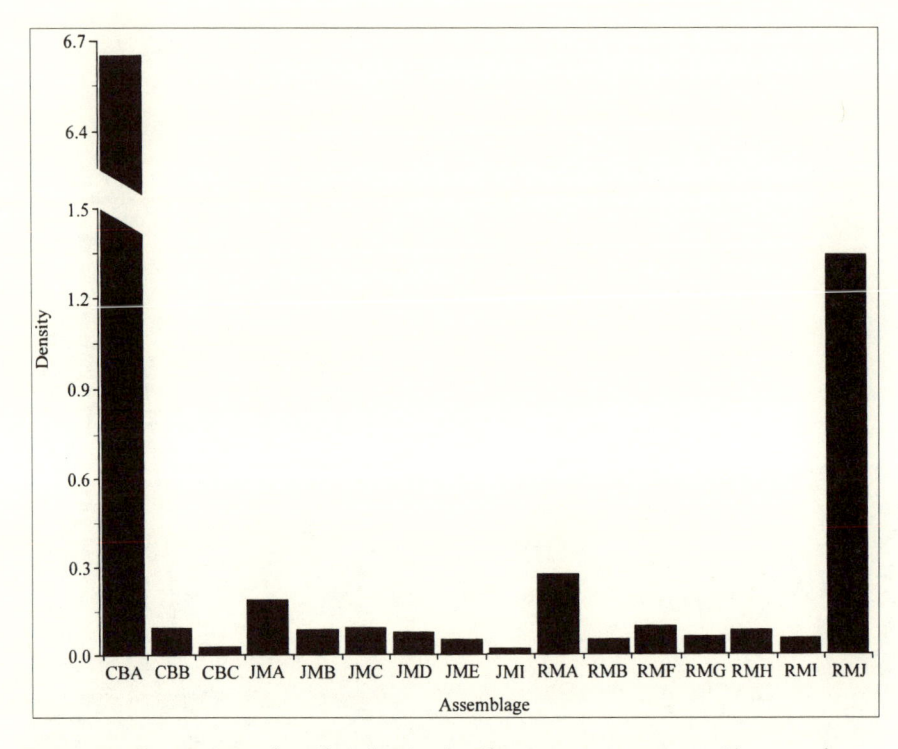

Figure 7-7. Comparison of artifact density (artifacts per 4 × 4-meter unit) across the clusters identified in the survey around Sandy Woods. Density estimates for clusters CBA, CBB, and RMA are adjusted and based on controlled surface collection at 50-percent sampling intensity. The estimate for Cluster RMJ should be considered a conservative estimate, as it is based on a 25-percent sample using prehistoric pottery and lithic material only.

The composition of the offsite record assists in monitoring potential biases in the survey data, especially those imposed by differential surface age with respect to portions of the prehistoric sequence represented in the sample. The current regional chronology is poorly suited for addressing questions of an evolutionary nature, much less the ad hoc hypotheses generated from current interpretations. However, existing ceramic and lithic typological systems (e.g., Justice 1987; May 1982; Morse and Morse 1983; Phillips 1970; Phillips et al. 1951; Williams and Brain 1983) are based on consistent chronological trends that enable assignment of some materials to broad periods (see below). This information serves as a useful point of departure for sorting out the age of materials present in different kinds of locations.

Bifaces and projectile points found in the lowest-lying areas, characterized by silty and clayey soils (representing the younger surfaces), are primarily fragments and tips. So far, projectile points assignable to the Middle Woodland period (ca. 250 B.C.–A.D. 450) and possibly to the Early Woodland period (ca. 600–250 B.C.) have been found on those surfaces. In intermediate areas, on surfaces characterized by fine sands in depressions, points from the Late Archaic period (ca. 3000–600 B.C.) (some are possibly from the Middle Archaic period [ca. 5000–3000 B.C.]) through the Mississippian period have been found. As the area covered in the survey increases, it will be possible to estimate which portions of the prehistoric sequence might be obscured by Holocene deposition. This will require a degree of redundancy in the chronological association of materials and the age of surfaces on which they occur. To be sure, land-use patterns changed significantly throughout the prehistoric sequence, and I expect this to be reflected in the age of materials found in different contexts and on different kinds of surfaces. Overall, however, the information will determine which portions of the prehistoric sequence are likely to be buried in different contexts and to what extent the surface record represents different portions of the sequence. Preliminary results based on the most conservative typological assignments suggest that Middle Woodland–period through Mississippian-period materials are represented on all the surfaces examined.

The third observation is that the composition of offsite assemblages is different from that of assemblages found within the clusters. For example, the ratio of bifaces to debitage is generally much higher for the offsite record (Figure 7-8). The ratio of bifaces to debitage will vary across space and through time as a consequence of prehistoric land-use patterns, formation processes, and recovery techniques, and differentiating among the contributions of each of these factors will require larger samples. Land-use patterns in which the ratios for the offsite record are generally high appear to dominate the data. The only exception to this is Cluster CBC. This is an interesting case, because the high biface/debitage ratio probably reflects the depositional context of the materials found on this very small, sandy, high spot in the middle of North Cut Swamp (see Figure 7-3). As of now, there are not enough samples from this kind of location to interpret these data further.

The ratio of pottery (excluding nonvessel ceramic objects such as daub and fragments of Poverty Point objects) to lithic debitage also reflects differences in assemblage composition (Figure 7-9). Variation in these ratios can also be expected to reflect changes in land-use patterns through time, formation processes, and/or recovery strategies. Some clusters do not include any pottery, which is known to have become an increasingly more important part of prehistoric tool assemblages through time. Still, the values for the ratios of pottery to debitage for the offsite assemblages are among the lowest discovered.

The fourth observation is that variation in the pottery/debitage ratios among the various clusters reveals two important features. With two excep-

162 | *Teltser*

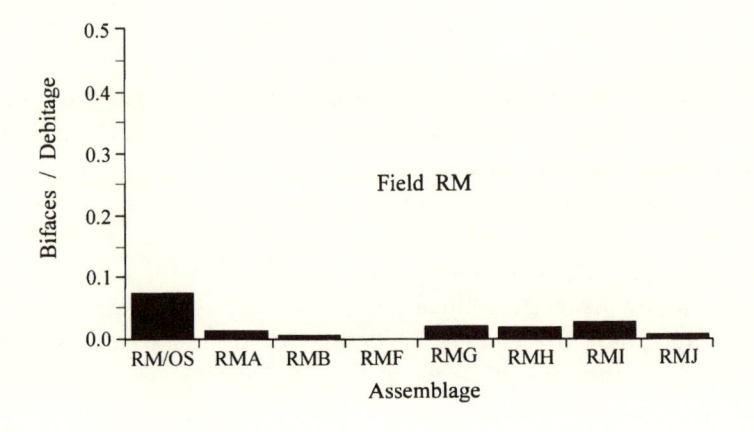

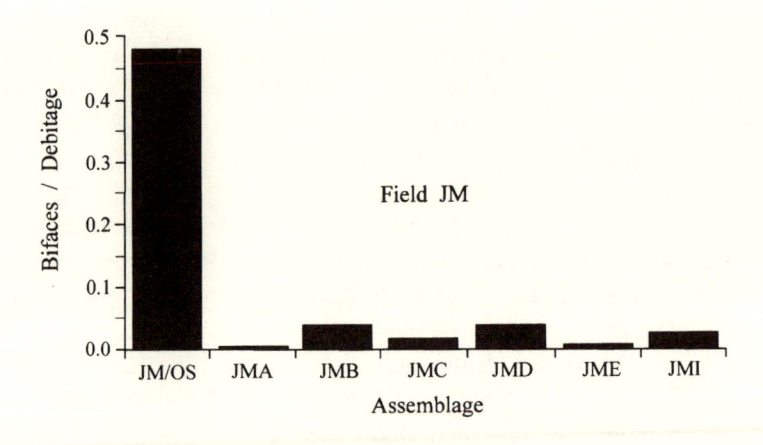

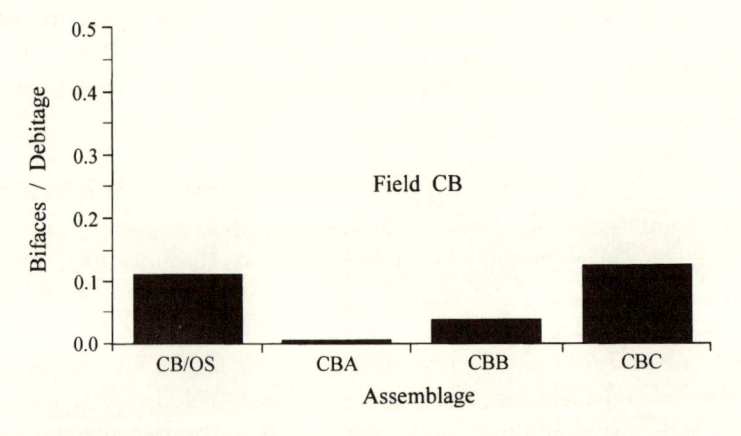

Figure 7-8. Biface-to-debitage ratios for assemblages from fields RM, JM, and CB at Sandy Woods. The offsite assemblages are in the leftmost column and are designated *OS*.

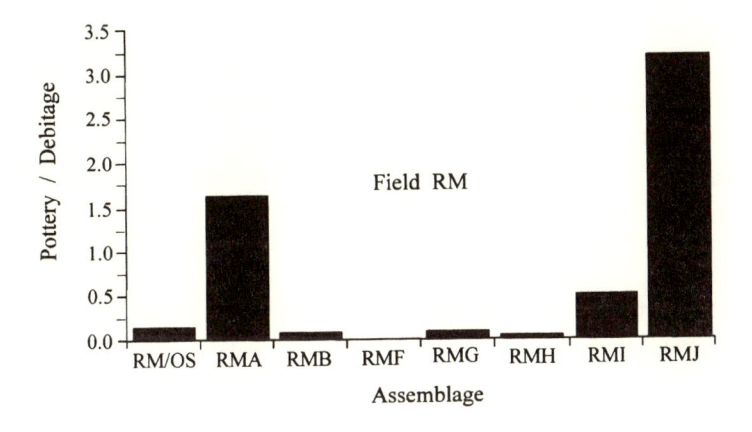

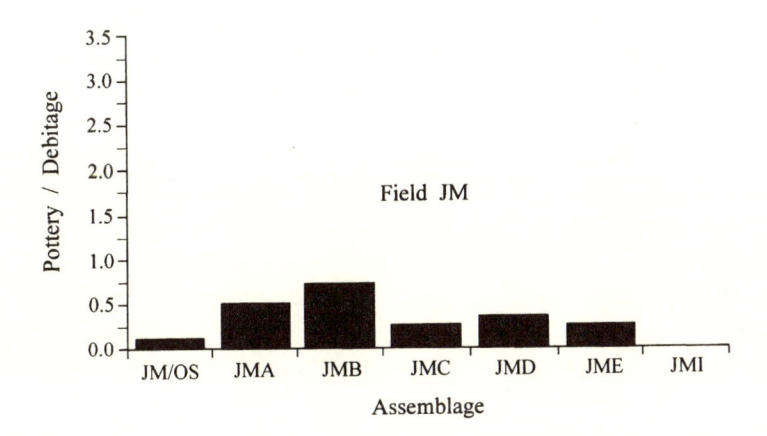

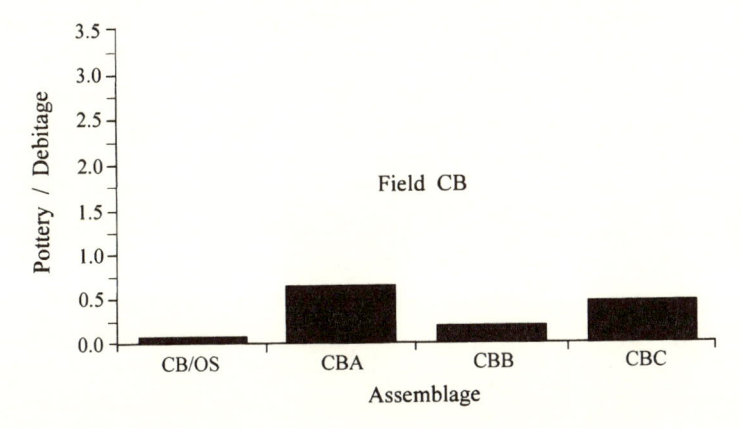

Figure 7-9. Pottery-to-debitage ratios for assemblages from fields RM, JM, and CB at Sandy Woods. The offsite assemblages are in the leftmost column and are designated OS.

tions, ratios are less than one—that is, there is more debitage than pottery. The exceptions are Cluster RMJ, in which the ratio is greater than 3.0, and Cluster RMA, in which the ratio is greater than 1.6. As previously mentioned, RMJ, a relatively high-density cluster, would probably be recorded as a site. Importantly, the ratio of pottery to debitage in Cluster CBA is 0.59 and indicates that general assemblage composition—that is, whether there is a significant amount of pottery or lithic material—is not necessarily correlated with artifact density.

Variation in the pottery/debitage ratios has some relevance to land-use patterns. For example, even though the density of Cluster RMA is relatively low (see Figure 7-7), there is a relatively high ratio of pottery to debitage. This could very well reflect the presence of a Mississippian component, in which pottery is a much more important part of the tool assemblage. At County Line (23SO166), a site on the edge of the Malden Plain in Stoddard County, Missouri, that contains evidence of both Woodland- and Mississippian-period occupations (Teltser 1992), the ratio of all pottery to debitage recovered was 1.7:1. If this does not appear to be a particularly useful comparison in light of the large, aggregated nature of the County Line settlement context, consider the ratio of pottery to debitage in the surface assemblages recovered from two much smaller, low-density clusters in the vicinity of Cummins Mound (23DU2), located on the Malden Plain in Dunklin County, Missouri. Those clusters, which also contained Mississippian-period materials, exhibited ratios of 6.9:1 and 18.6:1 (Teltser 1988).

The fifth observation is that of the sixteen clusters in the three fields shown here, fourteen produced sherds, and all produced materials that can be assigned broadly to the Woodland period on the basis of the presence of sand-tempered pottery. In the absence of a Woodland pottery sequence, this does not provide a great deal of information, given the broad temporal span of the Woodland period. Still, the nature of the deposits is unlike any so far described for the Cairo Lowland Woodland sequence, and the ubiquity of the record deserves attention. Indeed, judging from the results of the work discussed here, Woodland deposits are far more common across the landscape than are materials of Mississippian age.

Of the fourteen clusters with pottery, ten produced shell-tempered pottery, but of those ten, only five exhibited percentages of shell-tempered pottery in excess of 15 percent: CBC (four of twenty-one sherds; 19 percent), JMC (twenty-six of seventy-three sherds; 36 percent), JMD (eleven of sixty-one sherds; 18 percent), RMA (134 of 667 sherds; 20 percent), and RMH (seven of seven sherds; 100 percent). The presence of shell-tempered pottery is an extremely liberal definition for identifying the presence of a Mississippian-period occupation. Previous work on the Malden Plain suggests that other changes in pottery technology (e.g., low-oxygen firing technology [Dunnell and Feathers 1991; Feathers 1989, 1990a, 1990b, 1994]), subsistence (e.g., a reliance on intensive maize agriculture [Lynott et al. 1986; Greenlee, Chapter 13]), and settlement (e.g., aggregation [Dunnell and Feathers 1991; Morse and Morse 1983]) did not occur until well after the appearance of shell-tempered pottery. Given this, along with the fact that only two clusters (CBC and JMC) included any further supporting evidence for Middle Mississippian–period (ca. A.D. 1200–1400) domestic contexts (e.g., later slipped pottery, handle fragments, and so forth), these survey data support, in a qualitative way, the proposition that materials of Mississippian age have a more confined distribution than those of the Woodland period (see Dunnell and Simek 1995 for data on the Malden Plain). These distributions appear to conform to our current, albeit general, understanding of Woodland- and Mississippian-period subsistence practices. Materials dating to the Woodland period, when a more generalized set of subsistence strategies was followed, would have broader and more extensive distribution than those of the Mississippian period, when a more specialized strategy based on maize agriculture was followed. Only with a better understanding of chronological ordering of Woodland and Mississippian materials will it be possible to examine the sources of this variation in any detail.

Concluding Remarks

Two important and interrelated issues emerge from the preliminary results of the survey conducted near Sandy Woods. First, it should be quite clear how a poorly developed pottery-based chronology greatly reduces our ability to make any but the most general inferences regarding the demographic history of the area. Second, when the formation of the archaeological record is given serious consideration, we cannot assume that the assemblages from even the small, low-density clusters represent historically related assemblages from single occupational events (of whatever duration), much less settlements in the traditional sense of the term. In short, the inferential basis of "settlement pattern" is a complex issue.

Consider shell-tempered pottery, used here as a provisional indicator of Mississippian-period occupations. Because the use of shell as temper appears to have preceded other changes in pottery technology, subsistence, and settlement (see references above), shell-tempered pottery is a very broad temporal indicator. Still, the assemblage from Cluster RMA is instructive. Approximately 20 percent of the sherds collected contain shell temper. The assemblage also includes a sherd that is most likely from a bottle neck (a vessel shape associated with the Middle Mississippian period but only rarely with the Early Mississip-

Table 7-1. Frequency of Eroded Sherds from Cluster RMA by Temper

Temper	Eroded	Noneroded	Total	Percent Eroded
Shell	38	18	56	68
Sand	113	90	203	56
Grog	60	106	166	36
Shell and grog	9	10	19	47
Shell and sand	16	30	46	35
Sand and grog	62	102	164	38
Shell, sand, and grog	1	12	13	8

pian period), but there is no shell temper visible in the sherd, even though other kinds of artifacts considered "diagnostic" of Mississippian-age contexts, such as Mill Creek "hoe chips," are in the collection. Because it is quite likely that the assemblage includes materials from more than one discrete occupation, sorting the pottery on the basis of shell temper alone may be adequate for monitoring the areal extent of Mississippian-period land use in a qualitative way, but not for assessing occupation in a quantitative way.

The assemblage from Cluster RMA suggests an additional problem involved in tracking Mississippian-age materials in the region. Analysis of the assemblage is preliminary—the presence or absence of shell, sand, and grog has been noted, but temper-particle size and temper-particle abundance have not been measured. Sherds from the cluster are generally in poor condition, and many of them are badly eroded (Table 7-1). The highest frequency of eroded sherds is among those containing shell temper, which experimental work has shown to be tougher than those tempered with sand and thus less likely to break catastrophically (Dunnell and Feathers 1991; Feathers 1989, 1990b). Consequently, one would expect sand-tempered vessels, when reduced to sherds, to break into larger numbers of smaller pieces. This feature alone has obvious implications for using absolute numbers of sherds to measure density or intensity of occupation unless it can be shown that other postdepositional factors such as plowing will reduce all sherds, regardless of composition, to similar size distributions.

Using sherd quantities to measure occupational intensity is further complicated by the fact that the strength and integrity of shell- and sand-tempered pottery are compromised in different ways as a result of postdepositional factors. Even though pottery tempered with coarsely crushed shell is stronger than pottery tempered with finely crushed shell or sand (Feathers 1989; Feathers and Scott 1989), it is subject to far greater degradation because of the chemical weathering of shell in acidic soils.

The effect of postdepositional alteration is only one of the many problems that must be assessed if the quantity of typologically (and compositionally) different pottery is to be used to estimate density of settlement. It may well have been the case that a greater number of sand-tempered sherds than shell-tempered sherds were deposited at the Cluster RMA location. Certainly the amount of time during which sand-tempered pottery was manufactured and used (perhaps 1200 years) was far longer than that for shell-tempered pottery (no more than about 700 years). Of significance here is that at least some portion of what was originally a low-density Mississippian-period record could have been rendered even less visible as a result of postdepositional factors.

In conclusion, our current understanding of the origin, development, and decline of Mississippian societies in the central Mississippi River valley has been formulated on the basis of monitoring a variety of general indicators such as large population aggregates, mound complexes, and shell-tempered pottery. These dimensions can no longer be used without regard for the range of variation represented in those variables. Recent laboratory research has demonstrated that the nature of Mississippian ceramic technology was far more involved than the simple use of shell temper. The survey results presented here show that the manifestation of this variation in the archaeological record is complicated by a variety of depositional and postdepositional factors affecting the visibility of Mississippian occupations. This issue of visibility can be extended to any of the traits traditionally associated with the Mississippian period and used to monitor developments during that period. For example, we cannot simply use *large* population aggregates to track the decline in Mississippian occupation of a region; rather, we must use *all* population aggregates.

The Mississippian-period sequence in the Cairo Lowland may well include a fourteenth-century abandonment, or it may include an abandonment only of the large population aggregates. So far, the means by which we have monitored the sequence are too heavily influenced by visibility and ease of discovery according to nineteenth-century survey standards to know very much about these important changes.

Acknowledgments

Much of the fieldwork was conducted through a joint field school program through Southeast Missouri State University, Murray State University, and Southern Illinois University at Carbondale. I am particularly indebted to E. Claycolmb, J. Merrick, and D. Wagner of Scott County, Missouri, who provided access to their farms. I also thank M. J. O'Brien, R. C. Dunnell, M. B. Schiffer, and L. Wandsnider for comments on previous versions of the manuscript.

8 | Powers Fort
A Middle Mississippian–Period Fortified Community in the Western Lowlands of Missouri
Timothy K. Perttula

POWERS FORT (23BU10) is the civic-ceremonial center of the Middle Mississippian–period Powers phase (Price 1978; Smith 1978a), a short-lived manifestation of Mississippian society present in the Western Lowlands of the Mississippi River valley between about A.D. 1200 and A.D. 1350.[1] Here I summarize what is known about Powers Fort, which is one of the less well known Mississippian fortified communities in the central Mississippi Valley (Chapman et al. 1977; Price and Fox 1990; Teltser 1992). I pay special attention to local and regional shifts in settlement patterns and the use by the Powers-phase population of sand ridges in the Little Black River valley of the Western Lowlands (Figure 8-1). Those shifts appear to be contemporaneous with the evolution of intensive maize agricultural subsistence by Mississippian peoples (e.g., Buikstra 1992; Fritz 1990; Hastorf and Johannessen 1994; Lynott et al. 1986; Scarry 1993; see also Greenlee, Chapter 13).

My other principal concern is to present a comprehensive view of the major Powers-phase material-culture assemblage from Powers Fort, because the abundant remains recovered since the early 1900s provide a good accounting of the artifactual content of a Mississippian-period civic-ceremonial center occupied for only a short period. I also discuss the long history of investigations at the site, beginning with the work of Col. Philetus W. Norris of the Bureau of (American) Ethnology in 1882 (Perttula and Price 1984), continuing through unpublished work by personnel connected with the Powers Phase Project in the 1960s, and ending with more-recent examinations of the site.

Environmental Setting

Powers Fort is in the Western Lowlands of the Mississippi River valley, about 2 kilometers east of the Ozark Escarpment and the current channel of the Little Black River (Figures 8-1 and 8-2). Landforms in the Little Black River watershed were greatly influenced by events that occurred well before human occupation of southeastern Missouri (O'Brien and Dunnell, Chapter 1). Large

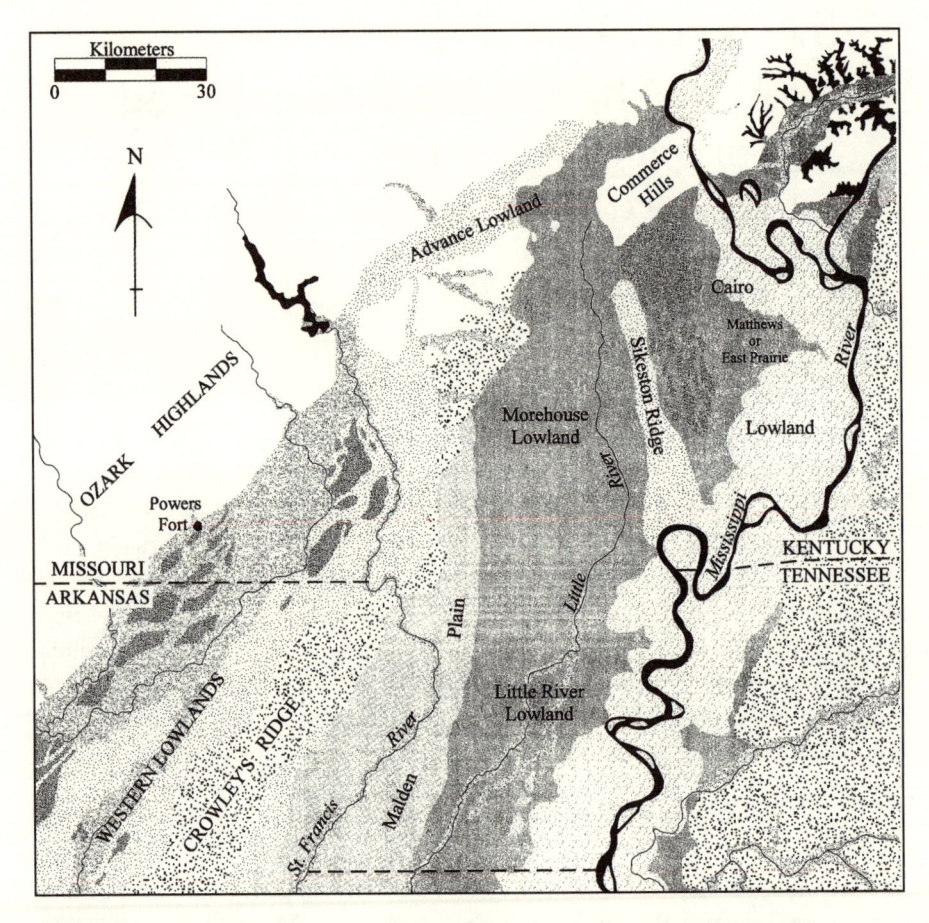

Figure 8-1. Location of Powers Fort relative to physiographic features in southeastern Missouri.

sand ridges—remnants of Early Wisconsin-age natural levees—were formed when the braided channel of the Mississippi River ran along the edge of the Ozark Highlands. The broad and relatively flat sand ridges are separated from each other by narrow, relict braided-stream channels.

This area of ridges and channels extends from the Ozark Escarpment to Cane Creek, which occupies a relict channel of the St. Francis River, and south into northeastern Arkansas (Price 1978:figure 8-3). Powers Fort is situated at the northeastern edge of one of the largest of the sand ridges in the southeastern-Missouri portion of the Little Black River watershed (Figure 8-2), opposite the point at which the Little Black River exits the Ozark Highlands and enters the Western Lowlands. Barfield Ridge is about 5 kilometers long and 1.2 to 2 kilometers wide, and its crest is 4.5 to 6 meters above the relict stream channels.

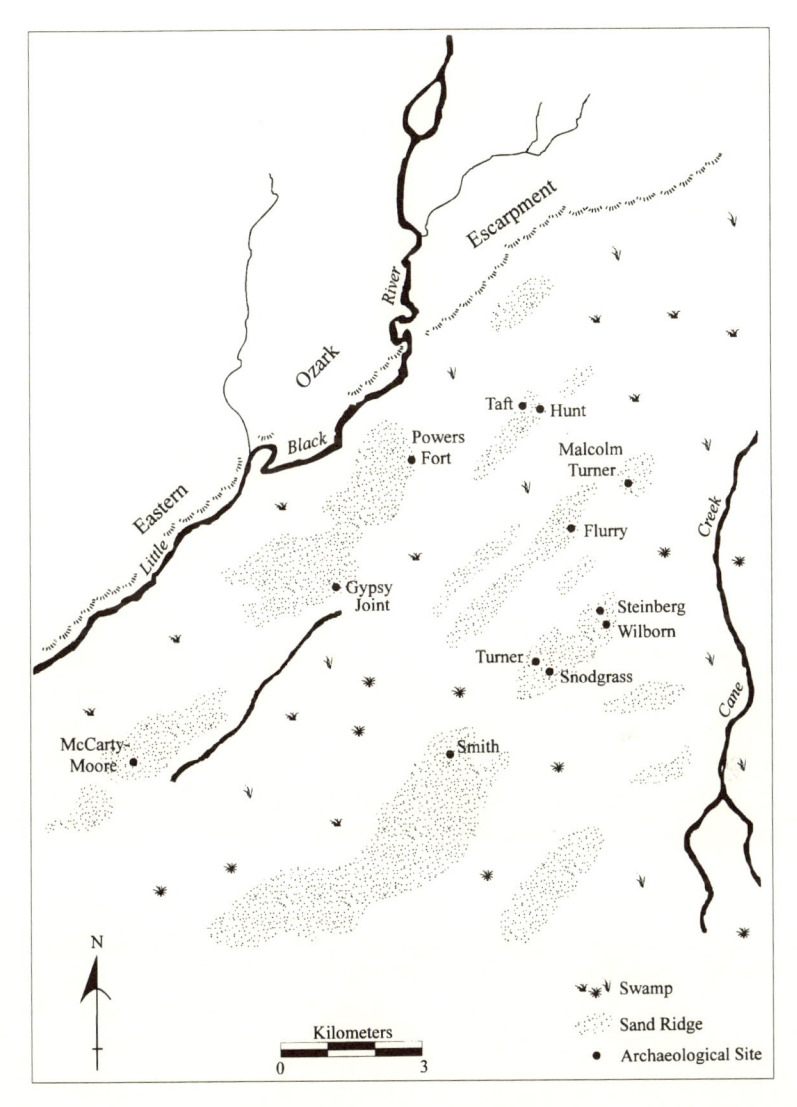

Figure 8-2. Map of the sand-ridge system in the Little Black River watershed in the vicinity of Powers Fort showing locations of Powers-phase sites.

Dotting the surface of the ridge are large and small aeolian sand dunes formed during the Late Pleistocene (Saucier 1978).

The Little Black River watershed below the Ozark Escarpment has minimal vertical relief. Other than the sand ridges, sand dunes, natural levees, and terraces of the Little Black River itself, the rest of the area was a seasonally inundated floodplain and swamp before it was drained in the early 1900s. Powers Fort is located at an elevation of 91.5 to 94.5 meters above mean sea level; areas below about 88 meters would likely have been seasonally if not permanently flooded (Price 1978:206).

Soils of the sand ridges are members of the Beulah-Brosely association—well to excessively drained but easily worked—and support oaks, hickory, and sweet gum on the level and sloping ridges. Backswamp areas such as the relict channels originally contained cypress and tupelo, while the natural levees and terraces along the Little Black probably had a cottonwood-and-willow overstory near the riverbank. Along the Ozark Escarpment, a mature oak-hickory forest probably was present; sugar maple, bitternut hickory, and white oak covered the more mesic habitats along the Little Black River in the Ozark Highlands. Sediment cores from the Powers Fort swale/cypress swamp indicate that about A.D. 1350 there was considerable land clearance and cultivation of the ridge adjacent to the site. Ragweed pollen peaked around that time, and maize pollen made its appearance—both denoting prehistoric anthropic disturbances of the environment.

The fauna in the Ozark Escarpment/Western Lowlands area has been considered in detail by Smith (1975). Except for possible differences between the Mississippi River meander belt and the Little Black River area in abundance of animal species and the availability of migratory waterfowl (Smith 1975:203–4), it is reasonable to suggest that the same range and type of terrestrial and aquatic species were present throughout southeastern Missouri during the Mississippian period.

Archaeological Investigations at Powers Fort

I subdivide this summary of the century-plus of work at Powers Fort into five sections: (1) the work by Norris in the nineteenth century, (2) agriculture-related activities of landowner Walter Koehler throughout much of the twentieth century, (3) excavations by James E. Price in 1964 and 1965, (4) the work of the Powers Phase Project in 1969, and (5) subsequent investigations.

Col. Philetus W. Norris

Col. Philetus W. Norris, an ethnological assistant of the Bureau of (American) Ethnology, was the first to recognize that Powers Fort was an important and major archaeological site. He was appointed by the bureau's director, John W. Powell, in August 1882 and was one of the first three regular assistants to Cyrus Thomas (the others being Edward Palmer and James D. Middleton) (Smith 1985) during Thomas's mound-survey project (Thomas 1894). Norris's interest in archaeology began in the 1850s when he recorded mounds in Pipestone County, Minnesota, and strengthened after a sojourn to Yellowstone National Park in the 1870s. Because of his efforts to publicize the park, he was appointed its second superintendent—a position he held from 1877 to 1881.

When his superintendency ended, he began working for the Bureau of (American) Ethnology.

Norris reached Powers Fort on November 24, 1882, after excavating in the Poplar Bluff, Harviell, and Doniphan areas of Butler and Ripley counties, Missouri. He left a rather detailed journal (for the time) of his work at the site (Norris 1883; see Perttula and Price 1984). What first caught his attention were the easily demarked earthen embankments on the north, south, and west sides of the site; the east side faced a cypress swamp.[2] The site plan (Figure 8-3) indicates a square that is oriented approximately north-south, with the four mounds oriented northeast-southwest in the northern and western quadrants of the site. Two borrow pits were visible at the northwest and southwest corners of the ditch and embankment. Both were more than 5 feet deep and contained standing water. The ditch was described by Norris as "from 3 to 4 feet deep, twice as wide."

Norris partially excavated each of the mounds using a plow-and-strip team, and he also hand-excavated a series of pits, but he spent most of his time working on Mound 1. He removed more than half the mound, which was 150 × 200 feet in area and 20 feet high. Thomas, in discussing the houses of the "moundbuilders," paraphrased from the notes made by Norris during the Mound 1 excavations:

> The construction [of the mound] was found to be somewhat peculiar.... The bottom layer, 1 [Figure 8-4], is a circular platform about one hundred feet in diameter and two feet high, formed of yellow sand, similar to the original surface beneath and around it. The next layer, marked 2, is only six inches thick and consists of dark blue adhesive clay or muck from the swamp, which by long use has become very hard. It was strewn over with burnt clay, charcoal, ashes, fragments of split bones, stone chips, fragments of pottery and mussel shells.
>
> The next layer, 3, is eight feet thick at the central point of what appears to have been the original mound of which it was the top stratum. But it is not uniform, and although showing no distinct layers was not all formed at one time, as in it were found at least three distinct fire-beds of burnt earth and heavy accumulations of ashes, charcoal and charred animal bones. In this layer, somewhat south of the center, at m, were found the charred fragments of long poles and small logs all lying horizontally, and also a post (A), probably of locust wood, six inches thick and five feet long, still erect, but the upper end shortened by fire and the lower end haggled off by some rude implement.
>
> Layer number 4 is an addition to the original plan, but here the original platform is continued with the same sandy material and same height: then the layer number 4 was built of blue muck similar to that of number 2 in the original mound. Having obtained the desired form, layer 5, which is 6 feet thick and of blue clay mixed with sand, was thrown over the whole. But this was evidently formed after an interval of usage of the original double mound, as northwest of the center and in the lower part of this layer (at n) were found charred timbers lying horizontally, and one post (B) standing erect, resembling the timber post found in number 3. (Thomas 1884:113)

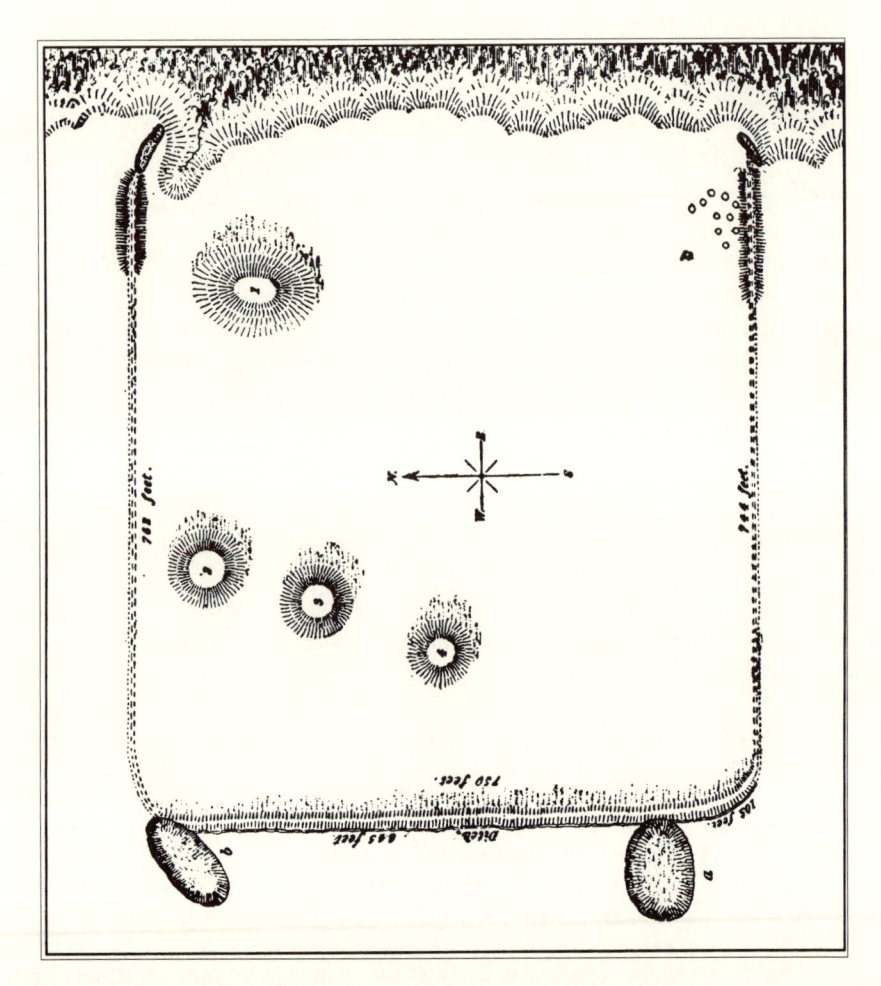

Figure 8-3. Plan map of Powers Fort made by Col. Philetus W. Norris for the Bureau of (American) Ethnology, Division of Mound Exploration. Norris excavated in all four mounds, uncovering burials and artifacts (from Thomas 1894).

These descriptions by Norris and Thomas are sufficient to indicate that Mound 1 was a pyramidal, flat-topped mound that served as the foundation for a number of different structures. The mound was constructed in a number of stages, and these apparently capped the remnants of burned structures marked by the different "fire-beds" present in the mound.

Burials were noted in association with at least three of the burned structures in the mound: one or more burials near the base of the mound in Stratum 2, another midway in the mound in Stratum 3, and a third in Stratum 5. According to Norris (1883), the burials were of adults placed in extended position under "fire-beds," with heads to the south and west, and they were not clearly

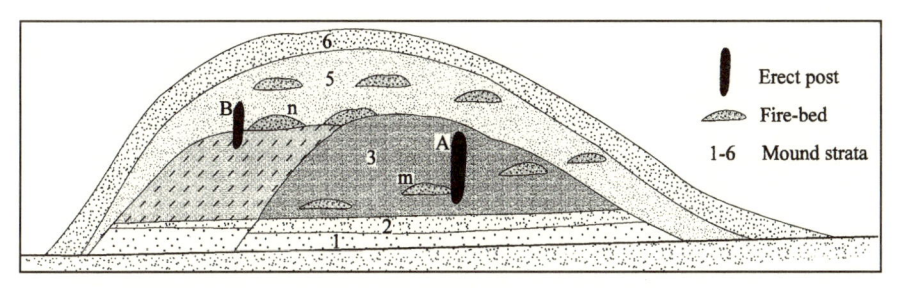

Figure 8-4. Cross section of Mound 1 at Powers Fort as depicted by Col. Philetus W. Norris. Numbers 1 through 6 represent mound strata (after Thomas 1894).

accompanied by any specific grave goods other than "the ordinary stone spalls, mussel-shells, fragments of pottery, one very rude lance head, and some small smoothe yellow stones (apparently natural) . . . found near them."

The erect wooden posts mentioned in mound strata 3 and 5 are of particular interest. It is possible that these posts were only remnants of house walls, but they also might have represented isolated posts either in or adjacent to the mound public structures that served as solar devices or markers (Smith 1992) or as poles for hanging the deer and elk skulls discovered in Stratum 5 (Norris 1883).

Norris (1883) found that human bone was common in mounds 2 and 4, whereas Mound 3 contained "fire-beds, patches of bone, charcoal ashes, fragments, etc.," but no human bone. His descriptions, unfortunately, are unclear as to the contexts of the human bones. Were they scattered bones or burials? Both Mound 3 and Mound 4 were called burial mounds by Norris, but Mound 2 can also be included within this class of mounds. In any case, functional differences in mound use seem likely at those secondary mounds.

Thomas described the other mounds as follows:

> Mound No. 2 is much smaller than No. 1, not exceeding 100 feet in diameter and 6 feet in height, and is flat on top. It consisted of four layers, the first or upper stratum of sandy soil, 2 feet thick, mixed with fragments of pottery: the second, about the same thickness, chiefly yellow sand, with patches of blue clay, charcoal, ashes, fragments of pottery, and human bone mostly unbroken but soft as pulp; the third, 6 inches thick, was made up of blue clay and fragments of pottery; and the fourth, 18 inches thick, of yellow sand, well filled with decayed human bones, though some of them were plump and soft. Scattered among them were charcoal and ashes.
>
> Mound No. 3, also flat on top, 80 feet in diameter and 4 feet high, was without regular layers; but the base was found to be composed chiefly of yellow sand, containing fire-beds, patches of bones, charcoal, ashes, fragments of pottery, etc.
>
> Mound No. 4 resembled No. 3 in form, size, composition, and contents. (Thomas 1894:194)

Within the enclosure, particularly in the southeast corner (see Figure 8-3), Norris (1883) noted that pottery, lithic tools, and lithic debris were common. This observation is borne out by the quantity of primarily Late Archaic–period (3000–600 B.C.) lithic artifacts recovered from the surface in Area A of the site (see below). Norris also described the base of a pottery vessel that apparently was fabric marked as "a fragment showing very clearly the art work of the basket in which it was baked."[3]

Walter A. Koehler, 1908–1978

Walter A. Koehler purchased the Powers Fort property in 1908 and farmed it regularly for row crops until the late 1960s. After that, the property was only shallowly disked until it was purchased by The Archaeological Conservancy in 1978. Over the years, Koehler surface collected more than 1500 projectile points and stone tools, and, while excavating for fence posts and constructing farm buildings, he discovered several human burials and whole vessels south of Mound 4. These were recorded and excavated by James E. Price (see below). Because Koehler never allowed indiscriminate digging at Powers Fort, the site escaped the fate of most large Mississippian sites in the Mississippi Valley that saw destructive pothunting (Harrington 1991).

Interviews with Koehler by Price indicated that the site embankments and ditches were still visible in 1908. The western embankment was evidenced by a band of white swamp clay containing "buckshot" (iron concretions) that extended in a southwest-northeast direction across his field. This contradicts Thomas's (1894) map, which illustrates the embankments and ditches running in the cardinal directions. Koehler's observations are likely correct, because all mapped villages of the Powers phase have an orientation of 25 to 30 degrees east of magnetic north (see Price and Griffin 1979:table 2). Furthermore, the three subsidiary mounds at Powers Fort (mounds 2 through 4) form a line with an orientation similar to that of the villages (Figure 8-5).[4] The southern embankment was oriented northwest-southeast and cut across the southern half of the farmyard to continue onto the property to the south. Koehler's description of the embankment and ditch indicates that the embankment was on the outside of the ditch, rather than on the inside, and that it was composed of white clay and yellow sand. Koehler also remembered when Mound 1 was near its original height. It has subsequently been reduced to 3.6 meters in height because of twentieth-century farming practices. The large borrow pits at the western corners of Powers Fort contained water until Koehler had them filled.

Excavations by James E. Price, 1964 and 1965

James E. Price conducted excavations in the farmyard and Area A (see Figure 8-5) while he was an undergraduate at the University of Missouri–Columbia. The 1964 excavations (250 square feet) comprised a discontinuous trench

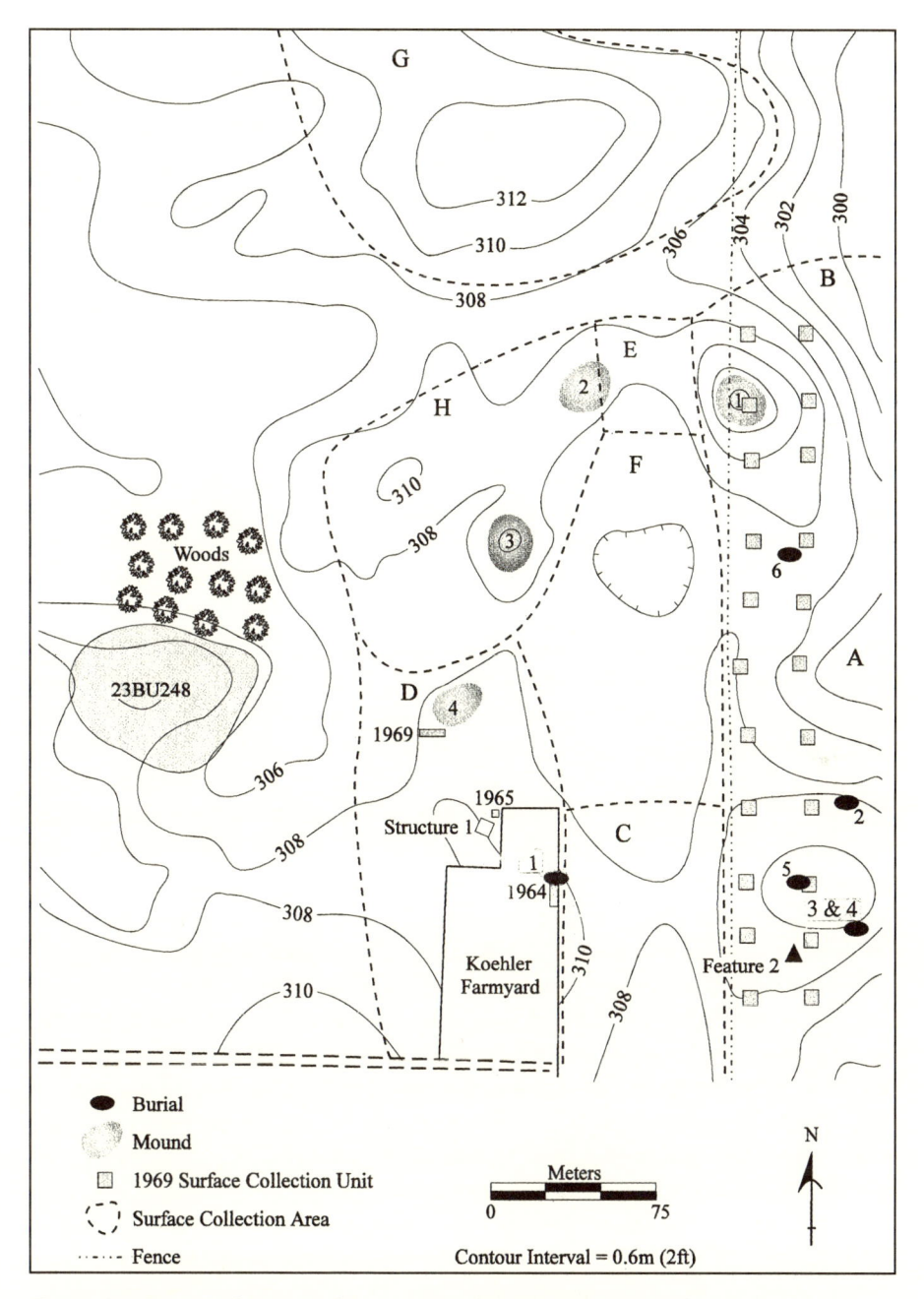

Figure 8-5. Topographic map of Powers Fort showing mounds, surface-collected areas, locations of excavations in the 1960s, and burials 2 through 6.

southeast of Mound 4. An extended adult burial—referred to here as Burial 1—together with half of a wall-trench structure and a small refuse pit were recorded in the chicken yard. An approximately 30-centimeter-thick midden with animal bones, sherds, and decayed human bone was present in the northern half of the trench. Surface evidence suggested this midden covers about a hectare south and southeast of Mound 4 and is in the midst of a residential area. Burial 1 had been placed in the midden, just south of the structure. According to Black (1979:44), this was a rearticulated burial of an approximately thirty-year-old male who had been shot from behind; a chert projectile point was found lodged in one femur. Included in the burial was a poorly fired long-neck water bottle placed above the right shoulder and a small, tapered fired-clay object that ended up in the rib column (Figure 8-6, *a*, and Table 8-1).

The wall-trench structure uncovered in 1964 was oriented 27 degrees east of north, like other Powers-phase structures (Price and Griffin 1979:50), and was burned. Broken charred poles and architectural remains, including the upper portion of the wall trench and structure floor, were exposed at a depth of 28 centimeters. The western profile revealed a layer of charred poles and grass thatch on the floor of the structure. Most of the burned wood on the structure floor was present along its northern and southern edges. Portions of two broken pottery vessels lay on the floor; they were left in place until the structure could be completely excavated. From the test-trench profiles and plan views, the structure measured approximately 4.7 meters on a side.

In 1965, Price excavated a 10 × 10-foot area about 40 meters southeast of Mound 4. This unit was in the same Powers-phase midden deposit exposed in the 1964 excavations, and it overlay the corner of a house structure that contained sherds, lithic artifacts, and well-preserved animal remains. Two wall trenches and a corner of the structure basin were exposed in cross section, but the orientation of the structure could not be determined. Evidence suggested the structure was rebuilt at least once; it is unknown whether it burned.

Several human burials were excavated in 1965 after they had been disturbed by cultivation. Burial 2, containing the remains of a sixty-five- to seventy-year-old male, was found near the cypress swamp; a metacarpal of a child was also included in the burial pit (Black 1979:45) (Figure 8-6, *c*). A large number of artifacts was associated with Burial 2 (Table 8-1), principally corner-notched arrow points around the head, chert flakes and tools by the shoulders, worked quartz crystals by the left arm, and a plain-surface, shell-tempered water bottle touching the left side of the cranium. Incidental inclusions in the grave fill included five shell-tempered Mississippi Plain (Phillips 1970) sherds (including one strap handle) and two Woodland-period sand-tempered Barnes (Williams 1954) sherds, one of which was cordmarked.

Burials 3 and 4 were in the same grave (Figure 8-6, *d*). Burial 3 (Black [1979:45] labeled this burial 3A) was of a sixty- to sixty-five-year-old male ex-

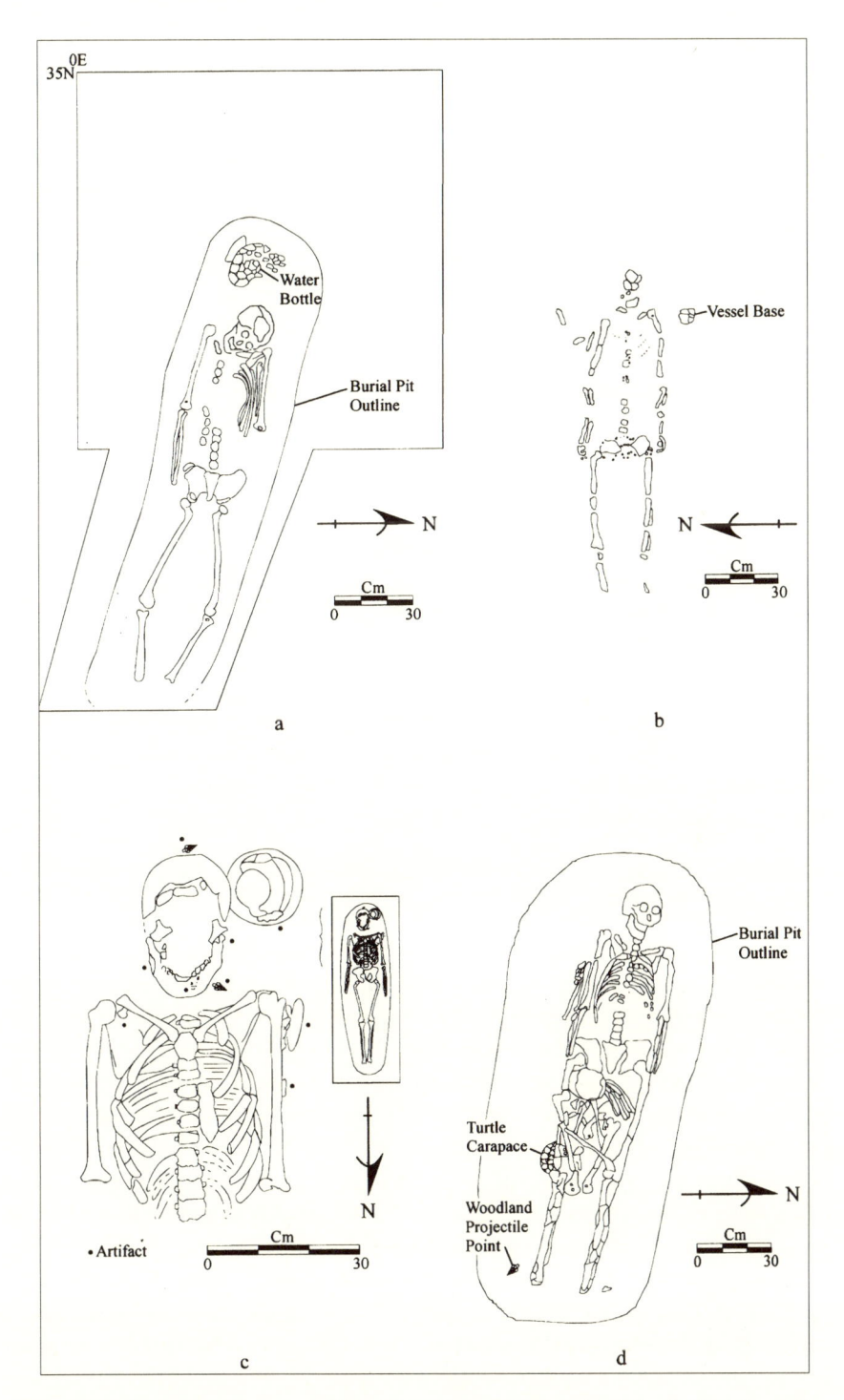

Figure 8-6. Plan maps of excavated burials at Powers Fort: *a*, Burial 1; *b*, Burial 5; *c*, Burial 2 (the *dots* indicate associated burial goods, including five arrow points, a scraper, four chert flakes, an antler tool, two quartz crystals, a bone fishhook, and a short-neck bottle); *d*, burials 3 and 4.

Table 8-1. Position, Orientation, Age, Sex, and Associated Artifacts of Powers Fort Burials

Burial Number	Burial Area	Burial Position	Orientation	Age	Sex	Associated Artifacts
Burial 1	C	Extended	W–NW	~30	Male	Long-necked water bottle, fired-clay object
Burial 2	A	Extended	S	65–70	Male	Five arrow points, bone fishhook, 4 flakes, hammerstone, antler flaking tool, 2 crystals, 1 scraper, 1 bottle
Burial 3	A	Extended	W–NW	60–65	Male	Turtle carapace, 2 dart points
Burial 4	A	Bundle	—	Adult	Male	None
Burial 5	A	Extended	E	Adult	Female	Pottery vessel
Burial 6	B	Extended	W	Adult	Female	None
Burial 7[a]	D	Extended	W	Infant	—	None
Burial 8	D	Extended	S	Infant	—	None
Burial 9	D	Extended	W	Infant	—	Large sherd

Source: Data from Black (1979).
[a]Burials 7 through 9 in Structure 1.

tended with the head to the west, and Burial 4 (Black [1979:45] labeled this burial 3B) was a bundle burial of an older adult male. The skeleton had been placed between the legs of Burial 3, with the head upside down at the west side of the bundle. The mandible was under the main part of the bundle of long bones, the ribs lay to the north of the head, and some of the ankle and feet bones of Burial 4 were placed at the right shoulder of Burial 3. A turtle carapace, probably a rattle, was placed at the distal end of the femur of Burial 3, and two Woodland-period projectile points were placed near the feet. Wilson's (1993) analysis of stable-carbon and nitrogen isotopes from Burial 3 indicates that maize comprised approximately 50 percent of the diet and that terrestrial herbivores (probably in large part deer) were important food items.

Bundle burials and multiple burials were a common form of interment in the Powers phase (Black 1979:table 39), with up to five individuals per grave noted at the nearby Turner site (see Figure 8-2). In each case, bundle burials were only of adults, and they always occurred in multiple arrangements. At least at Turner, no artifacts were intentionally placed with bundle burials.

Burial 5 was found in a residential area about midway between Burial 2 and burials 3 and 4 (Figure 8-5).[5] The burial was that of a female probably more than twenty-one years old. The base of a large shell-tempered vessel had been placed near the left shoulder (see Figure 8-6, *b*).

Powers Phase Project, 1969

As part of the Powers Phase Project (Price and Griffin 1979:xi–xiii), Price conducted excavations at Powers Fort in May 1969. Excavations were confined to three areas of the site: (1) Structure 1, south of Mound 4; (2) a trench of unspecified size north and west of Structure 1 in what was thought to be the approximate area of the palisade and ditch; and (3) three 5 × 5-foot units southeast of Mound 1 (located just off the map shown in Figure 8-5).[6]

STRUCTURE 1

Structure 1 was excavated between May 22 and July 7, 1969, by a crew of five students under the supervision of John Walthall. Techniques employed in the excavation of Structure 1 and in the excavation of pits located inside and outside the houses were similar to those described for the Snodgrass site (see Price and Griffin 1979:27–28). Eight hundred fifty-two specimens were recovered from the structure, which was demarcated by a dark, organic stain below the sandy plow zone. The dark stain was from ash and charcoal produced when the structure burned, as well as from midden soil dumped and/or washed into the structure basin. The structure had been built in a 30-centimeter-deep basin, the fill from which probably was piled against the structure walls (Price 1969). Unlike the structures excavated at Snodgrass and Turner (Figure 8-2), Structure 1 at Powers Fort showed extensive evidence that it had been rebuilt (Figure 8-7). On the basis of the number of wall trenches on the north and south sides, there were at least four rebuilding episodes. Wall trenches crosscut wall trenches; apparently when the structure was rebuilt, some wall trenches were abandoned whereas others were reused.

Only two wall trenches were present on the west side, and a single wall trench ran parallel to the structure basin wall on the east side. A single wall trench extended from the structure center to the east side, where it was bisected by a north-south wall trench. This trench may have served as a base for an internal partition during one occupational episode. Wall trenches were 21 to 39 centimeters wide and about 13 centimeters deep. Individual posts were set vertically in the trenches; the posts were about 7 centimeters in diameter and spaced irregularly. No definite interior support posts were recorded, but Pit 1 and the larger posts in the northeast and southeast corners might have represented such roof supports (Figure 8-7).

The structure basin was oriented approximately 25 degrees east of north and measured 6.5 × 5.3 meters. The size of the structure, at least during the initial rebuilding stages, was roughly comparable to those of the larger and more permanent structures constructed inside the white wall compound at

182 | Perttula

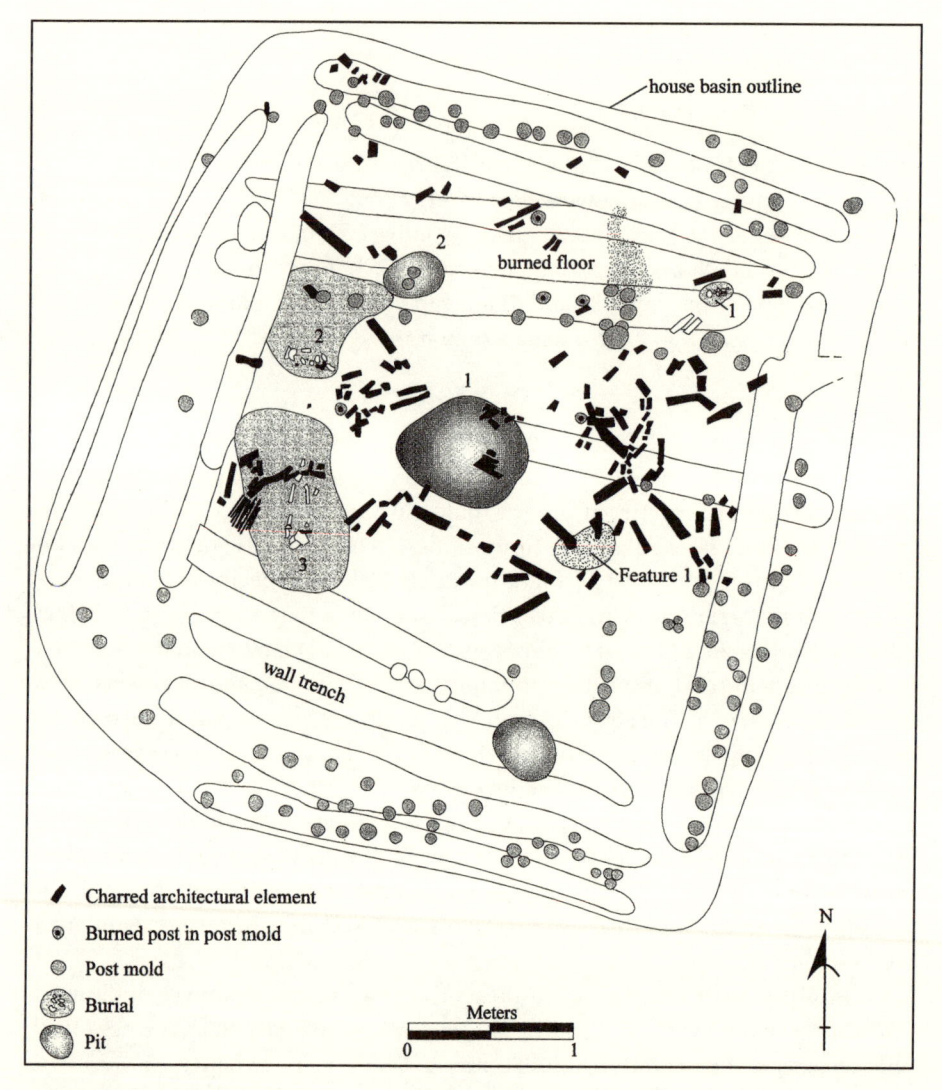

Figure 8-7. Plan map of Structure 1 at Powers Fort.

Snodgrass, where the mean size of the structures was about 29 square meters. The last structure to occupy the house basin at Powers Fort measured only about 4.9 × 4.1 meters.

Charred poles, logs, cane, grass, and post butts were preserved and lay on the structure floor. The direction and distribution of architectural elements suggest that the north and west walls collapsed inward toward the southeast corner when the structure burned. Cane from the base of the house walls was preserved along the west wall, and charred elements lay primarily between the northernmost wall trench and the third wall trench from the south. Charcoal extended from the second trench from the west across to the eastern trench (Figure 8-7).

The structure contained three pits, three infant burials, and a hearth. Two pits contained sherds, animal bone, and lithic items, and one (Pit 2) contained a thin layer of charcoal. The hearth was in the southeast quadrant of the structure basin, which is characteristic of Powers-phase houses (Price and Griffin 1979). It consisted of burned, oxidized sand, with small pieces of fire-cracked rock around it. The three burials (burials 1 through 3 on Figure 8-7 and burials 7 through 9 in Table 8-1) were all of infants less than six months of age. Burial 3 had a large shell-tempered sherd under the head. Two pits were outside the north and west walls, and both contained an assortment of midden refuse (fire-cracked rock, bone, and sherds). Both pits had layers of charcoal in the uppermost levels of fill, which indicates they had been filled prior to the time the structure burned.

Five radiocarbon dates were derived from wood charcoal from Structure 1 (Price and Griffin 1979:appendix D). Using the calibration curve of Stuiver and Pearson (1993), the mean of the five dates is A.D. 1340, with a standard-error range of A.D. 1310–1390 (rounded to the nearest 5/0). These dates fall comfortably within the range of radiocarbon dates from other Powers-phase sites (Price and Griffin 1979; Smith 1978a). Lynott (1987) reported that the average of thirty-one uncorrected radiocarbon dates from Powers-phase samples was A.D. 1361 ± 18.

The spatial distribution and association of different artifact classes within Mississippian structures can tell us something about the location and nature of activities within a house, provided that deposit-formation processes are understood (e.g., Pauketat 1989:290–94). This is particularly true with Powers-phase structures, which appear to have been burned deliberately (Price and Griffin 1979:54–138).

On the basis of the findings of three broken in situ vessels in the structure, the numbers of ceramic cones around the hearth (the cones may have been used to support vessels over the fire [Price 1969:20]), and a concentration of smaller artifacts (sherds, animal bone, and lithic debris) along the periphery of the hearth where they might have been swept, the floor and below-floor artifact assemblage from Structure 1 best represents a "behavioral assemblage" (Pauketat 1989:291). Price and Griffin note that at Snodgrass:

> Other than refuse and lost artifacts, most small articles such as axes, hoes, and vessels were either removed prior to the fire or were salvaged after it. Articles left behind include large jars, bowls, water bottles, ceramic cones, grinding slabs, and hammerstones, and predictably, artifacts that had been buried in the floor remain. Thus, it would appear that the inhabitants expected the fire and may actually have set it intentionally, since they had removed small vessels that would have been broken in the collapsing structures. Broken exam-

Table 8-2. Vertical Distribution of Cultural Materials in Structure 1 at Powers Fort

Context	Sherds	Bone	Shell	Cones	Projectile Points	Fire-Cracked Rock
Above floor	134	55	1	19	5	38
Floor	60	49	4	15	3	33
Below floor	95	102	8	24	10	56
Total	289	206	13	58	18	127

ples of such vessels are common in the refuse pits, and the paucity of whole specimens found in the burned structures indicates that most were removed prior to the fire. (Price and Griffin 1979:53)

Activities on the floor within Structure 1 centered around the hearth and interior Refuse Pit 1. Except for a concentration of deer mandibles and scapulas in the northeast quadrant along the wall (as at Gypsy Joint [Smith 1978a:137], located a few kilometers to the southwest of Powers Fort [Figure 8-2]), areas along the walls were relatively free of artifacts. Large grinding slabs, along with jars and ceramic cones, were near the hearth. The majority of artifacts from within the structure occurred in the fill above the floor as opposed to below it. Sherds, animal bone, and stones (including fire-cracked rocks) were the most common artifacts in the fill (Table 8-2). However, the densest concentration of sherds, mussel shell, cones, projectile points, and fire-cracked rock occurred within a few centimeters of the floor (Table 8-3). The above-floor cultural materials may have been the result (1) of the discard of midden in the structure basin after it had burned and/or (2) of materials washed in or carried in by plowing in modern times.

Table 8-3. Concentration Indices of Excavated Artifacts from Structure 1 at Powers Fort

Context	Sherds	Bone	Shell	Cones	Projectile Points	Fire-Cracked Rock	Total
Above floor	268	280	2	38	10	76	674
Floor	300	245	20	75	15	165	820
Below floor	106	117	8	25	11	59	326

Note: Numbers represent artifacts per cubic meter of deposit.

SURFACE COLLECTIONS

Twenty-two 20 × 20-foot units were surface collected on the east side of the site fronting the cypress swamp between Mound 1 and the Koehler property line (see Figure 8-5). The ground apparently had not been plowed specifically for the surface collection, but field notes imply that surface visibility was relatively uniform. Another six collection units were laid out in an area outside the embankment/ditch (an area labeled as site 23BU248), but most of the cultural material recovered there appears to date primarily to the Woodland period.

The surface distribution of cultural materials was highly patterned on the east side of the site and appears to correlate closely with topography. Powers-phase sherds were concentrated on the crest of the high, sandy knoll in Area A, southeast of the plaza (Area F on Figure 8-5), and considerably south of Mound 1. There was a substantial residential occupation of Area A. Another small surface concentration of Powers-phase pottery was identified just south of Mound 1, probably marking the location of a structure. Burial 6 was in the same approximate area (Figure 8-5). Because the surface collections were not contiguous, more-specific intrasite spatial patterns of structures and other features cannot be identified with the 1969 surface-collection data.

PALISADE/DITCH EXCAVATION

A trench was excavated about 46 meters north and 18 meters west of Structure 1 (Figure 8-5) to search for the embankment and ditch along the west side of Powers Fort; the exact location of the trench is unknown. A white-clay area about 2.1 meters wide was exposed (but not profiled or further excavated) in the western end of the trench and probably represents the base of the embankment.

OTHER EXCAVATIONS

Three 5 × 5-foot units were excavated southeast of Mound 1. A dark soil stain 87 centimeters thick was exposed in one of the test units, but it was unclear whether the stain was from a structure or a refuse midden. Burial 6 (an adult female) was uncovered in the area, and, according to Black (1979:45–46), a large piece of bone was missing from the cranium, which may be indicative of osteitis that resulted from scalping. Stable-carbon-isotope and nitrogen-isotope values obtained by Wilson (1993:126) from the skeleton suggest the individual did not consume much, if any, maize. Perhaps Burial 6 relates to an earlier occupation at the site, before maize contributed to the diet.

Subsequent Investigations

After the 1969 work at Powers Fort, Price subdivided the site into eight areas (A through H) for purposes of provenience control in further surface-collection activities (Figure 8-5). Of special note are Area B, which included Mound 1;

Area D, containing Mound 4 and a large midden south of the mound; Area E, a small area between mounds 1 and 2 where a large structure stain had been noted along with a concentration of nonlocal, or "status," artifacts (Price 1978:217–18); Area F, the plaza; and Area H, containing mounds 2 and 3.

Surface collections of artifacts have been made periodically from 1970 to the present in each of these areas. The collections are best characterized as "grab samples" in that only selected cultural items (e.g., rim and/or decorated sherds, projectile points, and other complete stone tools) have been collected. In 1979 and 1980, however, total surface collection was done in areas A and B after they had been plowed. Although a wide variety of Powers-phase lithic and ceramic artifacts has been collected from those areas since 1970 (see below), the overall density of cultural material on the surface of the site is quite low compared with that of other Mississippian-period civic-ceremonial centers in southeastern Missouri (e.g., Chapman et al. 1977; Leeds 1979; Teltser 1992).

Additional information has been generated from inspection of the site surface. Cultivation of the site prior to its purchase by The Archaeological Conservancy continually yielded soil stains that appeared to be evidence of house structures (Price and Griffin 1979). The stains were darker than the surrounding soil, and Mississippian-period artifacts were concentrated in them. Unfortunately, information about the intrasite settlement of Powers Fort is principally anecdotal in nature, as no maps exist that provide house locations or note the number of house rows that were observed over the years. With these caveats in mind, current settlement data available from Powers Fort based on surface exposures include the following:

1. An uncertain number of rows of structure stains are present in areas A, B, D, G, and H.
2. There are thought to be six rows of structures running 25 degrees east of north between Area A and Mound 1. Each row may have about forty structures, and the structures are spaced evenly along the rows. The rows also appear to be evenly spaced, but the distance between rows is unknown. Possible internal wall compounds (based on white-clay stains) are present in Area A that are probably analogous to those recorded at Snodgrass (Price and Griffin 1979).
3. A large midden area is visible on the surface in Area D.
4. The large area bounded by the mounds is void of Powers-phase artifacts, suggesting the location of a plaza.
5. Polished, painted, and engraved sherds are present northwest of Mound 1 in Area E. These are associated with a large soil stain that might mark a possible specialized residence or community structure.

Material Culture

Artifacts of numerous material classes have been surface collected and excavated at Powers Fort during the past several decades. Here I focus exclusively on ceramic and lithic items.

Ceramic Artifacts

More than 4240 ceramic sherds, 15 vessels, several ear plugs and earspools, a pottery trowel, and a single clay bead have been collected from various proveniences at Powers Fort over the years, along with small amounts of daub and pieces of ceramic cones. I estimate that 99 percent of the ceramic items are from the Middle Mississippian–period Powers-phase occupation, with much smaller amounts of pottery associated with Woodland or Early Mississippian occupations.

The Woodland occupation is represented by fifty-four sand-tempered Barnes sherds, most of which are from Area A ($n = 39$), with a few from areas B through D and G. Area A is where Norris (1883) had noted a number of cord-marked or fabric-impressed sherds. As Morse and Morse (1983:139–40) note, Barnes pottery includes large conical-based jars and simple bowl forms. The small sample of jars from Powers Fort has cordmarked surfaces and punctations and exterior bosses and is similar to other Woodland-period assemblages from the Naylor, Missouri, area (Price 1986). The amount of cordmarking in the assemblage is also comparable to that in the assemblage from McCarty (3PO467), located in Poinsett County, Arkansas, and suggested by Lynott et al. (1986) and Morse (1986) to date about 300 B.C.

Mississippian-period pottery at Powers Fort is shell-tempered; many sherds exhibit evidence of extensive leaching. The vessels have several different forms and, apparently, different functions. Except for a few simple stamped sherds and an occasional red-slipped body sherd, all the sherds are compatible with Mississippi Plain as described by Phillips (1970:130–35). Almost all of the shell-tempered pottery belongs to the Powers-phase occupation (Table 8-4).

The simple stamped sherds have a shell-sand paste and may be debris from a Late Woodland–Early Mississippian Buckskull- or Scatters-phase occupation (e.g., Price and Price 1981:498). Price and Price (1984:88–91) include this type of ceramic treatment within the Owls Bend tradition, which Lynott (1989, 1991) dates about A.D. 700–1000.

Red-slipped sherds are found in both Early Mississippian and Middle Mississippian ceramic assemblages in the Western Lowlands. Red slipping occurs on shell-tempered jars with recurved rims in Varney-tradition sites found throughout southeastern Missouri, extreme northeastern Arkansas, and several interior eastern-Ozark valleys (Lynott 1989; D. F. Morse and P. [A.] Morse 1990; Price and Price 1984). Red-slipped bottles, effigy bowls, and simple flared-rim

Table 8-4. Frequencies of Shell-Tempered Sherds and Other Ceramic Items from Powers Fort

| | Excavations ||| Provenience ||||||||
Class	1964	1965	1969	CSC[a]	A[b]	B	C	D	E	F	G	Gen[c]
Plain rim	20	14	12	10	74	12	3	20	3	2	15	48
Rim/strap handle	4	-	1	1	12	-	-	4	1	-	-	4
Rim/lug handle	-	-	-	1	1	-	-	-	-	-	-	-
Rim/loop handle	-	-	-	-	1	-	-	1	-	-	-	-
Scalloped rim	-	-	-	1	2	-	-	-	-	-	-	-
Noded rim	1	-	-	-	-	-	-	-	-	-	-	1
Notched rim	-	-	-	2	2	-	-	-	-	-	-	-
Tabtail	-	-	-	-	1	-	-	-	-	-	-	-
Effigy	1	-	-	-	-	-	-	-	-	-	-	-
Incision	-	-	1	-	-	-	-	-	-	-	-	1
Appliquéd	-	-	1	-	-	-	-	-	-	-	-	-
Punctated	-	-	-	1	-	-	-	-	-	-	-	-
Painted sunburst	-	-	1	-	-	-	-	-	1	-	-	-
Painted black	-	-	-	-	-	-	-	-	-	-	-	1
Interior engraved	-	-	-	-	-	-	-	-	-	-	-	1
Stamped	-	-	-	-	-	-	-	-	-	-	-	2
Fabric impressed	-	-	-	-	-	-	-	-	-	-	-	1
Red filmed	-	2	1	5	4	-	1	3	2	-	1	8
Plain body, bottle	-	-	-	-	3	-	-	-	-	-	-	-
Plain body	213	151	353	378	1430	95	87	349	175	28	202	397
Base	-	-	-	-	13	-	-	-	-	-	1	-
Disc	-	-	-	-	1	-	-	-	-	-	-	-
Trowel	-	-	-	-	-	-	-	-	-	-	-	1
Shell-and-sand-tempered, body	-	-	-	-	-	3	-	-	-	-	-	-
Total	239	167	370	399	1544	110	91	377	182	30	219	465

[a]Controlled surface collection.
[b]Surface-collected area.
[c]General surface collection.

bowls—vessel forms that are well represented in Powers-phase ceramic collections as well as in assemblages from contemporaneous sites (e.g., Moore 1910; Morse and Morse 1983:258)—are classifiable as Old Town Red (Phillips et al. 1951:129–32).

Small flared-rim bowls and undecorated large and small jars with strap handles are the most common vessel forms in Powers-phase domestic contexts (Table 8-5). Conversely, large flared-rim bowls and decorated jars (regardless of size) are uncommon in these contexts and are generally recovered only from burials (Black 1979:table 57; see also Price and Griffin 1979). Other types of ves-

Table 8-5. Occurrence of Vessel Forms, Rim and Body Decoration, and Appendages and Bases in the Powers Phase Ceramic Assemblages

	Jars		Bowls				Bottles		
			Flared Rim		Effigy	Incurved			
	Large	Small	Large	Small		Rim	Short	Medium	Long
Rim and body decoration									
Notching[a]	X	X	O	X	-	O	-	-	-
Incising[a]	O	O	-	X	O	-	-	O	-
Punctating[a]	-	X	-	O	-	-	-	O	-
Painting	-	O	-	X	-	-	-	-	O
Noding	-	O	-	O	-	X	-	-	-
Scalloping	-	-	-	X	-	-	-	-	-
Engraving	-	-	-	O	-	-	-	-	-
Appliquéing	-	O	-	-	-	-	-	-	-
Appendages and bases									
Loop handle	-	O	-	-	-	-	-	-	-
Strap handle	X	X	-	-	-	-	-	-	-
Lug handle	O	-	-	-	-	-	-	-	-
Tabtail	-	-	-	-	X	O	-	-	-
Effigy	-	-	-	-	X	-	-	-	-
Ring/tripod/ annular base	-	-	-	-	-	-	-	X	X
Flat base	-	-	X	X	O	-	-	-	-
Round base	-	-	-	-	-	-	O	-	-

Note: X, frequent; O, present.
[a]Notching occurs exclusively on rims, while incising and punctations occur on the shoulders of jars and on the interior and/or exterior of flared rim bowls.

sel forms, such as bottles, effigy bowls, and incurved-rim bowls, are also rare in domestic contexts and are most likely to be found in burial contexts; bottles with medium to long necks are restricted to Powers-phase burials.

Incised jar sherds are not common in the Powers Fort collection; the few provenienced sherds were found in Area D, the large midden southeast of Mound 4 (Table 8-6). Incising on large and small jars from other Powers-phase sites generally is restricted to three lines in a rectilinear, chevron design placed on the vessel shoulders (Price and Griffin 1979:plate 14; Smith 1978a:plate VII, *g, h*). These sherds and vessels belong in the category Matthews Incised, *var.*

Table 8-6. Decorative Elements on Shell-Tempered Pottery from Powers Fort

Decorative Element	N	%	A	B	C	D	E	F	G	General
Noded rim	2	4.2				X				X
Notched lip	4	8.3	X							
Tabtail	1	2.1	X							
Effigy	1	2.1				X				
Incision	2	4.2				X				X
Applique	1	2.1				X				
Punctation	1	2.1	X							
Painted sunburst	2	4.2				X	X			
Black painted	1	2.1					X[a]			
Interior engraved	1	2.1					X[a]			
Stamped	2	4.2								X
Fabric impressed	1	2.1								X
Red filmed	29	60.4	X		X	X	X		X	
Total	48	100.2								

[a]Reported from Area E (Price 1978:217–18).

Matthews (D. F. Morse and P. [A.] Morse 1990; Phillips 1970). Punctated sherds of the type Manly Punctated (Phillips et al. 1951:147) are from small jars decorated on the upper shoulders. The decorative motifs represented include rows of punctations bordered by vertical incised lines. An interior-engraved, flared-rim bowl sherd, probably of O'Byam Incised (Phillips 1970:144), was found on the surface in Area E. Vessels of this type were common in the Cairo Lowland during the Middle Mississippian period (see Lewis 1982, 1990).

Sherds with exotic painted red sunbursts and painted black sherds have been found only in areas D and E. It is possible that vessels with this kind of elaborate surface treatment originated in northeastern Arkansas (Belmont and Williams 1981; Morse and Morse 1983), but ceramic-provenience studies with petrographic or chemical analyses have not been conducted. Painted sunburst and sun-circle designs are found on Carson Red-on-Buff (Phillips et al. 1951:132–33) and Nodena Red-and-White (Phillips et al. 1951:133–34) bottles. A complete Carson Red-on-Buff bottle was excavated by Koehler from a burial within the ditched area, but its exact provenience is unknown.

Other decorated sherds are primarily from Area A (Table 8-6); that area also yielded the largest sherd sample from Powers Fort (Table 8-4). Several sherds from Area A exhibit rim notching, which is the most common decorative element in the Powers Fort ceramic assemblage. This observation also holds true for the ceramic assemblage from Snodgrass (Price and Griffin 1979:116–38). A large notched-rim jar was also recovered at Gypsy Joint in the fill of Structure 2 (Smith 1978a:57).

In addition to the two bottles and single jar recovered from burials 1, 2, and 5 excavated by Price, the Koehler collection includes a jar with a single perforated lug handle, a flared-rim bowl with rim notches (type 1 notching [Price and Griffin 1979:117, figure 63, *a*]), nine bottles, and a globular-body miniature bottle only 7.8 centimeters high (Figure 8-8). Long-neck bottles are more common in the collection than are short-neck bottles. The former generally have flattened bodies and bases, and the latter have globular bodies and round bases. Measurements of the whole vessels from Powers Fort (as well as vessel-size data from other Powers-phase sites) indicate that body diameter ranges from 12 centimeters to 16 centimeters for both bottle forms; height varies from 14 centimeters to 17 centimeters for short-neck forms and from 18 centimeters to 27 centimeters for long-neck forms. One of the bottles is of the type Carson Red-on-Buff (Figure 8-8, *c*) and has a carinated body, a flat circular base, and a long, narrow neck. There are sun circles on the body, in conjunction with painted vertical lines on the lower panel, and sun circles on the upper body panel. On the bottle neck, the lower panel has sun circles and the upper panel has vertical red lines.

Other types of ceramic artifacts occur in the Koehler collection from Powers Fort. These include a flat-handled pottery trowel, a single-holed pottery disc, earspools, and a single clay bead.

Lithic Artifacts

Stone does not occur naturally in the lowland sector of the Little Black River watershed. Chert, quartzite, and sandstone are, however, locally available in gravel deposits and outcrops of the Ordovician Gasconade, Roubidoux, and Jefferson City formations (Ray 1985:229–35) and could have been collected along the Ozark Escarpment. Cherts from these formations are sometimes grainy in texture, and there are frequent vugs, quartz crystals, and quartzose patches that limit their uses (McCutcheon and Dunnell, Chapter 11). Quartzite from the Roubidoux formation likewise has a grainy texture, though there is considerable variability in knapping quality. Rhyolite and igneous greenstone from Precambrian deposits in southeastern Missouri probably occur naturally in small quantities in the Little Black and Black river gravels (Perttula 1984; Ray 1985). These local raw materials account for more than 97 percent of the stone tools and debris in the Powers Fort lithic assemblage (Table 8-7).

Lithic raw materials clearly of nonlocal derivation have been found only in limited quantities at Powers Fort. While some of this exotic material has not been identified to particular source areas, Pitkin and Mill Creek cherts are rep-

192 | Perttula

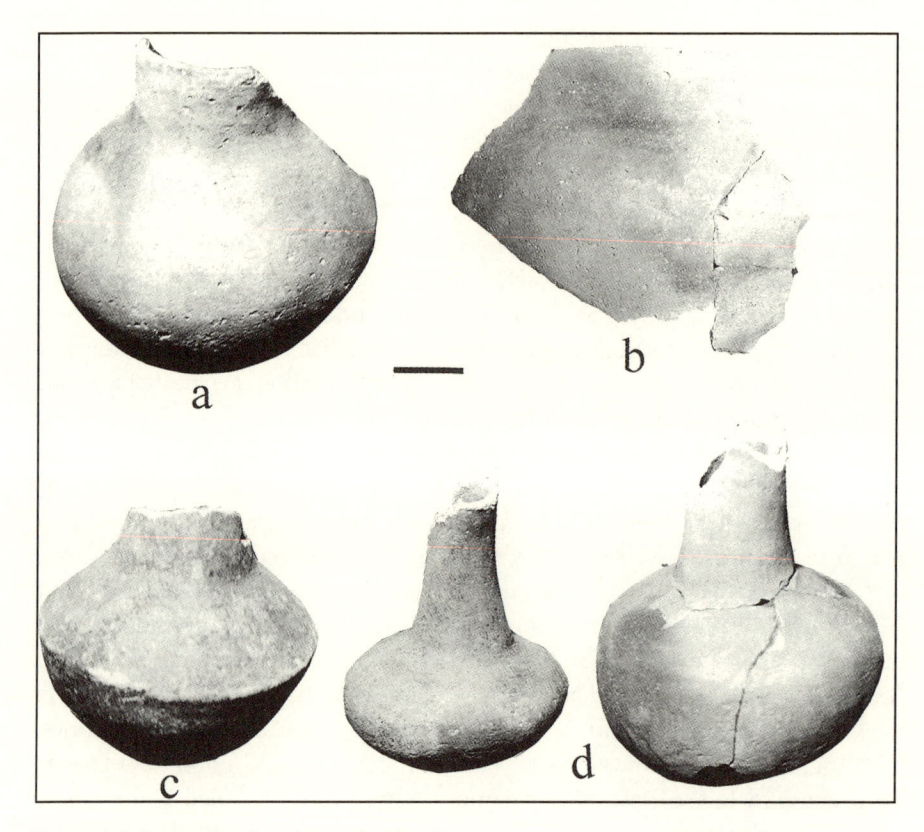

Figure 8-8. Large sherd and vessels from Powers Fort: *a*, short-neck, shell-tempered bottle; *b*, plain, shell-tempered jar rim from Structure 1; *c*, Carson Red-on-Buff bottle; *d*, long-neck, shell-tempered bottles. Specimens *a, c,* and *d,* Koehler collection; *b*, general surface collection. *Scale bar* = 5 centimeters.

resented in the debris (Table 8-7) and tool assemblage. The highest use of quartzite and rhyolite occurred during the Late Archaic period in the Ozark border area. About 3 percent of the Powers-phase arrow points were made from quartzite; no points were made from rhyolite.

Between 1 and 3 percent of the dart points and arrow points from the site were manufactured from nonlocal Pitkin and Dover chert, and several hoe chips and a reworked hoe are of Mill Creek chert, the source area for which is in Union County, Illinois (Philips 1900), more than 150 kilometers away. Pitkin chert occurs in outcrops across the Ozark Highlands area of northeastern Arkansas. Dover chert is found in Mississippian-age formations in the lower Tennessee and Cumberland valleys of Tennessee and Kentucky.

Material used to manufacture one of the side-notched arrow points in the Koehler collection closely resembles Sallisaw chert, common in lithic sources in the western Ozark Highlands and in the Arkansas Basin of Oklahoma (Banks

Table 8-7. Percentages of Raw Materials in Lithic Assemblages from Five Surface-Collected Areas at Powers Fort

Area	Chert Unidentified	Chert Mill Creek	Chert Pitkin	Quartzite	Rhyolite	Quartz	Greenstone
A	78	T	T	21	1	T	T
B	72	-	-	25	-	-	3
C	83	-	-	17	-	-	-
D	76	-	-	24	-	-	T
G	77	T	-	22	-	-	T

Note: T, Less than 1 percent.

1990). However, Price and Price (1984:40) note the presence of an apparently local high-quality, light-gray chert in the lithic-artifact assemblage from the Late Woodland–Early Mississippian–period Shell Lake site on the St. Francis River northeast of Powers Fort.

Lithic artifacts from excavated Powers-phase contexts at Powers Fort include a variety of chipped-stone and groundstone tools and debris (Table 8-8). Unmodified cobbles, tested cobbles, cores, and relatively abundant lithic debris indicate that the procurement and reduction of locally available lithic raw materials for the production of stone tools were important activities in Middle Mississippian–period times at the site.

The chipped-stone tools produced include arrow points (from flake arrow-point preforms), cylindrical drills, and used flakes, along with bifacially flaked, willowleaf-shaped knives (Price and Griffin 1979:21–22). Hoes of Mill Creek and Dover chert were obtained by Powers-phase groups in completed form, and hoe chips and reworked tools (small chisels and adzes) of these materials are present in limited amounts in the Powers Fort surface collections.

Greenstone (or green granite) celts, axes, and hoes are present in the groundstone-tool assemblage from the site; they may have been used for such tasks as wood working and cultivation. Although there may be some ice-rafted greenstone boulders in the Powers-phase area, the extremely limited amount of greenstone lithic debris (Table 8-7) suggests these tools were brought to Powers Fort in completed form.

Anvil stones, pitted cobbles, ground cobbles, and grooved abraders used in food preparation and tool production and maintenance activities were made of the locally available Ozark Highlands sandstone. These tools are common in Powers-phase household contexts (see Price 1969:13–15; Price and Griffin 1979) but are also present in Early Mississippian, Woodland, and Archaic deposits in the Little Black River area.

Table 8-8. Lithic Artifacts from Excavated Contexts at Powers Fort

Artifact Class	1964	1969	Burials 2–4
Unmodified cobbles	-	7	-
Tested cobbles	8	1	-
Lithic debris	48	148	4
Cores	1	7	-
Thin bifaces	2	2	-
Dart points	3	4	3
Arrow points	1	20	5
Arrow-point preforms	-	1	-
Unifaces	-	2	-
Drills	-	3	1
Hammerstones	-	3	-
Anvil stones	-	1	-
Pitted cobbles	-	1	-
Ground cobbles	1	4	-
Grooved abraders	1	-	-
Total	65	204	13

On the basis of the kinds of lithic tools found in extensive excavations at other Powers-phase sites in the Naylor area (Lynott 1991; Price and Griffin 1979; Smith 1978a), some 435 lithic tools from the surface of Powers Fort can reasonably be assigned to the Middle Mississippian Powers-phase occupation (Table 8-9). Excluding those from general provenience, the highest frequencies of tools are from two different domestic contexts—areas A and D (Figure 8-5). Few tools have been recovered from mounds (areas B and H), the plaza (area F), or the ridge between mounds 1 and 2 (Area E). Areas C and G, known to have Powers-phase structures, produced few tools and low numbers of arrow points compared with areas A and D. Analogous tool distributions from Snodgrass led Price and Griffin (1979:58) to suggest that "the scarcity of projectile points... would indicate that either very little hunting activity was conducted... or that this area was occupied for such a short time that very few projectile points were lost or discarded." Alternatively, the small number of projectile points might simply reflect the low likelihood of loss-in-use in certain residential areas.

Arrow points, arrow-point preforms, and unifacial tools comprise about 84 percent of the Powers-phase lithic tools from surface contexts. Drills and used flakes (and possibly the microlith) represent another 8 percent, with the remain-

Table 8-9. Powers Phase Lithic Tools from Surface Contexts at Powers Fort

Artifact Class	A	B	C	D	E	F	G	General	Koehler	1969 CSC
Hoes[a]	2	-	-	-	-	1	1	-	-	-
Adzes	1	-	-	-	-	-	-	-	9	1[b]
Celts	1	-	-	-	-	-	1	-	1	-
Axes	1	-	-	-	-	-	-	-	4	-
Grooved abraders	1	-	-	-	-	-	-	-	-	-
Arrow points	14	2	2	2	1	-	-	42	218	-
Arrow-point preforms	10	1	-	3	-	-	1	-	26	5
Drills	3	-	1	-	-	-	-	1	12	-
Microliths	1	-	-	-	-	-	-	-	-	-
Used flakes	-	-	1	1	-	-	1	-	-	-
Unifacial tools	26	2	-	14	-	3	1	-	8	8
Discoidals	-	-	-	-	-	-	-	-	1	-
Total	60	5	4	20	1	4	5	43	279	14

Note: CSC, controlled surface collections.
[a]Hoe chips from Mill Creek chert hoes.
[b]From reworked Mill Creek chert hoe.

der comprising groundstone tools and hoe chips. The arrow points are quite similar to those from Snodgrass (Price and Griffin 1979) and Turner (Lynott 1991) in that they have corner notches; serrated, ovate blades; and comparable lengths, blade lengths, and neck widths. At Snodgrass, 5 percent of the 156 arrow points are triangular, 1 percent are willowleaf shaped, 34 percent are stemmed, and 60 percent are corner notched (Price and Griffin 1979:appendix C). Lynott's (1991) analysis of the 185 Turner arrow points shows more diversity: approximately 3 percent are triangular, 59 percent stemmed, 9 percent side-notched, and 29 percent corner-notched. Forms represented among the 197 arrow points from Powers Fort are triangular (8 percent), willowleaf shaped (less than 1 percent), stemmed (33 percent), side notched (12 percent), and corner notched (47 percent).

Discussion

Powers Fort is the westernmost of the large Middle Mississippian–period sites in southeastern Missouri that contain mounds and/or palisades (Figure 8-9). Powers Fort, at 4.4 hectares, is the smallest of the sites, with only Peter Bess

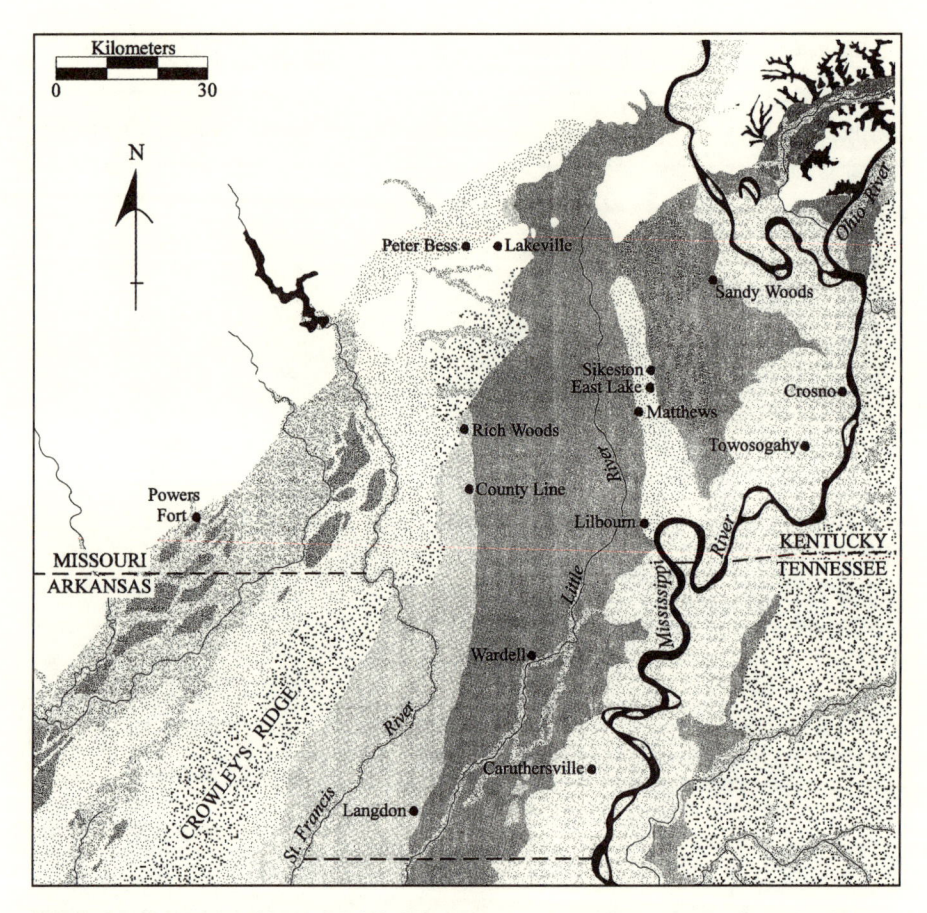

Figure 8-9. Locations of large Middle Mississippian–period sites in southeastern Missouri that contain mounds and/or palisades.

(4.8 hectares) and Lakeville (6.4 hectares), both in the Advance Lowland (Figure 8-1), being of similar size. The Powers phase is represented by a number of contemporaneous villages, hamlets, farmsteads, and hunting-gathering camps spread over a 5- to 15-kilometer area around Powers Fort (see Price and Griffin 1979:figure 3), the larger of which are shown in Figure 8-2. The villages and subsidiary sites were occupied for only short periods—perhaps less than five years for even the large villages such as Snodgrass and Turner—and then were cyclically abandoned and burned. Powers Fort, on the other hand, appears to have maintained a substantial population for the entire span of the Powers phase (ca. A.D. 1250–1350).

Prior to the Powers-phase occupation, the sand ridges in the alluvial lowlands of the Little Black River area were not heavily exploited or settled by local populations. Archaic through Early Mississippian groups maintained camps, houses, and small villages principally along the Little Black River, on the flanks of the Ozark Escarpment, and for some distance along the major valleys draining into the Western Lowlands, such as those of the Current, Eleven Point, and Black rivers (Lynott 1989, 1991; Price and Price 1981, 1984).

As Lynott (1991) recently noted, the Middle Mississippian–period settlement of the sand ridges after about A.D. 1250 closely corresponded with an apparent abandonment of the Eastern Ozarks by Mississippian groups and with "the florescence of Mississippian towns and ceremonial centers in the Bootheel region of southeast Missouri" (Lynott 1991:198). Furthermore, A.D. 1250 was approximately the beginning of the period when maize cultivation by Mississippian peoples attained dietary significance (Lynott et al. 1986; Rose et al. 1991; see also Greenlee, Chapter 13). Thus, it appears to be the case that the development of maize-based agricultural economies in the central Mississippi Valley led local communities to select residential locations in the Western Lowlands where the soil was suitable, at least initially, for agricultural pursuits. Such areas included sand ridges in the Little Black watershed and river levees in areas to the south, west, and east (D. F. Morse and P. [A.] Morse 1990; Price 1974).

The formation of nucleated communities such as those in the Powers phase may have drawn from several population sources, including Early Mississippian populations already in the Western Lowlands and peoples "who moved out of the hills [Eastern Ozarks] to become farmers in the towns and hamlets of the Powers phase" (Lynott 1991:198). Price and Griffin (1979:3) propose that the Powers-phase settlement was a colonization of "fully developed" Middle Mississippian groups from the central Mississippi Valley (the Cairo Lowland) as opposed to an indigenous development. This position, while not without challenges (see Morse and Morse 1983), is consistent with the relatively limited and dispersed Late Woodland–Early Mississippian population in the local area and with the apparently rapid and considerable population increases documented in the Western Lowlands after about A.D. 1250.

Evidence of a substantial population at Powers Fort is provided by the several hundred house stains that have been noted informally in areas A, D, G, and H and the presence of a large midden area in Area D. As a rule, midden deposits are virtually nonexistent in Powers-phase villages and hamlets because of their short occupations. Although only portions of three structures have been excavated at Powers Fort, two of them yielded evidence for two to four rebuilding episodes, suggesting that certain structures at the site had occupation spans upwards of 40 to 80 years (see Pauketat 1989). The lack of structure repair or rebuilding at Snodgrass and Turner is notable (Price and Griffin 1979:53).

On the basis of the placement of mounds, the surface evidence for houses and middens, limited excavations of houses and burials, and the character of stone and ceramic artifacts from various areas of the site, the internal structure of the Powers Fort site appears clear. First, residential and domestic use of the

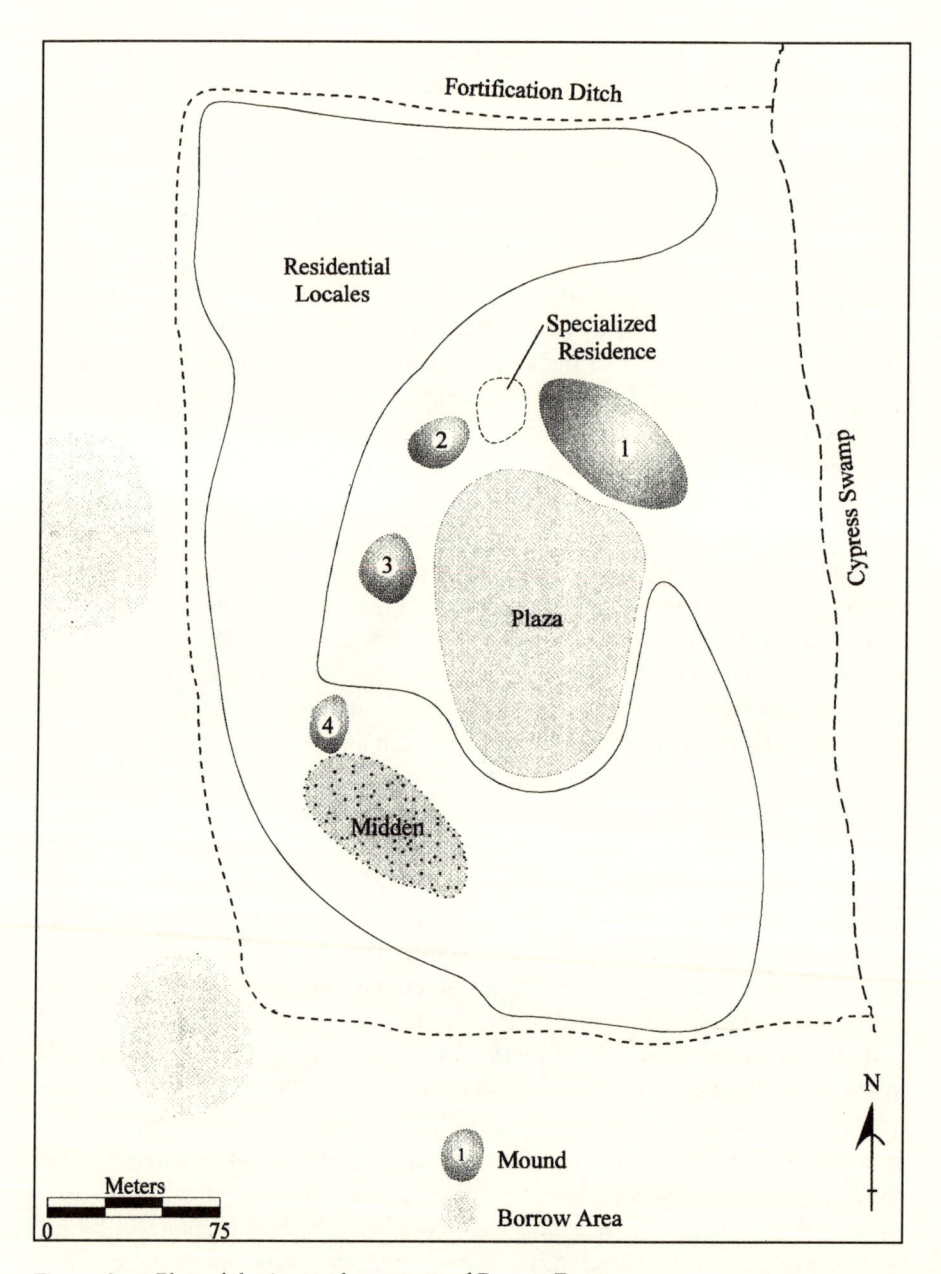

Figure 8-10. Plan of the internal structure of Powers Fort.

site was apparently concentrated in several bands from the embankment/ditch to near the mounds, primarily in areas A, D, G, and H (Figure 8-10). The structures are believed to have been in rows that visually were aligned with mounds 2 through 4 and the embankment/ditch. Price estimated conservatively that some 400 domestic structures might be present at the site, and these would probably be surrounded by refuse pits, areas of midden, and burials. The large midden area in Area D, adjacent to Mound 4, might represent refuse from activities conducted during the latter end of the Powers-phase occupation, or it might indicate that the residential occupation of Area D was principally early in the phase.

The large platform mound and three subsidiary mounds flank an apparent plaza covering about 100 × 60 meters; despite years of surface collecting, little Powers-phase refuse has been recovered from that area. In addition to the specialized structures apparently present on several platform stages within Mound 1 (see Figure 8-4), another large specialized structure might have been present on a narrow sand ridge between mounds 1 and 2 (Price 1978). It is possible that there also were structures in mounds 2 through 4, since descriptions by Norris (1883) of the human remains and burials within those mounds suggest that the burials were disarticulated. Extended and bundle burials of adults are known from the residential sectors, and infant burials have been recovered from Structure 1 in Area D.

This summary should make plain that, at best, only the broadest understanding of the development and internal temporal and functional character of Powers Fort has been realized. Systematic recording is needed of the often-reported surface evidence for structures, structure rows, compound walls, middens, and features. Then, those settlement data can be better associated with the distribution of material culture remains within the fortified center. Because the site was well protected by the landowner from 1908 to 1978 and is now an archaeological preserve, the site still holds tremendous research possibilities.

Acknowledgments

J. E. Price provided me the opportunity to study the Powers Fort collection in 1980-1982 and made available all notes and files on Powers Fort. Many of the figures in this chapter were redrafted by G. Blow from originals prepared by Price. B. D. Smith supplied information about possible Powers Fort artifacts in the Smithsonian Institution, and R. C. Dunnell provided aerial information about the site and commented on earlier versions of this chapter. I am grateful to D. E. Wilson for providing me with a copy of her master's thesis on the Powers phase.

9 | The Langdon Site, Dunklin County, Missouri
Robert C. Dunnell

LANGDON IS A large Mississippian-period, fortified settlement on the edge of the Malden Plain in southern Dunklin County, Missouri. The Malden Plain is an erosional remnant of Pleistocene braided-stream deposits (O'Brien and Dunnell, Chapter 1) that flanks the eastern edge of Crowley's Ridge, extending from Dexter, Missouri, well into Arkansas, where the deposits are buried by more-recent alluvium of the meandering Mississippi River. Standing as much as 5 meters above the Mississippi floodplain, the Missouri portion of the plain was a fairly dry haven in an otherwise swampy morass. Consequently, it attracted settlement during both the prehistoric and historical periods (Van Frank 1891). The archaeological record of the Malden Plain is not particularly well known. The area was isolated from settlement and commerce related to the Mississippi River by as much as 50 kilometers of swamp until drainage ditches and the first hard-surfaced road to Hayti, in Pemiscot County, Missouri, were completed in 1917 (Bratton 1926).

Before that time, connection with the outside world was principally by boat through the Little River–St. Francis river systems for southern Dunklin County and, after 1877, by rail by way of Dexter for Stoddard County, Missouri, and northern Dunklin County (Bradley 1951). As a result of this isolation, archaeological resources of the area were overlooked by most early investigators. Following Crowley's Ridge south, Cyrus Thomas's archaeological scouts, in this area I. H. Thing, recorded two important sites: Rich Woods, an enormous Mississippian site with at least thirty-two mounds (Figure 9-1), and County Line, a ditched Mississippian enclosure apparently without mounds (Thomas 1894:174–83; see also Leeds 1979; Teltser 1988, 1992) (Figure 9-1). Despite the obvious promise of the region, Thing found conditions in southeastern Missouri and northeastern Arkansas too unbearable to persist, as witnessed by his correspondence with Thomas: "As the water there was very high, I abandoned work there entirely. I was obliged to take my specimens to the railroad in a dug out.... I could have found some whole pots there (Webb Place), but as soon as I dug a hole it would fill with water and I could not see what I was doing" (Thing to Thomas 1883[1]). Indeed, everywhere Thing went he was faced with water, and all of his letters to Thomas make mention of the problems for collecting and transporting thus posed.

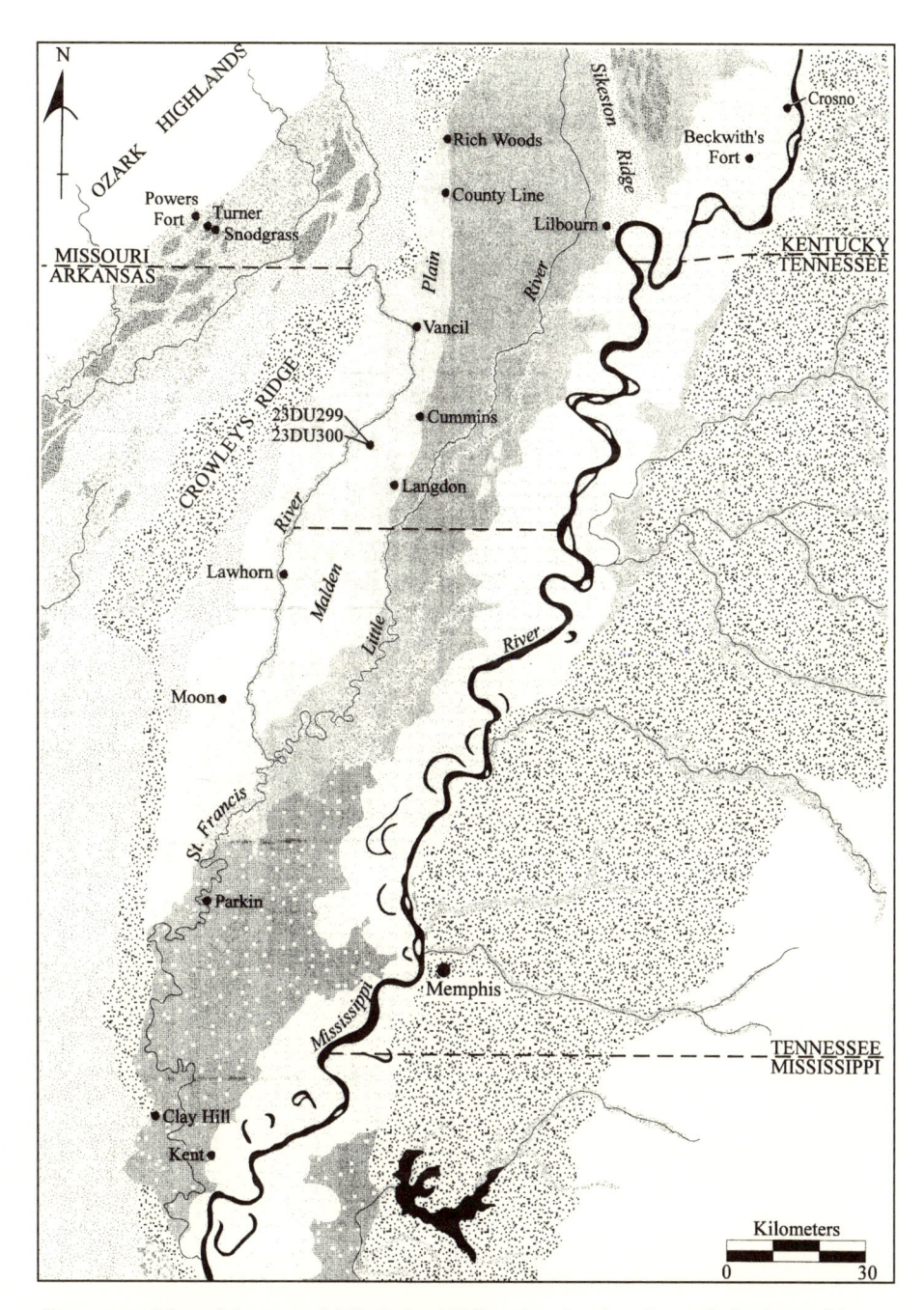

Figure 9-1. Map of the central Mississippi Valley showing locations of physiographic features and archaeological sites mentioned in the text.

The Malden Plain likewise was spared the attentions of Clarence B. Moore, though the reasons, albeit related to the isolated nature of the area, were somewhat different:

> It was not possible to take on the St. Francis above its union with the Little River.... Our quest... on Little River... came to an end owing to the hostility against negroes, entertained by the natives along the river above Lepanto, who maintained a negro deadline, permitting no colored person go among them. As this race prejudice has resulted in the murder of a number of negroes, we did not deem it fair to expose to slaughter men who had served us faithfully for years. (Moore 1910:256)

Langdon was well known locally from the earliest European settlement in the 1830s. The site was bisected by the main north-south road connecting Kennett, the county seat, and Hornersville, the "port" of the county and the northernmost navigable point on Little River. The main pyramidal mound at Langdon lay only a few meters east of the thoroughfare and from the 1880s onward was the site of the residence of one of south Dunklin County's leading families. Local histories (e.g., Smith-Davis 1896:12) take note of all major mound groups, including Langdon. The first extralocal account of Langdon and other major sites of the southern Malden Plain, however, was published in Louis Houck's *A History of Missouri* (1908). Houck commissioned two men, Lewis M. Bean and D. L. Hoffman, to "accurately and definitively locate every mound and settlement of the[se] prehistoric denizens of the state" (Houck 1908:41) before they were obliterated by "the plowshare and the ignorance of destroying man" (Houck 1908:41). All of the Dunklin County works are relegated to a single footnote, where the Langdon site occasions little more description than "abundant pottery," "5 mounds," and an accurate Public Lands System location (Houck 1908:64).

The Missouri Historical Society in St. Louis accepted a small lot of pots from Langdon shortly after 1892, only three of which have been located as of this writing. Although the circumstances of discovery do not appear in the records unearthed to date, pothunters seem the only likely source. There is no reason, however, to suppose that Langdon was ever "mined" for its pottery, as were so many southeastern-Missouri sites in the late nineteenth and twentieth centuries (O'Brien and Dunnell, Chapter 1). Such an event surely would not have escaped family notice, and there is no tradition of such activity. (By way of contrast, the nearby Vancil site [Figure 9-1], of comparable age and size, is reported to have been rented in the winter during the 1960s by commercial collectors from St. Francisville, Arkansas.) Various family members potted the site over the years, resulting in the dispersal of small collections to various locations; at most, a few afternoons of digging are indicated. Everett J. Langdon, owner of the eastern two-thirds of the site from the 1920s until his death in 1990, kept a collection of items encountered on the surface of the site during farming, but when his collection was stolen in the early 1950s, his interest waned as did his tolerance of even "off-season" collectors, effectively protecting the main body of the site for the past 40 years. The owners of the western portion of the site, the W. L. Davidsons, also were aggressive protectors of the resource.

The first mention of Langdon in the archaeological literature proper is a reference in passing to "spectacular mound groups in Southeast Missouri" by Robert M. Adams and Winslow Walker (1942:7): "five miles north of the Arkansas border, in Dunklin County, lies a large mound group, the Langdon site. It is on a sand ridge between the Little and St. Francis Rivers. This is a large mound group, the largest mound, a truncate, having been cut down for the construction of a farm house." Characterizing the Malden Plain as "a sand ridge between the Little and St. Francis Rivers," makes it clear that Adams and Walker received their initial information from Houck (1908), where that very phrase, more appropriate to a statewide scale, is used. Notation of the presence of a house and that the mound had been cut down to accommodate it suggests they actually visited the site and spoke with then-owner E. J. Langdon. (Langdon confirmed to me that the top of the mound was removed by his father, C. V. Langdon, around 1884. More was removed when the house was rebuilt to its present form in 1923; the basement, which occupies much of the mound, was apparently dug somewhat later.) Langdon recalled that personnel from the Works Progress Administration (which employed Adams) visited the site in the late 1930s, seeking permission to excavate, but their request was denied.

Despite being characterized as a large and spectacular mound group, there is only one map of the site, this being a sketch map in Stephen Williams's doctoral dissertation (Williams 1954:180) made some 125 years after Langdon had first been put into continuous cultivation. Williams's sketch map (Figure 9-2) is too crude to place the site on the modern landscape (e.g., the county road is over a hundred feet wide if the scales are to be believed; the escarpment does not turn west north of the site), but it suggests the presence of five separate mounds around a "plaza." Williams was also the first person to attempt to quantify the epithet "large" applied to Langdon by early commentators. He characterized it as the largest site on the southern Malden Plain and set its extent at approximately 27 acres. Although the means by which the measurements were made were not given, Williams's map also supplies heights for all of the mounds. Williams made collections at most sites he reported from the general area, but no collections are reported from Langdon. It was Langdon's quaint recollection that "the Harvard boys did not get far from the car." In the subsequent forty years, although occasionally mentioned, nothing substantial has been added to our knowledge of this major Mississippian-period settlement.

204 | Dunnell

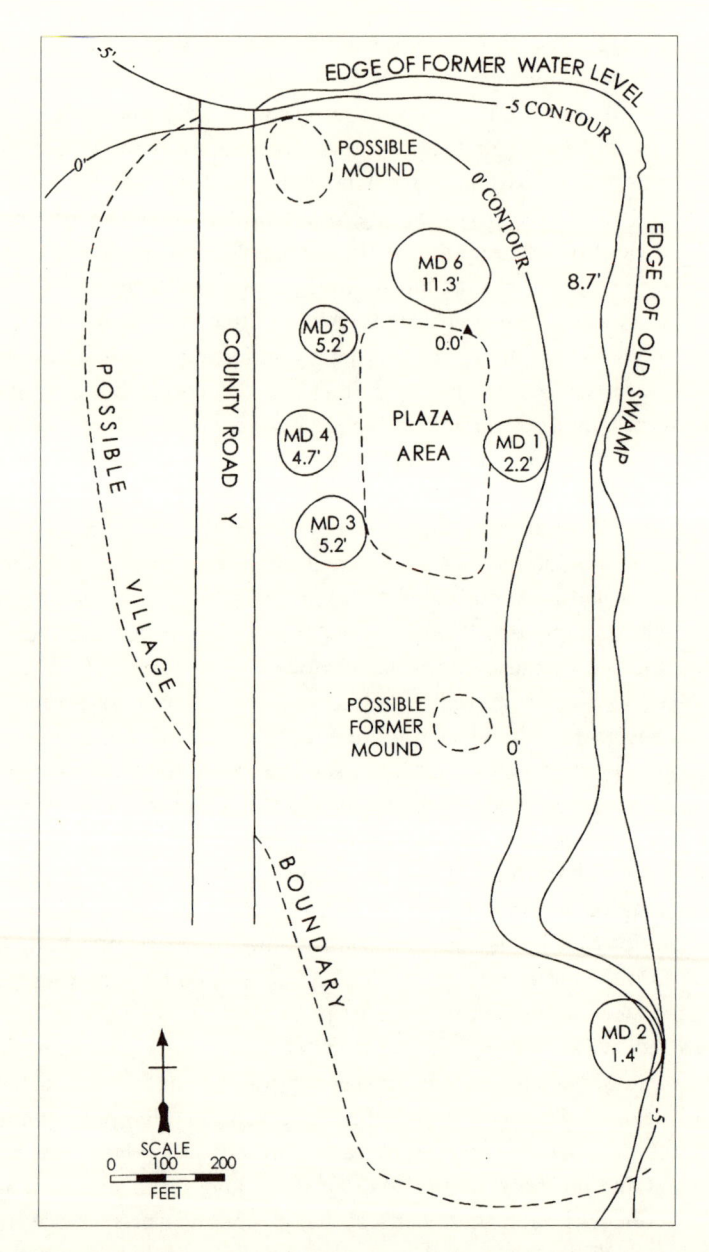

Figure 9-2. Stephen Williams's map of the Langdon site, 1954. From Williams's discussion and map (1954:180, figure 44), it is unclear whether his Mound 2 is actually part of the Langdon group or is the isolated mound south of the group extant today. E. J. Langdon recalled having the edge of the escarpment leveled, not so much to remove the mounds as to obtain fill for developing ravines.

Recent Investigations

My own investigations of the Langdon site began in 1983 after my wife and I acquired the western third of the site. The major effort ceased in 1987. An average of two and a half days with four assistants was spent at Langdon in each of five years. Brief efforts since then have been directed at filling minor gaps in the data generated between 1983 and 1987. Except for the extraction of a number of small-diameter cores, these investigations have been entirely noninvasive. Because it was not clear that access to the eastern property would be forthcoming after it passed from E. J. Langdon, the main effort was directed at acquiring the maximum amount of information as quickly as possible. This worry has proved to be unfounded, as the present owner, Joe S. Langdon, has been extraordinarily generous and patient with my archaeological work; nonetheless, the result has been that data acquisition has far outstripped analysis.

The primary task in this "salvage" setting was to create a topographic map of the site as it now exists, after some 160 years of continuous cultivation (Figure 9-3). In addition, several areas of the site were surface collected (all units were 4 × 4 meters) (Figure 9-3). Much higher artifact densities (frequently more than 1000 artifacts per collection unit) on the east side of the road—perhaps reflecting more-intensive occupation (or trash disposal) there—made extensive collection impractical. Transects were used in the hope of generating data on spatial structure, but being transects, they are wholly inadequate to estimate artifact-population parameters, even though well over 25,000 artifacts are involved in the collection-unit data.

Both the eastern and western sides of the site were traversed by sediment-sample transects (Figure 9-3). Samples from eastern transects weighed 0.5 to 1.5 kilograms each; given the large numbers of artifacts present, they can be used to make density estimates for the main components of the midden (bone, shell, pottery, architectural debris, and lithic material). In addition, several magnetometry transects were placed across the edges of the site as well as across interior features (Figure 9-3). The only subsurface data consist of thirty-four three-quarter-inch-diameter cores that were taken to ascertain the structure and depth of both the midden and the smaller mounds (Figure 9-3).

Site Structure

The most informative source of data on the nature of Langdon is aerial photographs, mostly 1:20,000 black-and-white coverage by the Soil Conservation Service. Coverage began in 1937 (Figure 9-4). Although there are directional changes evident in the photographs, most differences are seasonal or pertain to specific moisture/crop conditions. Langdon still has a striking soil signature, particularly on the northern edge where the underlying sediments are sandy,

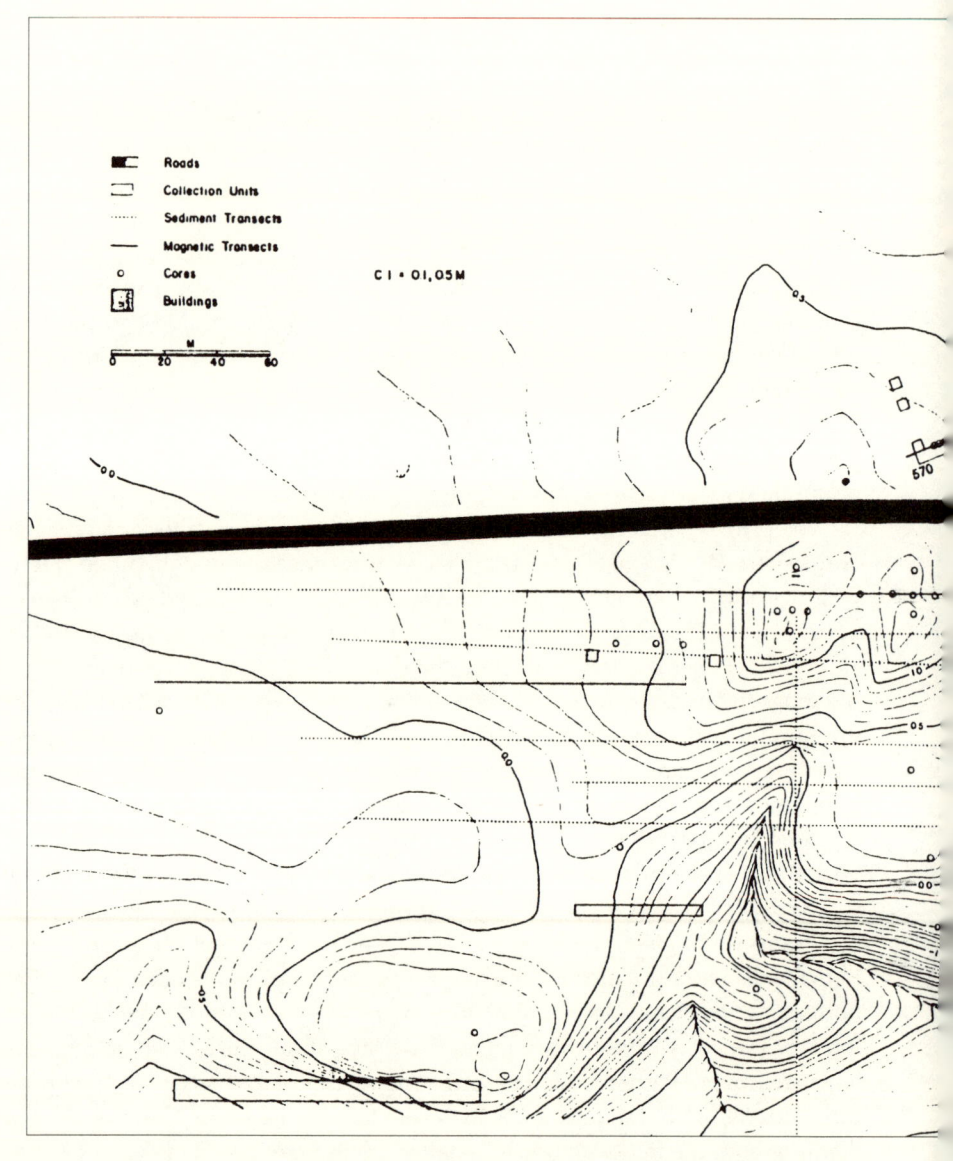

Figure 9-3. The 1985–1987 Langdon topographic map showing the location of recent investigations. Note that the contour interval (C.I.) is 0.1 meter except on the main mound where it is 0.5 meter.

but in most photographs (Figure 9-5) one sees a crop signature caused by enhanced phosphorus, mostly generated by decomposed bone (Dunnell 1993).

The photographs leave little doubt about the general nature of the site. It is a rectangular, fortified settlement, with the long axis oriented with the Malden Plain escarpment, which forms its eastern boundary. Wet-field photographs

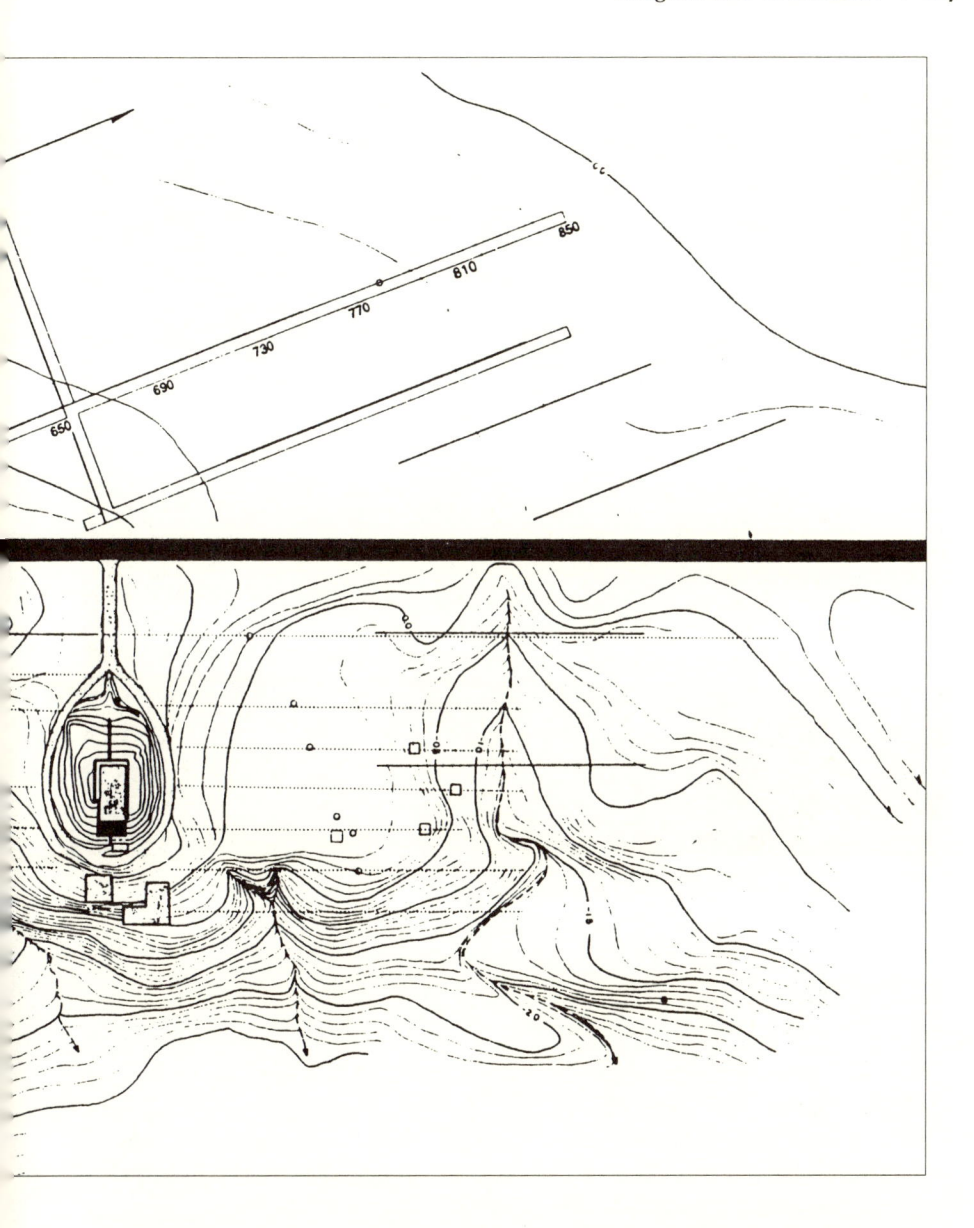

(Figure 9-5, *b*) show the site to be raised above its surroundings; the former ditch is still marked by a series of puddles. The aerial pattern is consistent with an exterior ditch and an interior wall—an exterior dark strip followed by a lighter band and then by the dark body of the settlement per se.

Data on the distribution of artifacts along the long north-south transect of the west field confirm these general observations (Figure 9-6). There is an abrupt increase in the amount of artifactual material as one crosses the boundary of the site as seen in the aerial photographs, at approximately meter 770 in the tran-

Figure 9-4. June 1937 Soil Conservation Service black-and-white aerial photograph (north at *top;* scale is 1:20,000) showing Langdon as a walled rectangle. Note the abandoned channel of the Little River just east of the escarpment; rendition is a mixed soil-and-crop mark.

sect. There is a strong peak in burned sediment (labeled *Blumps* on Figure 9-6) at the boundary, corresponding to the light band marking the fortifications, which apparently were burned at that location. There is another strong peak in Blumps, correlated with a daub peak, where one would anticipate houses. Since daub is differentiated from burned sediment in the analysis shown in Figure 9-6 solely by the presence of wattle impressions on the former, the lower daub/Blumps ratio in the peripheral band indicates either that the daub on the fortifications was much thicker than that on house walls or that support construction differed somewhat between the two kinds of structures. In some but not all locations, there is a strong magnetic signature as well, the strength of which is probably controlled by the presence or absence of burning. A circular dark/light structure seen at the southwest corner of the town may be a gate; more likely it is a natural feature. It has yet to be investigated.

In many regards, Langdon is an example of the "St. Francis-type settlement" of Phillips et al. (1951), differing only from the classic settlements of the lower St. Francis River by encompassing a much larger area while being less elevated. Some ad hoc observations on artifact-size distributions help to clarify this element. In the western part of the enclosure, where the topographic differences are smallest, degradable-artifact (shell, bone, sherds) size is typically small, with occasional patches of larger artifacts. This distribution is consistent with a shallow midden now wholly or nearly contained within the plow zone. The patches of large objects mark subsurface features (Dunnell and Simek 1995). In many areas east of the road, however, large sherds and bones abound, bespeaking a deep midden continually supplying new material to the plow zone. In most places, the edge of the escarpment is somewhat rolling, but within the enclosure it is quite level (allowing for recent erosion arising from cultivation of the berm). These observations suggest that trash was used constructionally to raise the level of the ground near the edge of the escarpment and to level topographic inequities. This may well be a common phenomenon among Mississippian sites in the central Mississippi Valley and would explain why sites such as Crosno, in Mississippi County, Missouri (Figure 9-1) (Fox, Chapter 2), and Clay Hill, in Lee County, Arkansas (Figure 9-1) (House 1991:199), show evident layering in deep middens but without any marked or systematic differences in artifact content from top to bottom. The same photographs that reveal Langdon as a high topographic feature on a water-sodden terrain also supply a plausible rationale for such construction effort.

The mounds, save the principal mound, are not prominent features in the earliest aerial photographs. As plowing gradually reduced their height, it also exposed lighter-colored, finer-grained sediments in their cores so that they are increasingly well marked in later photographs (Figure 9-5). There are three apparent mounds just east of the road and south of the large mound. The light aerial signatures match the topographic highs quite closely and suggest, unlike the modern topography, that all three were more or less rectangular structures. Collectors reported the occurrence of considerable architectural debris associated with the northernmost mound summit, and this phenomenon is still evident today. Results of a magnetic survey across the mound are consistent with the presence of a burned structure (Figure 9-7). The same collectors reported finding unusually thick blocks of daub that contained human bones. Although there is no particular reason to doubt the reports, at least to the extent that some kind of bones were found in the daub, I have not been able to locate such a specimen in any collection, nor have such items come to light in the field.

Partly to explore these issues, six cores were driven through the northernmost structure in 1985 (Figure 9-3). The analysis of the cores is incomplete, but the central and longest core in this mound supplies some interesting information (Figure 9-8).[2] It is apparent that there are vertical differences in compo-

210 | *Dunnell*

Figure 9-5. Soil Conservation Service black-and-white aerial photographs (north at *top*; scale is 1:20,000) showing the Langdon site: *a,* November 1950—this rendition is almost entirely a soil mark, and although the contrast is subtle compared to that evident in Figure 9-4, it shows much more internal detail; *b,* July 1959—showing Langdon as a dry rectangle in otherwise wet fields. Note the water in the fortification ditches on the west and south.

sition, registered in particle size, chemistry (particularly carbonate, phosphorous, aluminum, iron, calcium, and potassium), and organic matter. While it is tempting to see constructional stages in this record, the same effects could have been brought about by loading in a single-stage construction. Correlation with other cores, which might have resolved this question, has proved difficult because most of them were taken from what probably were slopes of the structure. The most interesting result is that what looks to be an old surface in the lowermost four units of the core is well below the apparent base of the mound as indicated topographically. Indeed, it most closely corresponds to the general level of the occupation area, some 70 centimeters lower. Considering this evidence and topographic data (Figure 9-3), it appears that the three western mounds might all be part of the same structure; that is, although there are three separate platforms, they appear to have been built on a much larger platform, itself already a meter or so high. It might be argued that this is a spurious result caused by the agriculturally accelerated erosion of three mounds located close together. This can be ruled out, however, because the platform is perfectly evident on the west side of the road as well, and that field has not been connected to the east field for well over 160 years.

The main mound, while still the major topographic feature in southern Dunklin County, is nonetheless a shadow of its former self. As already noted, it was cut down twice to increase the size of the top for a house and yard (as well as to reduce the climb). Some claims for the reduction in height (e.g., 12 feet [3.7 meters]) are plainly fanciful. Minimally, the mound is a little more than 4 meters high today. Interestingly, it was constructed so as to have the appearance of being 8 meters high when approached from the open (east) side of the enclosure, because its eastern slope blends into the escarpment. To judge from the area said to have been filled with the spoil, it is reasonable to suppose that as much as 1.5 meters of the mound might have been removed. In any case, it is apparent that the mound was relatively tall for its base, more like the big mound

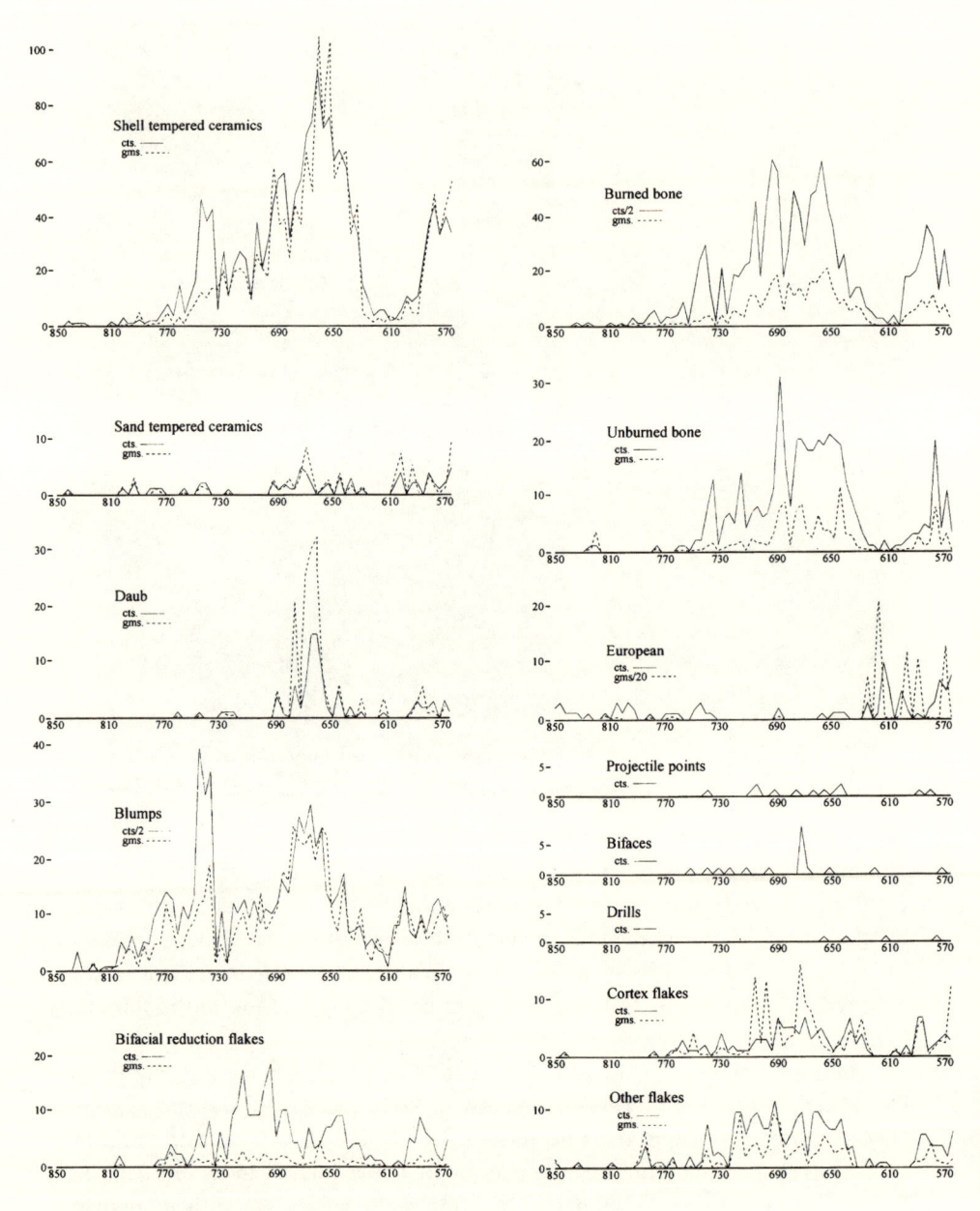

Figure 9-6. Artifact frequencies along the south-to-north transect west of the road at Langdon. The discrepancy between counts (*cts.*) and weights from X = 850 to X = 734 results from a misinterpretation of field protocol on the part of one collecting team (not done from standing position).

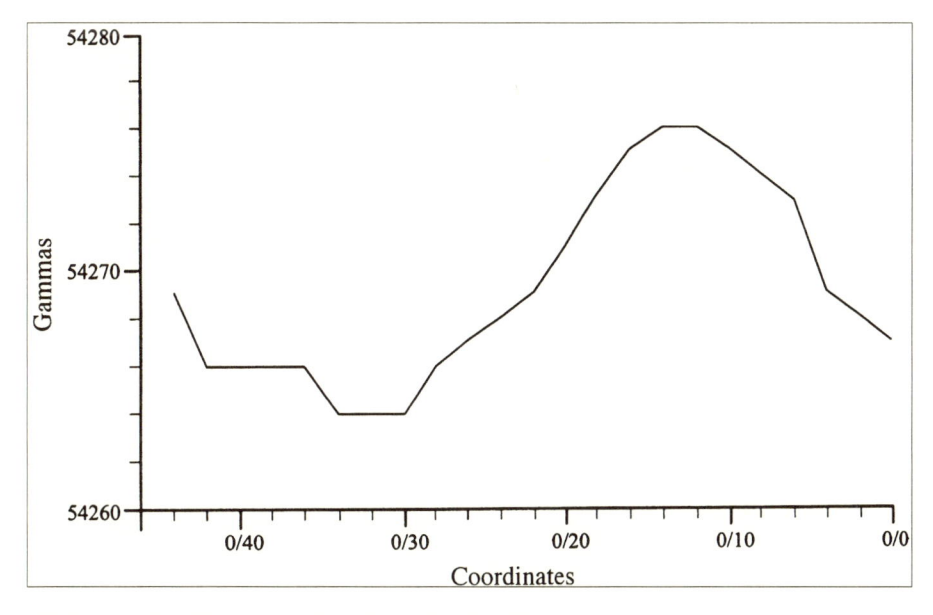

Figure 9-7. Magnetic transect (in meters) across the northernmost mound in the three-mound structure at Langdon (see Figure 9-3 for location of transect). That the mound shows as a large positive anomaly is undoubtedly a consequence of the large quantity of daub and other burned materials within the structure.

at Parkin, farther south in the St. Francis system (Figure 9-1) (Morse 1981), or the main mounds of the Kent phase (House 1991:252) than like the Cairo Lowland mounds such as those at Lilbourn (Chapman et al. 1977) and Beckwith's Fort (Price and Fox 1990) (Figure 9-1).

Typical of his generosity and intellectual curiosity, E. J. Langdon removed a section of his basement wall so that observations could be made on the remaining intact structure of the main mound. There is a persistent story, well distributed among Langdon family members and local residents, that a column (layer?) of ash was discovered in the center of the excavation for the basement. Even taking into account the extremely dry conditions, the exposure provided no evidence of such a feature. The exposure showed that the approximately 2-meter-high segment that could be viewed was the product of loading; the segment showed no obvious evidence of construction stages. Significantly, Middle Mississippian–period sherds (hard, grayish-white, reduced Mississippi Plain [Phillips 1970:130–35; Neeley's Ferry Plain of Phillips et al. 1951:105–10],[3] taken to be post–A.D. 1100) were fairly abundant in the cut face. This makes it clear that even the lower part of the mound was built *after* a fairly substantial amount of Middle Mississippian–period debris had already accumulated. Column samples were taken so more details of construction can be developed with additional analysis.

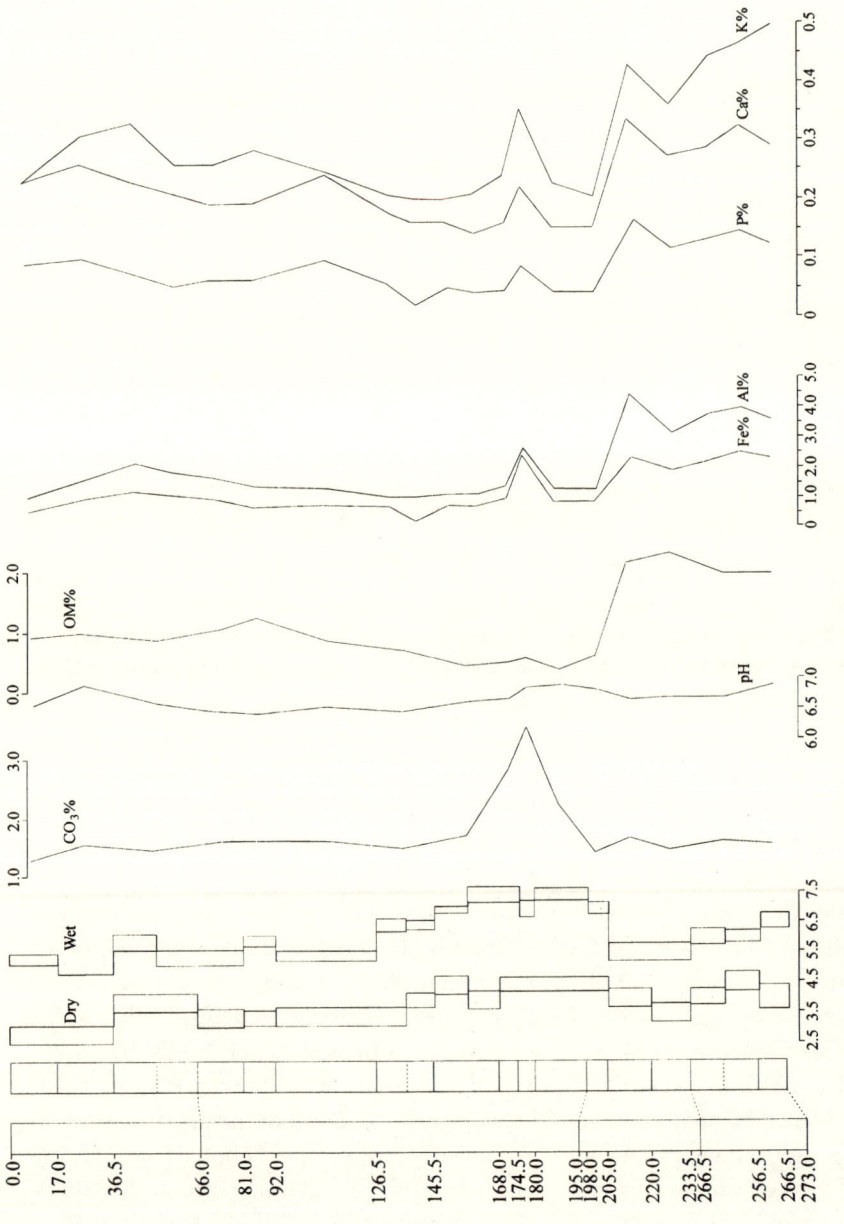

Figure 9-8. Grain-size and chemical characteristics of a core through the northernmost mound in the three-mound structure at Langdon. First column, core depth; second column, core segments; third and fourth columns, color (all samples 10YR hue, abscissa records chroma, column width records value); fifth column CO₃ as LOI at 1000° C; sixth column, pH; seventh column, organic matter as LOI at 500° C; eighth through twelfth columns, elemental percentage weights determined by ICP analysis of perchloric acid digestions.

There are no other mounds or identifiable mound remnants at Langdon today. There may well have been a mound due east of the three-pyramid complex—Williams's Mound 1 (Figure 9-2)—as all early reports mention five mounds. However, E. J. Langdon removed the eminence in this general location for fill in an attempt to stop berm erosion in the 1960s. A core in that location revealed no obviously artificial deposition remains. The edge of the escarpment has occasional natural bar-like features, and it is possible that the "mound" might have been such a feature. In view of the otherwise highly sculpted landscape within the enclosure, an artificial structure or at least an artificially modified natural structure at Williams's Mound 1 location seems quite likely. The 1966 aerial photograph (not shown) shows a circular signature that is otherwise similar to the known mound signatures. Beyond Williams's Mound 1, there is no evidence of additional mounds.

Williams's map (Figure 9-2) labels a substantial area bordered by the three-mound complex, the main mound, and the missing Mound 1 as a "plaza" void of artifacts. Today there is an area immediately south of the main mound that lacks surface artifacts, but the bulk of the area designated "plaza" is densely covered with architectural debris, pottery, and bone. In fact, individual buildings may be resolved in several of the aerial photographs. If there is a plaza, it is small, perhaps 70 × 50 meters. I say "if" because it is quite possible that the apparent absence of surface material in that location is attributable at least in part to slope wash from both the three-mound complex and the main mound. There is clearly a ring of slope wash around the north side of the main mound. Interestingly, additional small plazas may be indicated. In the western transect (Figure 9-3), there is a discrete break in the distribution of daub, sherds, and bone about 40 meters across near the southern end (Figure 9-6). This suggests a small "plaza" northwest of the three-mound group. Impressionistically, there is a similar gap in artifacts due north of the northwest corner of the main mound. While we certainly do not have good data on internal structure, the existence of a single larger plaza in the center of the town seems unlikely; more likely are several much smaller openings in an enclosure otherwise fairly cramped by buildings. In this, Langdon resembles the much smaller Snodgrass site in the Western Lowlands (Figure 9-1) (Price and Griffin 1979).

Age

As other authors of this volume note (e.g., Fox, Chapter 2; Kreisa, Chapter 3; Teltser, Chapter 7), the chronology for most of the Mississippian period is a patchwork of assumption, typology, and very few dates of even modest associational veracity. Although our situation is far from ideal, we are somewhat better off at Langdon because we have made extensive use of thermoluminescence dating (TL) (Dunnell 1989). TL has two enormous advantages in a context such as this. First, a specific heating event is dated, doing away with the need for "association" that characterizes methods that date nonarchaeological events. Also, with careful attention paid to possible effects of contamination (see below), surface sherds are not only usable but also in many ways superior to buried samples (Dunnell and Feathers 1994). Second, much of the crucial time period for Mississippian archaeology is subject to major variations in the atmospheric-carbon reservoir, creating serious ambiguities in ^{14}C dates (Stuiver 1982). TL is unaffected by these uncertainties. Because it is much more complex, TL is inherently less precise (though not less accurate) than radiocarbon dating; however, given the two observations just made, it often is possible to obtain a more precise archaeological chronology from TL than from ^{14}C for the late prehistoric period (Dunnell and Readhead 1988).

Unfortunately, the Malden Plain has not proved ideal as a candidate for TL. Many sherds have poor TL characteristics, and analyses must be abandoned for want of an adequate plateau test. Langdon has proved a modest exception. Six analyses have been done, five of which are technically secure and warrant chronological inference. Dates range from A.D. 1233 ± 51 to A.D. 1609 ± 34, falling mostly in the fourteenth century A.D. Although the 400-year span certainly seems reasonable on other grounds, the dates in general seem a bit too late. Indeed they are. Routine TL analysis assumes that radioactive decay chains are in equilibrium—that is, no decay products are lost/added, which would change the amounts of subsequent products. Feathers's (1993) work has demonstrated that this assumption is not met as widely as is assumed; further, my work has shown (Dunnell and Feathers 1994) that disequilibrium is linked closely to sample porosity. Because the Langdon samples are not very porous, the effect is small. Nonetheless, the initial "dates" must be regarded as minimum ages; correction based on porosity correlations would fix the occupation range between A.D. 1100 and A.D. 1500. All but one sherd dated are of the type Mississippi Plain; consequently, the range may be biased toward the earlier part of the occupation. Effort is under way to measure the disequilibrium directly for each of these samples, and while this will allow the dates to be reported with proper error terms, it likely will not affect the age range materially.

Artifacts

Difficulties in securing representative samples from large Mississippian sites that have complex depositional histories, complicated internal functional and stylistic structure, and an abundance of materials of different sizes are enormous and routinely underestimated. To make matters worse, the small amount of collecting done at Langdon has been specifically structured to ends other than estimating the relative abundance of different classes of artifacts. Consequently, the artifact data should be treated conservatively and viewed as little more than nominal-scale information.

Mississippian-period projectile points from Langdon are predominantly of the Madison and Nodena types, including both elliptical and Banks varieties (Justice 1987:230–32) (Figure 9-9), many of which are serrated. Alba Barbed (Justice 1987:235–36) and Scallorn (Justice 1987:220–22) points are relatively infrequent. Hoes are made from both Dover and Mill Creek cherts in apparently similar amounts. The lithic assemblage thus looks late for a Mississippian assemblage in the central valley (Morse and Morse 1983:271–73). The low frequency of stemmed points and the relative abundance of Nodena varieties set this assemblage off from those of the apparently earlier (ca. A.D. 1300) Moon and Lawhorn sites nearby in Arkansas (Benn, Chapter 10 [see also Benn 1992]; Moselage 1962).

Relatively narrow chipped and ground adzes/chisels are also a prominent feature of the lithic assemblages and are regarded as late markers (e.g., Morse and Morse 1983:272–74; O'Brien and Marshall 1994:169, 172). Although many of these were manufactured from recycled Dover and Mill Creek hoe fragments (Dunnell et al. 1994), some were made from other exotic materials. Another distinctively Mississippian tool class found in abundance at Langdon is the fine-grain-sandstone abrader. Such tools are also prominent in the Lawhorn assemblage (Moselage 1962). Although not yet the subject of detailed analysis, on cursory examination they appear to have been used in the manufacture of wood and bone tools rather than in honing groundstone implements. This is consistent with the myriad microtools—tiny scrapers and backed flakes—that make up the bulk of the cutting tools. Manos and metates are relatively infrequent, so much so that their occurrence might relate to earlier occupation at the Langdon locality, as both Woodland and Archaic artifacts have been found in small numbers.

The ceramic assemblage is overwhelmingly plain, the majority of the sherds being of the Mississippi Plain type (Phillips 1970:131–35) (Figures 9-10 and 9-11). In the southeastern transect, for example, coarse-shell paste characterizes 97 percent of the sherds; various fine pastes, including combinations of shell, grog, and sand—the so-called Bell paste (Williams 1954:208–9; see also Phillips 1970:58–61; Phillips et al. 1951:122–26; Teltser 1988:190–96)—occur in only 3 percent of the sherds. These figures probably vary from one part of Langdon to another, but the overwhelming dominance of the coarse-shell paste is clear and in this respect the assemblage resembles those of the Parkin phase, located farther south in the St. Francis basin (Morse 1981; but see O'Brien 1995).

Forms associated with the coarse-shell-tempered paste include large jars with short straight or slightly outcurving necks; a variety of bowls, including a large salt-pan form; and bottles, including short-neck forms, tall narrow-neck forms, and hooded effigy bottles (Figure 9-11). Handles are straps, often pierced by a single hole, and frequently are quite large. The smallest jars have loop-like

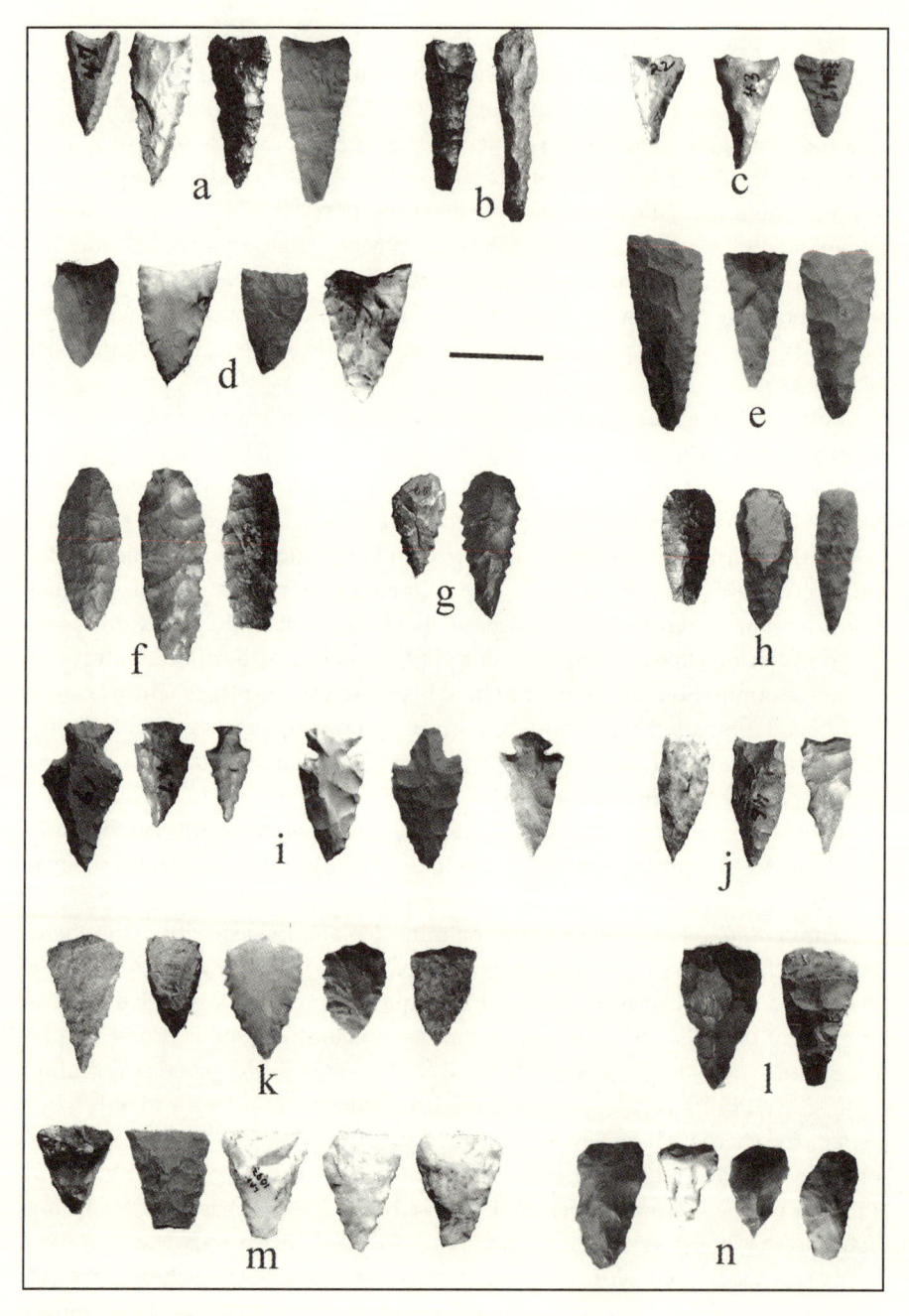

Figure 9-9. Projectile points from Langdon: *a, c, d, e, k, l, m,* and *n,* Madison points and variants thereof; *b,* drill and drill-like point; *f, g, h,* Nodena points, including Nodena, *var. Banks* (*h*), and Nodena, *var. Elliptical* (*f*); *i,* various small stemmed forms including Scallorn (first three) and Alba (last three); and *j,* forms intermediate between Madison and Nodena, *var. Banks. Scale bar* = 2 centimeters.

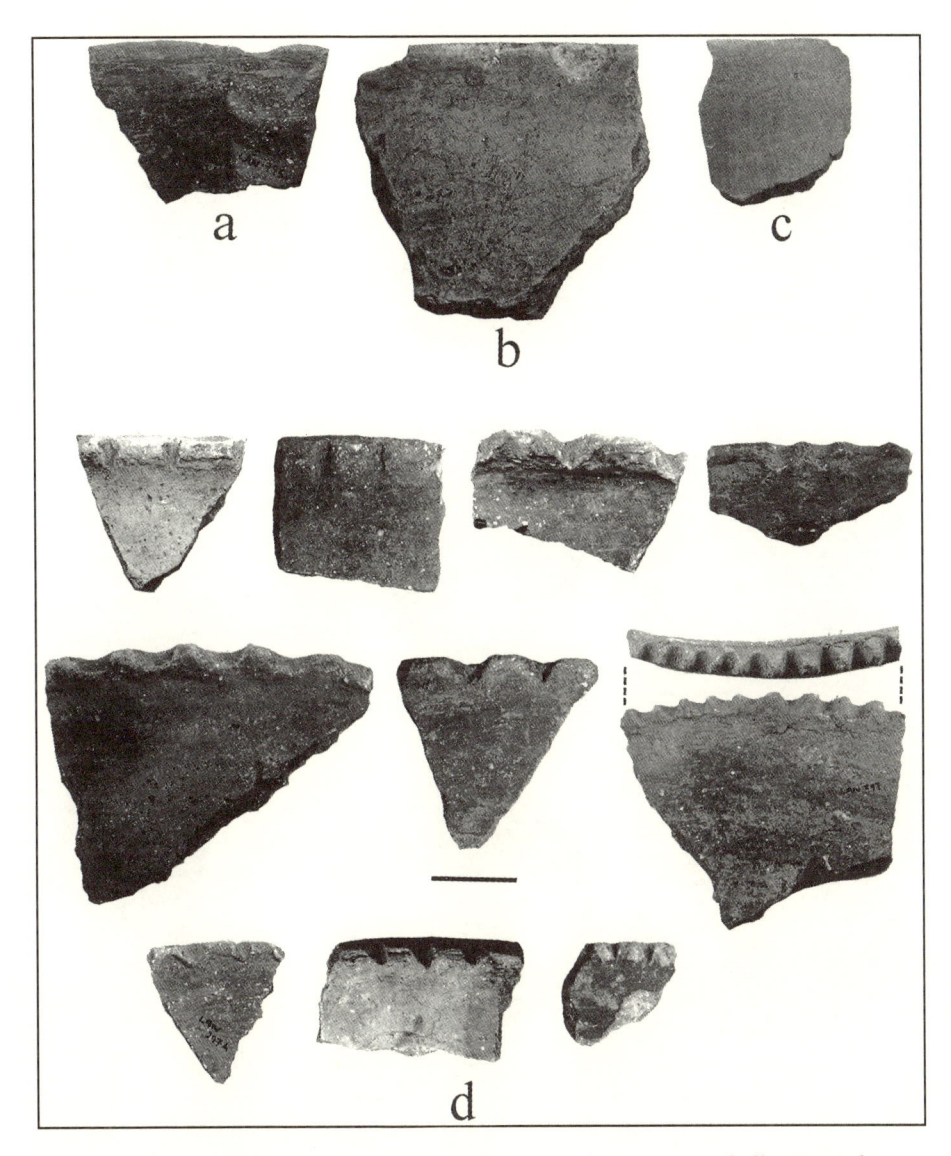

Figure 9-10. Plain shell-tempered rimsherds from Langdon: *a*, coarse-shell-tempered, bowl; *b*, coarse-shell-tempered, jar; *c*, Bell paste, bottle; *d*, notched and/or scalloped bowl rims, last one black-slipped.

handles that are more decorative than functional. Most small vessels have round bases, but ring bases, both attached and free-standing, as well as feet—probably from effigy bottles—also occur. Zoomorphic effigy heads adorn bowl rims; these include relatively complex forms such as a hollow vulture head with rattle beads and a black-slipped head with inlaid eyes. Small medallion faces are common bowl features and occur at or just below the rim. The majority of un-

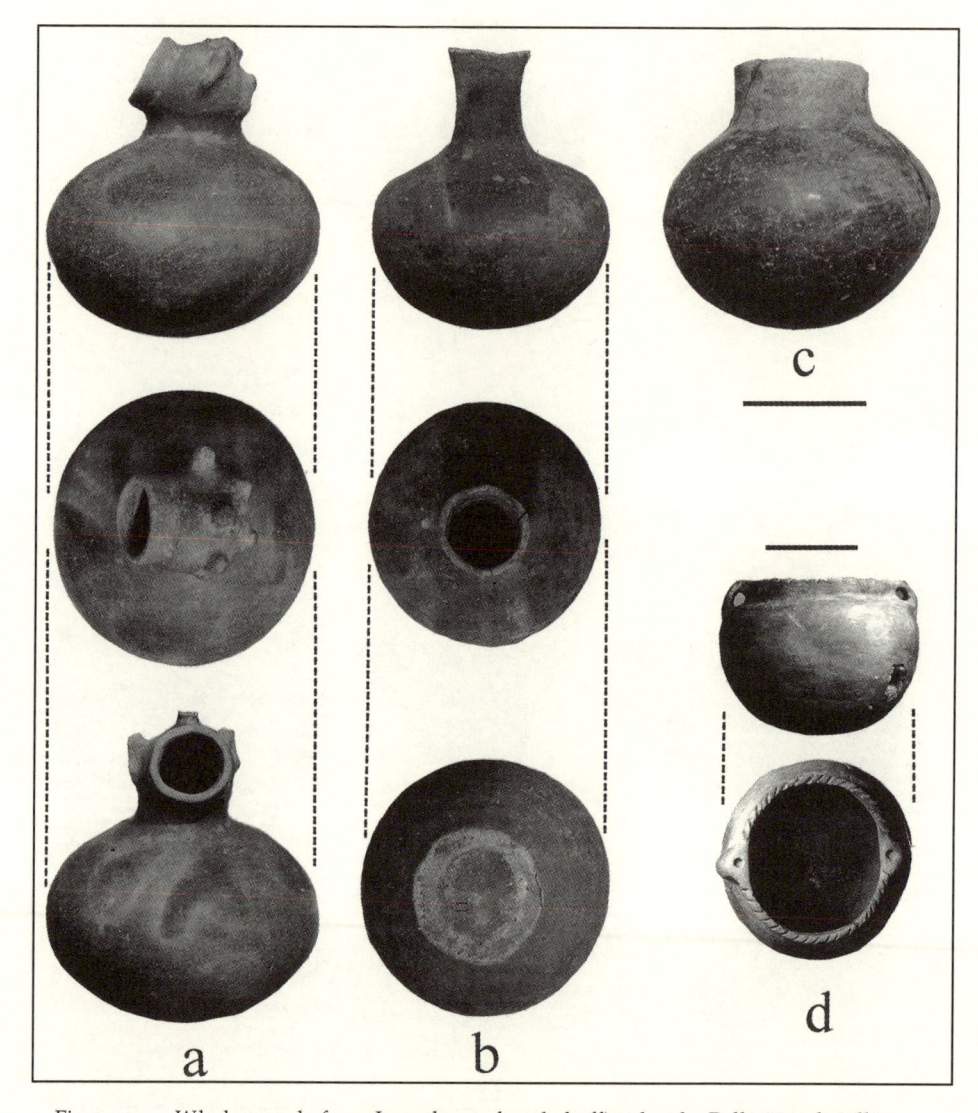

Figure 9-11. Whole vessels from Langdon: *a*, hooded effigy bottle, Bell paste; *b*, tall-necked bottle, coarse-shell-tempered paste (note there was an attached foot ring); *c*, short-necked bottle, coarse-shell-tempered paste; *d*, small jar, Bell paste (note dimples in the handles where holes would be located on full-size handles).

adorned bowl rims are notched and/or scalloped; jar and bottle rims are always plain.

Decorations on the coarse paste are limited to incision and punctation. Incision occurs in two locations. On body sherds it meets O'Brien and Fox's (1994) definition of Wallace Incised for southeastern Missouri (see also Phillips 1970:168–69; Phillips et al. 1951:134–36). On sherds from the neck-shoulder junction the incision is a curvilinear variation of Matthews Incised (Phillips 1970:127–28) and Manly Punctated (Phillips et al. 1951:146–47; but see Phillips 1970:128). On both, curvilinear arcades embellish the upper shoulders of jars. Rectilinear designs are notable by their complete absence, as is the guilloche. Punctation is nearly always done with a hollow punch, and multiple rows rather than one or two rows of punctations are the rule. This contrasts with the arcuate solid punch (fingernail impressions) characteristic of Parkin Punctated (Phillips 1970:150–52; Phillips et al. 1951:110–14) to the south, virtually precluding any confusion between the two types even for small sherds. Parkin Punctated thus appears to be absent or extremely rare at Langdon. The only red-slipped, coarse-shell-tempered pottery takes the form of salt pans. This pottery is not recognized in any of the classifications of Mississippian ceramics in wide use but is readily distinguished by many minor characters from Varney Red, an Early Mississippian type that Phillips (1970:167) associates exclusively with the salt-pan form. The absence of any major Early Mississippian occupation within the Langdon enclosure also makes any confusion with Varney Red unlikely. There also are several sherds that have hard, black-slipped surfaces, which impart the appearance of Bell Plain to the coarse-tempered paste (Dunnell and Jackson 1992). The sherds appear to be from bottles and bowls.

Sherds in the Bell-paste group are more frequently decorated than those in the coarse-paste group, but the decoration is almost always painting/slipping or engraving rather than incising. Sherds of both Old Town Red and Nodena Red-and-White occur in some numbers. The latter material has been the subject of special study and was reported earlier (Dunnell and Jackson 1992), but it is worth noting here that Nodena Red-and-White at Langdon (and generally on the Malden Plain) is *always* white paint on a red slip, applied to the interior of bowls only. In contrast to the types of designs used with incised decoration, both rectilinear and curvilinear designs are evident, the former dominating. There are also an attractive black-slipped pottery and odd (e.g., blue and orange) polychrome pieces. Surface-manipulated decoration is less common on sherds in the Bell-paste group. Only one Manly design is known on this paste; Mound Place Incised (Phillips 1970:135–36; Phillips et al. 1951:147–48) and O'Byam Incised (Phillips 1970:144; Williams 1954:222) are more typical. Engraving also occurs on Bell paste, where it is found on bottle exteriors and conforms closely to Walls Engraved (Phillips 1970:169–71; Phillips et al. 1951:127–29; Dye, Chapter 4) and on the interior of bowl lugs, where it is better attributed to O'Byam Engraved (Williams 1954:223). A number of appliquéd sherds are known and, since all appear to be from straight necks or near rims, they can be referred to as Campbell Appliqué (Chapman and Anderson 1955:42–44; O'Brien and Fox 1994a:41). A solid horizontal band of punctations at the base of such a neck probably represents Campbell Punctated (Chapman and Anderson 1955:42–44, 45–46; O'Brien and Fox 1994a:40). Bell-paste forms include bottles, bowls, and jars, with jars being quite infrequent in contrast to the coarse-paste group, where they are the predominant form.

As with the projectile points, the sherds reflect a long span of occupation within the Mississippian period, omitting any Early Mississippian deposition but extending well within Late Mississippian times, as suggested by the TL dates. It is the presence of late types such as Nodena Red-and-White, Walls Engraved, and Campbell Appliqué that sets the Langdon ceramic assemblage apart from that from Lawhorn, where those types are conspicuously absent (only a single Nodena Red-and-White sherd was reported in an assemblage of more than 20,000 sherds [Moselage 1962]). In decoration and form, the Langdon ceramic assemblage appears to be intermediate between those of the Cairo Lowland phase to the northeast and contemporary phases farther to the south.

Settlement Context

Late Mississippian–period regional settlement systems are poorly known in the central Mississippi Valley with the exception of the Parkin phase studied by Morse (1981) and, to a lesser extent, the Kent phase studied by House (1991). The Powers phase (Price 1978; Price and Griffin 1979; see also Perttula, Chapter 8) is the only comparably studied unit in Missouri and would definitely appear to predate the bulk of the Langdon occupation as well as the Parkin and Kent phases. Systematic survey around Langdon is still quite limited, but some suggestion of the larger settlement system is beginning to emerge from judgmental and haphazard surveys.[4]

Recent surveys immediately around Langdon itself have revealed numerous earlier archaeological deposits relating to the escarpment and to a small northeast-southwest-trending slough that passes just north of the Langdon fortifications. There is nothing to indicate a halo of smaller occupations coeval with and surrounding the Mississippian town. In this regard, Langdon appears more similar to Parkin (Morse 1981:41–42) than to Powers Fort (Price 1978:figure 8.9; see also Perttula, Chapter 8). On the other hand, there is clear evidence that for at least part of its duration, Langdon was the paramount node in a hierarchical settlement system that included at least two other levels. At the bottom in terms of size, density, and complexity are distributions of late-period pottery (reduced, hard, fine-tempered) a few tens of meters in diameter. Such distributions—one of which, 23DU300, is shown in Figure 9-1—were recorded only because they overlie much larger artifact concentrations of earlier age. As Teltser argues in Chapter 7, these kinds of phenomena have not been systematically identified. Consequently, they might be widely distributed and numerous, but there is no way of knowing this without systematic surveys designed to recover low-density artifact clusters. Only a fraction of Late Mississippian assemblages is typologically distinct, and repeated collection at such locations is required to generate assemblages large enough to contain specimens of rarer pottery types in reliable numbers (see O'Brien and Fox 1994b).

Intermediate between these isolated, household-size clusters and Langdon are settlements, rectangular or ovoid, roughly half the size (ca. 250 × 150 meters) of Langdon. These settlements apparently lack mounds. One such settlement (23DU299 [Figure 9-1]) is currently under investigation in southern Dunklin County. A single TL date of A.D. 1400 ± 45, the dominance of Madison and Nodena points over Scallorn points (Morse and Morse 1983:271-73), and the general character of the ceramic assemblage all indicate that 23DU299 was contemporaneous with the main phase of occupation at Langdon. Surface artifact distributions indicate the presence of one or more rows of buildings arrayed around a relatively large (compared to Langdon), centrally located plaza that is void of artifacts. It is unclear from artifact distributions and aerial photographs whether 23DU299 was surrounded by a moat and stockade. Although dense in comparison with the non-Langdon record in the region, artifact density is only a fraction of that seen at Langdon, and there is no topographic buildup of debris. Benn (Chapter 10) has described what appears to be an earlier but otherwise similar settlement in northeastern Arkansas, the Moon site. Turner and Snodgrass, the nearly completely excavated second-order settlements around Powers Fort (Figure 9-1), while smaller than 23DU299, appear to have been more complexly organized.

The grossly different sample sizes available for 23DU299 and Langdon make comparing the assemblages difficult. Impressionistically, the 23DU299 assemblage contains all the functional classes that occur at Langdon except for the rarest classes, which would be expected to be absent in the smaller sample. Likewise, although little decorated pottery is known from 23DU299, the low frequency with which decorated pottery occurs at Langdon makes its near absence from the 23DU299 assemblage predictable. Thus, while it is tempting to spin tales of elite artifacts, hierarchic social structures, and the like, all of the assemblage differences now known can probably be accounted for solely by sampling error. Clearly, larger samples from the second-order communities (Benn, Chapter 10) are needed. At this stage in the research, however, the only apparent differences between the two settlement types lie in the absence of mounds at 23DU299 and the differences in size and internal organization.

Because no systematic surveys have been undertaken, there is no way of knowing how many localities similar to 23DU299 exist on the southern Malden Plain or what spatial relations they might bear to Langdon on the one hand and to the smaller, hamlet-size clusters on the other. One Late Mississippian hamlet (23DU300) lies only a few hundred meters away from 23DU299, but dating of such small assemblages is currently too imprecise (small sample size) to claim the pair was contemporaneous.

Summary

Langdon is a large, fortified, dense Middle to Late Mississippian–period settlement on the Malden Plain escarpment overlooking the Little River Lowland. Although displaying similarities in form to settlements farther south in the St. Francis drainage, the artifact assemblage has more in common with assemblages from the Cairo Lowland, at least during the early portion of the Mississippian occupation. In many respects, however, Langdon, along with similar sites such as Vancil (Figure 9-1), is distinctive in its own right. Compact, fortified settlements such as Langdon and Vancil represent a major change in settlement pattern from the complex and sprawling Mississippian settlement systems that preceded them in the Malden Plain (Leeds 1979; Teltser 1988). Unlocking the answers to questions such as why settlement configuration changed—as well as placing Langdon more firmly in the regional context—awaits more thorough analysis of the data at hand.

Acknowledgments

Thanks are due to E. J. Langdon for access to the site and for his support, memory of events, and good-natured encouragement. Many other members of the Langdon family provided information and access to artifacts or pictures of them, as did the Missouri Historical Society, St. Louis. A great many people, some of whom not only survived but have gone on to fame and fortune, assisted in the field: H. Aiken, M. S. Allen, S. K. Campbell, S. Cole, J. K. Feathers, D. M. Greenlee, R. Holmberg, T. L. Hunt, M. E. Madsen, V. Martinez, P. T. McCutcheon, D. Morey, C. Pierce, J. F. Simek, B. Sorhan, P. A. Teltser, J. Tyler, J. Villarias, L. A. Wandsnider, and F. E. Hamilton. Much of the initial laboratory work was done by R. Vercruysee and B. Hildebrant. M. D. Dunnell helped turn the manuscript into English. National Science Foundation grant BN-58504394A02 to R. C. Dunnell and T. G. Stoebe supported the TL work in part.

10 | Moon
A Fortified Mississippian-Period Village in Poinsett County, Arkansas
David W. Benn

THIS CHAPTER SUMMARIZES excavations at the Moon site (3PO488), a Middle Mississippian-period (A.D. 1200–1400) village in Poinsett County, Arkansas (Figure 10-1). Named for the landowner, James Moon, the site was excavated by personnel from the Center for Archaeological Research, Southwest Missouri State University, under contract to the Arkansas Highway and Transportation Department.[1] The Moon site was declared potentially eligible for the National Register of Historic Places in 1988 following testing by Arkansas Highway and Transportation Department archaeologists, and Southwest Missouri State University conducted excavations from fall 1989 to spring 1990.

A lengthy history of archaeological investigations in eastern Arkansas preceded work at Moon (see Klinger et al. 1983:36; Morse and Morse 1983:17–30). The modern age of archaeology opened in northeastern Arkansas in 1939, when Philip Phillips, James A. Ford, and James B. Griffin began their survey of the Lower Mississippi River valley (Phillips et al. 1951), an important product of which was a ceramic typology that, with one major revision (Phillips 1970), continues in use today (Fox, Chapter 2; O'Brien and Dunnell, Chapter 1). The 1960s and 1970s witnessed a series of large-scale excavations in the central Mississippi Valley, mostly salvage efforts on large Mississippian-period towns. Some of this work has been published, but much of it is either unpublished or published only in cursory form (e.g., the 1977 report of Chapman et al. on Lilbourn, a large fortified center in New Madrid County, Missouri [Figure 10-1]). Several such projects took place in northeastern Arkansas, most of them focusing on sites that were in imminent danger of destruction or severe modification. These included Parkin in Cross County (Davis 1966; Klinger 1977b; P. A. Morse 1981, 1990); Hazel, located just south of Moon in Poinsett County (Davis 1973; D. F. Morse 1973a; Morse and Morse 1983; Morse and Smith 1973); and Nodena (D. F. Morse 1973b, 1990) and Knappenberger (Klinger 1974), both located in Mississippi County (Figure 10-1).

Beginning in the 1970s, the cultural-resource management revolution raised the level of concern for project impacts on all types of archaeological

226 | Benn

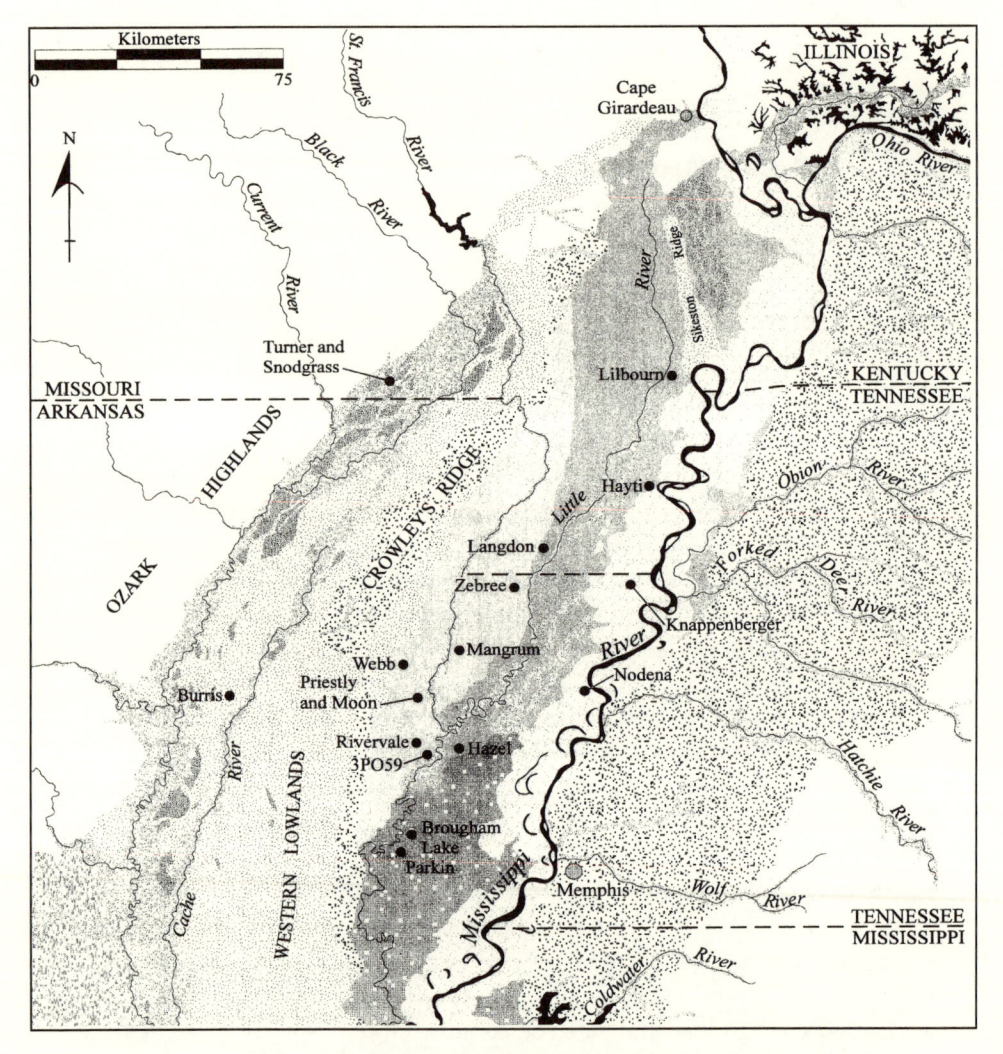

Figure 10-1. Map of the central Mississippi River valley showing physiographic features and the location of Moon and other archaeological sites mentioned in the text.

properties, including small sites. Sections of the St. Francis Basin in Poinsett and Craighead counties, Arkansas, were surveyed by Klinger and Mathis (1978), resulting in the recording of nine small sites and two small villages. Subsequently, the villages were excavated—Mangrum (3CG636) by Klinger (1982b) and Rivervale (3PO395) by G. P. Smith (1978) (Figure 10-1). The project with the greatest impact on the archaeology of northeastern Arkansas was the excavation of Zebree, a Late Woodland and Early Mississippian village in Mississippi County (Morse 1968, 1975; Morse and Morse 1977; P. [A.] Morse and D. F. Morse 1990) (Figure 10-1).

Work at Zebree stimulated a plethora of research questions (e.g., Morse 1982) that ostensibly could be investigated by large-scale village excavations. Consequently, Klinger's (1982b) excavations at Mangrum, located about 25 kilometers northeast of Moon, and at Brougham Lake (Klinger et al. 1983), located about 40 kilometers south of Moon (Figure 10-1), entailed defining a series of "problem domains," or research questions, that might be answerable by excavating Late Woodland and Mississippian components at these sites. Those investigations were followed by excavations at Priestly (3PO490), an Early Mississippian–period hamlet with a charnel structure (Benn 1990) located 3 kilometers north of Moon (Figure 10-1). Priestly and Moon represent consecutive occupations of the same general locality by Mississippian peoples.

The excavation of villages resulted in a burst of reporting, much of which is only now appearing in print. Many of these works consist of overviews of various regions within the central Mississippi Valley (e.g., Dunnell and Feathers 1991; Dye and Cox 1990; Marshall 1985; Morse and Morse 1983, 1989, 1990; Price and Price 1984) and tend to be problem specific (e.g., Late Woodland–period settlement patterns, the development of towns and villages, the Varney Red pottery tradition, and the emergence of shell-temper technology). At least one work (Morse and Morse 1983) covers the entire central valley. Other collections of papers (e.g., Emerson and Lewis 1991; Smith 1990b) extend consideration of the Mississippian period beyond the central Mississippi Valley proper.

Background Information

Vegetation patterns reconstructed from the 1845 General Land Office (GLO) survey (Figure 10-2) show there were three kinds of forest communities around Moon. The three communities, described in Klinger (1982b:29–34), follow the categorizations in Steyermark's (1963) study of southeastern-Missouri flora. One community consisted of the cypress-hardwood association in combination with the cottonwood-willow-sycamore association. The marker tree in this community, bald cypress (*Taxodium distichum*), is associated with standing water. The seasonally inundated low bottoms supported hardwoods such as ash (*Fraxinus* spp.), sweet gum (*Liquidambar styraciflua*), maples (*Acer* spp.), cottonwood (*Populus heterophylla*), willow (*Salix* spp.), sycamore (*Platanus occidentalis*), and elm (*Ulmus* spp.). The GLO notes place most of the cypress trees along Big Bay, about 3.2 kilometers west of Moon. No standing water was recorded within or on the margins of Section 22, which contains the Moon site. The land around Moon probably was seasonally inundated and supported mixed stands of the cottonwood-willow-sycamore plant association, which requires better-drained soils.

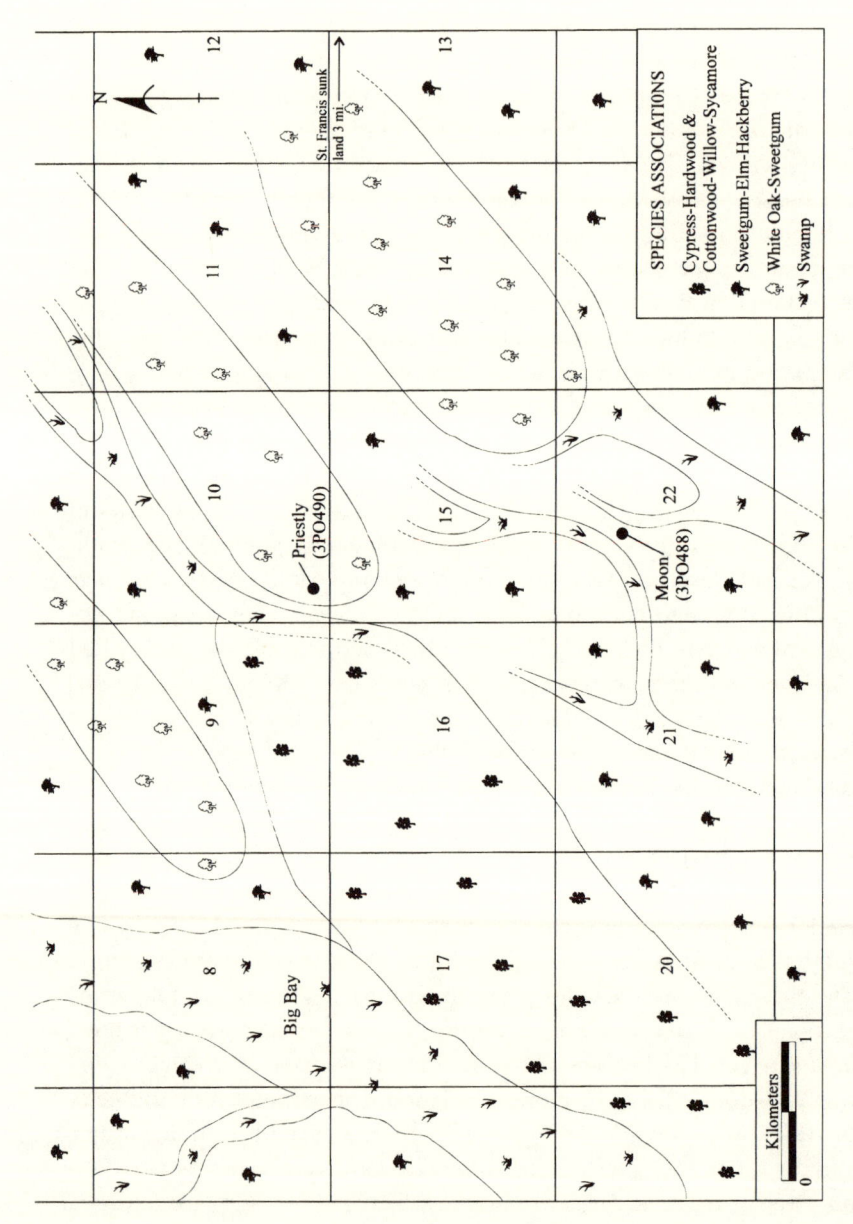

Figure 10-2. Environmental setting of Moon and Priestly based on modern soil surveys and GLO survey notes: the communities present are (1) cypress-hardwood association and cottonwood-willow-sycamore association; (2) sweet gum–elm–hackberry association; and (3) white oak–sweet gum association. *Numbers* in the middle of the 1-mile-square blocks are section designations.

Well-drained land around Moon was covered by trees of the sweet gum–elm–hackberry association. This community inhabited sandy rises (termed "first-rate" land in the GLO notes) that are only occasionally and briefly inundated by high water. In addition to the marker-tree species, the community also included oaks (*Quercus* spp.), walnut (*Juglans nigra*), hickories (*Carya* spp.), persimmon (*Diospyros virginiana*), dogwood (*Cornus* spp.), and sumac (*Rhus* sp.). The GLO notes describe "bushes, vines and greenbriers" at most mapping points, indicating understory vegetation was fairly thick. On the highest ground that did not flood, such as knolls and ridges of valley-train deposits, the white oak–sweet gum association was the dominant community. This association included several oak species (e.g., *Quercus alba*), ash (*Fraxinus* spp.), hickories, pecan (*Carya illinoensis*), and walnut. One expanse of the white oak–sweet gum community, which trended northeast-southwest (parallel to the relict channel system), occurred less than a kilometer northeast of Moon. The general impression one derives from the patchwork of forest communities is that of a region of high carrying capacity for hunters and gatherers (see Morse and Morse 1983:9, 203).

Weathering in the soil profile is the dominant natural process that has affected evidence of cultural activity at Moon. The soil on the site is mapped as Dundee silt loam (Gray and Ferguson 1977:15), which typically occurs on the lower slopes of natural levees. The soil profile at Moon consists of a reddish-brown loamy sand with structure developed to a meter or more of depth but with little evidence of clay movement in the profile. Its modern pH is near neutral at 6.5, but decades of liming agricultural fields probably have made the soil less acidic than it was under the prehistoric forest. This profile exhibits more oxidized color and less evidence for clay movement than the type description for the Dundee soil, so the soil should be judged as well drained. Under these soil conditions, cultural materials would have been subjected to intensive leaching. Poor preservation of animal bone, the absence of mussel shell, and leached shell temper in pottery are the general rule across Moon.

A backhoe trench was opened across the sandy rise containing the site (Figure 10-3) to assist in reconstructing the natural soil profile. This revealed that the rise was a mere 0.5 to 0.6 meters above the adjacent swales and relict channels when the village was occupied. In other words, the village was situated on an inconspicuous rise in a landscape of intersecting relict channels and swamps. The residents of Moon modified most of the upper solum (A, B_1 horizons) of the sand ridge during their occupation. Cultural debris was suffused throughout the B_1 soil horizon, and all previously existing Woodland features (presumably there had been some, given the number of Woodland artifacts recovered [see below]) were destroyed by the Mississippian residents. Postoccupational effects of the New Madrid earthquake of 1811–1812 were primarily mechanical (Saucier 1992). The quake liquefied the sandy substratum throughout

230 | Benn

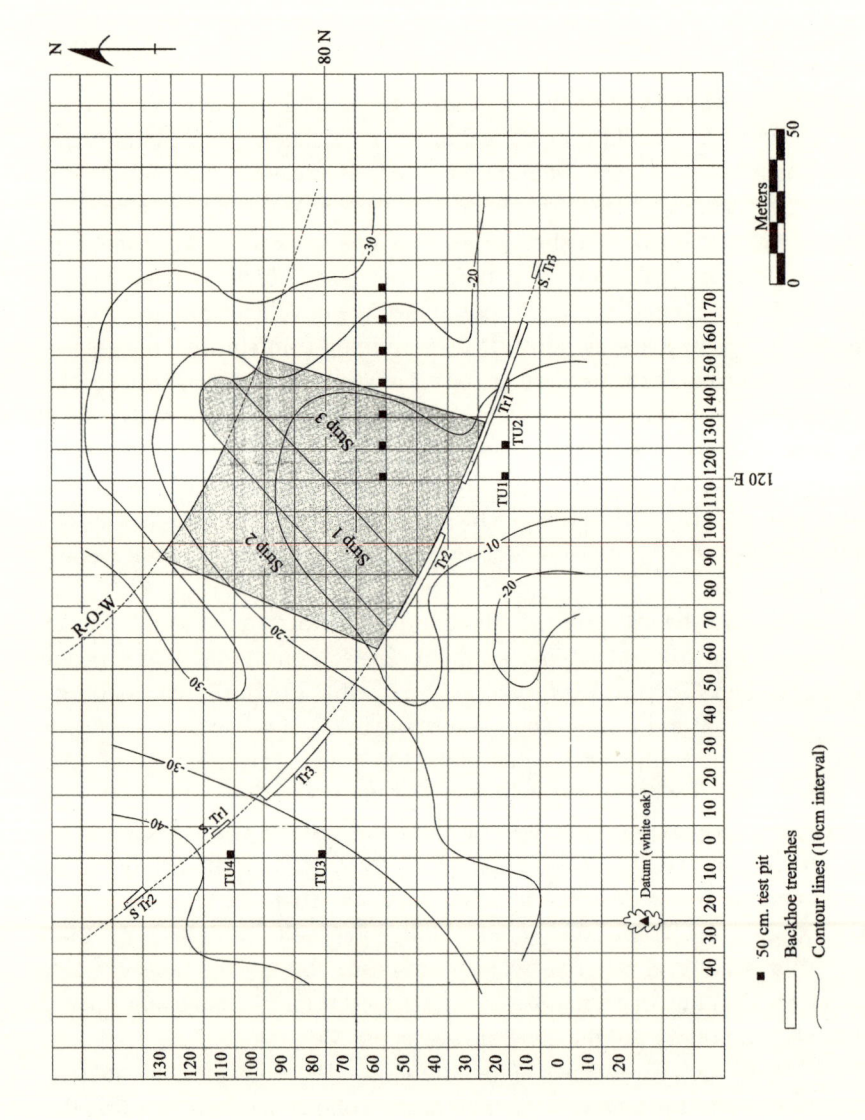

Figure 10-3. Excavation plan of Moon (November 1989) superimposed on the 10-meter grid.

Table 10-1. Radiocarbon Dates from Moon

Laboratory Number[a]	Date B.P.	Corrected Date[b]	Feature Number/ Structure Number	Wood Species
34405	870 ± 60	A.D. 1175	56/42	Red oak group
43957	780 ± 60	A.D. 1259	465/435	Cf. cottonwood
43958	780 ± 50	A.D. 1259	481/463	Red oak group
43954	730 ± 50	A.D. 1272	/254	Red oak group
43956	670 ± 60	A.D. 1285	432/440	Red oak group
35402	660 ± 60	A.D. 1287	/15	Red oak group
35403	610 ± 60	A.D. 1350	71/51	Red oak group
43955	600 ± 50	A.D. 1351	425/414	Cedar

[a]Beta Analytic, Coral Gables, Florida.
[b]Calibration done with CALIB 3.0.2 (Stuiver and Pearson 1986:805–38).

the region, causing cracks to open at the ground surface, which displaced sediments into the swales. Four large sand blows completely destroyed a relatively few archaeological features.

Samples for radiocarbon dating came from burned posts within buildings. Post wood was examined to identify the species and to ensure that pieces of small diameter were used for dating. The consistency of the samples is evident in the tight clustering of the eight dates. Moon was occupied for slightly less than 200 years, between the late twelfth century and the mid-fourteenth century A.D. (Table 10-1). The earliest mean date, A.D. 1175, came from Structure 42 in the Courtyard 1 grouping, the oldest and most established portion of the village (see below). The late end of the sequence is represented by Structure 414, with a mean date of A.D. 1351. This house was outside the inner (earlier) palisade line and represents a late building phase of the village.

Excavation of the Community

When the crew arrived at Moon in early November 1989, the site was in cotton stubble, with 60- to 100-percent visibility of the ground surface. The first order of business was to establish a 10-meter grid encompassing a rectangular area of 220 × 160 meters (35,200 square meters) over the site. This grid was oriented to magnetic north and centered on the sand ridge at stake 80N 120E (Figure 10-3). The first three days of fieldwork consisted of obtaining a controlled surface collection from 343 10-meter-square units laid out across the sand ridge and adjacent swales. Each unit was collected by walking between every row of cotton plants for up to fifteen minutes and picking up all objects larger than naturally occurring sediments. The distribution of surface-collected artifacts then was used to structure the excavations (Figure 10-4).

Earlier testing by the highway department (Miller 1988:36) had shown that shell-tempered pottery was concentrated on the northeastern portion of the sand ridge and that grit- and grog-tempered (Woodland) pottery was concentrated on the southwestern half of the site. This observation was confirmed by the surface collection, which showed an extensive scatter of shell-tempered pottery within the right-of-way and a much smaller concentration at the southwestern side of the site near the grid origin (Figure 10-5). The smaller sherd concentration also produced fragments of human bone and may have represented a cemetery. The distribution of daub fragments (Figure 10-6) more or less paralleled that of the shell-tempered sherds in the northeastern half of the site, suggesting that a Mississippian habitation area was within the right-of-way. Projectile-point locations were plotted as an additional check on the distribution of stone materials. The resulting map (Figure 10-7) showed that most Mississippian-age projectile points were in the northeastern half of the scatter, whereas Woodland and Archaic dart points were scattered everywhere on the site. The presence of so many dart points in the Mississippian village area was thought to be evidence for the recycling of lithic tools, a practice found at the Priestly site (McGrath et al. 1990).

After the surface collection had been analyzed, an earth-moving machine was used to strip the plow zone in the right-of-way (Figure 10-3). Then, shovel skimming was used to define features including post molds, pits, basins, burned houses, and patches of midden for mapping. All of the features, except for most of the thousands of post molds, were excavated by cross sectioning. The resulting village plan (Figure 10-8) turned out to correlate positively with the distribution of surface-collected shell-tempered pottery (Figure 10-5) and daub fragments (Figure 10-6). The village limits were fairly well defined by the surface artifact scatter, and even the empty plaza showed up north of the 80N grid line in Figures 10-5 and 10-6.

Finding a close spatial correspondence between surface and subsurface evidence on a heavily cultivated Mississippian site depends entirely on carrying out an intensive, controlled surface collection, not merely on collecting grab samples of sherds. In many locations in the central Mississippi Valley, especially those that have been subjected to continuous plowing and disking, artifacts are extremely small and hence are easily missed during random grab sampling. For example, Conner (1995:28) commented on the small number of artifacts (eighty-eight) collected from the surface of the Hayti site (23PM572) in Pemiscot County, Missouri (Figure 10-1), though the low number might have been predicted on the basis of the collection technique. Similarly, Price and Griffin (1979:53) found few shell-tempered sherds during the initial pass over the Snodgrass site in Butler County, Missouri (Figure 10-1). Later, controlled surface collecting of Snod-

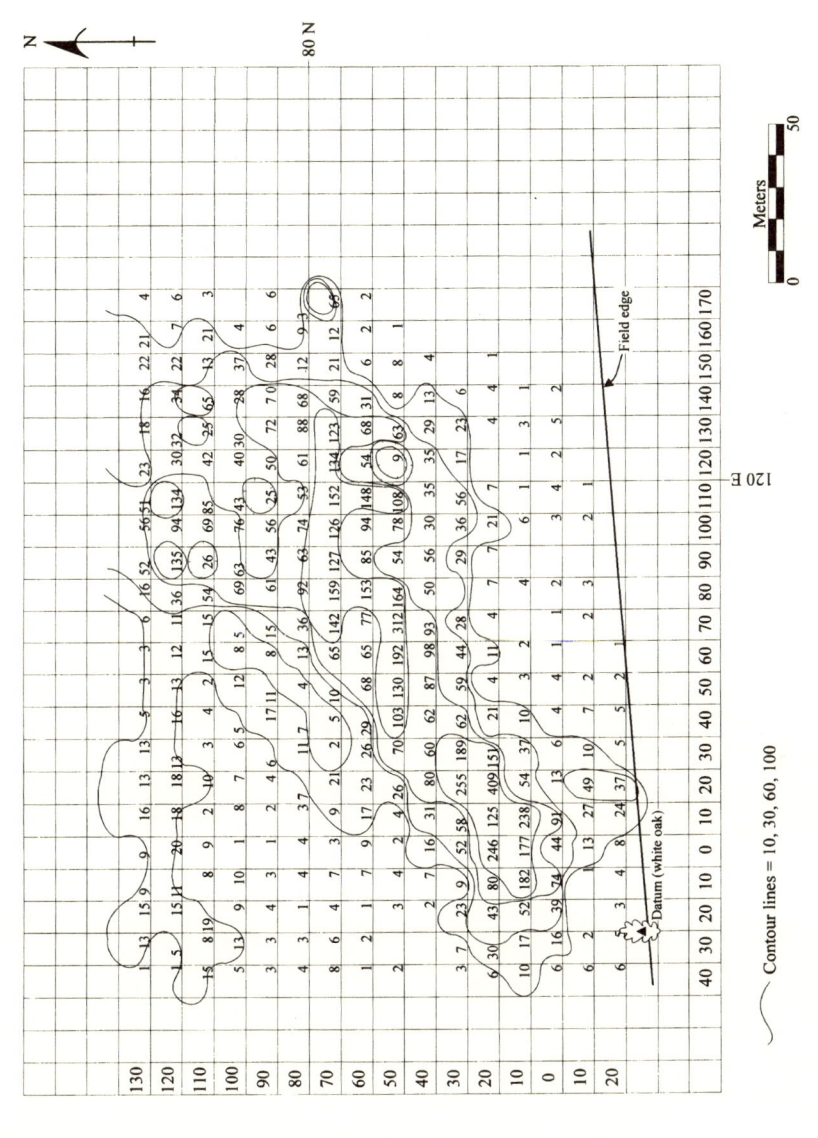

Figure 10-4. Density (objects per 10 × 10-meter unit) of surface-collected artifacts in all classes at Moon.

234 | Benn

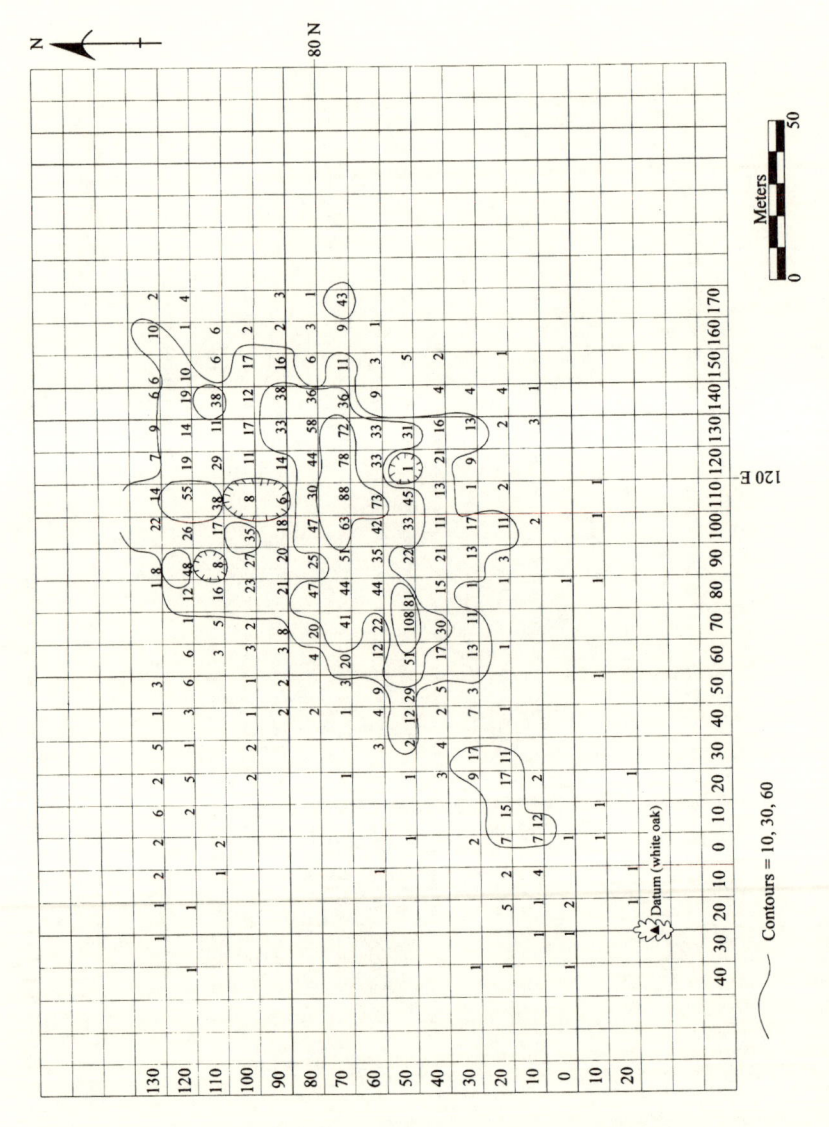

Figure 10-5. Density (objects per 10 × 10-meter unit) of surface-collected shell-tempered sherds at Moon.

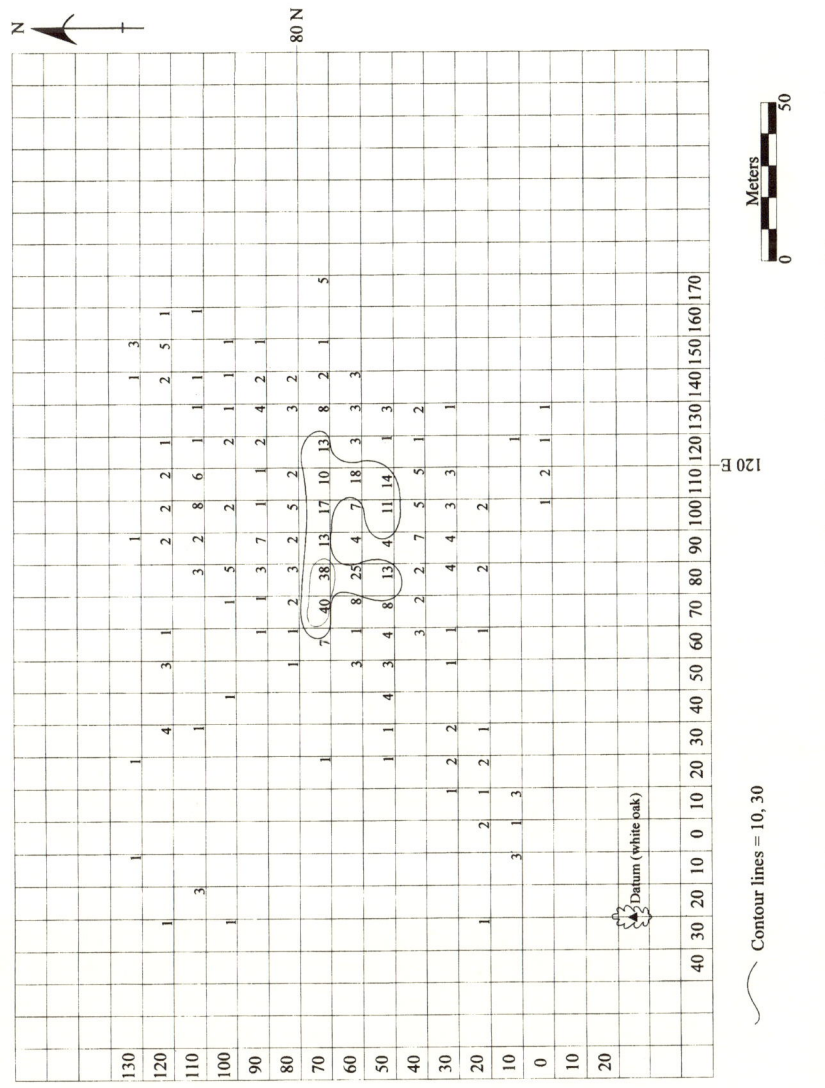

Figure 10-6. Density (objects per 10 × 10-meter unit) of surface-collected daub at Moon.

236 | Benn

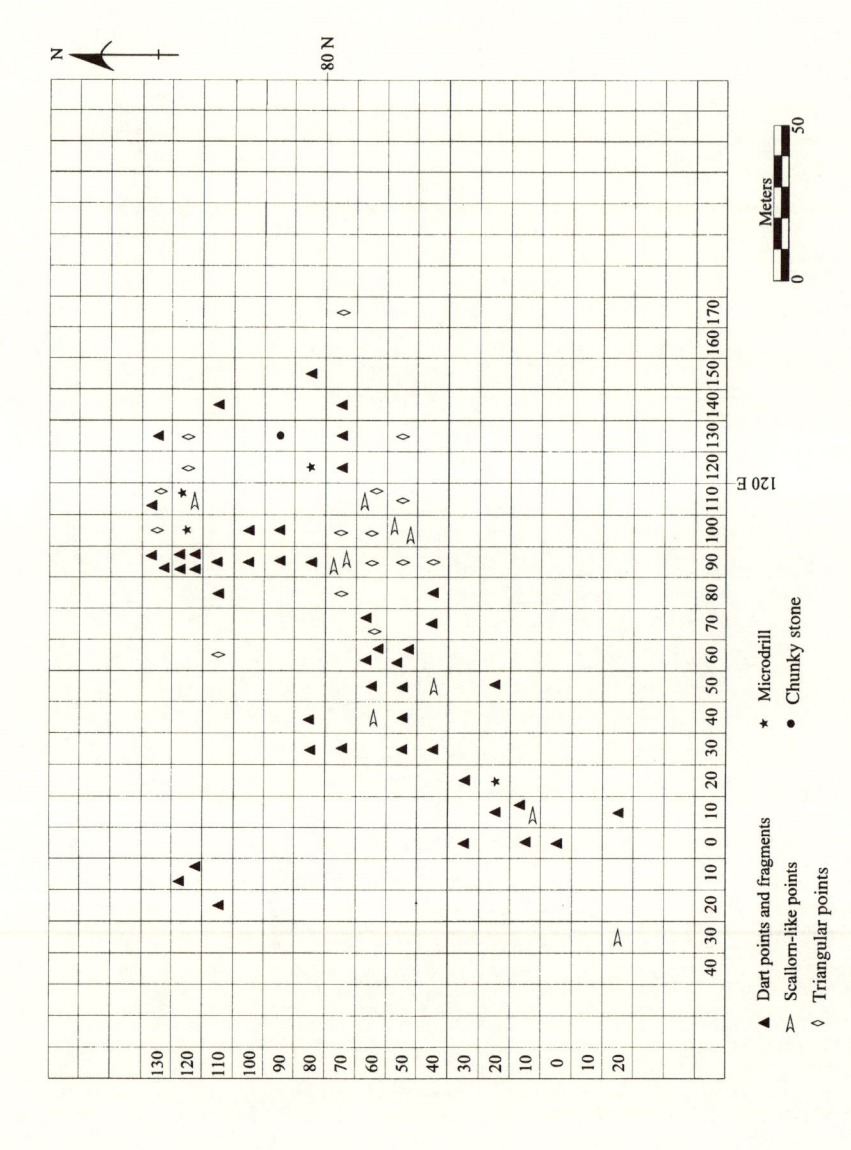

Figure 10-7. Locations of projectile points and other lithic artifacts in 10 × 10-meter surface-collection units at Moon.

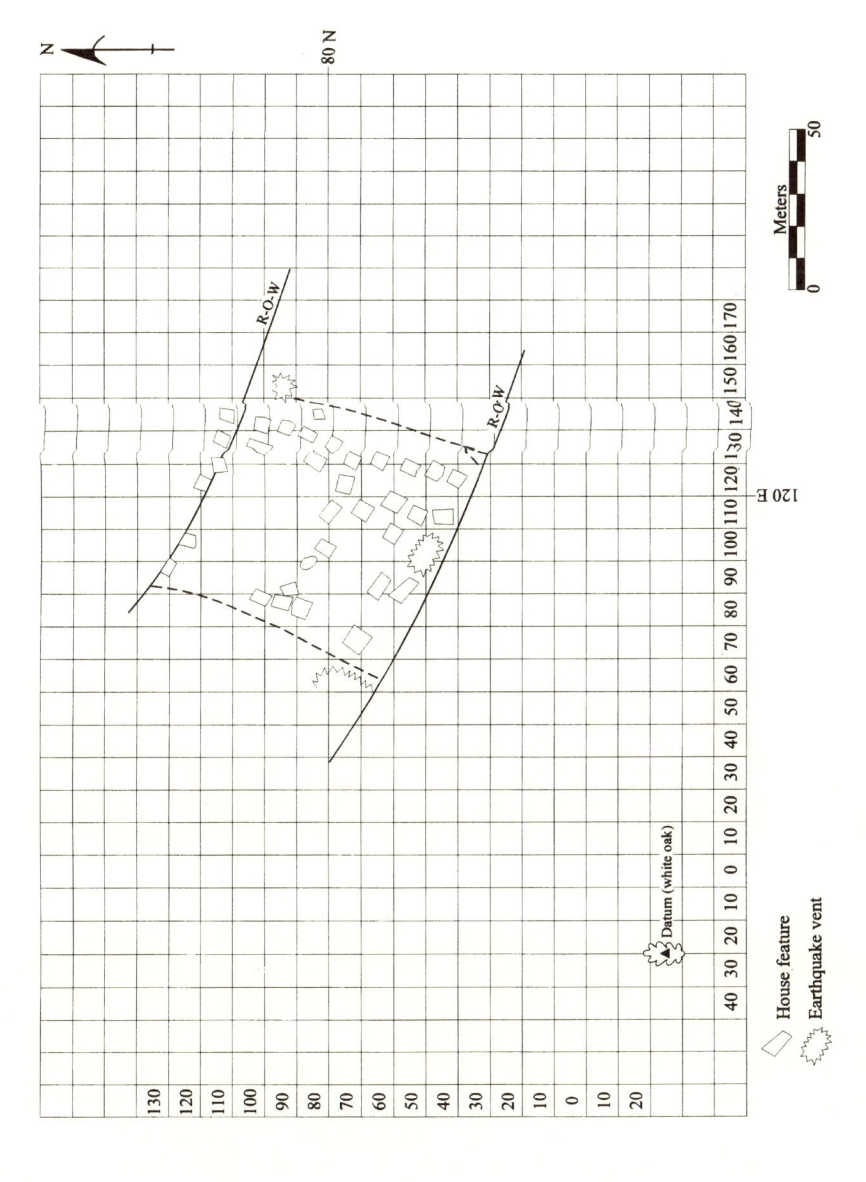

Figure 10-8. The excavated Moon community pattern superimposed on the 10 × 10-meter grid.

grass produced indications of the site limits and interior courtyards (Price and Griffin 1979:10).

Structures

Thirty-three domestic structures were identified at Moon (Figure 10-9), though the archaeological evidence for the structures was by no means uniform. The manner in which the evidence for structures was expressed on the machined surface depended on whether the building had burned or rotted, whether it was placed within a basin, the intensity of weathering throughout the feature, and how deep the plow and earth-mover had cut into the feature.

Rectangular domestic structures were represented in three features. The clearest example was Structure 15, a burned structure with dimensions of 7.6 × 3.4 meters (Figures 10-9 and 10-10). This building had 10- to 20-centimeter-diameter wall posts of red oak set at the edges of a shallow (10 centimeters below the machined surface) basin. No evidence of wall trenches was found. The building also had internal support posts but in no obvious pattern.

There were twenty-eight square wall-trench structures, all of which had 20- to 50-centimeter-wide wall trenches with open corners. Sometimes a small post occurred in the corner gap between wall trenches. Posts, usually not larger than 10 centimeters in diameter, were spaced at intervals greater than their diameters within wall trenches to form the house walls. Most wall posts in square structures formed a single line, but because of their small size it was assumed they did not support the roof. Some structures had preserved evidence for larger-diameter posts (ca. 20 centimeters) along the inside edges of the walls, seemingly for support of the roof, but most support posts (ca. 20 to 40 centimeters in diameter) occurred inside the structures, either in a four-post arrangement or as a center post. In the better-preserved burned structures, the absence of wall posts in the middle of the east-southeast walls indicated locations of doorways.

Daub fragments and mud dauber–nest fragments were very common in and around Moon structures. Many chunks of daub had pole and thatch impressions, but only one square structure (453) contained sheets of daub as clear evidence that at least one wall had been plastered. Considering the lack of contiguous layers of daub on the walls of many burned structures, it is likely that daub was used more often on special areas of houses (e.g., around the smoke hole, at the base of walls, and for patching) and that mats might have covered the walls. A sample of daub from Structure 453 was submitted for grain-size analysis and proved to be made of a sandy loam almost identical in texture to natural sediments comprising the sand rise on which the site is located.

Large sections of a palisade surrounding the village were found just two weeks before the end of the field season, which barely left enough time to delineate the palisade while finishing the excavations of pits and structures. Discovery of the palisade walls was fortuitous because the post stains were a very

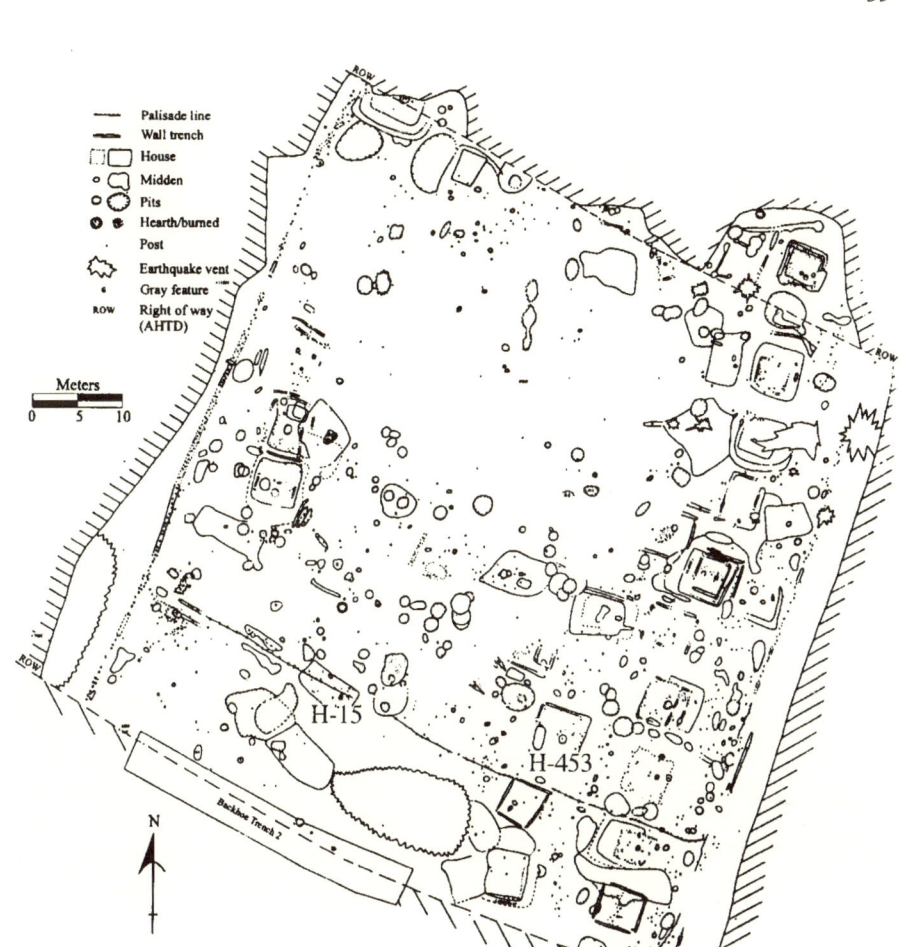

Figure 10-9. Plan of all features at Moon. *AHTD*, Arkansas Highway and Transportation Department.

240 | Benn

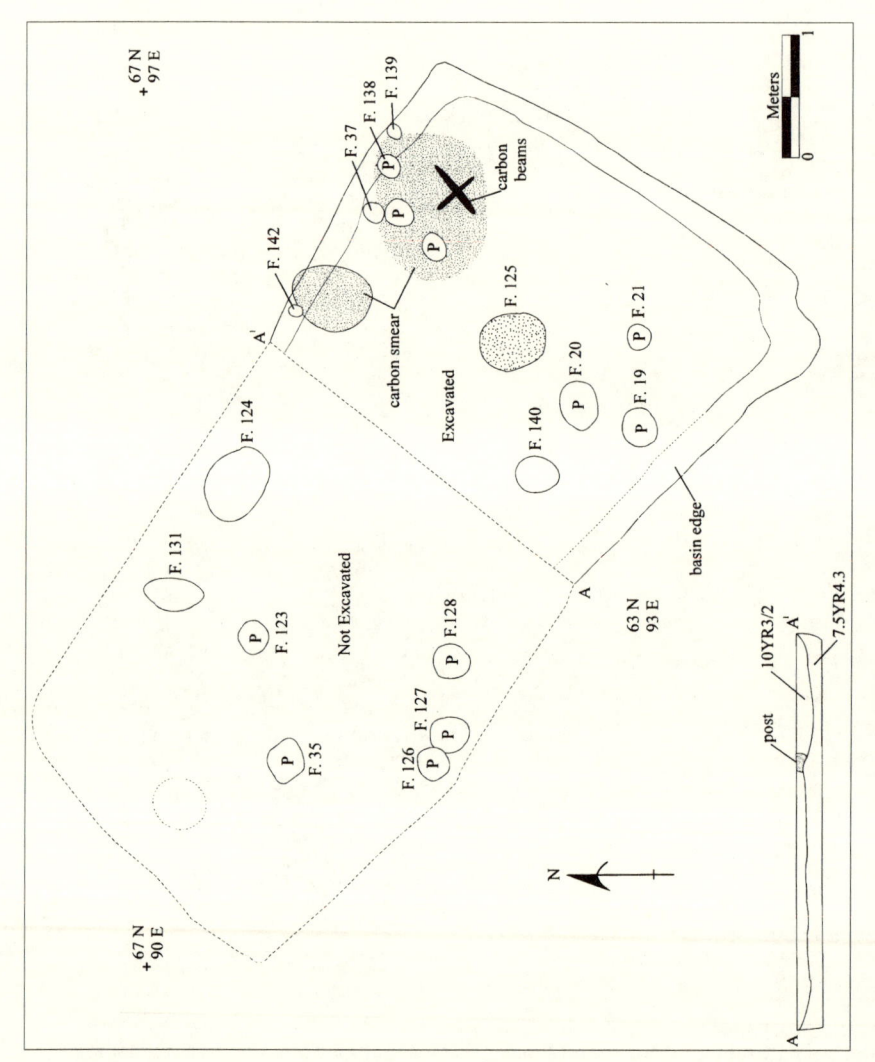

Figure 10-10. Plan of rectangular Structure 15 at Moon showing the location of carbon smears, pits, and post molds (*P*).

pale gray—a subtle color that went unnoticed for many weeks amid the patchwork of brightly colored burned structures, pits, posts, and oxidized root stains in the midden deposit.

A palisade surrounded each of two building phases of the village (Figure 10-9). The lines of posts delineated on the east and west sides of the village at the edges of the sand ridge were part of a palisade that surrounded the entire village during its latest and most expansive stage of occupation. The rest of this palisade on the north and south sides of the village lay outside the right-of-way and was not excavated. The outer palisade comprised a single line of posts 25 to 30 centimeters in diameter and placed 8 to 20 centimeters apart. There were several gaps of more than 20 centimeters between posts, but the gaps probably represented places where post stains could not be identified because of disturbance from roots and rodent runs. Sections of the western palisade showed traces of a 40-centimeter-wide trench holding the line of posts. It is uncertain how deep the trench or the post molds extended below the original habitation surface, since earthquake effects and cultivation modified the elevation of the landform.

Traces of a second, inner palisade were identified across the southern half of the village (Figure 10-9). The gray-stained post molds of this palisade had been superimposed by structures and village midden, and portions of the post line were obliterated by aboriginal digging. The inner palisade connected the east and west sides of the outer palisade and enclosed an earlier, smaller village. Post diameters varied from 20 centimeters to 30 centimeters. Most of the posts making up the inner palisade were spaced at intervals of more than 30 centimeters, with some gaps of as much as a meter. Although large gaps might have resulted from some of the post molds being missed, it appears that this earlier palisade had more widely spaced posts than the outer palisade.

Both palisades had possible entryways. The clearest example was on the inner palisade in the southwestern quadrant of the village (Figure 10-9). This entryway consisted of parallel 40-centimeter-wide wall trenches spaced a meter apart. Although partially destroyed by machine stripping of the plow zone, the entryway was more than 3.5 meters long. The other entry was situated on the east palisade near structures 435 and 463. There, a 7-meter-long wall trench was set a meter outside the palisade post line. Both entryways were designed the same way—that is, as long, narrow passageways placed parallel to and on the outer side of the palisade wall. Lafferty (1973:157) identified this type of entryway as a common form on Middle Mississippian and Late Mississippian sites.

The Moon Community Pattern

Moon was a planned, palisaded community (Figure 10-9). The initial village was 70 meters square (4900 square meters), assuming the northern edge was correctly estimated from the surface-collection map. Later, the village

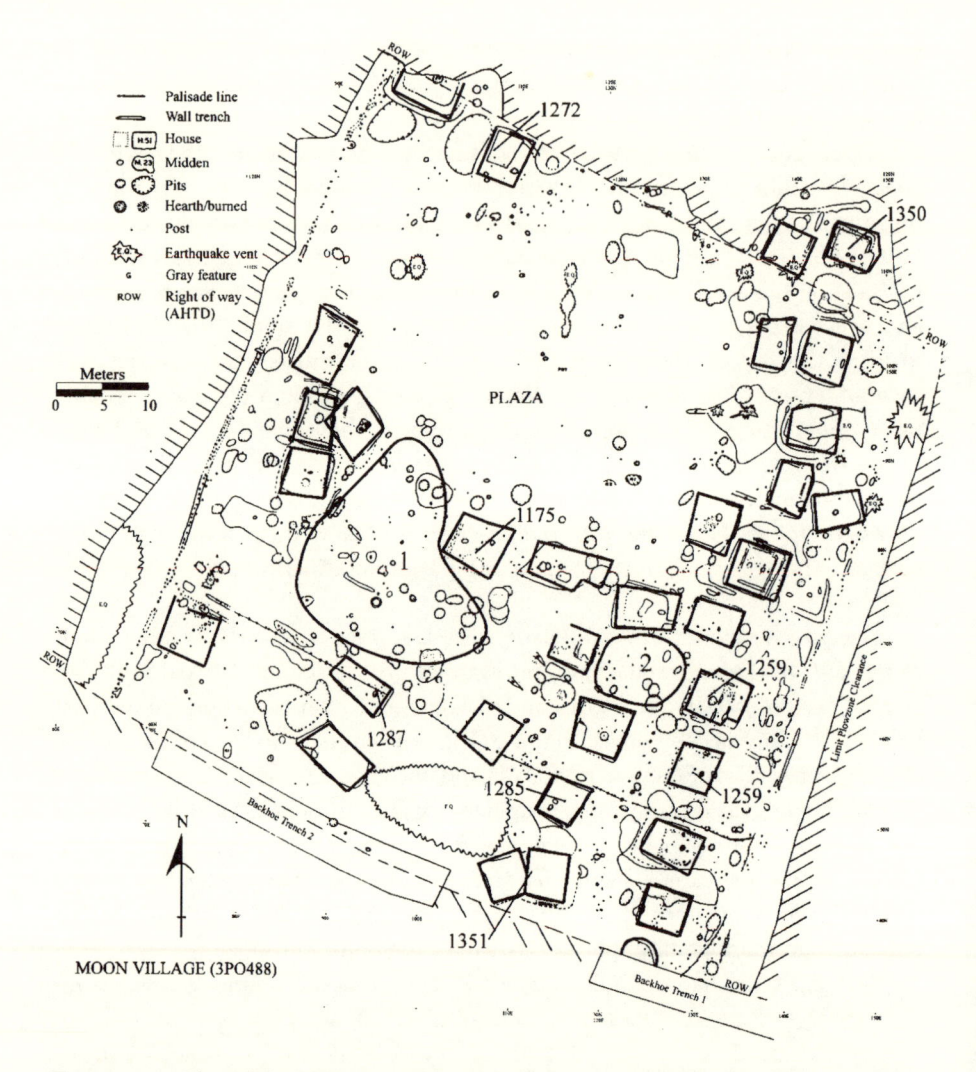

Figure 10-11. Plan of the Moon site showing locations of structures, courtyards 1 and 2, and radiocarbon-dated wood samples (mean corrected dates shown). *AHTD,* Arkansas Highway and Transportation Department.

expanded into a rectangle of the same width and approximately 95 meters in length (6650 square meters). The village orientation was 23 degrees east of north. The plaza in the northern half of the village may have been square (962 square meters) and parallel to the palisade and rows of houses, though the archaeological map makes it appear round. The plaza contained widely scattered post molds and a few pits, including one with a well-preserved human skeleton and another pit with a crudely formed bowl, but there were no other unusual materials or a large "village" post. Judging by the excellent condition of the skeleton in contrast to the marginal preservation of animal bones in the rest of the site, the plaza burial might postdate the main occupation. Midden was conspicuously absent from the plaza; indeed, in the course of shovel skimming the area, Woodland sherds and dart points of the preceding occupation period were encountered more often than were Mississippian materials.

Domestic structures were organized in two patterns that were integrated to form a cohesive village. The first pattern comprised houses that were in rows aligned with the village walls, and some houses within rows were organized around open areas, or courtyards (Figure 10-11). There were two rows of houses on the east side of the village, rows of houses enclosing the plaza, and a row alignment on the west side of the village. The most common distance separating houses within rows was 5 meters. The intervening spaces between houses contained storage pits, large basins, and, judging by concentrations of posts, probably structures such as granaries, drying racks, and canopies. The second pattern consisted of houses grouped around open areas at Courtyard 1 (structures 296, 244, 3, 1152, 119, and 42) and Courtyard 2 (structures 453, 463, 1066, 1044, and 1153). Within Courtyard 2, there were several post molds and large pits containing some polished and decorated pottery (see below). Courtyard 1 encompassed a pit complex that contained polished and decorated pottery (features 1, 4, 61, and 69) and two large hearths (features 6 and 13). The positioning of houses around courtyards is a pattern that shows up throughout the developmental sequence of Mississippian villages in the American Bottom of western Illinois (Kelly 1990b; Mehrer and Collins 1995).

Nearly all houses had the same orientation as the palisade. The long axis of the village had a mean orientation of 20.3 degrees east of north (10 to 30 degrees east of north; standard deviation, 5.5 degrees; $n = 21$). House sizes were quite regular, with square wall-trench structures having an average of 19.4 square meters of interior floor space and a mode of 20.25 square meters (standard deviation, 4.5 square meters; range, 9.75 to 26.5 square meters; $n = 20$). Three rectangular, single-post structures were too poorly preserved to delineate their exact dimensions, but two of them were larger than the third, being roughly 22 to 29 square meters. Regularity in the patterning of the houses extended through several rebuilding phases. Most houses were reconstructed over the same deep basins (Figures 10-11 and 10-12); thus, organizational patterns established at the inception of the village were carried through to the end of the occupation. Rebuilding houses on the same locations was a notable pattern of the Stirling phase in the ICT-II tract at Cahokia (Mehrer and Collins 1995:44).

Little information exists on the village construction sequence because of the limited superposition of artifact-bearing pits and our inability to detect temporal changes in the ceramic inventory. One observation relating to the development of the village is that deep basins with structures must have been built relatively early in the sequence because other house structures were superimposed on them. Further, the burned houses must represent the last major occupation of the village, because a conflagration of the magnitude suggested by the evidence would have ignited all thatched buildings in the village. Therefore, beginning with the map of deep-basin structures (Figure 10-13), we see that the eastern rows of houses were established during an early stage of the occupation and that those rows transect the interior palisade. This means the earlier, square village preceded erection of the long eastern row of deep-basin houses and might have consisted of houses in shallow basins, like those in the western half of the village (Figure 10-13). Parts of this earliest village (e.g., Structure 1066 [Figure 10-9]) were almost obliterated by the building of the deep-basin structures on the east side. Because the majority of radiocarbon dates from all parts of the village fall in the thirteenth century, the complete rectangular community must have been extant during the majority of the proposed 200-year occupation. The distribution of burned houses (Figure 10-14) suggests that all portions of the community were occupied until around the mid-fourteenth century.

Other Community Patterns in Northeastern Arkansas

Rectangular, single-post houses from the Early Mississippian period were found at Zebree (Morse 1975; Morse and Morse 1977, 1983). Those structures were about 2 to 4 meters on a side (average internal size of 8.5 square meters) and had small-diameter (6 to 8 centimeter) posts spaced 2 to 30 centimeters apart. One house was in a shallow basin. Zebree also contained a Middle Mississippian hamlet of up to three houses that was occupied more or less at the same time as Moon (Morse 1975; Morse and Morse 1983:253). Two of the later houses with wall trenches and lines of posts were 4.2 × 5 meters (21 square meters) and 4.1 × 5.2 meters (21.3 square meters).

Although no well-defined houses or house basins were uncovered at the nearby Priestly site, reconstructed evidence from post patterns indicated houses may have been rectangular, single-post structures with dimensions as large as 6 to 8 meters on a side (Benn 1990:70–71). This seems very large for Early Mississippian houses, but posts at Priestly averaged almost 22 centimeters in diameter and many were 40 to 50 centimeters in diameter. Compared with the smaller-diameter posts in Moon houses, such large posts must have supported substantial structures. Linear post patterns at Priestly, presumed to represent houses, were oriented 10 to 40 degrees from cardinal north, in the manner of those at Moon. There are no topographic factors at either Priestly or Moon that would have dictated a specific house orientation.

Other Middle Mississippian components in northeastern Arkansas (Figure 10-1) consist of excavated farmsteads or hamlets and destroyed villages from which uneven information has been collected. For example, Morse and Morse (1983:255) reported four wall-trench houses varying in size from 17.6 to 42 square meters that were excavated or salvaged by Arkansas State University per-

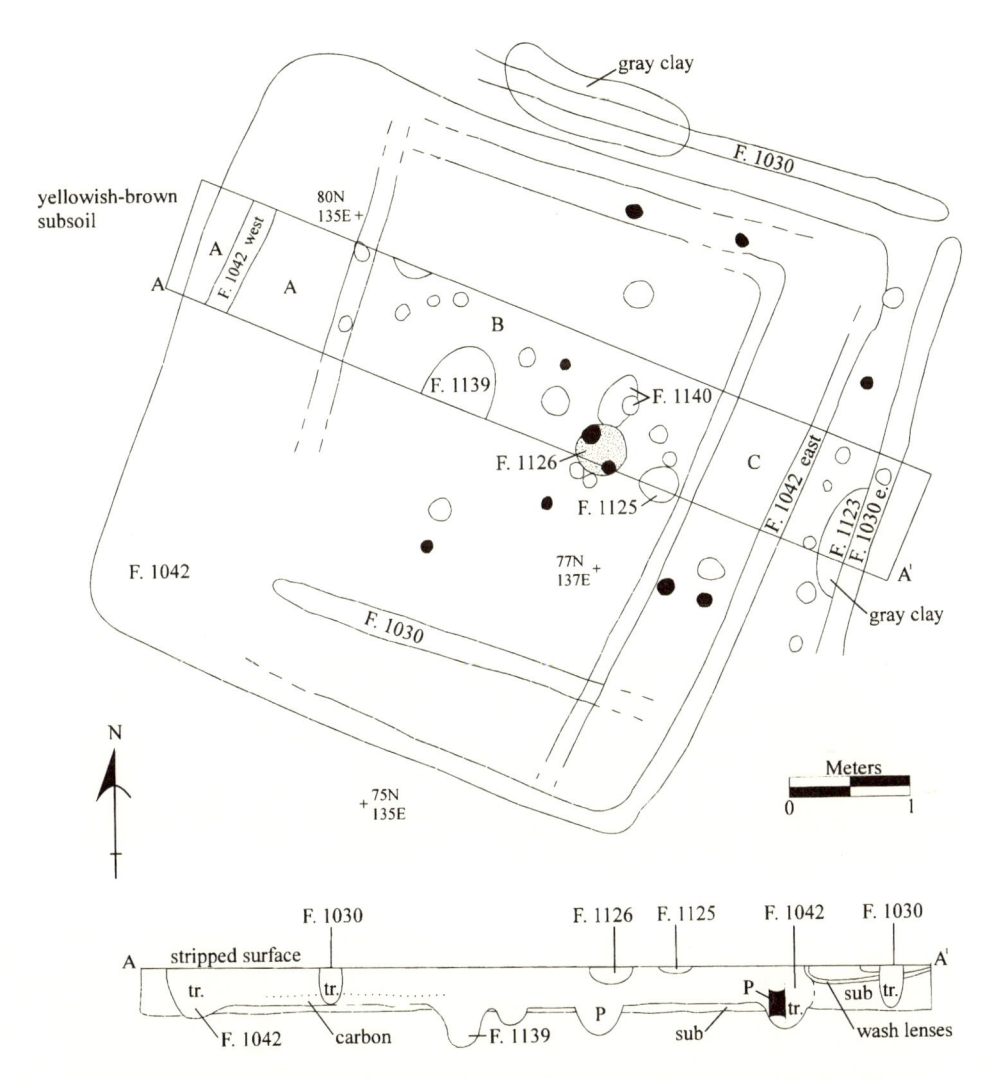

Figure 10-12. Excavation plans of square wall-trench structures 1030/1042 (*left*) and 1036 (*right*) at Moon.

sonnel. At Burris (3CG218), a village on the Cache River in Craighead County (Figure 10-1), a wall-trench structure with internal dimensions of 5.4 × 5.9 meters (32 square meters) was oriented 15 degrees east of north and probably dated to the mid-fourteenth century (Jeter 1988). Two wall-trench structures identified a Middle Mississippian–period farmstead at Brougham Lake (3CT98), in Crittenden County (Figure 10-1) (Klinger et al. 1983:344–45). The small structure had interior dimensions of 2.4 × 4.4 meters (10.6 square meters) and was oriented 26 degrees east of north. The larger building contained two rooms and

246 | Benn

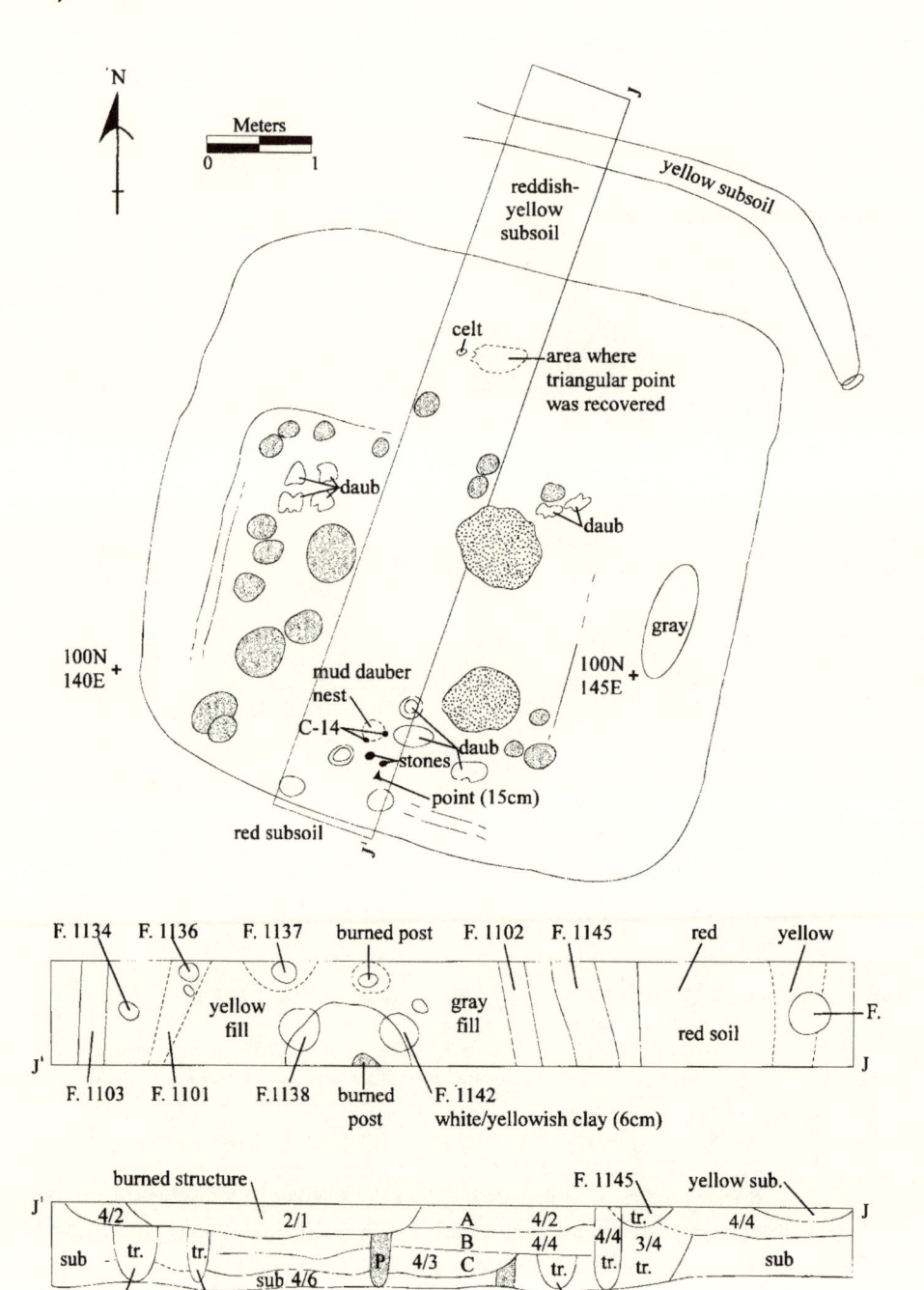

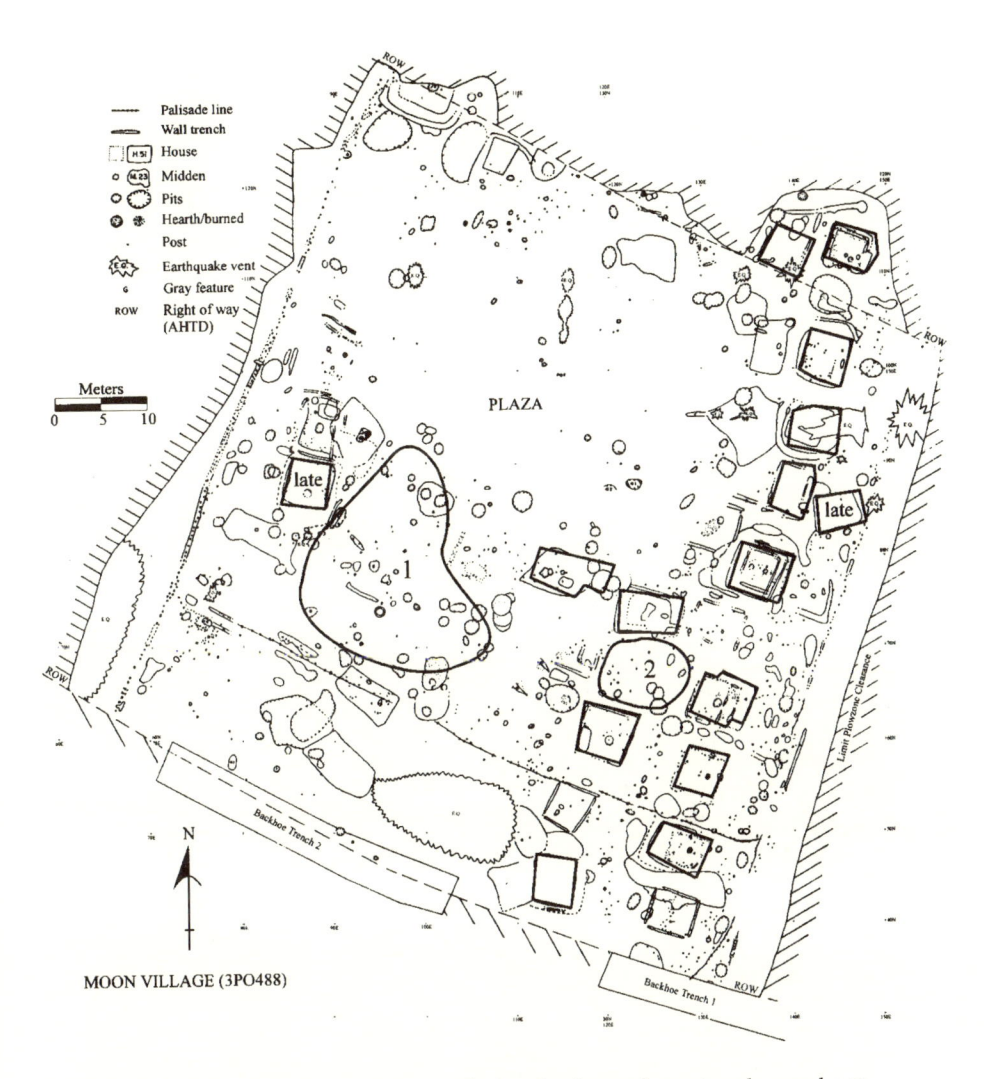

Figure 10-13. Locations of structures with deep basins and courtyards 1 and 2 at Moon. *AHTD*, Arkansas Highway and Transportation Department.

had a combined interior area of 23.3 square meters; it was oriented 63 degrees east of north. Other Middle Mississippian sites the size of Moon or larger include 3PO59 (Morse 1968) and Hazel (3PO6) (Morse and Smith 1973), both near Marked Tree, Arkansas (Figure 10-1). Site 3PO59 was mapped only from house stains in a plowed field, but structures appeared to have been in rows, and there was a plaza. At Hazel, which had a thick midden and a large mound, the exposed portion of the Middle Mississippian component contained more than two dozen structures in as many as six rows (Morse and Smith 1973). Daub was uncommon in the Hazel structures, some of which appeared to have been quite

248 | Benn

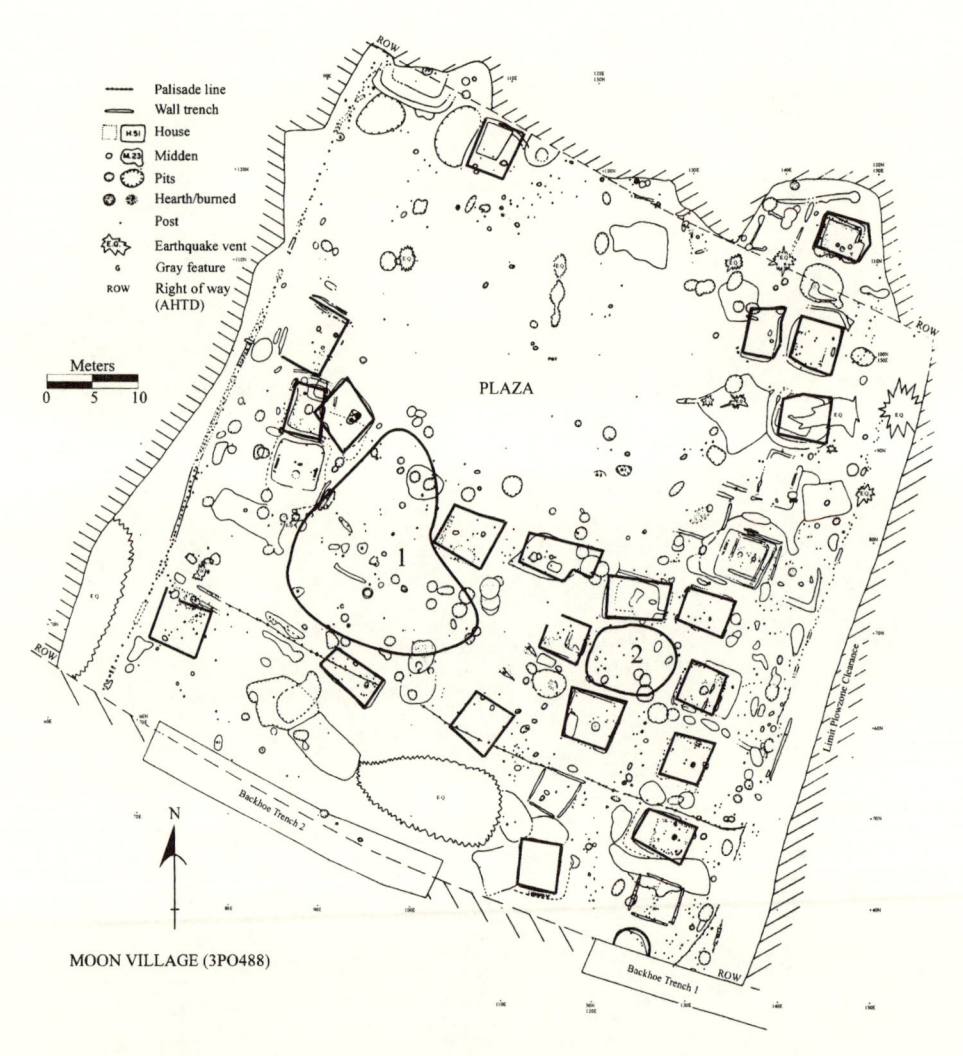

Figure 10-14. Locations of burned structures and courtyards 1 and 2 at Moon. *AHTD*, Arkansas Highway and Transportation Department.

large (6 to 7 meters on each side). Most structures and rows of structures were oriented 28 to 30 degrees east of north.

Snodgrass, in Butler County, Missouri (Figure 10-1), is the most completely excavated Middle Mississippian village in the central Mississippi Valley (Price and Griffin 1979). A century or more of occupation there overlapped with the time Moon was occupied (Perttula, Chapter 8). Snodgrass was larger than Moon, with roughly three times as many houses and three courtyards serving three segments of the village. The most prominent segment consisted of thirty-eight houses in four rows and a courtyard surrounded by a white-clay wall in the southwestern area of the village. The orientation of palisade walls and house rows ranged from 27 to 30 degrees east of north, and average house size ranged from 15.5 square meters in Segment 2, to 17.9 square meters in Segment 3, to 30.0 square meters in prominent Segment 1 (Price and Griffin 1979:51, 156). Snodgrass houses were of the square, wall-trench type and were set in basins; they had mat-and-cane walls and thatched roofs.

The preceding descriptions are too few to draw any compelling conclusions about trends in house size during the Early Mississippian and Middle Mississippian periods in northeastern Arkansas and southeastern Missouri, though the temporal continuity of the square or rectangular house type, as well as similarity in mode of construction and orientation between houses of the two periods, is striking (see Morse and Morse 1983:256–66). The significant change detected in these data occurs in the structure of community organization. From the Early Mississippian period to the Middle Mississippian period there was a trend toward fortified, consolidated villages, with houses arranged in rows.

Pottery Distribution

Excavated-feature proveniences at Moon yielded 24,855 Mississippian-period sherds in addition to a few dozen other ceramic items such as earspools, cones, discoidals, disks, beads, pipe fragments, and abraders (Benn 1992).[2] In terms of established types, the overwhelming majority of sherds—99.9 percent—were of Mississippi Plain (Phillips 1970:130–35). Sherds of Bell Plain (Phillips 1970:58–61), containing burnished surfaces, reduced colors, and a characteristic temper of finely pulverized grog and shell (Million 1975), made up the remaining 0.1 percent of the sherds. All Mississippi Plain rims were from jars; Bell Plain rims were exclusively from bowls and plates. Using rimsherds ($n = 466$) as a proxy for vessels, 98.6 percent of the vessels from Moon were of Mississippi Plain and 1.4 percent were of Bell Plain. The proportion of vessel forms for both types in the collection was roughly 52 percent jars, 26 percent bowls, 20 percent plates, and 2 percent bottles. Only thirty of 24,820 (0.1 percent) Mississippi Plain sherds and five of thirty-five (14 percent) Bell Plain sherds from excavated feature contexts were decorated by trailing, incising, modeling, or painting/slipping. The decorated pottery types in the Moon collection were as follows (see Phillips [1970] for type descriptions): among coarse-shell-tempered paste (Mississippi Plain) vessels, types included Barton Incised, *var. Barton* (one vessel), Carson Red-on-Buff (three), Mound Place Incised, *var. Mound Place* (one), Nodena Red-and-White (one), O'Byam Incised, *var. O'Byam* (fourteen), Old Town Red, *var. Old Town* (one), and Rhodes Incised (two); among fine-shell-tempered paste (Bell Plain) vessels, types included Mound Place Incised, *var. Mound Place* (two vessels), Mound Place Incised, *var. Chickasawba* (one), O'Byam Incised, *var. O'Byam* (one), and Rhodes Incised (one). The proportion of decorated and Bell Plain sherds in the Moon assemblage is significantly lower than the percentages reported for village assemblages from Late Mississippian sites in the region (Morse 1981; O'Brien 1994a).

We can use decorated pottery and/or finer-paste (Bell Plain) pottery, even though the sherds occur in low frequency, to examine spatial patterns that might have mirrored social patterns at Moon. A similar spatial analysis was done by Price and Griffin (1979) using more-numerous materials from the Snodgrass excavations. What propels this analysis is the assumption that decorated and fine-paste pottery (regardless of whether it was decorated) was produced and exchanged in low quantity because it was used in special contexts (e.g., ritual presentations of food, burial offerings, and the like). Therefore, its distribution within the village should reflect social standing among the residents of house clusters as well as intravillage interactions. Of course, factors that intervene between the evidence for social interaction and the archaeological record are numerous (e.g., Schiffer 1987). In the case of Moon, we are concerned with artifacts in secondary contexts—trash-filled pits and back-filled house pits—that have been subjected to weathering. What we are seeking in the Moon data are concentrations of special artifacts within spatially clustered houses and features, as well as refits of artifacts that reveal intravillage connections.

For the purpose of plotting the distribution of ceramics and special objects, features in the Moon community were grouped into seven zones (see Figures 10-9 and 10-14): (1) northwest quadrant (grid 90–120E), (2) northeast quadrant (100–120 N), (3) East Plaza (72–95N), (4) Courtyard 2, (5) southeast quadrant (south of interior fortification), (6) Courtyard 1, and (7) southwest quadrant (Table 10-2). The percentages in the far right column of Table 10-2 clearly depict that the majority of material came from Courtyard 1 (29.1 percent) and from the trash-filled pits and house basins surrounding Courtyard 1 in the southwest quadrant (28.2 percent). The cluster of Courtyard 2 and surrounding houses is a distant second with 16.4 percent of the items, and the northeast quadrant produced 12.7 percent of the objects. One artifact concentration in and around Courtyard 1 consisted of ceramic earspools (six of seven earspools occurred in that area). Earspools are items of personal adornment that would be expected to be associated with a particular set of individuals sharing a relationship within the community (Price and Griffin 1979:97, 101) (e.g., a kinship group, an economic class, or a social organization). Other artifacts with more than half their numbers within and around the Courtyard 1 cluster are bottle sherds (eleven of eighteen sherds), decorated sherds (eighteen of thirty-two), and microdrills (thirteen of sixteen). Microdrills are the sole potential piece of evidence for shell-bead production (among other possible uses) at Moon; shell, if it once was present, was not preserved. The one artifact class lacking an area of concentration (Table 10-2) is the discoidal.

The significance of the Courtyard 1–southwest house cluster in the context of the whole village can be visualized by plotting the distribution of sherds of

Table 10-2. Decorated Pottery and Special Artifacts from Moon

Location	Decorated Sherds	Bell Plain Sherds	Bottle Sherds	Ear-spools	Discoidals	Micro-drills	Percent of total
NW Quadrant							
Eight features	3	1	0	0	1	1	5.5
NE Quadrant							
Seven features	2	7	3	0	2	0	12.7
East Plaza							
Three features	0	0	2	1	1	0	3.6
Courtyard 2							
Sixteen features	9	5	1	0	1	2	16.4
SE Quadrant							
Four features	0	2	1	0	2	0	4.5
Courtyard 1							
Eight features	12	4	4	3	0	9	29.1
SW Quadrant							
Fifteen features	6	8	7	3	3	4	28.2
Total	32	27	18	7	10	16	100% of 110 items

burnished Bell Plain and other decorated pottery types. If pottery usually was disposed in trash facilities adjacent to houses, then it is apparent that some households in all but one house cluster had access, albeit unequal, to use of the finer pottery. For example, the Courtyard 2–southeast house cluster (structures 435 and 463, adjacent pits, and basin 464) contained the second-largest amount ($n = 16$) of burnished and decorated sherds. Nine sherds came from Structure 51 and from one of the large trash basins (Feature 171/178/200) next to that house in the northeast cluster. Sherd refits help trace some of the disposal patterns of the thirty sherds from the Courtyard 1–southwest cluster. A group of pits (1, 4, 61, and 69 [Figure 10-9]) on the east side of Courtyard 1 yielded the largest number of special items on the site: nine decorated sherds, four Bell Plain sherds, three bottle fragments, nineteen burnished sherds, two earspools, and nine microdrills. There are sherd refits from this cluster to the East Plaza (Feature 361) cluster and to Feature 40—a pit located on the edge of the plaza at the center of the village that contained five fine-paste sherds. Another refit from the features 1, 4, 61, and 69 group goes to the complex of trash-filled house basins in the southwest quadrant (features 3, 88, and 154), which contained nine special items and two refits to other areas of the village.

In sum, with the majority of special pottery and other artifacts, the Courtyard 1–southwest cluster is the best candidate for the location of a preeminent segment of the Moon community. By coincidence, a Courtyard 1 feature yielded the earliest radiocarbon date for Moon; the feature was located in the plaza, within the palisade marking the oldest portion of the village. This organizational pattern is very similar to the community pattern found at Snodgrass, where the most-prominent segment of the village, at least as distinguished by artifact distributions, also was in the southwestern part of the village and was separated from the other residences by a wall (Price and Griffin 1979:139).

Community and Settlement Patterns

The Early Mississippian–period Priestly site had a community pattern consisting of a row of about a half dozen rectangular or square single-post houses on a sand ridge next to a water source. Also present was an unusually large (16 × 18 meters), round, roofless charnel structure that appeared to be too large to have been built solely by the small number of Priestly residents and probably served a dispersed community beyond that hamlet (Benn 1990:74). This pattern is similar to that of many Late Woodland and Early Mississippian communities in the American Bottom (e.g., Emerson 1991; Kelly, Ozuk et al. 1984)—that is, the pattern of permanent residences clustered around a courtyard or grouped along the edge of an oxbow lake and sometimes associated with a ritual structure, such as groups of four pits and large buildings (Kelly 1990a). Small sites such as these, termed hamlets or small villages, remained part of the Mississippian culture pattern at least until A.D. 1400 (Smith 1978c, 1995) and perhaps into the historical period (Morse 1981).

Small Early Mississippian–period settlements were dispersed across the alluvial landscape of the central Mississippi Valley, much as Late Woodland–period settlements were dispersed in other parts of the Midwest (Braun and Plog 1982:515; House 1982; Kelly, Finney et al. 1984:126; Morse and Morse 1983:184). Yet, we do not know whether the Late Woodland populations were sedentary, which we assume Early Mississippian populations were. Broad survey data from northeastern Arkansas (Morse and Morse 1983:183) and southeastern Missouri (Dunnell and Feathers 1991:39) indicate there were many small sites with Late Baytown (Late Woodland) and Early Mississippian components at the same locations. Morse and Morse (1983:183) interpreted their survey data from Mississippi County, Arkansas, which showed fewer numbers of Mississippian-period than Baytown-period sites, as evidence for population nucleation during the Mississippian period. Their interpretation of survey data depended on relatively equal preservation of sand- and shell-tempered sherds. Because this is not necessarily the case, we cannot be certain when or if population nucleation took place during the Early Mississippian period. Nevertheless, it is clear that Late Woodland and Early Mississippian peoples occupied the same alluvial environment. The coincidence of Late Woodland–period and Early Mississippian–period sites has been observed in the Ozark Highlands as well (Price and Price 1984). I interpret this association of components to mean that Woodland and many Early Mississippian communities maintained similar relations with their environmental setting, principally as hunters, gatherers, and simple horticulturists living in small, dispersed communities.

Zebree (Figure 10-1) was a fortified, 1.15-hectare village, which made it one of the largest Early Mississippian sites in northeastern Arkansas (Morse 1975; Morse and Morse 1977; Morse and Morse 1983). Zebree might have had a plaza, but its houses were clustered with associated midden and storage areas rather than being arranged in rows. Other Early Mississippian sites of this size exist in the northwestern lowlands of the central Mississippi Valley (see D. F. Morse and P. [A.] Morse 1990), and their appearance may prove to be a characteristic that distinguishes Early Mississippian from Late Woodland villages. Other equally important elements of the Early Mississippian communities in northeastern Arkansas include building structures with the same orientation, grouping structures around a plaza or courtyards, and constructing public facilities such as the charnel structure at Priestly. Kelly's (1990a, 1990b) reconstructions of the Range-site communities in the American Bottom suggest that the process of village reorganization happened gradually over approximately 350 years: a plaza and four ceremonial pits appeared during the Late Woodland Patrick phase; a large structure was added during the Early Mississippian Dohack phase; houses were organized linearly during the Range phase; and, finally, a nucleated village was created during the George Reeves phase. It seems likely that similar changes were taking place in the community pattern of Early Mississippian–period sites in northeastern Arkansas (see Morse and Morse 1983:202–33).

The next significant development in community patterning was the emergence of planned communities and ceremonial centers with conspicuous mounds after about A.D. 1000. This happened about the same time among people in central and southern Arkansas (House and House 1985:131; Rolingson 1982), in the central Mississippi Valley (Dunnell and Feathers 1991:37; D. F. Morse and P. [A.] Morse 1990; Nassaney 1987:141), along the Black Warrior River in Alabama (Peebles 1978), and in the American Bottom (Kelly 1990b:135; Milner 1985:198). Opinions vary about the degree of population nucleation that occurred at that time. Dunnell and Feathers (1991:37) observed that areas of the Malden Plain with Early Mississippian–period Dunklin-phase and Big Lake-phase settlements lacked Middle Mississippian–period villages, thereby implying that a population relocation had occurred. House sizes increased in some places in the central Mississippi Valley (Morse and Morse 1977) and in the American Bottom (Milner 1985)—a change apparently related to increases in the size of the residential unit.

Outlying settlements in many sections of the Southeast are inferred to have been integrated into a political and exchange hierarchy associated with ceremonial centers, yet there is no indication that all groups actually moved to the centers (Peebles 1978; Steponaitis 1978:436). Isolated farmsteads and hamlets remained part of the settlement system in the central Mississippi Valley until well past the twelfth century A.D. (Lewis 1982). Thus the term population *nucleation* does not adequately describe all of the relations inherent in the process of consolidating the Mississippian settlement pattern—this is more or less the same point made by Teltser in Chapter 7. If there was a general trend toward the population being reorganized into nucleated settlements, the consequences of this change should be evident at the small villages as well as at large ceremonial centers (Paynter 1989:385). Being relatively small and lacking mounds, Moon is one place to observe how the organizational effects of Middle Mississippian-period social and settlement systems affected ordinary people.

Moon was a planned, palisaded village from inception to demise. Houses were organized in rows around courtyards and the plaza. The house compound with the most ceremonial items was the Courtyard 1 cluster in the southwest quadrant of the village, and the plaza was slightly west of center. When the village expanded and houses were rebuilt, the original village pattern was followed down to details, such as rebuilding the same types of structures, positioning houses in the locations of previous ones, and maintaining roughly the same spacing (5 meters) between houses. House size varied, with the modal size at 20.25 square meters (six of twenty-six houses). No house cluster contained structures that were much larger than houses in any other cluster—just the opposite of what Price and Griffin (1979:156) found at Snodgrass. Moon was abandoned as a unit after about A.D. 1350, and most standing structures, except the palisade, burned. Exactly why the palisade did not burn is unknown. A village-wide conflagration also destroyed the houses at Snodgrass.

Another aspect of the planned-village pattern at Moon was the orientation of the palisade walls and house rows at roughly 23 degrees east of north. This orientation is at one end of the range of site alignments (24 to 33 degrees east of north) for five Powers-phase sites reported by Price and Griffin (1979:51)—an alignment tendency that they speculatively called an "astronomical phenomenon." Kay (1990) has reasoned that building house walls so they faced away from the cardinal directions would have functioned to reduce the impact of solar radiation during the summer. However, physical orientation of houses would not have mattered much for control of solar heat if the thatched roofs hung over enough to insulate the walls and/or if the houses were partially submerged in earthen basins. Returning to the suggestion of Price and Griffin, I would note that where the evidence existed at Moon, doorways were located on the southeastern wall. This alignment would have allowed the rays of the rising sun at the winter solstice to enter the houses.

By establishing this planned village with an orientation and internal organization similar to those of other villages in the Eastern and Western Lowlands of the central Mississippi Valley, Moon residents might have been participating in a socioeconomic and political process of consolidation. Comparison of the Priestly and Moon villages illustrates my argument. Although Moon and Priestly shared many aspects of house construction type, structure spacing, and household clustering—a basic Mississippian social model—the two settlements were not established in the same manner. Priestly was a small cluster of houses strung along an undefended sand ridge; Moon was established as a planned, compact village with houses organized in rows. Moon exhibited a kind of uniform spatial organization that packed more people behind palisade walls—an arrangement entirely unlike that at Priestly. Moon fits comfortably within the pattern of small and medium-sized palisaded villages in the Powers phase of southeastern Missouri (Price 1978). Powers-phase villages, such as Turner and Snodgrass (Figure 10-1), were elements of an integrated regional settlement pattern that also included limited-activity sites, farmsteads, hamlets, and one civic-ceremonial center (Price and Griffin 1979:9; see also Perttula, Chapter 8).

The absence of a ceremonial building at Moon is another element that distinguishes it from Priestly, which contained a charnel structure. Recently, another village site (3PO555) about the size of Moon but containing a mound was found a little more than a kilometer north of Priestly by David Williamson of the Arkansas Highway and Transportation Department. Surface material indicates the site might date to the Early Mississippian period. Apparently, by the Middle Mississippian period the locus of public spectacle associated with charnel buildings and mounds had shifted from an ordinary village such as Moon to civic centers such as Langdon (Dunnell, Chapter 9), in Dunklin County, Missouri. Candidates for the regional ceremonial center that oversaw the Moon residents include the Webb, or Bay, mounds and village (Thomas 1894:201), located 10 kilometers north of Moon (Figure 10-1), and two larger villages with mounds located around Marked Tree, about 30 kilometers south of Moon (Morse and Morse 1983:249).

The process of settlement consolidation continued into the Late Mississippian period (Morse and Morse 1983; Nassaney 1987:141; Williams 1990). After the Moon village was abandoned about A.D. 1350, numerous settlements appeared along the St. Francis and Tyronza rivers to the south—the heartland of the Parkin phase (Morse 1981). Perhaps the Moon residents moved elsewhere as they were brought under the influence of Parkin—a site that had a 6.5-meter-high mound and a village that was at least twice as large as any other in the region (Morse 1981:56–57). In all likelihood, it was the preeminent civic-ceremonial center in the region. There were three more gradations of settlements in the Parkin system, ranging from 4-hectare villages with mounds to small villages the size of Moon. No farmsteads have been located around the Parkin site, and all of the villages were linked by the routes of the St. Francis and Tyronza rivers (Morse 1981). Settlement configurations represented by the Late Mississippian–period Parkin phase and other contemporary phases in the central Mississippi Valley, such as the Nodena phase (Morse 1973b, 1990), represent massive consolidations of the population (D. F. Morse and P. [A.] Morse 1990:169), which may have contributed to formation of the hypothetical "vacant quarter" (Williams 1980, 1982, 1990).

Concluding Remarks

Moon represents one of many small, palisaded villages in the central Mississippi Valley that lacked mounds, large public buildings, and other symbols of the presence of an elite class of leaders. We know the Moon residents participated in a regional cultural system because their planned village organization, ceramic styles, and everything they manufactured adhered to the Mississippian pattern. The integrating process of Mississippian culture systems has been investigated both in the Mississippi Valley (e.g., Bareis and Porter 1984:7; Morse and Morse 1983) and elsewhere (e.g., Steponaitis 1983) by tracing the development of the Mississippian community out of a Late Woodland base (e.g., Kelly 1990b). These studies suggest that as a generalized Mississippian culture pattern emerged about A.D. 1000, some of the population coalesced into more densely populated communities. However, this coalescence did not signal abandonment of all previously occupied villages. In fact, the organization of domestic (community) life probably was kept fairly intact at some levels and was simply reproduced around a litany of ceremonial systems (Howard 1968; Hudson 1976; Knight 1989). The type of social and political system that promoted penetration of Mississippian beliefs (whatever they might have been) to the village/hamlet level has been termed a "chiefdom" (Knight 1990; Morse and Morse 1983:202; Peregrine 1992:9–26).

Although some aspects of daily life remained intact, the tendency toward population nucleation during the Middle Mississippian period must have, on some plane, represented a fundamental contradiction for a population that prior to that period had made a secure living in smaller communities by relying on a varied subsistence base of hunting, gathering, and native-seed horticulture. My analysis of the contradiction is this: Moon was located within a patchwork of vegetation and aquatic communities, an optimal habitat for pursuing a strategy of selective harvesting of natural resources (Smith 1975:138). Yet, compared to the Priestly folks, the Moon residents reduced the diversity of their subsistence base, relying more heavily on hickory nuts and maize, apparently at the expense of producing large amounts of native-seed crops such as maygrass or exploiting fish and water fowl (Kelly 1992; Pearsall 1992). Moon residents imported at least one Mill Creek chert hoe (there were resharpening chips in the site collections [Sellars et al. 1992]), though we might wonder what difference in efficiency one hoe would make for an entire village.

I suspect the imported hoe had a more important function, namely signifying the influential standing of its owner within the Moon community. Likewise, the reliance on specific resources had a political dimension. Although bone preservation at Moon was poor, it is probable, on the basis of the work of B. D. Smith (1975) and others, that deer was a vital resource (e.g., for meat, hides, tallow, and antler). Maize and nuts, which likewise are found at many sites in the central Mississippi Valley, were productive crops that grew in fixed stands. In an environment where villages were palisaded and movement likely was determined by political interactions, those resources were primary candidates for territorial control by the leaders of a palisaded community. The argument has already been advanced that maize, which requires substantial expenditures of labor, was the choice resource for authority figures to promote in order to support a system of surplus production (Nassaney 1987:141; Nassaney and Cobb 1991:295). Under crowded community conditions, access to certain stands of natural resources can be manipulated in the same fashion through political coercion and raiding. In one sense, D. F. Morse and P. [A.] Morse (1990:170) might be correct in citing "land stewardship" (access to the most productive land, both natural and agricultural) as a factor that promoted nucleation of Middle Mississippian communities. I would add that *political* power as manifest through the productive and reproductive power of kin structures (Peregrine 1992) was the basis for allocations of natural and agricultural resources. Thus an imported Mill Creek hoe could have functioned as a symbol of control over production of a vital resource such as maize. Chiefdoms derive power by concentrating people at the locations of basic production, then inspiring the labor force to transform part of their surplus production into prestige goods, which the elite absorb to reproduce their power base. It appears to me that the challenge for prehistorians lies in connecting the evidence from communities such as Moon to the larger contexts of regional settlement systems, always cognizant of the fact that the power schemes of political leaders reflect from the centers of administration back to the smaller communities where basic production takes place.

11 | Variability in Crowley's Ridge Gravel
Patrick T. McCutcheon and Robert C. Dunnell

For those interested in prehistoric lithic technology, the central Mississippi River valley presents an interesting situation. Although chert and other lithic raw materials are abundant in the surrounding Paleozoic uplands and in the glacial-till sheet to the north, the alluvial-valley surface itself, which in places is more than 150 kilometers wide, lacks rock of even gravel size. Upon entering the valley, streams draining the bedrock source areas lose their competency to transport gravel-size and larger materials. The only major exception to this general picture is Crowley's Ridge, a long, narrow erosional remnant that bisects the valley in a north-south direction (Figures 1-1 and 11-1) (Autin et al. 1991; Fisk 1944; Saucier 1974). The ridge comprises a series of stratified Plio-Pleistocene gravels, mostly chert and orthoquartzite (both part of the widespread Lafayette gravels), and Eocene clays, capped in most places by Pleistocene loess of variable thickness (Autin et al. 1991; Call 1891; Guiccione et al. 1986; Markewich 1993; Potter 1955). Small streams expose the gravels throughout the 280-kilometer length of the ridge. Not surprisingly, throughout prehistory the gravels were the major source of raw material for groups living in much of the central Mississippi Valley. Even so, the use of stone typically was parsimonious away from the margins of the valley (Dunnell et al. 1994; Lewis 1990).

Although archaeologists have come to recognize common rocks occurring in the gravels (e.g., House 1975; Sellars et al. 1992), no quantitative studies of Crowley's Ridge gravel as a source of raw material have been done. Secondary sources are troublesome subjects compared to bedrock sources. Gravel deposits, such as Crowley's Ridge, can contain rock from many bedrock sources, and although this feature made the deposits especially attractive as sources to prehistoric consumers, it also makes them complex analytically. Further, gravel deposits display the added complication of transport variables. Consequently, secondary sources are generally understudied (e.g., Lavin and Prothero 1992; Luedtke 1992; but see Ray 1982; Shelley 1993). Not knowing the composition and size characteristics of the Crowley's Ridge source greatly limits the analysis of lithic artifacts produced from the gravels, and without a quantitative compositional baseline, identifying the attributes that drive material selection is impossible (cf. Andrefsky 1994). For example, because of the relative diversity in the

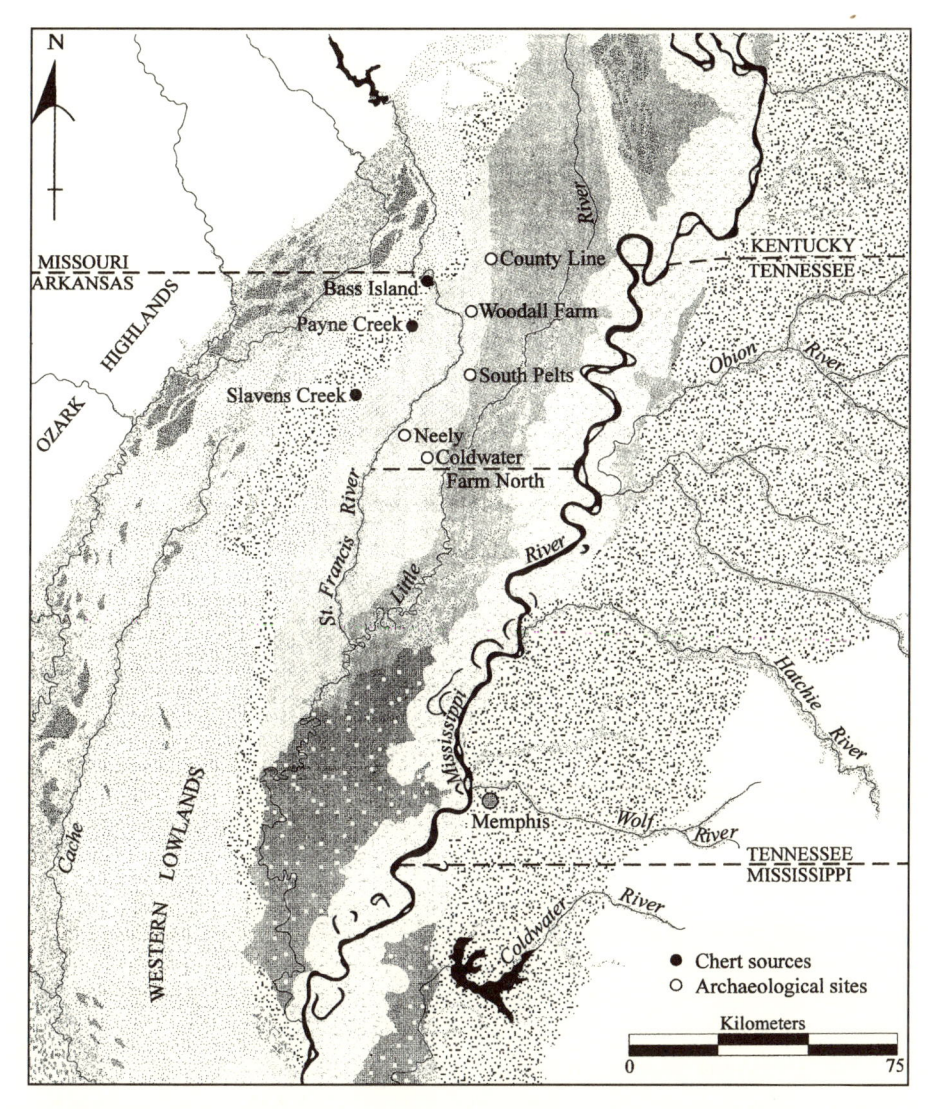

Figure 11-1. Map of the central Mississippi River valley showing the locations of physiographic features, chert-gravel sources that were sampled, and sites mentioned in the text.

raw materials in early lithic assemblages, it sometimes is supposed that Archaic-period people either undertook forays into the uplands or engaged in trade with such areas to acquire raw material. Yet if the bedrock source for such rocks lies in either the Mississippi or Ohio drainage system, the possibility exists that the archaeological source was Crowley's Ridge. Differences in the richness of rock types in archaeological assemblages might simply be a result of variable procurement strategies exploiting the same complex source (e.g., Dunnell and Whittaker 1988; cf. Dunnell and Whittaker 1994).

To address such issues, it is necessary to generate quantitative data on gravel composition. In support of archaeological research in southeastern Missouri, we assembled a number of samples from the Crowley's Ridge source (Figure 11-1). Here we report our initial findings based on an analysis of some of those samples, emphasizing within-source variation in composition and size as well as in the fracture toughness of the common rock types as potential causes of differential exploitation—a phenomenon demonstrated by comparisons of Crowley's Ridge gravel samples with archaeological assemblages from the nearby Malden Plain.

Research Design

We address two broad questions. First, are prehistoric lithic assemblages random samples of Crowley's Ridge gravels? Second, if gravel exploitation was not random, what were the lithic properties responsible for the nonrandom pattern? To answer these questions requires documentation of Crowley's Ridge gravel-size distribution and composition. Both properties may vary from exposure to exposure within the ridge, necessitating multiple samples of the source. Since object size interacts with both our collection methods and those of our prehistoric precursors, we also need to know if, and to what degree, composition and size are correlated (Figure 11-2).

If Crowley's Ridge gravels vary geographically, then the appropriate source/assemblage comparisons ought to pair prehistoric assemblage with the nearest exposure of the gravels. If no compositional differences are found among exposure samples, then source samples can be pooled for comparison with archaeological assemblages. In either case, the null hypothesis to be tested is that prehistoric assemblages are random samples of Crowley's Ridge gravels.

In the event the null hypothesis can be rejected, we are in a position to pursue the second question: What properties of rocks that make up the Crowley's Ridge gravel deposits account for the nonrandom selection? This question requires documentation of the physical properties of the rocks. Potentially critical variables include fracture toughness, gravel size, and response to heat treatment. Fracture toughness is a fundamental property that determines how easily a rock breaks (for a more detailed treatment see McCutcheon and Dunnell 1991) and is therefore directly pertinent to chipped-stone-tool use and manufacture. Gravel size is relevant because it limits the maximum size of tools and affects the energetics of collection and transport. Gravel size can also influence the choice of technology (e.g., bipolar technology [Crabtree 1972; Kuijt and Russell 1993; Shelley 1993; Shott 1989]). Finally, rock may have been selected not for

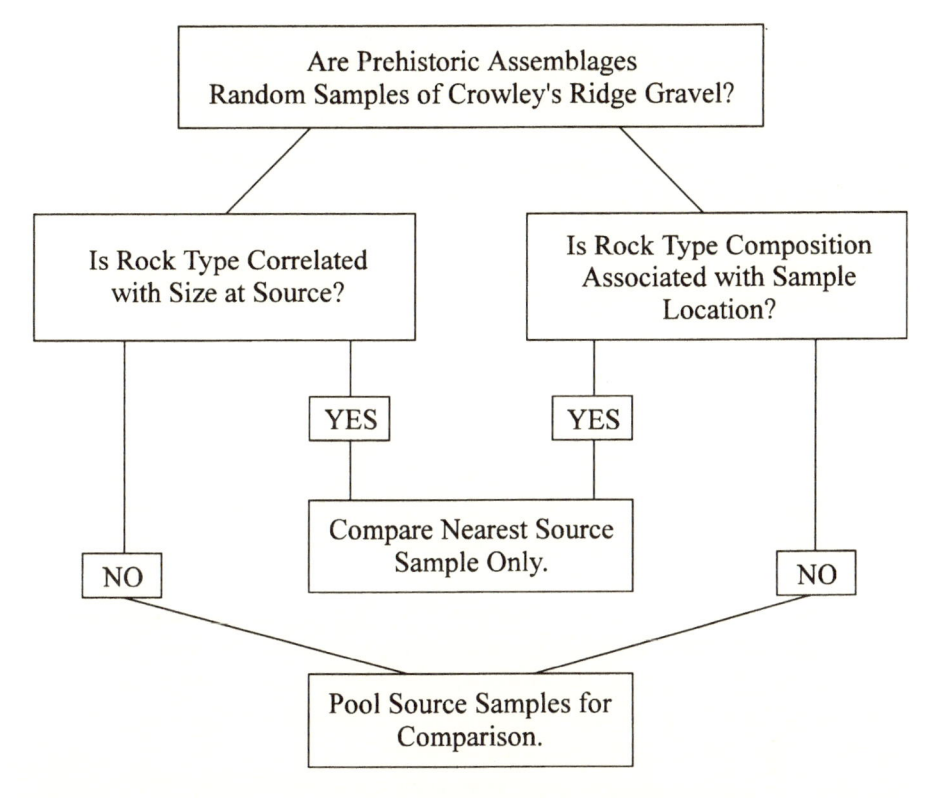

Figure 11-2. Research design used to examine Crowley's Ridge gravels.

properties that influence flaking directly but for its behavior under heat treatment. Heat treatment is a common, but variable, technology in central Mississippi Valley assemblages (Dunnell et al. 1994; House 1975; Morse and Morse 1983; Stanfill 1986), and different rocks may vary substantially in their responses to heating (e.g., Hunt 1994; Luedtke 1992; McCutcheon and Afonso 1994). While experiments are under way that will allow potential for heat treatment to be assessed, they are not sufficiently complete to address that parameter here. Consequently, we deal only with the first two variables, fracture toughness and size.

Classification

Size of rock can be treated metrically; *kind* of rock with respect to fracture toughness cannot be treated as a continuous variable, which thus necessitates the use of classes. The classes used to describe rock composition play a critical role here. In an earlier study (Bangs 1991), a twenty-four–class system was used that considered color, texture, inclusions, and structure. The intent of this classification was to help distinguish sources of raw material. As the variability in Crowley's Ridge gravel had yet to be established, a "splitter" strategy was used. Since Crowley's Ridge gravel is a secondary deposit that was derived from many bedrock sources, our initial sort overdifferentiated among samples. Examination of hundreds of gravels in subsequent studies led us to collapse the original twenty-four classes (nineteen cherts and five orthoquartzites) into twelve classes (seven cherts and five orthoquartzites), eliminating those types known to co-occur within the same rock. These categories did not correspond to the bedrock sources of the gravel, since the bedrock sources overlap in most properties used in the classification (Ray 1985). The classification still mixed attributes relevant to provenance with those pertinent to the fracture properties of rock. Subsequent to the initial presentation of the data used here (McCutcheon and Dunnell 1993), all materials, both geological and archaeological, were identified with a new classification that uses rock properties relevant to stone-tool manufacture and that are uncompromised by source characteristics.

Much experimental work that could provide the basis for selecting criteria pertinent to fracture properties has been carried out at the microscale level, at which materials are often homogeneous (see Luedtke 1992 for a summary of work). Although these kinds of studies have many advantages, not the least of which is their high reproducibility, they often are irrelevant to lithic technology directly. At the millimeter and larger scales—that is, at the scales at which people manipulate rock in lithic technologies—rock is not a homogeneous material, and large-scale flaws play an important role (e.g., Howarth 1987; Whittaker et al. 1992). In an earlier report (McCutcheon and Dunnell 1991), we showed that microtest results did not correlate well with macroscale properties. The vast majority of Crowley's Ridge rock displays one or more inhomogeneities. Consequently, our classification had to focus on macroscale properties that might affect fracture properties.

In *An Archaeologist's Guide to Chert and Flint,* Luedtke (1992) devoted an entire chapter to physical properties that are relevant to the mechanical behavior of rock (see also Cotterell and Kamminga 1979, 1987, 1990; Lawn and Marshall 1979). We need to be able to categorize rocks so that classes are more or less uniform with regard to (1) the energy required to produce macroscale fracturing (fracture toughness) and (2) the predictability of the fractures so produced. Potential measures of the latter include (1) standard deviation of the energy required to cause fracture and (2) variation in the amount of rock removed in fracture.

Crack propagation is heavily influenced by particle shape and size (Lawn and Marshall 1979). In most materials, cracks propagate around particles, increasing the surface area of the crack and thus the applied force necessary to produce and sustain a crack. Color differences are caused typically by the substitution of metal ions in the silica lattice or by fine-grain inclusions (Rossman 1994), both of which set up stresses internal to the rock and which may either retard or expedite fracturing, depending on their orientation relative to the applied force. As a result, physical properties employed here consist of three dimensions: groundmass, inclusions, and distribution of inclusions (Table 11-1).

Groundmass (Bates and Jackson 1984) is divided into six attribute classes. Three address patterns: *bedded,* in which the planes of the original sedimentary rock have been inherited by the chert; *banded,* in which concretionary growth has resulted in color/textural concentric differences; and *mottled,* in which apparent compositional and/or textural differences are irregularly but ubiquitously distributed. Three other classes address textural differences in homogeneous materials: *uniform,* characterizing specimens in which no grains are apparent at magnifications of 40× or less; *granular,* describing specimens in which angular and subangular particles are joined by a fine matrix; and *oolitic,* characterizing specimens in which rounded, often concentrically banded particles are cemented by fine material.

Inclusions are inhomogeneities that occur at a second, higher scale and are distinguished from textural properties of the groundmass in that they are more or less widely separated from other groundmass particles. Three modes are employed: *solid inclusions, void inclusions,* and *no inclusions.* Voids, which always act to impede fracturing by increasing the surface area of the crack and thereby the applied force needed to propagate it, are distinguished from solid inclusions, which may or may not retard crack growth, depending on their own composition and how well cemented they are to the groundmass. It would have been desirable to separate quartzose inclusions, which are similar to the groundmass in fracturing properties, from nonquartzose inclusions, which are more likely to behave as voids. Identifying the material constituting the inclusions would have proved prohibitive at this stage in the classification development. To ensure consistent tabulation, inclusion content is separated into two dimensions—void inclusions and solid inclusions—each of which has only two modes, present and absent.

The distribution of inclusions is treated with four modes: *random,* denoting distributions without apparent pattern at the scales observed; *uniform,* denoting a distribution in which inclusions are regularly spaced and oriented; *structured,* in which inclusions are concentrated to form bands, planes, and/or patterns; and *none.* By changing the force required to propagate a crack, patterns in the distribution of inclusions can be expected to influence both fracture toughness and fracture predictability. Random distributions decrease predictability, whereas uniform and structured distributions guide fractures in particular directions and increase predictability. Since inclusions are divided into voids and solids, the distributions are likewise divided.

Table 11-1. Dimensions and Attributes for the Rock Physical-Properties Classification

Groundmass
1. Uniform (Gm1): a consistent and unvarying structure, in which the distribution of color, texture, or luster is even.
2. Bedding Planes (Gm2): linear striae superimposed upon and parallel to one another. Individual stria can be distinct in color and/or texture.
3. Concentric Banding (Gm3): concentric layers of different color and/or texture.
4. Mottled (Gm4): abrupt and uneven variations (e.g., swirled or clouded) in color or texture.
5. Granular (Gm5): a consistent structure composed of many individual grains joined by a fine matrix.
6. Oolitic (Gm6): the matrix is composed of small round or ovoid grains cemented together by fine material.

Solid Inclusions
1. Present (SI+): particles present that are distinct from the rock body (e.g., isolated filled cracks, grains, fossils, minerals).
2. Absent (SI-): particles are absent from the rock body at 40X magnification or lower.

Void Inclusions
1. Present (VI+): areas devoid of any material are present in the rock body (e.g., vugs, fossil and mineral casts, unfilled cracks).
2. Absent (VI-): areas devoid of any material are absent from the rock body at 40X magnification or lower.

Distribution of Solid Inclusions
1. Random (SD1): the distribution of inclusions is irregular and not patterned in any fashion.
2. Uniform (SD2): the distribution of inclusions is unvarying and even throughout the rock body.
3. Structured (SD3): the distribution of inclusions is patterned or isolated within the rock body.
4. None (SD4): inclusions are absent from the rock body at 40X or lower magnification.

Distribution of Void Inclusions
1. Random (VD1): the distribution of inclusions is irregular and not patterned in any fashion.
2. Uniform (VD2): the distribution of inclusions is unvarying and even throughout the rock body.
3. Structured (VD3): the distribution of inclusions is patterned or isolated within the rock body.
4. None (SD4): inclusions are absent from the rock body at 40X or lower magnification.

Methods and Materials

Since our interests lie in southeastern Missouri, we did not attempt to sample the whole of Crowley's Ridge but rather confined our samples to those from three exposures in the northern part of the ridge: Bass Island, Payne Creek, and Slavens Creek (Figure 11-1). Inasmuch as prehistoric exploitation can be expected to vary over time, we selected five archaeological assemblages spanning the past 3000 years or so (Figure 11-1).

Gravel Samples

The bedrock sources for *common* cherts and orthoquartzites cannot lie at great distances from gravels. Plumley (1949) showed that for the Black Hills (South Dakota) terrace gravels, only quartzose rocks, such as chert and quartzites, were present in the 16- to 32-millimeter size class after 80 kilometers of transport. Other, softer rock is abraded to sand-size particles after that distance. On the basis of the occasional presence of sandstone in the northern end of Crowley's Ridge and the similarity in lithology among Crowley's Ridge chert gravels and Paleozoic upland cherts, Potter (1955) suggested that the source for at least some Crowley's Ridge gravel lay less than 160 kilometers from the periphery of the central Mississippi Valley. The identification of particular sources for the gravels is much enhanced by Ray's (1985) excellent account of the chert and other lithic sources for southern Missouri. Fossils, texture, and structure make it clear that the bulk of Crowley's Ridge cherts and orthoquartzites originated in the Ozark Highlands immediately north of the northern end of Crowley's Ridge. The most prominent materials appear to be Ordovician cherts and orthoquartzites, particularly those in the Roubidoux formation (Heller 1954) and to a lesser extent those in the Gasconade and Jefferson City formations. The occurrence of fenestrated bryozoan and large crinoid fossils, however, indicates a Mississippian Burlington chert contribution as well. More precise identification of provenance is unlikely because, as Ray (1985) notes, isolated fragments can often be allocated only to broadly defined Ordovician or Mississippian groups, and even those assignments can be ambiguous.

Importantly, some potentially archaeologically significant materials, such as St. Francis rhyolite (Perttula 1984) and the particularly uniform and highly tractable Burlington-chert variant from the Crescent Hills region near St. Louis, have not been found in any Crowley's Ridge sample to date. Potter (1955) suggested that the rhyolite (pre-Cambrian deposits in Missouri) was not a source of gravel because igneous and metamorphic rocks are not as resistant to abrasion as are chert and other quartzose rocks. Similarly, Burlington chert may be too brittle to survive transport in particle sizes larger than sand.

Although various exposures of Crowley's Ridge gravel occur (gravel quarries), we restricted our sampling to natural exposures that would have been available in the prehistoric past. At Payne Creek, in Clay County, Arkansas, two 1-meter squares were laid out on a gravel bar within the channel of Payne Creek where it emerges from Crowley's Ridge onto the Malden Plain. All gravels greater than or equal to 2 centimeters in their longest dimension were collected. At Bass Island, also in Clay County, two 1-meter squares were laid out on gravel bars within the channel of a small ephemeral stream that drains from the ridge into an old oxbow meander (Bass Island) of the St. Francis River. There, all gravels greater than or equal to 3 centimeters in their longest dimension were collected from two quadrants of each grid unit. At Slavens Creek, in Greene County, Arkansas, a single 2 × 2-meter unit was laid out on a gravel bar within the channel of the creek. All cobbles greater than or equal to 4 centimeters in their longest dimension were collected from two quadrants, while all cobbles greater than 8 centimeters in their longest dimension were collected from the remaining two quadrants. Because the size criterion used in each collection differed, if composition correlated with size, there would be serious biases in any composition analysis unless the effects were corrected by using only cobbles of a size range consistent across all collections. This kind of correction requires looking at the Payne Creek, Slavens Creek, and Bass Island gravels between 4 and 8 centimeters.

Gravel Size/Shape

Since Crowley's Ridge gravels have weathered and often stained exterior surfaces, it was necessary to break each cobble included in the study in order to assign it to the appropriate material class. Prior to breakage, the weight and maximum length of each cobble was recorded. In an earlier study (Bangs 1991), the shape of the cobble was traced and then subjected to a partly automated image analysis to determine shape attributes such as length/width ratio, equivalent diameter sphere, and roundness. That study, which used the collection from the Payne Creek locality, showed that statistically significant shape differences occurred only between orthoquartzite and chert cobbles (Bangs 1991); no significant differences were found within the orthoquartzite and chert classes. Further, there was no significant correlation between shape and size, and consequently, shape analysis was dropped in later studies. Results reported here suggest this decision may have been premature, though the amount of information lost is small and appears not to be of general relevance. Weight and maximum length were used to examine the heterogeneity of gravel size as well as potential variables influencing differential use.

Fracture Toughness

Mechanical-toughness testing was done on a single-pendulum, dynamic-impact loader modified to break samples. A minimum of six specimens measuring 20 × 20 × 5 millimeters were cut from gravels of each major composition type. The dynamic-loading mechanism employed a 156.5-gram blunt indenter. A vice held each cube at a 45-degree angle to the indenter at point of impact and the sample was struck 1 millimeter below the edge at the middle of the edge. Each cube could be used for four tests, one on each side. The distance from the specimen at which the indenter was released allows an ordinal-scale (potentially interval-scale) measurement of the load required to produce catastrophic failure.

Results

Gravel Size

Our first concern is whether rock physical properties correlate with gravel size, because the results of this examination determine what samples can be used in subsequent analyses. The null hypothesis is that there is no difference in mean dimensions of gravels of different composition within the same collections. Looking at each class in the rock physical-property classification would have introduced spurious rejections because of the large number of combinations and would have been invalid in any case because many classes had values of zero or less than five. Consequently, we examined dimensions of variation one at a time (groundmass, solid and void inclusions, and inclusion distribution). We tested mean weight and mean length, each a slightly different measurement of size. A two-sample *t*-test (assuming unequal variances) was used. One hundred *t*-tests (Payne Creek and Slavens Creek, thirty-six tests each; Bass Island, twenty-eight tests) were performed using a .05 significance level. The results are shown in Table 11-2. In the Bass Island collection, some of the modes were not represented, and as a result comparisons were not made, which explains the fewer number of *t*-tests for this collection. In Table 11-2, each matrix compares modes of a single dimension. For example, in the first matrix the different modes for the dimension "groundmass" are compared, where the mean weight of uniform groundmass (Gm_1) is compared with mean weight of bedded groundmass (Gm_2), and so on. In this case, the null hypothesis is Gm_1 is equal to Gm_2. All comparisons that resulted in rejection of the null hypothesis are labeled with an *R*.

Even with the reduced number of comparisons, a few (ca. five at the .05 significance level) spurious rejections of the null hypothesis are to be expected. Both the pattern of rejections evident in the tables and the redundancy among all six suggest that the presence/absence of void inclusions affects cobble size as measured by both mean weight and length in all three gravel collections. Two cases of the rejected null hypotheses consist of one in the Bass Island collection between mean weight of bedded (Gm_2) cherts compared with mottled (Gm_4) cherts and one in the Slavens Creek collection in mean length between mottled (Gm_4) and granular (Gm_5) cherts. Although plausible explanations of each

268 | McCutcheon and Dunnell

Table 11-2. Results of *t*-Tests for Gravel Collections Comparing Size to Rock Physical-Properties-Classification Dimensions

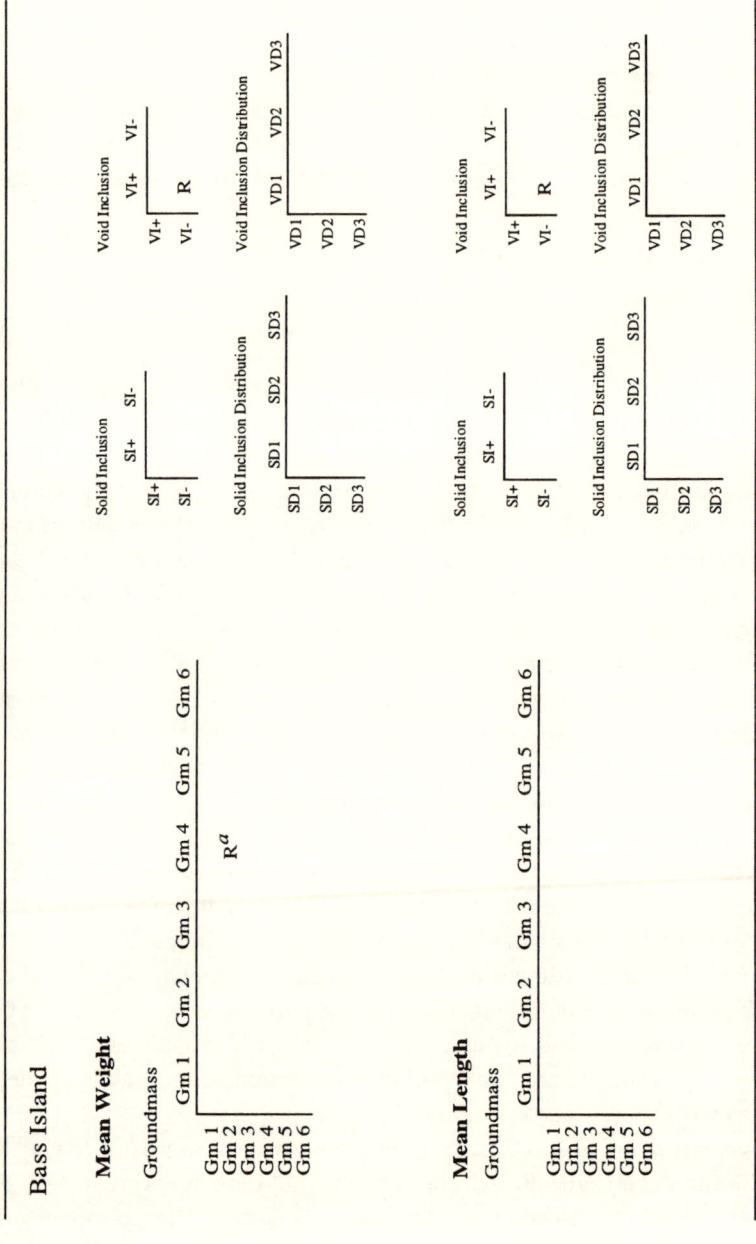

Bass Island

Mean Weight

Groundmass

	Gm 1	Gm 2	Gm 3	Gm 4	Gm 5	Gm 6
Gm 1						
Gm 2						
Gm 3						
Gm 4			R^a			
Gm 5						
Gm 6						

Solid Inclusion

	SI+	SI−
SI+		
SI−		R

Solid Inclusion Distribution

	SD1	SD2	SD3
SD1			
SD2			
SD3			

Void Inclusion

	VI+	VI−
VI+		
VI−		R

Void Inclusion Distribution

	VD1	VD2	VD3
VD1			
VD2			
VD3			

Mean Length

Groundmass

	Gm 1	Gm 2	Gm 3	Gm 4	Gm 5	Gm 6
Gm 1						
Gm 2						
Gm 3						
Gm 4						
Gm 5						
Gm 6						

Solid Inclusion

	SI+	SI−
SI+		
SI−		R

Solid Inclusion Distribution

	SD1	SD2	SD3
SD1			
SD2			
SD3			

Void Inclusion

	VI+	VI−
VI+		
VI−		R

Void Inclusion Distribution

	VD1	VD2	VD3
VD1			
VD2			
VD3			

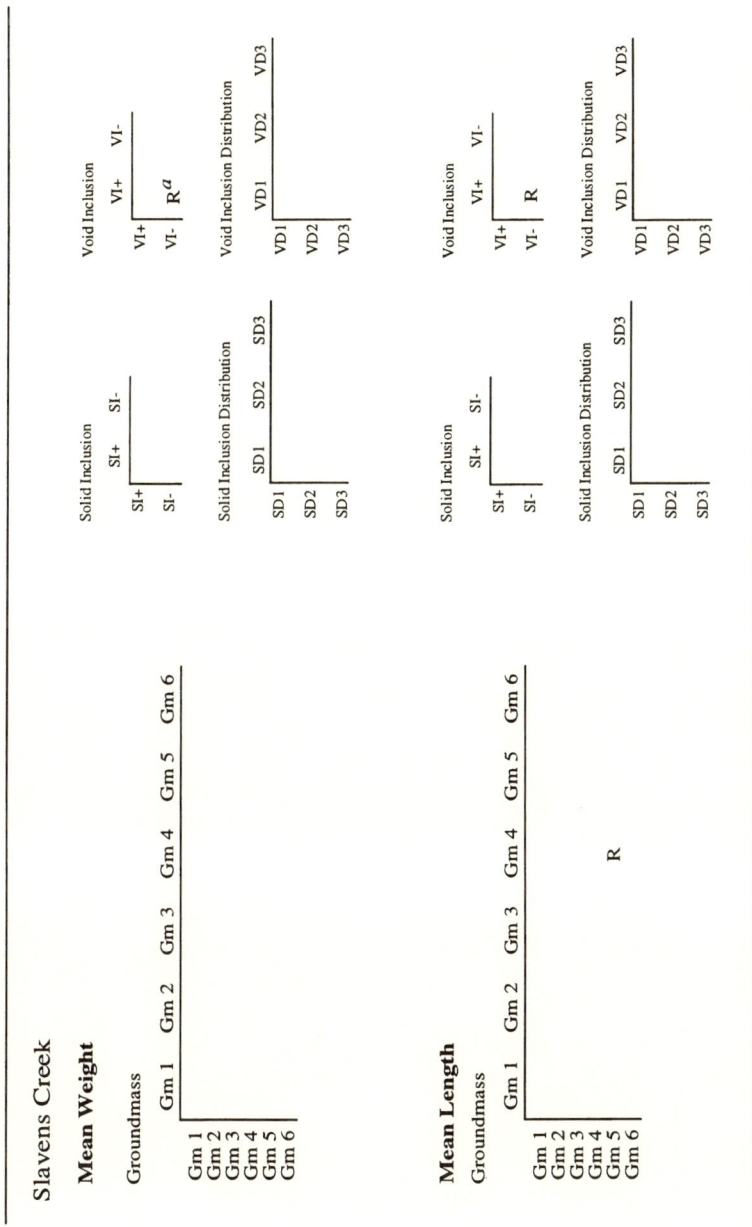

Table 11-2. (cont.)

Slavens Creek

Mean Weight

Groundmass

	Gm 1	Gm 2	Gm 3	Gm 4	Gm 5	Gm 6
Gm 1						
Gm 2						
Gm 3						
Gm 4						
Gm 5						
Gm 6						

Solid Inclusion

	SI+	SI-
SI+		
SI-		

Solid Inclusion Distribution

	SD1	SD2	SD3
SD1			
SD2			
SD3			

Void Inclusion

	VI+	VI-
VI+		
VI-		R[a]

Void Inclusion Distribution

	VD1	VD2	VD3
VD1			
VD2			
VD3			

Mean Length

Groundmass

	Gm 1	Gm 2	Gm 3	Gm 4	Gm 5	Gm 6
Gm 1						
Gm 2						
Gm 3						
Gm 4				R		
Gm 5						
Gm 6						

Solid Inclusion

	SI+	SI-
SI+		
SI-		R

Solid Inclusion Distribution

	SD1	SD2	SD3
SD1			
SD2			
SD3			

Void Inclusion

	VI+	VI-
VI+		
VI-		

Void Inclusion Distribution

	VD1	VD2	VD3
VD1			
VD2			
VD3			

Table 11-2. (cont.)

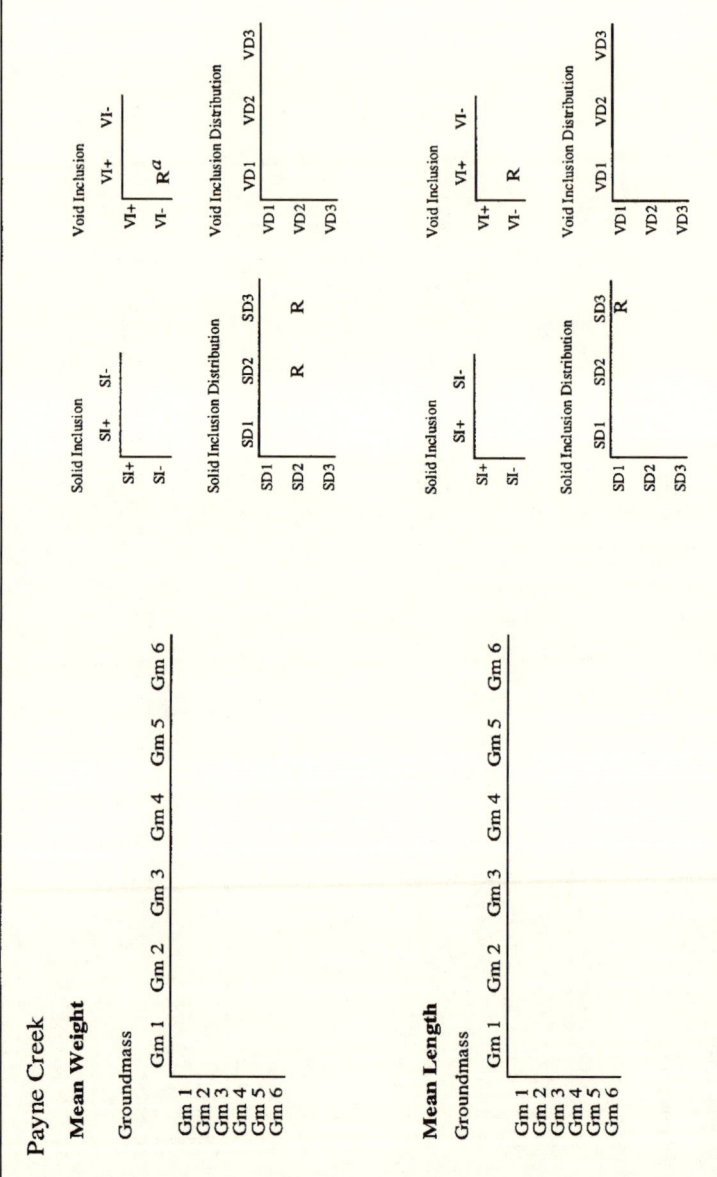

Payne Creek

Mean Weight

Groundmass

	Gm 1	Gm 2	Gm 3	Gm 4	Gm 5	Gm 6
Gm 1						
Gm 2						
Gm 3						
Gm 4						
Gm 5						
Gm 6						

Solid Inclusion

	SI+	SI-
SI+		
SI-		

Void Inclusion

	VI+	VI-
VI+		
VI-		R[a]

Solid Inclusion Distribution

	SD1	SD2	SD3
SD1			
SD2		R	
SD3			R

Void Inclusion Distribution

	VD1	VD2	VD3
VD1			
VD2			
VD3			

Mean Length

Groundmass

	Gm 1	Gm 2	Gm 3	Gm 4	Gm 5	Gm 6
Gm 1						
Gm 2						
Gm 3						
Gm 4						
Gm 5						
Gm 6						

Solid Inclusion

	SI+	SI-
SI+		
SI-		

Void Inclusion

	VI+	VI-
VI+		R
VI-		

Solid Inclusion Distribution

	SD1	SD2	SD3
SD1			
SD2			R
SD3			

Void Inclusion Distribution

	VD1	VD2	VD3
VD1			
VD2			
VD3			

Note: Abbreviations as given in Table 11-1.
[a] Reject the null hypothesis that the means are equal

might be adduced (e.g., bedding planes influence weathering), the lack of generality of these rejections—that is, they do not hold in all or most samples—coupled with an expectation of a few spurious rejections with a hundred t-tests precludes putting any significance on these rejections of the null hypothesis.

Rocks with voids are larger in terms of mean weight and length in all three gravel collections. The consistency of this pattern suggests that the presence/absence of void inclusions is interacting with gravel size and therefore that gravel size is dependent on gravel composition. Thus, our gravel samples could not be pooled for further comparison. As a result, comparisons with archaeological assemblages had to be made between particular assemblages and the nearest gravel sample.

Archaeological Assemblages

Our two northernmost assemblages, Woodall Farm (23DU269) and County Line (23SO166)—the former in Dunklin County, Missouri, and the latter in Stoddard County, Missouri (Figure 11-1)—were compared to the Bass Island sample. Woodall Farm has a major Late Woodland/Early Mississippian (ca. A.D. 500–1200) component and a minor, but still significant (at least in terms of amount of pottery), Middle Mississippian (A.D. 1200–1400) component (Hostetler and Hostetler 1986). Six hundred ninety-two flakes were made available by Charles Hostetler from his controlled surface collection of the site. County Line is a relatively short-term, fortified settlement dating from the late half of the Middle Mississippian period (post–ca. A.D. 1300) (Teltser 1988, 1992). A Woodland-period Barnes occupation is also present at County Line, but lithic artifacts are such a small element of Barnes occupations (see below) that the Woodland lithic artifacts have been swamped numerically by the later material (e.g., Price 1980). We used a sample of 1436 flakes from County Line that came from Patrice Teltser's controlled surface collections (Teltser 1988).

The South Pelts (23DU296) assemblage, from Dunklin County (Figure 11-1), is compared to the Payne Creek gravel sample. South Pelts represents a Woodland-age occupation, and, in contrast to many other sites on the Malden Plain, contains little later material. Because lithic artifacts are a minor part of Woodland assemblages, two semicontrolled surface collections—one made by Dunnell in 1982 and a second by us in 1991—had to be pooled to muster a modest sample of 131 flakes.

Finally, the Slavens Creek gravel sample is used as the standard against which assemblages from Neely (23DU326) and Coldwater Farm North (23DU272), both in Dunklin County (Figure 11-1), are compared. The Neely assemblage is a 212-flake random sample of a much larger assemblage of flakes acquired by controlled surface collection in 1992 and a spatially uncontrolled but "total" collection in 1991. Neely is predominantly a terminal Late Archaic site (probably dating ca. 1000–600 B.C.), though there also are a few Woodland-period artifacts present. Again, because Woodland assemblages have so little in the way of lithic items and the Barnes occupation is represented at Neely by only a few sherds, the pre-Mississippian-period contribution to the lithic assemblage from the site is regarded as negligible. Coldwater Farm North (Dunnell 1985b, 1988, 1992) represents a small Woodland occupation, probably somewhat later in time than that at South Pelts. The modest sample of 153 flakes represents a systematic collection of the locality in 1985 and semicontrolled collections made in 1989 and 1991.

Gravel Sample and Archaeological Assemblage Comparisons

The Crowley's Ridge samples were used to generate sets of expected frequencies against which the archaeological assemblages could be assessed using chi-square tests. Since our objective was to ascertain the nature of selection criteria, if any, in the use of the Crowley's Ridge gravel, the non–Crowley's Ridge materials were subtracted from the archaeological assemblages (both Archaic and Mississippian assemblages have significant amounts of nonlocal stone, whereas the Barnes-age [Woodland] assemblages do not). Thus, for these comparisons we had the following numbers of pieces in the samples: Coldwater Farm North, 148; County Line, 1272; Neely, 166; South Pelts, 107; and Woodall Farm, 667.

In Table 11-3, each archaeological assemblage is compared to the nearest gravel sample across the rock physical-properties-classification (RPPC) dimensions. In all five assemblages, the presence/absence of solid inclusions does not depart significantly from the composition of the nearest gravel sample. In contrast, all other dimensions, with the exception of solid-inclusion distributions for the South Pelts and Neely assemblages, depart significantly from the composition of the nearest gravel assemblages. Again, one does not want to interpret unpatterned rejections of the null hypothesis, but consistent rejection of solid inclusions is significant. Clearly, prehistoric stone-tool artisans were rejecting rocks because of groundmass, inclusion distribution, and presence of voids. They did not, however, make selections on the basis of the presence of solid inclusions. This is intuitively plausible for three reasons: (1) solid inclusions are present in 85 to 95 percent of all gravels sampled; (2) the presence of solid inclusions is less likely to have an impact on workability than any other physical property dimension of rock; and (3) the presence of solid inclusions may have been difficult to detect given the weathered nature of the cobbles.

Because the chi-square results give no hint as to the magnitude of difference, a set of Brainerd-Robinson (BR) coefficients (Robinson 1951) was calculated for each assemblage/source pair by RPPC dimensions (Table 11-4). A BR coefficient of 200 is scored if an assemblage and gravel sample are identical, whereas a BR coefficient of 0 is scored if the assemblage and gravel sample are

Table 11-3. Chi-Square Results Comparing Archaeological Assemblages to Nearest Gravel Sample along Rock Physical-Properties-Classification Dimensions

Site	Structure[a]	Solid Inclusions[b]	Void Inclusions	Solid-Inclusion Distribution[c]	Void-Inclusion Distribution
Bass Island					
23SO166	232.28	**0.59**	567.40	49.42	574.37
23DU269	152.46	**10.41**	302.62	52.20	298.21
Payne Creek					
23DU296	58.21	7.11	117.30	**11.88**	64.06[b]
Slavens Creek					
23DU326	103.83	**0.88**	66.55	9.36	74.14[d]
23DU272	75.62	7.11	106.61	22.33	94.65

Note: Boldface numbers are less than critical chi-square values.
[a] $p = .001$, d.f. = 5, $\chi^2 = 18.467$.
[b] $p = .001$, d.f. = 1, $\chi^2 = 10.828$.
[c] $p = .001$, d.f. = 3, $\chi^2 = 16.266$.
[d] $p = .001$, d.f. = 2, $\chi^2 = 13.816$.

completely different. Boldface numbers in Table 11-4 are the coefficients for archaeological assemblages and their nearest gravel sample.

Although the overall similarity between archaeological sample and nearest source sample might be low in consequence of prehistoric-artisan selection, the highest scores ought to be between the nearest source–assemblage pair. This is generally not the case, nor was it the case for the solid-inclusion dimension, in which no apparent selection is present. This result strongly suggests that (1) none of our source samples represents an actual source exploited by the people represented by our five archaeological assemblages or (2) gravel was obtained typically from more than one locality. While nonrandom use of secondary sources makes identification of the actual source used problematic, a more thorough sampling of Crowley's Ridge gravel would improve our abilities in this regard. Until actual sources can be pinpointed with some degree of accuracy, only the most general and strongest selection criteria can be detected; more subtle manipulation of the resource will be missed.

Gravel Fracture Toughness

The mean and standard deviation for failure load (Pa) and amount of material removed (grams) were measured for seventeen rocks (Table 11-5), though

Table 11-4. Brainerd–Robinson Coefficients for Rock Physical-Properties-Classification Dimensions Comparing Archaeological Assemblages and Gravel Samples

	Site				
	23SO166	23DU269	23DU296	23DU326	23DU272
Groundmass Dimension					
Bass Island	**126.67**	**133.06**	126.73	130.63	127.18
Payne Creek	118.53	125.11	**118.60**	122.39	119.18
Slavens Creek	112.61	119.20	112.68	**116.36**	**113.54**
Solid-Inclusion Dimension					
Bass Island	**196.61**	**188.07**	188.05	191.72	191.38
Payne Creek	190.45	181.91	**181.89**	197.88	185.22
Slavens Creek	194.64	186.10	186.08	**193.68**	**189.42**
Void-Inclusion Dimension					
Bass Island	**79.55**	**85.19**	73.87	103.33	80.11
Payne Creek	87.44	93.09	**81.76**	111.22	88.00
Slavens Creek	94.06	99.71	88.38	**117.84**	**94.62**
Solid-Inclusion-Distribution Dimension					
Bass Island	**161.61**	**148.12**	160.50	164.36	134.98
Payne Creek	168.43	160.11	**167.33**	170.61	146.98
Slavens Creek	181.73	166.32	153.19	**178.90**	**173.51**
Void-Inclusion-Distribution Dimension					
Bass Island	**79.55**	**85.19**	73.87	103.33	80.11
Payne Creek	87.44	93.09	**81.76**	111.22	88.00
Slavens Creek	94.06	99.71	88.38	**117.84**	**94.62**

Note: Boldface numbers are nearest archaeological assemblage and gravel sample.

only twelve had adequate weight-loss data. As noted above, groundmass and the presence or absence of inclusions affect both the load necessary to cause failure and the variability of the load causing failure. Test results were plotted for each dimension of the RPPC. Even so, small sample size renders our results suggestive rather than definitive.

Plotting mean failure load by groundmass (Figure 11-3) reveals that our sample size is reasonable only for comparisons between mottled and granular groundmass rocks. Although the range of mean failure loads overlaps, granular

Table 11-5. Mean and Standard Deviation of Failure Loads and Weight Loss for Crowley's Ridge Gravel Specimens

Specimen	Mean Load (Pa)	Standard Deviation of Load (Pa)	Mean Weight Loss (gm)	Standard Deviation of Weight Loss (gm)
QGS 004	0.1560	0.0155	*[a]	*
PC 033	0.0572	0.0025	*	*
PC 012	0.1100	0.0038	*	*
PC 017	0.1786	0.0339	*	*
PC 026-B	0.1320	0.0353	*	*
SC 260	0.2086	0.0414	0.0052	0.0057
QGS 013	0.1360	0.0385	0.0026	0.0012
PC 032	0.1010	0.0413	0.0050	0.0076
PC 001	0.1875	0.0399	0.0010	0.0017
PC 021	0.1743	0.0355	0.0086	0.0136
SC 251	0.1655	0.0311	0.0022	0.0044
QGS 011	0.1800	0.0340	0.0065	0.0070
QGS 008	0.1200	0.0009	0.0009	0.0009
QGS 007	0.1578	0.0338	0.0176	0.0327
PC 026-A	0.1457	0.0378	0.0011	0.0010
PC 044	0.1187	0.0033	0.0032	0.0033
QGS 010	0.1480	0.0328	0.0056	0.0064

[a]Weight-loss data were not collected systematically.

rocks (orthoquartzites) have consistently lower mean failure loads. Within each class there is a large range of variation. Plotting standard deviation of failure load shows that specimens for each dimension vary at about the same magnitude, with the exception of granular rocks, in which the average variation is nearly an order of magnitude less than that of cherts. This may occur as a function of the low loads necessary to initiate a failure in granular rocks. Weight-loss data were generated for only one granular-rock specimen, precluding further analyses at this point. This is unfortunate because it reduces our sample size further. Impressionistically, the amount of material removed differed systematically between the cherts and orthoquartzites, with the fragments of orthoquartzites being much smaller.

As noted previously, Crowley's Ridge rocks without solid inclusions are rare in our gravel samples; hence, specimens without solid inclusions are not well represented in our sample of impact specimens (Figure 11-4). Specimens with inclusions required an approximately 50-percent greater load to effect frac-

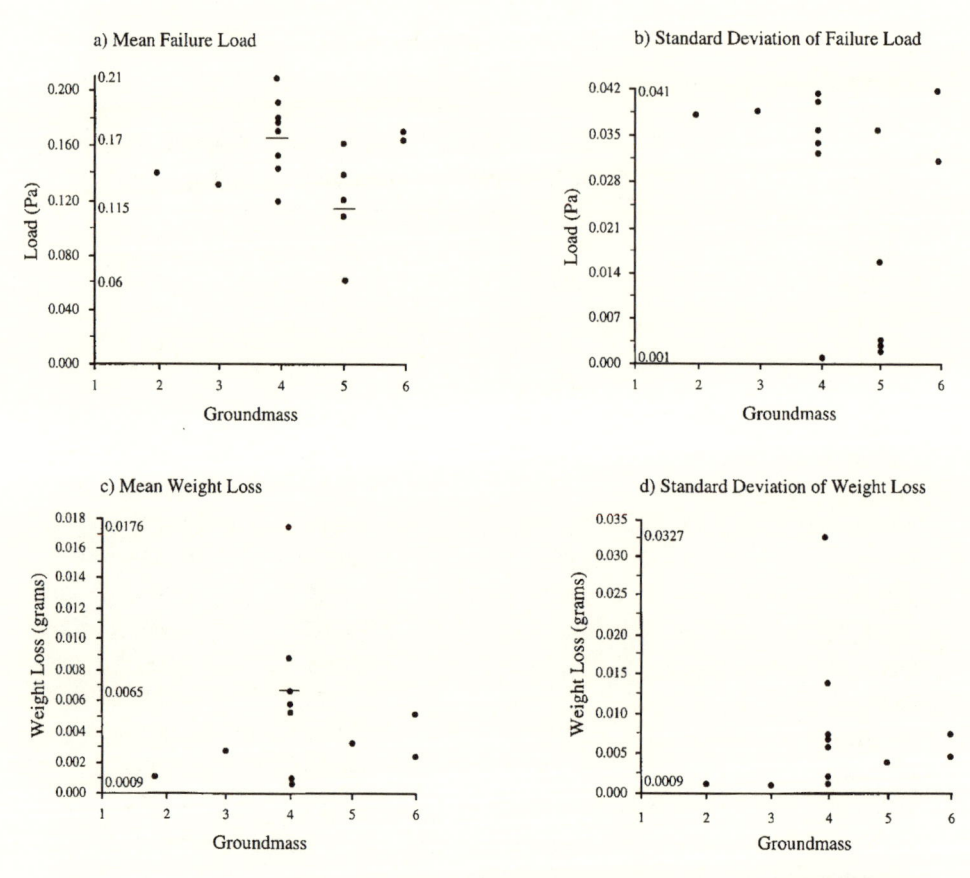

Figure 11-3. Plots of impact-testing results by rock groundmass: 1, uniform; 2, bedding planes; 3, concentric banding; 4, mottled; 5, granular; 6, oolitic. The mean failure-load values are indicated as *bars*, and the associated values are located inside the left axis, as are minimum and maximum values.

ture than those without—an entirely reasonable result given the mechanics of crack propagation in brittle solids (Lawn and Marshall 1979). Variability is about the same in both groups. This result suggests strongly that the lack of selection apparent along this dimension in the archaeological assemblages resulted from an inability to detect the difference in raw gravels and/or the limiting effect of the materials without inclusions.

The presence/absence of void inclusions does not affect the range of mean failure loads (Figure 11-5). Regardless of the presence/absence of void inclusions, rock specimens have a similar range of mean failure loads. A plot of the standard deviation of failure loads suggests two groups, a high and low, for both rocks with and those without void inclusions. This results from the sharp difference in mean failure loads of chert and orthoquartzite. As might be expected,

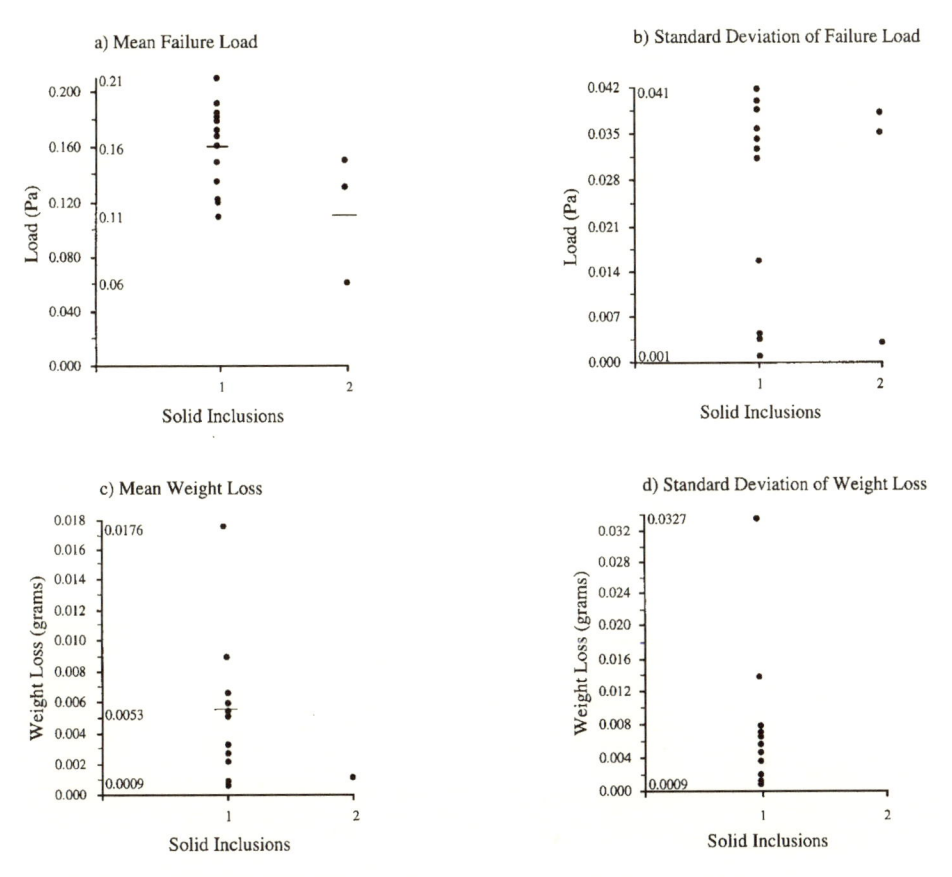

Figure 11-4. Plots of impact-testing results by solid inclusions: *1,* present; *2,* absent. The mean failure-load values are indicated as *bars,* and the associated values are located inside the left axis, as are minimum and maximum values.

voids appear to result in the detachment of smaller pieces (Figure 11-5, *c*). Again, the distribution of weight loss is decidedly nonnormal, limiting the interpretation of the small sample. Predictability of weight loss (Figure 11-5, *d*) is closely linked to magnitude of weight loss. The distributions of both kinds of inclusions (Figures 11-6 and 11-7) show similar patterns (compare mean values in Figures 11-6, *a,* and 11-7, *a*), consistent with mechanical considerations (no inclusions < uniform < random < structured inclusions), though the magnitudes are too small to be significant in these samples. The standard deviations (Figures 11-6, *b* and *d,* and 11-7, *b* and *d*) are even more variable, obscuring any patterns in predictability that might emerge from a larger sample.

The principal finding evident in our small sample is that, because of macroscale heterogeneity, any particular RPPC dimension exhibits a broad range of failure loads and amounts of material removed. One clear pattern is

278 | McCutcheon and Dunnell

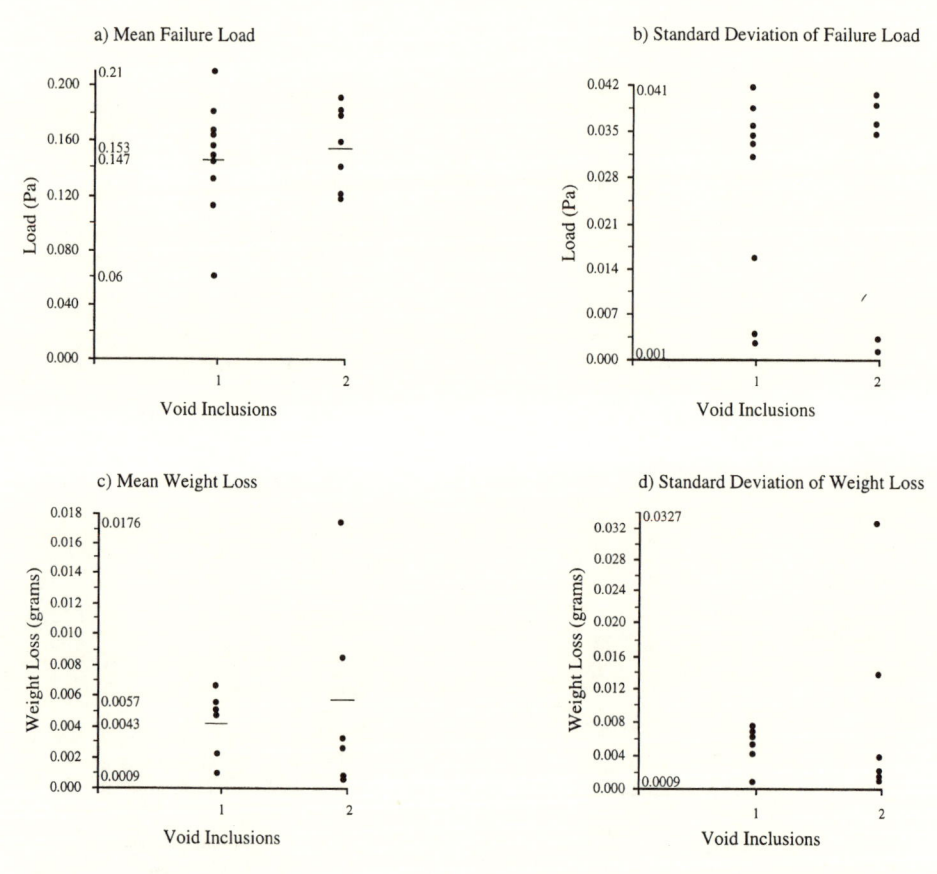

Figure 11-5. Plots of impact-testing results by void inclusions: *1*, present; *2*, absent. The mean failure-load values are indicated as *bars*, and the associated values are located inside the left axis, as are minimum and maximum values.

that rocks that have granular groundmass (orthoquartzites) break at lower mean loads than those required for all other rocks (cherts). This probably means (if mean weight loss proves to be smaller, as it seems to) that orthoquartzites have a tendency to crumble. This would account for the bias against these materials in the archaeological assemblages. Strong differences detected in failure loads between rocks with and without solid inclusions are well founded in fracture mechanics. The absence of any archaeological selection is enigmatic; resolution of this finding is an important goal of future research.

Summary

The rocks comprising Crowley's Ridge gravels vary in size and composition at all locations sampled. As a result, much more detailed analysis of this impor-

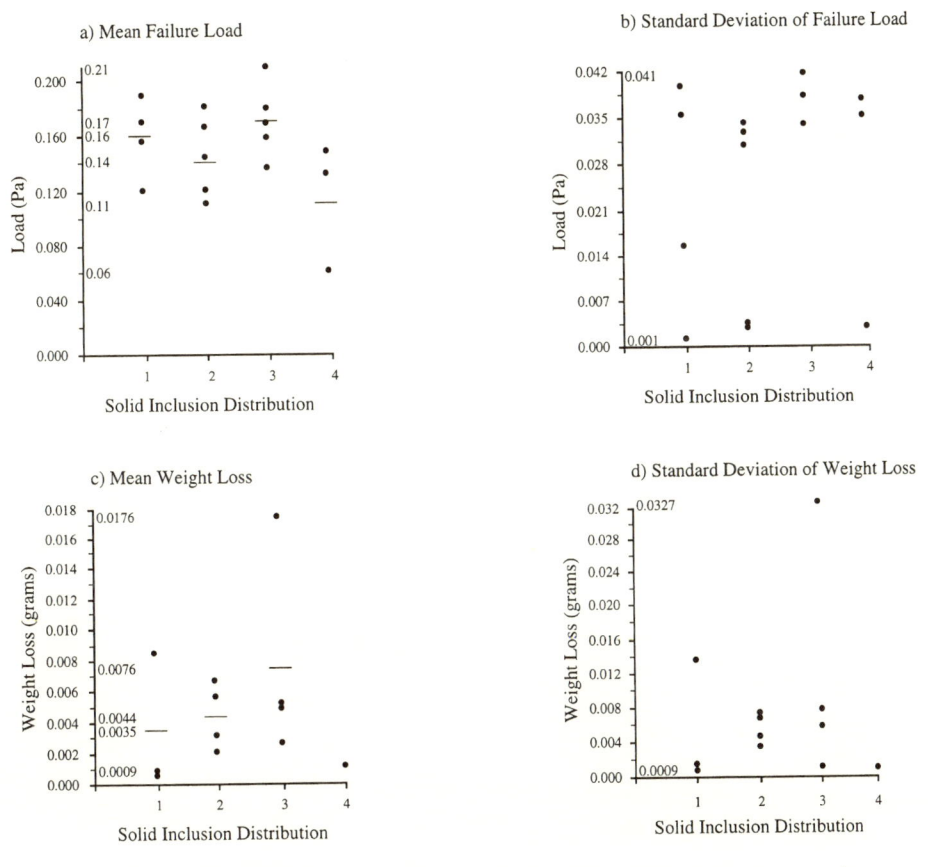

Figure 11-6. Plots of impact-testing results by solid-inclusion distributions: *1*, random; *2*, uniform; *3*, structured; *4*, none. The mean failure-load values are indicated as *bars*, and the associated values are located inside the left axis, as are minimum and maximum values.

tant lithic source is required before its archaeological use can be understood. Our preliminary examination of archaeological assemblages suggests only that orthoquartzites were discriminated against universally. Also, there was a strong tendency to avoid cherts containing internal voids. Inasmuch as orthoquartzites cannot be distinguished from cherts by cortex, this implies that cobbles were tested at the collection points, even though the high frequency of cortex flakes in archaeological assemblages suggests most reduction took place at the point of use. The range of variation in fracture toughness of Crowley's Ridge cherts is so great that any differential exploitation among them cannot be detected in the small sample we used. Heat treatment, present throughout the archaeological sequence but particularly important during the Mississippian period, was not examined. This parameter might provide a basis for differential use of

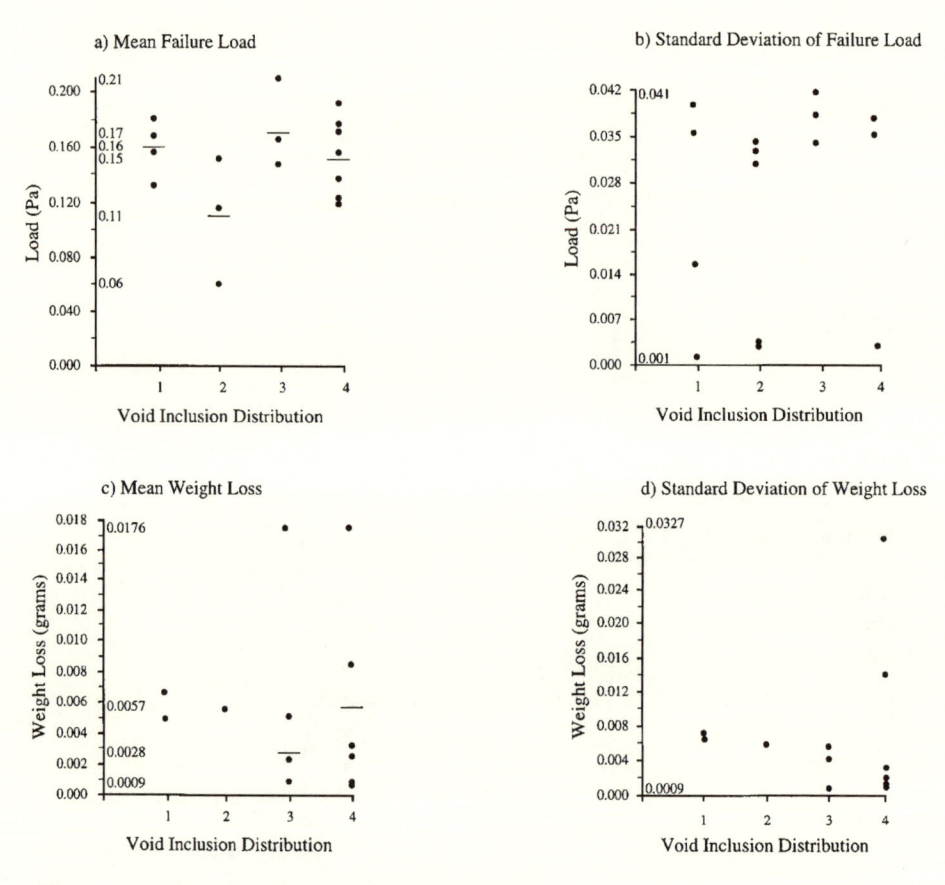

Figure 11-7. Plots of impact-testing results by void-inclusion distributions: *1*, random; *2*, uniform; *3*, structured; *4*, none. The mean failure-load values are indicated as *bars*, and the associated values are located inside the left axis, as are minimum and maximum values.

cherts, with selection criteria being based on the response of a particular rock type to heating. Data are being generated on the heat-treatment response of different Crowley's Ridge cherts by one of us (PTM), so this hypothesis can be evaluated in the future.

Acknowledgments

We acknowledge P. A. Teltser and C. Hostetler for allowing us to use their lithic assemblages from County Line and Woodall Farm, respectively. We also acknowledge the many people who participated in the Varney River project and collected the other assemblages used here. M. D. Dunnell read the manuscript and removed a great many literary errors.

12 | Blade Technology and Nonlocal Cherts
Hopewell(?) Traits at the Twenhafel Site, Southern Illinois

Carol A. Morrow

MIDWESTERN ARCHAEOLOGISTS TRADITIONALLY view evidence for use of prismatic-blade technology and nonlocal cherts, particularly blue-gray cherts, as being Middle Woodland (ca. 250 B.C.–A.D. 400) in age and Hopewellian in terms of cultural manifestation. Odell (1994:117), for example, argues that blade technology developed alongside Hopewell mortuary ritual and ended when those practices were abandoned at the end of the Middle Woodland period. I examine these assumptions using data from Twenhafel, a Mississippi River floodplain village in southern Illinois (Figure 12-1) occupied during the Middle Woodland and early Late Woodland periods, approximately 200 B.C.–A.D. 600. Data presented here suggest that the use of both prismatic-blade technology and nonlocal cherts actually *preceded* the appearance of typical Hopewellian traits and then persisted into post-Hopewell times.

The Hopewell "horizon," characterized by archaeological evidence of widespread movement of exotic raw materials, stylistic concepts, and finished goods, began perhaps as early as 100 B.C. (at least in southern Ohio), reached its zenith about A.D. 100, and then disappeared within about a hundred years. Core Hopewell areas were in the central Ohio River valley (Ohio Hopewell) and the lower Illinois River valley (Havana Hopewell), but Hopewellian artifacts are found throughout the Midwest and portions of the southeastern United States. Distinctively decorated ceramic vessels perhaps are the most characteristic Hopewellian artifacts, but finely made prismatic blades and pieces of high-quality, nonlocal chert also are commonly interpreted as Hopewellian items. A specific question addressed in this chapter is whether these two traits, blades and nonlocal cherts, correspond precisely with the appearance of Havana Hopewell pottery at Twenhafel or whether they preceded and/or postdated that appearance.

During the Middle Woodland period, chert was shaped through various distinctive manufacturing technologies, including blade-core technology, biface

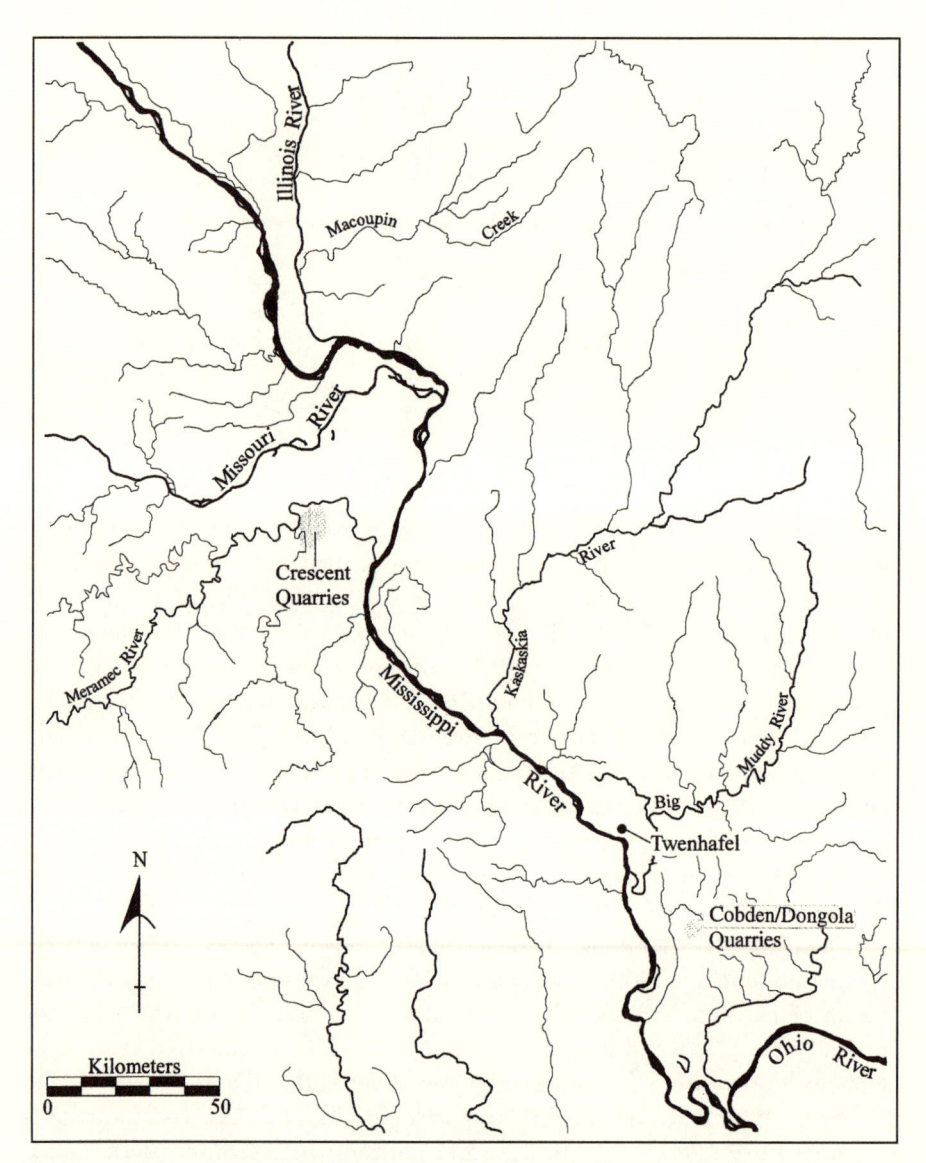

Figure 12-1. Map of western Illinois and eastern Missouri showing the locations of Twenhafel and chert quarries mentioned in the text.

technology, and amorphous-core technology, the latter also referred to as unstructured, or expedient, core reduction (Parry and Kelly 1987). Each technology produced a different type of debitage, debris, by-products, and end products. By studying these materials, it is possible to track the form in which chert was brought to a site, to examine patterns of chert usage, and to explore issues of recycling and reuse by later occupants of the site. An important issue is determining whether the archaeological deposits of blades and pieces of nonlocal chert represent (1) primary-use objects, (2) materials reused by later inhabitants of the site, or (3) a mix of the two. I examine the organization of specific manufacturing technologies used to shape chert into stone tools and employ the resulting information to argue that at Twenhafel blade manufacture and nonlocal-chert use continued much later than expected, with the latest deposits representing reuse or recycling of the materials by later inhabitants.

Research Area

Twenhafel (Figure 12-1), located in extreme southwestern Illinois on the alluvial plain near the junction of the Big Muddy and the Mississippi rivers, has traditionally been placed in what is termed the Crab Orchard tradition. The distribution of Crab Orchard pottery extends northward into the lower Kaskaskia, Saline, and Big Muddy River valleys and west, south, and east into portions of the Mississippi, Ohio, and Wabash river drainages (Butler and Jefferies 1986:524; see Muller 1986 for discussion and comparison of the Crab Orchard and Baumer traditions). Twenhafel is the largest and apparently most complex Crab Orchard site, covering approximately 40 hectares and containing twenty-five mounds and several habitation areas (Hofman 1979).

Early archaeological work at the site was done by the mound-exploration division of the Bureau of (American) Ethnology (Thomas [1894] referred to the site as the Vogel Mound Group). In the 1950s, archaeologists from the Illinois State Museum worked at the site for two field seasons. Illinois State Museum archaeologist Melvin Fowler worked at Twenhafel's Weber Mound in 1957, documenting that it was a Hopewell burial mound, and Joseph Caldwell worked approximately 610 meters southwest of that mound in 1958. Caldwell's work revealed the presence of numerous trash and storage pits and at least four major periods of occupation from the Early Woodland period (ca. 600–250 B.C.) through the Mississippian period (post–A.D. 900). The history of research at the site has been reported by Hofman (1979, 1980a, 1980b).

As Hofman (1980a:185) noted, Twenhafel's location in the central Mississippi River valley is a strategic position relative to resource exploitation and distribution. His research on the Twenhafel artifact collections indicated connections between Twenhafel and Havana-tradition sites in the Illinois Valley area (Hofman 1980a:187) and between Twenhafel and Copena and related complexes in the Midsouth (Hofman 1980a:185–95). Classic Hopewellian materials recovered from Twenhafel include figurines, copper artifacts, sheet mica, galena cubes, marine-shell artifacts, quartz and obsidian chips, and large numbers of prismatic blades of nonlocal cherts.

Blades and Nonlocal Cherts as Middle Woodland/Hopewell Markers

Blades, often referred to as flake knives, were part of the early diagnostic trait list developed by Cole and Deuel (1937:222) for the Hopewell phase in Fulton County, Illinois. The typical Hopewell flake knife was defined as "a slender flake having a single scar on one face and two to four longitudinal primary scars on the other" (Cole and Deuel 1937:281). Although early archaeological attention relative to chipped-stone material was focused on projectile points, the association between blades and Middle Woodland Hopewell sites was noted by researchers working at the larger Woodland sites (e.g., Byers et al. 1943; Griffin and Morgan 1941; Griffin et al. 1970; McGregor 1958; Montet-White 1963, 1968; Morse 1963). The characteristic blade-and-core industry of the Middle Woodland period was a highly developed technology that produced standardized blades, crested flakes, platform-rejuvenation flakes, and pyramidal (conical) cores (Greber et al. 1981; Montet-White 1963, 1968; Pi-Sunyer 1965; Reid 1976; Sanger 1970; various papers in Brose and Greber 1979 and in Johnson and Morrow 1987). As Hofman (1987:88) noted, hundreds of midwestern Middle Woodland sites have yielded blades and cores, though relatively few have yielded large numbers of those items.

The association between Middle Woodland sites and nonlocal lithic materials also is well documented (Cantwell 1980, 1987; Wiant and McGimsey 1986; Winters 1984; see also references in Hofman 1987 and in Morrow 1987, 1988). Struever (1973:61) was one of the earliest archaeologists to note that surface remains in the Illinois River valley can be identified as Hopewell simply on the basis of the presence of heat-treated Crescent chert from quarries along the Meramec River southwest of St. Louis and a blue-gray chert that we now know as Cobden/Dongola (but see below). Crescent, also known as Burlington or Burlington/Crescent (Ives 1975, 1984, 1985; Luedtke 1978, 1979; Meyers 1970), is a fine-quality, white or sometimes pink chert that was widely used across the Midwest. Cobden/Dongola also was widely used, particularly during the Late Archaic and the Middle Woodland periods. Artifacts made from that distinctive chert are found in a variety of forms and contexts ranging from Late Archaic caches of finely made items to blades, cores, flakes, and disks in Middle Woodland midden deposits and burials. Interest in this high-quality chert dates back more than a century (Bell 1943; Farrell 1883; Fowke 1894, 1902, 1928; Guernsey 1937; May 1981, 1982, 1984; Snyder 1877, 1883, 1893a, 1893b, 1895a, 1895b, 1910; Thomas 1894; Titterington 1937), and many of the early (erroneous) statements made about the sources of the cherts have entered the literature without critical examination (Morrow 1991; Morrow et al. 1992).

Winters (1984) provided an important overview of the procurement and exchange of chert during the Middle Woodland period in Illinois. In his view, chert, specifically Cobden/Dongola and Crescent, was "the most plentiful durable import" (Winters 1984:12) into the central Illinois Valley during the Havana phase of the Middle Woodland period (see also Cantwell 1980, 1987). More than 16,000 blue-gray disks have been found in different caches in a 25-kilometer radius of Beardstown, Illinois. Winters assumed that the disks were probably of Cobden/Dongola chert obtained from southern Illinois. However, first-hand examination of some of these large caches, for example, the one from the Baehr Mound, revealed that in some cases a *local* blue-gray chert, known as LaMoine River, was used (Morrow 1991, 1993). Despite this observation, there are indeed large numbers of blue-gray chipped-stone disks found in the area that were made from nonlocal cherts that resemble Cobden/Dongola and Wyandotte (southern Indiana).

Another important observation made by Winters (1984) on Havana chert use was that groups associated with the Crab Orchard and Allison traditions of southern Illinois and Indiana were the manufacturers and purveyors of the chert disks, while Havana populations were the recipients. Twenhafel generally has been considered to be the primary site that funneled southern-Illinois Cobden/Dongola blue-gray cherts out of the local area. Winters also suggested that Havana groups were manufacturing disks but that they were using materials from closer sources, including Grimes Hill, a raspberry-colored chert that lithologically is similar to Crescent. They distributed the disks within the Havana region and perhaps to the Crab Orchard and Allison regions as well. Twenhafel, despite its location near the source area for Cobden/Dongola chert, has yielded clear evidence of both of those nonlocal cherts (Crescent and Grimes Hill).

Blue-gray cherts, presumably nonlocal in derivation, are also found on Middle Woodland and early Late Woodland sites in the American Bottom near St. Louis (Bareis and Porter 1984; Fortier et al. 1984; Munson 1971). Published accounts of sites in the Kaskaskia River drainage (Conrad 1966; Fowler 1961; Kuttruff 1972; Morrell 1965; Salzer 1963) indicate that Cobden chert also was brought into that region, and Roper (1979:37), in her survey of the Sangamon drainage of central Illinois, noted that Cobden chert is a marker for Middle Woodland sites. There also is some evidence for the use of these blue-gray cherts in Middle Woodland sites in the Southeast. For example, blades of chert visually identified as Cobden/Dongola have been reported as far south as Middle Woodland–period Marksville sites in the upper Sunflower River region of Mississippi (Johnson and Hayes 1995).

High-quality blue-gray cherts associated with the Middle Woodland period are well suited for the manufacture of blades. Several researchers working with Illinois materials have argued for some type of relation between high-quality cherts such as Cobden/Dongola and Middle Woodland blade technology. Cantwell (1980) noted a "consistent relationship" between the two and suggested that fine-quality chert was a technological necessity for blade production. Griffin (1989:xxi) made the same point. Although not denying a strictly technological importance, I have argued (Morrow 1987, 1988) that Cobden/Dongola chert was an important part of Havana Hopewell for social reasons. Regardless, there appears to have been selection of blue-gray cherts during the Middle Woodland period, with a strong association between chert selection and blade technology.

The Chipped-Stone Sample: Context and Dating

The Twenhafel materials I used were excavated from a "village" area of the site by Caldwell in 1958 (Hofman 1980a, 1980b). The excavations were in a midden area that contained Middle Woodland, Late Woodland, and Mississippian deposits. Some degree of mixing of materials from more than one period occurred in many of the pits. In most cases, the presence of later-period (post–Middle Woodland) pottery was interpreted as evidence that pit construction had occurred during that later period, even if 90 percent or more of the pottery in the fill was Middle Woodland in age. This division is somewhat at odds with Hofman's (1980a) earlier seriation procedure and accounts for some temporal-assignment discrepancies between this study and an earlier pilot analysis (Hofman and Morrow 1984). Only materials from pits of presumed brief use were employed. Several criteria were used to select the pits. Initially, all pits that lacked Mississippian sherds were selected. Then, pits were deleted if they contained sherds from more than one period or if they lacked sufficient ceramic information (see below). All remaining features that contained *any* amount of chipped stone were retained. The final sample consisted of 628 pieces of chipped stone from thirty-four pits.

As a check on the dating of pits containing chipped stone used in this analysis, David Braun examined pottery from those contexts relative to his time-series analysis of sherds from western Illinois (see Braun 1985a, 1985b, 1987 for details). Materials then were assigned to one of five periods. The earliest period, early Middle Woodland (150 B.C.–A.D. 50), was represented by forty-five pieces of chipped stone from three pits. The dominant pottery type in those pits was Crab Orchard Fabric-Impressed. A few sherds of Havana ware (Havana Plain and Havana Zoned) also were present, but Hopewell/Baehr materials were absent. The second period, middle Middle Woodland (A.D. 50–250), was represented by 236 pieces of chipped stone from nine pits. The ceramic assemblage was dominated by sherds of Crab Orchard Fabric-Impressed, but Hopewell/Baehr pottery was present as well, as were a few sherds of the Havana series. The third period, late Middle Woodland (A.D. 250–350), was represented by forty-four pieces of chipped stone from four pits. The pits exhibited a shift in pottery from a dominance by Crab Orchard Fabric-Impressed to a dominance by Raymond. Sherds of both thick Raymond and thin Crab Orchard Fabric-Impressed were present, as were late Middle Woodland sherds exhibiting exterior brushing and punctation. The fourth period, early Late Woodland (A.D. 350–600), was represented by 251 pieces of chipped stone from thirteen pits. Those pits contained thick Raymond sherds but no Crab Orchard Fabric-Impressed sherds. The fifth period, late Late Woodland (post–A.D. 600), was represented by fifty-two pieces of chipped stone from five pits. Those pits contained thin-wall late Raymond sherds exhibiting fine cordmarking and finely ground temper.

Methodological Considerations: Lithic-Production Technology

The analytical framework used to examine the interrelated processes of chert procurement, use, and disposal is the concept of lithic-production technology—literally, the organization of the design and manufacture of chipped-stone tools. Explanation of basic concepts at this point will facilitate understanding the general goals of my research. *Lithic technology* refers to all aspects of the manufacture and use of stone tools. My research here focuses only on manufacturing practices, hence the term *production technology,* which refers to both the organization of the design and the process of manufacture of chipped-stone tools. The general concept of production technology can be subdivided into more-specific concepts. First, we need a precise answer to the question of what a chipped-stone tool is. The definition used here is that such a tool is any piece of chipped stone that has been culturally modified for potential use and that directs force through its edges. A chipped-stone tool is the product of a specific manufacturing trajectory that might be as simple as the production of sharp flakes or as complex as the manufacture of finely shaped prismatic blades. Both design and manufacturing principles are merged into consideration of the production technology involved in the manufacture of such items.

Although understanding design principles is an implicit part of technological analyses, it is rarely discussed in the literature. The concept of organization of design is used to consider how specific tool needs are met. Chipped-stone-tool needs are the basic work-involved needs, examples of which include cutting, piercing, and scraping. For example, are cutting needs met through the manufacture of quick, expedient flakes from amorphous cores, or is this need fulfilled by the manufacture of prismatic blades through a prepared-core technology? Recent discussion of this problem suggests that how such needs are met can inform us about issues as varied as mobility and sedentariness (Bamforth 1986; Johnson 1982, 1987, 1989; Kelly 1988; Koldehoff 1987; Morrow and Jefferies 1989; Parry and Kelly 1987; various papers in Torrence 1989) and social signaling (Clark 1987; Morrow 1987).

Manufacturing trajectory refers to the sequence of stages of manufacture involved in producing a tool and is the basis for the study of production. The concept of stone-tool production as a technological system with distinct stages was first developed by Holmes (1894, 1919), but it was not until the early 1970s that it was developed as a means for interpreting the archaeological record (Callahan 1974; Collins 1975; Muto 1971; Newcomer 1971; see Johnson 1993 for historical overview). In the late 1970s and early 1980s, several studies refined and applied staging concepts in terms of manufacturing processes (discussed below) as useful models for explaining human adaptive strategies (Ammerman and Andrefsky 1982; Arnold 1983; Goodyear 1979; Hofman 1987; Hofman and Morrow 1984; Jefferies 1976, 1982a, 1982b, 1983; Johnson 1979, 1981a, 1981b, 1982, 1984; Johnson and Morrow 1987; Johnson and Raspet 1980; Morrow and Jefferies 1989; Raab et al. 1979; Raspet 1979). Building on this body of research, archaeologists are beginning to look at the implications of different approaches to stone-tool manufacture in order to address more complex issues of social interaction and behavior (Arnold 1983, 1985a, 1985b; Johnson 1983, 1985; Johnson and Morrow 1987; Parry 1983).

A manufacturing trajectory can be broken into units such as early stage, late stage, and finished tool. Although these divisions are analytical constructs, some stages appear to represent prehistoric practice. Using such a construct, it is possible to categorize chipped-stone remains as finished tools, as unfinished tools in various stages of completeness, or as debris and by-products of manufacture. The categorization of chipping debris allows the analyst to determine whether on-site manufacture occurred, whether finished materials were brought into a site, or whether some combination of these processes occurred. This information should tell us something about specific processes of chert procurement and use.

Analytical Design

My objective was to generate data that tracked the presence or absence of three specific manufacturing technologies: conical-core blade manufacture, biface production, and amorphous-core reduction. These three technologies can be used to describe virtually all the chipped stone in the Twenhafel sample.

CONICAL-CORE BLADE TECHNOLOGY

This technology is marked by the presence of blades, blade-like flakes, core-rejuvenation flakes, other core flakes, and blade cores and core fragments. Because of the highly structured and distinctive nature of this technology, it probably is the most accurately monitored technology.

BIFACE TECHNOLOGY

Biface-thinning flakes and bifacial-tool forms are used to determine the presence of biface technology. This technology is probably the most underrepresented of the three technologies because the earliest stages of manufacture are not accounted for in the chipping debris.

AMORPHOUS-CORE TECHNOLOGY

This technology is tracked by the presence of broad platform flakes, flakes not assigned to the other two technologies, and all other cores in addition to those associated with conical-core reduction. Clearly, the potential problem here is overestimation of this technology. There is some amount of overlap between the materials assigned to amorphous-core production and biface production. If broad platform flakes and general flakes—that is, those assigned to amorphous-core technology—are produced during biface manufacture, they would have been produced during the early stages. If large numbers of broken early-stage bifaces, manufacturing rejects, and biface thinning flakes co-occur, then distinguishing between the two technologies would require more detailed categories. However, the scarcity of evidence for early-stage biface manufacture at Twenhafel indicates little debitage from this source.

Clearly, it is impossible to assign accurately every piece of stone to one of these technologies. This results in inflated estimates of the importance of the amorphous-core group and deflated estimates for the other two, especially for the biface system. Therefore, it is not argued that the tabulations presented reflect the actual proportions of debris and finished products of each technology used by the occupants of the site. However, given that this analysis is internally consistent—that is, the same criteria were used for all of the sample—the presence, absence, degree, and change in frequency of these three technologies can be monitored relative to each other if ambiguous classes of products are not used to generate the estimates. For example, although the amount of biface technology measured by this analysis is quite likely less than is actually present, the method of measurement remains constant; hence, it is possible to observe and compare how this technology was used by the Woodland inhabitants of Twenhafel over an 800-year span. Additionally, the problem actually may be less than stated, as the Twenhafel collection contains little evidence of very-early-stage reduction, such as the presence of large numbers of cortex-bearing flakes or early-stage bifaces (Morrow 1984).

Figure 12-2 illustrates the identification protocol that was used to sort all chert objects. The initial form of an object, noted in capital letters on the figure, refers to the shape of an object after it was initially produced but prior to its modification into a tool. Tabulating the initial form of objects provides information on manufacturing stages as represented by debris categories, selection of specific raw materials and forms for use in expedient technologies, and the presence or absence of specific manufacturing technologies. The identification key in Figure 12-2 is not a model of any particular manufacturing trajectory. Information derived from it can be used to detect the presence of different trajectories, depending on the presence or absence of specific categories in an actual assemblage. Sometimes an artifact is so modified that its initial form—

290 | Morrow

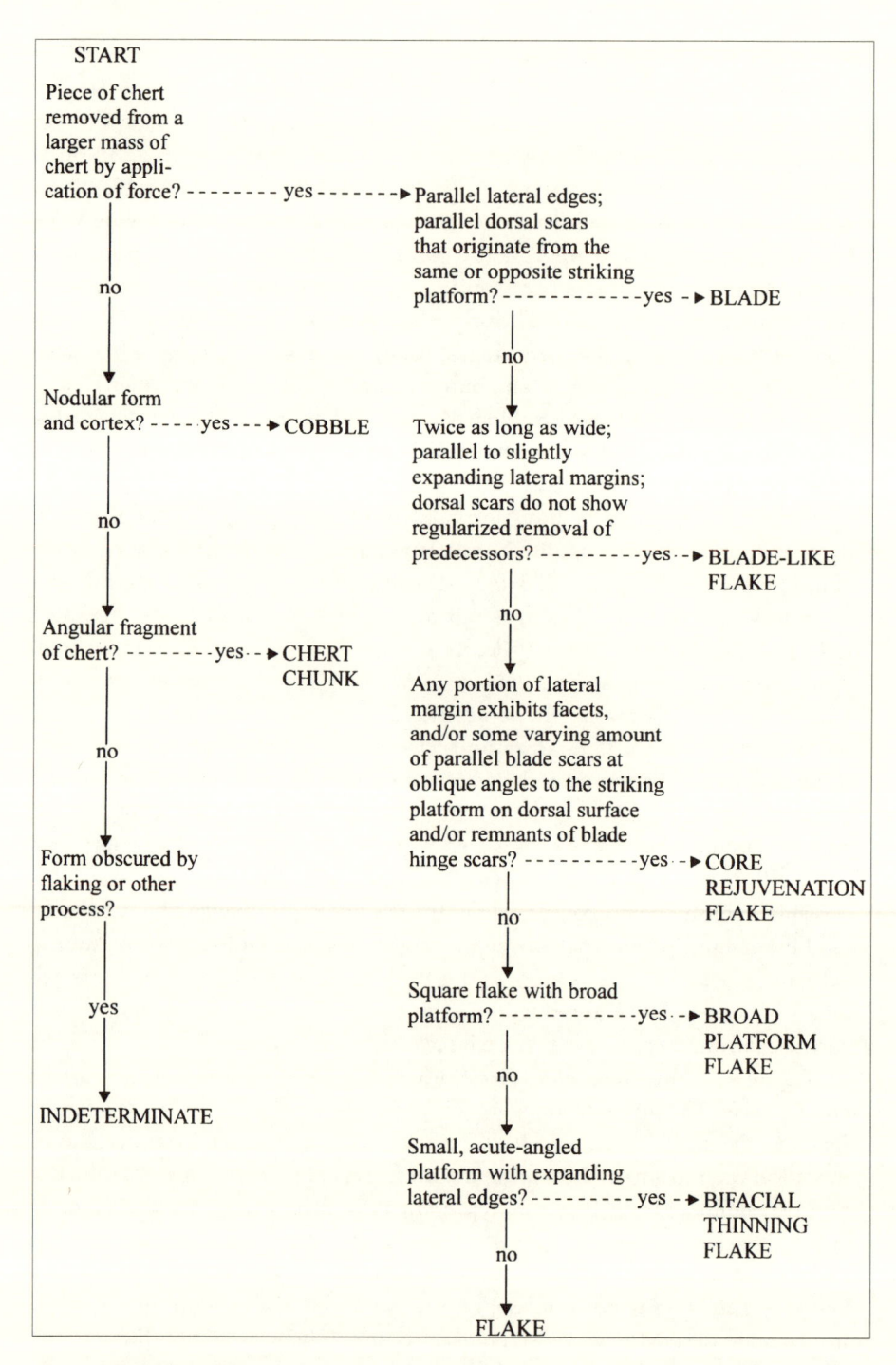

```
START
Piece of chert
removed from a
larger mass of
chert by appli-
cation of force? -------- yes ------▶ Parallel lateral edges;
       |                               parallel dorsal scars
       |                               that originate from the
      no                               same or opposite striking
       |                               platform? ------------yes -▶ BLADE
       ▼                                      |
Nodular form                                 no
and cortex? ----- yes ---▶ COBBLE             ▼
       |                               Twice as long as wide;
      no                               parallel to slightly
       |                               expanding lateral margins;
       ▼                               dorsal scars do not show
Angular fragment                       regularized removal of
of chert? --------yes --▶ CHERT        predecessors? ---------yes --▶ BLADE-LIKE
       |                 CHUNK                |                       FLAKE
      no                                     no
       |                                      ▼
       ▼                               Any portion of lateral
Form obscured by                       margin exhibits facets,
flaking or other                       and/or some varying amount
process?                               of parallel blade scars at
       |                               oblique angles to the striking
       |                               platform on dorsal surface
       |                               and/or remnants of blade
      yes                              hinge scars? ----------yes -▶ CORE
       |                                      |                      REJUVENATION
       ▼                                     no                      FLAKE
INDETERMINATE                                 ▼
                                       Square flake with broad
                                       platform? ------------yes --▶ BROAD
                                              |                      PLATFORM
                                             no                      FLAKE
                                              ▼
                                       Small, acute-angled
                                       platform with expanding
                                       lateral edges? --------yes -▶ BIFACIAL
                                              |                      THINNING
                                             no                      FLAKE
                                              ▼
                                            FLAKE
```

Figure 12-2. Identification protocol used to sort chert artifacts from Twenhafel.

blade, core-rejuvenation flake, general flake, and so forth—cannot be determined. Consequently, modified forms were identified using another key, which is not discussed here. The only relevant class of chipped-stone object from this second sorting process is that of biface—an object that was flaked on two planes to create a form with bifacial symmetry. The collapsed category used here contains early-stage, late-stage, and finished-stage bifaces (Morrow 1984). Bifaces are a minority category in the Twenhafel assemblage.

Results

Table 12-1 presents the basic data on manufacturing technologies at Twenhafel. The general technological trends at Twenhafel can be illustrated in several ways. Figure 12-3 presents the data in Table 12-1 as a line graph. Blade and biface technologies were used most during the early Middle Woodland period, then declined steadily in relative importance through time. By contrast, amorphous-core technology had its lowest percentage of use (40 percent) in the early Middle Woodland period and increased steadily thereafter, until it accounted for approximately 71 percent of the late Late Woodland sample.

Patterns of Chert Use

The most common chert used at Twenhafel, Cobden/Dongola, is a fine-quality blue-gray *local* chert. Cobden/Dongola sources are located about 25 kilometers south of Twenhafel and produced most of the chert used in the region (Morrow et al. 1992). As noted previously, this chert was widely used throughout the midwestern United States during the Middle Woodland period. As also noted earlier, Twenhafel is presumed to have been the "portal" through which much of this material was funneled out of southern Illinois. Table 12-2 illustrates the frequency of this chert in the different manufacturing technologies through time at Twenhafel.

Table 12-3 compares percentages of Cobden/Dongola chert used in each technology with the overall percentage of use of each technology for each of the five components. Cobden/Dongola chert was used in each technology in amounts roughly equivalent to the overall proportion that each technology was used. For example, during the early Middle Woodland period, 37 percent of the Cobden/Dongola chert was used for blade manufacture, 26 percent for biface manufacture, and 37 percent for amorphous-core reduction. During that time, about 36 percent of the entire early Middle Woodland sample was a result of blade technology, 24 percent of biface technology, and 40 percent of amorphous-core technology. This general pattern holds throughout the five Twenhafel components, with a small deviation seen in the late Middle Woodland sample. An inference drawn from these data is that there was no association of particular technologies with this fine-quality blue-gray chert during any of the Woodland

Table 12-1. Frequencies of Lithic Pieces by Period at Twenhafel

Lithic Class	Early Middle Woodland	Middle Middle Woodland	Late Middle Woodland	Early Late Woodland	Late Late Woodland
Blade technology					
Blades	7	48	8	45	10
Blade-like flakes	8	24	2	15	1
Core-rejuvenation flakes	1	4	1	8	-
Other core flakes	-	2	-	1	-
Cores	-	1	1	1	1
Biface technology					
Thinning flakes	11	42	4	21	3
Bifaces	1	6	1	6	1
Amorphous technology					
Broad platform flakes	7	28	6	56	11
Flakes	8	70	17	62	20
Chunks	2	5	4	16	3
Cores	-	-	-	5	2
Other/indeterminate	-	6	-	15	-
Total	45	236	44	251	52

periods. Other locally available cherts, in much smaller amounts, were used in a similar manner to the Cobden/Dongola chert (see Morrow 1988:205–60 for a detailed discussion of those cherts).

Only two (presumably) nonlocal cherts—Crescent and Grimes Hill—were used in appreciable amounts. Recall that Crescent is a fine-quality, white or pinkish-white chert found in outcrops southwest of St. Louis. Grimes Hill chert is a fine-quality, mottled-raspberry-colored chert that presumably is nonlocal (source area unknown). Given the abundance of the local Cobden/Dongola chert, and the importance of that chert in the Midwest, it seems remarkable that nonlocal cherts should appear in the Twenhafel assemblage in any abundance. The timing of the occurrence of those cherts and the technologies used to modify the raw materials are of particular interest here. Both nonlocal cherts (Crescent and Grimes Hill) display patterns of use different from those noted for local cherts. Table 12-4 presents general technological data for the use of those cherts.

Crescent chert at Twenhafel dates from the early Middle Woodland period on and is strongly associated with the production of blades. A comparison of the structure of this blade-technology sample with that for Cobden/Dongola chert reveals the low incidence of blade-like flakes of Crescent chert. The pres-

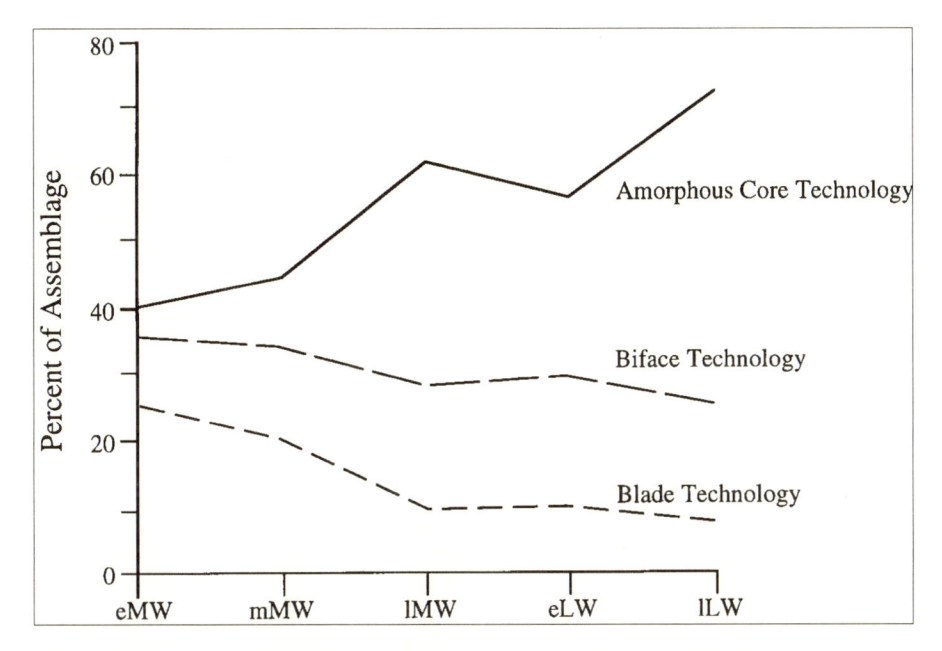

Figure 12-3. Line graph showing general technological trends in assemblages from Twenhafel: *eMW*, early Middle Woodland period (150 B.C.–A.D. 50); *mMW*, middle Middle Woodland period (A.D. 50–250); *lMW*, late Middle Woodland period (A.D. 250–350); *eLW*, early Late Woodland period (A.D. 350–600); *lLW*, late Late Woodland period (post–A.D. 600).

ence of a single blade-like flake, combined with the presence of core-rejuvenation flakes and a blade core, indicates that initial stages of blade manufacture are missing from the nonlocal-chert sample. However, note that in the large samples—those from the middle part of the Middle Woodland period and from the early Late Woodland period—blades made from nonlocal cherts are almost as common as Cobden/Dongola blades.

One plausible interpretation of these data is that prepared cores, rather than unmodified blocks, of Crescent chert were brought to the site. The occurrence of Crescent chert in the amorphous-core-reduction sample and its almost complete absence in the biface-manufacturing classes is consistent with the interpretation that prepared cores were the usual form—perhaps the only form—in which Crescent chert was brought to Twenhafel. Exhausted cores could have been used for amorphous-core reduction but would not have been useful for biface manufacture (Morrow 1984). Hofman (1987) presents a detailed examination of the differences in manufacturing techniques used to produce the Twenhafel blades.

Crescent chert occurs in the Twenhafel collection as both blade and amorphous-core technologies through the early Late Woodland period. Only a single

Table 12-2. Technological Use of Cobden/Dongola Chert through Time at Twenhafel

Lithic Class	Early Middle Woodland	Middle Middle Woodland	Late Middle Woodland	Early Late Woodland	Late Late Woodland
Blade technology					
Blades	4	22	5	20	8
Blade-like flakes	8	19	2	12	1
Core-rejuvenation flakes	1	1	1	6	-
Other core flakes	-	2	-	1	-
Cores	-	-	1	-	-
Biface technology					
Thinning flakes	8	33	2	11	2
Bifaces	1	4	1	4	1
Amorphous technology					
Broad platform flakes	6	20	1	33	4
Flakes	7	48	8	39	17
Chunks	-	4	-	4	-
Cores	-	-	-	1	1
Total	35	153	21	131	34

blade of Crescent was found in late Late Woodland pits, even though this particular chert type accounts for 12 percent of the late Late Woodland chert. The major use of Crescent chert during the late Late Woodland period was in amorphous-core reduction. Recycling of Crescent cores by later inhabitants might account for this difference (see below).

Table 12-3. Percentage of Cobden/Dongola Chert Used in Each Technology by Period at Twenhafel

Period	Percentage Present	Percentage Blade	Percentage Biface	Percentage Amorphous
Early Middle Woodland	77	37 (36)	26 (24)	37 (40)
Middle Middle Woodland	67	29 (33)	24 (22)	46 (44)
Late Middle Woodland	48	43 (27)	14 (11)	43 (61)
Early Late Woodland	57	30 (28)	11 (11)	58 (56)
Late Late Woodland	63	26 (23)	9 (8)	66 (71)

Note: Values in parentheses are the overall percentages of each technology present in each sample.

Table 12-4. Frequencies of Items of Crescent and Grimes Hill Chert in Each Technology by Period at Twenhafel

Lithic Class	Early Middle Woodland	Middle Middle Woodland	Late Middle Woodland	Early Late Woodland	Late Late Woodland
Blade technology					
Blades	2	16(5)	2	17(4)	1
Blade-like flakes	-	1	-	-	-
Core-rejuvenation flakes	-	3	-	2	-
Other core flakes	-	-	-	-	-
Cores	-	-	-	1	-
Biface technology					
Thinning flakes	-	-	-	3	-
Bifaces	-	1	-	-	-
Amorphous technology					
Broad platform flakes	-	3	4	5(1)	2
Flakes	-	1	-	8	2
Chunks	-	1	-	2	1
Cores	-	-	-	2	-
Total	2	26	6	40	6

Note: Numbers in parentheses are frequencies of Grimes Hill chert.

The pattern of use of Grimes Hill chert is interesting. Table 12-4 shows that it occurs almost exclusively in blade form. The only nonblade form is a single broad platform flake found in an early Late Woodland pit. The lack of evidence of manufacture of Grimes Hill blades, and the lack of this chert in the amorphous-core-reduction category, suggest that only finished blades of this material were brought to Twenhafel.

Recycling

Data already presented can be used to evaluate the initiation of use of the various cherts and how they were used through time at Twenhafel. It is more difficult, however, to evaluate the duration of these activities because of the possibility that later residents found and recycled chert left by earlier residents. Also, churning of the midden, through either human- or nonhuman-related actions, could have resulted in the incorporation of earlier materials into younger features. Data on the differences between blade and amorphous-core markers provide the clearest example of how it is possible to determine whether the material found in a sample represents the results of a primary use of a technology versus the presence of scavenged material (recycling).

Evidence of blade manufacture in the form of blade-like flakes, core-rejuvenation flakes, and other flakes from cores, as well as actual cores, is found throughout the entire sequence *until* the late Late Woodland period. A single blade-like flake, a potential marker of on-site manufacture, as well as a potentially useful tool, is present in the late Late Woodland sample. Although that sample is small, both the early Middle Woodland and the late Middle Woodland samples are slightly smaller still and yet they yielded evidence of blade manufacture. Several different interpretations of these data are plausible. Least likely is that although blade manufacture had ceased by A.D. 600, blades were still being brought to the site. Mixing of late Late Woodland features is another possible interpretation. However, the late Late Woodland materials do not appear to be a hodgepodge of earlier materials. There are specific materials missing—such as blade-manufacturing debris—while others are present—such as blades and numerous amorphous-core flakes. I interpret these data to indicate that blade manufacture had ceased at Twenhafel by A.D. 600 but that blades were "mined" and reused by later occupants.

The recycling argument can be developed further by observing the marked increase in the use of amorphous-core technology. Although blade manufacture apparently had ceased, other manufacturing technologies were being used by later occupants. However, the general trend throughout the Midwest appears to have been an increase during the Late Woodland period in the use of amorphous-core technology—either expedient-core technology or unstructured-core technology. Parry and Kelly (1987) correlate this shift with increased sedentariness and the capacity to stockpile chert supplies. This kind of tool-manufacturing technology does not require large pieces of chert and is particularly suited for recycling and reducing chunks of chert that are not useful for producing more standardized tool forms (see Hofman and Morrow 1984:176-77 for an earlier argument of this sort). After hundreds of years of occupation and hundreds of thousands of acts of chipped-stone manufacture and use, Twenhafel was surely a rich source of raw materials for Late Woodland groups.

Finally, there is the evidence discussed by Hofman and Morrow (1984:176-77) in favor of the argument that if the later material represents recycling activities, then the pieces of chipped stone in the later sample should be smaller than those found in earlier samples. We found that this was indeed the case: chipped-stone pieces from the late Late Woodland period were skewed in favor of smaller sizes (Morrow 1988)—a trend that characterized pieces manufactured from both local and nonlocal cherts.

All these lines of evidence suggest that chipped-stone pieces from the late Late Woodland sample do not represent primary use and deposition of the chert found in the pits used in this analysis. However, the evidence is congruent with recycling or scavenging activities rather than with simply postdepositional mixing. The strongest pieces of evidence are the marked dominance of one specific manufacturing technology—amorphous-core technology—and increased rates of use. Mixing would have resulted in a random group of materials assigned to different technologies as well as to random rates of use.

Discussion

The purpose of this chapter is to evaluate the working assumptions of most midwestern archaeologists that the appearance of prismatic-blade technology and an increased use of nonlocal cherts were coeval with other Hopewellian traits. These assumptions were tested by examining whether those two traits were restricted to the period A.D. 1–200. The analysis here demonstrates that the appearance and use of blades and nonlocal cherts at Twenhafel occurred earlier and lasted much longer than that time span.

Elsewhere (Morrow 1987, 1988, 1989), I have argued that blade production and the use of nonlocal cherts were markers of social relationships and interaction rather than general utilitarian strategies during the Middle Woodland period. There are several lines of evidence to support this proposition. First, the inhabitants of Twenhafel clearly had no need to import high-quality chert from hundreds of kilometers away. The major local chert was high-quality Cobden/Dongola, which itself was exchanged. In utilitarian terms, the import of Crescent chert would have been redundant. But, not coincidentally, Crescent is highly distinctive in appearance compared to the local Twenhafel cherts. This fine-quality, white, marble-like chert does not remotely resemble any local materials. It is common in the Havana region, particularly throughout the lower Illinois Valley, and I suggest that its use during the Middle Woodland period at Twenhafel, at least to some degree, was as a marker of social interaction with groups to the north. The high visibility factor of Crescent chert would have served to illustrate the ability to negotiate exchange across relatively large distances.

Second, this analysis has revealed that Crescent chert was brought to Twenhafel in prepared blade-core form. The design implications of the use of prismatic-core blade technology indicate that it maximizes the use of a chert resource in terms of producing the maximum amount of working edge per weight of raw material. This technology also allows the knapper/user to create highly specialized tool forms. However, blade-core technology is inflexible in that it cannot be used to manufacture a wide range of tool forms. Tool forms are restricted to blades and the specialized forms manufactured on blades.

Middle Woodland blades appear to have been simple cutting and/or scraping tools. Generally, they were not used as slender preforms for finely shaped projectile points, as seems to have been the case with Paleoindian points, nor do they appear to have been microliths used for drilling and engraving, as was the case during the Mississippian period. Essentially, the Hopewell blade technology functioned to produce large numbers of simple cutting and/or scraping tools. However, amorphous-core technology can produce functionally similar tools within a much simpler manufacturing strategy.

Use-wear analyses by Odell (1985, 1988) of some lower Illinois Valley artifacts reveal that blades were used as general tools for a wide variety of cutting and scraping activities. Smiling Dan (Stafford and Sant 1985), a Middle Woodland habitation site on the west bank of the Illinois River (Smiling Dan, Napoleon Hollow [see below], and Elizabeth [see below] are all located just off the northern edge of the map shown in Figure 12-1), yielded large numbers of blades that appear to be multipurpose tools with no special functional niche (Odell 1994:106). However, blades exhibiting a more restricted range of uses were found at Napoleon Hollow (Wiant and McGimsey 1986), particularly on the slope below the Elizabeth mound group. The suggested activities for these blades were hide scraping, cutting, and limited woodworking. Odell (1994) suggests these activities were most likely related to the production of funerary objects. Interestingly, blades were found in association with the remains of an elderly female at Elizabeth (Charles et al. 1988), perhaps suggesting the production or use of the blades was a female activity (Morrow 1988:339).

The study discussed here has documented evidence for the appearance of prismatic-blade-core technology and the use of nonlocal cherts prior to and after the Hopewell tradition. Perhaps what we are monitoring is the early beginnings of the movement of ideas and materials on a very modest, utilitarian sort of level. Evidence for late blades at Twenhafel is interpreted as resulting from recycling or reuse of the materials by later inhabitants rather than as a continuation of those traits into the late Late Woodland period.

13 | Prehistoric Diet in the Central Mississippi River Valley
Diana M. Greenlee

THE SYSTEMATIC RECOVERY and analysis of archaeobotanical remains has demonstrated convincingly that maize farming was not the exclusive basis for all sedentary, nucleated settlements in North America (Wymer 1987, 1990) and that native plants continued to play a variable role in subsistence systems after maize became the primary dietary focus (e.g., Rindos and Johannessen 1991; Rossen and Edging 1987; Wagner 1987). Comparisons of stable-carbon-isotope ratios have shown that the timing, rate, and degree to which maize was incorporated into prehistoric subsistence systems varied from region to region (e.g., Buikstra 1992; Buikstra et al. 1988; Greenlee 1991) and that dietary dependence on maize was not a prerequisite for the appearance of Hopewellian or Mississippian cultural phenomena (Bender et al. 1981; Lynott et al. 1986). Thus, long-held commonsensical assumptions about the nature of prehistoric subsistence systems, dietary change, the relation between subsistence and settlement, and the relation between cultural elaboration and maize agriculture are all open to question.

Nowhere have the old views been challenged more directly than in the central Mississippi River valley, the traditional epicenter of Mississippian culture. On the one hand, postdepositional environments and excavation strategies in some cases have precluded the recovery of items (e.g., archaeobotanical and faunal remains) relevant to understanding prehistoric subsistence in the Mississippi Valley, but on the other hand, there have been successful attempts at generating dietary information through the chemical analysis of archaeological human bone from the region. As research results have continued to document that late prehistoric–period diet in the region was highly variable, it has become increasingly clear that more work is necessary to explain the dietary variation documented thus far. This chapter reviews the current knowledge about prehistoric diet in the central Mississippi Valley, presents and integrates new dietary data based on analysis of skeletal samples from southeastern Missouri, and suggests directions for future research.

Bone Chemistry and Diet

Although several different sources of information, such as paleopathological observations, tooth microwear, and botanical and faunal remains, are often treated by archaeologists as reflecting diet, the linkage is indirect and inferential. Bone, of particular interest to archaeologists because it is frequently preserved, is one tissue that reflects dietary intake (e.g., Ambrose and DeNiro 1986; Ambrose and Norr 1993; Bender et al. 1981; Chisholm et al. 1982; DeNiro and Epstein 1978a, 1978b, 1981; DeNiro and Schoeninger 1983; Hare et al. 1991; Lambert and Weydert-Homeyer 1994; Mills 1970; Price et al. 1985, 1986; Schoeninger 1979; Schoeninger and DeNiro 1984; Schoeninger and Peebles 1981; Sealy and Sillen 1988; Tanaka et al. 1981; Tieszen et al. 1983; Underwood 1977; Vogel 1978). Because the biochemical sources and metabolic processes involved in the synthesis of the organic and mineral phases of bone differ, they provide different kinds of information about dietary intake, and they interact with the geochemistry of the depositional environment in different ways, thus creating a number of difficult issues for archaeological analyses. Although the relation between diet and tissue composition in archaeological specimens can be disrupted by postmortem chemical alterations, bone chemistry remains our only potential source of direct information about prehistoric diet; clearly, care must be taken to ensure that we do not mistake postmortem geochemical sources of bone composition for antemortem biological ones.

Stable-Carbon-Isotope Analysis in the Central Valley

Stable-carbon-isotope ratios ($^{13}C/^{12}C$) in the organic fraction of human bone are the primary source of dietary information currently used by archaeologists working in eastern North America. This is so for two reasons. First, stable-carbon-isotope ratios provide direct information regarding maize consumption. In terrestrial ecosystems, the stable-carbon-isotope ratios of plants reflect the biochemical pathway of atmospheric carbon dioxide (CO_2) in photosynthesis. The native vegetation of the Eastern Woodlands relies primarily on the C_3 (Calvin-Benson) photosynthetic pathway, which produces $\delta^{13}C$ values ranging from $-35°/_{oo}$ to $-20°/_{oo}$ (Deines 1980; O'Leary 1981, 1988; Smith and Epstein 1971).[1] A few plants in the region (e.g., species of Gramineae, *Amaranthus*, *Atriplex*, *Setaria*, and *Carex*) are known to operate in the C_4 (Hatch-Slack) photosynthetic mode (Downton 1975; Smith and Epstein 1971); C_4 plants have $\delta^{13}C$ values on the order of $-16°/_{oo}$ to $-7°/_{oo}$ (Deines 1980; O'Leary 1981, 1988; Smith and Epstein 1971). That C_4 plants are relatively rare in this environment is also reflected in $\delta^{13}C$ values for the local fauna. Because the isotopic composition of a plant is passed on to its animal consumers with some fractionation (DeNiro and Epstein 1978b; Teeri and Schoeller 1979; Vogel 1978), $\delta^{13}C$ values for the local fauna range from $-20°/_{oo}$ to $-23°/_{oo}$ (Bender et al. 1981; Boutton et al. 1991; Conard 1988; Katzenberg 1988, 1989). The $\delta^{13}C$ values would be enriched considerably, up to about $-7°/_{oo}$, for fauna in an environment dominated by C_4 plants (Vogel 1978).

Maize, an introduced plant of tropical origin, is thus a virtually unique resource in this area with its C_4 (Hatch-Slack) photosynthetic mode. This is not to say that it is the only potential C_4 resource in the diet of prehistoric human populations in the region. Of the other floral resources suggested from other evidence to have been consumed in significant amounts by populations in the Eastern Woodlands (including *Chenopodium berlandieri, Phaseolus vulgaris, Phalaris caroliniana, Polygonum erectum, Cucurbita, Helianthus annuus,* and various sources of mast), none is identified as a C_4 plant (Buikstra et al. 1988; Smith and Epstein 1971). Thus, large differences in $\delta^{13}C$ values between individuals are almost certainly reflections of differences in maize consumption. As I argue below, slight variations in $\delta^{13}C$ values, especially from contexts that predate the appearance of maize farming, might reflect differences in the isotopic background of the local environment and its exploitation and therefore merit further study.

The second reason stable-carbon-isotope ratios in the organic fraction of human bone constitute the primary source of dietary information for the prehistoric East is that the organic fraction of bone tends to be better preserved than the mineral fraction in temperate environments. This situation makes understanding prehistoric diet slightly more complex than it might otherwise be, since the isotopic composition of the organic fraction, dominated by the protein collagen, reflects primarily the protein component of the diet, whereas the mineral phase better reflects an average of the whole diet (Ambrose and Norr 1993; Tieszen and Fagre 1993). Thus, although dietary differences can be identified, archaeologists cannot rely on simple transforms to reconstruct dietary composition quantitatively.

The first and largest analysis of stable-carbon-isotope ratios of human skeletal material from the central Mississippi River valley was conducted to examine the relation between the appearance of Mississippian cultural elaborations and maize consumption (Boutton et al. 1984; Lynott et al. 1986). Toward that end, "collagen"[2] was analyzed from the remains of nineteen individuals from thirteen sites that range in age from 3200 B.C. to A.D. 1880 (Figures 13-1 and 13-2; individuals from the eastern Ozarks and historical-period contexts are excluded here). On the basis of their analysis, the authors concluded that (1) populations did not consume significant amounts of maize until after the "Emergent Mississippian" period, that is, until after about A.D. 1000; (2) the incorporation of maize as a major component of the diet occurred relatively rapidly; and (3) maize remained a major contributor to prehistoric diet in the region until contact with Euroamericans.

A later analysis of stable-carbon-isotope data from fifteen individuals from six more archaeological sites in southeastern Missouri and northeastern Arkansas (Boutton et al. 1991; Greenlee and Dunnell 1990; Rose et al. 1985, 1991), though not substantially altering the above conclusions, documented the existence of considerable regional dietary variation across occupations of similar age. Relative to data sets from other regions, the published central Mississippi Valley isotope data display both a lower commitment to and a greater variation

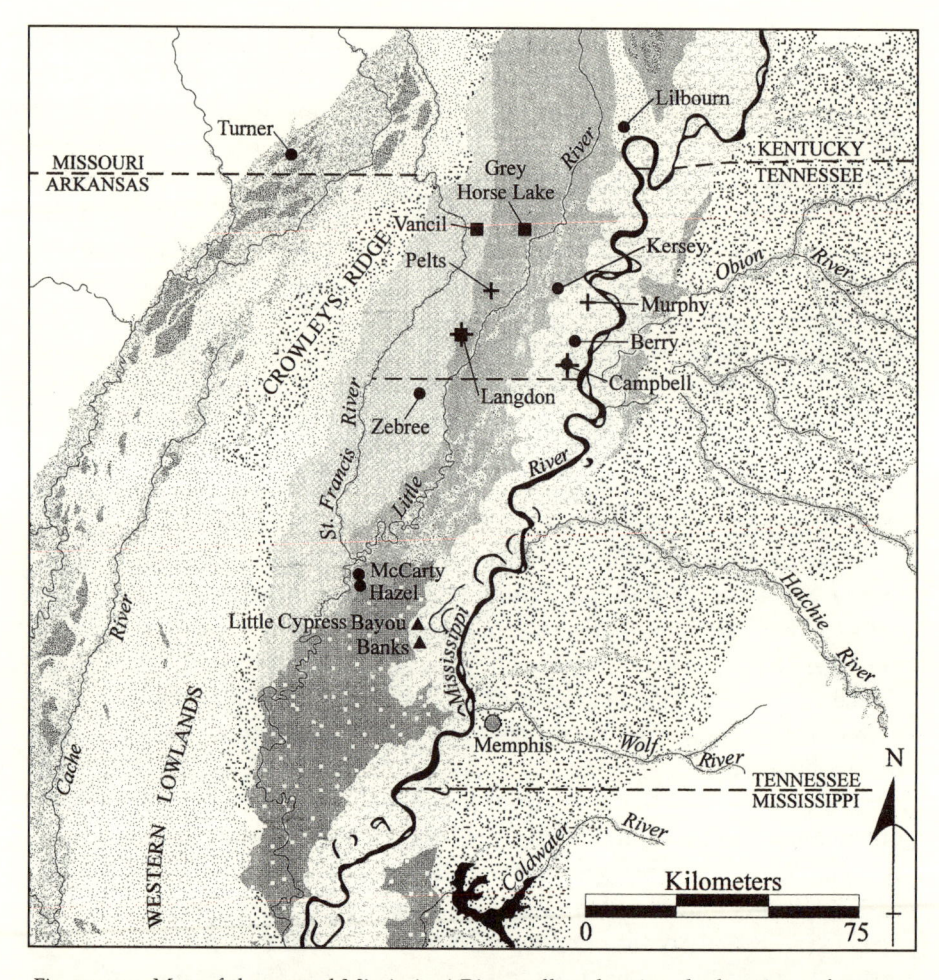

Figure 13-1. Map of the central Mississippi River valley, showing the locations of previously acquired (*circles,* Boutton et al. 1984; Lynott et al. 1986, 1991; *triangles,* Rose et al. 1985, 1991; *squares,* Greenlee and Dunnell 1990) and newly acquired (*crosses*) stable-carbon-isotope data.

in maize consumption, which has been suggested (Greenlee 1991; Greenlee and Dunnell 1990) to reflect the greater environmental diversity of the central Mississippi Valley. Data are too sparse to evaluate this hypothesis, however.

Attempts to explain the isotopic record of subsistence change toward increased maize consumption in the valley (Lynott et al. 1986; Rose et al. 1985, 1991) have regarded maize farming as just one aspect of the Mississippian phenomenon. Rose et al. (1991) further suggest that maize, as one of the trappings of "Mississippianization," was initially grown to be consumed only by certain special individuals at religious ceremonies and/or social events. Then, as large nucleated sedentary settlements were established and population density increased, greater stresses were placed on the resources of the local environment,

Prehistoric Diet | 303

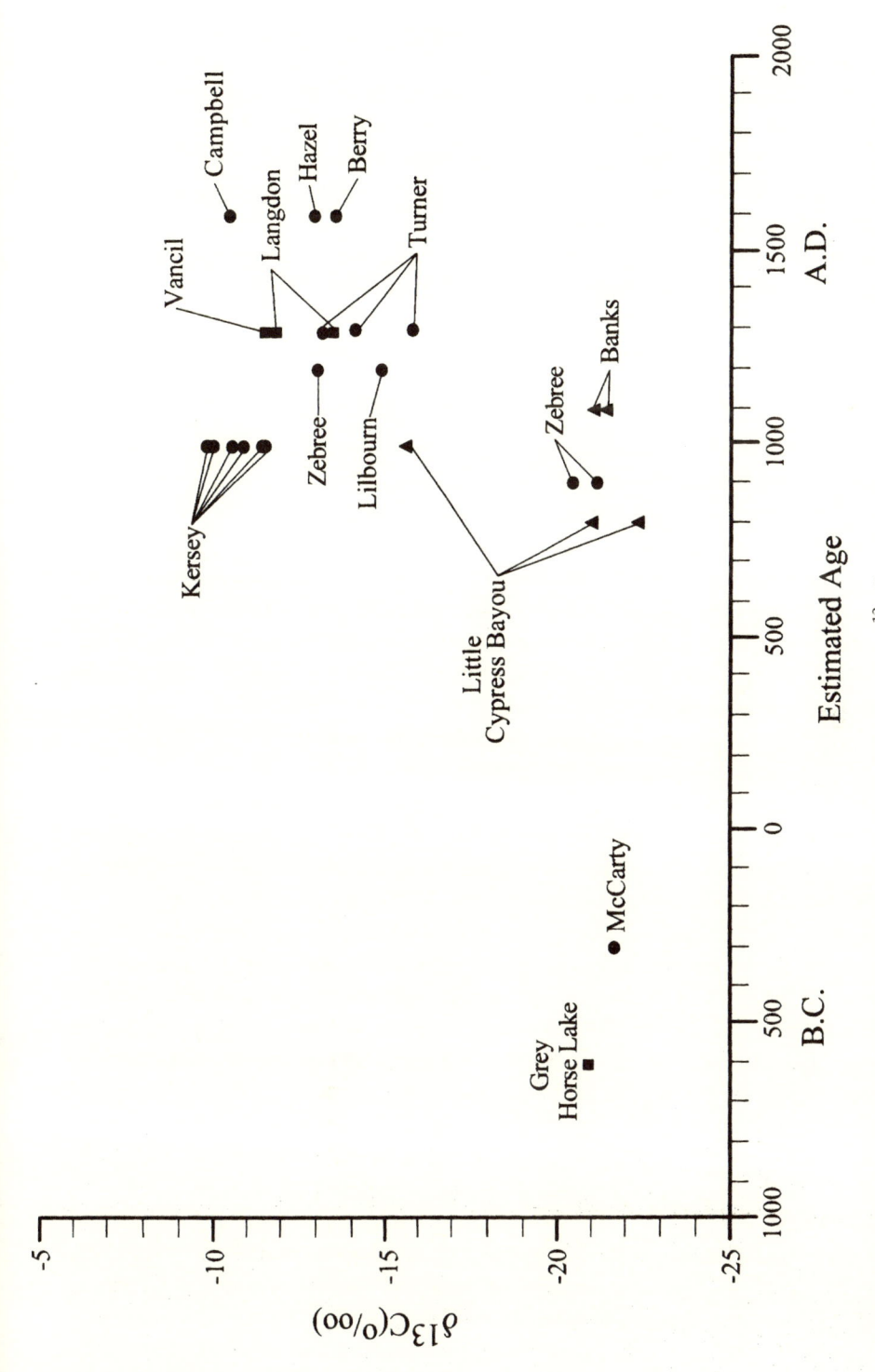

Figure 13-2. Plot showing previously acquired stable-carbon-isotope ratios ($\delta^{13}C$ ‰ PDB) versus estimated age. Symbols are the same as in Figure 13-1.

"necessitating" the eventual adoption of maize as a dietary staple by the entire population.

This scenario might have intuitive appeal, but as an explanation it suffers from what has been termed "demographic determinism" (Rindos 1984). That is, it assumes that increased population density, resulting at least in part from settlement reorganization, preceded the adoption of maize as a dietary staple. This may indeed have been the case, but, as Teltser points out in Chapter 7, the resolution (temporal, demographic, and isotopic) necessary to demonstrate that sequence of events has not been achieved. It is more likely that higher population density was a *consequence* of increased agricultural productivity associated with the incorporation of maize into the existing subsistence system.

Trace-Element Analysis in the Central Mississippi Valley

The first and only application of trace-element analysis to dietary problems in the central Mississippi Valley was conducted by Duncan (1977; cited in Powell 1980). Atomic-absorption analysis was used to measure copper, iron, manganese, strontium, and zinc concentrations in the mineral-hydroxyapatite phase of human bone from the Big Lake–phase (A.D. 800–1100) occupation at the Zebree site in Mississippi County, Arkansas. Although the results of this initial study have been interpreted by some to indicate "that the Zebree inhabitants ate less red meat than a comparative sample from Mound 72 at Cahokia" (P. [A.] Morse and D. F. Morse 1990:61), both Duncan and Powell caution that the local geochemistries need to be examined and taken into account.

This caution is supported by more-recent trace-element work undertaken by Greenlee and Dunnell (1993) at several Mississippi Valley locations. Electron-microbeam analysis was used to identify those elements linked to black and reddish-brown staining in the mineral matrix of human bone from twenty-three individuals from six Archaic- and Mississippian-period deposits. The chemistry of these archaeological specimens was concluded to be quite variable and, for some elements (e.g., manganese, iron, and barium) at least, it appears to be structured by the local postdepositional environment. A better understanding of postdepositional alteration in bone hydroxyapatite content is required before conclusions can be drawn about prehistoric diet on the basis of the trace-element composition of archaeological bones.

Assessing the Dietary Record

The archaeological record of the central Mississippi River valley has been the focus of a considerable amount of dietary research, particularly involving stable-carbon-isotope analysis of bone "collagen." When plotted against time as in Figure 13-2, published $\delta^{13}C$ values do show a general increase in maize consumption after A.D. 1000, but there is clearly considerable variation. One or more factors (e.g., local environment, temporal resolution, settlement system, community composition, individual metabolic or behavioral differences, preservation, "collagen"-extraction techniques) are certainly reflected in the data. Unraveling the contribution of these variables is hampered by small sample size, but it is extremely important to consider how such factors might influence stable-carbon-isotope values from central Mississippi Valley skeletons.

Preservation

As bone interacts chemically with the surrounding burial environment, the organic fraction deteriorates. Collagen becomes fragmented and leaches away, with some residues being preferentially retained as a result of charge interactions with the mineral-hydroxyapatite phase. As a result, the total protein content drops, and the relative amino-acid composition changes (Hare 1980; Masters 1987). At the same time, amino acids from more stable noncollagenous proteins may survive, and amino acids and/or other carbonous materials (e.g., humic and fulvic acids) from exogenous sources may become incorporated into the organic mass. Because amino acids have different stable-carbon-isotope ratios (Abelson and Hoering 1961; Hare and Estep 1983; Hare et al. 1991; Macko et al. 1983, 1987; Stafford et al. 1988; Tuross et al. 1988), as do humic and fulvic acids, the $\delta^{13}C$ value of the extracted "collagen" will not accurately reflect the original biological signature. To evaluate the possibility of diagenetically altered isotope ratios, archaeologists use one or more assessment strategies: extract yield, percent carbon and percent nitrogen, elemental carbon/nitrogen (C/N) ratios, and amino-acid composition.

About 22 percent of modern bone is organic by weight. Approximately 90 percent of that is collagen, so bone is roughly 20 percent collagen. The amount of "collagen" remaining in archaeological bones is highly variable, however, and depends on the nature of postdepositional processes. Empirically, there appears to be a threshold of about 2 percent: when the concentration of "collagen" extracted from archaeological materials is 2 percent or less, other indicators (e.g., C/N ratios, amino-acid composition) suggest that the bone is severely altered and the extract is no longer representative of its original composition (Ambrose 1990; DeNiro and Weiner 1988). This observation may simply reflect that when collagen yields are this low, small amounts of noncollagenous proteins or contaminants can make substantial contributions to the composition of the extract. Additionally, Tuross et al. (1988) note that high yields may result when exogenous materials survive the extraction process; thus "collagen" concentration should not be used as the exclusive criterion for evaluating the integrity of the extract.

Modern collagen is approximately 45 percent carbon and 15 percent nitrogen (by weight) and has atomic C/N ratios ranging from 2.9 to 3.6. This range of C/N ratios was determined empirically for modern animals by DeNiro (1985) and others (e.g., Ambrose 1990; Nelson et al. 1986; Schoeninger and DeNiro 1984). More-recent estimates calculated from the C/N ratios of amino acids and their measured frequencies in modern collagen range from 3.21 (Ambrose 1993) to 3.9 (Schoeninger et al. 1989). The C/N ratio is thus a potential measure of the collagenous origin of carbon in the extract. In support of his argument that C/N ratios act as measures of the degree to which inorganic and organic impurities are included in archaeological "collagen" extracts, DeNiro (1985) found that samples with C/N ratios outside the reported modern range have aberrant stable-isotope ratios. Masters (1987) suggests that C/N ratios slightly higher than the known range might reflect preservation of noncollagenous proteins rather than collagen, whereas extremely high ratios (in the range of 10 to 20) probably reflect extensive diagenesis or high levels of exogenous carbon contamination. Indeed, Ambrose (1990) found that C/N ratios of "collagen" samples of less than 2-percent yield were highly variable and consistently well outside the range of modern collagen.

Concentrations of carbon and nitrogen in collagen extracts have been identified by Ambrose (1990) as effective criteria for assessing "collagen" preservation and diagenetic alteration. In his study of prehistoric human bones, Ambrose (1990) found virtually no relation between carbon and nitrogen concentration and sample yields greater than 5 percent, a systematic decrease in the 2- to 5-percent yield range, and an abrupt drop below 2 percent. In arguing against the exclusive use of C/N ratios for assessing "collagen" integrity, Ambrose notes that seemingly good samples with C/N ratios fortuitously within the "acceptable" range and high apparent yields (resulting from incomplete removal of salts and other inorganic residues) can be identified as diagenetically altered on the basis of low carbon and nitrogen concentrations.

Collagen molecules have a unique amino-acid composition—about 33 percent glycine with high amounts (relative to other proteins) of proline and hydroxyproline (Woodhead-Galloway 1980). Because of this, amino-acid composition is a good indicator of preservation. The amino-acid composition of a sample will reflect (1) differential loss of amino acids during collagen diagenesis, (2) intrusive amino acids from an exogenous source, and (3) differential survival of amino acids from noncollagenous proteins. Studies (e.g., Hare 1980; Masters 1987) have identified systematic changes in the amino-acid composition of collagen as it degrades: hydroxyproline and proline are lost; glycine, alanine, serine, and threonine levels decrease; and aspartic and glutamic acid levels increase. Because the amino acids each have different C/N and stable-isotope ratios, collagen degradation will affect both of those ratios in the extract.

Of the published isotope ratios shown in Figure 13-2, none is accompanied by information about extract yield. C/N ratios are available for twenty-one individuals, and all fall within the range of modern collagen (Boutton et al. 1991; Greenlee and Dunnell 1990). For three individuals, two from Langdon and one from Vancil, both located in Dunklin County, Missouri (Figure 13-1), carbon and nitrogen concentrations are known and are characteristic of collagen, thereby complementing the C/N ratios. Lynott et al. (1986) report that carbon concentrations of their extracts were variable, ranging from 20 to 45 percent; because they do not provide those data for specific samples, it is impossible to identify which ones might contain significant inorganic contamination. Amino-acid compositions are reported for two individuals, one from McCarty (Poinsett County, Arkansas) and the other from Campbell (Pemiscot County, Missouri) (Figure 13-1) (Boutton et al. 1984, 1991); relative abundances of the amino acids are consistent with the composition of human bone collagen. Overall, these indicators suggest that diagenetic alteration has not significantly affected the composition of the "collagen" in at least some of the samples considered here. The general similarity of depositional conditions leads one to hope, at least, that diagenesis is *not* a major factor for the rest. In any case, variation in the isotope ratios is not simply a product of preservation conditions.

"Collagen"-Extraction Techniques

Several approaches to "collagen" extraction are currently in use by different research programs. While efforts to compare different extraction techniques (e.g., Chisholm et al. 1983a; Gurfinkel 1987; Schoeninger et al. 1989; Stafford et al. 1987; Tuross et al. 1988) have shown that the extract quality and resulting $\delta^{13}C$ values vary, systematic evidence in support of conclusions about the effects of procedural variations is lacking. Fortunately, the same basic extraction strategy was used by researchers to obtain the isotope ratios of interest here; the primary source of variation lies in efforts to remove humic substances. Boutton et al. (1984, 1991), Lynott et al. (1986), and Rose et al. (1985) used a 1.0 molar (M) sodium-hydroxide treatment for the removal of humic substances, whereas Greenlee and Dunnell (1990) did not. This reflects disagreement in the literature regarding sodium-hydroxide pretreatment (e.g., Ambrose 1990, 1993; Ambrose and Norr 1992; Chisholm 1989; Chisholm et al. 1983a, 1993; Häkansson 1976; Katzenberg 1989; Katzenberg et al. 1995; Liden et al. 1995; van Klinken and Hedges 1995), which, although it may remove humic materials, also reduces "collagen" yield and alters the amino-acid composition, potentially altering the $\delta^{13}C$ value of the extract. In environmental situations in which C_3 plants dominate, as in the Eastern Woodlands, the inclusion of humates in "collagen" will decrease the measured $\delta^{13}C$ value. The isotope data in Figure 13-2, at any rate, do not show a *systematic* pattern across results from different researchers that might suggest differences caused by varying extraction procedures.

Other potential sources of error, in addition to systematic errors resulting from different sample extraction techniques, need to be considered. Errors such as those introduced during sample preparation and measurement must be estimated before differences in the $\delta^{13}C$ values of individuals can be evaluated.

Comparing measurements for replicate samples from the same bone is one way to estimate such errors. The error terms of replicate extractions reflect several sources of error, including those associated with mass spectrometry, sample preparation, and sample homogeneity. Unfortunately, the results of replicate extractions are not typically reported, if indeed they are measured, which thus makes it difficult to assess how great a difference between individuals is required for significance. Boutton et al. (1984; see also Lynott et al. 1986) note that the standard deviations for all replicate extractions were less than 0.5°/oo, whereas two replicates of Rose et al. (1985) had standard deviations of 0.07°/oo and 0.57°/oo, and the standard deviations for replicates of Greenlee and Dunnell (1990) ranged between 0.01°/oo and 0.07°/oo. As a rule, intralaboratory error associated with mass spectrometry is negligible compared with that resulting from sample heterogeneity and preparation, which in itself appears to be considerably less than interlaboratory mass-spectrometer calibration error, estimated to be on the order of 1.0°/oo (Chisholm 1989; Chisholm et al. 1983a; Mann 1982). Thus, unless the results of replicate extractions are reported, it is probably safe to assume that intralaboratory differences in $\delta^{13}C$ values between individuals that exceed 0.5°/oo and interlaboratory differences that exceed 1.0°/oo can be considered significant. If intralaboratory errors are reported, smaller differences between individuals may be significant.

Individual Metabolism

Metabolic differences might also contribute to the variability seen in $\delta^{13}C$ values. To document this, researchers have examined both intraindividual and interindividual variation in the isotopic composition of bone collagen. DeNiro and Schoeninger (1983) examined variation in $\delta^{13}C$ values of collagen between different bones of the same individual. The stable-carbon-isotope ratios of collagen extracted from multiple bones of three rabbits and fifteen minks raised on monotonous diets varied by more than 0.5°/oo and 1.0°/oo, respectively. In a later study, Chisholm (1989) reported a mean difference of 0.2°/oo between different bones of the same individual for four individuals, with even less variation (0.1°/oo) in isotopic composition between different parts of the same bone. These results indicate that (1) isotopic differences between the bones in the body are not significant compared with other sources of error in current protocols and (2) collagen extracted from any bone represents the entire skeleton adequately.

Variation in $\delta^{13}C$ values has also been documented between individuals of modern animal populations eating the same diet (DeNiro and Epstein 1978b; DeNiro and Schoeninger 1983; Hobson and Schwarcz 1986; Tieszen et al. 1989). Not unexpectedly, wild populations tend to exhibit greater variation than laboratory animals raised on controlled diets (Hobson and Schwarcz 1986). Overall, however, the animal data fail to suggest any metabolic sex or age effect on stable-carbon-isotope ratios. Results of cross-sectional studies of isotope ratios in hair from modern Japanese (Minagawa 1992) conform to the animal model—that is, they show a lack of metabolic age or sex effect on $\delta^{13}C$ values. Also conforming to the animal model are findings from several archaeological human populations assumed to have consumed relatively uniform diets (Boutton et al. 1991; Lovell et al. 1986; White and Schwarcz 1989). Taken together, these data suggest that when age- or sex-related differences in $\delta^{13}C$ values are documented for archaeological human populations, they probably reflect behavioral (dietary) rather than metabolic differences.

A potential source of variation in $\delta^{13}C$ values that has received little attention is illness, which disrupts an individual's metabolism. Currently, there are no data on this issue. Clinical research using ^{13}C-labeled substrates to diagnose conditions such as intestinal malabsorption or liver dysfunction (e.g., Klein and Klein 1985; Schoeller et al. 1977, 1980, 1981; Solomons et al. 1977) is not designed to provide information regarding isotopic discrimination during metabolism, nor do the results reveal the long-term effects of these conditions on the isotopic composition of tissues. One example, however, that might lend support to the notion that at least some physiological conditions might produce different isotope ratios is discussed by Schoeller et al. (1980). Compared with results in normal infants tested under the same conditions, breath tests of infants with cystic fibrosis, who have abnormal fat oxidation because of impaired pancreatic function, showed significantly different levels of $^{13}CO_2$ after six hours. Unfortunately, it is not known how mass balance is achieved in these individuals, though research on healthy rats has shown that breath $^{13}CO_2$ level is a good predictor of hydroxyapatite and, to a lesser extent, collagen $\delta^{13}C$ values (Tieszen and Fagre 1993).

The extent to which the stresses that produce skeletal pathologic conditions also influence the incorporation of $\delta^{13}C$ into bodily tissues is unknown, but because indicators of physiological stress are frequently found in archaeological skeletal populations (e.g., Buikstra 1992; Buikstra et al. 1988; Cassidy 1984; Norr 1991; Perzigian et al. 1984; Rose et al. 1991), this question is worth considering. The skeletal pathologic conditions that are found (e.g., Harris lines, linear enamel hypoplasias, and porotic hyperostoses) are not attributable to particular physiological stresses. In some cases they may be associated with nutritional deficiency and in others disease. Because collagen-turnover rates are on the order of 10 to 20 years, the condition would need to be either chronic or severe to be detectable in stable-carbon-isotope ratios of collagen. Currently, there is *no* evidence that the variation in $\delta^{13}C$ values documented for the central Mississippi Valley is a result of illness-related metabolic differences.

Individual Behavior

It is well documented that many animal species display dietary differences with age, sex, size, geographic location, season, reproductive status, or social standing (Ambrose and DeNiro 1986; Boutton et al. 1980, 1983; Schell 1983; Tieszen and Imbamba 1980). Indeed, differences in stable-carbon-isotope ratios between different age groups in archaeological populations have been argued to reflect age-related dietary differences (Chisholm et al. 1983b; Katzenberg and Saunders 1990; Katzenberg et al. 1993; Reed 1995; Sealy and van der Merwe 1988). The central Mississippi Valley sample includes only one subadult skeleton thus far, that of a twelve-year-old recovered from an unusual burial context at Little Cypress Bayou (Crittenden County, Arkansas; Figure 13-1) (Rose et al. 1985, 1991). This individual had a significantly greater $\delta^{13}C$ value than two other individuals from that location. The reason for the difference, however, is not entirely clear; it might reflect a different juvenile diet, a different time period (one Mississippian-period sherd and a radiocarbon date of A.D. 1000 obtained from associated wood charcoal [Dicks and Weed 1985, cited in Rose et al. 1991] suggest that this individual might date to a later occupation than the others), or, as the analysts imply, a different social status.

Status differences are frequently invoked as an explanation for dietary variation (e.g., Bender et al. 1981; Blakely and Beck 1981; Hatch and Geidel 1985; Reed 1995; Rose et al. 1991; Schoeninger and Peebles 1981; Schurr 1989). Although some might argue that differences in burial treatment reflect status in life (e.g., Balter 1995; O'Shea 1984; Peebles 1971), this is an untestable inference made with little empirical basis. To the extent they are empirically based, however, "social-status" explanations of dietary differences can be reduced to differences in individual behavior. Reconstructions aside, the critical question is whether dietary change occurs sympatrically—that is, do *all* individuals change their diet—or allopatrically—that is, do only *some* individuals change their diet? If we are to explain dietary change, we must understand the underlying mechanism of change. Thus, documenting the range of dietary variation and tying that to specific individuals are critical. Data to do that are not yet available.

Temporal Resolution

Assigning dates to individuals of isotopic interest is of primary importance when the goal is understanding and explaining dietary change. Unfortunately, dates are often based on associations of varying reliability. Association arguments are particularly problematic in the central Mississippi Valley because many locales have been sites of sporadic, if not nearly continuous, occupation from the Archaic through the Late Mississippian periods.

In the best of all research worlds, radiocarbon dates would be determined directly for the same individuals that are studied isotopically. This is rarely feasible. Of the twenty-seven skeletons for which we currently have $\delta^{13}C$ values, only three have been directly dated: one each from McCarty and Hazel (Poinsett County, Arkansas) (Lynott et al. 1986) and one from Grey Horse Lake (Pemiscot

County, Missouri) (R. C. Dunnell, pers. comm., 1993) (Figure 13-1). The radiocarbon age of the McCarty individual, however, was rejected by Lynott et al. (1986) as being 500 years too young. The authors provide no specific reason for dismissing that date, but it is important to note that a 500-year difference in a specimen of the age they posit requires the inclusion of approximately 25-percent modern contamination. Presumably the source of contamination was removed for the stable-isotope analysis. One can readily appreciate how different Figure 13-2 might look if some of the age estimates were off by even a couple of hundred years, which is not unreasonable given the complexity of the archaeological record in the region. Unfortunately, the kinds of information required to assess the correctness of the published age assignments are unavailable.

Environment

The prehistoric environment of the central Mississippi Valley was a rich and diverse hardwood swamp (O'Brien 1994b; O'Brien and Dunnell, Chapter 1) comprising topographically created microenvironments. The richness, evenness, and productivity of the local environment, as well as the resource-extraction technology, can be expected to influence the subsistence and diet of the people living there. Indeed, differences in the composition of the local environment, as well as differences in how the environment was exploited, may give rise to variation in stable-carbon-isotope ratios, independent of maize consumption. In the Mississippi Valley, the abundance of C_4 grasses has been documented to vary with July minimum temperature (Teeri and Stowe 1976), generating a potentially variable isotopic environmental backdrop.

General Land Office survey notes document the presence of prairies throughout southeastern Missouri (O'Brien 1994b), and large Mississippian settlements have been found associated with those expanses (R. C. Dunnell, pers. comm., 1993). Beyond notation of their existence, there are no good descriptions of the grasslands because they were among the first areas disturbed by Euroamerican agriculture. This has hampered our ability to determine their age, reason of origin, and economic potential. If they are Altithermal remnants, they would have been available for exploitation by Archaic and later populations. If the prairies are an agricultural artifact—that is, if they formed in areas sufficiently disturbed by farming that forest could not be reestablished—then they would be a post-Mississippian phenomenon. In the first scenario, they potentially provide a source of dietary variability for prehistoric inhabitants of the region; in the second, they do not. Thus, there is good reason to document dietary variation in pre-Mississippian populations. In Figure 13-2, individuals from Grey Horse Lake and McCarty, both considerably older than any maize in the eastern United States, appear to differ isotopically; however, these differences are not significant given the magnitude of interlaboratory calibration error (Chisholm 1989; Chisholm et al. 1983a; Mann 1982).

The local environment would also have had consequences for maize farmers. In fact, local microenvironmental productivity has been used by archaeologists attempting to explain both why heavy maize consumption occurred relatively late in the valley (Lynott et al. 1986) and why maize consumption was lower and more variable relative to that in other areas of the Eastern Woodlands (Greenlee and Dunnell 1990). As noted earlier, sufficient data to assess environmental variation in $\delta^{13}C$ values are unavailable.

Settlement System

Little can be said about the nature of pre-Mississippian settlement systems in the central Mississippi Valley (Dunnell and Feathers 1991, 1994) because, as Lafferty points out in Chapter 6, little effort has been made to survey the distribution of settlement in a consistent fashion. In addition, recent work has shown that Mississippian settlements in the valley do not conform to traditional models, instead displaying considerable variation (Teltser 1988, Chapter 7). How people distribute themselves, both through the annual seasonal cycle and across the landscape, is influenced by the availability and productivity of exploitable resources and, in turn, will influence the nature of their subsistence systems. Thus, dietary variation might well be explicable, in part, by the structure of the settlement system involved. When the isotope data in Figure 13-2 are considered in light of available settlement information, no clear patterns emerge, but a larger sample, controlled for age and environmental context, might well show definitive patterning.

Community Composition

Archaeologists consistently speculate that prehistoric peoples moved between different communities—that is, individuals might live and/or die among different populations as adults than the ones within which they were born and/or raised—and use this notion to explain the distribution of various characteristics (e.g., Ericson 1985; Greenlee 1990; Lane and Sublett 1972; Schurr 1989; Spence 1974; Verano and DeNiro 1993; Walker and DeNiro 1986). However, persuasive independent evidence to that effect is only rarely forwarded. If diet varies geographically, then individuals raised in a population different from the one with which they are buried likely consumed a different diet over part of their lifetime and may have $\delta^{13}C$ values that differ significantly from those of the remainder of the burial population. Thus, the occurrence of the enriched skeleton of the twelve-year-old at Little Cypress Bayou, rather than reflecting ritual maize consumption by elites (Rose et al. 1985, 1991), might just as reasonably reflect that juvenile's immigrant status (Buikstra 1991). This might also explain a portion of the variation in some of the Mississippian-period samples from the central Mississippi Valley, since there is strong evidence that some women joined communities as adults from elsewhere (Black 1979; Holland 1991, 1993, 1994; O'Brien and Holland 1994).

Summary

Several potential variables may have significance for the stable-carbon-isotope record in the central Mississippi River valley. All these factors may play varying roles in the isotopic variation documented thus far, some more important in certain circumstances and some more important in others. Clearly, a larger, better-documented sample will be required to determine the contribution of these variables to the record of dietary change in the region.

Recent Stable-Carbon-Isotope Analyses

As of this writing, I am addressing these potential sources of variation in $\delta^{13}C$ values. Bone samples have been selected for $\delta^{13}C$ and radiocarbon analyses from contexts that reflect a range of temporal, environmental, and settlement situations. Some early results, based on examination of eleven individuals from four archaeological deposits, are included here (Figure 13-1 and Table 13-1). I briefly describe the archaeological context from which these samples have been collected, the "collagen"-extraction techniques, sample-quality evaluation, and results of the isotopic analyses.

Five samples are from two Mississippian localities (see below) situated on the Malden Plain in Dunklin County, Missouri. All of the specimens originate from the surface. Acidic soil conditions in the region preclude the preservation of bone except where anthropogenic deposition has raised soil pH. Thus, corresponding to the major episodes of occupation, the samples are almost certainly from Mississippian or Euroamerican contexts. Given that historical-period cemeteries are well defined and undisturbed in this area, and that associated mandibles exhibit classic shovel-shaped incisors, a Mississippian-period attribution of these skeletal materials seems appropriate.

Langdon, 23DU1, dating approximately A.D. 1250–1550 (Dunnell, Chapter 9), is the largest Mississippian site in southern Dunklin County (Figure 13-1). The Mississippian occupation is represented by a fortified settlement with pyramidal mounds and a palisade. Samples from four individuals are analyzed here; when added to the two reported elsewhere (Greenlee and Dunnell 1990), they create one of the largest samples (equal to that from Kersey) for southeastern Missouri. Pelts, 23DU29, is located north of Langdon (Figure 13-1) on the eastern edge of the Malden Plain (Teltser 1988). It is smaller than Langdon, probably occupied somewhat earlier, and lacks the mounds, fortifications, and fancy pottery present at Langdon. One individual from Pelts is included here.

The remaining six individuals analyzed here are from burial contexts at

Table 13-1. Summary of Skeletal Specimens from Southeastern Missouri Included in the Analysis

Burial/Catalog Number	Element	Sex	Age (years)	Cranial Deformation
Langdon 297A 1	right distal humerus	nd	adult	nd
Langdon 297A 3	occipital	nd	nd	nd
Langdon 303	left humerus diaphysis	nd	adult	nd
Langdon 2004	left femur diaphysis	nd	adult	nd
Pelts 31	left parietal	nd	nd	nd
Murphy 26A	right fibula diaphysis	male	36-40	no
Murphy 28	left fibula diaphysis	male	36-40	no
Campbell 20	right fibula diaphysis	female	36-40	yes
Campbell 54	right fibula diaphysis	female	41-45	no
Campbell 64W	left fibula diaphysis	female	41-45	yes
Campbell 65W	left fibula diaphysis	female	46-50	yes

Note: nd, no data

two Pemiscot Bayou locales—Murphy and Campbell (Figure 13-1). Two individuals are from Murphy (23PM43), a large village and cemetery that dates approximately A.D. 1200-1400 or perhaps even later. The ninety-one skeletons recovered displayed a range of temporally sensitive interment modes, from cremations to bundle burials (placed both vertically and horizontally) to extended burials (O'Brien and Marshall 1994). Campbell (23PM5) is a large Late Mississippian village and cemetery located along the former southern shoreline of Cagle Lake (Chapman and Anderson 1955; O'Brien and Holland 1994). Between the mid-1950s and the late 1960s, 218 skeletons were excavated, four of which were randomly selected for inclusion here. These will be added to the single specimen, Burial 52 (a thirty- to thirty-five-year-old male), previously analyzed by Boutton et al. (1984, 1991; Lynott et al. 1986).

The skeletal materials newly analyzed and discussed here are only a sample of those scheduled for analysis. From the brief descriptions offered above, the temporal, settlement, and environmental variation represented can be readily appreciated. In addition, the burial assemblages from Campbell and Murphy include a large number of artificially deformed crania, the age distribution of which suggests the immigration of women to Campbell as adults (Holland 1991, 1993, 1994; O'Brien and Holland 1994). These data will ultimately enable us to assess how much variation is added to a community by the inclusion of immigrants to that community. Before these factors can be considered, variability associated with "collagen" preservation and extraction/measurement techniques must be documented.

"Collagen" Extraction

For "collagen" extraction, sediments, rootlets, and other foreign matter were first mechanically removed from the bone with brushes, then the bone was subjected to an ultrasonic bath with repeated changes of water until the water remained clear. Next, the hydroxyapatite fraction was dissolved and washed away using 0.25 M hydrochloric acid (HCl) at room temperature, with several acid changes and rinses, over several days. This left an insoluble protein fraction for further purification procedures. When completely demineralized, the bone pseudomorph (depending on degree of preservation) was translucent in appearance and bendable, and the acid remained clear with a pH of less than 1.0 maintained between changes. This demineralized bone was placed into slightly acidic water (0.01 M HCl) and heated to 60° C for twenty hours. This was followed by filtering the solution through fine glass-fiber filters to remove precipitates and other residues such as rootlets and sediments. The solution was partially evaporated in a low-temperature drying oven (approximately 50° C), followed by lyophylization (freeze-drying) in carbon-clean glass scintillation vials. This process was repeated to provide two replicate samples from each bone. One of the two replicates from each bone was randomly chosen for carbon-hydrogen-nitrogen and amino-acid analyses.

YIELD

Table 13-2 and Figure 13-3 present collagen-extract yields (milligrams extract/milligrams dry bone) of the samples analyzed here. The error terms in Table 13-2 are smaller than the points on Figure 13-3; thus, they are not shown on the graph. As might be expected, there is a significant, positive relation ($y = 0.981x + 0.767$; $r^2 = .87$) between the "collagen" yields of the two independent replicate extractions. Variation of the data along the regression line reflects interbone variation in "collagen" preservation; variation perpendicular to that line reflects intrabone variation in "collagen" preservation and error associated with the extraction and weighing procedures. That the slope of the regression line is less than 1 and the intercept is greater than 0 suggests that, for the lower-yield samples, the second extraction typically gives a larger yield. The bone of the second extraction, being located farther toward the interior along the diaphysis in relation to the first in several samples, might be slightly better preserved. The largest difference between two replicates here was 2.9 percent. These yield data indicate that the samples are above the empirical threshold and should comprise primarily "collagen." Accordingly, one would expect the other measures of extract quality discussed below to indicate excellent "collagen" integrity.

Table 13-2. Collagen-Extract Yield, Percent Carbon, Percent Nitrogen, and Carbon/Nitrogen Ratios for New Samples from Southeastern Missouri

Burial/Catalog Number	Replicate	Percent Yield ±1 SE	Percent Carbon	Percent Nitrogen	Carbon/Nitrogen Ratio
Langdon 297A 1	A	5.176 ± 0.003			
	B	4.856 ± 0.002	43.868	14.795	3.458
Langdon 297A 3	A	5.341 ± 0.002			
	B	8.241 ± 0.004	41.545	13.413	3.612
Langdon 303	A	3.688 ± 0.004	43.827	14.725	3.471
	B	4.728 ± 0.002			
Langdon 2004	A	3.898 ± 0.004	40.142	16.338	2.865
	B	4.859 ± 0.004			
Pelts 31	A	5.507 ± 0.002			
	B[a]	5.009 ± 0.002	45.273	13.657	3.866
			44.531	14.088	3.686
Murphy 26A	A	11.313 ± 0.003	44.261	15.466	3.337
	B	11.121 ± 0.004			
Murphy 28	A	10.314 ± 0.002	43.994	15.389	3.334
	B	12.469 ± 0.003			
Campbell 20	A	9.992 ± 0.003			
	B	10.953 ± 0.002	43.098	13.486	3.727
Campbell 54	A	9.750 ± 0.006	43.971	15.217	3.370
	B	10.550 ± 0.002			
Campbell 64W	A	14.470 ± 0.002	45.041	16.030	3.277
	B	15.374 ± 0.003			
Campbell 65W	A	8.851 ± 0.004			
	B	6.927 ± 0.000	44.818	15.344	3.406

Note: SE, Standard error.
[a]Duplicate analyses of same extract.

C/N RATIOS, PERCENT CARBON, AND PERCENT NITROGEN

Approximately 1 milligram of each collagen extract was weighed in carbon-clean silver boats and loaded, with standards and blanks, onto a Carlo Erba CHN microanalyzer. Each sample was combusted in sequence, and the gases were separated chromatographically and counted. Thus far, the Pelts 31 sample has been analyzed twice to determine errors associated with duplicate measurements. Table 13-2 presents the C/N ratios and carbon and nitrogen concentrations for recently analyzed samples from the central Mississippi Valley.

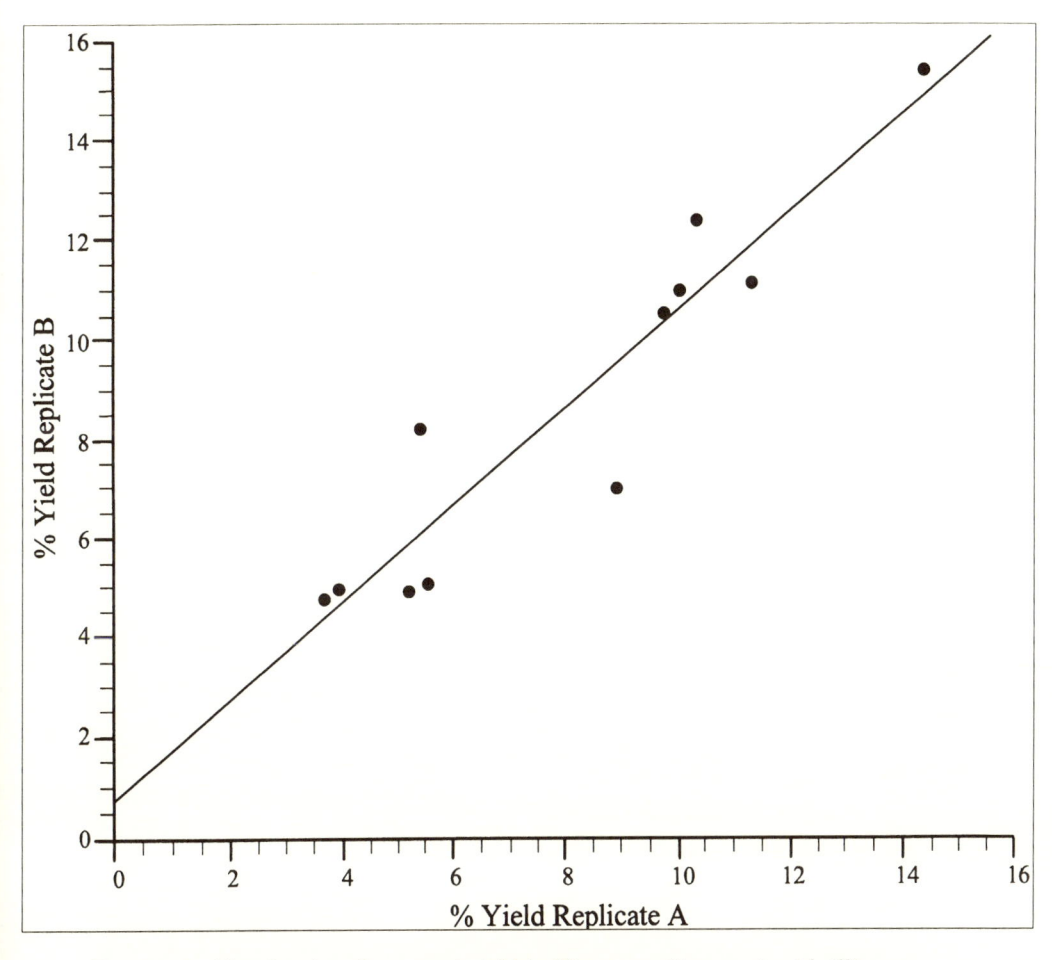

Figure 13-3. Plot showing the percent yield (milligrams collagen extract/milligrams dry bone × 100) for the two independent replicate extractions. The *line* is a least squares regression line that summarizes the relation between the two extractions.

As Figure 13-4 shows, there is no relation between yield and C/N ratio; most values are clearly within the range (2.9 to 3.6) identified by DeNiro (1985) as reflecting unaltered "collagen"; the two that exceed the upper limit are within two standard deviations of 3.6. Figure 13-5 shows carbon and nitrogen concentrations plotted against yield for the same samples. Again, no relation with yield is apparent, nor is there a noticeable decrease associated with samples yielding less than 5-percent extract as seen by Ambrose (1990). These carbon and nitrogen concentrations are easily within the range of modern collagen, lending additional support for the hypothesis that the material extracted is indeed primarily collagen.

318 | Greenlee

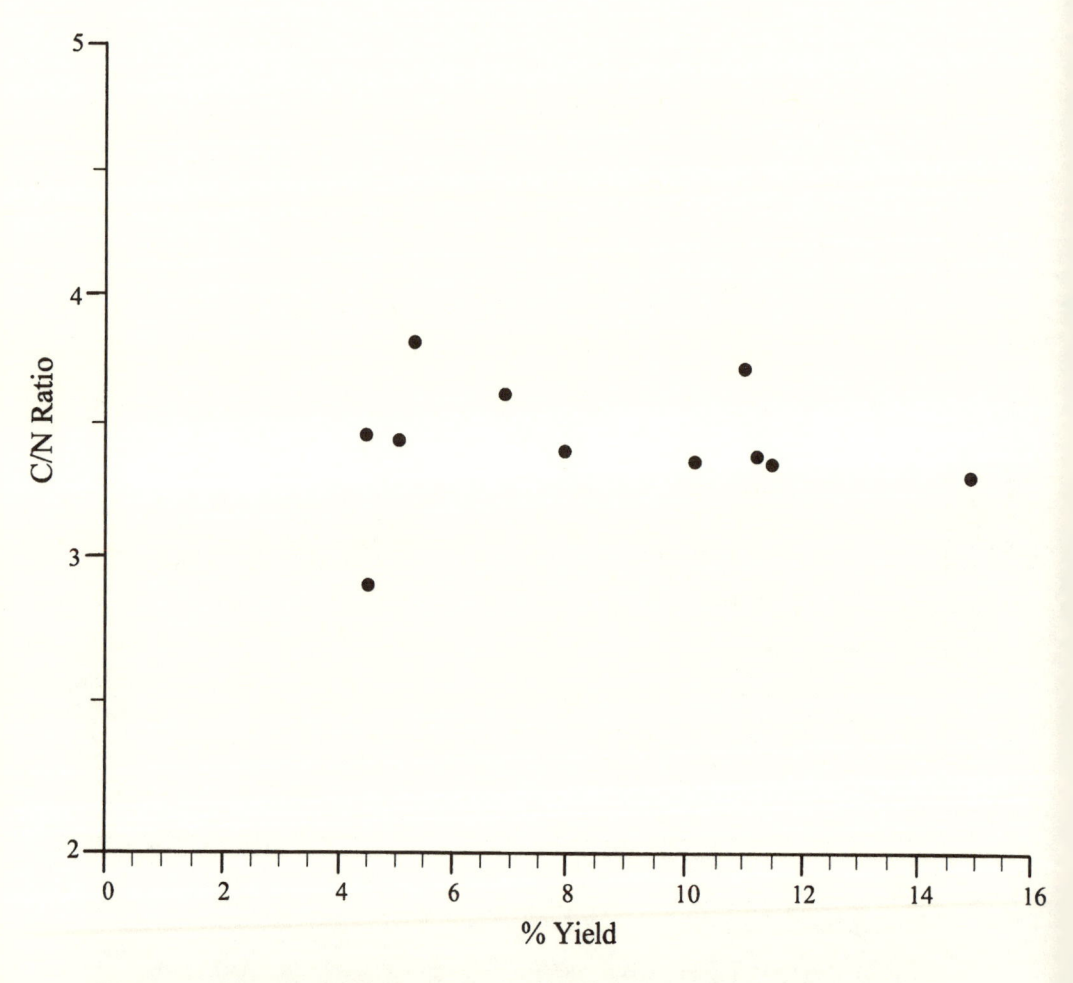

Figure 13-4. Atomic carbon/nitrogen ratios of "collagen" plotted against the mean extract yield of replicate extractions.

AMINO-ACID COMPOSITION

For amino-acid analysis, approximately 0.2 milligrams of extract was weighed and placed in an ampule with 2 milliliters 6.0 M HCl, a crystal of phenol, mercaptoethanol, and 100 micromoles of norleucine (an amino acid not present in collagen) standard. The ampule was evacuated and flushed with argon repeatedly, sealed, and hydrolyzed at 115° C for twenty hours. Following evaporation and solubilization in lithium buffer, the samples were loaded onto a model 7300 Beckman Amino Acid Analyzer with System Gold software for amino-acid analysis. The standard error associated with multiple analyses is approximately 2 percent. All of the samples have results within 10 percent of the modern composition, suggesting that diagenetic alteration of the "collagen"

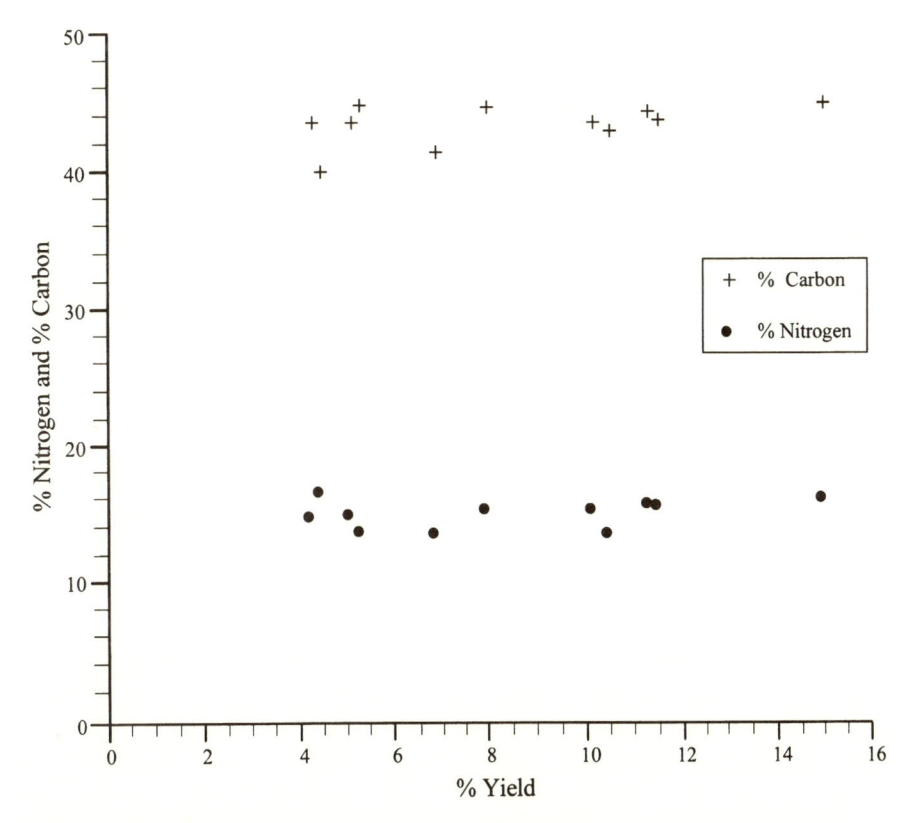

Figure 13-5. Carbon and nitrogen concentrations in "collagen" plotted against the mean extract yield of replicate samples.

has not been sufficient to significantly alter the isotopic composition of the sample.

CONCLUSION

The results presented above are generally in line with expectations of collagen from the current literature. These archaeological human bone samples are relatively well preserved, with reasonably high "collagen" concentrations, and the C/N ratios, carbon and nitrogen concentrations, and amino-acid profiles are generally characteristic of modern values. Thus, diagenesis can be eliminated as a significant source of variability in stable-carbon-isotope ratios of these collagen extracts. Values should be reflective of biological levels at the time of death.

Stable-Carbon-Isotope Analysis

Ten milligrams of collagen extract from each replicate was weighed into a clean Vycor boat along with manganese (IV) dioxide, copper (II) oxide, and silver. Each boat was placed in a clean Vycor ampule, evacuated, and sealed before being subjected to combustion at 900° C for one hour. Carbon dioxide in the combusted samples was purified cryogenically prior to isotopic measurement on a Micromass 903 mass spectrometer in the Quaternary Isotope Laboratory at the University of Washington.

RESULTS

Newly obtained $\delta^{13}C$ values are presented in Table 13-3 and Figure 13-6. Error introduced during sample preparation and measurement must be estimated before differences in the $\delta^{13}C$ values of individuals can be assessed. One source of measurement error is associated with the mass spectrometry. Measurements of a cellulose standard over the duration of the analysis produced a standard error of 0.03°/oo.

Two measurements were obtained for each collagen carbon dioxide sample analyzed; the standard deviation of duplicate measurements ranged from 0.00°/oo to 0.16°/oo. Error associated with sample preparation can be estimated by comparing measurements for replicate samples from the same bone. The mean difference (±1 standard error) in $\delta^{13}C$ values between replicates in this study is 0.04°/oo ± 0.04°/oo. A paired-sample *t*-test showed no significant difference exists between sample replicates at $\alpha = 0.05$ ($t = -0.833$; $n = 11$; $0.40 < p < 0.50$). A 95-percent confidence interval around the mean replicate difference ($0.06 > -0.04 > -0.13$) provides an estimate of variation due to error introduced by sample preparation and measurement. Differences in $\delta^{13}C$ values between individuals must exceed this error to be considered significant.

Discussion

Consistent with other data from post–A.D. 1000 occupations in the region, the $\delta^{13}C$ values of the samples analyzed here are enriched, indicating significant C_4 (in this area, probably maize) consumption. Indeed, the new values bracket the existing data points obtained for Campbell by Boutton et al. (1984) and Lynott et al. (1986) and for Langdon by Greenlee and Dunnell (1990).

Although such a small sample precludes the establishment of any conclusive statements with regard to maize consumption by southeastern-Missouri Mississippian populations, three patterns merit further investigation. First, the data support the observation (Greenlee and Dunnell 1990) that the stable-carbon-isotope ratios of the central Mississippi River valley are, in general, less enriched and more variable than those of communities in many other areas of the Eastern Woodlands. Second, significant interpopulational differences exist in isotopic variation among central Mississippi Valley communities (Figure 13-7). Of particular interest are the Kersey and Campbell samples, from two populations with suspected immigrants (Holland 1991, 1994; O'Brien and Holland 1994), in comparison with the Langdon sample, in which immigration is un-

Table 13-3. $\delta^{13}C$ Values for New Skeletal Samples from Southeastern Missouri

Burial/Catalog Number	Replicate	$\delta^{13}C \pm 1$ SD	Mean $\delta^{13}C \pm 1$ SE[a]
Langdon 297A 1	A	-13.79 ± 0.13	-13.85 ± 0.12
	B	-13.90 ± 0.13	
Langdon 297A 3	A	-9.41 ± 0.00	-9.41 ± 0.04
	B	-9.40 ± 0.08	
Langdon 303	A	-12.27 ± 0.11	-12.28 ± 0.06
	B	-12.29 ± 0.04	
Langdon 2004	A	-12.84 ± 0.04	-12.74 ± 0.13
	B[b]	-12.65 ± 0.05	
Pelts 31	A	-13.55 ± 0.04	-13.55 ± 0.04
	B	-13.55 ± 0.08	
Murphy 26A	A	-10.46 ± 0.01	-10.44 ± 0.06
	B	-10.42 ± 0.10	
Murphy 28	A	-8.55 ± 0.04	-8.55 ± 0.02
	B	-8.55 ± 0.01	
Campbell 20	A	-9.88 ± 0.11	-9.74 ± 0.23
	B	-9.59 ± 0.16	
Campbell 54	A	-10.30 ± 0.06	-10.21 ± 0.13
	B	-10.11 ± 0.01	
Campbell 64W	A	-9.71 ± 0.00	-9.75 ± 0.08
	B	-9.79 ± 0.11	
Campbell 65W	A	-10.94 ± 0.09	-11.00 ± 0.09
	B	-11.06 ± 0.00	

[a]The standard error (SE) is calculated as follows:

$$SE = \sqrt{\sigma_{\bar{x}}^2 + \frac{\sigma_A^2 + \sigma_B^2}{n}}$$

where σ_A and σ_B are standard deviations of replicates A and B, respectively; $\sigma_{\bar{x}}$ is the standard deviation of the mean of replicates A and B; n is the number of measurements made.

[b]The mean of two independent measurements of this extract.

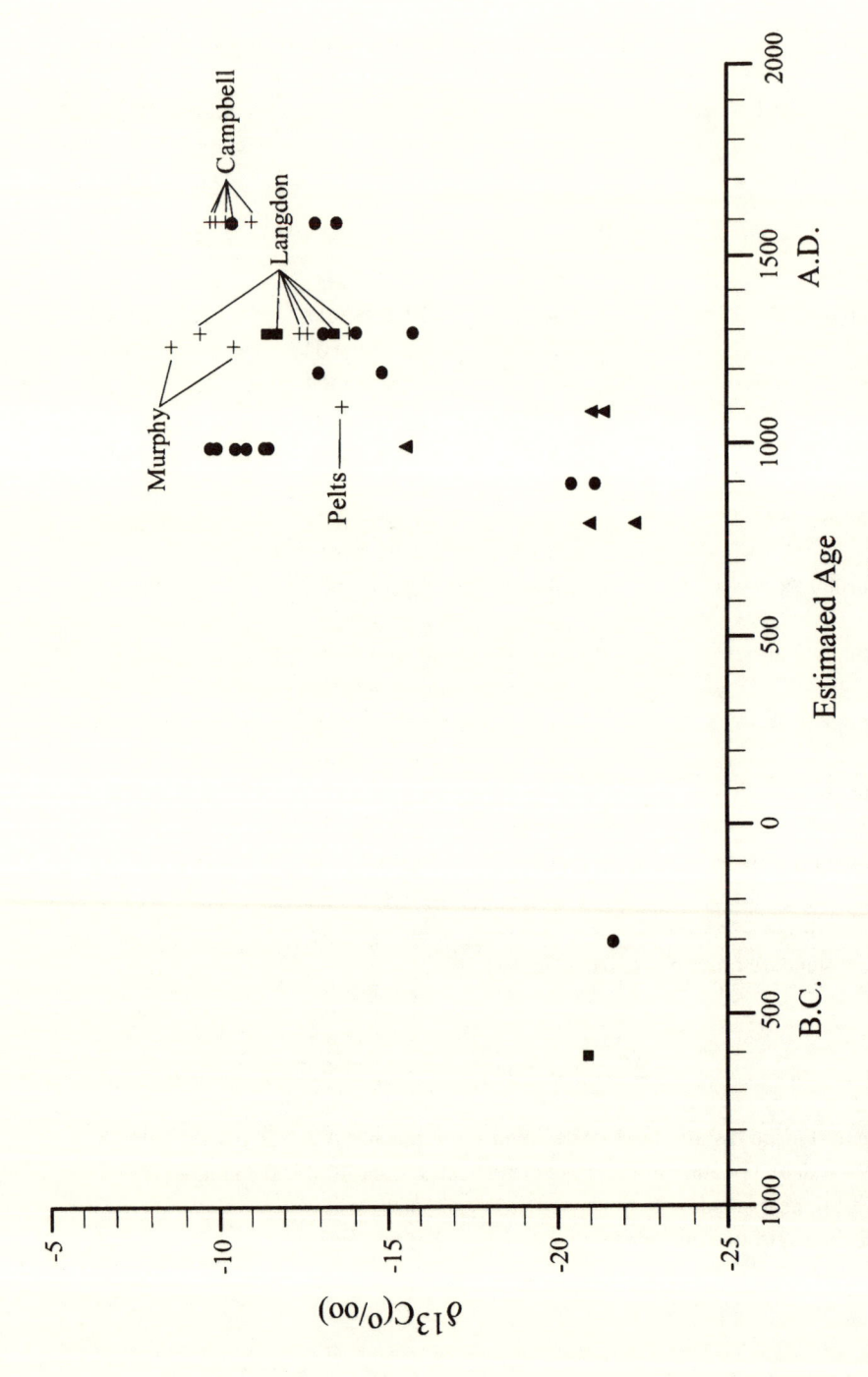

Figure 13-6. Newly (and previously) acquired stable-carbon-isotope ratios ($\delta^{13}C$ °/oo PDB) versus estimated age. Symbols are the same as in Figure 13-1.

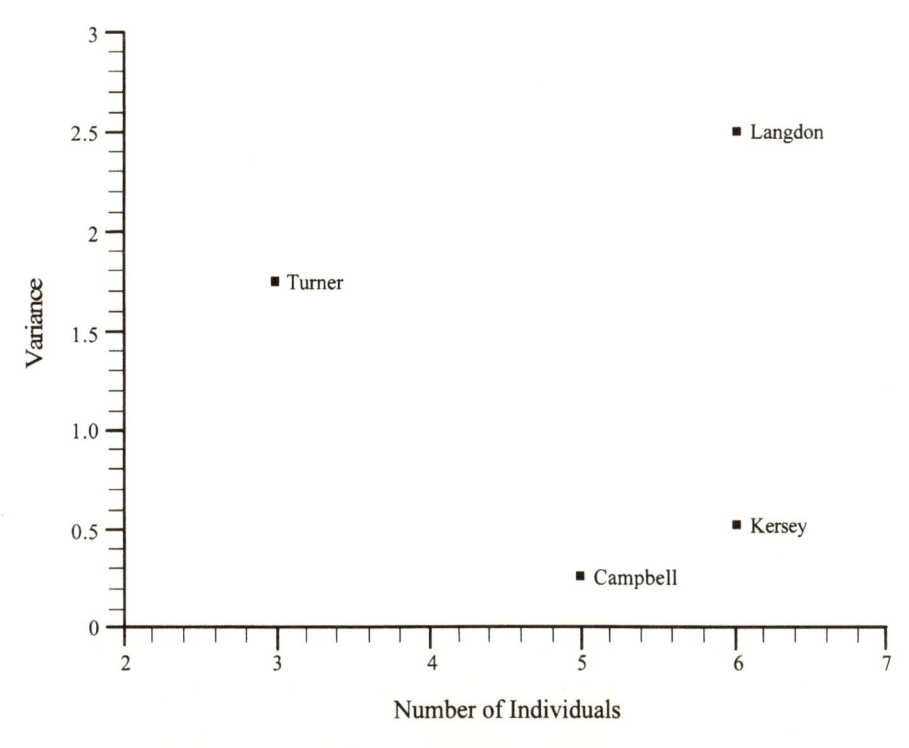

Figure 13-7. Variance in stable-carbon-isotope ratios versus number of individuals for four central Mississippi Valley skeletal samples.

documented. The variance of the Langdon sample far exceeds that of the other two, even though the Campbell sample probably reflects at least two populations (based on the occurrence of cranial deformation). Third, these data suggest that environment may indeed have significantly influenced prehistoric diet. Findings in individuals from the Pemiscot Bayou locales (Kersey, Murphy, and Campbell) tend to be more enriched and less variable than findings in individuals from Langdon, which is on the Malden Plain. Clearly, though, these observations can only be viewed as hypotheses to be evaluated with the collection of additional data.

Future Directions

Documenting variation is the key to a scientific explanation of prehistoric dietary change. In the central Mississippi River valley, this task has only just begun. Analyzing larger samples from a suite of environmental and temporal contexts will contribute greatly to our understanding of how and why dietary change occurred when and where it did. I offer here some suggestions for future research.

Better temporal control of samples analyzed is crucial for pinpointing the timing and tempo of dietary change throughout the region. Rough estimates of the age of skeletal materials, based on associated materials and without information to allow reevaluation, will not provide the temporal resolution necessary to resolve issues such as the relations among dietary change, settlement reorganization, and population growth. Future research must include ^{14}C determinations on individuals from which stable-carbon-isotope ratios are obtained.

To avoid dealing with the possibility that there may be age-related physiological changes in carbon metabolism, most archaeological dietary studies restrict their analyses to adults. While this practice is safer for comparative purposes (despite a lack of evidence for age-related metabolic effects), it might actually make achieving the goal of documenting dietary change more difficult. Because growth and modeling in subadults results in the incorporation of a larger proportion of dietary carbon than remodeling in adults, the skeletons of subadults may be more sensitive indicators of dietary change. In other words, depending on turnover rates, it may take longer for the collagen of an adult to signal a dietary change than it does for that of a rapidly growing subadult. Hence, it may be profitable to sample subadults as well as adults.

There has been little effort to document the effects of environmental variation on δ^{13}C values in human populations of the central Mississippi Valley. For example, do differences in the isotope ratios of Late Mississippian individuals from Pemiscot Bayou and Malden Plain localities (Figure 13-2) reflect different local subsistence systems?

Finally, the potential of understanding the effect of immigration on intrapopulational and interpopulational dietary variation is enticing. Future research with the use of DNA and/or trace elements might allow us to determine whether individuals in addition to those with cranial deformation originated in other populations. This information, in conjunction with dietary data, can provide real insight into community composition, reproduction, and dietary change.

Acknowledgments

I thank R. C. Dunnell and M. J. O'Brien for making samples available for this analysis, offering patient encouragement throughout the process, and providing valuable comments on earlier drafts of this chapter. I am also greatly indebted to L. H. and N. R. Ericsson of AAA Laboratory, Mercer Island, Washington, for their help with the amino-acid analyses and to P. Reimer, T. Saling, and M. Stuiver of the Quaternary Isotope Laboratory, University of Washington, for their assistance with mass spectrometry.

Notes

Chapter 1

1. Putnam (1875a) usually is listed as Swallow (1875). However, the entry in the *Eighth Annual Report of the Peabody Museum* was written by Putnam, who abstracted portions of Swallow's manuscript that accompanied the collection. Putnam (1875b) is identical to Putnam (1875a) except for the addition of a short introductory remark and the addition of woodcuts from Foster (1873).
2. Apparently East Lake was never mapped.

Chapter 2

1. Remarks made in the symposium "Archaeological Ceramic Investigations in Mid-Continental North America" at the 58th Annual Meeting of the Society for American Archaeology, St. Louis, May 1993.
2. Neeley's Ferry Plain and Bell Plain basically are default categories for any nondecorated sherds. As such, their totals will almost always far outweigh those of any other type. Since decorated sherds are the basis for most pottery types constructed for the Mississippi Valley, it seems reasonable to remove the plainwares from consideration.

Chapter 3

1. Note that Feature 4, located in Unit 2, and the lower zone of Unit 4 both produced identical radiocarbon dates—a result of the irregularity of the recognized midden zones.

Chapter 5

1. All recovered cultural materials from Graves Lake and Richardson's Landing, as well as relevant field records, are housed in the TDOA curation facility at Pinson Mounds State Archaeological Area, Pinson, Tennessee. The later-referenced collections from Campbell and Berry, both located in Pemiscot County, Missouri, are curated by the Arkansas Archeological Survey at Arkansas State University, Jonesboro.

Chapter 6

1. See Porter and Guccione (1994) for a lengthy discussion of the radiocarbon dating of landforms in the project area.

Chapter 7

1. There is little consensus on the dating of the Mississippian period in the central Mississippi River valley. Some archaeologists use a starting date of about A.D. 900; others, such as Morse and Morse (1983), use about A.D. 700. The ending date is equally ambiguous, though most archaeologists extend it into the historical period—that is, after the de Soto entrada in 1541.

Chapter 8

1. The location also evidences periodic prehistoric occupation ranging from the Dalton to the Early Mississippian period, as well as that of more recent Anglo-American settlement, but these are not considered herein in any great detail.
2. Parts of this cypress swamp are still preserved on the property purchased by The Archaeological Conservancy.
3. A few artifacts at the Smithsonian Institution are thought to derive from Norris's work at Powers Fort (B. D. Smith, pers. comm., 1982). The material (catalog nos. 71724–71725 and 71848–71851) was transferred from the Bureau of (American) Ethnology in 1883. These artifacts appear to have been incorrectly cataloged, since the materials (primarily sherds of clay-tempered Baytown [Woodland]-period types such as Mulberry Creek Cordmarked, Larto Red Filmed, Kimmswick Fabric-Impressed, and Baytown Plain) are distinctly foreign to the Western Lowlands and the Powers phase. On two catalog cards, the collection locality was originally marked as "Mound on Beckwith's Fort, Mo." Beckwith's Fort (Chapman et al. 1977; Price and Fox 1990) is located east of Powers Fort in the Cairo Lowland (Mississippi County, Missouri).
4. Examination of 1960s aerial photographs of the Powers Fort area generally confirms Koehler's observations, as the western ditch does not run north-south (R. C. Dunnell, pers. comm., 1982).
5. Feature 2 was recorded near Burial 5 and consisted of thirteen large sherds from a shell-tempered jar. This vessel probably sat on the floor of a house and had been brought to the surface by plowing. Powers-phase house stains are common in the southeast quadrant of the site.
6. No exact proveniences are available for the three test units, and the cultural materials from the squares and the hand-excavated trench were unaccounted for when this study was undertaken (1980–1982). I presume they were lost.

Chapter 9

1. I am indebted to David J. Meltzer for locating this correspondence and for providing me with copies of the key letters.
2. J. Tyler, in preparation for a senior honor's thesis, did much of the analysis reported here. Unfortunately, he did not complete the thesis.

3. Inasmuch as neither Phillips's categories (1970) nor those of Phillips et al. (1951) are founded on a direct knowledge of southeastern-Missouri pottery, varietal names are omitted.

4. In 1971, I proposed a systematic survey—consisting of a mile-wide transect crossing the Malden Plain east to west—that not only would have included the immediate environs of Langdon but also would have sampled all of the diverse settings of the north-northeast–south-southwest-trending landscape. The National Science Foundation declined to fund the project because, in the words of one reviewer, "farmers already know where all the sites are." D. F. Morse has since put such a plan into effect in a section of northeastern Arkansas, but the results have been published only in cursory form (Morse and Morse 1983).

Chapter 10

1. I served as principal investigator and co–field director with Jack Ray. Archaeological work at Moon was mandated by construction of U.S. Highway 63 from Payneway (Poinsett County), Arkansas, to Jonesboro (Craighead County), Arkansas.

2. The complete Moon pottery collection, including surface material, contained almost 32,000 sherds. Approximately 2500 sherds belonged to Woodland-period types, such as Barnes Plain, Barnes Cordmarked, and Baytown Plain, and nineteen sherds were identified as Varney Red Filmed.

Chapter 13

1. Isotope ratios of samples are expressed as delta (δ) values in parts per thousand ($°/_{oo}$) relative to the isotopic composition of a standard:

$$\delta^{13}C = \frac{{}^{13}C/{}^{12}C \text{ sample} - {}^{13}C/{}^{12}C \text{ standard}}{{}^{13}C/{}^{12}C \text{ standard}} \times 1000$$

In the case of carbon, the standard (PDB) is CO_2 produced by reaction of marine carbonate (belemnite) from the Peedee Formation of South Carolina with phosphoric acid (H_3PO_4), which by convention has a $\delta^{13}C$ value of $0°/_{oo}$ (Craig 1957). Most substances have lower concentrations of ^{13}C than the standard; hence, their $\delta^{13}C$ values are negative. Readers interested in details about the fundamentals of stable-carbon-isotope analysis and its application to archaeology are encouraged to refer to any of several excellent reviews of the subject (e.g., Ambrose 1993; DeNiro 1987; Pate 1994; Schoeninger and Moore 1992; Schwarcz and Schoeninger 1991; van der Merwe 1982).

2. Because collagen in archaeological bones may have undergone profound postdepositional changes, the residue or extract that archaeologists obtain is not usually the protein collagen. The product is mostly collagenous protein, but it also contains varying amounts of other indigenous biological, exogenous organic, and ex-

ogenous inorganic materials; additionally, it may have undergone differential loss or preservation of amino acids. To reflect its different chemistry, the extract is called "collagen," gelatin, organic residue, protein remnants, or collagen extract (e.g., Ambrose 1990; Brown et al. 1988; DeNiro and Weiner 1988).

References

Abelson, P. H., and T. C. Hoering
1961 Carbon Isotope Fractionation in Formation of Amino Acids by Photosynthetic Organisms. *Proceedings of the National Academy of Sciences, U.S.A.* 47:623–32.

Adams, R. M., and W. M. Walker
1942 Archaeological Surface Survey of New Madrid County, Missouri. *The Missouri Archaeologist* 8(2):1–23.

Aldenderfer, M. S., and R. K. Blashfield
1984 *Cluster Analysis.* Quantitative Applications in the Social Sciences Series No. 44. Sage Publications, Beverly Hills, California.

Ambrose, S. H.
1990 Preparation and Characterization of Bone and Tooth Collagen for Isotopic Analysis. *Journal of Archaeological Science* 17:431–51.
1993 Isotopic Analysis of Paleodiets: Methodological and Interpretive Considerations. In *Investigations of Ancient Human Tissue: Chemical Analyses in Anthropology,* edited by M. K. Sandford, pp. 59–130. Gordon and Breach, Langhorne, Pennsylvania.

Ambrose, S. H., and M. J. DeNiro
1986 The Isotope Ecology of East African Mammals. *Oecologia* 69:395–406.

Ambrose, S. H., and L. Norr
1992 On Stable Isotopic Data and Prehistoric Subsistence in the Soconusco Region. *Current Anthropology* 33:401–4.
1993 Experimental Evidence for the Relationship of the Carbon Isotope Ratios of Whole Diet and Dietary Protein to Those of Bone Collagen and Carbonate. In *Prehistoric Human Bone: Archaeology at the Molecular Level,* edited by J. B. Lambert and G. Grupe, pp. 1–37. Springer Verlag, Berlin.

Ammerman, J. J., and W. Andrefsky, Jr.
1982 Reduction Sequences and the Exchange of Obsidian in Neolithic Calabria. In *Contexts for Prehistoric Exchange,* edited by J. E. Erikson and T. L. Earle, pp. 149–72. Academic Press, New York.

Anderson, D. G.
1990 Stability and Change in Chiefdom-Level Societies: An Examination of Mississippian Political Evolution on the South Atlantic Slope. In *Lamar Archaeology: Mississippian Chiefdoms in the Deep South,* edited by M. Williams and G. Shapiro, pp. 187–213. University of Alabama Press, Tuscaloosa.

Andrefsky, W., Jr.
1994 The Geological Occurrence of Lithic Material and Stone Tool Production Strategies. *Geoarchaeology* 9:375–92.

Anonymous
1964 Excavation of a Baytown Period House at the Hoecake Site. *Missouri Archaeological Society Newsletter* 179:2.

Arnold, J. E.
1983 *Chumash Economic Specialization: An Analysis of the Quarries and Bladelet Production Villages of the Channel Islands, California.* Ph.D. dissertation, Department of Anthropology, University of California–Santa Barbara.
1985a Economic Specialization in Prehistory: Methods of Documenting the Rise of Lithic Craft Specialization. In *Lithic Resource Procurement: Proceedings from the Second Conference on Prehistoric Chert Exploitation,* edited by S. C. Vehik, pp. 37–58. Southern Illinois University at Carbondale, Center for Archaeological Investigations, Occasional Paper No. 4.
1985b The Santa Barbara Channel Islands Bladelet Industry. *Lithic Technology* 14:71–80.

Autin, W. J., S. F. Burns, B. J. Miller, R. T. Saucier, and J. I. Snead
1991 Quaternary Geology of the Lower Mississippi Valley. In *The Geology of North America.* Vol. K-2, *Quaternary Nonglacial Geology: Coterminous U.S.,* edited by R. B. Morrison, pp. 547–82. Geological Society of America, Boulder, Colorado.

Balter, M.
1995 Masters and Slaves in an Iron Age Cave? *Science* 268:1132–33.

Bamforth, D.
1986 Technological Efficiency and Tool Curation. *American Antiquity* 51:38–50.

Bangs, E.
1991 Crowley's Ridge Gravels: An Archaeological Perspective. Senior honors thesis, Department of Anthropology, University of Washington.

Banks, L. D.
1990 *From Mountain Peaks to Alligator Stomachs: A Review of Lithic Sources in the Trans-Mississippi South, the Southern Plains, and Adjacent Southwest.* Oklahoma Anthropological Society, Memoir No. 4. Norman.

Bareis, C. J., and J. W. Porter, eds.
1984 *American Bottom Archaeology: A Summary of the FAI-270 Project Contribution to the Culture History of the Mississippi River Valley.* University of Illinois Press, Urbana.

Bass, Q. R. II
1984 Preface. In *Duck River Cache: Tennessee's Greatest Archaeological Find* (reprint), edited by H. C. Brehm, pp. iii–vi. Mini-Histories Reprint, Nashville.

Bates, R. L., and J. A. Jackson
1984 *Dictionary of Geological Terms.* Doubleday, Garden City, New York.

Beckwith, T.
1887 Mounds in Missouri. *The American Antiquarian* 9:228–32.

Bell, R. E.
1943 Lithic Analysis as a Method in Archaeology. M.A. thesis, Department of Anthropology, University of Chicago.

Belmont, J. S., and S. Williams
1981 Painted Pottery Horizons in the Southern Mississippi Valley. *Geoscience and Man* 22:19–42.

Bender, M., D. Baerreis, and R. L. Steventon
1981 Further Light on Carbon Isotopes and Hopewell Agriculture. *American Antiquity* 46:346–53.

Benn, D. W., ed.
- 1990 *Excavations at the Priestly Site (3PO490), an Emergent Mississippian Community in Northeastern Arkansas.* Southwest Missouri State University, Center for Archaeological Research, Report No. 740. Springfield.
- 1992 *Excavations at the Moon Site (3PO488), a Middle Mississippian Village in Northeastern Arkansas.* Southwest Missouri State University, Center for Archaeological Research, Report No. 780. Springfield.

Black, T. K. III
- 1979 *The Biological and Social Analyses of a Mississippian Cemetery from Southeast Missouri: The Turner Site, 23BU21A.* University of Michigan, Museum of Anthropology, Anthropological Papers No. 68. Ann Arbor.

Blakely, R. I., and L. A. Beck
- 1981 Trace Elements, Nutritional Status, and Social Stratification at Etowah, Georgia. *Annals of the New York Academy of Science* 376:417–31.

Boutton, T. W., M. A. Arshad, and L. L. Tieszen
- 1983 Stable Isotope Analysis of Termite Food Habits in East African Grasslands. *Oecologia* 59:1–6.

Boutton, T. W., P. D. Klein, M. J. Lynott, J. E. Price, and L. L. Tieszen
- 1984 Stable Carbon Isotope Ratios as Indicators of Prehistoric Human Diet. In *Stable Isotopes in Nutrition,* edited by J. R. Turnlund and P. E. Johnson, pp. 191–204. American Chemical Society Series No. 258. American Chemical Society, Washington, D.C.

Boutton, T. W., M. J. Lynott, and M. P. Bumsted
- 1991 Stable Carbon Isotopes and the Study of Prehistoric Human Diet. *Critical Reviews in Food Science and Nutrition* 30:373–85.

Boutton, T. W., B. N. Smith, and A. T. Harrison
- 1980 Carbon Isotope Ratios and Crop Analyses of *Arphia* (Orthoptera: Acrididae) Species in Southeastern Wyoming Grassland. *Oecologia* 45:299–306.

Bradley, H. H.
- 1951 History of Hornersville. *Dunklin County Historical Society* 1:175–92. Thrower, Kennett, Missouri.

Brain, J. P.
- 1988 *Tunica Archaeology.* Harvard University, Peabody Museum of American Archaeology and Ethnology, Papers 78. Cambridge, Massachusetts.

Bratton, S. T.
- 1926 *The Geography of the St. Francis Basin.* University of Missouri Studies 1(3). Columbia.

Braun, D. P.
- 1985a Ceramic Decorative Diversity and Illinois Woodland Regional Integration. In *Decoding Prehistoric Ceramics,* edited by B. A. Nelson, pp. 128–53. Southern Illinois University Press, Carbondale.
- 1985b Absolute Seriation: A Time Series Approach. In *For Concordance in Archaeological Analysis: Bridging Data Structure, Quantitative Technique, and Theory,* edited by C. Carr, pp. 509–39. Westport, Kansas City, Missouri.
- 1987 Coevolution of Sedentism, Pottery Technology, and Horticulture in the Central Midwest, 200 B.C.–A.D. 600. In *Emergent Horticultural Economies of the Eastern Woodlands,* edited by W. F. Keegan, pp. 153–81. Southern Illinois University at Carbondale, Center for Archaeological Investigations, Occasional Paper No. 7.

Braun, D. P., and S. Plog
1982   Evolution of "Tribal" Social Networks: Theory and Prehistoric North American Evidence. *American Antiquity* 47:504–25.

Brigham, C. S.
1936   Clarence Bloomfield Moore. *American Antiquarian Society, Proceedings* 46:12–13.

Brose, D. S.
1980   How Capt. Riggs Hunted for Mound Builders' Relics: An Historical Investigation of Some Influences on C. B. Moore. *Southeastern Archaeological Conference, Bulletin* 22:145–52.

Brose, D. S., and N. Greber, eds.
1979   *Hopewell Archaeology: The Chillicothe Conference.* Kent State University Press, Kent, Ohio.

Brown, C. S.
1926   *Archaeology of Mississippi.* Mississippi Geological Survey, University.

Brown, J. A., R. A. Kerber, and H. D. Winters
1990   Trade and the Evolution of Exchange Relations at the Beginning of the Mississippian Period. In *The Mississippian Emergence,* edited by B. D. Smith, pp. 251–80. Smithsonian Institution Press, Washington, D.C.

Brown, T. A., D. E. Nelson, J. S. Vogel, and J. R. Southon
1988   Improved Collagen Extraction by Modified Longin Method. *Radiocarbon* 30:171–77.

Buikstra, J. E.
1991   Out of the Appendix and Into the Dirt: Comments on Thirteen Years of Bioarchaeological Research. In *What Mean These Bones? Studies in Southeastern Bioarchaeology,* edited by M. L. Powell, P. S. Bridges, and A. M. W. Mires, pp. 172–88. University of Alabama Press, Tuscaloosa.
1992   Diet and Disease in Late Prehistory. In *Disease and Demography in the Americas,* edited by J. W. Verano and D. H. Ubelaker, pp. 87–101. Smithsonian Institution Press, Washington, D.C.

Buikstra, J. E., W. O. Autry, E. Breitburg, L. Eisenberg, and N. van der Merwe
1988   Diet and Health in the Nashville Basin: Human Adaptation and Maize Agriculture in Middle Tennessee. In *Diet and Subsistence: Current Archaeological Perspectives,* edited by B. V. Kennedy and G. M. LeMoine, pp. 243–59. Proceedings of the 19th Annual Conference of the Archaeological Association of the University of Calgary.

Butler, B. M.
1977   *Mississippian Settlement in the Black Bottom, Pope and Massac Counties, Illinois.* Ph.D. dissertation, Department of Anthropology, Southern Illinois University at Carbondale.
1991   Kincaid Revisited: The Mississippian Sequence in the Lower Ohio Valley. In *Cahokia and the Hinterlands: Middle Mississippian Cultures of the Midwest,* edited by T. E. Emerson and R. B. Lewis, pp. 264–73. University of Illinois Press, Urbana.

Butler, B. M., and R. W. Jefferies
1986   Crab Orchard and Early Woodland Cultures in the Middle South. In *Early Woodland Archaeology,* edited by K. B. Farnsworth and T. E. Emerson, pp. 523–34. Center for American Archeology, Kampsville Seminars in Archeology 2. Kampsville, Illinois.

Byers, D. S., F.-C. Cole, and W. C. McKern
1943 First Archaeological Conference on the Woodland Pattern. *American Antiquity* 8:393–400.

Call, R. E.
1891 *The Geology of Crowley's Ridge.* Annual Report of the Geological Survey of Arkansas for 1889. Woodruff, Little Rock.

Callahan, E.
1974 A Guide for Flintworkers: Stages of Manufacture. In *Ape #3, Experimental Archaeology Papers*, edited by E. Callahan, pp. 185–92. Manuscript on file, Department of Sociology and Anthropology, Virginia Commonwealth University, Richmond.

Cambron, J. W., and D. C. Hulse
1983 *Handbook of Alabama Archaeology.* Part 1, *Point Types.* Archaeological Research Association of Alabama, University.

Cande, R. F., and R. H. Lafferty III
1991 *Archaeological Survey of Undeveloped Portions at Eaker Air Force Base, Mississippi County, Arkansas.* Mid-Continental Research, Investigations No. 90-3. Springdale, Arkansas.

Cantwell, A.-M.
1980 *Dickson Camp and Pond: Two Early Havana Tradition Sites in the Central Illinois Valley.* Illinois State Museum, Reports of Investigations No. 36. Springfield.
1987 Havana Tradition Patterns of Chert Procurement: Economic and Political Implications for the Central Illinois Valley and Beyond. *Wisconsin Archeologist* 68:22–43.

Cassidy, C. M.
1984 Skeletal Evidence for Prehistoric Subsistence Adaptation in the Central Ohio River Valley. In *Paleopathology at the Origins of Agriculture,* edited by M. N. Cohen and G. J. Armelagos, pp. 307–45. Academic Press, New York.

Chapman, C. H.
1952 Culture Sequence in the Lower Missouri Valley. In *Archeology of Eastern United States,* edited by J. B. Griffin, pp. 139–51. University of Chicago Press, Chicago.
1980 *The Archaeology of Missouri, II.* University of Missouri Press, Columbia.

Chapman, C. H., and L. O. Anderson
1955 The Campbell Site: A Late Mississippi Town Site and Cemetery in Southeast Missouri. *The Missouri Archaeologist* 17(2–3).

Chapman, C. H., J. Cottier, D. Denman, D. Evans, D. Harvey, M. Reagan, B. Rope, M. Southard, and G. Waselkov
1977 Investigation and Comparison of Two Fortified Mississippi Tradition Archaeological Sites in Southeast Missouri: A Preliminary Comparison. *The Missouri Archaeologist* 38.

Charles, D. K., S. R. Leigh, and J. E. Buikstra
1988 *The Archaic and Woodland Cemeteries at the Elizabeth Site in the Lower Illinois Valley.* Center for American Archeology, Kampsville Archaeological Center, Research Series 7. Kampsville, Illinois.

Childs, T.
1993 Variations of Walls Engraved and Rhodes Incised Pottery. *The Arkansas Archeologist* 32:139–52.

Chisholm, B. S.
1989   Variation in Diet Reconstructions Based on Stable Carbon Isotopic Evidence. In *The Chemistry of Prehistoric Human Bone,* edited by T. D. Price, pp. 10–37. Cambridge University Press, New York.

Chisholm, B., M. Blake, and M. W. Love
1993   More on Prehistoric Subsistence in the Soconusco Region: Response to Ambrose and Norr. *Current Anthropology* 34(4):432–34.

Chisholm, B. S., D. E. Nelson, K. A. Hobson, H. P. Schwarcz, and M. Knyf
1983a Carbon Isotope Measurement Techniques for Bone Collagen: Notes for the Archaeologist. *Journal of Archaeological Science* 10:355–60.
1983b Marine and Terrestrial Protein in Prehistoric Diets on the British Columbia Coast. *Current Anthropology* 24(3):396–98.

Chisholm, B. S., D. E. Nelson, and H. P. Schwarcz
1982   Stable-Carbon Isotope Ratios as a Measure of Marine versus Terrestrial Protein in Ancient Diets. *Science* 216:1131–32.

Clark, J. E.
1987   Politics, Prismatic Blades, and Mesoamerican Civilization. In *The Organization of Core Technology,* edited by J. K. Johnson and C. A. Morrow, pp. 259–84. Westview Press, Boulder, Colorado.

Clay, R. B.
1961   *Excavations at the Tinsley Hill Village, 1960.* Manuscript on file, Office of State Archaeology, University of Kentucky, Lexington.
1963a Ceramic Complexes of the Tennessee-Cumberland Region in Western Kentucky. Unpublished M.A. thesis, Department of Anthropology, University of Kentucky, Lexington.
1963b *Tinsley Hill Village, 1962.* Report submitted to the National Park Service, Richmond, Virginia.
1976   Tactics, Strategy, and Operations: The Mississippian System Responds to its Environment. *Midcontinental Journal of Archaeology* 1:137–62.
1979   A Mississippian Ceramic Sequence from Western Kentucky. *Tennessee Anthropologist* 4:111–28.
1984   Morris Plain: And Other West Kentucky Ceramic Smoking Guns. *Tennessee Anthropologist* 9:104–13.
1991   Summary and Conclusions. In *Excavations at Andalex Village, (15Hk22), Hopkins County, Kentucky,* edited by C. M. Niquette, pp. 142–63. Cultural Resource Analysts, Contract Publication Series No. 91-03. Lexington, Kentucky.

Clay, R. B., S. Hilgeman, and K. W. Wesler
1991   Lower Ohio Valley Mississippian Ceramic Sequence. Paper presented at the Ceramic Workshop, Kentucky Heritage Council Archaeological Conference, Bowling Green.

Cobb, C. R.
1989   An Appraisal of the Role of Mill Creek Chert Hoes in Mississippian Exchange Systems. *Southeastern Archaeology* 8:79–92.

Cole, F.-C., and T. Deuel
1937   *Rediscovering Illinois: Archaeological Investigations in and around Fulton County.* University of Chicago Press, Chicago.

Collins, M. B.
1975   Lithic Technology as a Means of Processual Inference. In *Lithic Technology:*

Making and Using Stone Tools, edited by E. Swanson, pp. 15-34. Mouton, The Hague.

Conant, A. J.
1878   Archaeology of Missouri. *Transactions of the Academy of Science of St. Louis* 3:353-68.

Conard, A. R.
1988   Analysis in Dietary Reconstruction. In *A History of 17 Years of Excavation and Reconstruction: A Chronicle of 12th Century Human Values and the Built Environment,* Vol. 1, edited by J. M. Heilman, M. C. Lileas, and C. A. Turnbow, pp. 112-56. Dayton Museum of Natural History, Dayton, Ohio.

Conner, M. D., ed.
1995   *Phase III Investigations of the Hayti Bypass Site (23PM572), Pemiscot County, Missouri.* Southwest Missouri State University, Center for Archaeological Research, Report No. 932. Springfield.

Conrad, L. A.
1966   *Archaeological Survey of the Lower Kaskaskia Canalization Project.* Southern Illinois University Museum, Archaeological Salvage Reports No. 26. Carbondale.

Cotter, J. L., and J. M. Corbett
1951   *Archaeology of the Bynum Mounds, Mississippi.* U.S. Department of the Interior, National Park Service, Archaeological Research Series No. 1. Washington, D.C.

Cotterell, B., and J. Kamminga
1979   The Mechanics of Flaking. In *Lithic Use-Wear Analysis,* edited by B. Hayden, pp. 99-112. Academic Press, New York.
1987   The Formation of Flakes. *American Antiquity* 52:675-708.
1990   *Mechanics of Pre-industrial Technology.* Cambridge University Press, Cambridge, England.

Cottier, J. W.
1972   *Plaza Excavations at Towosahgy State Archeological Site.* Manuscript on file, Museum of Anthropology, University of Missouri–Columbia.
1977a   The 1972 Investigations at the Lilbourn Site. *The Missouri Archaeologist* 38:123-54.
1977b   Continued Investigations at the Lilbourn Site, 1973. *The Missouri Archaeologist* 38:155-85.

Cottier, J. W., and M. D. Southard
1977   An Introduction to the Archeology of Towosahgy State Archeological Site. *The Missouri Archaeologist* 38:230-71.

Cowgill, G. L.
1982   Clusters of Objects and Associations between Variables: Two Approaches to Archeological Classes. In *Essays in Archeological Typology,* edited by R. Whallon and J. Brown, pp. 30-55. Center for American Archeology Press, Evanston, Illinois.
1990   Why Pearson's r Is Not a Good Similarity Coefficient for Comparing Collections. *American Antiquity* 55:512-20.

Crabtree, D. E.
1972   *An Introduction to Flintworking.* Idaho State University Museum, Occasional Paper No. 28. Pocatello.

Craig, H.
1957 Isotopic Standards for Carbon and Oxygen and Correction Factors for Mass-Spectrometric Analysis of Carbon Dioxide. *Geochimica et Cosmochimica Acta* 12:133-49.

Croswell, C.
1878 Mound Explorations in Southeast Missouri. *Academy of Science of St. Louis, Transactions* 3:531-38.

Cummings, L.
1994 Pollen Analysis for Four Cores from the Mississippi Alluvial Valley near Charleston, Missouri. In *Cairo Lowland Archeology: The Second Step*, by R. H. Lafferty III, M. C. Sierzchula, R. F. Cande, M. T. Oates, M. Dugan, D. Porter, M. J. Guccione, L. Cummings, and K. M. Hess, pp. 183-200. Draft report submitted to the U.S. Army Corps of Engineers, Memphis District.

Curren, C.
1984 *The Protohistoric Period in Central Alabama*. Alabama-Tombigbee Regional Commission, Camden, Alabama.

Dancey, W. S.
1973 *Prehistoric Land Use and Settlement Patterns in the Priest Rapids Area, Washington*. Ph.D. dissertation, Department of Anthropology, University of Washington.

Davis, H. A.
1966 An Introduction to Parkin Prehistory. *Arkansas Archeologist* 7:1-40.
1973 The Hazel Site, Historical Background. *Arkansas Archeologist* 14(2-4):21-31.

Deetz, J. J. F., and E. Dethlefsen
1965 The Doppler Effect and Archaeology: A Consideration of the Spatial Aspects of Seriation. *Southwestern Journal of Anthropology* 21:196-206.

Deines, P.
1980 The Isotopic Composition of Reduced Organic Carbon. In *Handbook of Environmental Isotope Geochemistry*, Vol. 1, edited by P. Fritz and J. C. Fontes, pp. 329-406. Elsevier, Amsterdam.

DeNiro, M. J.
1985 Postmortem Preservation and Alteration of *In Vivo* Bone Collagen Isotope Ratios in Relation to Paleodietary Reconstruction. *Nature* 317:806-9.
1987 Stable Isotopy and Archaeology. *American Scientist* 75:182-91.

DeNiro, M. J., and S. Epstein
1978a Carbon Isotopic Evidence for Different Feeding Patterns in Two *Hyrax* Species Occupying the Same Habitat. *Science* 201:906-8.
1978b Influence of Diet on the Distribution of Carbon Isotopes in Animals. *Geochimica et Cosmochimica Acta* 42:495-506.
1981 Influence of Diet on the Distribution of Nitrogen Isotopes in Animals. *Geochimica et Cosmochimica Acta* 45:341-51.

DeNiro, M. J., and M. J. Schoeninger
1983 Stable Carbon and Nitrogen Isotope Ratios of Bone Collagen: Variations within Individuals, between Sexes, and within Populations Raised on Monotonous Diets. *Journal of Archaeological Science* 10:199-203.

DeNiro, M. J., and S. Weiner
1988 Chemical, Enzymatic and Spectroscopic Characterization of "Collagen"

and Other Organic Fractions from Prehistoric Bones. *Geochimica et Cosmochimica Acta* 52:2197-2206.

Dicks, A. M., and C. S. Weed, eds.
1985 *Archaeological Investigations of the Little Cypress Bayou Site (3CT50), Crittenden County, Arkansas.* Report submitted to the Memphis District, U.S. Army Corps of Engineers.

Downton, W. J. S.
1975 The Occurrence of C_4 Photosynthesis among Plants. *Photosynthesis* 9(1):96-105.

Duncan, J. E.
1977 *Zebree: An Example of Trace Element Analysis in Archeology.* Manuscript on File, Department of Anthropology, University of Arkansas, Fayetteville.

Dunnell, R. C.
1971 *Systematics in Prehistory.* Free Press, New York.
1978 Style and Function: A Fundamental Dichotomy. *American Antiquity* 43:192-202.
1982 Current Research, Missouri. *American Antiquity* 47:225-26.
1984 23DU270: A Limited Activity Site in Dunklin County, Missouri. *Missouri Archaeological Society Quarterly* 1:8-10, 16-18.
1985a Archaeological Survey in the Lower Mississippi Alluvial Valley, 1940-1947: A Landmark Study in American Archaeology. *American Antiquity* 50:297-300.
1985b The Interpretation of Low Density Archaeological Records from Plowed Surfaces. Paper presented at the 50th Annual Meeting of the Society for American Archaeology, Denver.
1988 Low-Density Archaeological Records from Plowed Surfaces: Some Preliminary Considerations. *American Archaeology* 7:29-38.
1989 Four New TL Dates for Southeast Missouri Mississippian. *MAPA Newsletter* 1(1):7-9.
1990 The Role of the Southeast in American Archaeology. *Southeastern Archaeology* 9(1):11-22.
1992 The Notion Site. In *Space, Time, and Archaeological Landscapes*, edited by J. Rossignol and L. Wandsnider, pp. 21-41. Plenum, New York.
1993 Chemical Origins of Archaeological Aerial Signatures. In *Looking into the Future with an Eye to the Past, ASPRS Technical Papers, Remote Sensing*, edited by A. J. Lewis, pp. 65-75. American Society for Photogrammetry and Remote Sensing No. 2. Bethesda, Maryland.

Dunnell, R. C., and W. S. Dancey
1983 The Siteless Survey: A Regional Scale Data Collection Strategy. In *Advances in Archaeological Method and Theory* 6:267-87.

Dunnell, R. C., and J. K. Feathers
1991 Later Woodland Manifestations of the Malden Plain, Southeast Missouri. In *Late Woodland Stability, Transformation, and Variation in the Greater Southeast*, edited by M. Nassaney and C. R. Cobb, pp. 21-45. Plenum, New York.
1994 Thermoluminescence Dating of Surface Archaeological Materials. In *The Dating of Archaeological Surfaces*, edited by C. Beck, pp. 115-37. University of New Mexico Press, Albuquerque.

Dunnell, R. C., M. Ikeya, P. T. McCutcheon, and S. Toyoda
- 1994 Heat Treatment of Mill Creek and Dover Cherts on the Malden Plain, Southeast Missouri. *Journal of Archaeological Science* 21:70–89.

Dunnell, R. C., and M. K. Jackson
- 1992 Technology of Late Mississippian Polychromes. Paper presented at the 49th Annual Meeting of the Southeastern Archaeological Conference, Little Rock.

Dunnell, R. C., and M. Readhead
- 1988 The Relation of Dating and Chronology: Comments on Chatters and Hoover (1986) and Butler and Stein (1988). *Quaternary Research* 30:232–33.

Dunnell, R. C., and J. Simek
- 1995 Artifact Size and Plowzone Processes. *Journal of Field Archaeology* 22:305–19.

Dunnell, R. C., and F. H. Whittaker
- 1988 The Late Archaic of the Little River Lowlands and its Regional Relations. Paper presented at the 45th Annual Meeting of the Southeastern Archaeological Conference, New Orleans.
- 1994 The Late Archaic of the Eastern Lowlands and Evidence of Trade. *Louisiana Archaeology* 21:13–37.

Dye, D. H., and C. A. Cox, eds.
- 1990 *Towns and Temples along the Mississippi.* University of Alabama Press, Tuscaloosa.

Edging, R.
- 1990 *The Turk Site: A Mississippi Period Town in Western Kentucky.* Kentucky Heritage Council, Frankfort.

Eisenberg, L. E.
- 1989 On Gaming Pieces and Culture Contact. *Current Anthropology* 30:345.

Emerson, T. E., and R. B. Lewis, eds.
- 1991 *Cahokia and the Hinterlands: Middle Mississippian Cultures of the Midwest.* University of Illinois Press, Urbana.

Ericson, J. E.
- 1985 Strontium Isotope Characterization in the Study of Prehistoric Human Ecology. *Journal of Human Evolution* 14:503–14.

Evers, E.
- 1880 The Ancient Pottery of Southeastern Missouri. In *Contributions to the Archaeology of Missouri, by the Archaeological Section of the St. Louis Academy of Science.* Part 1, *Pottery*, pp. 21–30. Bates, Salem, Massachusetts.

Farrell, F. M.
- 1883 Ancient Remains near Cobden, Illinois. *Smithsonian Institution, Annual Report* (1881):584.

Feathers, J. K.
- 1989 Effects of Temper on Strength of Ceramics: Response to Bronitsky and Hamer. *American Antiquity* 54:579–88.
- 1990a An Evolutionary Interpretation for the Predominance of Shell Tempering in Late Prehistoric Southeastern Missouri Ceramics. Paper presented at the 55th Annual Meeting of the Society for American Archaeology, Las Vegas.
- 1990b *Explaining the Evolution of Prehistoric Ceramics in Southeastern Missouri.*

Ph.D. dissertation, Department of Anthropology, University of Washington, Seattle.
1993 Thermoluminescence Dating of Southeast Missouri Pottery and the Problem of Radioactive Disequilibrium. Manuscript in possession of the author.
1994 Function and History of Ceramic Change: The Case of Shell Tempering in Southeast Missouri. Manuscript in possession of the author.

Feathers, J. K., and W. D. Scott
1989 Prehistoric Ceramic Composite from the Mississippi Valley. *Ceramic Bulletin* 68:554–57.

Festervand, D. F.
1981 *Soil Survey of Cape Girardeau, Mississippi, and Scott Counties, Missouri.* U.S. Soil Conservation Service, Washington, D.C.

Fisk, H. N.
1944 *Geological Investigation of the Alluvial Valley of the Lower Mississippi River.* U.S. Army Corps of Engineers, Vicksburg, Mississippi.

Ford, J. A.
1935a Outline of Louisiana and Mississippi Pottery Horizons. *Louisiana Conservation Review* 4(6):33–38.
1935b *Ceramic Decoration Sequence at an Old Indian Village Site near Sicily Island, Louisiana.* Louisiana Department of Conservation, Anthropological Study No. 1. Baton Rouge.
1936 *Analysis of Indian Village Site Collections from Louisiana and Mississippi.* Louisiana Geological Survey, Department of Conservation, Anthropological Study No. 2.
1938 A Chronological Method Applicable to the Southeast. *American Antiquity* 3:260–64.
1952 *Measurements of Some Prehistoric Design Developments in the Southeastern States.* American Museum of Natural History, Anthropological Papers 44(3). New York.

Ford, J. A., and J. B. Griffin
1937 [A proposal for a] Conference on Pottery Nomenclature for the Southeastern United States. Mimeographed. Reprinted (1970) in *Newsletter of the Southeastern Archaeological Conference* 7(1):5–9.
1938 Report of the Conference on Southeastern Pottery Typology. Mimeographed. Reprinted (1970) in *Newsletter of the Southeastern Archaeological Conference* 7(1):10–22.

Ford, J. A., P. Phillips, and W. G. Haag
1955 *The Jaketown Site in West-Central Mississippi.* American Museum of Natural History, Anthropological Papers 45(1). New York.

Ford, J. A., and Quimby, G. I., Jr.
1945 *The Tchefuncte Culture, an Early Occupation of the Lower Mississippi Valley.* Society for American Archaeology, Memoirs No. 2. Washington, D.C.

Ford, J. A., and G. R. Willey
1940 *Crooks Site, a Marksville Period Burial Mound in La Salle Parish, Louisiana.* Louisiana Department of Conservation, Anthropological Study No. 3. Baton Rouge.

1941   An Interpretation of the Prehistory of the Eastern United States. *American Anthropologist* 43:325–63.

Ford, J. L., M. A. Rolingson, and L. D. Medford
1972   *Site Destruction Due to Agricultural Practices.* Arkansas Archeological Survey, Research Series No. 3. Fayetteville.

Fortier, A. C., T. E. Emerson, and F. A. Finney
1984   Early Woodland and Middle Woodland Periods. In *American Bottom Archaeology: A Summary of the FAI-270 Project Contribution to the Culture History of the Mississippi River Valley,* edited by C. J. Bareis and J. W. Porter, pp. 59–103. University of Illinois Press, Urbana.

Foster, J. W.
1864   Ancient Relics in Missouri. *Smithsonian Institution, Annual Report* (1863):383–84.
1873   *Pre-historic Races of the United States of America.* Griggs, Chicago.

Fowke, G.
1894   Material for Aboriginal Stone Implements. *The Archaeologist* 2:328–35.
1902   *Archaeological History of Ohio.* Ohio State Archaeological and Historical Society, Columbus.
1910   *Antiquities of Central and Southeastern Missouri.* Bureau of American Ethnology, Bulletin 37. Washington, D.C.
1928   Archaeological Investigations (part 2). *Bureau of American Ethnology, Annual Report* 44:399–540.

Fowler, M. L.
1961   *Carlyle Reservoir Site No. 1: The Gus Krebs Site.* Southern Illinois University Museum, Archaeological Salvage Report No. 7. Carbondale.

Fox, G. L.
1992   *A Critical Evaluation of the Interpretive Framework of the Mississippi Period in Southeast Missouri.* Ph.D. dissertation, Department of Anthropology, University of Missouri–Columbia.

Fritz, G. J.
1990   Multiple Pathways to Farming in Precontact Eastern North America. *Journal of World Prehistory* 4:387–435.

Galloway, P. K., ed.
1989   *The Southeastern Ceremonial Complex: Artifacts and Analysis.* University of Nebraska Press, Lincoln.

Goodyear, A. C.
1974   *The Brand Site: A Techno-Functional Study of a Dalton Site in Northeast Arkansas.* Arkansas Archeological Survey, Research Report No. 7. Fayetteville.
1979   *A Hypothesis for the Use of Cryptocrystalline Raw Materials among Paleo-Indian Groups of North America.* University of South Carolina, Institute of Archaeology and Anthropology, Research Manuscript Series No. 156. Columbia.

Graham, R. W.
1990   The Extinct Stout-Legged Llama (*Palaeolama mirifica*) in the Lower/Central Mississippi River Valley. In *Field Guide to the Mississippi Alluvial Valley, Northeast Arkansas and Southeast Missouri,* edited by M. J. Guccione and E. M. Rutledge, pp. 207–9. Friends of the Pleistocene, Southeast Cell, Fayetteville, Arkansas.

Gray, J. L., and D. V. Ferguson
- 1977 *Soil Survey of Poinsett County, Arkansas.* U.S. Department of Agriculture, Soil Conservation Service, Washington, D.C.

Greber, N., R. S. Davis, and A. S. Du Fresne
- 1981 The Micro Component of the Ohio Hopewell Lithic Technology: Bladelets. In The Research Potential of Anthropological Museum Collections, edited by A.-M. Cantwell, J. B. Griffin, and N. A. Rothschild. *Annals of the New York Academy of Sciences* 376:489–528.

Greenlee, D. M.
- 1990 Environmental and Temporal Variability in $\delta^{13}C$ Values in Late Prehistoric Subsistence Systems in the Upper Ohio Valley. Unpublished M.A. paper, Department of Anthropology, University of Washington, Seattle.
- 1991 Patterns in Late Prehistoric Subsistence through Mass Spectrometric Analysis. Paper presented at the 56th Annual Meeting of the Society for American Archaeology, New Orleans.

Greenlee, D. M., and R. C. Dunnell
- 1990 Carbon Isotope Ratios from Three Southeast Missouri Localities. *Missouri Association of Professional Archaeologists Newsletter* 2(2):7–9.
- 1993 Understanding Post-depositional Processes through Electron Microbeam Analysis of Archaeological Bone from SE Missouri. In *Materials Issues in Art and Archaeology III*, edited by P. B. Vandiver, J. R. Druzik, G. S. Wheeler, and I. C. Freestone, pp. 883–88. Materials Research Society, Symposium Proceedings 267. Pittsburgh.

Griffin, J. B.
- 1946 Cultural Change and Continuity in Eastern United States Archaeology. *R. S. Peabody Foundation for Archaeology, Papers* 3:37–95, 307–48.
- 1949 The Cahokia Ceramic Complexes. *Proceedings of the Fifth Plains Conference for Archeology* 44–58. Lincoln, Nebraska.
- 1952 Prehistoric Cultures of the Central Mississippi Valley. In *Archeology of Eastern United States*, edited by J. B. Griffin, pp. 226–38. University of Chicago Press, Chicago.
- 1967 Eastern North American Archaeology. *Science* 156:175–91.
- 1981 The Acquisition of a Little-Known Pottery Haul from the Lower Mississippi Valley. In Traces of Prehistory: Papers in Honor of William G. Haag, edited by F. H. West and R. W. Neuman. *Geoscience and Man* 22:51–55.
- 1985 An Individual's Participation in American Archaeology, 1928–1985. *Annual Review of Anthropology* 14:1–23.
- 1989 Foreword. In *The Holding Site: A Hopewell Community in the American Bottom (11-Ms-118).* Vol. 19, American Bottom Archaeology, FAI-270 Site Reports, by A. C. Fortier, T. O. Maher, J. A. Williams, M. C. Meinkoth, K. E. Parker, and L. S. Kelly, pp. xvii–xxii. University of Illinois Press, Urbana.

Griffin, J. B., R. E. Flanders, and P. F. Titterington
- 1970 *The Burial Complexes of the Knight and Norton Mounds in Illinois and Michigan.* University of Michigan, Museum of Anthropology, Memoir No. 2. Ann Arbor.

Griffin, J. B., and R. G. Morgan, eds.
- 1941 Contributions to the Archaeology of the Illinois River Valley. *Transactions of the American Philosophical Society* 32(part 1).

Griffin, J. B., and A. C. Spaulding
1952   The Central Mississippi River Valley Archaeological Survey, Season 1950: A Preliminary Report. In *Prehistoric Pottery of Eastern United States*, edited by J. B. Griffin, pp. 1–7. University of Michigan Museum of Anthropology, Ann Arbor.

Guccione, M. J.
1987   Geomorphology, Sedimentation, and Chronology of Alluvial Deposits, Northern Mississippi County, Arkansas. In *A Cultural Resources Survey, Testing, and Geomorphic Examination of Ditches 10, 12, and 29, Mississippi County, Arkansas*, by R. H. Lafferty III, M. J. Guccione, L. J. Scott, D. K. Aasen, B. J. Watkins, M. C. Sierzchula, and P. F. Bauman, pp. 67–99, D1–D38. Report submitted to the U.S. Army Corps of Engineers, Memphis District.

Guccione, M. J., R. H. Lafferty III, and L. S. Cummings
1988   Environmental Constraints on Human Settlement in an Evolving Holocene Alluvial System, the Lower Mississippi Valley. *Geoarchaeology* 3:65–84.

Guccione, M. J., W. L. Prior, and E. M. Rutledge
1986   *The Tertiary and Quaternary Geology of Crowley's Ridge: A Guidebook*. Arkansas Geological Commission, Little Rock.

Guccione, M. J., and E. M. Rutledge, eds.
1990   *Field Guide to the Mississippi Alluvial Valley, Northeast Arkansas and Southeast Missouri*. Friends of the Pleistocene, Southeast Cell, Fayetteville, Arkansas.

Guernsey, E. Y.
1937   Certain Southern Indiana Sources of Lithic Artifact Material. *Proceedings of Indiana Academy of Science* 46:47–52.

Gurfinkel, D. M.
1987   Comparative Study of the Radiocarbon Dating of Different Bone Collagen Preparations. *Radiocarbon* 29:45–52.

Haag, W. G.
1939   Description of Pottery Types. *News Letter of the Southeastern Archaeological Conference* 1(1).

Häkansson, S.
1976   University of Lund Radiocarbon Dates IX. *Radiocarbon* 18:290–320.

Hare, P. E.
1980   Organic Geochemistry of Bone and Its Relation to the Survival of Bone in the Natural Environment. In *Fossils in the Making: Vertebrate Taphonomy and Paleoecology*, edited by A. K. Behrensmeyer and A. P. Hill, pp. 208–19. University of Chicago Press, Chicago.

Hare, P. E., and M. L. F. Estep
1983   Carbon and Nitrogen Isotopic Composition of Amino Acids in Modern and Fossil Collagens. *Carnegie Institution of Washington, Yearbook* 82:410–14.

Hare, P. E., M. L. Fogel, T. W. Stafford, Jr., A.D. Mitchell, and T. C. Hoering
1991   The Isotopic Composition of Carbon and Nitrogen in Individual Amino Acids Isolated from Modern and Fossil Proteins. *Journal of Archaeological Science* 18:277–92.

Harrington, S. P. M.
1991   The Looting of Arkansas. *Archaeology* 44(3):22–31.

Hastorf, C. A., and S. Johannessen
- 1994 Becoming Corn-eaters in Prehistoric America. In *Corn and Culture in the Prehistoric New World*, edited by S. Johannessen and C. A. Hastorf, pp. 427–43. Westview Press, Boulder, Colorado.

Hatch, J. W., and R. A. Geidel
- 1985 Status-Specific Dietary Variation in Two World Cultures. *Journal of Human Evolution* 14:469–76.

Hathcock, R.
- 1976 *Ancient Indian Pottery of the Mississippi Valley*. Hurley, Camden, Arkansas.
- 1983 *The Quapaw and Their Pottery: A Pictorial Study of Proto-historic Pottery of the Quapaw Indians, 1650–1750 a.d.* Hurley, Camden, Arkansas.
- 1988 *Ancient Indian Pottery of the Mississippi River Valley* (2nd ed.). Walsworth, Marceline, Missouri.

Heller, R. L.
- 1954 *Stratigraphy and Paleontology of the Roubidoux Formation of Missouri*. Missouri Geological Survey and Water Resources, Rolla.

Hobson, K. A., and H. P. Schwarcz
- 1986 The Variation in $\delta^{13}C$ Values in Bone Collagen for Two Wild Herbivore Populations: Implications for Palaeodiet Studies. *Journal of Archaeological Science* 13:101–6.

Hoffman, M. P.
- 1981 The Father of Us All: S. C. Dellinger and the Beginning of Arkansas Archeology and Anthropology. Paper presented at the 38th Annual Meeting of the Southeastern Archaeological Conference, Asheville, North Carolina.

Hofman, J. L.
- 1979 Twenhafel: A Prehistoric Community on the Mississippi, 500 B.C.–A.D. 1500. *The Living Museum* 41:34–38.
- 1980a Twenhafel Archaeology: 1958 Excavation in the Village Area (11Jv87) and a Preliminary Definition of Ceramic Phases. Manuscript on file, Illinois State Museum, Springfield.
- 1980b Twenhafel Archaeology: The Southeastern Connection. *Tennessee Anthropologist* 5:185–201.
- 1987 Hopewell Blades from Twenhafel: Distinguishing Local and Foreign Core Technology. In *The Organization of Core Technology*, edited by J. K. Johnson and C. A. Morrow, pp. 87–118. Westview Press, Boulder, Colorado.

Hofman, J. L., and C. A. Morrow
- 1984 Chipped Stone Technologies at Twenhafel: A Multicomponent Site in Southern Illinois. In *Lithic Resource Procurement: Proceedings from the Second Conference on Prehistoric Chert Exploitation*, edited by S. C. Vehik, pp. 165–82. Southern Illinois University at Carbondale, Center for Archaeological Investigations, Occasional Paper No. 4.

Holland, T. D.
- 1991 *An Archaeological and Biological Analysis of the Campbell Site*. Ph.D. dissertation, Department of Anthropology, University of Missouri–Columbia.
- 1993 Bioarchaeology of Southeast Missouri. Paper presented at the 58th Annual Meeting of the Society for American Archaeology, St. Louis.
- 1994 Skeletal Analysis. In *Cat Monsters and Head Pots: The Archaeology of Mis-*

souri's Pemiscot Bayou, by M. J. O'Brien, pp. 307-47. University of Missouri Press, Columbia.

Holmes, W. H.
1884a Illustrated Catalogue of a Portion of the Collections Made by the Bureau of Ethnology during the Field Season of 1881. *Bureau of Ethnology, Annual Report* 3:427-510.
1884b Ancient Pottery of the Mississippi Valley: A Study of the Collection of the Davenport Academy of Sciences. *Davenport Academy of Sciences, Proceedings* 4:123-96.
1886 Ancient Pottery of the Mississippi Valley. *Bureau of Ethnology, Annual Report* 4:361-436.
1894 Natural History of Flaked Stone Implements. *International Congress of Anthropology, Chicago, 1894, Memoirs* 120-39.
1903 Aboriginal Pottery of the Eastern United States. *Bureau of American Ethnology, Annual Report* 20:1-201.
1919 *Handbook of Aboriginal American Antiquities* (part 1). Bureau of American Ethnology, Bulletin 60. Washington, D.C.

Hopgood, J. F.
1967 The Burkett Site (23MI-20). In *Land Leveling Salvage Archaeological Work in Southeast Missouri: 1966*, by J. R. Williams, pp. 293-304. Report submitted to the National Park Service, Midwest Archeological Center, Lincoln, Nebraska.
1969a Continuity and Change in the Baytown Pottery Tradition of the Cairo Lowland, Southeast Missouri. M.A. thesis, Department of Anthropology, University of Missouri-Columbia.
1969b *An Archaeological Reconnaissance of Portage Open Bay in Southeast Missouri.* Missouri Archaeological Society Memoir No. 7. Columbia.

Hostetler, C. H., and B. A. Hostetler
1986 Woodall Farm, 23DU269: A Late Woodland/Early Mississippian Site. *Missouri Archaeological Society Quarterly* 3(3):10-15.

Houck, L.
1908 *A History of Missouri* (3 vols.). Donnelley, Chicago.

House, J. H.
1975 Prehistoric Lithic Resource Utilization in the Cache Basin: Crowley's Ridge Chert and Quartzite and Pitkin Chert. In *The Cache River Archeological Project: An Experiment in Contract Archeology*, assembled by M. B. Schiffer and J. H. House, pp. 81-91. Arkansas Archeological Survey, Research Series No. 8. Fayetteville.
1982 Evolution of Complex Societies in East-Central Arkansas: An Overview of Environments and Regional Data Sets. In *Arkansas Archeology in Review*, edited by N. S. Trubowitz and J. D. Jeter, pp. 37-47. Arkansas Archeological Survey, Research Series No. 15. Fayetteville.
1991 *Monitoring Mississippian Dynamics: Time, Settlement, and Ceramic Variation in the Kent Phase, Eastern Arkansas.* Ph.D. dissertation, Department of Anthropology, Southern Illinois University at Carbondale.
1993a Decoding Mississippian Ceramic Art in the Central Mississippi Valley. *The Arkansas Archeologist* 32:153-56.
1993b Dating the Kent Phase. *Southeastern Archaeology* 12:21-32.

House, J. H., and R. B. House
1985   Investigating Early Mississippi Period Occupation in the Lower St. Francis Basin, Eastern Arkansas. In *The Emergent Mississippian: Proceedings of the Sixth Mid-South Archaeological Conference*, edited by R. A. Marshall, pp. 122–36. Mississippi State University, Cobb Institute of Archaeology, Occasional Papers No. 87-01. State College.

Howard, J. H.
1968   *The Southeastern Ceremonial Complex and Its Interpretation*. Missouri Archaeological Society, Memoir No. 6. Columbia.

Howarth, D. F.
1987   The Effect of Pre-existing Microcavities on Mechanical Rock Performance in Sedimentary and Crystalline Rocks. *International Journal of Rock Mechanics and Mining Science* 24:223–33.

Hudson, C.
1976   *The Southeastern Indians*. University of Tennessee Press, Knoxville.

Hunt, T.
1994   Luster and Surface Texture of Heat-treated Cherts. Manuscript in possession of the author.

Ives, D. J.
1975   *The Crescent Hills Prehistoric Quarrying Area*. University of Missouri, Museum of Anthropology, Brief No. 22. Columbia.
1984   The Crescent Hills Prehistoric Quarrying Area: More Than Just Rocks. In *Prehistoric Chert Exploitation: Studies from the Midcontinent*, edited by B. M. Butler and E. E. May, pp. 187–96. Southern Illinois University at Carbondale, Center for Archaeological Investigations, Occasional Paper No. 2.
1985   Chert Sources and Identification in Archaeology: Can a Silk Purse Be Made from a Sow's Ear? In *Lithic Resource Procurement: Proceedings from the Second Conference on Prehistoric Chert Exploitation*, edited by S. C. Vehik, pp. 211–24. Southern Illinois University at Carbondale, Center for Archaeological Investigations, Occasional Paper No. 4.

Jefferies, R. W.
1976   The Lookout Valley Research Project: A Micro-regional Approach to Locational Analysis in Settlement Archaeology. *Southeastern Archaeological Conference, Bulletin* 19:14–18.
1982a   Debitage as an Indicator of Intraregional Activity Diversity in Northwest Georgia. *Midcontinental Journal of Archaeology* 7:99–132.
1982b   Archaeological Overview of the Carrier Mills District. In *The Carrier Mills Archaeological Project: Human Adaptation in the Saline Valley, Illinois*, edited by R. W. Jefferies and B. M. Butler, pp. 1461–509. Southern Illinois University at Carbondale, Center for Archaeological Investigations, Research Paper No. 33.
1983   Intraregional Behavioral Variability: A Regional Approach to Lithic Analysis. Paper presented at the 11th International Congress of Anthropological and Ethnological Sciences, Vancouver.

Jennings, J. D.
1985   River Basin Surveys: Origins, Operations, and Results, 1945–1969. *American Antiquity* 50:281–96.

Jermann, J. V.
1981   Surface Collection and Analysis of Spatial Pattern: An Archeological Example from the Lower Columbia River Valley. In *Plowzone Archeology: Contributions to Theory and Technique*, edited by M. J. O'Brien and D. E. Lewarch, pp. 71–118. Vanderbilt University, Nashville, Tennessee, Publications in Anthropology No. 27.

Jeter, M. D., ed.
1988   *The Burris Site and Beyond*. Arkansas Archeological Survey, Research Report No. 27. Fayetteville.

Johnson, J. K.
1979   Archaic Biface Manufacture: Production Failures, a Chronicle of the Misbegotten. *Lithic Technology* 8(2):25–35.
1981a   Chronological Trends in the Prehistoric Settlement of the Yellow Creek Uplands in Northeastern Mississippi. *Tennessee Anthropologist* 6:172–79.
1981b   *Lithic Procurement and Utilization Trajectories: Analysis*. University of Mississippi, Center for Archaeological Research, Archaeological Papers No. 1. University.
1982   Archaic Period Settlement Systems in Northeastern Mississippi. *Midcontinental Journal of Archaeology* 7:185–204.
1983   Biface Production Trajectories in Mississippi: A Regional Perspective. Paper presented at the 11th International Congress of Anthropological and Ethnological Sciences, Vancouver.
1984   Measuring Prehistoric Quarry Site Activity in Northeastern Mississippi. In *Prehistoric Chert Exploitation: Studies from the Midcontinent*, edited by B. M. Butler and E. E. May, pp. 225–35. Southern Illinois University at Carbondale, Center for Archaeological Investigations, Occasional Paper No. 2.
1985   Patterns of Prehistoric Chert Procurement in Colbert Ferry Park, Northwest Alabama. In *Lithic Resource Procurement: Proceedings from the Second Conference on Prehistoric Chert Exploitation*, edited by S. C. Vehik, pp. 153–64. Southern Illinois University at Carbondale, Center for Archaeological Investigations, Occasional Paper No. 4.
1987   Complex Core Technology in the Midsouth. In *The Organization of Core Technology*, edited by J. K. Johnson and C. A. Morrow, pp. 187–206. Westview Press, Boulder, Colorado.
1989   The Utility of Production Trajectory Modeling as a Framework for Regional Analysis. In *Alternative Approaches to Lithic Analysis*, edited by D. O. Henry and G. H. Odell, pp. 119–38. American Anthropological Association, Archaeological Papers No. 1. Washington, D.C.
1993   North American Biface Production Trajectory Modeling in Historic Perspective. *Plains Anthropologist* 38:151–62.

Johnson, J. K., and F. Hayes
1995   Long Distance Contacts during the Middle Woodland Period in the Yazoo Basin, Mississippi. In *Native American Interactions: Multiscalar Analysis and Interpretations in the Eastern Woodlands*, edited by M. S. Nassaney and K. E. Sassaman, pp. 100–121. University of Tennessee Press, Knoxville.

Johnson, J. K., and C. A. Morrow, eds.
1987   *The Organization of Core Technology*. Westview Press, Boulder, Colorado.

Johnson, J. K., and C. A. Raspet
1980   Delta Debitage. *Mississippi Archaeology* 15:3–11.

Jones, G. T., and C. Beck
- 1992 Chronological Resolution in Distributional Archaeology. In *Space, Time, and Archaeological Landscapes*, edited by J. Rossignol and L. Wandsnider, pp. 167-92. Plenum, New York.

Justice, N. D.
- 1987 *Stone Age Spear and Arrow Points of the Midcontinental and Eastern United States*. Indiana University Press, Bloomington.

Katzenberg, M. A.
- 1988 Stable Isotope Analysis of Animal Bone and the Reconstruction of Human Palaeodiet. In *Diet and Subsistence: Current Archaeological Perspectives*, edited by B. V. Kennedy and G. M. LeMoine, pp. 307-14. Proceedings of the 19th Annual Conference of the Archaeological Association of the University of Calgary.
- 1989 Stable Isotope Analysis of Archaeological Faunal Remains from Southern Ontario. *Journal of Archaeological Science* 16:319-29.

Katzenberg, M. A., and S. R. Saunders
- 1990 Age Differences in Stable Carbon Isotope Ratios in Prehistoric Maize Horticulturalists. *American Journal of Physical Anthropology* 81:247.

Katzenberg, M. A., S. R. Saunders, and W. R. Fitzgerald
- 1993 Age Differences in Stable Carbon and Nitrogen Isotope Ratios in a Population of Prehistoric Maize Horticulturalists. *American Journal of Physical Anthropology* 90:267-81.

Katzenberg, M. A., H. P. Schwarcz, M. Knyf, and F. J. Melbye
- 1995 Stable Isotope Evidence for Maize Horticulture and Paleodiet in Southern Ontario, Canada. *American Antiquity* 60:335-50.

Kay, M.
- 1990 A Regional Assessment of Huntsville Mounds in the Western Ozark Highland. Paper presented at the 55th Annual Meeting of the Society for American Archaeology, Las Vegas.

Kelly, J. E.
- 1990a Range Site Community Patterns and the Mississippian Emergence. In *The Mississippian Emergence*, edited by B. D. Smith, pp. 67-112. Smithsonian Institution Press, Washington, D.C.
- 1990b The Emergence of Mississippian Culture in the American Bottom Region. In *The Mississippian Emergence*, edited by B. D. Smith, pp. 113-52. Smithsonian Institution Press, Washington, D.C.

Kelly, J. E., F. A. Finney, D. L. McElrath, and S. J. Ozuk
- 1984 Late Woodland Period. In *American Bottom Archaeology: A Summary of the FAI-270 Project Contribution to the Culture History of the Mississippi River Valley*, edited by C. J. Bareis and J. W. Porter, pp. 104-27. University of Illinois Press, Urbana.

Kelly, J. E., S. J. Ozuk, D. K. Jackson, D. L. McElrath, F. A. Finney, and D. Esarey
- 1984 Emergent Mississippian Period. In *American Bottom Archaeology: A Summary of the FAI-270 Project Contribution to the Culture History of the Mississippi River Valley*, edited by C. J. Bareis and J. W. Porter, pp. 128-57. University of Illinois Press, Urbana.

Kelly, L. S.
- 1992 Moon Site Faunal Analysis. In *Excavations at the Moon Site (3PO488), A Middle Mississippian Village in Northeastern Arkansas*, edited by D. W. Benn,

pp. 225-48. Southwest Missouri State University, Center for Archaeological Research, Report No. 780. Springfield.

Kelly, R. L.
1988   Three Sides of a Biface. *American Antiquity* 53:717-34.

King, J. E., and W. H. Allen
1977   A Holocene Vegetation Record from the Mississippi River Valley, Southeast Missouri. *Quaternary Research* 8:307-23.

Klein, P. D., and E. R. Klein
1985   Applications of Stable Isotopes to Pediatric Nutrition and Gastroenterology: Measurement of Nutrient Absorption and Digestion Using ^{13}C. *Journal of Pediatric Gastroenterology and Nutrition* 4:9-19.

Klinger, T. C.
1974   Report on the 1974 Test Excavations at the Knappenberger Site, Mississippi County, Arkansas. *Arkansas Archeologist* 15:45-75.
1977a   Assembler. *Contract Archeology in the Lower Mississippi Valley of Arkansas: Miscellaneous Papers.* Arkansas Archeological Survey, Research Report No. 12. Fayetteville.
1977b   Parkin Archeology: A Report on the 1966 Field School Test Excavations at the Parkin Site. *Arkansas Archeologist* 16-18:45-80.
1982a   Assessing the Arkansas Contract Program: Its Trials and Tribulations, Its Accomplishments and Prospects. In *Arkansas Archeology in Review,* edited by N. L. Trubowitz and M. D. Jeter, pp. 316-26. Arkansas Archeological Survey, Research Report No. 15. Fayetteville.
1982b   *The Mangrum Site: Mitigation through Excavation and Preservation.* Arkansas Archeological Survey, Research Series No. 20. Fayetteville.

Klinger, T. C., S. M. Imhoff, and R. J. Cochran
1983   *Brougham Lake.* Historic Preservation Associates, Report No. 83-7. Fayetteville, Arkansas.

Klinger, T. C., and M. A. Mathis, assemblers
1978   *St. Francis II.* Arkansas Archeological Survey, Research Report No. 14. Fayetteville.

Klippel, W. E.
1969   The Hearnes Site: A Multicomponent Occupation Site and Cemetery in the Cairo Lowland Region of Southeast Missouri. *The Missouri Archaeologist* 31.

Knight, V. J., Jr.
1989   Some Speculations on Mississippian Monsters. In *The Southeastern Ceremonial Complex: Artifacts and Analysis,* edited by P. Galloway, pp. 205-10. University of Nebraska Press, Lincoln.
1990   Social Organization and the Evolution of Hierarchy in Southeastern Chiefdoms. *Journal of Anthropological Research* 46:1-23.

Koldehoff, B.
1987   The Cahokia Flake Tool Industry: Its Cultural Context within and Socioeconomic Implications for Late Prehistory in the Central Mississippi Valley. In *The Organization of Core Technology,* edited by J. K. Johnson and C. A. Morrow, pp. 151-86. Westview Press, Boulder, Colorado.

Kreisa, P. P.
1988   *Second-order Communities in Western Kentucky: Site Survey and Excavations at Late Woodland and Mississippi Period Sites.* University of Illinois at Ur-

bana-Champaign, Department of Anthropology, Western Kentucky Project Report No. 7.
- 1990 *Organizational Aspects of Mississippian Settlement Systems in Western Kentucky.* Ph.D. dissertation, Department of Anthropology, University of Illinois at Urbana-Champaign.
- 1991 *Mississippian Sites of the Lower Ohio River Valley in Kentucky.* University of Illinois at Urbana-Champaign, Department of Anthropology, Western Kentucky Project Report No. 9.
- 1995 Mississippian Secondary Centers along the Lower Ohio River Valley: An Overview of Some Sociopolitical Implications. In *Kentucky Heritage Council, Annual Volume on Kentucky Archaeology,* pp. 161–77. Frankfort.

Kreisa, P. P., and R. Edging
- 1990 Ceramic Assemblage. In *The Turk Site: A Mississippi Period Town in Western Kentucky,* by R. Edging, pp. 34–54. Kentucky Heritage Council, Frankfort.

Kruskal, J. B., and M. Wish
- 1978 *Multidimensional Scaling.* Sage Publications, Beverly Hills, California.

Kuijt, I., and K. W. Russell
- 1993 Tur Imdai Rockshelter, Jordan: Debitage Analysis of Historic Bedouin Lithic Technology. *Journal of Archaeological Science* 20:667–80.

Kuttruff, L. C.
- 1972 *The Marty Coolidge Site, Monroe County, Illinois.* Southern Illinois University Museum, Southern Illinois Studies Series No. 10. Carbondale.

Lafferty, R. H. III
- 1973 An Analysis of Prehistoric Southeastern Fortifications. M.A. thesis, Department of Anthropology, Southern Illinois University at Carbondale.

Lafferty, R. H. III, M. J. Guccione, L. J. Scott, D. K. Aasen, B. J. Watkins, M. C. Sierzchula, and P. F. Baumann
- 1987 *A Cultural Resources Survey, Testing and Geomorphic Examination of Ditches 10, 12, and 29, Mississippi County, Arkansas.* Mid-Continental Research, Investigations No. 86-5. Springdale, Arkansas.

Lafferty, R. H. III, and J. E. Price
- 1996 Southeast Missouri. In *Prehistory of the Mississippi Valley,* edited by C. H. McNutt, pp. 1–45. University of Alabama Press, Tuscaloosa.

Lafferty, R. H. III, L. G. Santeford, P. A. Morse, and L. M. Chapman
- 1984 *A Cultural Resources Survey and Evaluation in the Tyronza River Watershed Phase I Area, Mississippi County, Arkansas.* Mid-Continental Research, Investigations No. 84-2. Springdale, Arkansas.

Lafferty, R. H. III, M. C. Sierzchula, R. F. Cande, M. T. Oates, M. Dugan, D. C. Porter, M. J. Guccione, J. Toney, L. Cummings, and K. M. Hess
- 1995 *Cairo Lowland Archeology: The Second Step.* Report submitted to the U.S. Army Corps of Engineers, Memphis District.

Lafferty, R. H. III, C. S. Spears, P. A. Morse, and H. N. Gillespie
- 1985 *A Cultural Resources Survey, Testing and Predictive Model in the Tyronza River Watershed Phase II Mississippi and Poinsett Counties, Arkansas.* Mid-Continental Research, Investigations No. 85-1. Springdale, Arkansas.

Lambert, J. B., and J. M. Weydert-Homeyer
- 1994 The Fundamental Relationship between Ancient Diet and the Inorganic Constituents of Bone as Derived from Feeding Experiments. *Archaeometry* 35:279–94.

Lane, R. A., and A. J. Sublett
- 1972   Osteology of Social Organization: Residence Patterns. *American Antiquity* 37:186–201.

Lavin, L., and D. R. Prothero
- 1992   Prehistoric Procurement of Secondary Sources: The Case for Characterization. *North American Archaeologist* 13:97–114.

Lawn, B. R., and D. B. Marshall
- 1979   Mechanisms of Microcontact Fracture in Brittle Solids. In *Lithic Use-Wear Analysis,* edited by B. Hayden, pp. 99–112. Academic Press, New York.

Lawrence, W. L., and Mainfort R. C., Jr.
- 1992   40LK4, a Protohistoric Site in the Reelfoot Basin, Lake County, Tennessee. Paper presented at the Annual Meeting of the Kentucky Heritage Council, Murray.
- 1995   Otto Sharp: A Protohistoric Site in the Reelfoot Basin, Lake County, Tennessee. In *Current Archaeological Research in Kentucky,* Vol. 3, edited by J. F. Doershuk, C. A. Bergmann, and D. Pollack, pp. 205–77. Kentucky Heritage Council, Frankfort.

LeeDecker, C. H.
- 1979   *A Survey Level Report of the Ditch 24 Enlargement Project.* Report submitted to the U.S. Army Corps of Engineers, Memphis District.

Leeds, L. L.
- 1979   *Surface Sampling and Spatial Analysis: The Study of a Major Mississippian Ceremonial Center at the Rich Woods Site in Southeast Missouri.* Ph.D. dissertation, Department of Anthropology, University of Washington, Seattle.

Lewarch, D. E., and M. J. O'Brien
- 1981   Effect of Short Term Tillage on Aggregate Provenience Surface Pattern. In *Plowzone Archeology: Contributions to Theory and Technique,* edited by M. J. O'Brien and D. E. Lewarch, pp. 7–49. Vanderbilt University, Publications in Anthropology No. 27. Nashville, Tennessee.

Lewis, R. B.
- 1974   *Mississippian Exploitative Strategies: A Southeast Missouri Example.* Missouri Archaeological Society, Research Series No. 11. Columbia.
- 1982   *Excavations at Two Mississippian Hamlets in the Cairo Lowland of Southeast Missouri.* Illinois Archaeological Survey, Special Publication No. 2. Urbana-Champaign.
- 1984   An Examination of the Vacant Quarter Hypothesis in the Northern Lower Mississippi Valley. Paper presented at the 49th Annual Meeting of the Society for American Archaeology, Portland.
- 1986   *Mississippian Towns of the Western Kentucky Border: The Adams, Wickliffe, and Sassafras Ridge Sites.* Kentucky Heritage Council, Frankfort.
- 1988   Old World Dice in the Protohistoric Southern United States. *Current Anthropology* 29:759–68.
- 1990   The Late Prehistory of the Ohio-Mississippi Rivers Confluence Region, Kentucky and Missouri. In *Towns and Temples along the Mississippi,* edited by D. H. Dye and C. A. Cox, pp. 38–58. University of Alabama Press, Tuscaloosa.
- 1991   The Early Mississippi Period in the Confluence Region and its Northern Relationships. In *Cahokia and the Hinterlands: Middle Mississippian Cultures*

of the Midwest, edited by T. E. Emerson and R. B. Lewis, pp. 274-94. University of Illinois Press, Urbana.

Liden, K., C. Takahashi, and D. E. Nelson
- 1995 The Effects of Lipids in Stable Carbon Isotope Analysis and the Effects of NaOH Treatment on the Composition of Extracted Bone Collagen. *Journal of Archaeological Science* 22:321-26.

Lineback, J. A., compiler
- 1979 *Quaternary Deposits of Illinois* (map). Institute of Natural Resources, Illinois State Geological Society, Urbana.

Lovell, N. C., D. E. Nelson, and H. P. Schwarcz
- 1986 Carbon Isotope Ratios in Palaeodiet: Lack of Age or Sex Effect. *Archaeometry* 28:51-55.

Luedtke, B. E.
- 1978 Chert Resources and Trace Element Analysis. *American Antiquity* 43:413-23.
- 1979 The Identification of Sources of Chert Artifacts. *American Antiquity* 44:744-57.
- 1992 *An Archaeologist's Guide to Chert and Flint.* Institute for Archaeology, University of California, Los Angeles.

Lumb, L. C., and McNutt, C. H.
- 1988 *Chucalissa: Excavations in Units 2 and 6, 1959-67.* Memphis State University, Anthropological Research Center, Occasional Papers No. 15.

Lyman, R. L., M. J. O'Brien, and R. C. Dunnell
- 1997 *The Rise and Fall of Culture History.* Plenum, New York.

Lynott, M. J.
- 1987 Thermoluminescence Dating of Prehistoric Ceramics in Southeast Missouri: A Progress Report. *Society for Archaeological Sciences Newsletter* 10(2):2-5.
- 1989 *An Archeological Evaluation of the Gooseneck and Owls Bend Sites, Ozark National Scenic Riverways, Southeast Missouri.* National Park Service, Midwest Archeological Center, Occasional Studies in Anthropology No. 23. Lincoln, Nebraska.
- 1991 Identification of Attribute Variability in Emergent Mississippian and Mississippian Arrow Points from Southeast Missouri. *Midcontinental Journal of Archaeology* 16:189-211.

Lynott, M. J., T. W. Boutton, J. E. Price, and D. E. Nelson
- 1986 Stable Carbon Isotopic Evidence for Maize Agriculture in Southeast Missouri and Northeast Arkansas. *American Antiquity* 51:51-65.

Lyon, E. A.
- 1996 *A New Deal for Southeastern Archaeology.* University of Alabama Press, Tuscaloosa.

McCutcheon, P. T., and J. A. Afonso
- 1994 Quantifying the Mechanical Behavior of Chert from the Central Mississippi River Valley and Southeast Iberia, Spain. Poster presented at the 59th Annual Meeting of the Society for American Archaeology, Anaheim, California.

McCutcheon, P. T., and R. C. Dunnell
- 1991 Mississippian Lithic Exchange, Heat Treatment, and Fracture Toughness.

Paper presented at the 48th Annual Meeting of the Southeastern Archaeological Conference, Jackson, Mississippi.

1993   Quantifying Lithic Raw Material Variability of Crowley's Ridge Gravel, Southeast Missouri. Paper presented at the 58th Annual Meeting of the Society for American Archaeology, St. Louis.

McGimsey, C. R. III, and H. A. Davis

1968   Modern Land Use Practices and the Archeology of the Lower Mississippi Alluvial Valley. *The Arkansas Archeologist* 9:28-36.

1977   Editors. *The Management of Archaeological Resources: The Airlie House Report.* Society for American Archaeology, Washington, D.C.

McGrath, K. C., J. H. Ray, and D. W. Benn

1990   Lithic Analysis. In *Excavations at the Priestly Site (3PO490), an Emergent Mississippian Community in Northeastern Arkansas,* edited by D. W. Benn, pp. 215-326. Southwest Missouri State University, Center for Archaeological Research, Report No. 740. Springfield.

McGregor, J. C.

1958   *The Pool and Irving Villages: A Study of Hopewell Occupation in the Illinois River Valley.* University of Illinois Press, Urbana.

McKern, W. C.

1939   The Midwestern Taxonomic Method as an Aid to Archaeological Culture Study. *American Antiquity* 4:301-13.

1940   Application of the Midwestern Taxonomic Method. *Archaeological Society of Delaware, Bulletin* 3:18-21.

McNerney, M.

1978   *An Intensive Cultural Resources Survey and Assessment of Proposed Levee Modification at Item No. R-950, Wyatt Berm, Mississippi County, Missouri, and Item R-892, Hubbard Lake Berm, New Madrid County, Missouri.* Fischer-Stein, Cultural Resources Management Report No. 48. Carbondale, Illinois.

McNutt, C. H., ed.

1996   *Prehistory of the Central Mississippi Valley.* University of Alabama Press, Tuscaloosa.

Macko, S. A., M. L. F. Estep, P. E. Hare, and T. C. Hoering

1983   Stable Nitrogen and Carbon Isotopic Composition of Individual Amino Acids Isolated from Cultured Microorganisms. *Carnegie Institution of Washington, Yearbook* 82:404-9.

Macko, S. A., M. L. Fogel, P. E. Hare, and T. C. Hoering

1987   Isotopic Fractionation of Nitrogen and Carbon in the Synthesis of Amino Acids by Microorganisms. *Chemical Geology* 65:79-92.

Mainfort, R. C., Jr.

1991   An Overview of Late Mississippian Sites in West Tennessee. Paper presented at the Southeastern Archaeological Conference, Jackson, Mississippi.

1992   *Report on Archaeological Investigations in Lower Hatchie National Wildlife Refuge, Tennessee.* Report submitted to the U.S. Fish and Wildlife Service, Atlanta.

1994   *Archaeological Investigations in the Obion River Drainage: The West Tennessee Tributaries Project.* Report submitted to the U.S. Army Corps of Engineers, Memphis District.

Mann, W. B.
1982   An International Reference Material for Radiocarbon Dating. Paper presented at the 11th International Radiocarbon Conference, Seattle.

Marcher, M. V.
1962   *Geology of the Dover Area, Stewart County, Tennessee.* Tennessee Department of Conservation and Commerce, Division of Geology, Report of Investigations No. 16. Nashville, Tennessee.

Markewich, H. W.
1993   *Progress Report on Chronostratigraphic and Paleoclimatic Studies: Middle Mississippi River Valley; Eastern Arkansas and Western Tennessee.* U.S. Geological Survey, Atlanta.

Marshall, R. A.
1965   *An Archaeological Investigation of Interstate Route 55 through New Madrid and Pemiscot Counties, Missouri.* Missouri State Highway Department, Highway Archaeology Report No. 1. Columbia.
1966   Highway Salvage Archaeology at Two Village Sites in Pemiscot and New Madrid Counties, Missouri, 1965. Manuscript on file, University of Missouri, Museum of Anthropology, Columbia.
1985   Editor. *The Emergent Mississippian: Proceedings of the Sixth Mid-South Archaeological Conference.* Mississippi State University, Cobb Institute of Archaeology, Occasional Papers No. 87-01. State College.
1988   The Burial Pattern in Story Mound I: Hoecake Site, Southeast Missouri. In *Middle Woodland Settlement and Ceremonialism in the Mid-South and Lower Mississippi Valley,* edited by R. C. Mainfort, Jr., pp. 117–31. Mississippi Department of Archives and History, Archaeological Report No. 22. Jackson.

Marshall, R. A., and J. F. Hopgood
1964   A Test Excavation at Hoecake, 23MI-8, Mississippi County, Missouri. *Missouri Archaeological Society Newsletter* 177:3–6.

Masters, P. M.
1987   Preferential Preservation of Noncollagenous Protein During Bone Diagenesis: Implications for Chronometric and Stable Isotopic Measurements. *Geochimica et Cosmochimica Acta* 51:3209–14.

May, E. E.
1981   Archaeological Geology: Problems in the Identification of Chert Types and Source Areas. *Southeastern Archaeological Conference Bulletin* 24:109–13.
1982   Analysis of Carrier Mills Projectile Points. In *The Carrier Mills Archaeological Project: Human Adaptation in the Saline Valley, Illinois,* edited by R. W. Jefferies and B. M. Butler, pp. 1349–79. Southern Illinois University at Carbondale, Center for Archaeological Investigations, Research Paper No. 33.
1984   Prehistoric Chert Exploitation in the Shawnee Hills. In *Cultural Frontiers in the Upper Cache Valley, Illinois,* by V. Canouts, E. E. May, N. H. Lopinot, and J. D. Muller, pp. 68–91. Southern Illinois University at Carbondale, Center for Archaeological Investigations, Research Paper No. 16.

Medford, L. D.
1972   *Site Destruction due to Agricultural Practices in Northeast Arkansas.* Arkansas Archeological Survey, Research Series No. 3. Fayetteville.

Mehrer, M. W., and J. M. Collins
1995   Household Archaeology at Cahokia and in its Hinterlands. In *Mississip-*

pian Communities and Households, edited by D. Rogers and B. D. Smith, pp. 32–57. The University of Alabama Press, Tuscaloosa.

Meltzer, D. J., and R. C. Dunnell, eds.
 1992 *The Archaeology of William Henry Holmes*. Smithsonian Institution Press, Washington, D.C.

Meyers, J. T.
 1970 *Chert Resources of the Lower Illinois Valley*. Illinois State Museum, Reports of Investigations No. 18. Springfield.

Miller, J.
 1988 *Test Excavations at the Moon Site (3PO488), Poinsett County, Arkansas*. Manuscript on file, Environmental Division, Arkansas Highway and Transportation Department, Little Rock.

Million, M. G.
 1975 Ceramic Technology of the Nodena Phase People. *Southeastern Archaeological Conference Bulletin* 18:201–8.

Mills, C. F., ed.
 1970 *Trace Element Metabolism in Animals*. Proceedings of the WAAP/IBP International Symposium, Aberdeen, Scotland. Livingstone, Edinburgh.

Milner, G. R.
 1985 Cultures in Transition: The Late Emergent Mississippian and Mississippian. In *Proceedings of the Sixth Mid-South Archaeological Conference*, edited by R. A. Marshall, pp. 194–211. Mississippi State University, Cobb Institute of Archaeology, Occasional Papers No. 87-01. State College.
 1990 The Late Prehistoric Cahokia Cultural Systems of the Mississippi River Valley: Foundations, Florescence, and Fragmentation. *Journal of World Prehistory* 4:1–43.

Milner, G. R., T. E. Emerson, M. W. Mehrer, J. A. Williams, and D. Esarey
 1984 Mississippian and Oneota Period. In *American Bottom Archaeology: A Summary of the FAI-270 Project Contribution to the Culture History of the Mississippi River Valley*, edited by C. J. Bareis and J. W. Porter, pp. 158–86. University of Illinois Press, Urbana.

Minagawa, M.
 1992 Reconstruction of Human Diet from ^{13}C and ^{15}N in Contemporary Japanese Hair: A Stochastic Method for Estimating Multi-source Contribution by Double Isotopic Tracers. *Applied Geochemistry* 7:145–58.

Monteith, S. E.
 1990 *Soil Survey of Lauderdale County, Tennessee*. U.S. Department of Agriculture, Soil Conservation Service, Washington, D.C.

Montet-White, A.
 1963 Analytic Description of the Chipped Stone Industry from Snyders Site, Calhoun County, Illinois. In *Miscellaneous Studies in Typology and Classification*, by A. M. White, L. R. Binford, and M. L. Papworth, pp. 1–70. University of Michigan, Museum of Anthropology, Anthropological Papers No. 19. Ann Arbor.
 1968 *The Lithic Industries of the Illinois Valley in the Early and Middle Woodland Period*. University of Michigan, Museum of Anthropology, Anthropological Papers No. 35. Ann Arbor.

Moore, C. B.
- 1910 Antiquities of the St. Francis, White and Black Rivers, Arkansas. *Academy of Natural Sciences of Philadelphia, Journal* 14:255–364.
- 1911 Some Aboriginal Sites on Mississippi River. *Academy of Natural Sciences of Philadelphia, Journal* 14:367–478.
- 1916 Additional Investigation on Mississippi River. *Academy of Natural Sciences of Philadelphia, Journal* 16:493–508.

Morrell, L. R.
- 1965 *The Texas Site, Carlyle Reservoir, Clinton County, Illinois.* Southern Illinois University Museum, Archaeological Salvage Reports No. 23. Carbondale.

Morrow, C. A.
- 1984 A Biface Production Model for Gravel-based Chipped Stone Industries. *Lithic Technology* 13:20–28.
- 1987 Blades and Cobden Chert: A Technological Argument for Their Role as Markers of Regional Identification during the Hopewell Period in Illinois. In *The Organization of Core Technology,* edited by J. K. Johnson and C. A. Morrow, pp. 119–50. Westview Press, Boulder, Colorado.
- 1988 *Chert Exploitation and Social Interaction in the Prehistoric Midwest, 200 B.C.– 600 A.D.* Ph.D. dissertation, Department of Anthropology, Southern Illinois University at Carbondale.
- 1989 Middle Woodland Chert Exchange at Macoupin: Multiple Levels of Interaction in the Lower Illinois River Valley. In Research Trends in Midwest Archaeology, edited by K. McGowan, P. Kreisa, and R. Edging. *Steward Anthropological Society, Journal* 18(1-2):72–86.
- 1991 Baehr Mound Chert Disks: Archival Research on the American Museum of Natural History's Collections. *Illinois Archaeology* 3:77–92.
- 1993 Blue-gray Chipped Stone Disks: Middle Woodland Thingamabobs. Poster presented at the 58th Annual Meeting of the Society for American Archaeology, St. Louis.

Morrow, C. A., M. Elam, and M. Glascock
- 1992 The Use of Blue-gray Chert in Midwestern Prehistory. *Midcontinental Journal of Archaeology* 17:166–97.

Morrow, C. A., and R. W. Jefferies
- 1989 Curational Theory as a Means of Determining the Role of Lithic Material in Cultural Systems. In *Time, Energy, and Stone Tools,* edited by R. Torrence, pp. 27–33. Cambridge University Press, Cambridge, England.

Morse, D. F.
- 1963 *The Steuben Site and Mounds: A Multicomponent Late Hopewell Site in Illinois.* University of Michigan, Museum of Anthropology, Anthropological Papers No. 21. Ann Arbor.
- 1968 Mapping a Mississippian Community near Marked Tree. *Arkansas Archeological Society Bulletin* 9(3–4):37–40.
- 1973a The Hazel Site: Archeological Salvage on the Pyramidal Mound, August 19, 1968. *Arkansas Archeologist* 14(2–4):32–35.
- 1973b Editor. *Nodena.* Arkansas Archeological Survey, Research Series No. 4. Fayetteville.
- 1975 *Report of Excavations at the Zebree Site, 1969.* Arkansas Archeological Survey, Research Report No. 4. Fayetteville.

1979 A Wilson Phase House Pattern at 3CG218 in Northeast Arkansas. *Arkansas Archeological Society Field Notes* 167:6-8.
1982 Regional Overview of Northeast Arkansas. In *Arkansas Archeology in Review*, edited by N. L. Trubowitz and M. D. Jeter, pp. 20-36. Arkansas Archeological Survey, Research Series No. 15. Fayetteville.
1986 McCarty (3-Po-467): A Tchula Period Site near Marked Tree, Arkansas. In *The Tchula Period in the Mid-South and Lower Mississippi Valley*, edited by D. H. Dye and R. C. Brister, pp. 70-92. Mississippi Department of Archives and History, Archaeological Report No. 17. Jackson.
1989 The Nodena Phase. In *Nodena: An Account of 90 Years of Archeological Investigation in Southeast Mississippi County, Arkansas*, edited by D. F. Morse, pp. 97-113. Arkansas Archeological Survey, Research Series No. 30. Fayetteville.
1990 The Nodena Phase. In *Towns and Temples along the Mississippi*, edited by D. H. Dye and C. A. Cox, pp. 69-97. University of Alabama Press, Tuscaloosa.

Morse, D. F., and P. A. Morse
1977 Editors. *Zebree Archeological Project*. Report submitted to the U.S. Army Corps of Engineers, Memphis.
1983 *Archaeology of the Central Mississippi Valley*. Academic Press, New York.
1989 The Rise of the Southeastern Ceremonial Complex in the Central Mississippi Valley. In *The Southeastern Ceremonial Complex: Artifacts and Analysis*, edited by P. Galloway, pp. 41-44. University of Nebraska Press, Lincoln.
1990 Emergent Mississippian in the Central Mississippi Valley. In *The Mississippian Emergence*, edited by B. D. Smith, pp. 153-73. Smithsonian Institution Press, Washington, D.C.

Morse, D. F., and S. Smith
1973 Archeological Salvage during the Construction of Route 308. *Arkansas Archeologist* 14(2-4):36-78.

Morse, P. A.
1979 *An Archeological Survey of Portions of the Big Lake National Wildlife Refuge*. Manuscript on file, Arkansas Archeological Survey. Fayetteville.
1981 *Parkin*. Arkansas Archeological Survey, Research Series No. 13. Fayetteville.
1990 The Parkin Site and the Parkin Phase. In *Towns and Temples along the Mississippi*, edited by D. H. Dye and C. A. Cox, pp. 118-34. University of Alabama Press, Tuscaloosa.

Morse, P. [A.], and D. F. Morse
1990 The Zebree Site, an Emerged Early Mississippian Expression in Northeast Arkansas. In *The Mississippian Emergence*, edited by B. D. Smith, pp. 51-66. Smithsonian Institution Press, Washington, D.C.

Moselage, J.
1962 The Lawhorn Site. *The Missouri Archaeologist* 24.

Muller, J.
1983 The Southeast. In *Ancient North Americans*, edited by J. D. Jennings, pp. 373-420. Freeman, New York.
1986 *Archaeology of the Lower Ohio River Valley*. Academic Press, Orlando.

Muller, J. D., and J. E. Stephens
1991   Mississippian Sociocultural Adaptation. In *Cahokia and the Hinterlands: Middle Mississippian Cultures of the Midwest*, edited by T. E. Emerson and R. B. Lewis, pp. 297–310. University of Illinois Press, Urbana.

Munson, P. J.
1971   An Archaeological Survey of the Wood River and Adjacent Bottoms and Bluffs in Madison County, Illinois. In *Archaeological Surveys of the American Bottoms and Adjacent Bluffs, Illinois*, pp. 3–17. Illinois State Museum, Reports of Investigations 21. Springfield.

Muto, G. R.
1971   A Stage Analysis of the Manufacture of Stone Tools. In *Great Basin Anthropological Conference 1970: Selected Papers*, pp. 109–117. University of Oregon, Anthropological Papers No. 1. Eugene.

Nash, C. H.
1972   *Chucalissa: Excavations through 1963*. Memphis State University, Anthropological Research Center, Occasional Papers No. 6.

Nassaney, M. S.
1987   On the Causes and Consequences of Subsistence Intensification in the Mississippi Alluvial Valley. In *Emergent Horticultural Economies of the Eastern Woodlands*, edited by W. F. Keegan, pp. 129–52. Southern Illinois University at Carbondale, Center for Archaeological Investigations, Occasional Paper No. 7.

Nassaney, M. S., and C. R. Cobb
1991   Patterns and Processes of Late Woodland Development in the Greater Southeastern United States. In *Stability, Transformation, and Variation in the Late Woodland Southeast*, edited by M. S. Nassaney and C. R. Cobb, pp. 285–322. Plenum, New York.

Nelson, B. K., M. J. DeNiro, M. J. Schoeninger, D. J. De Paolo, and P. E. Hare
1986   Effects of Diagenesis on Strontium, Carbon, Nitrogen and Oxygen Concentration and Isotopic Composition of Bone. *Geochimica et Cosmochimica Acta* 50:1941–49.

Newcomer, M.
1971   Some Quantitative Experiments in Handaxe Manufacture. *World Archaeology* 3:85–93.

Newell, H. P., and A. D. Krieger
1949   *The George C. Davis Site, Cherokee County, Texas*. Society for American Archaeology, Memoirs No. 5. Washington, D.C.

Niemczycki, M. A. P.
1987   *Probability of Archaeological Site Occurrence in the Northern Portion of the Birds Point–New Madrid Floodway: An Analysis of the Distribution of Cultural Resources and Environmental Features*. Manuscript on file, U.S. Army Corps of Engineers, Memphis District.

Nixon, J. M.
1982   *An Archaeological and Historical Resource Survey of 21 Mississippi River Level Berm Items: The New Madrid Floodway, Component Four*. Fischer-Stein, Cultural Resources Management Report No. 48. Carbondale, Illinois.

Norr, L. C.
1991   *Nutritional Consequences of Prehistoric Subsistence Strategies in Lower Central*

America. Ph.D. dissertation, Department of Anthropology, University of Illinois, Urbana.

Norris, P. W.
1883   *Journal, 1882–1883.* Manuscript on file, National Anthropological Archives, Smithsonian Institution, Washington, D.C.

O'Brien, M. J.
1994a   *Cat Monsters and Head Pots: The Archaeology of Missouri's Pemiscot Bayou.* University of Missouri Press, Columbia.
1994b   The Physical Environment. In *Cat Monsters and Head Pots: The Archaeology of Missouri's Pemiscot Bayou,* by M. J. O'Brien, pp. 95–140. University of Missouri Press, Columbia.
1995   Archaeological Research in the Central Mississippi Valley: Culture History Gone Awry. *The Review of Archaeology* 16:23–36.
1996   *Paradigms of the Past: The Story of Missouri Archaeology.* University of Missouri Press, Columbia.

O'Brien, M. J., J. W. Cogswell, R. C. Mainfort, H. Neff, and M. D. Glascock
1995   Neutron-activation Analysis of Campbell Appliquéd Pottery from Southeastern Missouri and Western Tennessee: Implications for Late Mississippian Intersite Relations. *Southeastern Archaeology* 14:181–94.

O'Brien, M. J., and G. L. Fox
1994a   Sorting Artifacts in Space and Time. In *Cat Monsters and Head Pots: The Archaeology of Missouri's Pemiscot Bayou,* by M. J. O'Brien, pp. 25–60. University of Missouri Press, Columbia.
1994b   Assemblage Similarities and Dissimilarities. In *Cat Monsters and Head Pots: The Archaeology of Missouri's Pemiscot Bayou,* by M. J. O'Brien, pp. 61–93. University of Missouri Press, Columbia.

O'Brien, M. J., and T. D. Holland
1994   Campbell. In *Cat Monsters and Head Pots: The Archaeology of Missouri's Pemiscot Bayou,* by M. J. O'Brien, pp. 195–260. University of Missouri Press, Columbia.

O'Brien, M. J., and R. L. Lyman
n.d.   *Measuring the Flow of Time: James A. Ford and the Growth of Americanist Archaeology.* Manuscript in possession of the authors.

O'Brien, M. J., and R. A. Marshall
1994   Late Mississippian Period Antecedents: Murphy and Kersey. In *Cat Monsters and Head Pots: The Archaeology of Missouri's Pemiscot Bayou,* by M. J. O'Brien, pp. 141–94. University of Missouri Press, Columbia.

Odell, G.
1985   Microwear Analysis of Middle Woodland Lithics. In *Smiling Dan: Structure and Function of a Middle Woodland Settlement in the Illinois Valley,* edited by B. Stafford and M. Sant, pp. 298–326. Center for American Archeology, Kampsville Archeological Center, Research Series 2. Kampsville, Illinois.
1988   Preliminary Analysis of Lithic and Other Nonceramic Assemblages. In *The Archaic and Woodland Cemeteries at the Elizabeth Site in the Lower Illinois Valley,* edited by D. K. Charles, S. R. Leigh, and J. E. Buikstra, pp. 155–90. Center for American Archeology, Kampsville Archeological Center, Research Series 7. Kampsville, Illinois.

1994   The Role of Stone Bladelets in Middle Woodland Society. *American Antiquity* 59:102–20.

Odell, G. H., and Cowan F.
1987   Estimating Tillage Effects on Artifact Distributions. *American Antiquity* 52:456–84.

O'Leary, M. H.
1981   Carbon Isotope Fractionation in Plants. *Phytochemistry* 20:553–67.
1988   Carbon Isotopes in Photosynthesis. *BioScience* 38:328–36.

Orr, K. G.
1951   Change at Kincaid: A Study of Cultural Dynamics. In *Kincaid: A Prehistoric Illinois Metropolis,* by F.-C. Cole, R. Bell, J. Bennett, J. Caldwell, N. Emerson, R. MacNeish, K. Orr, and R. Willis, pp. 293–376. University of Chicago Press, Chicago.

O'Shea, J. M.
1984   *Mortuary Variability: An Archaeological Investigation.* Academic Press, New York.

Padgett, T. J.
1977   Poinsett Watershed: Contract Archeology on Crowley's Ridge. Arkansas Archeological Survey, Research Report No. 10. Fayetteville.

Parry, W. J.
1983   *Chipped Stone Tools in Formative Oaxaca, Mexico: Their Procurement, Production, and Use.* Ph.D. dissertation, Department of Anthropology, University of Michigan, Ann Arbor.

Parry, W. J., and R. L. Kelly
1987   Expedient Core Technology and Sedentism. In *The Organization of Core Technology,* edited by J. K. Johnson and C. A. Morrow, pp. 285–304. Westview Press, Boulder, Colorado.

Pate, F. D.
1994   Bone Chemistry and Paleodiet. *Journal of Archaeological Method and Theory* 1:161–209.

Pauketat, T. R.
1989   Monitoring Mississippian Homestead Occupation Span and Economy Using Ceramic Refuse. *American Antiquity* 54(2):288–310.

Paynter, R.
1989   The Archaeology of Equality and Inequality. *Annual Review of Anthropology* 18:369–99.

Pearsall, D. M.
1992   Analysis of Plant Remains from the Moon Site (3PO488). In *Excavations at the Moon Site (3PO488), A Middle Mississippian Village in Northeastern Arkansas,* edited by D. W. Benn, pp. 249–345. Southwest Missouri State University, Center for Archaeological Research, Report No. 780. Springfield.

Peebles, C. S.
1971   Moundville and Surrounding Sites: Some Structural Considerations of Mortuary Practices. In Approaches to the Social Dimensions of Mortuary Practices, edited by J. A. Brown. *Society for American Archaeology, Memoirs* 25:69–91.
1978   Determinants of Settlement Size and Location in the Moundville Phase.

In *Mississippian Settlement Patterns,* edited by B. D. Smith, pp. 369–416. Academic Press, New York.

Peregrine, P. N.
- 1992 *Mississippian Evolution: A World-System Perspective.* Monographs in World Archaeology No. 9. Prehistory Press, Madison, Wisconsin.

Perino, G.
- 1966 *The Banks Village Site, Crittenden County, Arkansas.* Missouri Archaeological Society, Memoir No. 4. Columbia.

Perttula, T. K.
- 1984 Prehistoric Use of Rhyolite in the Current River Valley, Eastern Ozark Highland, Southeast Missouri. *Missouri Archaeological Society Quarterly* 1:3, 11, 15.

Perttula, T. K., and J. E. Price
- 1984 The 1882 Investigations by Colonel P. W. Norris at the Powers Fort Site, 23BU10, Southeast Missouri. *Tennessee Anthropologist* 9:1–14.

Perzigian, A. J., P. A. Tench, and D. J. Braun
- 1984 Prehistoric Health in the Ohio River Valley. In *Paleopathology at the Origins of Agriculture,* edited by M. N. Cohen and G. J. Armelagos, pp. 347–66. Academic Press, New York.

Philips, W. A.
- 1900 Aboriginal Quarries and Shops at Mill Creek, Illinois. *American Anthropologist* 2:37–52.

Phillips, P.
- 1939 *Introduction to the Archaeology of the Mississippi Valley.* Ph.D. dissertation, Department of Anthropology, Harvard University.
- 1940 Middle American Influences on the Archaeology of the Southeastern United States. In *The Maya and Their Neighbors,* pp. 349–67. Appleton-Century, New York.
- 1958 Application of the Wheat-Gifford-Wasley Taxonomy to Eastern Ceramics. *American Antiquity* 24:117–25.
- 1970 *Archaeological Survey in the Lower Yazoo Basin, Mississippi, 1949–1955.* Harvard University, Peabody Museum of Archaeology and Ethnology, Papers 60. Cambridge, Massachusetts.

Phillips, P., and J. A. Brown
- 1978 *Pre-Columbian Shell Engravings from the Craig Mound at Spiro, Oklahoma* (2 vols.). Harvard University, Peabody Museum, Cambridge, Massachusetts.

Phillips, P., J. A. Ford, and J. B. Griffin
- 1951 *Archaeological Survey in the Lower Mississippi Alluvial Valley, 1940–1947.* Harvard University, Peabody Museum of American Archaeology and Ethnology, Papers 25. Cambridge, Massachusetts.

Phillips, P., and G. R. Willey
- 1953 Method and Theory in American Archaeology: An Operational Basis for Culture-Historical Integration. *American Anthropologist* 55:615–33.

Pi-Sunyer, O.
- 1965 The Flint Industry. In The McGraw Site: A Study in Hopewellian Dynamics, edited by O. H. Prufer. *Cleveland Museum of Natural History, Scientific Publications* 4:60–90.

Plog, S.
1980   *Stylistic Variation in Prehistoric Ceramics.* Cambridge University Press, New York.

Plumley, W. J.
1949   Black Hills Terrace Gravels: Study in Sedimentary Transport. *Journal of Geology* 56:526-77.

Porter, D. C., and M. J. Guccione
1994   Geomorphology of the Cairo Lowland. In *Cairo Lowland Archeology: The Second Step,* by R. H. Lafferty III, M. C. Sierzchula, R. F. Cande, M. T. Oates, M. Dugan, D. C. Porter, M. J. Guccione, J. Toney, L. Cummings, and K. M. Hess, pp. 53-82. Draft report submitted to the U.S. Army Corps of Engineers, Memphis District.

Potter, P. E.
1955   The Petrology and Origin of the Lafayette Gravel. *Journal of Geology* 63:1-38, 115-32.

Potter, W. B.
1880   Archaeological Remains in Southeastern Missouri. In *Contributions to the Archaeology of Missouri, by the Archaeological Section of the St. Louis Academy of Science.* Part 1, *Pottery,* pp. 1-19. Bates, Salem, Massachusetts.

Powell, M. L.
1980   The Big Lake People: Skeletal Population. In *Zebree Archeological Project,* edited by D. F. Morse and P. A. Morse. Manuscript on file, Arkansas Archeological Survey. Fayetteville.
1989   The People of Nodena. In *Nodena,* edited by D. F. Morse, pp. 23-1-24. Arkansas Archeological Survey, Research Series No. 30. Fayetteville.

Price, J. E.
1969   *A Middle Mississippian House.* University of Missouri, Museum of Anthropology, Museum Briefs No. 1. Columbia.
1973   *Settlement Planning and Artifact Distribution on the Snodgrass Site and Their Socio-political Implications in the Powers Phase of Southeast Missouri.* Ph.D. dissertation, Department of Anthropology, University of Michigan, Ann Arbor.
1974   Mississippian Settlement Systems of the Central Mississippi Valley. Manuscript presented at the Advanced Seminar on Mississippian Development, School of American Research, Santa Fe, New Mexico.
1976a   *An Archaeological Survey of Houck Park, Puxico, Stoddard County, Missouri.* Report on file, Missouri Department of Natural Resources, Jefferson City.
1976b   Prehistory of the Fourche Creek Watershed. In *An Assessment of the Cultural Resources of the Fourche Creek Watershed,* edited by J. E. Price, C. R. Price, and S. Harris, pp. 33-51. Report submitted to the U.S. Soil Conservation Service, Springfield, Missouri.
1978   The Settlement Pattern of the Powers Phase. In *Mississippian Settlement Patterns,* edited by B. D. Smith, pp. 201-31. Academic Press, New York.
1980   *Archaeological Investigation at 23DU244, a Limited Activity Barnes Site, in the City of Kennett, Dunklin County, Missouri.* Manuscript on file, Southwest Missouri State University, Center for Archaeological Research.
1986   Tchula Period Occupation along the Ozark Border in Southeast Missouri. In *Early Woodland Archeology,* edited by K. B. Farnsworth and T. E. Emer-

son, pp. 535-45. Center for American Archeology, Kampsville Seminars in Archeology No. 2. Kampsville, Illinois.

Price, J. E., and G. L. Fox
1990 Recent Investigations at Towosahgy State Historic Site. *The Missouri Archaeologist* 51:1-71.

Price, J. E., and J. B. Griffin
1979 *The Snodgrass Site of the Powers Phase of Southeast Missouri.* University of Michigan, Museum of Anthropology, Anthropological Papers No. 66. Ann Arbor.

Price, J. E., L. Morrow, and C. R. Price
1978 *A Preliminary Literature Review of the Prehistoric and Historic Cultural Resources for the Missouri and Arkansas Power Corporation Power Line Transect in New Madrid, Dunklin, and Pemiscot Counties, Missouri, and Mississippi County, Arkansas.* Manuscript on file, Southwest Missouri State University, Center for Archaeological Research. Springfield.

Price, J. E., and C. R. Price
1981 *Changing Settlement Systems in the Fourche Creek Watershed, Southeast Missouri and Northeast Arkansas: 1980.* Southwest Missouri State University, Center for Archaeological Research, Report No. 251. Springfield.
1984 *Phase II Testing of the Shell Lake Site, 23WE627, near Wappapello Dam, Wayne County, Missouri, 1984.* U.S. Army Corps of Engineers, St. Louis District, Cultural Resource Management Report No. 11.
1990 Protohistoric/Early Historic Manifestations in Southeastern Missouri. In *Towns and Temples along the Mississippi,* edited by D. H. Dye and C. A. Cox, pp. 59-68. University of Alabama Press, Tuscaloosa.

Price, T. D., M. Connor, and J. D. Parsen
1985 Bone Chemistry and the Reconstruction of Diet: Strontium Discrimination in White-tail Deer. *Journal of Archaeological Science* 12:419-22.

Price, T. D., R. W. Swick, and E. P. Chase
1986 Bone Chemistry and Prehistoric Diet: Strontium Studies of Laboratory Rats. *American Journal of Physical Anthropology* 70:365-75.

Pugh, T., and C. H. McNutt
1991 Julius Augustus Davies, M.D., an Early Contributor to Mississippi Archaeology. *Mississippi Archaeology* 26(2):1-6.

Putnam, F. W.
1875a [List of items from mounds in New Madrid County, Missouri, and brief description of excavations]. *Harvard University, Peabody Museum, Eighth Annual Report.* 16-46.
1875b The Pottery of the Mound Builders. *The American Naturalist* 9:321-38, 393-409.

Raab, L. M., R. Cande, and D. Stahle
1979 Debitage Graphs and Archaic Settlement Patterns. *Midcontinental Journal of Archaeology* 4:167-82.

Ramenofsky, A. F.
1987 *Vectors of Death: The Archaeology of European Contact.* University of New Mexico Press, Albuquerque.

Rands, R. L.
1956 Southern Cult Motifs on Walls-Pecan Point Pottery. *American Antiquity* 22:183-86.

Raspet, C. A.
   1979   A Production Stage Analysis of Lithic Artifacts from the Lightline Lake Site, Leflore County, Mississippi. M.A. thesis, Department of Anthropology, University of Mississippi.

Ray, J. H.
   1982   A Test for the Quality and Quantity of Chert Nodules in Stream Deposited Chert Sources. *Lithic Technology* 11(1):5-12.
   1985   An Overview of Chipped Stone Resources in Southern Missouri. In *Lithic Resource Procurement: Proceedings from the Second Conference on Prehistoric Chert Exploitation*, edited by S. C. Vehik, pp. 225-50. Southern Illinois University at Carbondale, Center for Archaeological Investigations, Occasional Paper No. 4.

Redfield, A.
   1971   *Dalton Project Notes*. University of Missouri, Museum of Anthropology, Museum Brief No. 20. Columbia.

Redfield, A., and J. H. Moselage
   1970   The Lace Place: A Dalton Project Site in the Western Lowland in Eastern Arkansas. *Arkansas Archeologist* 11:21-44.

Reed, D. M.
   1995   Maya Diets at Late Classic Copán. Poster presented at the 60th Annual Meeting of the Society for American Archaeology, Minneapolis.

Reid, K. C.
   1976   Prehistoric Trade in the Lower Missouri Valley: An Analysis of Middle Woodland Bladelets. In *Hopewellian Archaeology in the Lower Missouri Valley*, edited by A. E. Johnson, pp. 63-99. University of Kansas, Publications in Anthropology No. 8. Lawrence.

Rice, P. M.
   1987   *Pottery Analysis: A Sourcebook*. University of Chicago Press, Chicago.

Rindos, D.
   1984   *The Origins of Agriculture: An Evolutionary Perspective*. Academic Press, New York.

Rindos, D., and S. Johannessen
   1991   Human-Plant Interactions and Cultural Change in the American Bottom. In *Cahokia and the Hinterlands: Middle Mississippian Cultures of the Midwest*, edited by T. E. Emerson and R. B. Lewis, pp. 35-45. University of Illinois Press, Urbana.

Riordan, R.
   1975   *Ceramics and Chronology: Mississippian Settlement in the Black Bottom, Southern Illinois*. Ph.D. dissertation, Department of Anthropology, Southern Illinois University at Carbondale.

Ritchie, W. A.
   1961   Highway Construction and Salvage Programs. *Archaeology* 14:241-44.

Robinson, W. S.
   1951   A Method for Chronologically Ordering Archaeological Deposits. *American Antiquity* 16:293-301.

Rolingson, M. A., ed.
   1982   *Emerging Patterns of Plum Bayou Culture*. Arkansas Archeological Survey, Research Series No. 18. Fayetteville.

Roper, D.
1979   *Archaeological Survey and Settlement Pattern Models in Central Illinois.* Illinois State Museum, Scientific Papers 16. Springfield.

Rose, J. C., M. K. Marks, and L. L. Tieszen
1985   Bioarchaeology of the Little Cypress Bayou Site. Appendix IV in *Archaeological Investigations of the Little Cypress Bayou Site (3CT50), Crittenden County, Arkansas,* edited by A. M. Dicks and C. S. Weed. Report submitted to the U.S. Army Corps of Engineers, Memphis District, by New World Research, Inc.
1991   Bioarchaeology and Subsistence in the Central and Lower Portions of the Mississippi Valley. In *What Mean These Bones? Studies in Southeastern Bioarchaeology,* edited by M. L. Powell, P. S. Bridges, and A. M. W. Mires, pp. 7–21. University of Alabama Press, Tuscaloosa.

Rossen, J., and R. B. Edging
1987   East Meets West: Patterns in Kentucky Late Prehistoric Subsistence. In *Current Archaeological Research in Kentucky,* Vol. 1, edited by D. Pollack, pp. 225–34. Kentucky Heritage Council, Frankfort.

Rossignol, J., and L. Wandsnider, eds.
1992   *Space, Time, and Archaeological Landscapes.* Plenum, New York.

Rossman, G. R.
1994   Colored Varieties of the Silica Minerals. In *Reviews in Mineralogy.* Vol. 29, *Silica Physical Behavior, Geochemistry, and Materials Application,* edited by P. J. Heaney, C. T. Prewitt, and G. V. Gibbs, pp. 433–67. Mineralogical Society of America, Washington, D.C.

Rouse, I.
1964   Archaeological Approaches to Cultural Evolution. In *Explorations in Cultural Anthropology,* edited by W. Goodenough, pp. 455–68. McGraw-Hill, New York.

Royall, P. D., P. A. Delcourt, and H. R. Delcourt
1991   Late Quaternary Paleoecology and Paleoenvironments of the Central Mississippi Alluvial Valley. *Geological Society of America Bulletin* 103:157–70.

Rust, H. N.
1877   The Mound Builders in Missouri. *Western Review of Science and Industry* 1:531–35.

Rutledge, E. M., L. T. West, and M. Omakupt
1985   Loess Deposits on a Pleistocene Age Terrace in Eastern Arkansas. *Soil Science Society of America* 49:1231–38.

Salzer, R. J.
1963   *The Kerwin and Orrell Sites, Carlyle Reservoir, Clinton County, Illinois.* Southern Illinois University Museum, Archaeological Salvage Report No. 14. Carbondale.

Sanger, D.
1970   Mid-latitude Core and Blade Traditions. *Arctic Anthropologist* 7:106–14.

Saucier, R. T.
1964   *Geological Investigation of the St. Francis Basin, Lower Mississippi Valley.* U.S. Army Engineer Waterways Experiment Station, Technical Report No. 3-659. Vicksburg, Mississippi.
1968   A New Chronology for Braided Stream Surface Formation in the Lower Mississippi Valley. *Southeastern Geology* 9:65–76.

1970   Origin of the St. Francis Sunk Lands, Arkansas and Missouri. *Geological Society of America Bulletin* 81:2847–54.
1974   *Quaternary Geology of the Lower Mississippi Valley.* Arkansas Archeological Survey, Research Series No. 6. Fayetteville.
1978   Sand Dunes and Related Eolian Features of the Lower Mississippi River Alluvial Valley. *Geoscience and Man* 19:23–40.
1981   Current Thinking on Riverine Processes and Geologic History as Related to Human Settlement in the Southeast. *Geoscience and Man* 22:7–18.
1992   The Geomorphic Setting of the Moon Site (3PO488), Poinsett County, Arkansas. In *Excavations at the Moon Site (3PO488), A Middle Mississippian Village in Northeastern Arkansas,* edited by D. W. Benn, pp. 19–33. Southwest Missouri State University, Center for Archaeological Research, Report No. 780. Springfield.
1994   *Geomorphology and Quaternary Geologic History of the Lower Mississippi Valley* (2 vols.). U.S. Army Engineer Waterways Experiment Station, Vicksburg, Mississippi.

Saucier, R. T., and J. I. Snead, compilers
1989   *Quaternary Geology of the Lower Mississippi Valley* (Map at 1:1,100,000). Louisiana Geological Survey, Baton Rouge.

Scarry, C. M.
1993   Variability in Mississippian Crop Production Strategies. In *Foraging and Farming in the Eastern Woodlands,* edited by C. M. Scarry, pp. 78–90. University Press of Florida, Gainesville.

Schell, D. M.
1983   Carbon-13 and Carbon-14 Abundances in Alaskan Aquatic Organisms: Delayed Production from Peat in Arctic Food Webs. *Science* 219:1068–71.

Schiffer, M.
1987   *Formation Processes of the Archaeological Record.* University of New Mexico Press, Albuquerque.

Schiffer, M. B., and J. H. House
1975   Compilers. *The Cache River Archeological Project: An Experiment in Contract Archeology.* Arkansas Archeological Survey, Research Series No. 8. Fayetteville.
1977a   Cultural Resource Management and Archaeological Research: The Cache Project. *Current Anthropology* 18:43–68.
1977b   An Approach to Assessing Scientific Significance. In *Conservation Archaeology: A Guide for Cultural Resource Management Studies,* edited by M. B. Schiffer and G. J. Gumerman, pp. 249–57. Academic Press, New York.

Schoeller, D. A., P. D. Klein, W. C. MacLean, Jr., J. B. Watkins, and E. Van Santen
1981   Fecal ^{13}C Analysis for the Detection and Quantitation of Intestinal Malabsorption. *Journal of Laboratory and Clinical Medicine* 97:439–48.

Schoeller, D. A., P. D. Klein, J. B. Watkins, T. Heim, and W. C. MacLean, Jr.
1980 ^{13}C Abundances of Nutrients and the Effect of Variations in ^{13}C Isotopic Abundances of Test Meals Formulated for $^{13}CO_2$ Breath Tests. *The American Journal of Clinical Nutrition* 33:2375–85.

Schoeller, D. A., J. F. Schneider, N. W. Solomons, J. B. Watkins, and P. D. Klein
1977   Clinical Diagnosis with the Stable Isotope ^{13}C in CO_2 Breath Tests: Methodology and Fundamental Considerations. *Journal of Laboratory and Clinical Medicine* 90:412–21.

Schoeninger, M. J.
1979 Dietary Reconstruction at Chalcatzingo, a Formative Period Site in Morelos, Mexico. University of Michigan, Museum of Anthropology, Technical Report No. 9. Ann Arbor.

Schoeninger, M. J., and M. J. DeNiro
1984 Nitrogen and Carbon Isotopic Composition of Bone Collagen from Marine and Terrestrial Animals. *Geochimica et Cosmochimica Acta* 48:625-39.

Schoeninger, M. J., D. M. Moore, M. L. Murray, and J. D. Kingston
1989 Detection of Bone Preservation in Archaeological and Fossil Samples. *Applied Geochemistry* 4:281-92.

Schoeninger, M. J., and K. Moore
1992 Bone Stable Isotope Studies in Archaeology. *Journal of World Prehistory* 6:247-96.

Schoeninger, M. J., and C. S. Peebles
1981 Effects of Mollusc Eating on Human Bone Strontium Levels. *Journal of Archaeological Science* 8:391-97.

Schurr, M. R.
1989 *The Relationship between Mortuary Treatment and Diet at the Angel Site.* Ph.D. dissertation, Department of Anthropology, Indiana University, Bloomington.

Schwarcz, H. P., and M. J. Schoeninger
1991 Stable Isotope Analyses in Human Nutritional Ecology. *Yearbook of Physical Anthropology* 34:283-321.

Scott, L. J., and D. K. Aasen
1987 Interpretation of Holocene Vegetation in Northeastern Arkansas. In *A Cultural Resources Survey, Testing, and Geomorphic Examination of Ditches 10, 12, and 29, Mississippi County, Arkansas*, by R. H. Lafferty III, M. J. Guccione, L. J. Scott, D. K. Aasen, B. J. Watkins, M. C. Sierzchula, and P. F. Bauman, pp. 100-132. Report submitted to the U.S. Army Corps of Engineers, Memphis District.

Scully, E. G.
1953 Extinct River Channels as a Method of Dating Archaeological Sites in Southeast Missouri. *The Missouri Archaeologist* 15(1-2):84-91.

Sealy, J. C., and A. Sillen
1988 Sr and Sr/Ca in Marine and Terrestrial Foodwebs in the Southwestern Cape, South Africa. *Journal of Archaeological Science* 15:425-38.

Sealy, J. C., and N. J. van der Merwe
1988 Social, Spatial and Chronological Patterning in Marine Food Use as Determined by ^{13}C Measurements of Holocene Human Skeletons from the Southwestern Cape, South Africa. *World Archaeology* 20:87-102.

Sellars, J. R., J. H. Ray, and D. W. Benn
1992 Analysis of Chipped Stone and Other Lithic Artifacts. In *Excavations at the Moon Site (3PO488), a Middle Mississippian Village in Northeastern Arkansas*, edited by D. W. Benn, pp. 167-204. Southwest Missouri State University, Center for Archaeological Research, Report No. 780. Springfield.

Shelley, P. H.
1993 A Geoarchaeological Approach to the Analysis of Secondary Lithic Deposits. *Geoarchaeology* 8:59-72.

Shepard, A. O.
1956   *Ceramics for the Archaeologist.* Carnegie Institution of Washington, Publication No. 609.

Shott, M. J.
1989   Bipolar Industries: Ethnographic Evidence and Archaeological Implications. *North American Archaeologist* 10:681–87.

Smith, B. D.
1975   *Middle Mississippi Exploitation of Animal Populations.* University of Michigan, Museum of Anthropology, Anthropological Papers No. 57. Ann Arbor.
1978a   *Prehistoric Patterns of Human Behavior: A Case Study in the Mississippi Valley.* Academic Press, New York.
1978b   Editor. *Mississippian Settlement Patterns.* Academic Press, New York.
1978c   Variation in Mississippian Settlement Patterns. In *Mississippian Settlement Patterns,* edited by B. D. Smith, pp. 479–503. Academic Press, New York.
1985   Introduction to the 1985 Edition. In *Report on the Mound Explorations of the Bureau of Ethnology,* by C. Thomas, pp. 5–19. Smithsonian Institution Press, Washington, D.C.
1990a   The Division of Mound Exploration of the Bureau of Ethnology and the Birth of Modern American Archeology. In *Edward Palmer's Arkansaw Mounds,* edited by M. D. Jeter, pp. 27–37. University of Arkansas Press, Fayetteville.
1990b   Editor. *The Mississippian Emergence.* Smithsonian Institution Press, Washington, D.C.
1992   Mississippian Elites and Solar Alignments: A Reflection of Managerial Necessity, or Levers of Social Inequality. In *Lords of the Southeast: Social Inequality and the Native Elites of Southeastern North America,* edited by A. W. Barker and T. R. Pauketat, pp. 11–30. American Anthropological Association, Archeological Papers No. 3. Washington, D.C.
1995   The Analysis of Single-Household Mississippian Settlements. In *Mississippian Communities and Households,* edited by D. Rogers and B. D. Smith, pp. 224–49. University of Alabama Press, Tuscaloosa.

Smith, B. N., and S. Epstein
1971   Two Categories of $^{13}C/^{12}C$ Ratios for Higher Plants. *Plant Physiology* 47:380–84.

Smith, F. L., and R. T. Saucier
1971   *Geological Investigation of the Western Lowlands Area, Lower Mississippi Valley.* U.S. Army Engineer Waterways Experiment Station, Technical Report No. S-71-5. Vicksburg, Mississippi.

Smith, G. P.
1978   *Final Report, Archaeological Excavation, the Riverdale Site, 3PO395, Fall 1977, Poinsett County, Arkansas.* Manuscript on file, Arkansas Archeological Survey, Fayetteville.
1990   The Walls Phase and Its Neighbors. In *Towns and Temples along the Mississippi,* edited by D. H. Dye and C. A. Cox, pp. 135–69. University of Alabama Press, Tuscaloosa.

Smith-Davis, M. F.
1896   *History of Dunklin County, Mo. 1845–1895.* Nixon-Jones, St. Louis.

Snyder, J. F.
- 1877 Deposits of Flint Implements. *Smithsonian Institution, Annual Report* (1877):563–68.
- 1883 Buried Flints in Cass County, Il. *Smithsonian Institution, Annual Report* (1882):568–79.
- 1893a Buried Deposits of Hornstone Disks. *The Archaeologist* 1:181–86.
- 1893b Buried Deposits of Hornstone Disks. *American Association for the Advancement of Science, Proceedings* 42:318–24.
- 1895a A Group of Illinois Mounds (part 1). *The Archaeologist* 3:77–81.
- 1895b A Group of Illinois Mounds (part 2). *The Archaeologist* 3:109–13.
- 1910 Prehistoric Illinois: The Primitive Flint Industry. *Illinois State Historical Society, Journal* 3:11–25.

Solomons, N. W., D. A. Schoeller, J. B. Wagonfeld, D. Ott, I. H. Rosenberg, and P. D. Klein
- 1977 Application of a Stable Isotope (^{13}C)-labeled Glycocholate Breath Test to Diagnosis of Bacterial Overgrowth and Ileal Dysfunction. *Journal of Laboratory and Clinical Medicine* 90(3):431–39.

Spence, M. W.
- 1974 Residential Practices and the Distribution of Skeletal Traits in Teotihuacán, Mexico. *Man* 9:262–73.

Spyglass, Inc.
- 1991 *Transform* (Version 2.0). Spyglass, Champaign, Illinois.

Stafford, B. D., and M. B. Sant, eds.
- 1985 *Smiling Dan: Structure and Function of a Middle Woodland Settlement in the Illinois Valley.* Center for American Archeology, Kampsville Archeological Center, Research Series 2. Kampsville, Illinois.

Stafford, T. W., Jr., K. Brendel, and R. C. Duhamel
- 1988 Radiocarbon, ^{13}C and ^{15}N Analysis of Fossil Bone: Removal of Humates with XAD-2 Resin. *Geochimica et Cosmochimica Acta* 52:2257–67.

Stafford, T. W., Jr., A. J. T. Jull, K. Brendel, R. C. Duhamel, and D. Donahue
- 1987 Study of Bone Radiocarbon Dating Accuracy at the University of Arizona NSF Accelerator Facility for Radioisotope Analysis. *Radiocarbon* 29:24–44.

Stallings, R.
- 1989 Factors in Interpreting the Prehistoric Use of the Citronelle Gravels in Mississippi. *Mississippi Archaeology* 24:35–58.

Stanfill, A. L.
- 1986 Stages of Cobble Reduction and the Base Settlement/Specialized Activity Site Dichotomy: A Test Case with the 1976 Village Creek Collections. In *Village Creek: An Explicitly Regional Approach to the Study of Cultural Resources,* edited by T. C. Klinger, pp. 247–72. Arkansas Archeological Survey, Research Report No. 26. Fayetteville.

Steponaitis, V. P.
- 1978 Location Theory and Complex Chiefdoms: A Mississippian Example. In *Mississippian Settlement Patterns,* edited by B. D. Smith, pp. 417–53. Academic Press, New York.
- 1983 *Ceramics, Chronology, and Community Patterns.* Academic Press, New York.

Steyermark, J. A.
- 1963 *Flora of Missouri.* Iowa State University Press, Ames.

Struever, S.
- 1973 Chert Utilization in Lower Illinois Valley Prehistory. In *Variations in Prehistory*, edited by D. W. Lathrap and J. Douglas, pp. 61–73. Illinois Archaeological Survey, Urbana.

Stuiver, M.
- 1982 A High Precision Calibration of the AD Radiocarbon Time Scale. *Radiocarbon* 24:1–26.

Stuiver, M., and B. Becker
- 1986 A Calibration Curve for the Radiocarbon Timescale. *Radiocarbon* 28:863–910.

Stuiver, M., and G. W. Pearson
- 1986 High-precision Calibration of the Radiocarbon Time Scale, A.D. 1950–500 B.C. *Radiocarbon* 28:805–38.
- 1993 High-precision Bidecadal Calibration of the Radiocarbon Time Scale, AD 1950–500 BC and 2500–6000 BC. *Radiocarbon* 35:1–23.

Stuiver, M., and P. J. Reimer
- 1993 Extended ^{14}C Data Base and Revised CALIB 3.0 ^{14}C Age Calibration Program. *Radiocarbon* 35:215–30.

Sturdevant, C.
- 1981 *Preliminary Report: Cultural Resource Survey of the Mississippi County Spillway Watershed Ditch Improvement Project Areas and NRHP Evaluation of Sites Recovered within the Survey Zone.* Manuscript on file, U.S. Army Corps of Engineers, Memphis District.

Swallow, G. C.
- 1858 Indian Mounds in New Madrid County, Missouri. *Academy of Science of St. Louis, Transactions* 1:36.

Tanaka, G. I., H. Kawamura, and E. Nomura
- 1981 Reference Japanese Man. II: Distribution of Strontium in the Skeleton and in the Mass of Mineralized Bone. *Health Physics* 40:601–14.

Teeri, J. A., and D. A. Schoeller
- 1979 ^{13}C Values of an Herbivore and the Ratio of C_3 to C_4 Plant Carbon in Its Diet. *Oecologia* 39:197–200.

Teeri, J. A., and L. G. Stowe
- 1976 Climatic Patterns and the Distribution of C_4 Grasses in North America. *Oecologia* 23:1–12.

Teller, J. T.
- 1987 Proglacial Lakes and the Southern Margin of the Laurentide Ice Sheet. In *The Geology of North America.* Vol. K-3, *North America and Adjacent Oceans during the Last Deglaciation*, edited by W. F. Ruddiman and H. E. Wright, Jr., pp. 39–69. Geological Society of America, Boulder, Colorado.
- 1990 Volume and Routing of Late-glacial Runoff from the Southern Laurentide Ice Sheet. *Quaternary Research* 34:12–23.

Teltser, P. A.
- 1988 *The Mississippian Archaeological Record on the Malden Plain, Southeast Missouri: Local Variability in Evolutionary Perspective.* Ph.D. dissertation, Department of Anthropology, University of Washington.
- 1992 Settlement Context and Structure at County Line, Missouri. *Southeastern Archaeology* 11:14–30.

1993 An Analytical Strategy for Studying Assemblage-scale Variation: A Case Study from Southeast Missouri. *American Antiquity* 58:530–43.

Thomas, C.
1884 The Houses of the Mound-builder. *Magazine of American History* (February):110–16.
1894 Report on the Mound Explorations of the Bureau of Ethnology. *Bureau of Ethnology, Annual Report* 12:3–742.

Tieszen, L. L., T. W. Boutton, W. K. Ottochilo, D. E. Nelson, and D. H. Brandt
1989 An Assessment of Long-term Food Habits of Tsavo Elephants Based on Stable Carbon and Nitrogen Isotope Ratios of Bone Collagen. *African Journal of Ecology* 27:219–26.

Tieszen, L. L., T. W. Boutton, K. G. Tesdahl, and N. A. Slade
1983 Fractionation and Turnover of Stable Carbon Isotopes in Animal Tissues: Implications for ^{13}C Analysis of Diet. *Oecologia* 57:32–37.

Tieszen, L. L., and T. Fagre
1993 Effect of Diet Quality and Composition on the Isotopic Composition of Respiratory CO_2, Bone Collagen, Bioapatite, and Soft Tissues. In *Prehistoric Human Bone: Archaeology at the Molecular Level*, edited by J. B. Lambert and G. Grupe, pp. 121–55. Springer Verlag, Berlin.

Tieszen, L. L., and S. K. Imbamba
1980 Photosynthetic Systems, Carbon Isotope Discrimination and Herbivore Selectivity in Kenya. *African Journal of Ecology* 18:237–42.

Titterington, P. F.
1937 Flint Quarries. *The Missouri Archaeologist* 3(1):3–6.

Torrence, R.
1989 *Production and Exchange of Stone Tools*. Cambridge University Press, Cambridge, England.

Toth, A.
1977 Early Marksville Phases in the Lower Mississippi Valley: A Study of Culture Contact Dynamics. Ph.D. dissertation, Department of Anthropology, Harvard University.
1979 The Marksville Connection. In *Hopewell Archaeology: The Chillicothe Conference*, edited by D. S. Brose and N. Greber, pp. 188–99. Kent State University Press, Kent, Ohio.

Tuross, N., M. L. Fogel, and P. E. Hare
1988 Variability in the Preservation of the Isotopic Composition of Collagen from Fossil Bone. *Geochimica et Cosmochimica Acta* 52:929–35.

Underwood, E. J.
1977 *Trace Elements in Human and Animal Nutrition*. Academic Press, New York.

van der Merwe, N. J.
1982 Carbon Isotopes, Photosynthesis, and Archaeology. *American Scientist* 70:596–606.

Van Frank, J. R.
1891 *Map of Topographic Survey of the Swamp Lands in South-east Missouri*. State of Missouri, Jefferson City.

van Klinken, G. J., and R. E. M. Hedges
1995 Experiments on Collagen-Humic Interactions: Speed of Humic Uptake, and Effects of Diverse Chemical Treatments. *Journal of Archaeological Science* 22:263–70.

Verano, J. W., and M. J. DeNiro
- 1993 Locals or Foreigners? Morphological, Biometric, and Isotopic Approaches to the Question of Group Affinity in Human Skeletal Remains Recovered from Unusual Archaeological Contexts. In *Investigations of Ancient Human Tissue: Chemical Analyses in Anthropology*, edited by M. K. Sandford, pp. 361–86. Gordon and Breach, Langhorne, Pennsylvania.

Vogel, J. C.
- 1978 Isotopic Assessment of the Dietary Habits of Ungulates. *South African Journal of Science* 74:298–301.

Wagner, G. E.
- 1987 *Uses of Plants by the Fort Ancient Indians*. Ph.D. dissertation, Department of Anthropology, Washington University, Seattle.

Walker, P. L., and M. J. DeNiro
- 1986 Stable Nitrogen and Carbon Isotope Ratios in Bone Collagen as Indices of Prehistoric Dietary Dependence on Marine and Terrestrial Resources in Southern California. *American Journal of Physical Anthropology* 71:51–61.

Walker, W. M., and R. M. Adams
- 1946 Excavations in the Matthews Site, New Madrid County, Missouri. *Academy of Science of St. Louis, Transactions* 31(4):75–120.

Waring, A. J., Jr., and P. Holder
- 1945 A Prehistoric Ceremonial Complex in the Southeastern United States. *American Anthropologist* 47:1–34.

Wesler, K. W.
- 1989 *Archaeological Excavations at Wickliffe Mounds, 15BA4: Mound D, 1987*. Murray State University, Wickliffe Mounds Research Center, Report No. 3. Murray, Kentucky.
- 1991a Ceramics, Chronology, and Horizon Markers at Wickliffe Mounds. *American Antiquity* 56:278–90.
- 1991b *Archaeological Excavations at Wickliffe Mounds, 15BA4: North Village and Cemetery, 1988–1989*. Murray State University, Wickliffe Mounds Research Center, Report No. 3. Murray, Kentucky.
- 1992 An Inside View of Chiefly Cycling at Wickliffe Mounds. Paper presented at the Ninth Annual Kentucky Heritage Council Archaeological Conference, Murray.

Westbrook, K. C.
- 1982 *Legacy in Clay: Pre-historic Ceramic Art of Arkansas*. Rose, Little Rock.

White, C. D., and H. P. Schwarcz
- 1989 Ancient Maya Diet: As Inferred from Isotopic and Elemental Analysis of Human Bone. *Journal of Archaeological Science* 16:451–74.

Whittaker, B. N., R. N. Singh, and G. Sun
- 1992 *Rock Fracture Mechanics: Principles, Designs, and Applications*. Elsevier, Amsterdam.

Wiant, M. D., and C. R. McGimsey, eds.
- 1986 *The Woodland Period Occupations of the Napoleon Hollow Site in the Lower Illinois Valley*. Center for American Archeology, Kampsville Archeological Center, Research Series 6. Kampsville, Illinois.

Wilkinson, L., M. A. Hill, J. P. Welna, and G. K. Birkenbeuel
- 1992 *SYSTAT Statistics*. Systat, Evanston, Illinois.

Willey, G. R., and P. Phillips
- 1955 Method and Theory in American Archaeology. II: Historical-Developmental Interpretations. *American Anthropologist* 57:723–819.
- 1958 *Method and Theory in American Archaeology.* University of Chicago Press, Chicago.

Williams, J. R.
- 1964 A Study of Fortified Indian Villages in Southeast Missouri. M.A. thesis, Department of Anthropology, University of Missouri–Columbia.
- 1967 *Land Leveling Salvage Archaeological Work in Southeast Missouri: 1966.* Report submitted to the National Park Service, Midwest Archeological Center, Lincoln, Nebraska.
- 1968 *Southeast Missouri Land Leveling Salvage Archaeology: 1967.* Report submitted to the National Park Service, Lincoln, Nebraska.
- 1971 *A Study of the Baytown Phases in the Cairo Lowland of Southeast Missouri.* Ph.D. dissertation, Department of Anthropology, University of Missouri–Columbia.
- 1972 *Land Leveling Salvage Archaeology in Missouri: 1968.* Report submitted to the National Park Service, Midwest Archeological Center, Lincoln, Nebraska.
- 1974 The Baytown Phases in the Cairo Lowland of Southeast Missouri. *The Missouri Archaeologist* 36.

Williams, S.
- 1949 An Archaeological Study of the Sandy Woods Site, Scott County, Missouri. Undergraduate thesis, Department of Anthropology, Yale University.
- 1954 *An Archeological Study of the Mississippian Culture in Southeast Missouri.* Ph.D. dissertation, Department of Anthropology, Yale University.
- 1956 Settlement Patterns in the Lower Mississippi Valley. In *Prehistoric Settlement Patterns in the New World,* edited by G. R. Willey, pp. 52–62. Viking Fund Publications in Anthropology No. 23. New York.
- 1957 James Kelly Hampson. *American Antiquity* 22:398–400.
- 1980 Armorel: A Very Late Phase in the Lower Mississippi Valley. *Southeastern Archaeological Conference Bulletin* 22:105–10.
- 1982 The Vacant Quarter Hypothesis: A Discussion Symposium. Paper presented at the 39th Annual Meeting of the Southeastern Archaeological Conference, Memphis.
- 1988 Time and Stratigraphy: The Eternal Search in the Southeast. Paper presented at the Annual Meeting of the Southeastern Archaeological Conference, New Orleans.
- 1990 The Vacant Quarter and Other Late Events in the Lower Valley. In *Towns and Temples along the Mississippi,* edited by D. H. Dye and C. A. Cox, pp. 170–80. University of Alabama Press, Tuscaloosa.

Williams, S., and J. P. Brain
- 1983 *Excavations at the Lake George Site, Yazoo County, Mississippi, 1958–1960.* Harvard University, Peabody Museum of Archaeology and Ethnology, Papers 74. Cambridge, Massachusetts.

Wilson, D. E.
- 1993 Diet, Health, and Social Status in the Mississippian Powers Phase Turner Cemetery Population. M.A. thesis, Department of Anthropology, University of Texas at Austin.

Winters, H. D.
- 1981 Excavating in Museums: Notes on Mississippian Hoes and Middle Woodland Copper Gouges and Celts. In The Research Potential of Anthropological Collections in Museums, edited by A.-M. Cantwell, J. B. Griffin, and N. A. Rothchild. *Annals of the New York Academy of Sciences* 376:17-34.
- 1984 The Significance of Chert Procurement and Exchange in the Middle Woodland Traditions of the Illinois Area. In *Prehistoric Chert Exploitation: Studies from the Midcontinent*, edited by B. M. Butler and E. E. May, pp. 3-21. Southern Illinois University at Carbondale, Center for Archaeological Investigations, Occasional Paper No. 2.

Woodhead-Galloway, J.
- 1980 *Collagen: The Anatomy of a Protein.* The Institute of Biology's Studies in Biology No. 117. Arnold, London.

Wymer, D. A.
- 1987 *The Paleoethnobotanical Record of Central Ohio—100 B.C. to A.D. 800: Subsistence Continuity and Cultural Change.* Ph.D. dissertation, Department of Anthropology, Ohio State University, Columbus.
- 1990 Archaeobotany. In *Childers and Woods: Two Late Woodland Sites in the Upper Ohio Valley, Mason County, West Virginia*, Vol. 2, edited by M. J. Shott, pp. 487-616. University of Kentucky, Program for Cultural Resource Assessment, Archaeological Report No. 200. Lexington.

Contributors

David W. Benn received his Ph.D. from the University of Wisconsin in 1976. He currently is research coordinator for Bear Creek Archeology, Inc., of Cresco, Iowa, a firm conducting resource-management studies in the upper Mississippi River basin. He has published two books, *Hadfields Cave* and *Woodland Cultures on the Western Prairies,* and numerous articles about the Woodland cultural periods. He continues to pursue two major programs—geoarchaeological research in Iowa and the political economy of Woodland and Oneota peoples.

Robert C. Dunnell received his Ph.D. from Yale University in 1967. He currently is professor of anthropology and adjunct professor of Quaternary studies at the University of Washington. He is also an affiliate curator of the Peabody Museum, Yale University. His earliest fieldwork was in the Ohio Valley, which included his dissertation research in Fishtrap, Kentucky. His current interests are in the central Mississippi Valley. He is probably best known for methodological and theoretical contributions in areas including classification, surficial field methods, and the use of evolutionary theory in archaeology.

David H. Dye received his Ph.D. from Washington University in St. Louis in 1980. He currently is associate professor of anthropology at the University of Memphis. He has conducted extensive research in the Mississippi River valley and written numerous articles on the region, especially pertaining to the Late Mississippian period. Along with Cheryl Ann Cox, he edited the often-cited *Towns and Temples along the Mississippi.*

Gregory L. Fox received his Ph.D. from the University of Missouri in 1992. He currently works at the Western Archeological and Conservation Center, National Park Service, Tucson, Arizona, where he manages the external archaeology program. He continues to do fieldwork in Arizona, California, Colorado, Oklahoma, and Texas for the park service.

Diana M. Greenlee is a Ph.D. candidate in the Department of Anthropology at the University of Washington. In her dissertation she uses scientific evolutionary theory to explain settlement, subsistence, and dietary change associated with the appearance of maize farming in the middle and upper Ohio River valley. She is particularly interested in the physical and chemical properties of bone, how they are altered by postdepositional processes, and how they can be used to document the life histories of individuals in archaeological skeletal populations.

Paul P. Kreisa received his Ph.D. from the University of Illinois in 1990. He currently serves as the program coordinator of the Public Service Archaeology Program, a sponsored-research program of the University of Illinois. His research interests have long centered on Mississippian-period cultures living around the confluence of the Mississippi and Ohio rivers.

Robert H. Lafferty III received his Ph.D. from Southern Illinois University at Carbondale in 1977. He is co-owner of Mid-Continental Research Associates, Inc., of Springdale, Arkansas. He has directed major archaeological excavations on fifteen different sites in the lower Mississippi Valley, the Tennessee Valley, and the Arkansas Ozarks. One of Lafferty's interests is the development and testing of predictive settlement models. He has authored or co-authored several books and more than seventy-five technical reports and papers.

Patrick T. McCutcheon received his Ph.D. from the University of Washington in 1997.. He has conducted several seasons of fieldwork in southeastern Missouri and northeastern Arkansas, much of which was directed toward understanding the relation between heat treatment and stone-tool use on the Malden Plain.

Robert C. Mainfort, Jr., received his Ph.D. from Michigan State University in 1977. He currently serves as a sponsored-research-program administrator in the Arkansas Archeological Survey and associate professor of anthropology at the University of Arkansas. He has published a number of articles and monographs on prehistoric and historical-period archaeology, as well as on Civil War history. His major research interests include mortuary studies and the emergence of ranked societies, particularly in the central Mississippi Valley.

Michael C. Moore received his M.A. from the University of Oklahoma. He currently serves as state-programs archaeologist with the Tennessee Division of Archaeology. Moore has authored several articles and reports on research in Oklahoma and Tennessee; his research interests include the Mississippian-period occupation of central Tennessee.

Carol A. Morrow received her Ph.D. from Southern Illinois University at Carbondale in 1988. She currently is assistant professor of anthropology at Southeast Missouri State University in Cape Girardeau. Her research interests center on various aspects of lithic technology, especially the procurement and use of exotic cherts during the Middle Woodland period. She has published numerous articles and books, including *The Organization of Core Technology*, which she edited with Jay Johnson.

Michael J. O'Brien received his Ph.D. from the University of Texas at Austin in 1977. He currently is professor of anthropology and associate dean of the College of Arts and Science at the University of Missouri–Columbia. His research interests include the late prehistoric-period record of the Mississippi River valley and the application of evolutionary theory to archaeology. He has authored numerous articles and books, including *Cat Monsters and Headpots: The Archaeology of Missouri's Pemiscot Bayou* and *Paradigms of the Past: The Story of Missouri Archaeology*.

Timothy K. Perttula received his Ph.D. from the University of Washington in 1989. He currently is an independent archaeological consultant living in Austin, Texas. Perttula has worked on archaeological projects in numerous states, including Missouri, Oklahoma, and Texas, where his research has focused on the archaeology and history of the Caddo Indians. He is the author of *The Caddo Nation: Archaeological and Ethnohistoric Perspectives*.

Patrice A. Teltser received her Ph.D. from the University of Washington in 1988. She currently is assistant professor at Lehigh University. Her primary research interests concern tracking regional-scale demographic and organizational changes during the Mississippian period from an evolutionary perspective. She has authored several articles on Mississippian materials from southeastern Missouri and edited a volume entitled *Evolutionary Archaeology: Methodological Issues*.

Index

Academy of Science of St. Louis, 13
Adams, R., 126, 203
Adams site (Kentucky), 60, 64, 65, 69, 70, 71, 77
Advance Lowland (Missouri), 196
Alabama Museum of Natural History, 16, 82
Alba Barbed points, 217
Allison tradition, 285
American Bottom, 148, 252, 253, 254, 285
Americanist archaeology, 3, 13, 19
Amino-acid composition, 305, 306, 307, 318, 319
Amorphous-core technology, 288, 289, 291, 293, 295, 296, 297, 298
Ancient Buried City. *See* Wickliffe Mounds
Antiquity of humans in North America, 13
Archaeobotanical remains, 299
Archaeological Conservancy, 176, 186, 326 (n. 8-2)
Archaeometry, 16
Archaic period, 132, 139, 144, 145, 146, 147, 161, 176, 193, 196, 271, 284, 310
Arkansas Archeological Survey, 24, 325 (n. 5-1)
Arkansas Basin (Oklahoma), 192
Arkansas Highway and Transportation Department, 225, 255
Arkansas River, 1, 4, 5, 89
Arkansas State University, 244
Armorel phase, 52, 54, 55, 56, 120
Avenue Polychrome, 97

Baehr Mound (Illinois), 285
Baldwin Plain, 111
Banks site (Arkansas), 93
Barfield Ridge (Missouri), 170
Barker site (Missouri), 43, 45
Barnes Cordmarked, 327 (n. 10-2)
Barnes occupations, 271, 272
Barnes Plain, 178, 187, 327 (n. 10-2)
Barnes Ridge (Missouri), 125, 128, 134, 139, 146
Barton Incised, 63, 64, 106, 110, 111, 122, 249
Bass Island (Arkansas), 265, 266, 267, 271

Baumer tradition, 283
Bay Mounds. *See* Webb Mounds
Baytown period, 19, 110, 127, 134, 252, 326 (n. 8-3)
Baytown Plain, 111, 112, 114, 145, 326 (n. 8-3), 327 (n. 10-2)
Bean, L. M., 202
Beck site (Arkansas), 93, 95
Beckwith, T., 13
Beckwith's Fort (Missouri), 13, 25, 43, 45, 48, 127, 213, 326 (n. 8-3)
Bell City–Oran Gap (Missouri), 8, 10
Bell Plain, 48, 55, 63, 71, 77, 80, 83, 106, 109, 111, 114, 121, 221, 249, 250, 251, 325 (n. 2-2)
Bell paste, 217, 221
Belle Meade site (Arkansas), 93
Berry site (Missouri), 120, 121, 325 (n. 5-1)
Biface technology, 288, 289, 291, 293
Big Lake phase, 54, 253, 304
Big Lake site (Arkansas), 10
Big Muddy River (Illinois), 29, 283
Birds Point (Missouri), 131, 134
Birds Point–New Madrid Set Back Levee (Missouri), 124, 128
Bishop site (Tennessee), 120
Black River (Arkansas and Missouri), 15, 191, 197
Black Warrior River (Alabama), 253
Brackinseik site (Arkansas), 93
Bradley site (Arkansas), 82, 93, 97
Braided-stream fluvial regime, 5, 8, 9, 10, 153, 170, 200
Brainerd-Robinson coefficient of similarity, 38, 272
Brand site (Arkansas), 25
Braun, D. P., 286
Brewer Lake (Missouri), 134
Brooks site (Missouri), 93, 97
Brougham Lake site (Arkansas), 227, 245
Brown, C., 82
Buckskull phase, 187
Buffalo Slough (Missouri), 9
Bureau of (American) Ethnology: Division of

379

Mound Exploration, 15, 81, 125, 126, 151, 169, 172, 173, 283, 326 (n. 8-3)
Burkett site (Missouri), 145, 146
Burlington chert. *See* Crescent chert
Burris site (Arkansas), 245
Byrd site (Missouri), 52, 53, 55

C_3/C_4 photosynthetic pathways, 300, 301
Cache River (Arkansas), 24, 245
Cagle Lake (Missouri), 314
Cagle Lake site (Missouri), 22, 45, 49, 52, 54, 55, 56
Cahokia site (Illinois), 243
Cairo, Illinois, 5, 10, 124, 132
Cairo Lowland (Missouri), 4, 27, 64, 124, 125, 127, 128, 139, 144, 146, 147, 148, 150, 151, 153, 154, 164, 190, 213, 224, 326 (n. 8-3)
Cairo Lowland phase, 31, 33, 41, 43, 45, 50, 52, 53, 55, 57, 85, 222
Caldwell, J., 283, 286
Callahan-Thompson site (Missouri), 52, 53, 55, 64
Campbell Appliqué, 27, 111, 118, 221, 222
Campbell phase, 54, 55
Campbell Punctated, 221
Campbell site (Missouri), 23, 45, 49, 52, 54, 55, 56, 93, 97, 120, 121, 307, 314, 320, 323, 325 (n. 5-1)
Canady site. *See* Kersey site
Cane Creek (Missouri), 170
Carson Red-on-Buff, 97, 190, 191, 249
Central Mississippi Valley Archaeological Survey, 20
Charleston Fan (Missouri), 132
Charleston site. *See* Hearnes site
Chemical analysis of bone, 299, 300
Chickasawba site (Arkansas), 97
Chucalissa site (Tennessee), 93, 110, 118
Chute site. *See* McCoy site
Clay Hill site (Arkansas), 209
Cluster analysis, 38, 57, 70
Cobdon/Dongola chert, 284, 285, 286, 291, 293, 297
Cockrum Landing site (Missouri), 45
Coldwater Farm North site (Missouri), 271, 272
Cole, F.-C., 284
Collagen, 305, 306, 317, 319; extraction, 307, 315; replicate extraction, 308, 315
Commerce Hills (Missouri), 10
Conant, A. J., 1, 13
Conical-core blade technology, 288
Cooter site. *See* Campbell site

Cormorant Cord-Impressed, 111, 112, 114
County Line site (Missouri), 164, 200, 271, 272
Crab-Orchard Fabric-Impressed, 286, 287
Crab Orchard tradition, 283, 285
Crescent chert, 265, 284, 292, 293, 294, 297
Crescent Hills (Missouri), 265
Crosno/Cahokia Cordmarked, 41
Crosno site (Missouri), 31, 33, 41, 42, 43, 45, 48, 50, 52, 53, 60, 209
Croswell, C., 13
Crowley's Ridge (Arkansas and Missouri), 4, 5, 8, 10, 24, 29, 148, 149, 200, 258, 259, 260, 262, 265, 266, 272, 273, 275, 278, 279, 280
Cultural research management (CRM), 24, 25, 122, 126, 225
Culture-history paradigm, 3, 17
Cummins Mound (Missouri), 164
Current River (Missouri), 197

Davenport Academy of Sciences, 81
Davies, J. A., 82
Davis place site. *See* Double Bridges site
DeJarnette, D. L., 82
DeJarnette, J., 82
Dellinger, S. C., 82
Demographic determinism, 304
Denton Mounds (Missouri), 22, 52, 54, 55
Deuel, T., 284. *See also* Cole, F.-C.
Distributional analysis, 115
Dohack phase, 253
Dorena phase, 63
Dorrah site (Missouri), 52, 54, 55
Dover chert, 113, 192, 193, 217
Double Bridges site (Missouri), 15
Duck River cache (Tennessee), 114
Duncan, J. E., 304
Dunklin Phase, 253

Early Wickliffe phase, 63
Eastern Lowlands (Arkansas and Missouri), 4, 8, 29, 255
East Lake site (Missouri), 13, 45, 325 (n. 1-2)
Effigy vessels, 111, 121, 187, 189, 217, 219
Elemental carbon/nitrogen (C/N) ratios, 305, 306, 307, 316, 317, 319
Eleven Point River (Missouri), 197
Elizabeth site (Illinois), 298
Essentialism, 20, 24, 27
Estes site (Missouri), 45
European trade goods, 23, 120
Evers, E., 13, 14
Extract yield, 305, 306

Fisk, H., 5, 127
Flake knives. *See* Prismatic-blade technology
Focus, 21
Ford, J. A., 3, 17, 18, 19, 20, 21, 23, 24, 59, 83, 225. *See also* Lower Mississippi Alluvial Valley Survey
Foster, J. W., 13
Fox, G. L., 21
Furrs Cordmarked, 111

George Reeves phase, 253
Gravel: composition, 260, 261; crack propagation, 262, 276; deposits, 258; distribution, 260; fracture toughness, 260, 261, 262, 266, 273, 278; groundmass, 263, 267, 274, 278; inclusions, 263, 267, 271, 272, 273, 274, 275, 276; size, 260, 261, 266, 267, 271, 278
Graves Lake site (Tennessee), 99, 102, 108, 110, 113, 114, 116, 118, 119, 120, 121, 122, 325 (n. 5-1)
Greenlee, D. M., 304
Grey Horse Lake site (Missouri), 310, 311
Griffin, J. B., 3, 17, 18, 19, 20, 21, 23, 24, 59, 83, 225, 232, 250, 254. *See also* Ford, J. A.; Lower Mississippi Alluvial Valley Survey
Grimes Hill chert, 285, 292, 295
Gypsy Joint site (Missouri), 184, 191

Hall, Capt. W. P., 82
Hampson, J. K., 16, 82. *See also* Middle Nodena site; Upper Nodena site
Hampson Museum, 121
Harris site. *See* Walls site
Hatchie site (Tennessee), 99, 121
Havana phase, 285
Havana Plain, 286
Havana region, 297
Havana tradition, 283, 286
Havana Zoned, 286
Hayes, J., 82
Hayti phase, 54
Hayti site (Missouri), 232
Hazel site (Arkansas), 225, 247, 310
Hearnes site (Missouri), 45
Heat treatment, 260, 261, 279, 284
Hess site (Missouri), 52, 53, 55, 64
Hillhouse site (Missouri), 131, 134, 145
Hoecake site (Missouri), 22, 23, 151
Hoffman, M. P., 202
Hofman, J. L., 283, 286, 293, 296
Holcomb site (Missouri), 45, 49
Holland site (Missouri), 52, 54, 55, 56
Hollywood White Filmed, 110

Holmes, W. H., 16, 81, 82, 95, 148, 288
Hopewell/Baehr pottery, 286
Hopewell materials, 29, 283
Hopewell period, 19, 281, 283, 284, 299
Horseshoe Lake (Arkansas), 93, 95, 97
Houck, L., 202, 203
Hull Engraved, 83, 84

Illinois River, 298
Illinois River valley, 281, 284, 285, 297, 298
Illinois State Museum, 283
Interlaboratory mass-spectrometer error, 308

Jackson phase, 63
James Bayou phase, 62
Jones Bayou site (Tennessee), 121
Jones, W. B., 82
Journal of the Academy of Natural Sciences of Philadelphia, 15, 82

Kaskaskia River (Illinois), 283, 285
Kelly, R. L., 296
Kennett site (Missouri), 45
Kent phase, 118, 213, 222
Kersey site (Missouri), 22, 45, 48, 49, 50, 52, 53, 54, 56, 320, 323
Kimmswick Fabric-Impressed, 41, 63, 64, 71, 73, 77, 78, 326 (n. 8-3)
Kinfolk Ridge site (Missouri), 45, 49
King, F., 16. *See also* Wickliffe Mounds
Knappenberger site (Arkansas), 225
Koehler, W., 172, 176, 190, 191

Lakeville site (Missouri), 45, 196
LaMoine River chert, 285
Land leveling, 22, 126, 127, 129, 153
Langdon, E. J., 202, 203, 205, 213, 215
Langdon site (Missouri), 28, 200, 202, 203, 205, 209, 215, 216, 217, 221, 222, 223, 224, 255, 306, 313, 320, 323
La Plant site (Missouri), 134
Larto Red Filmed, 326 (n. 8-3)
Late Wickliffe phase, 63, 64
Lawhorn site (Arkansas), 217, 222
L'eau Noire Incised, 81
Leland Incised, 64
Lewis, R. B., 61, 62, 64, 77, 78
Lilbourn site (Missouri), 13, 25, 45, 127, 213
Lithic technology, 287
Little Black River (Missouri), 25, 28, 169, 170, 171, 172, 191, 193, 196, 197
Little Cypress Bayou site (Arkansas), 310, 312
Little River (Missouri), 2, 10, 202

382 | Index

Little River Lowland (Missouri), 4, 8, 10, 224
Llama (*Palaeolama mirifica*), 9
Lower Mississippi Alluvial Valley Survey, 16–20, 59, 81, 85, 126, 225
Luedtke, B. E., 262

McCarty site (Arkansas), 187, 307, 310, 311
McCoy site (Missouri), 45, 49, 52, 54, 56
Madison points, 113, 122, 217, 223
Maize, 300, 304; agriculture, 169, 197, 256, 257, 299, 302; consumption, 301, 302, 311, 312, 320
Malden Plain (Arkansas and Missouri), 8, 9, 10, 28, 164, 165, 200, 202, 203, 206, 216, 221, 223, 224, 253, 260, 266, 271, 313, 323, 324, 327 (n. 9-4)
Malden Plain phase, 31, 45, 49, 50, 51, 54, 55
Mangrum site (Arkansas), 25, 226, 227
Manly Punctated, 190, 221
Mastodon (*Mammut americanum*), 9
Matthews Incised, 63, 71, 73, 77, 189, 221
Matthews site (Missouri), 13, 126
Meander-belt stream fluvial regime, 5, 10, 153
Medley phase, 63, 64
Meramec River, 284
Meyer's Mound (Missouri), 43, 45
Middle Wickliffe phase, 63
Middle Nodena site (Arkansas), 16, 25, 82, 225
Middleton, J. D., 172. *See also* Bureau of (American) Ethnology
Migration, 23
Mill Creek chert, 113, 166, 191, 192, 193, 217, 257
Mississippian period, 19, 22, 23, 25, 28, 29, 31, 52, 53, 60, 62, 83, 93, 99, 109, 122, 127, 134, 139, 145, 146, 148, 161, 164, 165, 167, 186, 187, 190, 193, 194, 195, 196, 197, 213, 221, 223, 224, 225, 226, 227, 243, 244, 245, 252, 253, 255, 256, 271, 272, 279, 283, 286, 298, 299, 301, 310, 311, 313, 314, 324, 326 (n. 7-1), 326 (n. 8-1); fortified communities, 13, 169, 200, 249, 313; settlement systems, 150, 154, 165, 222, 312
Mississippi Plain, 63, 71, 77, 80, 110, 111, 114, 122, 178, 187, 213, 216, 217, 249
Mississippi River, 2, 4, 8, 9, 10, 15, 29, 60, 65, 82, 124, 139, 146, 147, 153, 170, 200, 281, 283; channel reconstructions, 5, 127, 128, 131, 132, 134
Mississippi River valley, 1, 3, 11, 13, 15, 16, 17, 18, 19, 20, 22, 23, 24, 25, 28, 31, 80, 81, 83, 85, 99, 110, 113, 114, 118, 121, 126, 147, 148, 167, 169, 176, 197, 209, 222, 225, 232, 248, 252, 253, 254, 255, 256, 257, 258, 261, 265, 283, 299, 301, 302, 304, 310, 311, 312, 313, 320, 323, 324, 325 (n. 2-2), 326 (n. 7-1); physical environment, 4–10
Missouri Historical Society, 202
Moon site (Arkansas), 28, 29, 217, 223, 225, 227, 229, 231, 238, 241, 243, 245, 247, 248, 249, 250, 252, 254, 255, 256, 257, 327 (n. 10-1), 327 (n. 10-2), 327 (n. 10-2)
Moore, C. B., 15–16, 82, 99, 202
Morehouse Lowland (Missouri), 8
Morrow, C. A., 296. *See also* Hofman, J. L.
Morse, D. F., 16, 20, 25, 187, 252, 327 (n. 9-4)
Morse, P. A., 16, 20, 25, 187, 222, 252. *See also* Morse, D. F.
Mort site (Missouri), 52, 53, 55
Moundbuilders, myth of, 13
Mound Place Incised, 63, 221, 249
Moundville site (Alabama), 83, 84, 85, 98
Moxley site (Missouri), 134
Moxley Well (Missouri), 132
Mulberry Creek Cordmarked, 111, 145, 326 (n. 8-3)
Multidimensional scaling, 52, 55, 70
Murphy site (Missouri), 45, 49, 52, 54, 93, 314, 323

Nally site (Missouri), 131, 134, 145
Nashville Negative Painted, 63, 64
National Register of Historic Places, 225
Neeley's Ferry Plain, 48, 55, 213, 325 (n. 2-2)
Neely site (Missouri), 271, 272
New Madrid, Missouri, 8
New Madrid Floodway (Missouri), 124, 128, 146
Nickel site (Arkansas), 93
Nodena phase, 31, 45, 49, 50, 52, 54, 55, 256
Nodena points, 113, 122, 217, 223
Nodena Red-and-White, 97, 110, 190, 221, 222, 249
Nonlocal chert, 281, 283, 284, 292, 293, 297, 298. *See also* Cobdon/Dongola chert; Crescent chert; Dover chert; Grimes Hill chert; Mill Creek chert; Pitkin chert; Wyandotte chert
Nonsite survey, 154
Norris, Col. P. W., 169, 172, 173, 174, 175, 176, 187, 199, 326 (n. 8-3). *See also* Bureau of (American) Ethnology

O'Bryan Ridge (Missouri), 124, 128, 131, 132, 139

O'Byam Incised/Engraved, 41, 63, 64, 71, 73, 77, 80, 81, 190, 221, 249
Odell, G., 298
Ohio River, 5, 10, 60, 65, 126, 132
Ohio River Valley, 148, 281
Old Field site (Missouri), 10
Old Town Red, 63, 64, 71, 73, 77, 110, 187, 221, 249
Old Varney River (Missouri), 45, 48, 49, 50, 51, 52, 53, 54, 55, 56
Open Bayou. *See* Portage Open Bay
Otto Sharpe site (Tennessee), 85, 113
Owens Punctated, 64
Owls Bend tradition, 187
Ozark Escarpment, 8, 170, 171, 172, 191, 197
Ozark Highlands, 4, 25, 170, 172, 192, 193, 197, 253, 265

Palmer, E., 172. *See also* Bureau of (American) Ethnology
Parkin phase, 25, 52, 55, 56, 217, 222, 255, 256
Parkin Punctated, 27, 110, 111, 122, 221
Parkin site (Arkansas), 25, 52, 54, 55, 56, 93, 213, 225, 256
Parry, W. J., 296
Patrick phase, 253
Payne Creek (Arkansas), 265, 266, 267, 271
Peabody Museum (Harvard), 13, 85, 151
Pecan Point site (Arkansas), 82, 93, 95
Pelts site (Missouri), 313
Pemiscot Bayou (Arkansas and Missouri), 2, 10, 93, 95, 97, 323, 324
Pemiscot Bayou phase, 31, 45, 49, 50, 51, 52, 54, 55
Persimmon Grove. *See* Cagle Lake site
Peter Bess site (Missouri), 195
Phase, 3, 20, 21, 31, 33, 38, 43, 56, 59, 78, 79
Phillips, P., 3, 17, 18, 19, 20, 21, 23, 24, 59, 62, 78, 81, 82, 83, 84, 225. *See also* Ford, J. A.; Lower Mississippi Alluvial Valley Survey
Pinhook Ridge (Missouri), 127
Pitkin chert, 191, 192
Plumley, W. J., 265
Portage Open Bay (Missouri), 15
Porter site (Tennessee), 121
Pothunting, 23
Potter, W. B., 13, 14, 151
Pottery types, 3, 17, 18, 19, 31, 58
Pouncey Ridge Pinched, 111
Poverty Point objects, 139, 144, 161
Powell, J. W., 15, 172. *See also* Bureau of (American) Ethnology
Powers Fort (Missouri), 28, 169, 170, 171, 172, 173, 176, 181, 182, 184, 185, 186, 187, 189, 190, 191, 193, 194, 195, 196, 197, 199, 223, 326 (n. 8-3), 326 (n. 8-4)
Powers Fort Swale (Missouri), 8, 172
Powers phase, 169, 180, 183, 185, 186, 187, 188, 189, 192, 193, 194, 196, 197, 199, 222, 254, 255, 326 (n. 8-3)
Powers Phase Project, 25, 28, 172, 181
Price, J. E., 25, 172, 176, 178, 181, 185, 191, 199, 232, 250, 254
Priestly site (Arkansas), 227, 232, 243, 252, 253, 255, 256
Prismatic-blade technology, 281, 284, 285, 286, 287, 291, 292, 293, 296, 297, 298
Processual archaeology, 59
Production technology, 287

Radiocarbon-date calibration, 68, 116, 183
Raffety site (Missouri), 145
Ramey Incised, 63, 64
Ranch Incised, 110
Range phase, 253
Ray, J. H., 265, 327 (n. 10-1)
Raymond, 286, 287
Rhodes Incised, 80, 81, 111, 249
Rhodes site (Arkansas), 82
Richardson's Landing (Tennessee), 121, 122, 325 (n. 5-1)
Rich Woods site (Missouri), 45, 151, 200
Riggs, Capt. C. W., 82
Rim beveling, 119–121
Rinaud site (Missouri), 134, 144
Rivervale site (Arkansas), 226
Rose Mound (Arkansas), 82, 93, 97
Rowlandtown site (Kentucky), 60, 64, 65, 66, 70, 71, 73, 77
Rush Ridge (Missouri), 132
Rust, H., 13, 151

Saline River (Illinois), 283
Sallisaw chert, 192
Salvage archaeology, federally funded, 16, 22
Sand Mountain points, 113
Sandy Woods site (Missouri), 13, 27, 43, 45, 151, 153, 165
Sangamon River (Illinois), 285
Saucier, R. T., 8, 10
Scallorn points, 217, 223
Scatters phase, 187
Scroll motifs, 80, 95, 97
Seriation, 17, 18, 20
Shell Lake site (Missouri), 193
Sikeston Ridge (Missouri), 8, 124, 126, 127

Sikeston site (Missouri), 13, 43, 45
Slavens Creek (Arkansas), 265, 266, 267, 271
Smiling Dan site (Illinois), 298
Smithsonian Institution, 15, 81, 326 (n. 8-3)
Snodgrass site (Missouri), 25, 29, 181, 183, 186, 191, 194, 195, 196, 197, 223, 232, 248, 249, 250, 252, 254, 255
Snub-nosed end scrapers, 113, 118, 120
Sodium-hydroxide treatment, 307
Southeastern Ceremonial Complex, 83
Southern Cult, 83, 84
South Pelts site (Missouri), 271, 272
Southwest Missouri State University Center for Archaeological Research, 225
Spanish Grant site (Missouri), 45
Spiro Mound (Oklahoma), 84, 85
Stable-carbon-isotope analysis, 299, 300, 301, 304, 313, 319
Stateline site (Missouri), 97
St. Francis Basin (Arkansas and Missouri), 217, 226
St. Francis-Little River Basin (Arkansas and Missouri), 22, 200, St. Francis River, 2, 4, 5, 8, 9, 15, 82, 83, 84, 89, 119, 170, 193, 209, 224, 255, 256
St. Francis-type settlement, 209, 213
Stratigraphic excavation, 59
Struever, S., 284
Subsurface cores, 205, 209, 210, 215
Sugar Tree Ridge (Missouri), 125, 128, 134, 139, 146
Sunflower River, 15, 285
Surface-artifact density, 114
Survey site (Missouri), 45
Swallow, G. C., 13, 325 (n. 1-1)
Sweat site (Tennessee), 120, 121
Sycamore site (Arkansas), 93

Tchula period, 110, 112
Tennessee Division of Archaeology (TDOA), 99, 102, 103, 121, 122
Thebes, Illinois, 1, 4, 10
Thebes Gap (Missouri), 10, 132
Thermoluminescence dating (TL), 215, 216, 222, 223
Thing, I. H., 200. *See also* Bureau of (American) Ethnology
Thomas, C., 15, 151, 172, 174, 200. *See also* Bureau of (American) Ethnology
Tom Bird Blue Hole (Missouri), 124, 127
Trace-element analysis, 304
Twenhafel site (Illinois), 29, 281, 283, 285, 286, 289, 291, 292, 295, 296, 297, 298
Twin Mounds (Kentucky), 60, 64, 68, 70, 71

Turk site (Kentucky), 60, 64, 68, 70, 71, 77
Turnage site (Arkansas), 93
Turner site (Missouri), 25, 29, 180, 181, 195, 196, 197, 223, 255
Tyronza River (Arkansas), 255, 256

University of Arkansas Museum, 16, 82
University of Memphis, 103
University of Michigan, 20, 25; Ceramic Repository, 17
University of Missouri, 13, 22, 25
Upper Nodena site (Arkansas), 16, 25, 82, 93, 97, 225. *See also* Middle Nodena site
U.S. Army Corps of Engineers, 124

Vacant Quarter hypothesis, 28, 148, 149, 256
Vancil site (Missouri), 202, 224, 307
Variation in isotopic bone collagen, 308, 309; age related, 310, 324; status related, 310
Varney Red Filmed, 49, 221, 227, 327 (n. 10-2)
Varney tradition, 187
Vegetation patterns, 227
Vernon Paul Appliqué, 111, 118
Vogel Mound Group. *See* Twenhafel site

Wabash River, 283
Walker, W., 126, 203
Wallace Incised, 220
Walls complex, 80, 83
Walls Engraved, 27, 80, 81, 82, 83, 84, 85, 89, 93, 95, 97, 98, 111, 221, 222
Walls site (Mississippi), 82, 93, 95
Wardell site (Missouri), 45, 49
Webb Mounds (Arkansas), 255
Webb Place site (Missouri), 200
Weber Mound (Illinois), 283. *See also* Twenhafel site
Weems site (Missouri), 145, 146
Wesler, K. W., 61, 63, 64, 73, 77
Western Lowlands (Arkansas and Missouri), 4, 5, 8, 9, 10, 24, 28, 169, 170, 172, 187, 197, 255, 326 (n. 8-3)
West site (Mississippi), 93
White River, 15
Wickliffe Cordmarked, 41
Wickliffe Incised, 41
Wickliffe Mounds (Kentucky), 16, 61, 64
Wickliffe Plain, 41
Wickliffe Thick, 41, 63, 64, 71, 73, 77, 78
Wilder site (Tennessee), 121
Wilkins Island site (Missouri), 48, 49
Willey, G., 3, 21, 24, 62, 78. *See also* Phillips, P.
Williams, J. R., 22, 23, 24, 28

Williams, S., 20, 21, 23, 28, 31, 33, 41, 42, 43, 45, 50, 51, 52, 57, 121, 126, 153, 203
Williams Mound 1 (Missouri), 215
Winters, H. D., 284, 285
Winterville Incised, 64
Woodall Farm site (Missouri), 271, 272
Woodland period, 19, 29, 110, 139, 145, 146, 147, 161, 164, 165, 178, 180, 185, 187, 193, 226, 227, 243, 252, 253, 271, 272, 281, 283, 284, 285, 286, 287, 289, 291, 293, 294, 295, 296, 297, 298, 327 (n. 10-2). *See also* Baytown period; Hopewell period; Tchula period
Works Progress Administration, 203
Wyandotte chert, 285

Yazoo River (Mississippi), 15

Zebree site (Arkansas), 226, 227, 243, 253, 304